The Historiography of Economics

A. W. (Bob) Coats (1924–2007) made a unique contribution to the history of economic thought, economic methodology and the sociology of economics. Most of his work was in the form of articles, which are scattered throughout a wide range of journals, many of which are not easily accessible. The three volumes in *British and American Economic Essays* make his most important contributions widely available in permanent form.

The Historiography of Economics completes the collection, under the editorship of Roger E. Backhouse and Bruce Caldwell. The volume covers fields between which Coats, who described himself as an "economist watcher", never made any sharp distinction. These range from the writing of the history of economics to methodology and rhetoric. The volume includes essays on individual historians of economics, on the journal *History of Political Economy*, on Lakatos's methodology of scientific research programmes, and on diverse aspects of economic methodology. Coats developed many of his ideas through debating with others, and so the volume includes many of his most substantial book reviews. This selection is designed to complement the work on the history of economics and the economics profession contained in Volumes I and II of the series. The volume also includes a substantial biographical essay on A.W. (Bob) Coats, and interviews with him.

A. W. (Bob) Coats, who died in 2007, was formerly Head of the Department of Economic and Social History at the University of Nottingham, UK. Volume I of his collected papers was published in 1992, and Volume II in 1993.

Roger E. Backhouse is Professor of History and Philosophy of Economics at the University of Birmingham, UK.

Bruce Caldwell is Research Professor of Economics and Director of the Centre for the History of Political Economy, Duke University, USA.

British and American economic essays

1. On the History of Economic Thought
British and American economic essays, Volume I
A. W. (Bob) Coats

2. The Sociology and Professionalization of Economics
British and American economic essays, Volume II
A. W. (Bob) Coats

3. The Historiography of Economics
British and American economic essays, Volume III
A. W. (Bob) Coats; compiled and edited by Roger E. Backhouse and Bruce Caldwell

The Historiography of Economics

British and American economic essays

A. W. (Bob) Coats

Compiled and edited by Roger E. Backhouse and Bruce Caldwell

Routledge
Taylor & Francis Group
LONDON AND NEW YORK

First published 2014
by Routledge
2 Park Square, Milton Park, Abingdon, Oxfordshire OX14 4RN

Simultaneously published in the USA and Canada
by Routledge
711 Third Avenue, New York, NY 10017

First issued in paperback 2016

Routledge is an imprint of the Taylor & Francis Group, an informa business

British Library Cataloguing in Publication Data
A catalogue record for this book is available from the British Library

Library of Congress Cataloging in Publication Data
A catalog record has been requested for this book

ISBN 13: 978-1-138-24376-7 (pbk)
ISBN 13: 978-0-415-66264-2 (hbk)

Typeset in Times New Roman
by Cenveo Publisher Services

Contents

PART II
Book reviews **419**

Preface

Roger E. Backhouse and Bruce J. Caldwell

Bob Coats always planned to compile a third volume of the collected papers that he chose to subtitle "British and American Economic Essays" and that it should cover both the historiography and the methodology of economics. Unfortunately, we do not know which papers he planned to include. Michalis Psalidopoulos has told us that Bob kept a box into which he dropped copies of papers he wanted to include but we could not find this in his papers, which have been deposited at the University of Nottingham. Sonia Coats also assured us that he attached great importance to some of his book reviews, for the books he reviewed were major source of inspiration.

We approached the task of assembling this volume by compiling a list of his many articles and reviews, starting from a CV that Sonia gave us, and making use of the research assistance of Michael Thomas, a Fellow at the Center for the History of Political Economy at Duke University, for whose help we are very grateful. We then eliminated everything that was included in Volumes I and II. With articles that he could have included in those volumes, we had to decide whether their omission was because he thought they fitted better into the theme of Volume III, or because he did not consider the article sufficiently valuable to reprint. However, where we thought an article of sufficient interest, we decided to include it, even if he might have taken a more modest view of its merits. With book reviews we again used our own judgement, though generally opting for the longer reviews.

It is greatly to be regretted that this collection does not contain Bob's own introduction. In its place, we include an obituary that, together with Craufurd Goodwin and Malcolm Rutherford, we wrote for *History of Political Economy*, the journal that he did so much to support. We also include a publications list that is as complete as we could make it.

Our intention is that this volume will serve as a memorial to a scholar who, through his writings and his support for others, occupies an important place in the history of economics.

June 11, 2013

Sources of articles and reviews

Introduction "A. W. (Bob) Coats, 1924–2007." B. Caldwell, C. D. W. Goodwin and M. Rutherford, *History of Political Economy* 40(3): 421–46.

Part I: Articles

1. "Memoirs of an economist watcher," *Journal of the History of Economic Thought*, vol. 18, Fall 1996, pp. 250–70.

2. "A conversation with A. W. Bob Coats" (Interviewed by Grant Fleming) *History of Economic Ideas* 3(3), 1995, pp. 141–56.

3. "T. W. Hutchison as an historian of economics," in Warren Samuels, ed., *The Craft of the Historian of Economics* (Greenwich, CT: JAI Press, 1983), pp. 187–207.

4. "Half a century of methodological controversy in economics: as reflected in the writings of T. W. Hutchison," in A. W. Coats, ed., *Methodological Controversy in Economics: Historical Essays in Honor of T. W. Hutchison* (JAI Press: Greenwich, CT, 1983), pp. 1–42.

5. "What Mirowski's history leaves out," in Neil De Marchi ed., *Non-Natural Social Science: Reflections on the Enterprise of More Heat than Light, History of Political Economy*, Annual Supplement to volume 25 (Durham: Duke University Press, 1993), pp. 271–82.

6. "The pillars of economic understanding: a new magisterial history of economic thought?," *Journal of the History of Economic Thought*, vol. 22, September 2000, pp. 377–84.

7. "History of political economy: The AEA and the history of economics," *Bulletin of the History of Economics Society*, vol. 9, Fall 1987, pp. 61–6.

8. "Explanations in history and economics," *Social Research*, vol. 56, Summer 1989, pp. 331–60.

9. "Comments on Schabas: The nature and significance of the 'New' economic history 'Parmenides and the Cliometricians'," in Daniel Little, ed. *On the Reliability of Economic Models* (Boston: Kluwer, 1995) pp. 203–9.

10. "What is American about American economics?," in Malcolm Rutherford, ed. *The Economic Mind in America: Essays in the History of American Economics* (London: Routledge, 1998), pp. 9–17.

11. "Research priorities in the history of economics," *History of Political Economy*, vol. 1, Spring 1969, pp. 9–18.

12. "The first decade of *HOPE* (1968–79)," *History of Political Economy*, vol. 15, 1983, pp. 303–19.

13. "Economics, history and *HOPE*," *Bulletin of the History of Economics Society*, vol. 8, Winter 1987, pp. 1–20.

14. "Situational determinism in economics: The implications of Lastis's argument for the historian of economics," *British Journal of the Philosophy of Science*, vol. 25, 1974, pp. 285–8.

15. "Economics and psychology: The death and resurrection of a research programme," in Spiro J. Latsis, ed. *Method and Appraisal in Economics* (New York: Cambridge University Press, 1976), pp. 43–64.

16. "Economics and psychology: A resurrection story," in Peter Earl, ed. *Psychological Economics: Development, Tensions, Prospects* (Kluwer, 1987), pp. 211–25.

17. "Appraising economic theories," a review article on N. de Marchi and Mark Blaug, eds., *Appraising Economic Theories: Studies in the Methodology of Research Programs, History of Economics Review*, 1993, pp. 46–56.

18. "The influence of Veblen's methodology," *Journal of Political Economy*, vol. 62, December 1954, pp. 529–37.

19. "The politics of political economists: Comment," *Quarterly Journal of Economics*, vol. 74, November 1960, pp. 666–9.

20. "Value judgments in economics," *Yorkshire Bulletin of Economic and Social Research*, November, 1964, pp. 53–67.

21. "Methodology and professionalism in economics: A subordinate theme in Fritz Machlup's writings," in *Breadth and Depth in Economics: Fritz Malchlup – The Man and His Ideas*, ed. Jacob S. Dreyer (Lexington, Mass: Lexington Books D. C. Heath and Co., 1978), pp. 23–35.

22. (with Stuart Thompstone) "Against 'against convergence,'" *Cambridge Journal of Economics*, vol. 5, December 1981, pp. 383–6.

23. "The methodology of economics: Some recent contributions," *Kyklos*, vol. 35, May 1982, pp. 310–21.

24. "Economic methodology: Theory, practice and the current state of economics," *Kyklos*, vol. 39, February 1986, pp. 109–15.

25. "Reflections on the Austrian-institutionalism symposium," in Warren Samuels, ed. *Research in the History of Economic Thought and Methodology*, vol. 6 (JAI Press, 1989), pp. 101–6.

26. "Economics as a profession," in David Greenaway, Michael Bleaney, and Ian Stewart, eds. *Companion to Contemporary Economic Thought* (London and New York: Routledge, 1991), pp. 119–42.

27. "The past, present and future of economics," in Cosimo Perrotta and Vitantonio Gioia, eds. *Where is Economics Going? Historical Viewpoints* (Lecce: Universita Degli Studi de Lecce, 1994), pp. 7–18.

28. "Fusfeld and Economic Methodology," in Nahid Aslanbeigui and Young Back Choi, eds. *Borderlands of Economics: Essays in Honor of Daniel R. Fusfeld* (London: Routledge, 1997), pp. 32–46.

29. "Roundtable: The progress of heterodox economics," *Journal of the History of Economic Thought*, vol. 22, June 2000, pp. 145–8.

30. "Review article: Mary O. Furner's *Advocacy and Objectivity: A Crisis in the Professionalization of American Social Science*." *Journal of American Studies*, vol. 12 August 1978, pp. 227–33.

31. (co-author with Bruce Caldwell) "The rhetoric of economists: A comment on McCloskey," *Journal of Economic Literature*, vol. 22, June 1984, pp. 575–8.

32. (co-author with Steven Pressman) "Further comments on McCloskey's argument," *Eastern Economic Journal* vol. 13, July–September 1987, pp. 305–7.

33. "Economic rhetoric: The social dimension," in Arjo Klamer, Donald N. McCloskey, and Robert M. Solow, eds. *The Consequences of Economic Rhetoric* (Cambridge University Press, 1988), pp. 64–84.

Part II: Book reviews

1. "*History of economic analysis* by J. A. Schumpeter," *Economica*, vol. 22, May 1955, pp. 171–4.

2. "*The meaning and validity of economic theory: A historical approach* by Leo Rogin," *Economica*, vol. 24, May 1957, pp. 164–6.

3. "*A history of economic ideas* by Robert Lekachman," *Kyklos*, vol. 13, February 1960, pp. 134–6.

4. "*Founders of American economic thought and policy* by Virgle Glenn Wilhite," *Science and Society* vol. 24, Spring 1960, pp. 185–7.

5. "*The economic mind in American civilization, vols. IV and V: 1918–1933* by Joseph Dorfman," *Journal of Political Economy*, vol. 68, June 1960, pp. 311–12.

6. "*The economic mind in American civilization, vols. IV and V: 1918–1933* by Joseph Dorfman," *Bulletin of the British Association for American Studies*, 2 new series, March 1961, pp. 86–7.

7. "*Types of economic theory, from mercantilism to institutionalism. Vol. 1.* by Wesley C. Mitchell," *American Economic Review*, vol. 58, March 1968, pp. 206–8.

8. "*Events, ideology and economic theory. The determinants of progress in the development of economic analysis* by Robert V. Eagly," *History of Economic Thought Newsletter*, 2, April 1969, pp. 17–20.

9. "*Economic theory in retrospect (revised edition.)* by Mark Blaug," *Kyklos*, vol. 22, November 1969, pp. 781–3.

10. "*J. R. McCulloch: A study in classical economics* by Denis P. O'Brien," *Kyklos*, vol. 24, August 1971, pp. 605–7.

11. "*The correspondence of Lord Overstone* by Denis P. O'Brien (ed.)," *Kyklos*, vol. 26, January 1973, pp. 688–670.

12. "*The classical economists* by Denis P. O'Brien," *Kyklos*, vol. 28, November 1975, pp. 903–6 and "*The structure of classical economic theory* by Robert V. Eagley," *Kyklos*, vol. 28, November 1975, pp. 903–6.

13. "*The emergence of professional social science: The American Social Science Association and the nineteenth century crisis of authority* by Thomas L Haskell," *History of Political Economy*, vol. 11, Summer 1979, pp. 312–5.

14. "*Adam Smith's politic: An essay in historiographical revision* by Donald Winch," *Kyklos*, vol. 32, August 1979, pp. 603–5.

15. "*The organization of knowledge in modern America 1860–1980* by Alexandra Oleson and John Voss (eds.)," *Journal of American Studies*, vol. 15, December 1981, pp. 465–8.

16. "*Beyond positivism. Economic methodology in the twentieth century* by Bruce Caldwell," Kyklos, vol. 36, August 1983, pp. 487–9.

17. "*John Maynard Keynes: Hopes betrayed 1883–1920* by Robert Skidelsky," *Kyklos*, vol. 37, August 1984, pp. 511–3.

18. "*The intellectual and social organisation of the sciences. From knowledge to wisdom: a revolution in the aims and methods of science* by Richard Whitley," *History of Political Economy*, vol. 18, Winter 1986, pp. 683–6 and "*From Knowledge to Wisdom: A Revolution in the Aims and Methods of Science* by Nicholas Maxwell," *History of Political Economy*, vol. 18, Winter 1986, pp. 683–6.

19. "*Economic history and the modern economist* by William N. Parker (ed.)," *History of Political Economy*, vol. 20, Spring 1988, pp. 152–4.

20. "*Before Adam Smith: The emergence of political economy, 1662–1776* by Terence Hutchison," *The Economic History Review*, vol. 42, November 1989, pp. 631–3.

21. "*The Popperian legacy in economics. Papers presented at a symposium in Amsterdam, December, 1985* by Neil De. Marchi (ed.)," *Journal of Economic Literature*, vol. 27, December 1989, pp. 1678–9.

22. "*Economists and the economy. The evolution of economic ideas, 1600 to the present day* by Roger Backhouse," *History of Political Economy*, vol. 22, Winter 1990, pp. 760–2.

23. "*The state and economic knowledge: The American and British experiences* by Mary O Furner and Barry Supple," *The Economic Journal*, vol. 101, November 1991, pp. 1580–2.

24. "*More heat than light. Economics as social physics: Physics as nature's economics* by Philip Mirowski," *Kyklos*, vol. 44, February 1991, pp. 131–5.

25. "*The inexact and separate science of economics* by Daniel M. Hausman," *Kyklos*, vol. 46, February 1993, pp. 132–5.

26. "*The making of an economist* by Arjo Klamer and David Colander," *Research in the History of Economic Thought and Methodology*, vol. 11, 1993, pp. 163–70.

27. "*Economics – mathematical politics or science of diminishing returns?* by Alexander Rosenberg," *Economics and Philosophy*, vol. 11, October 1995, pp. 386–91.

28. "*Economic thought in communist and post-communist Europe* by Hans-Jürgen Wagener, ed.," *History of Economic Thought Newsletter*, 66, Summer 2001, pp. 3–8.

Introduction

A. W. (Bob) Coats, 1924–2007

Roger E. Backhouse, Bruce Caldwell
Craufurd Goodwin, and Malcolm Rutherford

Bob Coats was an exceptional scholar. His work covered a wide range of periods and places, from eighteenth-century Europe to the contemporary United States. Furthermore it spanned different disciplines – economic and social history, intellectual history, philosophy of science, and the sociology of knowledge. What makes him exceptional is the way he helped open new fields of research within these areas: the study of American economics, the professionalization of economics, and the recent internationalization of economics were all fields where his work dramatically broadened the agenda for subsequent scholars. Without work such as his, these fields would have been very different indeed.

Born Alfred William Coats, Bob, as he was always called, was one of a small but remarkable group of scholars whose work dominated the history of economic thought in Britain from roughly the 1970s to the 1990s (see Goodwin 2008). But while he was very much part of this group, there was a difference: he belonged not to an economics department but to a Department of Economic and Social History, which, in the British system, identified him as a historian rather than an economist. Yet, though he deprecated his qualifications as an economist, his interests were in economics as much as history, and he described himself (with typically excessive modesty) as a marginal member of the historians' guild. His attitudes were never constrained by disciplinary boundaries. Furthermore, in that his publications took the form of articles, edited volumes, and two collections of his own papers, the structure of his CV looked much more like that of an economist than a historian.

One reason for this is that he had an inexhaustible desire to engage with other scholars. Send him a paper and a reply would come back – often with several pages of detailed handwritten comments (he never took to the word processor or e-mail). His letters did not just correct mistakes but they clearly showed the way his mind was responding to your work, encouraging further engagement. His observations could easily lead to new conclusions or modifications of previously held ones. This urge to engage with other scholars continued to the end of his life. He loved to travel and to meet new people and this continued as long as he was physically capable of doing so. The last time he attended the British History of Economic Thought conference, in Brighton in September 2007, he had a long list of people with whom he wanted to catch up. Illness did not eliminate the aim of completing the third volume of his collected papers, though in alliance with his high standards, it eventually stopped him from doing so.

1. Career

Bob's own explanation of this puzzling career, written as the introduction to the first volume of his collected papers (published in 1992 when he was sixty-eight, though far from the end of his career), goes back to his undergraduate education, disrupted by the Second World War. He had a year at the University of Exeter before entering the Royal Air Force, during which he continued his studies by correspondence course, making use of the British Council Library in Cairo. The first mention of economics in this reflection was when he wrote that his intention was to drop the subject in favor of English literature. On the end of his military service, he returned to Exeter to complete his degree in eighteen months, graduating in 1948. He gave as his reason for returning to Exeter that LSE would take him only if he were willing to take their full three-year course. He graduated as an economist, albeit one who had taken papers in economic history as part of his degree, and proceeded to a highly unstructured master's degree that left him free to read widely in the "great books" of economics, eventually being examined on John Bates Clark. Bob offered no explanation of why he had made the very significant decision to study an American economist.

The next turning point was being offered an English Speaking Union Fellowship at the University of Pittsburgh for 1950–51. This was significant not simply as Bob's first exposure to the United States, but because he encountered Bela Gold, who had come to economics after taking a degree in engineering and who was interested in bringing insights from both disciplines to bear on industrial problems. Bob took Gold's classes in production economics, his seminar in industrial economics, and, crucially, a seminar on social science research methods. This raised what Bob later described in the introduction to the first volume of his papers as "a host of searching and disquieting questions about the nature and significance of economics and the other social science disciplines." Such questions preoccupied him for much of his career, but it was Gold who persuaded Bob to write his PhD dissertation, not on John Bates Clark, whom Gold did not find interesting, but on methodological controversies in American economics around 1900. This took him not only into methodology but also into Anglo-American comparisons and eventually comparative studies across many countries.

His doctoral thesis was not written in Pittsburgh, but at Johns Hopkins where he held a junior assistantship from 1951–53. In addition to taking classes that increased his exposure to technical economics (he later recalled with gratitude "the generous C grade" that Carl Christ awarded him in mathematical economics), he attended the History of Ideas Club established by Arthur O. Lovejoy in 1923. His supervisor was Fritz Machlup. But Bob claimed that Machlup, beyond instilling in him the importance of semantics, had much less influence on his thesis than the longserving department chair, George Heberton Evans, like Gold a business economist and historian. The only economic history lectures he

attended were from T. S. Ashton, who was visiting Johns Hopkins, on England in the eighteenth century.

On the strength of a supportive reference from Ashton, Bob's first academic post was as an assistant lecturer at the University of Nottingham with promotion to a lectureship a year later. Apart from a year on a Rockefeller Fellowship (1958–59),[1] a year at the newly established University of York (UK) in 1963–64, where he was promoted to reader, numerous visiting positions in the United States,[2] and a summer at the University of Western Australia, he remained at Nottingham until he took early retirement aged fifty-eight. When he returned from York to Nottingham in 1964 it was as professor and head of the department. His career at Nottingham reflects the fate of economic history as a discipline in Britain. In Britain, unlike in the United States, economic history had established an institutional presence that was distinct from both economics and history, in independent departments, and in the decades leading up to 1970, the subject experienced a remarkable expansion (see Coleman 1987, chap. 6). Bob came to Nottingham as this expansion was getting under way. His retirement was occasioned by the decision, in the wake of funding cuts, to merge his department with history, as happened in many universities in the 1980s and 1990s, a time when the number of posts in the subject shrank. It was while he was at Nottingham that he was involved in the moves by Bob Black (at Belfast) and Donald Winch (Sussex) to establish an institutional presence for the history of economic thought in

Britain with the History of Economic Thought conference, the first of which was organized by Winch at Sussex in 1968, and the *History of Economic Thought Newsletter.*[3] He became even more heavily involved in the parallel activities in the United States – the History of Economics Society in 1973 and *HOPE.*

Early retirement did not mean retirement in what was then the conventional sense of the term. He held a fellowship at the National Humanities Center in Research Triangle Park, North Carolina, in 1983–84, and in 1984 took a position as research professor at Duke University, becoming even more fully involved with *HOPE* and the historians of economics there, and teaching courses on slavery and the economic history of the American South. To allow both himself and his wife, Sonia, to follow their different careers, they began to spend half the year at Duke and the other half in Britain. That is, when Bob was not visiting Texas at Austin (1986), La Trobe (1987), Newcastle, Australia (1987), Victoria, British Columbia (1987), Alberta (1987), the Hebrew University (1988), São Paulo (1992), Wollongong (1994), and the Australian National University (1995). In many of these he taught courses on British and American economic history, the history of economic thought, and, increasingly, methodology. In 2001–3 he taught in Nottingham again, this time a final-year module, Explanation in Economics, taught with the experimental economist Chris Starmer. His CV also lists over one hundred universities in twenty-two countries, excluding those in which he had teaching appointments, where he gave occasional lectures and seminars, many of these being after his official retirement. Eventually, ill health forced him to slow down but he continued his academic work to the end of his life.

2. Historian of Anglo-American economics

Bob developed an early interest in American economics, but this interest was always combined with three other themes that were to be characteristic of his work – the methodology of economics; the professionalization of economics; and international comparisons, particularly Anglo-American comparisons. As the title of his PhD thesis, "Methodological Controversy as an Approach to the History of American Economics, 1885–1930," indicates, the work covered both the disputes between the "new school" of German-trained economists (including Richard T. Ely and Henry Carter Adams) and their "old school" opposition (including J. L. Laughlin, Simon Newcomb, and W. G. Sumner) that were concentrated in the 1880s and 1890s, and the later disputes between institutionalists, represented by Thorstein Veblen, Wesley C. Mitchell, and John R. Commons, among others, and their more "orthodox" critics that began in the 1890s and ran through to the early 1930s. The one direct offspring from his thesis work was his article "The Influence of Veblen's Methodology" (1954), which argued that Veblen's methodology, while influential among institutionalists, was both vague and incomplete and thus responsible for the heterogeneity of the institutionalist movement and its failure to produce a coherent evolutionary economics. In later essays on the history of American economics Bob continued to stress both the importance of institutionalism within that history *and* its theoretical weaknesses and failures. Bob's other early paper, "The Historist Reaction in English Political Economy, 1870–90" (1954), provided a contrast to the American case. Historism in England, which he distinguished from German "historicism," established economic history as a distinct area in English economics, but otherwise had a much smaller impact than in the United States.

Originally, Bob had planned to use his Rockefeller year (1958–59) to work on developing his thesis into a book. According to his autobiographical essay he abandoned this plan after having reread his thesis on the boat over and deciding that the work was too "divorced from the broader intellectual, social and cultural context," an impression only reinforced by the research he conducted during that year in the Adams, Ely, and American Economic Association archives. Bob became interested in the history of the AEA; the development of official governmental roles for economists; the numerous academic freedom cases in the United States in the late 1800s; and, more generally, with the professionalization of economics as it took place in America – again in contrast to the British case. During his year in the States, Bob also met and interviewed Clarence Ayres, Joseph Dorfman, and Walter Metzger. As he wrote in his autobiographical essay, he came away with the view that the "intensity and persistence of methodological controversy among American, as against British economists" was due less to any "epistemological preoccupations" among the former than to differences in "occupational security and cultural self-assurance."

As a result of this experience, the 1960s were an immensely productive time for Bob. He wrote two papers dealing with the formation and early history of the AEA, in which Ely had a major role: "The First Two Decades of the American Economic Association" (1960) and "The American Economic Association, 1904–29" (1964). He published a paper in 1961 on the Political Economy Club, which preceded the AEA and was comprised mainly of "old school" economists; a paper in 1969 detailing the early publications of the AEA; a major paper in 1968 on the career of Henry Carter Adams as a case study of the professionalization of American economics; and in that decade several other pieces dealing with aspects of American scholarship in this period, among them "Democracy and Education: The American Experience" and "The Origins of the 'Chicago School(s)'?" It should be noted here that Henry Carter Adams is a particularly interesting case. His movement from church to academia, his writing of a widely influential piece on the role of the state, his being the subject of an intellectual freedom case, and his becoming the chief statistician for the new Interstate Commerce Commission dealing with railroad accounting and regulation, all serve to make his career a particularly illuminating one in the history of American social science. Bob wrote a book-length study of Adams, for which he could not find a publisher.

Bob was always interested in contrasting the development of the economics profession in America with the path followed in England. These differences included the central, and highly authoritative, position of Marshall in English economics, for which there was no equivalent in the United States, and the much greater sense of continuity to be found in English economics. Bob's work on this subject can be found in "The Role of Authority in the Development of British Economics" (1964), in articles on the Royal Economic Society, and in articles introducing unpublished correspondence between Ely and Marshall and unpublished correspondence of Marshall concerning the early development of the London School of Economics.

In later work, Bob not only returned to these themes but significantly expanded on them. On the topic of institutional economics, Bob wrote a stream of book reviews. One of his most highly critical reviews was of Allan Gruchy's *Contemporary Economic Thought,* a review solicited and published by Warren Samuels in 1974 in the *Journal of Economic Issues.* This resulted in Gruchy's waging a long and bitter campaign to remove Samuels from the editorship of the *JEI.* Bob also contributed a chapter assessing Clarence Ayres's place in American economics to a commemorative volume, *Science and Ceremony* (Breit and Culbertson 1976) devoted to Ayres's institutionalism. Bob argued that while Ayres had attempted to provide a philosophical foundation for institutionalism, there was little evidence that the core ideas of Ayres's system – the instrumental (or technological) theory of value – was generating much interest among the many young economists expressing dissatisfaction with economic orthodoxy.

The paper on Ayres, it might be noted, is one of a comparatively small number of Bob's papers that focused on the work of one individual. For the most part his focus was on the profession. Bob's continuing work on this can be seen in his "Professionalization of American Social Science" (1978), "Culture and the Economists: Some Reflections on Anglo-American Differences" (1980), and his contribution to the centenary of the AEA, "The American Economic Association and the Economics Profession" (1985). The last of these discusses the role of the AEA in dealing with "certain problems arising in the professionalization process," including issues of nonpartisanship, academic freedom, academic communication, proposals for certification of economists, and treatment of "heterodox" groups.

Bob's work discussed in this section is intimately related to his other research endeavors, especially his work on the sociology of knowledge and his various large projects dealing with the role of economists in government, the role of economists in international agencies, and the internationalization of economics. This work is discussed below, as it was both later in time and broader in scope than the material central to his work on Anglo-American economics.

3. Economic and social historian

Bob started his career as an economist concerned with methodological problems relating to economics in the age of John Bates Clark. He was trained by economists, albeit including Bela Gold and George Heberton Evans, two "old-fashioned" economists with an interest in business institutions and business history. His training, as well as his commitment to the history of economic thought, helps explain his feeling marginal to the economic history profession, though it does not mean his perception was correct. But this all makes it significant that, in the introduction to the second volume of his collected papers, he describes the volume as representing "an economic and social historian's approach to the history of economics." Where did this come from?

Clearly, Bob's interest in economic history began as an undergraduate, his economic history course being the one course that he recalls taking, by correspondence, during the Second World War. He attributed his interest in eighteenth-century England to hearing T. S. Ashton's lectures while studying at Johns Hopkins. However, his more systematic study of economic history would appear to have come, not from his postgraduate work, but from his early teaching experience at Nottingham, preparation for which took, as he put it, "considerable time." There, he started out teaching The Development of the World Economy, 1850–1950, a standard course for those who took degrees in economic history during that era.[4] During this period he developed an interest in the relationship between economics and policy that resulted in his replacing this with a course on economic thought and policy, 1660–1848. Out of this emerged a series of articles. In 1958–60 he published articles on mercantilism, mid-eighteenth-century attitudes to labor, and eighteenth-century attitudes to the poor laws, in economic history journals (the *Scandinavian Economic History Review* and the *Economic History Review).* Another article from this period dealt with Adam Smith, but this was also aimed at historians, being published in *Renaissance and Modern Studies* in 1961. He also wrote about the importance of business records for the economic historian, perhaps reflecting the early influence of Gold and Evans.

As its title, "In Defence of Heckscher and the Idea of Mercantilism," suggests, Bob's first paper on mercantilism was a response to an ongoing debate, concerned not with uncovering new evidence but with reinterpreting the evidence that had been amassed by Eli Heckscher and others. Developing his ideas in this way, through responding to others, was typical of the way he worked. So too was his focus on the different perspectives through which historians, economists, and historians of economics would typically come to a problem. He presented his own perspective as being that of the intellectual historian. He believed more than most historians that ideas were important, concerned to find links between events and policies. But neither did he accept the economist's focus on the autonomous development of ideas: he believed that the mercantilists deserved more respect than most economists paid them. Mercantilism as a topic involving politics, economics, and economic ideas, was ideal for bringing out these general issues. Another theme that proved important for his subsequent work was his concern with what happened to economic ideas as they were applied to policy. There was, however, a marked difference in approach. The mercantilist period had been the subject of extensive, detailed historical research, with the result that Bob's analysis and his historical insights relied very much on the research that had already been undertaken on unearthing the primary materials. In contrast, the projects he organized on the twentieth century, because they were concerned with opening up new fields, often involved establishing basic facts (such as how many economists were employed in government) and developing new frameworks within which the material could be analyzed.

These various concerns were linked. Bob largely accepted the conclusion that if attention is confined to economic policy, the idea of mercantilism is unhelpful: there is no body of policy enactments that can be fitted under this label. Where it might make sense to talk of mercantilism is at the level of economic doctrines.

Though the relevant writings were prescientific and though events exerted a significant influence on policies, causing considerable variation across time and place, they were far from unsystematic. In the late-seventeenth-century literature on the East India Company, for example, he found it "striking," as he explained in the Heckscher essay, that certain "accepted maxims of trade" persisted "in the face of theoretical criticism and changing economic circumstances." Bob thus concluded that the important aspect of Heckscher's book was not that it answered but that it identified the questions that needed to be answered about how ideas and policy were linked. This conclusion was as much a criticism of traditional history of doctrine as of the refusal of historians to take ideas sufficiently seriously. Indeed, in his later writing, when he engaged more with historians of economics, his most critical remarks were directed against those who sought to read historical texts as they would read contemporary economics.

Around 1960 his interests began to move more squarely into intellectual history and the early history of the AEA, the result of the 1958 Fulbright scholarship that enabled him to supplement his thesis with more archival work in the United States.[5] In retrospect, despite his exposure to Arthur O. Lovejoy's intellectual history seminar at Johns Hopkins, he saw this year as a turning point in his attitude to the history of economic thought: this is when he began to view it, as he put it, from the viewpoint of an economic and social historian.

Bob's work on Anglo-American economics and the economics profession may have been legitimate work for an economic and social historian to undertake (T. S. Ashton encouraged it) but, as he acknowledged, it took him away from the mainstream of British economic history. Rather than continue the path toward becoming a leading authority on British economic history, he adopted a strategy of pursuing simultaneously his studies of Britain and the United States. As the pathbreaking American work developed, and as his Anglo-American comparisons took him more firmly into the history of economic thought and circles dominated by economists, his contributions to British economic and social history inevitably became more sporadic. During the 1960s he published an article on the classical economists and the laborer in a volume on the industrial revolution edited by two historians. In the early 1970s he edited a volume, *The Classical Economists and Economic Policy,* and published "Contrary Moralities: Plebs, Paternalists, and Political Economists" in an influential historical journal *(Past and Present);* Bob engaged with leading historians, E. P. Thompson and Elizabeth Fox-Genovese, and he edited a multivolume collection of primary sources on poverty in the Victorian age, but it is clear that he was moving in other directions. His publications for the 1960s appeared mostly in economics journals and, from 1969, there was *HOPE,* to which he contributed the first article and with which he became heavily involved.[6] Thus, although he continued to write on classical economists and policy, and occasionally published papers in the proceedings of economic history conferences, he wrote about the subject primarily in places such as a book edited by an economist at the Institute of Economic Affairs, and in *HOPE* or publications marking the bicentenary of the *Wealth of Nations.* He had become a professional historian of economics (albeit with the perspective of an economic and social historian) rather than an economic and social historian who also had an interest in the history of ideas.

If Bob's published research took him away from the mainstream of economic history in the United Kingdom, the same cannot be said of the many PhD theses he supervised at Nottingham, or of his broader professional activities. The one that is probably most familiar to readers of *HOPE,* and closest to Bob's own interests in the history of economics, is that of John Maloney on the professionalization of economics in the late nineteenth century (which formed the basis for Maloney 1985). But more typical of theses he supervised were "The Agrarian Revolution in N. Nottinghamshire, 1750–1900" (A. C. Pickersgill), "The Derby Borough Development Committee, 1906–1933" (J. M. Bonsall), "A History of Trade Unionism in the Hosiery Industry from the 18th Century to the Present Day" (R. I. Gurnham), and "The Economic and Social Development of the Leicestershire and S. Derbyshire Coalfield, 1550–1914" (C. P. Griffin). "Harvest Technology and Labour Supply in Britain, 1790–1870" (E. J. T. Collins) involved both unearthing new historical data and applying economic concepts. "Origins of Enterprise: A Study of Social Mobility in the Industrial Revolution" (K. Honeyman) fell squarely in the field of social history. He, together with Stanley Chapman, trained many of those who went on to staff Britain's economic history departments.[7] Given these interests, it is not surprising that he was a mainstay of the Midlands economic historians, and was close to business historians such as Peter Payne and Sidney Pollard.

4. Establishing a community of historians of economics

Early signs of a crisis looming in the history of economic thought appeared in the 1950s when Bob was still a graduate student in economics at Johns Hopkins University. By the end of the decade the subject seemed increasingly unwelcome at professional meetings and in the mainstream journals. Most troubling, several highly respected young scholars in the field were denied tenure in prominent economics departments, and the prospects for newly minted PhDs seemed dim. Even economic history, the subdiscipline most sympathetic toward the history of economic thought, was just entering the cliometric revolution and was growing increasingly uncomfortable with its "literary" cousin, something of which Bob was very conscious.[8]

In response to the challenge presented to the history of economic thought within the economics discipline, conversations began on both sides of the Atlantic about what could be done and how to mount a counterattack against the growing "disrespect." The objectives of the British and Americans were very similar but the strategy and style were rather different. In Britain improved networking and informal interaction were the main goals. The *HET Newsletter* was started by Bob Black, Bob Coats, and Donald Winch, and annual meetings, informal by American standards, began in 1968 with a conference organized by Winch at Sussex. Bernard Corry and Mark Blaug considered starting a journal but rejected the idea in part because it might lure the historians away from the mainstream of the discipline and justify the mainstream in excluding historians from its midst. The only substantial new publication that emerged from the ferment in Britain was a guide to archival resources for the history of economic thought in the United Kingdom, prepared by Paul Sturgess but stimulated very much by Coats.[9] In North America, by contrast, geographical dispersion seemed to call for more structure and a society was formed in 1973. The first issue of the first journal in the field, *HOPE,* appeared in 1969, with a lead article by Bob. A second journal *(History of Economics Society Bulletin,* which later became the *Journal of the History of Economic Thought)* was started later by the new society. It was determined that it was more important to direct available energies toward the actual collection of archival resources in North America than to the preparation of a North American guide, and the Economists Papers Project at Duke was a result.

By the 1960s Bob Coats was resolutely transatlantic, and he became distinctive by taking an active part in promoting and contributing to developmental efforts in the history of economic thought in the United States as well as in Britain. In addition to his extensive efforts in Britain, he was the first non-North American to be elected president of the History of Economics Society (1986), he was elected a Distinguished Fellow of the HES in 1996, and he was a founding member of the board of *HOPE.* From 1991 until 1994 he was an associate editor of *HOPE* while he held a parttime appointment at Duke. His influence on the journal was mainly as a frequent referee. He read a total of 340 papers for *HOPE* from 1968 through 2002, nearly one a month and almost 10 percent of the nearly 4,000 that have been received and refereed to date. This is a record unlikely to be equaled or exceeded by anyone any time soon. All referee correspondence received by *HOPE,* whether pertaining to rejected or accepted papers, is placed in the Rare Book, Manuscript, and Special Collections Library at Duke. This means that there are close to one thousand pages of comment from Coats over more than three decades, telling us as much about the referee and his views about the field in general as about the papers under review. (Referee reports are, when used judiciously, an exceptionally rich resource for the study of the history of the history of economic thought.)

Why did *HOPE* use Bob so much as a referee? Memory and a selective rereading of his reports suggest several reasons. First, he was remarkably eclectic in his tastes and amazingly widely read in the literature. He could comment knowledgeably on the mercantilists, the classical economists, American economics, British economics, the sociology and philosophy of economics, and the place of economists in government. His interest in these areas, and others, waxed and waned but he seldom put one totally aside. Many authors must have felt embarrassment to receive an anonymous report from Bob with a literature review of their subject much more thorough and penetrating than that contained in their paper. Second, although he was fearless about entering new areas of inquiry, stimulated sometimes by a paper to evaluate, he was always quick to say if he felt he was not competent to act as judge in particular cases. Third, he was prompt and reliable, qualities dearly beloved of editors as well as of authors. Fourth, he was firm but constructive in his appraisals. He always wrote a report suitable to be passed along to the author. *HOPE* has had from the start a policy of allowing authors to "face their accusers" rather than producing for the authors sugar-coated summaries. Bob's reports fitted well with this policy. He was concerned above all to help an author improve a manuscript; if he was critical he made clear why. Fifth, he was a tough but fair grader. Of the 340 papers he was sent for evaluation, he recommended that 57 be accepted outright and 159 be rejected. He returned 39 as beyond his competence and recommended serious revision of 85, usually with guidance as to how this should be done. This reflects a balance in the disposition of papers very close to that made by the journal overall during its existence.

What other reflections are stimulated by a perusal of the voluminous Coats correspondence with *HOPE?* His love for travel and new scenery stands out. His referee cards contain a string of address changes: always Nottingham as home base, but then Rhode Island, Atlanta, Western Australia, New South Wales, the Netherlands, Texas, British Columbia, and many more. He was always upbeat and optimistic; very little whining ever. He was endlessly curious and anxious to connect with young scholars so that he could see what was happening on the intellectual frontier. He was comfortable with a wide range of people, from senior political figures to big shots in economics and leaders of other disciplines.

5. Policy making and the sociology of the modern economics profession

Bob long had an interest in the sociology of economics, much of his work on American and British economics in the nineteenth century and earlier having been concerned with this, as parts 1 and 2 of the second volume of his collected essays clearly show. However, the first History of Economic Thought conference at Sussex marked a turning point in the style and coverage of Bob's research, toward exploring the role of economists in government from the Second World War onward, from where he went on to a series of collaborative international comparative projects on the modern economics profession. The first of these started from his own work on the role of economists in the British and Dutch governments, which he described, in a 12 March 1973 letter to Lionel Robbins, as "a by-product of that meeting."[10] The British side was financed for several years by the SSRC (which later became the ESRC) and involved a research assistant (Alan Booth) working in London to access government papers, covered by the Official Secrets Act. The Dutch side, which arose, in 1973, out of a fellowship that Bob held at the Netherlands Institute for Advanced Study, was funded by the Dutch research organization, ZWO, and the Ford Foundation, and it also involved a research assistant, Marie Bemelmans-Videc. One part of this research involved the idea, possibly suggested by Alec Cairncross or John Jewkes,[11] of bringing together all the economists who had been head of the Government Economic Service since its beginning in 1941, something that was then still possible. Thus in April 1973, at the Reform Club in London, there took place a dinner at which Lionel Robbins, James Meade, Robert Hall, John Jewkes, Alec Cairncross, and Douglas MacDougall discussed their experiences. It is perhaps worth noting that Robbins initially declined to come, on the grounds that he had already said what he had to say in his autobiography, but Bob persuaded him that the point was to foster discussion between those who had held this position at different times. The discussion was recorded and transcribed, but not published, though it no doubt fed into Bob's research.

In 1973 Bob published a short piece in the *HET Newsletter* outlining this project and its importance. Though much had been published on economists in government, he argued that there was a dearth of *systematic* research on the subject. "Unsystematic" research included the memoirs of those who had worked in government, such as Robbins. The questions he argued needed to be answered included finding out the skills that economists brought to bear on policy making, the extent to which economists constituted a quasi-autonomous professional group, and the influence on government economists of factors within and without the discipline. The questions that most concerned him, though, were what governments wanted from the economists they employed, and how they communicated with others in the administrative hierarchy.[12] He ended with a cry for help.

A year after the Reform Club dinner Bob organized, with Alec Cairncross, an international conference in Royaumont, near Paris, sponsored by the Ford Foundation, bringing together experienced policy makers from six countries. He had plans to publish the proceedings, but despite negotiations with several publishers, including discussions of publishing them in *HOPE* and with Duke University Press, these came to nothing. In November 1976 he described the process of finding a publisher as "dispiriting" in a letter seeking advice about publication from the SSRC. However, assisted by the Ford Foundation, Bob organized two further conferences, the first in Bellagio in 1977 and the second in Dubrovnik. These differed in approach. Whereas bringing together policy makers had helped define the questions that needed to be asked (and of course provided much information), in these conferences he turned to academics who would undertake research rather than practitioners who would reflect on their experiences.[13] Substantial fees ($900) were paid to contributors. As he wrote in a draft proposal to the Ford Foundation, "It is only Americans who expect large sums for such purposes. However we are prepared to adopt American standards where appropriate."[14] The results were published as *Economists in Government: An International Comparative Study* (1981).

His next two projects followed up some suggestions made while he had been preparing for this conference. As items in Bob's papers show, in November 1974 Craufurd Goodwin had suggested that he bring in less developed countries, and several months later David Bell, a senior officer of the Ford Foundation, had offered to Bob the following criticism of his project:

> The framework is almost exclusively national – how economists relate to their own governments. Would it not be appropriate to recognize that in today's world government economists do a lot of international work, and to bring that aspect of their involvement into prominence? I have in mind such things as the OECD committees at which economists from various governments explain (and defend) their governments' policies, GATT and other tariff negotiations, etc, etc.

Whether stimulated by this remark or not, Bob's second project focused on exactly this topic: the role of economists in international agencies. Again, he started with a conference, this time in Washington, D. C., in December 1983, at which were presented papers by economists with long experience of working in the IMF, the World Bank, GATT, the OECD, and the United Nations. The proceedings were published as *The Role of Economists in International Agencies: An Exploratory Study* (1986).

Bob's projects took a different turn in the 1990s, when he conceived the idea of investigating the internationalization of the economics profession, turning to academic economics as well as economists in government. As before, this took the form of a series of meetings, though this time sessions at HES meetings, where preliminary papers were presented so as to set the agenda for those contributions that had not yet been written. He exerted pressure on contributors to address common themes and to find ways to undertake statistical analysis. Over a period of years he agonized over whether the process under investigation should be called "internationalization" or "Americanization," his preferred title until near the end being "the international spread of American-style professional economics." It was eventually published in 1997 under the title *The Post-1945 Internationalization of Economics.* Although the United States was clearly central, the papers covered several continents: Britain, Australia, India, Japan, and Brazil. There was also an attempt to tie it in with previous projects through papers (by eminent practitioners) on the International Monetary Fund and the World Bank. It was followed up shortly afterward (after a conference of course) with a volume in 2000 that sought systematically to cover Western Europe.

Bob was not the first to organize themed academic conferences. However, he developed this method as a way of coordinating research, developing the questions, selecting participants, and trying to develop methods that would answer the questions he had posed. He had been involved, with R. D. Collison Black and Craufurd Goodwin, in organizing the conference on the marginal revolution, at Bellagio in 1971, the papers from which appeared in *HOPE* and as a book. With his projects on economists in government and, later, internationalization, he developed the technique of holding a small preliminary meeting to thrash out questions and methods, prior to the final meeting at which the final papers would be developed. It was a method that reflected his own passion for engagement with other people and their ideas. Throughout these projects, the questions that he posed related to the sociology of the profession, contributing to the opening up of that field.

6. Methodology

Though Bob's interest in methodology dated back to his dissertation days, professional interest in the area among historians of economic thought began to pick up in the late 1960s and early 1970s. At least part of the impetus was changes that were occurring within the philosophy of science, where the influence of positivism (or logical empiricism) was waning. Thomas Kuhn, Karl Popper, and

Imre Lakatos were offering alternative accounts to the "received view," each with varying emphases on description and prescription. In the mid-1970s new voices were added, as philosophers of science like Alex Rosenberg and Daniel Hausman began to analyze the structure and nature of theorizing in economics. By the 1980s journals like *Economics and Philosophy* and *Methodus* (later the *Journal of Economic Methodology)* began publication, and books and articles by economists writing about issues in methodology began appearing with increasing frequency.

Bob participated in the renaissance of methodology in a variety of ways. In the first instance he was a trend-spotter, or, at times, a path-breaker. Thus although he was not the first to introduce Thomas Kuhn's work to economists (he generously pointed out in his own article that Gordon 1965 took precedence), he was the first explicitly to put the question, "Is there a 'structure of scientific revolutions' in economics?" Though appreciative of the fact that Kuhn had provided an important new way to think about the development and nature of the scientific enterprise, Bob did not think that Kuhn's framework could be readily applied to economics. (The Keynesian revolution was the only episode that he thought fitted Kuhn's framework.) He was far more receptive to the potential applicability of Imre Lakatos's "methodology of scientific research programs" to economics, and again he recognized its importance early on. In 1972 Spiro Latsis, writing in a philosophy journal, had been the first to apply Lakatos's approach to an area of economics, the theory of the firm. Bob was among the first (the other commentator was Fritz Machlup) to comment on Latsis's paper and the applicability of the Lakatosian framework. Noting that Latsis's treatment was philosophical rather than historical, Bob thought that the Lakatosian framework could be useful in understanding certain historical episodes in economics, and offered as a brief example the early development of consumer choice theory in the United States.

He developed that example in much more detail in perhaps his most important methodological contribution, "Economics and Psychology: The Death and Resurrection of a Research Programme" (1976). The paper appeared in a book edited by Latsis and containing papers from a conference that specifically attempted to address the relevance of Lakatos's and Kuhn's work for economics. In his paper Bob traced the turn-of-the-century American debates over the relevance of psychology to the theory of choice, and offered a "rational reconstruction" of the "hard cores" and "positive heuristics" of the two major rival approaches. Bob's understanding of history of both British and American economics of the period enabled him to give an account that was historically insightful into the decline of psychology in economics as well as creating an exemplary Lakatosian reconstruction. This sort of work would be replicated by many others as the decade progressed, reaching its culmination perhaps in Mark Blaug's book, *The Methodology of Economics* (1980), the last third of which is given over to the reconstruction and assessment of various areas of economics along Lakatosian lines. But Bob's study was the first.

Another role that Bob played in the advancement of methodology was the prosaic but essential one of review writer. He wrote two major review articles, one published in *Kyklos* in 1982 that treated books by Mark Blaug, Homa Katouzian, and Ian Stewart, and another in 1986, also in *Kyklos*, that reviewed collections of articles edited by Bruce Caldwell, Daniel Hausman, Alfred Eichner, Peter Wiles, and Guy Routh, as well as a book by J. J. Klant. Two things stand out in the reviews. First, though Bob would of course offer penetrating assessments of the books under review, he also provided footnote citations to many other books and articles that spoke to whatever issue was at hand. His reviews were guides to the books under review, but they had the additional virtue of positioning those books within the wider literature. Second, it is clear from his responses to the books that he saw increased understanding and better communication to be the main goals of methodological work. As a result, he had little patience with writers whose principal use for methodology was as a cudgel to bash mainstream economics.

Another role was that of critical commentator on a particular position. The chief example here is Bob's reaction to Deirdre McCloskey's "rhetoric of economics" approach, a topic on which he wrote three times, in 1984 (with Bruce Caldwell), 1987, and 1988. As might be expected, Bob was not sympathetic. As he made clear in the 1987 article, he did not take well to McCloskey's "exaggerated and misdirected attack on economic methodology," that is, McCloskey's claim that all methodology was modernist and prescriptivist, and that the advent of the rhetorical approach meant the end of methodology. He viewed the study of economic rhetoric "as subordinate to the study of its intellectual content and the social and historical context in which it occurs." Bob thought that the rhetorical approach could benefit from integration with sociological work on the intellectual and social organization of science, and in this regard was a frequent promoter of the investigations that had been done by the sociologist Richard Whitley, especially Whitley 1984.

Bob's final role was to offer assessments of the contributions of various individuals to the methodological literature. He wrote appreciations for Fritz Machlup, T. W. Hutchison, and Daniel Fusfeld, the most substantial of these being his masterful forty-two-page paper on Hutchison, published in 1983. There Bob traced the development of Hutchison's ideas, but he also put his subject squarely within the context of his times, detailing the work both of his sources and of his opponents. The title of the paper tells it all: "Half a Century of Methodological Controversy in Economics as Reflected in the Work of T. W. Hutchison."

If anyone ever wanted to provide an historical account of the growth of interest in methodological thought that took place within economics in the second half of the twentieth century, or of the methodological debates that informed the period, the person would be well advised simply to study Bob Coats's articles, not neglecting his footnotes. He was a player but also always a chronicler, and a fair-minded one at that.

7. Conclusion

Bob described himself as an "economist watcher." This role aptly sums up much of his work. It captures the variety of perspectives from which he looked at economics – as historian, as sociologist, and as methodologist. But he did not just "watch" economists. He engaged with them, perhaps best illustrated by his bringing prominent policy advisers together to talk about their profession. This passion for engagement with others, reflected in the three hundred or so book reviews that he wrote, may be one reason, apart from his belief that it would raise productivity, for arguing that there was not enough joint authorship in the history of economics. It was not accidental that he considered conferences the way to get projects started and that he posed questions that were so large that collaborative work was a necessity.

He had a profound effect on the fields in which he worked, many of which were transformed or given new impetus by his work, and the breadth of his interests was such that few scholars will be able to appreciate the full picture. Much of his work, such as that on late-nineteenth-century American economics, has not been superseded. So much has been written on some of the fields he explored, including the study of the economics profession in the period since the Second World War, that it is hard to recall how much of an innovator he was. But what many of us will remember is not just his published work but the way he was always full of enthusiasm for new ideas, wanting to find out what we were doing and encouraging us to think in new ways and try new methods. His passion for engaging with other people was infectious and his comments and advice could change the direction of other people's research. This method of working made him many friends. He will be greatly missed.

Notes

Though we have all read and discussed the whole article, Backhouse bears prime responsibility for the opening paragraphs and sections 1, 3, and 5; Caldwell for section 6; Goodwin for a large part of section 4; and Rutherford for section 2. We are indebted to Alan Booth, Mary Morgan, and Donald Winch for valuable comments on previous drafts and to staff at the Manuscripts and Special Collections section at the University of Nottingham for providing access to materials held there.

1 During this year he met with Clarence Ayres, in Austin, Texas; studied Henry Carter Adams's papers in Michigan; consulted the AEA papers at Northwestern; and visited Columbia.

2 Summer visits to Columbia (1962) and Wisconsin (1963 and 1964), and longer visits to the University of Virginia (1962–63), Stanford (fall 1967), Texas at Austin (fall 1978), and Emory (winter-spring 1979).

3 HET in the United Kingdom appears unique in having an annual conference and a newsletter but without having any formal society.

4 American readers need to be reminded that British degrees were much more specialized than American ones, students typically choosing their major as part of their initial application to university. Undergraduate teaching could therefore reach a more advanced level.

5 See note 1 above.

6 See section 4.

7 Others include Colin Griffin and Peter Payne. A complete list has not been found, though his CV states that he supervised twenty PhD and seven MA theses.

8 When Bob met Craufurd Goodwin for the first time at an Economic History Association meeting in 1958, both were delighted to find a kindred spirit as they recognized the cool reception for their subject all around them.

9 On 12 October 1966, Bob wrote to Donald Winch seeking advice on a directory of "unpublished manuscripts."

10 The sense in which it was a by-product is not made clear.
11 Cairncross is the likely suspect, but there is one letter in Bob's papers from March 1972 suggesting it might have been Jewkes.
12 His research assistant, Alan Booth, recalls these being the key questions Bob would pose when he met him once a fortnight at the Treasury.
13 Participants at Bellagio included S. Ambirajan, William J. Barber, Trond Bergh, Franco Ferraresi, Paulo Roberto Haddad, Egon Kemenes, Ryutaro Komiya, A. Petridis, Craufurd Goodwin (then at the Ford Foundation), and Coats.
14 Given that he had complained that it was difficult to find people prepared to commit to undertaking research, perhaps this shows that he had learned from the subject he was studying, but to which he claimed to be an outsider. A condition for payment was that papers were circulated some weeks before the conference.

References

Black, R. D. C., A. W. Coats, and C. D. W. Goodwin, eds. 1972. *The Marginal Revolution in Economics.* Durham, N. C.: Duke University Press.

Blaug, M. 1976. Kuhn versus Lakatos, or Paradigms versus Research Programmes in the History of Economics. In *Method and Appraisal in Economics,* edited by S. Latsis, 149–80. Cambridge: Cambridge University Press.

____. 1980. *The Methodology of Economics: How Economists Explain.* Cambridge: Cambridge University Press.

Breit, W., and W. P. Culbertson Jr., eds. 1976. *Science and Ceremony: The Institutional Economics of C. E. Ayres.* Austin: University of Texas Press.

Caldwell, B., and A. W. Coats. 1984. Comment on McCloskey: The Rhetoric of Economics. *Journal of Economic Literature* 22:575–78.

Coleman, D. C. 1987. *History and the Economic Past: An Account of the Rise and Decline of Economic History in Britain.* Oxford: Clarendon Press.

Goodwin, C. D. W. 2008. History of Economic Thought. In *The New Palgrave: A Dictionary of Economics,* edited by S. Durlauf and L. Blume. 2nd ed. London: Palgrave.

Gordon, D. F. 1965. The Role of the History of Economic Thought in the Understanding of Modern Economic Theory. *American Economic Review* 55.1–2:119–27.

Latsis, S. 1972. Situational Determinism in Economics. *British Journal of the Philosophy of Science* 23:207–45.

Maloney, J. 1985. *Marshall, Orthodoxy, and the Professionalization of Economics.* Cambridge: Cambridge University Press.

McCloskey, D. N. 1983. The Rhetoric of Economics. *Journal of Economic Literature* 21:481–517.

Whitley, R. 1984. *The Intellectual and Social Organization of the Sciences.* Oxford: Oxford University Press.

Appendix 1:
Selected Bibliography of A. W. (Bob) Coats

[Note: Items marked with a single asterisk are also in *On the History of Economic Thought,* vol. 1 of Coats's *British and American Economic Essays* (London: Routledge, 1992); items marked with two asterisks are also in *The Sociology and Professionalization of Economics,* vol. 2 of Coats's *British and American Economic Essays* (London: Routledge,1993).]

1954

*The Historist Reaction in English Political Economy, 1870–90. *Economica,* n.s., 21.82:143–53.

The Influence of Veblen's Methodology. *Journal of Political Economy* 62.6:529–37.

1958

*In Defence of Heckscher and the Idea of Mercantilism. *Scandinavian Economic History Review* 2:73–87.

1960

**The First Two Decades of the American Economic Association. *American Economic Review* 50.4:555–74.

1961

**The Political Economy Club: A Neglected Episode in American Economic Thought. *American Economic Review* 51.4:624–37.

1962

*Adam Smith: The Modern Re-appraisal. *Renaissance and Modern Studies,* November, 25–48.

Democracy and Education: The American Experience. *Bulletin of the British Association for American Studies.*

1963

**The American Economic Association, 1904–29. *American Economic Review* 54.4, pt. 1, 261–85.

**The Origins of the 'Chicago School(s)'? *Journal of Political Economy* 71.5:487–93.

1964

**The Role of Authority in the Development of British Economics. *Journal of Law and Economics* 7:85–106.

1967

*The Classical Economists and the Labourer. In *Land, Labour, and Population in the Industrial Revolution,* edited by E. L. Jones and G. E. Mingay. London: Edward Arnold.

1968

*Henry Carter Adams: A Case Study in the Emergence of the Social Sciences in the United States, 1850–1900. *Journal of American Studies* 2.2:177–97.

**The Origins and Early Development of the Royal Economic Society. *Economic Journal* 78:349–71.

1969

**The American Economic Association's Publications: An Historical Perspective. *Journal of Economic Literature* 7.1:57–68.

**Is There a "Structure of Scientific Revolutions" in Economics? *Kyklos* 22: 289–96.

1971

The Classical Economists and Economic Policy. London: Methuen.

1972

Contrary Moralities: Plebs, Paternalists and Political Economists. *Past and Present* 54:130–33.

1973

The Interpretation of Mercantilist Economics: Some Historiographical Problems. *HOPE* 5.2:485–95.

The Role of Economists in Government. *History of Economic Thought Newsletter* 10:19–23.

Poverty in the Victorian Age: Debates on the Issue from Nineteenth Century Critical Journals, ed. 4 vols. Farnborough.

1974

Economic Ideas and Policy in England, c. 1550–1750. In *Proceedings of the Fifth International Congress of Economic History, Leningrad, 1970.* Vol. 1. Moscow.

Review of *Contemporary Economic Thought,* by A. G. Gruchy. *Journal of Economic Issues* 8.3:597–605.

Situational Determinism in Economics: The Implications of Latsis's Argument for the Historian of Economics. *British Journal of the Philosophy of Science* 25:285–88.

1975

*Adam Smith and the Mercantile System. In *Essays on Adam Smith*, edited by Andrew S. Skinner and Thomas Wilson. Oxford: Clarendon Press.

1976

Economics and Psychology: The Death and Resurrection of a Research Programme. In *Method and Appraisal in Economics,* edited by S. Latsis, 43–64. Cambridge: Cambridge University Press.

History and Theory in Adam Smith's Treatment of the Mercantile System. In *200 Jahre Adam Smith Reichtum der Nationen,* edited by P. Thal. Berlin: Akademic-Verlag.

1978

Method and Professionalism in Economics: A Subordinate Theme in Machlup's Writings. In *Breadth and Depth in Economics: Fritz Machlup, the Man and His Ideas,* edited by J. S. Dreyer, 23–35. Lexington, Va.: Lexington Books.

The Professionalization of American Social Science: A Review of *Advocacy and Objectivity,* by M. O. Furner. *Journal of American Studies* 12.2:227–33.

1980

**The Culture and the Economists: Some Reflections on Anglo-American Differences. *HOPE* 12.4:588–609.

1981

Economists in Government: An International Comparative Study, ed. Durham, N. C.: Duke University Press.

1982

The Methodology of Economics: Some Recent Contributions. *Kyklos* 35: 310–21.

1983

Half a Century of Methodological Controversy in Economics as Reflected in the Work of T. W. Hutchison. In *Methodological Controversy in Economics: Historical Essays in Honor of T. W. Hutchison,* edited by A. W. Coats, 1–42. Greenwich, Conn.: JAI Press.

1985

**The American Economic Association and the Economics Profession. *Journal of Economic Literature* 23.4:1697–727.

1986

Economic Methodology: Theory, Practice, and the Current State of Economics. *Kyklos* 39:109–15.

*The Role of Economists in International Agencies: An Exploratory Study*ed. New York: Praeger.

1987

Further Comments on McCloskey's Argument. *Eastern Economic Journal* 13 (July-September):305–6.

1988

Economic Rhetoric: The Social and Historical Context. In *The Consequences of Economic Rhetoric,* edited by A. Klamer, D. N. McCloskey and R. M. Solow, 64–84. Cambridge: Cambridge University Press.

1992

British and American Economic Essays. Vol. 1, *On the History of Economic Thought.* London: Routledge.

1993

British and American Economic Essays. Vol. 2, *The Sociology and Professionalization of Economics.* London: Routledge.

1997

Fusfeld on Methodology. In *Borderlands of Economics: Essays in Honor of Daniel R. Fusfeld,* edited by N. Aslanbeigui and Y. B. Choi. London: Routledge.

The Post-1945 Internationalization of Economics, ed. Durham, N. C.: Duke University Press. Supplement to vol. 28 of *HOPE.*

2000

The Development of Economics in Western Europe since 1945, ed. London: Routledge.

Part I

Articles

1 Memoirs of an economist watcher

A. W. Bob Coats

I. Family background; formative social and political attitudes

Oddly enough, my first clear recollection of an encounter with an economic proposition dates from the age of six or seven, when my father (who died suddenly from the pneumonia when I was eight) casually remarked that the Colman Mustard Company derived most of its profits from the residue people left on their plates. Unfortunately at the time I did not appreciate the analytical subtlety of this observation. Nor, I suspect, did my father, who probably only wanted to particularize the familiar maxim: waste not, want not. Nevertheless, the point evidently stayed in my mind, though I cannot claim it as the origin of my subsequent fascination with economics. The evolution of my attitudes to economics will be considered later. First, however, let me briefly sketch some relevant features of my personal and socio-economic background, which may shed some light on my subsequent intellectual activities.[1]

Though settled in an undistinguished London suburb, now a thriving center of Asian culture and politics, both my parents came from West country farming stock and had a practical, down-to-earth acceptance of the social as well as the natural world. To the best of my memory ours was an unanalytical, even unintellectual household, though book-loving, and – mainly through my mother – with a strong belief in the value of education at all levels. As a child I spent many family vacations on an uncle's farm; but despite occasional references to the farming community's hardships during the depression of the thirties, my parent's non-ideological Toryism was unshakable. I enjoyed a happy, modest but comfortable upbringing cushioned against contemporary economic distress by my father's pension and my mother's salary as a teacher. Real incomes were stable or rising for those in employment or on fixed incomes, owing to low or falling living cost and low interest rates, which fueled a significant housing boom.

As a schoolboy I was vaguely aware of poverty and hardships elsewhere, especially in the South Wales mining communities, for at school we periodically collected shoes, clothing, and other items for families suffering from unemployment. Yet although the conditions were conductive to open class conflict, especially in the so-called depressed areas, in my hometown there was remarkably little evidence of radicalism. The local populace was largely indifferent to or contemptuous of the vocal minority of Mosleyite "blackshirts;" and my closest personal encounter with communism came from an embittered uncle (ironically a skilled craftsman in the prosperous building trade) whose periodic outbursts against the capitalist system were generally treated by his family as tiresome irritants, if not evidence of mental imbalance!

Looking back, I am mildly embarrassed to realize how little impact contemporary economic, social, and political issues had on my adolescent outlook. The failure of the existing socio-economic order should have been obvious enough. But while struggling with my conventional Christian upbringing en route to a mature agnosticism, I had (and still have) little patience with doctrinaire socialism or communism. I have never been, nor ever will be, one of the "men of system," to cite Adam Smith's phrase. I recall reading, probably in the early 1940s, a number of outspoken indictments of the British governing class in the series of bright yellow-jacketed Left Book Club volumes published by Victor Gollanz. The volume in that series that impressed me most at that time was rather different, i.e. *The Socialist Sixth of the World* (1939), by Hewlett Johnson, the so-called 'Red Dean of Canterbury.' Possibly I was more impressed by his high ecclesiastical status than by the quality of his arguments and evidence. Although warning against the dangers of presenting "too rosy and optimistic [a] view of life in the Soviet Union" (ibid., p. 18), he nevertheless painted a glowing picture of an alternative form of society that was both more productive and morally superior to capitalism, which, he claimed, unlike the Soviet Union, involved the denial of justice, freedom, opportunities for creative living, and fellowship. Johnson's naive Christian Socialist plea for Anglo-Soviet cooperation was, of course, far more acceptable during the war once the Russians became our allies. And doubtless it provided an early stimulus to my thinking about comparative socio-economic systems.

During the 'thirties the evils of the Soviet regime were insufficiently publicized in Britain and, when publicized, insufficiently heeded. Likewise, far too little was known of the horrors and dangers of Nazism, other than its threatening territorial aggrandizement. Ours was a complacent, head-in-the-sand society, admirably characterized in the ironic adaptation of Kipling's poem: "If you can keep your head when all around you are losing theirs, ... maybe you haven't fully grasped the situation!" Eventually it became clear even to the government that war was both necessary and unavoidable. But unlike the Americans' protracted crisis and soul-searching over Vietnam, Britain's declaration of war in 1939 posed a profound moral dilemma only to confirmed pacifists. It was obviously a "just war." Fortunately, I was too young for military service when hostilities broke out. It never occurred to me to try to avoid enlistment, however, and in due course, after one year at university (of which more anon), I volunteered and was "called up" for aircrew training in the Royal Air Force (RAF), the least unattractive branch of His Majesty's armed forces.

II. Wartime experiences, postwar problems, democratic socialist beliefs

During my military service I travelled widely in Britain, South Africa, and the Middle East – no doubt in the process getting the bug that helps to explain my subsequent academic restlessness. The places I saw, the books I read, and the people I met in the years away from "civvy street" greatly expanded my mental horizons, but clarified and strengthened rather than transformed my overall political and social viewpoint. (There was, however, one significant exception, for despite the comparatively relaxed and unhierarchical atmosphere in the RAF I acquired an anti-establishment bias that I have retained, more or less intact, ever since.) Like so many of my generation looking to the future, I became convinced of Britain's need to break with the past and find a "middle way" between the extremes of so-called "free" market private enterprise capitalism and centralized economic planning, whether socialist or communist. The implementation of major, even fundamental postwar economic and social reforms designed to achieve a more just, equitable, and prosperous society seemed not merely desirable and necessary: it was also a moral obligation on those of us fortunate enough to have survived the greatest wartime dangers and sacrifices. The broad, enthusiastic wartime campaign to eradicate Want, Disease, Ignorance, Squalor, and Idleness, so vigorously promoted by Sir William Beveridge (himself a Liberal) and others, clearly pointed the way towards some form of democratic socialism, which I favored then, and still do. But in the early postwar years practical difficulties took precedence over ideological alignments. Despite the bitter battles between the Labour government and the Conservative opposition, politics seemed much less a problem than economics, for, unlike, the situation in some former belligerent countries, Britain's pre-war governmental, constitutional, legal and cultural structures remained essentially intact. And it was some time before I came to appreciate that this much-vaunted institutional stability and continuity was not just a source of pride, but also a serious obstacle to change. At the time the Labour party's reforms seemed to mark the dawn of a brave new era. In retrospect, however, they seemed more like a missed opportunity for genuinely radical reconstruction.

During the past half century the question of the role of the state in economic and social affairs has absorbed an enormous amount of intellectual energy, much of it unfortunately wasted owing to the activities of ideological polemicists and partisan hacks on both sides of the debate. Given capitalism's lamentable interwar performance in Britain it was surely inevitable that the balance of postwar opinion would support a significant increase in state ownership/control/regulation/management, or some combination of these; and, in the long run, the effects of this increase are still with us, notwithstanding periodic determined efforts to reduce governmental functions and responsibilities, to cut government expenditure drastically, and, as the propagandists put it, to "roll back the state," and "get government off our backs." On the whole, these efforts have had remarkably limited success, despite a dramatic recent shift in the ideological climate. The simplistic early postwar socialist faith in the desirability and efficacy of nationalization, to take one conspicuous example, has given way to even more uncritical devotion to privatization. Yet, contrary to the true believers in both camps, experience demonstrates that there are no panaceas. How much enhanced understanding and hope of solving major problems there might be were it generally recognized that all the interesting and important issues lie somewhere in the intractable difficulties of getting reliable evidence and balanced assessment of past experience, there has been little progress in economic thought and policy on these matters.

Both before and after World War II a number of British democratic socialist economists were endeavoring to formulate a theoretical rationale for what we now call a mixed economy – i.e., a combination of planning and the price mechanism.[2] This is not the place to assess their success or failure. At least their work was constructive, and not incompatible with the dominant post-war Keynesian economic ideas. By contrast, many of the critics of socialist economics were purely destructive. A prime example, unworthy of its author's deservedly high standing as an economist, methodologist, philosopher and intellectual historian, is Hayek's shrill polemic (1944). Ignoring the subtleties and practical policy significance of the issues, Hayek treated planning (a weasel word, if ever there was one) sweepingly as "the organization of everything;" described most planners as militant nationalists; identified what he termed the socialist roots of Nazism; and argued that Britain was already moving along the Germanic path (ibid., pp. 106, 135–36, 152). The choice, he claimed, lay between the impersonal forces of the market and dictatorial totalitarianism: there was no intermediate stopping point. I find it astonishing, and indeed appalling, that Hayek has recently been lauded as an accurate forecaster of things to come, notwithstanding all the evidence to the contrary.

III. Transatlantic economic education, 1942–53: "great books," and methodological controversy

My first formal encounter with economics occurred in wartime, initially in a suburban London state grammar-school sixth form and, a year later at the University College of the South West, Exeter. The contrast between the two could hardly have been greater. At school I received a clear and helpful if uninspiring introduction to economic history, and basic principles of economics via Benham's (1941) remarkably effective, durable, and widely used elementary text. At Exeter the instruction was genial but chaotic, for the temporary superannuated professor spent much of his time telling anecdotes about his long teaching career in India, and boasting of his ownership of a first edition of Smith's *The Wealth of Nations*. The examination papers were set by London University staff, and without Benham's lifeline I would surely have failed at my first examination hurdle.

Three and a half years later, after war service, I returned to Exeter to complete my London External B.Sc(Econ) degree, having already successfully passed two special papers in economic history by correspondence course, while in the R.A.F. This proved to be an efficient, but constricted and impersonal introduction to a rich and complex subject, and it helps to explain why for so long I have considered myself a less than fully paid up member of the economic and social historians' community. During my absence from Exeter, the university's student body and teaching staff had changed dramatically, and for the better. But it was not until six months before my finals, with the aid of competent instruction, that I began to appreciate the intellectual attractions of economics. Stigler 1947, though an elementary text, gave me my first taste of a more rigorous treatment of economic analysis, and Britain's postwar problems provided abundant stimuli for diagnosis and discussions, in which economics and politics were inextricably linked. Nevertheless, though immensely enjoying myself, I was acutely conscious of the limitations of my knowledge and understanding of economics, and when the opportunity to do postgraduate work arose I decided to concentrate on the history of economic thought as the most congenial way of learning the subject – that is, by studying the discipline's "great books."

This essentially literary approach to the acquisition of economic expertise will doubtless seem bizarre to present day readers, as indeed it does to me! Yet at the time it was reasonable enough for I was motivated solely by intellectual (I am tempted to say idle) curiosity, and a love of books. I had no thought of becoming an academic, and none of the Exeter economics staff ever suggested that my choice of subject might be inadvisable in career terms. My attitude towards economics had in fact changed substantially since my war service when, for a time, I became disenchanted with the subject and determined to switch to English Literature, taking the compulsory London University external examination paper in Latin, which I had not studied while at school. During that phase I read widely, becoming fascinated with the interpretation of texts, a problem that has since become fashionable in the social sciences, and even in economics. Dover Wilson's *What Happens in Hamlet?* (1937) was an influential exemplar and, incidentally, a study that permanently enhanced my appreciation of theatre. This "interpretive turn," to use recent jargon, carried over into my postgraduate and professional interest in the multiple interpretations of economic theories and policies, which stemmed partly from my psychological and intellectual reluctance to make firm doctrinal (or doctrinaire) commitments. This helps to explain why I have never been entirely persuaded either by orthodox or heterodox economics.

At Exeter in the late 1940s there were no facilities for advanced work in economics. I was the sole postgraduate student in the subject; there were no relevant lectures or seminars; I had no academic adviser; and I was firmly told that I could not write a postgraduate thesis. Instead, I prepared myself for three general examination papers in the history of economic thought for my London External M.Sc(Econ), plus a special paper on John Bates Clark, which I proposed in the hope that it might enhance my qualifications for further study in the U.S.A. Working alone, I ploughed through tome after tome on the reading list I had compiled with the aid of the available general textbooks on the history of economics, in the process forming, occasionally abandoning, and sometimes reforming my interpretations of the economic classics. No wonder I often felt lost amid the array of available concepts, theories, and approaches. To all intents and purposes I was an autodidact. Doubtless this contributed to my sense of being an outsider: an economist-watcher rather than an economist *proprement dit.*

Given my background and intellectual predilections, my first year in the U.S.A. as an English Speaking Union Fellow at the University of Pittsburgh (1950–51) proved to be crucial academically, quite apart from the culture shock. My initial intentions were modest and conventional – to remedy some of the deficiencies in my education by taking postgraduate courses in economics (hitherto I had had none), and to write a Ph.D. thesis on John Bates Clark, the leading American *fin de siècle* economic theorist. This topic, I believed, would enable me to combine economic analysis with biography and intellectual history, since I aimed to "place" Clark in relation to his contemporaries at home and abroad. However, I had counted without Bela Gold, an inspiring teacher and deeply penetrating critic, who gently persuaded me that there was much more to American economics than was dreamt of in Clark's philosophy, or his economics. Under Gold's influence, especially in his seminar on research methods in the social sciences, I soon scrapped my original plan. Seeking a broader and more challenging interdisciplinary subject, I decided to focus on the American economists' preoccupation with methodology in the period 1885–1930, a concern that had no real counterpart in British economics after the early 1890s. The reasons for this marked difference were various and in part obscure, and the problem had hitherto been almost entirely overlooked by historians of economics. It took me some years to work out my own interpretation, which extended beyond logic and epistemology, and the nature of economic theory, to the history of American academia and the position of the intellectual in American life. No wonder it took time to arrive at this interpretation! When I moved to Johns Hopkins the following year, my new thesis topic was accepted without demur, and after completing the required graduate courses (not without difficulty in the case of mathematical economics) I was able to devote a full year to my research.

In 1953, towards the end of my second year at Hopkins, when my doctoral thesis was nearing completion, I was fortunate to be appointed Assistant Lecturer in Economic History at Nottingham, for I was not able to be present for the interview normally regarded as essential in such circumstances. My wife, Sonia, and I had already decided to return to England at the end of my postgraduate period, largely for family reasons, and the short side-step into economic history (as it seemed to me) was determined by two very different circumstances. The first was negative: my manifest lack of the necessary intellectual motivation and capacity to keep abreast of the latest mathematical and quantitative developments in economics.[3] This seemed a poor match for my intellectual interests and aptitudes. I reached this conclusion as a result of my contacts with brilliant fellow graduates, rather than from my teachers. Neither group was brutal enough, however, to advise me to quit economics! But no doubt my enthusiasm for the history of methodological controversy in economics sufficed to mark me out as an eccentric, at the very least.

The second, and by far the more important factor shaping my career, was the enormous positive stimulus I derived from the series of seminars on English eighteenth century economic development given by the great economic historian, T. S. Ashton, who visited Hopkins during my first year. This was only the second, and in fact the last economic history course I ever attended, and Ashton's masterly combination of economic analysis and deep historical erudition was a revelation, quite apart from his personal modesty and charisma. Prior to his postwar move to the chair of Economic History at the London School of Economics, Ashton had for many years been teaching economics at Manchester while producing a series of major economic history writings. At Hopkins this background was apparent, especially in his treatment of economic fluctuations and monetary history. In the early postwar decades he was a major influence on a series of able students who became leaders in economic history in Britain and elsewhere during its "take-off" phase; and his acknowledgement that the subject provided only "a narrow window on the world" highlighted its function as an essential bridge between economics and history. As the great Cambridge economic historian, J. H. Clapham observed (1949, Introduction), "economic history is the most fundamental kind of history, not the most important: foundations exist to carry better things." *Mutatis mutandis,* this has been my conception of the history of economics.

IV. Teaching at Nottingham, 1953–82: historiography and methodology, slavery, the new economic history

Throughout my three decades in Nottingham – interspersed with leaves of absence in the U.S.A., and a two-year break (1962–64) in Virginia and York (UK) – none of my departmental colleagues was either well-trained in economics by the standards of the time, or much interested in that discipline. By contrast, my own distinctive position was characterized by a witty external examiner who dubbed me "that theoretical young man," a description that would have seemed odd to my Hopkins contemporaries. In addition to Ashton, W. W. Rostow was influential during the 1950s and 1960s in making British nineteenth century economic history more economic; and in my first lecture course I subjected my defenseless students to a heavy dose of Gayer, Rostow and Schwartz (1953).[4] This major theoretical and statistical study was, of course, more suitable for postgraduate students. But having diligently ploughed through it in the summer before I began my Nottingham teaching, I was obliged to make a good pedagogic use of my limited scarce resources! The important point, however, is that at the time economics was quietly and effectively infiltrating British economic history, rather than being forcefully imposed on it, as was the case in the U.S.A. during the 1960s and 1970s, by the fervent missionaries of the new economic history, or "cliometrics."[5]

Given my continuing interest in economic methodology and things American, it is hardly surprising that cliometrics fascinated me. I was able to keep in touch with its development through my reading, visits with American friends and colleagues, and through contacts with three of our outstanding Nottingham economic history graduates: Roy Church, Eric Jones, and Peter Payne, the first two of whom spent a year at Purdue, one of the principal shrines of the new evangelicalism. After my return to Nottingham from York in 1964, I was instrumental in scrapping the unsatisfactory compulsory final year general essay paper and substituting an ambitious, albeit disarticulated, collaborative series of seminars entitled "The Historiography and Methodology of Economic History." I firmly believed that our undergraduate honors economic history specialists should not go out into the so-called "real world" without having seriously thought about their subject's relationships with economics and history, and the arguments for and against the economic interpretation of history which was for some so potentially seductive a doctrine. Needless to say my colleagues, though mostly cooperative, were not wildly enthusiastic about the course, for they considered it was altogether too general, even philosophical.

My only published contribution to the new economic history originated in my effort to understand its nature and significance for the development of the discipline, and to explain it to my students. By the 1970s there was already a substantial, intensely controversial methodological literature, but "The Historical Context of the New Economic History,"[6] one of my favorite articles, was an idiosyncratic outsider's survey of the field combining intellectual and institutional history with economic methodology and the sociology of knowledge. I like to think that nobody else could have written it – or, perhaps, would have wanted to!

Inevitably, the new economic history figured prominently in the course on "Slavery and the Antebellum South" which I taught for about two decades, initially at Nottingham and subsequently at Duke (where the prefix "The Economics of ..." was added, lest the historians should suppose that an imperialistic economics department was encroaching on their domain!). As I was beginning, Robert Fogel's and Stanley Engerman's sensational *Time on the Cross* (1974) appeared, surely the most controversial book in economic history ever published. *Time on the Cross* was reviewed in the Times Literary Supplement several months before it became available in England, and I still vividly recall the combined sense of shock, excitement, and in part incredulity, with which I read the advanced copy Stan Engerman was kind enough to send me. *Time on the Cross* was by far the boldest and most ambitious attempt to apply static, microeconomic analysis and statistical methods to a unique phase in the American experience. Its initial impact was almost intimidatory, with its teams of researchers, acres of archives, and uninhibitedly inventive exploration of such sensitive topics as the age of first birth of slave females, the break-up of families by sale, miscegenation, and whipping, topics that had hitherto not been amenable to conventional historical methods. Could it be that like economics at Hopkins, economic history was in the process of becoming so theoretical and technical that I would be forced to retreat to intellectual history, or even sociology?

Slavery appealed to me as an academic subject not only because of its intrinsic fascination, the richness and controversial character of its sources and historiography, and my long-standing interest in the origins and development of American jazz, but also because the course provided an unusual interdisciplinary opportunity to move, within a distinctive geographical and historical framework, through economic analysis to social and cultural history. (I did not attempt to explore in any depth other dimensions such as politics, religion, and the history of ideas.) It provided an opportunity to test, though not in any narrowly econometric sense of the term, the historical uses and limitations of economic theory, and the validity of the economic interpretation of history. I found it a never failing educational experience, and undoubtedly some students – especially those from the American south – felt the same way.

As a contribution to scholarship *Time on the Cross* was deeply flawed. Serious errors and exaggerations were exposed by its critics, some of the most severe being new economic historians, and the emergence of hostilities within the ranks of the faithful constituted evidence that the movement had come of age. They no longer felt obliged to aim their weaponry exclusively at the older generation of scholars. Needless to say, most historians, especially those specializing on the history of the American South, intensely disliked the book. But like Stanley Elkin's *Slavery: A Problem in American Intellectual and Institutional Life* (1959), another brilliant but flawed work, *Time on the Cross* illustrates the dictum that fertile error is sometimes preferable to dull truth. Like Fogel's earlier massive counterfactual study of American railroads which, as one critic observed, revealed his "daredevil impulse," *Time on the Cross* significantly advanced the history of American slavery even for those who rejected many of its principal conclusions. From my standpoint it served as another major illustration of the limitations of economic theory and the plurality of plausible interpretations of complex historical subjects.

V. Linking economic and social policy with the history of economics

Largely owing to the diversity of my research interests I have never succeeded in fully integrating research and teaching, although a number of my published articles are direct by-products of teaching commitments.[7] The subject of my Ph.D. thesis (Coats 1953) was far too abstract and exotic to be suitable for undergraduate economic historians; and in a small department a conventional history of economic thought course was not a sufficiently high priority. As a compromise, however, for a good many years I taught a course on "Economic Thought and Policy 1660–1848" designed to explore linkages between economic ideas and their historical context. For a time I planned to write a monograph on changing attitudes to labor, poverty and social conditions, which would examine policy objectives, legislative enactments, and their effects against the general background of economic and social development. But unfortunately other research interests proved too seductive, especially the growth of knowledge in economics, the social and institutional history of the discipline, and professionalization.

As is well known, I have long regarded the history of economic analysis (or theory) as necessary, but insufficient activity, although I can understand its attractions for those fascinated by intellectual puzzles, and I enormously admire the energy, confidence, and brilliance of Mark Blaug's textbook (1968), a veritable tour de force of its species. Nevertheless, given my economic and social history background I feel a much stronger rapport with efforts to link economic ideas, events and policies, as in Leo Rogin's highly original but unsatisfactory volume (1953), or Wesley Mitchell's effort (1967) to portray the relevant historical context of classical economics – another commendable failure. As Terence Hutchison pointed out (1952), Mitchell was forced to abandon his Deweyite instrumentalist project once he got into and beyond the marginal revolution era (Mitchell 1969), as economic theory became increasingly autonomous and detached from its historical environment. Joseph A. Schumpeter (1954) too made an ambitious but somewhat schizophrenic effort to portray the "intellectual scenery" behind the "filiation" of ideas. But taken together, these and other grandiose ventures had little hope of success, although there was abundant scope for more limited specific studies of economic ideas and policy (for example, Coats 1960, 1968).

VI. The growth of knowledge movement; the sociology and professionalization of economics

Given this conclusion, I turned to other general themes – in particular the overall "shape" of the evolution of economics as a discipline or science; aspects of the social and institutional history of economics; and professionaliziation. The first of these themes was inspired by Thomas Kuhn's pathbreaking study of scientific revolutions (1962, 1970), an exciting and enourmously influential book that generated immensely stimulating discussions of the growth of knowledge in economics. Curiously enough, my modest six page contribution to this literature (Coats 1969), one of the first attempts to apply Kuhn to economics, has proved to be one of my most frequently cited publications. Together with Imre Lakatos's work on the methodology of scientific research programs and other writings in the philosophy of science (by scholars such as K. Popper, N. Hanson, M. Polanyi, and S. Toulmin), Kuhn's work contributed to a major shift away from positivism, and to the subsequent massive boom in economic methodology that still continues today. The growth-of-knowledge phase is too rich and complex to summarize briefly. Even though it did not yield either a general theory or philosophy of the development of economics, or a solution to the discipline's fundamental methodological problems, I still believe the search for comprehensive patterns was constructive. Whatever the outcome, for a decade or so I enjoyed the ride.

The second general theme – the sociology and professionalization of economics – has become my major interest during the past two decades. It covers an extraordinary variety of issues, such as: the emergence of economics as an academic discipline; the institutional environment that has shaped or inhibited more purely intellectual developments; the role of scholarly and other organizations of economists; the nature, structure and functions of the economics profession; and the study of what economists actually "do" – with special reference to their work in government and their contributions to policy formulation and implementation. Needless to say, this list is far from complete. Some of the topics have attracted the attention of researchers, while others have been almost entirely neglected – a source of regret to me, for when we take account of the opportunities for comparative studies of developments in different countries, the potential scope for research is extraordinary.[8] Certainly the history of economic thought has for too long been dominated by Anglo-Saxon viewpoints and interests; but that bias is now, at last, being substantially corrected.

As I suggested more than a quarter of a century ago in the first article in the first issue of *History of Political Economy*,[9] there is enough worthwhile work to be done to keep generations of historians of economics busy. Moreover, they can look forward to fruitful collaborations with scholars in a number of neighboring disciplines such fields as: intellectual history, the history and philosophy of science, the sociology of knowledge, the interaction of economics and politics, and – with help from experienced economist practitioners – the role of economic ideas and economists in policymaking.

VII. Concluding reflections

As is clear from the foregoing account, I have periodically changed the direction or extended the range of my intellectual interests, often more by chance than design. These changes have been stimulating, if sometimes worrying, for I have been conscious of the danger of spreading myself too thinly. In this highly specialized late twentieth-century academic world a would-be "jack of all trades" is liable to be master of none. Obviously a strong case can be made for cross-disciplinary "trespassing," to use Albert Hirschman's graphic term; but it calls for a certain independence of mind, and perhaps a measure of wilful nonconformity. Occasionally, however, in my sometimes lonely quest, I have had welcome reassurances from distinguished scholars. For example, when I suggested to Ashton that by specializing in the history of economics I might become too detached from mainstream British economic history, he dismissed my concern, advising me to go my own way – which I probably would have done anyway! Nevertheless, I knew him well enough to be able to respond that it was easy for an established professor to give that advice, but somewhat more risky for a young academic to act on it.

Some years later, when I happened to be driving Kenneth Boulding from Ann Arbor to the Detroit airport, he remarked that he might have achieved greater recognition from economists had he refrained from engaging in so many other academic activities. This seemed likely, for his earlier, highly original *The Reconstruction of Economics* (1950) required energetic promotion if its singular merits were to be appreciated. Yet by any standards Boulding's record was remarkable: as a prolific author; pioneer in several new disciplinary organizations, of which he became President; and as one of the three economists to be elected President of the prestigious American Association for the Advancement of Science. Moreover, not long after our meeting, he achieved the recognition from economists he desired, with his election as President of the American Economic Association.

Contact with Boulding certainly stimulated my imagination and widened my intellectual horizons, for he was an untiring innovator pursuing new ideas and ever expanding lines of inquiry, rarely returning to his earlier interests, and never wasting his energies replying to critics. There are obviously intellectual rewards as well as costs of trespassing.

Periodically in this essay I have made passing references to the limitations of economics, and it seems appropriate to conclude with some general reflections on this theme. As indicated in the early pages, my basic attitudes and temperament are anti-doctrinaire and anti-establishment, and in economics nowadays the latter means dissociation from and skepticism (even perhaps hostility) towards what is so widely and loosely termed neoclassical doctrine.[10]

Over time, my initial inchoate dissent became more explicit and coherent. This occurred, for example, under the influence of Gold's revelatory guidance, and later partially as a result of my immersion in Thorstein Veblen's writings while preparing my Ph.D. dissertation. The antipositivist movement in the philosophy of science was, I found, a valuable source of heterodox insights. I benefited from its teachings not only as they were expressed in the work of Kuhn and Popper, but especially as they were conveyed in Michael Polanyi's beautifully written and constructed book *Personal Knowledge; Towards A Post Critical Philosophy* (1958). Although Polanyi's work was not highly regarded by philosophers, or frequently cited by historians of economics or economic methodologists, I was captivated by his conception of science as a moral enterprise profoundly shaped by the individual scientist's personal aims and interests, as well as those of the scientific community to which he belongs and submits his research findings. (This conception of science is much more widely recognized now than it was in the 1960s).

Polanyi's influence underlies my article on "Value Judgments in Economics" (Coats 1964b) drawn from a monograph of the same title (1964a) that was written while I was a visitor at the University of Virginia. It marks the beginning of my serious interest in the sociology of science (economics) inspired by Schumpeter, Polanyi, Kuhn and others. The concluding sentences articulate a theme that was to become increasingly prominent in later economic methodology literature:

> "Positive" economics is, in other words, an ideal to which economists may aspire; it is not a state of grace that has already been attained. If economists blind themselves to the gap between the ideal and the actual, between methodological principle and methodological practice, they will only exacerbate the already formidable difficulties confronting them.[11]

In this "methodological decade" of the nineties, as Terence Hutchison suggests it should be called (Hutchison 1992, p. x), the conventional distinction between "positive" and "normative" economics appears far less clear cut than it did thirty years ago. Positivist (or modernist) philosophy of science is now discredited; Popperian falsificationism has lost its appeal for economic methodologists (Blaug and Hutchison excepted); and they are currently far more interested in studying what economists do than in prescribing correct methodological rules. From a methodological standpoint ours is a much more tolerant, pluralistic age; but this does not mean that the barbarians are at the gate, as some critics aver. There has indeed been a confusing proliferation of new approaches – such as causal holism, critical rationalism, deconstruction, discourse analysis, hermeneutics, holism, pluralism, postmodernism, realism, rhetorical analysis, storytelling, etc. – the list seems endless. But there has also been substantial progress towards a deeper understanding of the nature and limitations of economics and the social sciences generally. While these developments have opened up stimulating possibilities for historians of economics, especially those concerned with the relatively recent past, they have obviously complicated the tasks of historical interpretation.

However, whereas methodological discourse has become more open and multivocal, almost the opposite is true of the neoclassical mainstream. The core training of economics graduates, especially in the U.S.A., has become increasingly standardized, narrowly technocratic, and remote from the needs of society. The complacent findings of the American Economic Association's landmark Commission on Graduate Education in Economics (1991) reveal no interest whatsoever in the profession's responsibilities to the wider, non-academic public, including the vast numbers of professional economists in non-academic employment. Far too many academic economists nowadays are preoccupied with "good games," to cite J. R. Hicks's term – that is, intellectual pursuits that have no conceivable practical application or interest outside academia. This is a far cry from earlier times when the discipline's leaders viewed economics primarily as a body of knowledge dedicated to the prevention or cure of depressions and the alleviation of poverty and suffering. This was the message I received in my early ventures into economic literature; and while I do not deny the pleasures of studying economic and social history and the history of economics for their own sake, this has never been sufficient of itself. These fields have always seemed potentially relevant to practice, especially when economic ideas are viewed in context, and in relation to events and policies. Economic thought and policy, and the role of economists in government, are two distinct research areas which shed light on the question: Is economics useful, and if so how?

An intellectual autobiography is, of course, an ego trip, an exercise in self-exposure not without its dangers as well as its satisfactions. Given my long-standing fascination with the interrelationships between ideas, personalities, institutions, and historical conditions, I could hardly be expected to resist the editor's invitation, even though I am profoundly uneasy at the notion of discussing my "contribution" to the history of economics. Any contribution I have made stems from personal idiosyncrasies rather than formal training, for I have already described the marked peculiarities of my initiation into academic life, my first foray into the history of economics, and my distinctive (if not unique) intellectual perspective as an economic and social historian. Consciousness of these differences – which I may, of course, exaggerate – explains my self-description as economist watcher, rather than economist, a position that has obvious limitations as well as certain advantages. One can, for example, be a bird-watcher without being a bird.

My global travels in the four decades or so since I obtained my Ph.D. have enhanced my awareness of the wide variety of institutions of higher education, and my sense of detachment towards the academic profession generally. I have taught for periods of a semester or more in eleven different universities (seven in the U.S.A.; two in the UK and two in Australia) and for shorter spells in several more, e.g. Canada (two); Australia (two); Israel and Brazil. Like many other mature professors, I have also given occasional lectures in a wide variety of countries including Western Europe, Yugoslavia, Greece, Japan and New Zealand. Conference organizing has also been a major, albeit occasional activity, in connection with my international research projects, various history of economics groups (there is no formal history of economic thought society in the UK), and the quadrennial International Economic History Congress. This kind of administrative undertaking has been extremely satisfying, unlike most internal university administrative work.

Having been based in an independent economic and social history department for most of my career, my experiences as a postgraduate supervisor – a task I have always relished – have been with subjects far removed from the history of economics. The development of the pyrities industry, and eighteenth century professional women novelists are two of the more exotic examples. The one exception, and the notable one, is John Maloney, whose chosen subject was close to my heart; and I have also been at times both an official and an unofficial D.Phil supervisor at Oxford, with John Cunningham Wood and Alon Kadish. Some of the most penetrating and satisfying intellectual exchanges have been with an external examiner and a Ph.D. student who has already been told that his or her thesis has been accepted. On such occasions it has been unnecessary to pull one's punches in deference to a nervous candidate!

More generally, I have greatly enjoyed helping young scholars, either through the formal journal refereeing process, or more informally. Despite the time involved, the opportunity to shape an embryonic or emerging piece of work is almost invariably rewarding, both in personal and intellectual terms. By contrast, I have usually found writing both painful and frustrating, as in the present instance.

It would, perhaps, be appropriate to conclude with some general observations on the current state of economics, viewed in historical perspective; but I have, perhaps, already tried the reader's patience unduly. However, let me say that I believe economics (and perhaps the social sciences generally) are now undergoing changes of almost seismic magnitude. No brief summary will suffice, but insiders' efforts to strengthen the central corpus of neoclassical theory are undermining its foundations in at least three distinct but interrelated ways: i) by incorporating such complex but unescapable features of economic life as uncertainty, expectations, imperfect information, and the limits to human ability to make rational calculations; ii) by developing various species of disequilibrium analysis and nonlinear dynamics, incorporating path dependency, hysteresis, "real" historical time, irreversible processes, evolutionary change, and perhaps chaos; iii) by breaking down barriers between economics and her neighboring disciplines – e.g. by developing two-way interfaces with psychology, ethics, politics, anthropology and biology. That is the antithesis of economic imperialism, the one-way direct and uncritical application of conventional economic analysis to subjects customarily viewed as non-economic.

In many respects these developments give added weight to matters of deep and lasting concern to heterodox and dissenting economists, including the role of institutions, habits, and conventions in economic life; the historicity of economic processes; and the interrelations between economics and other disciplines that have to be taken into account in policymaking. This is not to claim that a grand synthesis or paradigm is in prospect, especially in view of economic orthodoxy's proven remarkable recuperative powers, and the disciplinary establishment's firm hold over the pedagogical (indoctrination?) process. As that sage Yogi Berra is said to have opined: "Prediction is difficult; predicting the future is especially difficult"; and I have no intention of getting involved in that dangerous game.

Nevertheless, we certainly live in interesting times!

Notes

1 I have deliberately kept the career facts to a minimum, given my introductory autobiography essay: "First kick up a dust ..." (Coats 1992). I have tried to minimize the amount of duplication; but as some readers will appreciate, I find it unrewarding to discuss "intellectual" matters in abstraction from the relevant historical context.

2 There is a thoughtful and balanced account of this episode in Durbin, 1985. James Meade was a notable member of the group, who carried the same torch throughout his long and distinguished career. However much the Marxists and libertarians protest, a mixed economy is what we have, and what we shall continue to have for the foreseeable future. Better by far to devote our intellectual efforts to devising and implementing workable solutions to the inescapable problems that arise in such real world economies.

3 I found it disconcerting when my peers occasionally dismissed as rubbish the technical papers I was struggling to comprehend. If I could not distinguish the chaff from the wheat, I was obviously in the wrong field.

4 These volumes, the first National Bureau of Economic Research studies focusing exclusively on Britain, were preceded by Rostow's heavily economic one (1948). Taken together, they represented a powerful combination of Keynesian-type economic analysis and massive statistical research.

5 Although over the years I taught a variety of courses on British and European economic history, the world economy, and economic thought and policy, I will mention only those most relevant to my evolving conceptions of economics and its history.

6 Coats 1980. I received valuable comments on early drafts from some of the pioneers of the movement.

7 See the essay referred to in note 1.

8 See, for example, Coats 1981, 1986, 1997. I have now launched a comparative multi-author study of the post-1945 development of economics in Europe. Another multi-author international comparative project to which I contributed is "The Institutionalization of Political Economy: Its Introduction and Acceptance into European, American, and Japanese Universities," which bore fruit in seven "country" studies. They are listed in footnote 35 in the essay cited above in note 1. Another is Barber 1988.

9 Coats 1969, 1983. See also the immediately following analysis of the contents of the journal by Neil de Marchi and John Lodewijiks (Coats 1993).

10 Incidentally, I strongly dislike the widespread current loose use of that term. When I began my lonely trek through the literature of economics, "neoclassical" meant Marshallian, and it was clearly distinguishable from Austrian and Walrasian economics. Nowadays all three are stuffed into the same doctrinal portmanteau, often together with other miscellaneous items.

11 (Coats 1964b, p. 67) The footnotes contain a representative selection from the then current philosophy of science literature. Although strongly critical of "positive" economics, the article concedes that many, perhaps most, economists regarded it as an ideal that made their discipline seem scientific.

References

Barber, William J. 1988. *Breaking the Academic Mould. Economists and American Higher Education in the Nineteenth Century*, Wesleyan University Press, Middletown.

Benham, Frederick. 1941. *Economics.* Pitman, London.

Blaug, Mark. 1962. *Economic Theory in Retrospect*; 4th ed., Irwin, Homewood, 1985.

Boulding, Kenneth. 1950. *The Reconstruction of Economics,* Wiley, New York.

Clapham, John H. 1949. *A Concise Economic History of Britain. From the Earliest Times to 1750,* Cambridge University Press, Cambridge.

Coats, A. W. 1953. *Methodological Controversy as an Approach to the History of American Economics, 1885–1930,* unpublished doctoral dissertation, Johns Hopkins University, Baltimore.

____. 1960. "Economic Thought and Poor Law Policy in the Eighteenth Century," *Economic History Review, 13,* August, 39–51.

____. 1964a. *The Role of Value Judgments in Economics,* Thomas Jefferson Center for Political Economy, Charlottesville, Virginia.

____. 1964b. "Value Judgments in Economics," *Yorkshire Bulletin of Economic and Social Research, 16,* November, 53–67.

____. 1968. "Political Economy and the Tariff Reform Debate of 1903." *Journal of Law and Economics, 11,* April, 181–229.

____. 1969a. "Is there a Structure of Scientific Revolutions in Economics?," *Kyklos, 22,* no.2, 289–95.

____. 1969b. "Research Priorities in the History of Economics," *History of Political Economy, 1,* April, 9–18.

____. 1980. "The Historical Context of the New Economic History," *Journal of European Economic History, 9,* Spring, 185–207.

____, ed. 1981. *Economists in Government. An International Comparative Study,* Duke University Press, Durham.

____. 1983. "The First Decade of *Hope (1968–1979)*," *History of Political Economy, 15,* Fall, 303–19.

____, ed. 1986. *Economists in International Agencies. An Exploratory Study,* Praeger International, New York.

____. 1992. "First kick up a dust ..." in A. W. Coats, ed., *On the History of Economic Thought. British and American Economic Essays, 1,* Routledge, London.

____. 1994. "Economics as a Policy Science," in C. Perrotta and V. Gioia, *Where is Economics Going? Historical Viewpoints,* Università Degli Studi di Lecce, Congedo editori.

____, ed. 1997. *The Post-1945 Internationalization of Economics,* Duke University Press, Durham.

Durbin, Elizabeth. 1985. *New Jerusalems. The Labour Party and the Economics of Democratic Socialism,* Routledge, London.

Elkins, Stanley. 1959. *Slavery: A Problem in American Intellectual and Institutional Life,* University of Chicago Press, Chicago.

Fogel, Robert and Engerman, Stanley. 1974. *Time on the Cross,* Little Brown, Boston.

Gayer, A. D., W. W. Rostow, and A. J. Schwartz. 1953. *The Growth and Fluctuation of the British Economy, 1790–1850,* 2 vols. Clarendon Press, Oxford.

Hayek, Friedrich A. von. 1944. *The Road to Serfdom,* University of Chicago Press, Chicago.

Hutchison, Terence W. 1952. "Historians of Economic Thought," in Arthur F. Burns, ed., *Wesley Clair Mitchell. Economic Scientist,* National Bureau of Economic Research, New York, 292–300.

____. 1992. *Changing Aims in Economics,* Blackwell, Oxford.

Johnson, Hewlett. 1939. *The Socialist Sixth of the World,* Gollancz, London.

Kuhn, Thomas S. 1962. *The Structure of Scientific Revolutions,* 2d ed., University of Chicago Press, Chicago.

Mitchell, Wesley C. 1967. *Types of Economic Theory. From Mercantilism to Institutionalism,* edited by Joseph Dorfman, *1*, Augustus M. Kelley, New York.

____. 1969. *Types of Economic Theory. From Mercantilism to Institutionalism,* edited by Joseph Dorfman, *2*, Augustus M. Kelley, N.Y.

Polanyi, Michael. 1958. *Personal Knowledge. Towards a Post-Critical Philosophy,* University of Chicago Press, Chicago.

Rogin, Leo. 1956. *The Meaning and Validity of Economic Theory,* Harper, New York.

Rostow, Walt W. 1948. *The British Economy in the Nineteenth Century,* Clarendon Press, Oxford.

Rutherford, Malcolm. 1994. *Institutions in Economics. The Old and the New Institutionalism,* Cambridge University Press, Cambridge.

Schumpeter, J. A. 1954. *History of Economic Analysis,* Oxford University Press, Oxford.

Smith, Adam. 1776. *An Inquiry into the Nature and Causes of the Wealth of Nations,* Cadell, London.

Stigler, George J. 1946. *The Theory of Competitive Price,* Macmillan, New York.

Wilson, John Dover. 1937. *What Happens in Hamlet?* Cambridge University Press, Cambridge.

2 A conversation with A.W. Bob Coats*

Grant Fleming

A.W. Bob Coats occupies a privileged position as an economist in that he has witnessed, and indeed participated in, the growth of the history of economics. Coats completed degrees in economic history in Britain before heading to America where he undertook a PhD on methodological controversies in the history of American economics under Fritz Machlup and George Heberton Evans at Johns Hopkins University. In a career spanning almost forty years he has held Professorships in Economic and Social History at Nottingham and in Economics at Duke University, Durham and visiting appointments in universities in Australia, Brazil, Israel and the United States of America.

In the introduction to the first volume of his collected essays Coats described his primary research interest as in the "development, dissemination and influence of economic ideas, events and policies; the historical and institutional (especially educational) context from which they have emerged; and the socioeconomic problems to which they have been addressed"[1]. Indeed, he has spent much of his academic life promoting interdisciplinary research in economics; the relevance of Kuhnian and Lakatosian frameworks to economics, economists in government and international agencies, the sociology of knowledge and the professionalisation of economics to name only a few. In this interview he talks about the early years and development of the history of economics, the several projects he was instrumental in establishing and the teaching and present state of the subject.

After your early training in Britain you set out on an English Speaking Union Fellowship to the University of Pittsburgh, where you mention in the introduction to your collected essays that you were greatly influenced by Bela Gold[2]. And then on to Johns Hopkins to do graduate work. Do you think it was a benefit going to Hopkins to work under Machlup?

It was tremendous; it was a revelation and I had a very, very bright group of contemporaries. It was a small department and the interaction between staff and students was very good. Carl Christ and Al Harberger were assistant professors, and they always had their doors open and people went in and out of there. I wasn't working on their sort of material but they were marvellous with the graduates. Evsey Domar was an extremely stimulating man who had a way of putting things upside down so that you saw them in a quite different light. And I made some very good, lasting friendships there.

Did you notice any differences, while you were at Johns Hopkins, between the American approach to the history of economics and the British approach to the history of economics?

This question of Americanization is in the background. I'm not up to date with what is going on in economics departments in England but I imagine the differences are a good deal narrower than they were earlier. There was an article years ago in the *Oxford Economic Papers* (1963) by Sargent called "Are American Economists Better?" which has some very interesting Anglo-American contrasts and there is this mathematical and technical preoccupation in the United States. There's much more intense competition in the atmosphere of American universities because of the structure of the careers, the need to publish, and the uncertainty in people's careers in the early stages.

Did you feel that this was the case when you were at Johns Hopkins?

Oh yes, I was aware of it. Feeling the pressure to publish was something quite new, because as a graduate student in England I was by myself and there was no basic comparison, really no one to talk to in connection with the work I was doing. But at Hopkins the constant encouragement to expose what you were writing and the practice of weekly departmental seminars which everyone was supposed to attend (one week it would be a visitor and the next week it would be a graduate student presenting); that was very good training. I remember Merton Miller saying that he went to an econometrics institute in Belgium for a year, the kind of criticism that went on in a typical Hopkins seminar shocked the Europeans. It was much too direct – the American penchant for open criticism was a very marked difference from the intellectual environment of England.

Your earlier positions were as an economist teaching economic history. Was your "hands-on" contact with economic history important in your early research in the history of economics?

Well, my research was really only loosely connected with economic history. What was clear was that although I was technically an amateur by American graduate economics standards, my economics was much more advanced and competent than my Nottingham colleagues – they were essentially historians. I found that they would ask me to read certain things they had written as though I would ask you to check a column of figures that might not add up, as though they had made some awful mistake. Most of the comments I made were by no means fundamental but they were unsure of their economics. On the other hand, they were excellent within their particular fields. For example, Robert Ashton, a seventeenth century specialist working on what we would call public finance before the English Civil War, was totally in control of what he was doing; and on the problems of the nature of the currency, of different types of currency, for example, he could run rings around any twentieth century economist.

Although he hadn't done economics for an undergraduate degree, he knew what he needed to know for the purposes of his research and that's true of good historians, I think.

So you didn't see much of a relationship between the history of economics and economic history?

Well, I wanted to bring them together. When I started at Nottingham I planned to do a detailed study of the relationship between economic ideas and parliamentary debates in the aftermath of the Napoleonic War. The density of parliamentary debates is just amazing, and I was confronted with the difficulty of extracting economic ideas in any abstract sense of the term. Later Barry Gordon wrote two books on this period, both of which I reviewed, which were to some extent the kind of thing I was aiming to do. But even so, he was more interested in the ideas than in the context. My notion was to look at how public policy was discussed in relation to the condition of the economy and what ideas were being used, so there was almost, in a sense, an added dimension to what I planned to do. Like most of the things I started, it was over-ambitious. I read several years of parliamentary debates and was uncertain about the direction of what I was doing; certainly about the scholarly returns in terms of the effort involved.

Do you think that today the historian of economics could learn something from economic history?

Oh I'm sure, yes – this is a more philosophical, a more epistemological, more technical question – I have no doubt whatever. Again the very best historians of economics are very good at dealing with the contemporary environment of economic thinkers. A classic example is Bob Black's book on *Economic Thought and the Irish Question,* which is a significant contribution to Irish economic history as well as an outstanding piece of work in the history of economics[3]. But there are degrees of this. Sometimes one feels that historians of economics could have gone a good deal more fully into not only the economic dimensions but also the social dimensions of their subject, because I have always thought that the economic and social are very much interactive. For example, you can take major figures like Marshall: to try to understand Marshall's economic analysis without reference to the man and the society, the morality and other dimensions – it's very impoverished.

Isn't there a trend in the history of economics toward a more revisionist or rational reconstruction of ideas?

I wouldn't personally go that far. The amusing thing is that when the major postwar movement in the history of economics started we had a conference in

Sussex in 1968 and I gave a paper – they knew something about my prejudices – which became the first paper in the first issue of HOPE and it was on research priorities in the history of economic thought. Well, ten years later or so Neil De Marchi and John Lodewijks wrote a piece in HOPE which showed perfectly well that what I thought were research priorities were not what people were doing; they didn't switch what they were doing to what I was doing or what I wanted them to do. It was very clear then the direction I'd have liked to see it go and there have been times when I think: "What! another bloody article on Ricardo or another bloody article on Keynes". There's just too much of it; it's scratching over and over the surface. It's like one of the Professors of English at Nottingham who said that in the English department in Swansea, whence he came, all the original works were in the basement but all the literary critics and "pulp versions" were on the main shelves. There is a danger in concentrating unduly on narrow aspects of the history of ideas from the point of view of economic theory, whereas I tend to favour the opposite extreme, which perhaps involves taking it too much the other way. A classic example of that is Wesley Mitchell's *Types of Economic Theory*[4]. Hutchison pointed out, in a very good review that he wrote of it, that Mitchell couldn't keep up his volume one approach when he got to volume two. In volume one there is masses of stuff about the social, political, and economic conditions in England, about the growth of democracy. How that is directly connected to the development of classical economics is a moot point; but if you're not careful you will develop a kind of encyclopedic approach. Somebody, I think it was Talcott Parsons, described institutional economics as encyclopedic sociology. Well, Mitchell's approach would be encyclopedic history of economics. One clearly has to draw a line somewhere, and it's not easy to say just where. It has been said that text without context is pretext. On the other hand, context can swamp text.

You mentioned the Sussex conference and the renewed interest in the history of economics in the 1960s. But your interests had begun much earlier than this. How did the American Economic Association and the RES react to someone wanting to examine their records and write on the professionalisation process in economics?

Well, the circumstances were very different in the two cases. It was Hal Williamson, a very good economic historian, who had become Secretary of the American Economic Association and was under some pressure to write the AEA's history. When I said I was interested at looking at the papers he was delighted. He wanted to get rid of this particular burden, and of course I never completed it. In Cambridge, UK, I got the sense very clearly from Austin Robinson, that it was deplorable that the younger people, in the sixties, were not interested in the history of economics or the early years of the Royal Economic Society. He was obviously sorry that it was an "outsider" who was interested; but an outsider was better than nobody. He welcomed my interest, but was a little bit surprised, I think. Actually looking at the society's records rather than the development of economic ideas as such again seemed a bit odd to some people. Terence Hutchison, whose work I greatly admire, once said I was doing the history of economists, not the history of economics. That struck me as fair comment. But it seemed odd to me that nobody had done it before. There seemed to be a legitimate and worthwhile field for exploration. I wanted to know more about the relationships among the various economists, what they wrote to each other; how they exchanged ideas, if they did; and of course that again becomes an indefinitely expansible field. When you look at the AEA archives that have not been sifted there is a vast amount of uninteresting stuff that falls into two categories of letters: (a) why haven't I received my journal? and, (b) yes, I have paid my subscription! If you cut these out about a third of the documentation disappears straight away. In other words, a lot of it is not very interesting but you have to plough through it – like a lot of historical research in archives, you plough through a lot of stuff to get a few nuggets here and there. One of the things I would have liked to have done more of, and it is difficult, is to look at the records of the editorship of major journals. I did write about the *American Economic Review,* for which there are very full records; and later on I made enquires about the availability of other records but they seemed to be very limited. Of course there are quite a lot of Keynes papers relevant to the management of the *Economic Journal* and Don Moggridge has written a valuable article on that.

We could turn now to the revival in interest in the history of economics and the early years of HOPE. You were present at the first British conference on the history of economics and no doubt kept up with American developments. Did you find any discernible difference in the approach of American as compared with British historians of economics?

It's difficult to generalise. The British conferences have always been very small. I doubt whether more than a couple of them have had more than thirty-five people. At one point I remember noting that there were people from nine different countries within this total. So there's a very high proportion of foreigners; non-British, including Americans of course, and the main thing – which is something I wrote about in the first article in HOPE – is that there were fewer papers delivered at the British meetings, but the average quality was very high and the discussions were very good.

In the States they have so many papers there's really no time for discussion: also some of the commentators are very poor in that they say, for example: "Well, in his paper Professor X said so and so and so and so" and summarise it, as though they didn't know much about it. Then they add: "But there's one question, one sentence which I didn't understand". That type of comment is absolutely pointless from the audience's point of view. Also there is the frustration that comes from having too many papers. One continually has to miss promising sounding papers because three or four sessions run concurrently and one inevitably misses a lot especially if one is chairing a session, acting as discussant, as well as giving a paper. When I came to run a HES conference I was very anxious to raise the quality. In fact it's very difficult to refuse papers that are either just a title or else four or five lines which may make it look quite interesting. The meetings are very enjoyable occasions. There are many people one enjoys meeting once a year or so, and one can learn a lot about what is going on. This helps given the current bewildering amount of stuff that's recently published or in prospect.

The scale of the British meetings is entirely different and there is much more attention to any given paper – though there has recently been some discussion of whether there should be parallel sessions. There are people in England who are thinking of turning this strictly informal sequence of annual conferences with no President, Executive or Secretary-Treasurer into a society. How it is to become a society and what the differences will be from the status quo, I can't say.

A feature of your work in the history of economics is its interdisciplinary nature; for example, your work in the sociology of economics, the application of Kuhn or Lakatos to the discipline, your interests in the "outer boundaries" of economics. Is this a fair comment?

Yes. I've been pulled along to some extent. Ronald Coase introduced me to Kuhn very early in the sixties, and I found him fascinating. I wasn't aware of wanting to adopt that kind of approach. The idea that there could be patterns of development of economics seemed to me fascinating, and a worthwhile thing. Two of the characteristics of my intellectual interest have been on the one hand an interest in particular facts and individual personalities, and on the other hand being drawn to these rather large abstractions. It is difficult to reconcile the two. I got into the sociology of economics quite unintentionally. When I did my thesis, which was on methodology as a way of looking at the differences between British and American economic thought, I realised it wasn't that the Americans spent a lot more time discussing methodology because either they were better or worse methodologists, but that there were deeper cultural reasons for their preoccupation. It became clear that there was a kind of self-satisfaction about the British; that they didn't feel the need to discuss methodology. They knew what they wanted to know. Five years later, when I went back to the U.S. to write up my thesis as a book, I realised there was a lot more to it than methodology and that I needed to learn a great deal more about the way universities functioned, and about the position of the intellectual in American society. That may sound a bit pretentious, but I was being pulled in that direction; and then that approach reacted back on the way I saw the British scene; and of course from there one could go on to do international comparisons *ad nauseam*. One of the things I'd like to think is that my contributions have helped to open out the subject to new perspectives and new types of research. But of course that goes far beyond anything I have ever been able to do. I didn't self-consciously go into these things: I was just drawn into them by reading and by thinking about what I wanted to do.

Focusing on your introduction to Kuhn's work, how did this new interest in methodology and the development of science fit in with your earlier work on economic methodology?

I didn't think of it either earlier or later so much as methodology, but as a sort of broad historical perspective of the way a "science" develops. There was the question: does economics fall into that pattern, or is it a different kind of subject, whether you call it science or not. Initially the philosophical implications of Kuhn didn't strike me. I just thought his book an intriguing way of looking at the historical development of ideas. In many ways a more interesting approach than Schumpeter's, for example, or Leo Rogin's. But these were different again. I mentioned Mitchell – his was another way of looking at the subject. Mitchell was very aware of the way economists and social scientists have ideas which constitute a species of expertise for society. So the kind of pragmatism people required in the judicious application of economics to real problems was the thing that motivated Mitchell. Kuhn's pattern struck me first as a way of looking at the history of science. Then as a source of questions about the differences between the 'natural' and the 'social' sciences, an oft-debated issue.

In the 1970s you turned your attention to the role of economists in government. And in 1981 you edited a special edition of HOPE on the economists in government in several countries. Was the project always conceived on this large scale?

There is an amusing history to this. When it started I already had an interest in the subject. The project started with the international economic history conference in Leningrad. Craufurd Goodwin came; of course, I already knew him, and he said he was going to the Ford Foundation for a couple of years, and that we could direct some of their money towards the history of economic thought. Well, what does one say to a proposal like that! One goes off and starts serious thinking. I met him in London several months later, having come up with the idea of making a careful and thorough Anglo-American comparative study. But he said well that wasn't any good because the Foundation didn't want to support Anglo-American studies; it wanted to be more European-focused. So we talked about it, and I suggested the project should start with a bilateral comparison. We both felt an Anglo-French study would be too difficult, and that it would be easier to start with an Anglo-Dutch study as I was going for a year to the Netherlands Institute for Advanced Study. There I found a Dutch graduate student from Leiden who did a study of wage-price policy in relation to the structure of government and the role of economists in the Netherlands. Unfortunately it came out as a nine hundred page thesis in Dutch, with only a very short English abstract and as far as I know it has never been published. Nevertheless, it was clear that there was scope for wider international comparisons. Craufurd and I talked about it again and the idea was launched. Initially, I had a rather bizarre scheme of getting studies of pairs of countries – Sweden and Norway, say; or Sweden and Denmark; the Netherlands and Belgium, etc. – pairs of countries that looked similar in some respects. There would also be a Commonwealth component including Canada, India and Australia.

However, while the Ford Foundation liked the general idea they didn't like the particular selection of countries. So in the end Hungary, Brazil, Japan, and Israel were included, and other nominees were dropped. It turned out to be extremely interesting and revealing. I hoped other people would follow it up but there hasn't been much additional work of this kind, partly, I suspect, because it is too time consuming.

Do you mean studies of other countries?

Or more detailed studies of the same countries. I think it has widened the international perspective on the development of economics because there's a logical sequence between that exercise, the study of economists in international agencies published in 1986, and the recent Duke conference on the post 1945 internationalisation of economics. That represents a different way of looking at the subject – incredibly broad and extremely vague – and it remains to be seen how coherent it is. I think it's a very interesting idea and only someone with gross over-ambitious ideas can undertake it. I've had support from people in Duke and I think they think it's a bit broad and a bit vague.

You kept intermittent contact with methodological issues throughout your career, from your PhD thesis to your current writings. Do you think there is a place for the study of methodology in today's economics degree?

I have some mixed feelings about this. In American departments of history they often have a course in historiography and/or historical methods so that students get to know something about patterns of development in historical writing. And obviously I would like to see something like that – a treatment of the relationship between methodology and the history of economics – as part of the training of economists. But I would place much more emphasis on the value – both instructional and entertainment value of a course on the role of economists in government, because the literature on this is absolutely fascinating. I have described it, and I think it's a fair way of putting it, as a sort of collective learning process on the part of the profession. It provides wonderfully illuminating and often amusing insights into the nature, uses, and limitations of economics as a 'science' and a profession. Now that, injected into graduate training, would give graduate students an idea that economics is a discipline which has had uses in a lot of different contexts, and that there are very different views about how it's used, and whether it has been used effectively or not. You could go from that to a more narrow and specific study of economic policy. That would, I think, help to correct some of the deficiencies resulting from a lack of the history of economic thought, and a lack of economic history in the graduate economics curriculum. If you ask economists, or if you read what economists say, about the current state of the discipline virtually anyone would say: "we wish we had more time for economic thought";

"we wish we had more time for economic history". But they are loath to say exactly where or how it should fit into the curriculum. What I have suggested is that we inject a different element which has an historical dimension and also has a methodological dimension. And coming back to Hutchison, one of the great things that he stressed was the importance of economists recognising the limitations of their knowledge. That takes you back to methodology in a more pragmatic sense. One of the important, but neglected, things that occurred to me about the value of looking at the way economists operate in government is that it depends very much where they are located in the government machine. The facile tendency is to assume that an economist is somebody who is called in, sits at the Prime Minister's right hand and tells him or her either to raise or lower the rate of interest. The reality is not like that at all. A lot of ideas come up from within the bureaucracy; whereas ideas introduced at the top are definitely shaped and modified as they move down the structure towards implementation. So there is a real interaction between organisational structure, ideas, and policy practice.

The final subject I want to touch on is the teaching of the history of economics, perhaps in relation to your comments above about the topic of economists in government. What are your views on the teaching of the history of economics?

Well, I think that to talk about the role of economists in policy context is one way of bringing graduate work closer to what you could call the real world (if there is such a thing)! Teaching the history of economic thought is a different matter. Most of my career I've not done that. I did teach a course which I called economic thought and policy 1660–1850, which was an attempt to bring economic thought and economic history together in a series of topics like Mercantilism, trade policy, poverty problems, etc. And the students enjoyed it. They were sometimes joint honours economics/economic history students or else straight economists, occasionally historians, not very large groups. It was clear you couldn't do this for the entire two hundred years. I had to focus on certain topics. I spent a lot of time on labour ideas and policy, on foreign trade, the poor law, and a number of additional early nineteenth century topics. Most of my teaching in the history of economic thought proper has been in the United States, as an occasional visitor; and of course when you are a visitor you can be relatively irresponsible! I do have some quite clear and slightly unusual ideas about the way the history of economics should be taught. If one is teaching graduate students in economics, rather than a group of intellectual historians (that's another subject: there is really a great dearth of the history of economic ideas in intellectual history; many intellectual historians are, I think, rather frightened of economics; it's a bit too complex and scientific for them), I have for a long time felt that the way to teach a first course, because of the enormous volume and variety of the literature, is to start with the present and to discuss basic questions, such as what is distinctive about economics as a subject; and then consider different conceptual approaches to the history of economics as a whole, for example, the absolutist versus relativist approaches, so as to provide some sort of framework. Here Kuhn is very useful, because you can set up Kuhn's model very quickly and can treat it as a useful tool. It has a lot of defects; but the course is not designed to examine the detail but to provide an instructive framework. Then you can go back to some point – for example, you could start with Adam Smith – and try and give a sense and the flavour of the literature. Of course, you do have to end up dealing with some of the major figures. You can't get away from that. The problem is how much time is there for reading in the originals? I have never felt that a very clear feeling for the history of economics would come from throwing a student into the middle of *The Wealth of Nations,* for example, because there is always the inevitable tendency to look at it simply in relation to contemporary price theory, distribution theory and so forth. That's inescapable and that's bound to happen, but one must counteract that tendency as far as possible.

The other thing I think is essential is to give some idea of the persistence of the stream of heterodox economics. Of course one can admit that heterodox writers, Marxists etc., haven't provided an alternative to neoclassical economics; and one can go into the reasons for that, ideological and other. Nevertheless, the persistence of these heterodox streams is very clear and it is seriously misleading to ignore them for the sake of concentrating on the history of economic theory. Mark Blaug's *Economic Theory in Retrospect* is an extraordinary book, but it seems to me very arid ultimately, unless you want to give people a reductionist history of the evolution of economics. Of course, he's quite unsympathetic towards non-orthodox economics. The history of economics is not simply a history of Popperian falsficationism in practice. One can, after all, adjust the course if one is doing it regularly, especially if it's not a crucial examinable part of graduate training.

Do you find differences in the different countries you have taught in with regards to teaching the history of economics?

Well again my experience is peculiar because when I have taught in the States I've usually been the only one teaching it and I have never had a clear idea what other people were doing in their courses. I think that over long periods big departments have thought it quite a good thing to have someone come in occasionally and teach the history of economics without having a faculty member to do it as a primary activity. There used to be a Readership in the history of economic thought at Manchester; and of course Hutchison had a Readership in the history of economic thought at the LSE (which was Robbins' direct influence). Then when he [Hutchison] went to Birmingham, obviously he was primarily a teacher of the history of economic thought. Thus, there are such posts, but there are very few of them. It's taught a lot more now than it used to be. One factor has been the development of various sub-fields like Post-Keynesian economics, Marxian economics and the neo-institutionalist movement; the latter is likely to promote a lot of interest in the history of institutional economics, both old and new.

And your perceptions of the state of the history of economics at the moment?

I find it difficult to believe that it will continue to grow as a field of research and publication at the rate it's being growing at recently. It's quite astonishing in terms of sheer quantity; and it's bewildering to some extent in terms of range of things now being done. Developments in methodology and the philosophy of economics linked to history have all sorts of intellectual potentialities. For example, someone could try write a deconstructionist history of economics though I doubt that could be done for the entire subject. Certainly, for example, histories of the theme of evolution in economics, of ethics and economics, and the relationship between economics and sociology – there are all sorts of possibilities like that. I think it's very encouraging that there has been this great expansion in the discipline, though I can't help feeling a bit bemused by it. There's the awful problem of what to read. There is the danger of minute overspecialisation, so that eventually those working in the field can hardly talk to or understand each other. If only people would just stop writing for awhile! I have said for some time, that if only we could shut down Routledge and Elgar and Cambridge and a couple of other publishers, and put Warren Samuels and Mark Blaug in a dungeon, we might have time to read more of the literature we have! What does one do about this? I've never been well disciplined in what I do. I'm very easily drawn in different directions, so one feels that one is simply a *dilettante*; one dabbles in this and in that.

As for the future, it's very open. If the current dissatisfaction with the core graduate training in economics grows to an extent where people feel we really must do something different from what is being done already, then the potential for a serious interest in the history of economics by practicing economists is almost infinite. The possibility is not the creation of lots and lots of teaching positions in the field but of bringing it closer to what economists actually do; and that I think is a very healthy sign. It's what Neil De Marchi has called 'recovering practice'. I think there is, however, a danger there; I mean, looking at what economists do in minute detail leads to a kind of descriptivism, a kind of naive empiricism. It is not necessary to go that far – but the more historians of economics are able to show intelligent economists that what they do has some bearing on what the economist does in his main professional activity, the more it will be constructive. For example, the recent work on the history of econometrics is a very exciting development; and Roy Weintraub's work on the history of mathematical economics is extremely good (I mean it helps me understand things I couldn't understand otherwise). For example, his article on the existence theorem in the *Journal of Economic Literature* is absolutely superb. If you read it there is correspondence between people talking about politics and all sorts of things. It's not simply straight history of mathematical economics. It's putting it in a rich historical context. And if that doesn't show conventional economists what historians of economics can do, then nothing will.

Notes

* This interview was conducted during A.W. Coats's visit to the Australian National University, Canberra, Australia, February 1995.

1 "Introduction: First kick up dust" *Just On the History of Economic Thought: British and American Economic Essays* Volume 1, London and New York: Routledge, 1992, pp. 1–26, at page 6.

2 "Introduction", pp. 4–5.

3 Black, R.D.C. *Economic Thought and the Irish Question: 1817–1870,* Cambridge: Cambridge University Press, 1960.

4 Mitchell, W.C. *Types of Economic Theory: from mercantilism to institutionalism,* (2 volumes), New York: Augustus M. Kelley, 1967–69, (ed) J. Dorfman.

3 T. W. Hutchison as a historian of economics[1]

> [The historical economists'] approach to the history of political economy and economics did much to raise scholarly and intellectual standards by inculcating a realisation that ... economics is a house of many mansions ... a subject to which there are many different approaches, a number of which possess both validity and interest as well as weaknesses and defects; and that economic truth is not the monopoly of some one particular school or method, or of some one particular academic or political group. Such an approach promotes the idea of synthesis and compromise rather than the lasting confrontations of revolutionary extremes.
>
> Hutchison (1978, pp. 236–237)

I

Terence Wilmot Hutchison (hereinafter referred to as TWH) is much more than merely a historian of economics. During the past five decades he has also made major contributions to the discussion of methodology and the philosophy of economics; the relations between economic theory, policy, and politics; and the increasingly important problems of the economist's professional ethics, standards, and responsibilities. As he has lived through dramatic changes in the prevailing intellectual, political, and socioeconomic climate during the great depression of the 1930s, World War II, and the long postwar boom and expansion of government activity up to the present crisis of capitalism, there have naturally been discernible changes in his views and in the focus and content of his work. Nevertheless, a systematic examination of his writings reveals a remarkable independent-mindedness, underlying unity, and consistency of mental outlook and purpose, from his first published note on "Tautologies and the Nature of Economic Theory" (1935) to his latest collection of essays, *The Politics and Philosophy of Economics: Marxists, Keynesians and Austrians* (1981), which contains a powerful and sustained attack on some of his former teachers and the Cambridge tradition in which he was reared (1981, pp. 46–107).

Given this unity and consistency, any attempt to treat his historical contributions and interests in isolation from other aspects of his work would necessarily be somewhat artificial and misleading. Nevertheless, in the following account attention will be concentrated mainly on that part of his output which has recently led no less an authority than Gottfried Haberler to describe TWH as "the foremost living historian of economic thought" (See Hutchison, 1980; also 1981, pp. 233–265).

II

TWH was born in London on August 13, 1912, and studied classics at Tonbridge School before entering Peterhouse College, Cambridge, in 1931, shortly after Britain left the gold standard. Partly under the influence of contemporary events, he took an active interest in politics and decided to switch from classics to economics at the end of his first year, despite some opposition from the college authorities who, having no suitable tutor among their numbers, were obliged to farm him out to a rising young scholar, Mrs. Joan Robinson. This move proved to be a significant turning point in his intellectual development, and those familiar with TWH's later writings may be surprised to find, in the preface to his first book, his tribute to her, and an acknowledgement of his "general indebtedness to the incomparable training in and stimulus to economic thinking" which he received in Cambridge.[2]

For a student of economics and politics this was, of course, one of the most exciting (and subsequently most intensively researched) periods in Cambridge University's history. In addition to the small so-called circus engaged in assisting John Maynard Keynes's epoch-making intellectual Odyssey from the *Treatise on Money* (1930) to the *General Theory of Employment, Interest and Money* [(1936); see his *Collected Writings* (1973–); also Patinkin and Leith (1977)], there was also another small coterie – even more sinister, some jaundiced anti-Keynesians would probably contend – including Anthony Blunt, Guy Burgess, Donald Maclean, and Harold (Kim) Philby, who were assiduously, but more covertly, creating what has since become known as a "climate of treason" (Boyle, 1979; Howarth, 1978). Sensationalists may be disappointed to learn that TWH belonged to neither of these privileged circles. Then, as often later, he was to some degree an outsider, perceptively observing the course of ideas and events and formulating his own independent viewpoint. He had a brief flirtation with Labour politics, but, more importantly, like so many others of his generation, he was profoundly disturbed by the manifest failure of the capitalist system and felt a keen urge to seek understanding and solutions for present discontents. Had he been more extraverted, TWH might have sought a political career, since he was then at least as interested in politics as in economics, and he has sometimes wondered whether political science would have been his true academic forte. Had he been at Oxford, rather than Cambridge, he would doubtless have switched to Modern Greats, or PPE – i.e., politics, philosophy, and economics – a much less specialized course than Cambridge economics, and who can judge which of these three might have become his chosen field? But as it transpired, he encountered Cambridge economics at a critical juncture, a time when the Marshallian hegemony was at last coming under serious challenge even from within the citadel, and this provided him with one of the central themes of his life's work, namely, the fundamental critical study of the nature, provenance, and limitations of economic science.

It was not Keynes, whose lectures he attended, but Joan Robinson whose lead he followed; and it was methodology, not history, that initially became the central focus of his intellectual quest. Evidence of the continuity and persistence of this exploration is provided by the presence of "basic postulates" in the title of his first book and "knowledge" or "philosophy" in the titles of his three most recent volumes. Like a number of distinguished predecessors and contemporaries, TWH quickly discovered that, while economics was more relevant to current affairs than classics, its teachings were a good deal less clear-cut and constructive than he had hoped. He first seriously encountered current scepticism in his tutor's provocative pamphlet *Economics Is a Serious Subject* (1932), and this was subsequently reinforced by parts of her more orthodox, yet pathbreaking and occasionally iconoclastic study *The Economics of Imperfect Competition* (1933). From outside Cambridge came Lionel Robbins's comparatively complacent and defensive *Nature and Significance of Economic Science* (1932), which, like Robbins's innovative lectures at the London School of Economics (LSE), introduced TWH and others to a number of methodological writings unfamiliar or completely unknown to most British economists. Joan Robinson probably exaggerated the differences when, in her pamphlet, she contrasted the "rough-and-ready common-sense English economists" with their continental counterparts "who are experts in methodology." Nevertheless there was substantial justification for her complaint about

> the bad habit of English economists of never giving a proper account of their assumptions. The search for Marshall's hidden assumptions has occupied a whole generation, and almost threatened at one time to turn English economists into a school of higher-critical theologians (1932, pp. 8–9).

Joan Robinson's particular brand of heresy was still rare among Cambridge insiders during TWH's undergraduate days, and doubtless it affected him deeply. And he was also profoundly influenced by another Cambridge contemporary, the philosopher Ludwig Wittgenstein, whose ideas underlay much of TWH's methodological thinking in the 1930s.[3] But by the time he completed his first book in 1937 he had encounted a variety of other important influences, initially after graduating from Cambridge, in 1934, during his two terms as an occasional student at LSE, where he met and heard Robbins and F. A. Hayek (for background, see Coats, 1982), and subsequently in Bonn, where he had ample time to immerse himself in the continental European literature on economics and philosophy. This location was undoubtedly significant, for it was well outside the mainstream of British economics in the heady revolutionary days of the mid- and late 1930s, thereby enabling – indeed obliging – TWH to develop his own detached but not neutral perspective on contemporary academic and real-world issues. It also gave him the opportunity to meet and marry a German girl, Loretta Hack, whose active and lively mind stimulated and enriched his already growing knowledge and understanding of European literature, life, and thought. This has indeed been one of the most distinctive features and strengths of his subsequent economic writings.

III

In studying TWH primarily as a historian of economics it is inappropriate to examine in detail either the content or the impact of his *Significance and Basic Postulates.* As its avowed purpose was "to help in elucidating the significance of that body of 'pure theory' the possession of which distinguishes Economics from the other social sciences" (1960, p. 3), history naturally occupied a subordinate place. Nevertheless, despite several rather unsympathetic reviews, there was praise of TWH's wide-ranging citations from the works of notable past great economists in several different languages. However, no reviewer remarked upon the budding historian's frank and perceptive admission that because

> too much 'originiality' ... in many cases seems probably to be dangerous fault in a scientific work ... I have therefore made in this book extensive references to and quotations from other writers to whom I am indebted *or would have been indebted had I happened to read their works earlier.* It seemed to me, further, more impressive and convincing, either in bringing support for my own conclusions or in the expositions of doctrines that seemed to me criticizable, to cite the actual works of authoritative writers (1960, p. xxv; italics supplied).

This unusually revealing passage, with its explicit references to originality and authority, displays TWH's youthful sensitivity to both the individual psychology and the sociology of the academic process, matters that were to figure much more prominently in his later writings. It also exemplifies the honesty, detachment, and independence which have characterized his work. A few lines later he acknowledged "the possible danger of misquotation or misrepresentation" in citing the works of previous writers to buttress a position initially arrived at by a priori reasoning or sheer prejudice. Of course all historians, indeed perhaps all scholars, encounter this problem of textual exegesis, a matter that cannot be fully explored here (Stigler, 1965). It is one that will, however, reappear when we consider some of TWH's more recent writings later (in Section IV).

TWH did not enter the mainstream of British academic life until 1946, when he became a Temporary Lecturer in Economics at Hull University. From 1938, when he left Germany, he was Professor of English and Social Studies at the Teacher's Training College in Baghdad, where he remained until he joined the Indian Army Intelligence Service. During that period he read comparatively little economics and had no contacts with professional economists and, again, it is tempting to speculate whether his subsequent ideas and attitudes might not have been rather different had he, like so many other economists of his generation, been employed in Whitehall during World War II. At Hull he taught the history of economics, keeping (as he recalls) one week ahead of the students by reading Alexander Gray's little textbook *The Development of Economic Doctrine,* originally published in 1931. At the end of that year Robbins invited him to join the LSE's staff, suggesting that he should lecture on the history of methodological controversy in economics, an idea he readily accepted. From this point his attention was devoted mainly to doctrinal history, and he wrote only several major book reviews and an article (1953a) on George Berkeley before publishing *A Review of Economic Doctrines, 1870–1939* (Hutchison, 1953b).

This volume assured TWH's position as one of the leading practitioners in the field. It is much more than an advanced textbook since it embodies the fruits of much original and perceptive research. As might be expected, given his background, it revealed TWH's intimate knowledge of continental European economic literature, his profound grasp of methodological issues, and his enduring interest in politics as well as conventional *Dogmengeschichte.* In the preface he explicitly denied any intention of providing a generalized interpretation of the development of economic thought whether "in terms of contemporary economic events, or in other terms" (ibid., p. vii), for, as an empiricist, he has always been chary of sweeping speculative systems.[4] Nevertheless he "especially tried" to present the leading economists' ideas "on the principles of economic policy and the role of the State in economic life," a theme reflecting his awareness of contemporary political and socioeconomic trends. While conceding that the volume focused mainly on "the 'internal' logical requirements of economic theory," he added that this did not imply

> any great confidence in the common liberal-professional assumption that intellectual progress in a particular subject arises simply out of professional intellectual ingenuity working purely on its own particular subject-matter as though in a vacuum

but rather the fact that

> in the earlier part of our period the development of economics as an academic specialism coincided with a period of *comparatively* stable politico-economic development in the Western world, during which economic reality did not force itself *too* brusquely or strikingly on the more detached student (*Ibid.,* p. vii, italics in original).

More recently, however, circumstances had been very different, and the historian's lens needed to be adjusted accordingly.

> Having enjoyed or endured so expensive an education in the Economics of Disturbance, Instability, and Insecurity, it would surely be stupid... conservatively to deny or obscure the great limitations of doctrines formulated for a different sort of world ... [and] even more disastrous practically....Applicability and significance, however, also depend on the economic world for which the doctrine is being formulated and applied. Therefore, some effort of the imagination must constantly be made not to forget that much of what may today seem to betray a lack of realism in what economists in, say 1890 took as their 'normal' model, is due simply to the immense differences in the economic

> world with which they were confronted, as contrasted with that of our own day (*ibid*., pp. ix–x).

These passages have been cited at length because they reveal TWH's fundamental outlook as a historian and announce themes that connect the *Review* with his first book and with his later writings. The element of historical relativism in the 1953 volume was foreshadowed two years earlier in his thoughtful review of Wesley Mitchell's *Types of Economic Theory*,[5] in which he argued that Mitchell's encyclopedic "externalist" treatment of economic thought worked comparatively well for the pre-1870 period but was much less suitable thereafter, as economics became so much more of a professional academic specialism. This insight may indeed have influenced TWH's decision to subdivide the *Review of Economic Doctrines* into Part I (individual economists and schools); Part II (various branches of economic theory); and Part III (the economics of instability and disturbance) – an arrangement which irritated several reviewers. As in his 1938 book TWH was, like Mitchell, concerned with both the practical and the methodologial status of economic theory, but he adopted a much more charitable view of orthodox "pure" theory in 1953 than in either his earlier or his later work. Nevertheless, as already noted, already in 1953, he emphasized its "limitations" and the "disastrous" consequences of attempts to apply "doctrines formulated for a different world," and this foreshadows one of the central messages of his most recent writings.

As with several of TWH's books, the reactions to the *Review* were mixed, but on the whole decidedly favorable. Reviewers expressed reservations about his "somewhat involved" style; his evident likes and dislikes [e.g., his treatment of Marshall was termed "niggling" or "somewhat carping" (Guillebaud, 1953, p. 364)]; his effort to cover too much material; and the idiosyncratic organization of subject matter. However, there was also high praise of the author's erudition; his range; the quality of his insights and interpretations; and his unusual capacity to discover and appreciate the value of significant contributions by hitherto unknown or neglected authors. Carl Uhr (1953, p. 936) described the *Review* as an "outstanding treatise," and H. W. Spiegel (1953, pp. 542–544) even more aptly, termed it:

> a gold mine which future authors of histories of economics will want to exploit ... [It is] lucid, urbane and subtle. This is one of the books which can be read from cover to cover with a great deal of sustained pleasure. It belongs in the hands of all economists whose horizon encompasses more than the narrow task of the day.

Only a few of the book's more conspicuous features can be mentioned here. It actually covers a far wider chronological range than the title suggests. This is largely the corollary of a strikingly novel feature insufficiently appreciated by reviewers, namely, the attention devoted to Say's Law, a concept featured more prominently here than in any previous English language doctrinal history text. When the *Review* appeared Keynes's influence was at or approaching its height, especially in Britain, and TWH did not conceal his own sympathies in declaring that "James Mill's dogmatic rigmarole about the impossibility of general overproduction" and the support it received from later classical economists like J. S. Mill, H. Fawcett, and J. E. Cairnes, "must surely represent the most successful and important campaign of intellectual aggression and terminological dogmatism in the history of economic thought."[6] TWH's distaste for Ricardian orthodoxy had already been revealed in his less than deferential review of the early volumes of Sraffa's great edition; and it was to be reiterated and reinforced in subsequent years (1951b, cf. 1978, pp. 26–57). His perceptive analysis of Bishop Berkeley's *Querist*[7] (published in the same year as the *Review*) formed part of the influential postwar reappraisal of pre-Smithian ideas inspired by Keynes's "Notes on Mercantilism," the penultimate chapter of the *General Theory.* Here, too, is evidence of TWH's essential consistency, for despite his later severely caustic attacks on the Keynesians' distortions and perversions of Keynes's teachings he has always admired and respected Keynes himself. Moreover, *On Revolutions and Progress in Economic Knowledge* contains a surprisingly favorable, even indulgent, account of Keynes's brilliant but occasionally cavalier forays into doctrinal history (1978, pp. 121–174).

In addition to Keynes's list of his own precursors, which included both pre-Smithian writers and such nineteenth century heretics as T. R. Malthus and J. A. Hobson, TWH drew attention to K. H. Rau, W. G. F. Roscher, H. K. E. Mangoldt, and others whose "steady and sensible" criticism of Say's Law of markets had paved the way for the more constructive analyses of crises and fluctuations examined in Part III of the *Review.* Like J. A. Schumpeter, whose work he greatly admired and respected (see Hutchison, 1982), TWH drew on his deep knowledge of European literature, which enabled him to provide a much broader and more detached perspective on British economics than most of his countrymen. Curiously enough, as in Schumpeter's magisterial *History of Economic Analysis,* published posthumously a year later, the *Review* displays an unconcealed tone of satisfaction derived from deflating some of the great figures and revealing

> how much of the most original and enduring work was due to complete outsiders unknown in orthodox circles; or at any rate to thinkers who met with very little recognition from other economists in their own day (1953b, p. 17).

Not surprisingly, TWH's assured handling of methodological issues is one of the *Review*'s many strengths, which is nowhere more evident than in the treatment of Carl Menger and the *Methodenstreit.* No other English-speaking economist had treated that turbulent episode so fully and fairly, notwithstanding TWH's obvious distaste for L. von Mises's methodological individualism in the 1938 book. Fifteen years later TWH reported that the battle over methods

> did not give rise to much positive methodological analysis, the problems of which lie rather in how empirical, analytical and 'practical' prepositions combine and apply to one another... for Menger was concerned with problems of methodological *norms* rather than with 'positive' methodological

> analysis or elucidation, that is, with trying to lay down what economists *ought* to aim at or study, and how they ought to study it, and with fixing the value of history and statistics as being simply auxiliary (*ibid.*, pp. 149–150; italics in original; sentence order reversed).

On Schumpeter's view that the *Methodenstreit* was essentially "a struggle for Luftraum oder Herrschaft (breathing-space or mastery):" he commented, caustically:

> Neither of these rather Teutonically conceived desiderata has much to do with the search for truth or the eradication of error. In fact, of course, they usually beckon in precisely the opposite direction.[8]

Of course, TWH appreciated that conflicts between doctrinal schools often involved personal, sociological, and even nationalistic considerations as well as strictly methodological issues, and the underlying prescriptive aims provided one of the central themes of his next book, *'Positive' Economics and Policy Objectives* (1964), in which he most effectively combined his skills in history and methodology.[9] This volume also revealed the widening range of his postwar interests, for in addition to providing an historical perspective on the perennial problem of the respective spheres of positive and normative economics he went on to examine the economist's role and responsibilities in the policymaking process, a motif which has been repeatedly echoed in his later writings.[10] Here, as earlier, he aimed to provide both clarification and understanding of one of the most sensitive yet intensely practical aspects of the economist's activities. His intention was both scholarly and present-minded, for as policy objectives had become more ambitious, wide ranging, quantitatively precise, and liable to be mutually inconsistent, he believed it was increasingly important to explicate the relevant value judgments or preference functions. Under present-day conditions, logical and methodological issues necessarily impinged on questions of professional ethics and "the functions, duties, and sphere of 'scientists,' economists 'as such,' experts, advisers, and University teachers who write, say, to *The Times*." Consequently, while he would "shrink in horror from attempting to lay down the law on questions of professional ethics," he could not excape the obligation to explicate the views implicit in the earlier chapters of his book (1964, p. 189). In so doing, he revealed the basic methodological and political convictions which have guided his work, especially during the postwar period.

At the risk of distorting TWH's position the following summary (*ibid.*, pp. 189–197) may be helpful:

1. Although economists have usually underestimated the difficulties involved, a clear distinction should as far as possible be maintained between positive and normative statements.
2. The aim of a scientific positive economics is neither impossible nor unattainable in principle. Although many seemingly descriptive statements have hidden value implications, and are therefore ambiguous, "there is no reason

why these should not yield to the critical processes of scientific procedure, like other mistakes in logic or mathematics."

3. Economists should not be expected to confine themselves to purely positive statements. But even here questions of professional ethics arise "with regard to indicating the evidence, the extent and results of testing, and the degree of consensus, regarding positive-empirical statements and theories," matters on which the individual scientist should be as vigilant, self-critical, and detached as possible.
4. While the role of value judgments in policy recommendations is generally recognized, it is far more complex and comprehensive than usually appreciated owing to the customary neglect of uncertainty factors. It is one thing to choose objectives and quite another to ascertain whether those objectives are in fact attainable. "Democratic theory seems to require that the role of the 'expert,' economic or otherwise, be as clearly defined and limited as possible, and that his function should, as nearly as possible, be confined to elucidating and interpreting choices, rather than proclaiming them or laying them down."

At first sight these broad, prescriptive methodological rules may seem both obvious (especially as summarized here) and unrelated to the craft of the historian of economics, but on closer inspection neither of these impressions is warranted. The foundations of scientific method are metaphysical, not scientific – as, for example, with the "demarcation principle," which TWH introduced into economics in 1938[12] – and "all formal rules of scientific procedure must prove ambiguous, for they will be interpreted differently according to the particular conceptions about the nature of things by which the scientist is guided" (Polanyi, 1958, p. 167). Not that scientific work is purely arbitrary, a matter of individual judgement or caprice, for its results are subject to what Ernest Nagel has termed "the self-corrective mechanisms of science as a social enterprise" (1961, p. 489). How far these mechanisms operate effectively in any discipline at any given time is, of course, itself a matter of judgment, one on which an historical perspective and training may be valuable, if not essential. Here lies the central connection between TWH's work as a methodologist and as an historian. As he was aware in the 1930s, in economics the authority of tradition is strong; well-defined standards of technical competence are lacking, and it is exceedingly difficult to devise conclusive empirical tests of the validity of economic hypotheses or statements. Under these circumstances the "self-corrective mechanisms of science as a social enterprise" are liable to function badly, if at all, and he believed this deficiency had become increasingly serious, both for the economics profession itself and the general public as the result of postwar developments, to which we must now turn.

IV

The underlying shift of focus and emphasis in TWH's postwar writings between the four main components – methodology, history, politics, and professionalism – can be depicted and accounted for in a number of different ways. Most pertinent to historians of economics, perhaps, is the approach outlined in his brief popular essay on the changing relationships between economics and politics in Britain since the early nineteenth century, "The Market Economy and the Franchise, or 1867 and All That" (1981, pp. 23–45).

Acknowledging that a shifting combination of "internal" and "external" influences had shaped the economists' agenda in different periods, TWH sought to direct attention away from economic events and developments, which have usually been recognized as important, to "changing political forces and changes in policy preferences and demands." Thus classical political economy in its prime was inevitably involved with political values and reform objectives because it was "concerned with the reshaping of the whole framework or constitution of the economy on competitive free-market principles," though the role of government as such was then far more limited than it is in this century. "In the neoclassical period, however, from its formative phase in the 1860's and 1870's onwards, these major political concerns largely disappeared," and in spite of extensions of the franchise the interactions of politics and economics were "at something of an all-time low" as the result of "a fleeting impermanent conjuncture, fundamentally one of politico-economic disequilibrium." With the development of academic economics, a justifiable departmental division of labor emerged between nonpolitical economics and political studies, but unfortunately "the justification for nonpolitical economics sometimes got mixed up with the case for a politically neutral, value-free economics" and the term "political" became increasingly equated with "normative" or "ethical," as though political behavior and processes could not be studied as positively or neutrally as economic processes (ibid., pp. 23, 33–34).

One important by-product of this supposedly nonpolitical attitude has been "the tremendous importance economists attach to one another's ideas, for better or worse, in the determination of economic policy," and this of course paved the way for the exaggerated overconfidence and collective professional hubris of the postwar Keynesian era. In juxtaposition to Keynes's own oft-quoted dictum on the ruling importance of economic ideas, TWH is fond of quoting John Stuart Mill's reminder that "Ideas, unless outward circumstances conspire with them, have in general no very rapid or immediate efficacy in human affairs" (1845, p. 503), and in TWH's recent writings the preponderant influence of outward circumstances is repeatedly emphasized. The post-1945 expansion of government has transformed both the nature and scale of interactions between political and economic processes: "Not only are economic processes substantially controlled or affected by political forces, but they react back on politics, through the ability of governments to improve their chances of holding on to political power by short-run economic manipulation." Of course, some economists, like the public choice theorists, have recognized the implications of these changes. Yet TWH has little hope of solutions from the so-called economic theory of politics, which, by relying on maximization analysis,

> shares with much traditional economic theorizing the limitations or problems, of (1) the extent of knowledge, ignorance and uncertainty with which a maximand is pursued, and (2) the content of the maximand.

While efforts in this direction may have some value in exposing the naive and crude politics concealed or embodied in much earlier political economy, on the whole TWH shares Herbert Simon's view that more drastic changes in the conventional approach are required. Thus, he maintains, "Political theorizing which takes account of ignorance, uncertainty and complex political maximands cannot avoid, methodologically, a 'long march through the institutions'" *(ibid.,* pp. 35–39). It is necessary to restore to economics its earlier concern with *Ordnungspolitik,* which primarily involves political and qualitative rather than narrowly economic and quantitative objectives, and to develop a new political economy, "not simply in normative terms in providing value-judgments and policy-objectives, but *also in positive terms* with regard to how institutions work and how political man behaves" (ibid., pp. 97, 162–163, cf. 1964, pp. 125–126). It is no longer feasible, as in the days of Alfred Marshall and A. C. Pigou, to assume a stable general culture or socioeconomic framework.

Underlying TWH's later writings on economics there is a deep concern about certain manifest postwar tendencies. This is clearly revealed, curiously enough, in the *Review*, in the previously quoted section on Menger. After commenting on Menger's belief in the general

> beneficence of spontaneous, 'unreflected' social phenomena, the result of no formally agreed plan or legislation, like language, the State itself, competition, or money

TWH added that

> Since Menger's day there has been an immense further growth in what may be called 'social self-consciousness,' with the spread or urbanisation, literacy, popular means of communication, and (usually on a somewhat higher level) social and economic statistics, which have together produced that state of 'fanaticised consciousness' that characterises the modern world. *Among the most profound transformers of the socially unconscious into the socially conscious are, of course, the economists and social scientists....*For society, as for an individual, a heightening of self-consciousness is obviously an irreversible step, at least in a democratic society with free distribution of increased social knowledge. There is no going back to a blissful unself-conscious childhood either for society or the individual, and each has to bear the burden easily, not to throw it off, which cannot be done except through madness or self-destruction.[13]

Irrespective of whether this passage reflected TWH's first-hand experience of German conditions in the late 1930s, there is no mistaking the parallels between his abhorrence of Nazi totalitarianism and his many scathing postwar references to socialist dictatorship. These sentiments largely explain his scorn and disgust at what he terms the "infallibist" and "apostolic" doctrines of Marxists and Keynesians, especially those of his Cambridge contemporaries Maurice Dobb and

Joan Robinson (1978, pp. 249, 265, 270; 1981, pp. 82–83, 83–88, 94–5, 98, 218). But while his adverse judgments will be familiar to readers of his more recent works, it may be more fruitful to consider the positive aspects of his beliefs, especially as revealed in his 1979 article on "Walter Eucken and the German Social-Market Economy." In this instance, he maintained, "we have an unusually unambiguous example of the beneficent effects of economists' ideas on economic policy" and quoted approvingly the views of those who identified Eucken as the "intellectual godfather" of this success story.[14]

For Eucken, *Ordnungspolitik,* in the form of a sound legal and institutional framework, was the essential basis for successful economic policies. Nevertheless he was no crude advocate of laissez-faire. On the contrary, he considered that:

> We still have no answer to the problem of how to organise an industrialised economy humanely and efficiently.... [However,] the problem will not solve itself simply by our letting economic systems grow up spontaneously. The history of the last century has shown this plainly enough. The economic system has to be consciously shaped (1981, p. 163).

The postwar German Federal Republic's success was directly associated with the combination of limited government economic and social interventionism and reliance on market principles, a conjuncture made possible by the strong reaction against the previous mixture of total economic control and political dictatorship, which had brought disaster. The circumstances differed profoundly from conditions in the United Kingdom and the United States at that time, yet TWH quotes with evident satisfaction the judgment that "West Germany's impressive recovery took place under policies that were in many respects the direct antithesis of post-Keynesian prescriptions for rapid economic growth" *(ibid.,* p. 169; cf. pp. 108–154, and 20).

This is not the place to examine either the validity of TWH's interpretation of the German "economic miracle" or his general views on economic policy – views which he has deliberately suppressed, on the grounds that this was necessary to his role as a scholarly historian and detached commentator. More directly pertinent here is the manner in which he has utilised what he aptly terms the "historical-contemporary tense" to demonstrate the relevance of the history of economics to such current issues as the training of apprentice economists, the activities of accredited professional practitioners, the scientific status of economics, and consequently its practical influence in the contemporary world. These matters are of central importance to this volume, for no other historian of economics has so effectively brought his specialist knowledge and skills to bear on the discipline's past, present, and prospective problems.

TWH's first sustained undertaking in this area was his pathbreaking *Economics and Economic Policy in Britain: Some Aspects of their Interrelations* (1966), a book that outraged some of his professional peers and raised important issues of historiographic principle. By analyzing systematically a large number of ephemeral sources such as newspapers, popular magazines, radio talks, and speeches, in addition to the more usual scholarly periodicals and books designed for professional and student audiences, TWH had no difficulty in showing that some well-known economists had not only been guilty of error, vagueness, and inconsistency – all of which are, up to a point, pardonable – but also that in some cases they had been guilty of evasiveness, gross overconfidence, arrogance, irresponsibility, and even perhaps dishonesty.

Predictably some of his victims responded angrily, accusing him of misquotation or misrepresentation by selecting isolated passages out of context, a danger to which he had already been sensitive when he produced his first book. But in his vigorous defense he emphasised that selection was obviously unavoidable and challenged his critics to provide evidence of misquotation – which none of them was either able or willing to do – and commented wryly on the curious snobbery which treats eighteenth and nineteenth century published ephemera as suitable material for serious scholars yet denies this role to exactly comparable up-to-date equivalents. Beyond this, he retorted that those who preferred to laugh off or neglect such "cutting jobs" or "scissors and paste efforts" as unworthy or irrelevant might really "be simply seeking to ward off *any* genuinely critical methodological appraisal of economists' policy pronouncements by discrediting the basic empirical evidence which is available."[15] But for those who were unwilling to take this easy way out, the results of this volume, and a later study entitled "Economists on Devaluation and Europe, 1964–74" (1977b, pp. 98–143), were acutely embarrassing not only to some of those more frequently cited but also, more seriously, for the economics profession at large. It was not simply that the evidence revealed profound and persistent disagreements on matters of principle, theory, and practice – important though these undoubtedly were; more fundamental still were the underlying doubts engendered about "what economists know and how they know it, as contrasted with what they think or assume they know, and what, on the other hand, they don't know" *(ibid.*, p. 101). As he had perspicaciously observed in '*Positive' Economics and Policy Objectives*, in commenting on the view that the arguments for and against Britain's entry into the European Economic Community (EEC) were "evenly balanced," there is

> a vital distinction between a confident belief on convincing evidence that the balance of advantages is about even, or is likely only to veer very slightly either way, and a belief that in view of the extensive ignorance of many of the factors affecting the various kinds of advantage and disadvantage involved, a fifty-fifty toss-up is as rational a method of decision as any other (1964, p. 99).

All too often economists' forecasts weighed the factors involved in such a way as to generate conclusions in conformity with their own social or political prejudices, or, in conformity with the prevailing consensus at the time. In order to be both more reputable and more effective as forecasters or assessors of economic trends and tendencies it was necessary to specify (1) the kinds of issues on which economists' (or some kinds of economists') guesses are better than other people's and (2) what exactly it is in their equipment or qualifications which, on some reasonably clearly defined issues, will justify one in holding that economists' (or some kinds of economists), guesses *are* better than other people's (1966, p. 260).

TWH did not attempt to supply these specifications in detail for he was well aware of the difficulties involved and he was naturally disinclined to appear either dogmatic or unduly prescriptive. However, despite the absence of agreed "assessments as to who the best guessers are, or what their 'batting averages' have been" *(ibid.*, p. 262), he did tentatively suggest that, on the basis of his analysis of the British evidence, successful predictions were, generally, negatively correlated with

1. ideological dogmatism and party-political fervor, and
2. subservience to fashion; at best neutrally or perhaps negatively correlated with
3. mathematical and geometric facility; and positively correlated with
4. institutional experience,
5. knowledge of historical cases and processes in economic policy, and the critical study of theories and policies relevant to economic policy, and
6. knowledge of administrative and political processes which should help in the appreciation of the gulf which yawns between bright ideas and successful legislation or policies.[16]

These are clearly issues of immense professional and public importance since they constitute the principal basis on which the economists' base their claims to expertise and, consequently, their employment opportunities outside the academic sphere (and it is worth noting that TWH was already voicing these concerns in the mid 1960s, well before it became fashionable to lament the existence of a "crisis" in economics). The connection between these practical concerns and the underlying methodological principles is abundantly clear in TWH's later contention that

> if the economists *cannot go on to predict at all, or improve or assist in forming less inaccurate predictions, as to the effects of possible policies by which objectives can be approached, then his contribution hardly matches up to the traditional aims and claims to promote the wealth of nations and reduce poverty and unemployment* (1977b, p. 9; italics in original).

As will appear below, the deliberate reference to the title of Smith's great classic is a direct clue to the balanced blend of predictivism and history underlying TWH's mature programmatic pronouncements.

TWH's *On Revolutions and Progress in Economic Knowledge* (1978) provides yet another original and provocative example of how he has endeavored to utilize history in the education of economists. By means of extensive studies of the discipline's historiography (see Chap. 5, 8, and 9), TWH was able to show how often economists from Smith to Keynes and after have reinterpreted doctrinal history in order to discredit rival ideas and approaches and demonstrate convincingly the revolutionary significance of their own innovations or favored doctrines.

From these exercises few reputations have emerged unscarred, and TWH has been unsparing in exposing and denouncing "the evil intent of apologetic" in each literature. Nevertheless, here too his intention has not been simply destructive, for he has emphasized that

> *these persuasive and justificatory 'scenarios,' devised as a prestigeful framework for advancing of their [authors'] theories and ideas, may, in some cases, have had a valuable contribution to make to the history of the subject.*[17]

Toward the end of his historiographic survey TWH maintained that a more disciplined study of the history of economics might make a valuable contribution to raising scholarly and scientific standards throughout the subject. Indeed,

> it is probably the case that the standards generally maintained in writing the history of economics, including its contemporary history, may be taken as a reflection, or indicator, of how far economics is being pursued as a serious subject *(ibid.,* p. 276).

If this is in fact the case, there is perhaps some hope for economics, given the vigorous renaissance of *Dogmengeschichte* during the past decade or so.

V

This is a large claim, more ambitious in its scope and pretensions than most historians or economists might assert. Yet, as shown earlier, TWH's practice of history has consistently been both scholarly and pragmatic. He has studied the past not only "for its own sake" – whatever that may signifiy – but also as a means of illuminating the present and raising current and prospective professional standards.

As Neil De Marchi has noted in an excellently perceptive review of *On Revolutions and Progress in Economics*, "what is called progress in economics is going to depend on which methodological rules one prefers" (1979, pp. 1021–1023), and this remark provides a further link between TWH's early convictions and his later historical work. In the concluding chapter of his first book he declared that "Advance in economic knowledge depends ultimately on discovering, however limited, provisional, and tentative they may be, such [empirical] regularities" in the behavior of economic actors under differing circumstances (1960, p. 164). Exactly 40 years later, in a less "naturalistic" frame of mind, under radically changed circumstances, and with the benefit of hindsight, he still held that "The steady growth of historical and statistical material might well he regarded as the most solid basis for a belief in the progress of economic knowledge" (1978, p. 318), although he was also prepared to acknowledge the evidence of progress in mathematical and statistical techniques. By this time, however, he had come to believe that the development of ever more general, abstract theories or models had become distinctly counterproductive. Consequently,

> instead of waiting for Newton, or a new Keynes, it may be more promising to seek to restore the historical, institutional and psychological components of the subject, so masterfully incorporated in *The Wealth of Nations.*[18]

In pursuing this line of argument TWH formulated the most original and provocative theme of *On Revolutions and Progress in Economic Knowledge* – his attack on the James Mill-Ricardo "methodological revolution," on the grounds that it had "removed or destroyed the historical dimension of the subject which was so vital and pervasive for Adam Smith,"[19] who is one of TWH's heroes. He maintained that the costs of the practice, introduced by Ricardo, of cultivating "ever more precise, and frequently extremely abstract, maximising, self-equilibrating 'models'" had been excessive and damaging

> in terms of the kind of empirical, predictive, policy-relevant content, which economists have usually and traditionally aimed at and claimed....Perhaps the programme, or 'paradigm' based on these kinds of abstract 'models' should now be phased out, or relegated to a minor role in a new kind of 'consultant-administrative' economics, which in a primitive form had been dominant in the seventeenth and eighteenth centuries.[20]

To many historians of economics, and especially those economists who are defenders of the orthodox mainstream in the discipline, TWH's attack on the Mill-Ricardo tradition has seemed unwarranted and excessive. This is true, for example, of George J. Stigler, who has described TWH as "a devoted student of the history of economics" who "has been unfailingly honest, deeply and widely read, and frequently completely dissatisfied with the literature of which he is so completely a master." While granting that Ricardo often carried abstraction too far, Stigler nevertheless emphasized (as most commentators probably would) Ricardo's invaluable contribution "to the development of a tight logical structure which is the essential strength of economics today." Beyond this, Stigler reiterated his personal disagreement with TWH's preference for "insight" over "logic," saying (1978, pp. 396–399):

> Consider what that rule would do to a science: logic, which is at least and at once verifiable, should give way to insight, the validity of which can only be confirmed after the time when it has been successfully incorporated into a system of coherent theory!

In general, Stigler considered that while there were still abundant targets for TWH's charges of anti-empiricism, formalism, and overhasty views on policy, he had nevertheless underestimated the extent and accelerating pace of the cumulative progress in microeconomics *(ibid.,* p. 599).

In De Marchi's apt review of *On Revolutions and Progress,* cited earlier, he referred to TWH's

> Knack for choosing interesting questions, impeccable scholarship, sharp but substantiated criticism, disdain of fashion, distaste for everything that smacks of centralising attempts to circumscribe individual freedom of choice, and an ease with words which makes reading a delight (1979, p. 1021).

Although TWH's style is often cautious and somewhat hesitant, as though betraying an undue anxiety to weigh his words carefully, there is clear evidence of his classical training, his unusually wide reading – in philosophy, politics, and literature, as well as innumerable contemporary newspapers, magazines, etc. – and continuing emphasis on the precision and clarity of language. In addition to his capacity for sustained logical argument and his exceptional skill in selecting apt and telling quotations even from the most familiar economic classics, behind his restrained language there is evidently a passionate concern for what he has termed the "square," "old fashioned" academic and scientific values. Even his warmest admirers concede that at times the tone is too passionate – for example, in his critique of his former Cambridge colleagues and Ricardo; and doubtless some readers have stronger objections to his persistent baiting of modern Marxists and authoritarian regimes of all ages. Against his chief opponents he can muster a devastating scorn, consummate polemical ability, and mordant wit, and when this is combined, as is often the case, with his disclaimer of personal political or policy commitments and insistence on his role as a neutral observer, there is an irresistible temptation to compare him with that other notable economic outsider, Thorstein Veblen.

Whether the economics profession will listen more carefully, and follow more closely the advice proffered, however cautiously, by this equally penetrating critic remains to be seen. However, a sustained look at the persistence of certain perennial weaknesses in the literature of economics and in the conduct of economists does not, it must be concluded, inspire much optimism.

Notes

1 This is a revised and extended version of a paper delivered at the History of Economics Society's annual conference at East Lansing, Michigan, in May 1981.

2 Hutchison (1938). It had, as TWH put it, "another little run for Mr. Kelley's money," with a revealing new Preface, in a New York 1960 reprint. Here the reference to Joan Robinson and Cambridge appears on p. xxvi. All subsequent references are to this edition (1960a). The new Preface contains TWH's reflections on subsequent methodological discussion, especially Karl R. Popper's notion of the "demarcation criterion," first introduced into economics by TWH. While conceding certain "crudities and inadequacies" in his 1938 dichotomy between "tautologies" and testable (or falsifiable) empirical statements, and admitting that he had perhaps "concentrated too exclusively on fitting economic statements into one or other of these two categories" (p. xxi), he nevertheless stoutly defended himself against such critics as Fritz Machlup, Kurt Klappholz, and Joseph Agassi. Years later he commented that while the book was "in many ways a sceptical work by the standards of 1938, its optimistic 'naturalism' seems now indefensible" (1977, p. 151).

3 Wittgenstein (1921). It was the subject of vigorous debate in Cambridge during the 1930s. This is not the place to examine TWH's philosophical views. However, in reply to Frank Knight's fierce review (1941), TWH declared his general allegiance to the "Anglo-Saxon" as against the "Teutonic" tradition, referring specifically to John Locke, David Hume. J. S. Mill, and the contemporary philosophers Bertrand Russell, Ludwig Wittgenstein, Ernst Mach, M. Schlick, and Rudolf Carnap (Hutchison, 1941, p. 735). This article demonstrates TWH's devasting polemical ability. Professor W. D. Grampp recalls that some of his Chicago graduate contemporaries considered Knight's review both ill-judged and unfair to TWH.

4 See, for example, his cautious and qualified "definitions and conclusions" in the final, overview chapter of *On Revolutions and Progress ...* (1978, pp. 286–320).

5 Hutchison (1951a); reprinted in Burns (1952, pp. 292–300). Mitchell would have sympathized with TWH's emphasis on the practical social significance of economic doctrines and would probably have agreed that "these static or 'stationary' self-adjusting models had far greater justification when compared with the economic life of the last quarter of the nineteenth century than they can have today" (1953b, p. viii). The neglect of this issue is one of TWH's principal complaints about contemporary mathematical economics. (See, especially, 1977b, pp. 62–97).

6 Hutchison (1953b, p. 348; also pp. 238–239, 354–358, et. seq.). The tone of this passage recalls Keynes's remark: "Ricardo's doctrine that it was impossible for effective demand to be deficient ... conquered England as completely as the Holy Inquisition conquered Spain" (1936, p. 32).

7 Hutchison (1953b, pp. 32–77). For an effective critique, arguing that TWH had overstated the Keynesian features of Berkeley's work, cf. Ward (1959, pp. 31–40) and TWH's reply (1960, pp. 302–307).

8 Hutchison (1953b). The *Methodenstreit,* TWH remarked, had "a certain sombre instructive value as an extreme example of the consequences of intolerant normative methodologising." (See also 1973, pp. 15–37).

9 Hutchison (1964). Two chapters reviewed the changing conceptions of the positive/normative distinction and the objectives of economic policies, from Sir James Stewart, Adam Smith, and Jeremy Bentham through to the post-1945 period; and two chapters focused on the sources and roles of value judgments and bias, and the formulation of policy objectives and preferences.

10 This theme was foreshadowed in the Appendix on "Some Postulates of Economic Liberalism" in Hutchinson (1960a) and in his *Review* (1953b, p. 150): "Whether or not it is in the province of the economist as such to lay down for the citizen and politician what ought to be the aims of economic policy, it is even much more doubtful whether he should be trying to lay down what other adult students ought to be aiming at or ought to be interesting themselves in." By the later 1960s and 1970s this order of emphasis was modified – and even reversed.

11 For TWH's reply to critics of his 1938 classification, see the 2nd ed. (1960a, especially pp. xvi-xxiii). Also note 2, *supra.*

12 Hutchison (1938) contains several references to Popper's *Logic der Forschung* (1934), subsequently translated as *Logic of Scientific Discovery* (1959; see especially pp. 37–38). (See also TWH's Preface to the 1938 ed.).

13 Hutchison (1953b, pp. 150–151; italics added). Is there a personal reference in another sentence in this paragraph: "Sudden accessions of self-consciousness are notoriously apt to produce crises in individual lives, and presumably also in societies"?

14 Hutchison (1981, pp. 157–164). He had earlier translated Eucken (1948, 1950).

15 Hutchison (1977b, p. 99). There is an instructive parallel here with TWH's reaction to F. A. Hahn's effort to discredit technical and methodological criticisms of general equilibrium theory on the grounds that the critics were incompetent – notwithstanding the manifest inconsistencies in Hahn's own views *(ibid.*, p. 81 ff). See also the devasting use of this technique in comparing quotations from Joan Robinson's and Nicholas Kaldor's earlier and later works *(ibid.,* pp 74–79).

16 Hutchison (1964). For Pigou's appreciation of the temptations open to the economist in the policy sphere, (see *ibid.*, p. 275). TWH admitted his predilection for what he termed "square, "old fashioned" academic virtues *(ibid.*, p. 276).

17 Hutchison (1978, p. 215; italics in original). Some commentators, after reading TWH'S account, may well feel that this is a somewhat indulgent judgment.

18 Hutchison (1978, p. 320); see also 1977b, especially p. 88, on the "exhaustion of intellectual opportunities" in the analysis of maximization under certainty.

19 Hutchison (1978, p. 294). For a similar general argument see 1977b, pp. 62–97: "'Crisis' in the Seventies: The Crisis of Abstraction." TWH notes that not all academic work needs to be justified in terms of its practical or policy-oriented utility. "Academics must always retain the right to pursue studies which are not of any immediate or discernible practical significance – a right which is essential and fundamental for academic freedom" (ibid., p. 90).

20 Hutchison (1978, pp. 319–320): cf. 1977b. p. 92: "To use a favourite term of Keynes, it may sometimes be easier to 'bamboozle' the student with abstractions, or at any rate to get him to accept, or make the willing suspension of disbelief, than it is subsequently to 'debamboozle' him or her by bringing home the full extent of the limitations for real-world relevance and policy which the nature and degree of the abstractions employed have inevitably imposed." Some advanced undergraduate analysis "may even be actively misleading, for those trying to use economics in government or business." See also his telling citations from the E. H. Phelps Brown, G. D. N. Worswick, and K. E. Boulding.

References

Boyle, Andrew, *The Climate of Treason,* London: Hutchison, 1979.

Burns, A. R. (ed.) *Wesley Clair Mitchell. The Economic Scientist*, New York: National Bureau of Economic Research, 1952.

Coats, A. W. "The L.S.E. ethos in the inter-war years," *Atlantic Economic Journal* (March) 1982, 10, 18–30.

Eucken, Walter, "On the Theory of a Centrally Adminstered Economy: An analysis of the German Experiment," *Economica* N.S. (May and August) 1948, 79–100; 173–93.

___, *The Foundations of Economics. History and Theory in the analysis of economic reality*, London: W. Hodge, 1950.

Guillebaud, C. W., Review of T. W. Hutchison, *A Review of Economic Doctrines, 1870–1939.* In *Economica* N. S. 20 (November) 1953, 364.

Heertje, Arnold (ed.), *Schumpeter's Vision, Capitalism, Socialism and Democracy after Forty Years*, Eastbourne: Praeger Holt-Saunders, 1982.

Howarth, T.E.B., *Cambridge Between Two Wars*, London: Collins, 1978.

Hutchison. T.W., "Tautologies and the Nature of Economic Theory," *Review of Economic Studies* (February) 1935, 2, 159–61.

___, *The Significance and Basic Postulates of Economic Theory*, London: Macmillan, 1938; 2nd ed. New York: Augustus Kelley, 1960a.

___, "A Reply to Professor Knight." *Journal of Political Economy*, (October) 1941, 49, 732–50.

___, "Review of Lecture Notes on Types of Economic Theory," *Economic Journal* (March) 1951a, 61, 123–30.

___, "Some Questions About Ricardo," *Economica,* N.S. (August) 1951b, 19, 415–32.

___, "Berkeley's *Querist* and the Economic Thought of the Eighteenth Century," *British Journal for the Philosophy of Science*, (May) 1953a, 4, 52–77.

___, *A Review of Economic Doctrines, 1870–1939* Oxford: Clarendon Press, 1953b.

___, "George Berkeley as an Economist," *Journal of Political Economy* (June) 1960b, 68, 302–7.
___, *'Positive' Economics and Policy Objectives* London: Allen and Unwin, 1964.
___, *Economists and Economic Policy in Britain: Some Aspects of Their Interrelations*, London: Allen and Unwin, 1966.
___, "Some Themes from Investigation into Method'." In J. R. Hicks and W. Weber (eds.), *Carl Menger and the Austrian School of Economics*, Oxford: Clarendon Press, 1973, 15–37.
___, *Keynes* v *the 'Keynesians'...?* London: Institute of Economic Affairs, 1977a.
___, *Knowledge and Ignorance in Economics*, Oxford: Basil Blackwell. 1977b.
___, *On Revolutions and Progress in Economics*, Cambridge: Cambridge University Press, 1978.
___, *The Limitations of General Theories in Macroeconomics,* Washington, D.C.: American Enterprise Institute, 1980.
___, *The Politics and Philosophy of Economics: Marxists, Keynesians and Austrians,* Oxford: Basil Blackwell, 1981.
___, Review of *Schumpeter's Vision. Capitalism, Socialism and Democracy after Forty Years,* by Arnold Heertje, *Times Literary Supplement, 5. (February)* 1982.
Keynes, J. M., *The General Theory of Employment Interest and Money*, Macmillan, 1936.
___, *The Collected Writings of John Maynard Keynes,* Vols. XII, XIV, and XXIX London, Macmillan, 1973–9.
Knight, Frank H., "What is 'Truth' in Economics?'', *Journal of Political Economy* (February) 1940, 48, 1–32; "Rejoinder," *ibid.,* (October) 1941, 49, 750–3.
Marchi, Neil de, Review of *On Revolutions and Progress in Economics,* by T. W. Hutchison, *Journal of Economic Literature*, (September) 1979, 17, 1021–3.
Mill, John Stuart, "The Claims of Labour," *Edinburgh Review*, (October) 1845, 82, 498–525.
Nagel, Ernest, *The Structure of Science, Problems in the Logic of Scientific Explanation,* London: Routledge, Kegan Paul, 1961.
Patinkin, Don, and Leith, J. Clark (eds.) *Keynes, Cambridge and the General Theory*, London: Macmillan, 1977.
Polanyi, Michael, *Personal Knowledge. Towards a Post-Critical Philosophy*, Chicago: University of Chicago Press, 1958.
Popper, Karl R., *Logic of Scientific Discovery*, London: Hutchison, 1959.
Robbins, Lionel, *The Nature and Significance of Economic Science*, London: Macmillan, 1932.
Robinson, Joan, *Economics Is a Serious Subject,* Cambridge: Heffer and Sons, 1932.
___, *The Economics of Imperfect Competition,* London: Macmillan, 1948.
Roll, Eric, Review of T.W. Hutchison, *A Review of Economic Doctrines 1870–1939.* In *Economic Journal*, (June) 1954, 64, 361–4.
Spiegel, H. W., Review of T. W. Hutchison, *A Review of Economic Doctrines, 1870–1939.* In *Journal of Political Economy* (December) 1953, 43, 542–4.
Stigler, George J., "Textual Exegesis as a Scientific Problem," *Economica* N.S., (November) 1965, 32, 447–50.
___, "The History of Economics Through Professor Hutchison's Spectacles," *Minerva,* (Winter) 1978, 16, 596–99.
Uhr, Carl, Review of T. W. Hutchison, *A Review of Economic Doctrines, 1870–1939.* In *American Economic Review*, (December) 1953, 43, 936–9.
Wittgenstein, Ludwig, *Tractatus Logico-Philosophicus*, London: Routledge and Kegan Paul, 1951; originally published in 1921.
Ward, Ian D.S., "George Berkeley: precursor of Keynes or moral economist on underdevelopment?", *Journal of Political Economy*, (February) 1959, 67, 31–40.

4 Half a century of methodological controversy in economics

As reflected in the writings of T. W. Hutchison

In the most widely quoted English language economic methodology book published this century, Lionel Robbins confidently declared that economic science contained "a body of generalisations whose substantial accuracy and importance are open to question only by the ignorant or the perverse" and that questions of method or "how Economics should be pursued... may be regarded as settled as between reasonable people."[1]

If Robbins was correct we must, unfortunately, conclude that during the intervening 50 years ignorance and perversity have generally prevailed over reasonableness, for there has been almost continuous and intermittently intense methodological controversy in economics. Moreover, economists now seem to be a good deal less certain about the precise nature and significance of their science than Robbins then was; and as we are currently in the midst of a fresh spate of methodology books and articles it is an appropriate time for some retrospective stocktaking.

To review the entire history of methodological controversy in economics during the past half century would require a lengthy monograph rather than an essay, and the present exercise makes no pretensions to completeness. Nevertheless, many of the main developments and central issues in dispute will be considered here by reference to the writings of T. W. Hutchison (hereinafter referred to, for brevity, as TWH), who has been the most consistently effective, penetrating, and professionally relevant contributor to the methodology of economics during the period. His first published article, a critique of Robbins, appeared in 1935,[2] about the same time as the second edition of *The Nature and Significance of Economic Science,* and his initial interest in methodology had been inspired both by Robbins's work and by the writings of Joan Robinson, his Cambridge tutor. Since that time his methodological preoccupations have included: the nature and significance of the basic postulates or assumptions of economics; the relationship between analytical (theoretical) and synthetic (empirical) propositions; the respective roles of positive and normative statements (or value judgments); the importance of testing or falsification – an issue he was the first to introduce into the literature of economics; the epistemological, methodological, and practical differences between the social and the natural (or physical) sciences; the relations of economic theory (or science) to policy; and the economist's professional responsibilities to the public as a scholar, as a contributor to policymaking, and as a citizen. On all these major topics TWH has been a powerful, consistent, vigorous and independent-minded critic and commentator, whose writings have displayed a remarkable combination of historical knowledge, philosophical and logical grasp, and an urgent sense of relevance to contemporary affairs. No attempt will be made in this essay to survey that part of his output which recently led no less a figure than Gottfried Haberler to describe TWH as "the foremost living historian of economics."[3] Instead, attention will be focussed on the development of his methodological ideas from the publication of his path-breaking *The Significance and Basic Postulates of Economic Theory* (1938) to his most recent collection of essays, *The Politics and Philosophy of Economics: Marxists, Keynesians and Austrians* (1981). As the latter's title suggests, the attempt to detach TWH's methodological ideas from his historical writings is somewhat artificial, for he has repeatedly emphasized the combination of methodology and history as essential tools of the economists' trade, especially where questions of professional functions, knowledge, and responsibilities arise. Indeed, he has stated that

> no kind of ignorance can be more dangerous than ignorance regardimg the limits and limitations of one's knowledge. In so far as he may be able to combat and reduce this kind of ignorance, the student of the methodology and history of economics has a task which is of considerable social and political importance, as well as a worthy scholarly and philosophically interesting pursuit. *In fact, to promote clarification of the extent and limits of economic knowledge and ignorance may well do much more to reduce dissatisfaction with current economic policies and their results, than do many or most of the contributions to confused and undisciplined wrangles and debates on particular policy problems....* [E]conomists are only preparing disappointment and disillusionment for politicians, the public, and themselves, if they demand, like prophets, to be fired by impressive or exciting inspirations.[4]

The concern expressed in this passage is fully justified, given the dramatic changes in the scale and importance of the economics profession since the beginning of TWH's career in the 1930s. After a phase of sustained growth and professional confidence – hubris, some would aver – in the first two postwar decades, there has been a substantial shift of opinion and a widespread questioning, both within the profession and without, of the scientific status of economics as an academic discipline with pretensions to influence on public policy. The following review of methodological controversy is designed to shed light on the question whether, as often claimed, there is a crisis in economics or whether there has indeed been genuine progress toward scientific respectability during the past half century.

II

In assessing any major contribution to the methodology of economics it is advisable to consider both the historical context and the author's polemical orientation. TWH began his undergraduate studies in Cambridge in 1931 shortly after Britain had gone off the gold standard, and being interested in contemporary politics and acutely aware of the extent of poverty and unemployment he sought a more "relevant" subject than the "classics," to which he was initially committed. Like a number of eminent predecessors and contemporaries he hoped that economics could offer explanations and perhaps remedies for present discontents, and he was somewhat disillusioned to find the discipline much less clear, helpful, and constructive than he had anticipated, partly owing to significant disagreements among some of the leading practitioners.

TWH first became aware of this situation when he read his tutor's challenging pamphlet, *Economics is a Serious Subject* (1932), and his skepticism was reinforced by sections of Joan Robinson's basically Marshallian but nevertheless path-breaking analysis of *The Economics of Imperfect Competition* (1933). From these he proceeded to Lionel Robbins's classic, quoted earlier, which provided a comparatively complacent and defensive view of the state of the art, and this aroused his interest in a number of European methodological works unfamiliar to British readers. Robbins's reliance on continental sources, which became one of the major intellectual virtues of the London School of Economics (LSE) tradition in the 1930s,[5] was markedly in contrast with the prevailing insularity of Cambridge teaching in economic theory and must have added piquancy to Robinson's somewhat exaggerated contrast between the "rough and ready common-sense English economists" and their continental counterparts "who are experts in methodology."[6] There was, indeed, substantial justification for her complaint about

> the bad habit of English economists of never giving a proper account of their assumptions. The search for Marshall's hidden assumptions has occupied a whole generation, and almost threatened at one time to turn English economists into a school of higher-critical theologians[7]

engaged in the exegesis and elaboration of themes in Marshall's *Principles,* their sacred text. Her contention that "Continental economists ought to have learned by now not to take an Englishman's word about what he is assuming, but to go behind his back and ask his technique"[8] indicated the path that TWH was to follow, though he quickly became concerned with more than mere assumptions and techniques.

Despite some oversimplification, Robinson was essentially correct in implying that British economists, unlike their European and American contemporaries, had displayed a marked distaste for methodology and that this can be regarded, as TWH subsequently emphasized, as a characteristic manifestation of Anglo-Saxon insularity and complacency not confined to Cambridge.[9] But there especially, under the combined influence of the Marshallian hegemony and John Neville Keynes's influential *Scope and Method of Political Economy* (1890), it had become generally accepted that methodology in general, and especially methodological disputation, was a waste of time and energy, a diversion from the investigation of "puzzles" posed by the Marshallian "paradigm" – to cite T. S. Kuhn's now familiar terminology. It may be noted parenthetically that one of the few Cambridge-trained economists to take an interest in methodology during the 1920s was Philip Sargent Florence, subsequently a colleague of TWH's at Birmingham, who had pursued graduate studies in the United States, where he came under the influence of Wesley C. Mitchell, himself a former student of that arch-iconoclast and methodological subversive, Thorstein Veblen.[10] Joan Robinson's critique suggests that by the early 1930s the Marshallian tradition was losing some of its former hold, so that a strong-minded individual reared in that stable could pose searching questions about its limitations, perhaps even with impunity. And her comments, though tantalizingly brief and inadequately developed, can now be seen to have anticipated the critiques of two eminent Europeans – Wassily Leontief, who complained of Cambridge economists' "Implicit theorizing," and Tjalling C. Koopmans, who referred to what he called "The Diplomatic Style of Discourse" among British economists.[11]

The fact that Robinson's heresies were unusual probably enhanced their impact on TWH, who – in his 1938 classic – paid her a glowing tribute for having introduced him to its subject matter and for her part in "the incomparable training in and stimulus to economic thinking" which he had received in Cambridge.[12] By the time he had graduated in 1934 (with a "first," despite his "disastrous" initial year in classics) he was determined to pursue his methodological investigations, if possible in Germany. And even before he left England in 1935 his first article, published while he was an "occasional" postgraduate student at LSE, clearly revealed the direction his ideas were taking.

Robbins had maintained that, although "Economic Science knows no way of predicting what will be the given data at any particular point in time," economic analysis has "very considerable prognostic value" because, "given the data in a particular situation, it can draw inevitable conclusions as to their implications."[13] TWH flatly disagreed, pointing out that Robbins had failed to distinguish between inevitable implications, or tautologies (of the form: "if p, then q") – which can "no more prognosticate anything than can the multiplication table" – and inferences (of the form "since p, therefore q"), which "requires some data to be known in order to establish a 'since'." Instead of confusing purely "formal connections" with statements about the real world it was necessary to recognize that "successful hypotheses of prognostic value may often be *inductively* formed" in economics as in physics, though in the former case it is more difficult. Nevertheless, "the necessary fundamental assumption of all scientists is that there are some regularities about the facts of the world which allow of successful inductive hypotheses" and, TWH implied, economists should adopt this approach instead of making excessive claims on behalf of purely deductive theories.[14]

In retrospect it may seem remarkable that the issues raised in the concluding page of TWH's first brief article should have become the subject of intensive, if intermittent, debate with a series of economists and philosophers over the next four decades.[15] Of course, some basic methodological questions are hardy perennials, unlikely ever to be settled conclusively or definitively, and TWH's criticisms of Robbins were to be generalized both clearly and cogently three years later in his oft-quoted *Significance and Basic Postulates of Economic Theory*. Nevertheless, it is appropriate to ask at this juncture: Why did these questions arise in the mid 1930s in this particular form? How did TWH develop them in his book? Why did subsequent critics and commentators view them as important? And what, if anything, is the current consensus on these matters?

III

In depicting the historical context of methodological discussion in economics during the first half of the 1930s it is sufficient for the present purpose to recall that Robbins's *Nature and Significance* provoked a storm of criticism, especially from those who regarded his conception of the subject as excessively narrow, rigid, formalistic, defensive, and prescriptive. In the second edition, published in 1935, he "endeavoured to eliminate certain manifestations of high spirits no longer in harmony with present moods" – a remark presumably conceding that by then economists had comparatively little to be complacent about. But although he substantially modified parts of the text, especially the chapter on the nature of economic generalizations, he anticipated that the changes would not mollify the critics but would, rather, make the book even "more difficult and more contentious."[16] While TWH's initial response stemmed from an entirely different philosophical background from Robbins's, Fritz Machlup undoubtedly overstated the case somewhat when he described TWH as an "ultra-empiricist" and placed Robbins near the opposite end of the spectrum, as one of the "pure, exact, aprioristic" economists.[17] Robbins certainly did not embrace Ludwig von Mises's extreme apriorism, for he maintained that the fundamental postulates of economics were "assumptions involving in some way simple and indisputable facts of experience."[18] But, on the other hand, he defined "Economic Generali[z]ations proper" as those generalizations "which have the character of certainty," as opposed to historical, sociological, or other inductive generalizations "which only have a high degree of probability,"[19] thereby implying that the inductive approach had nothing to contribute to economic science.

TWH's conception of the role of inductive generalizations in economics was in accord with the contemporary school of logical positivists, and his concept of "tautology" was derived from his early reading of Ludwig Wittgenstein's immensely influential *Tractatus logico-philosophicus* (1921), which was being actively debated in Cambridge during his undergraduate days. Some years later, in response to Frank Knight's demand that he should disclose his "philosophical position," TWH declared his general allegiance to the "Anglo-Saxon" as against the "Teutonic" philosophical position, specifically referring to Locke, Hume, and J. S. Mill, and the contemporary authors Russell, Wittgenstein, Mach, Schlick, and Carnap (not all of whom can strictly speaking be regarded as Anglo-Saxon).[20] The last three, whose works he probably encountered only after his first article, were members of the immensely influential so-called Vienna Circle, a group who refused to answer the traditional philosophical questions of metaphysics, ethics, and epistemology, preferring instead to concentrate on "scientific" problems, to which the German idealists were basically hostile. The Vienna Circle held that the idealists were not merely wrong in philosophical terms but had used their doctrines illegitimately in defence of the status quo, and TWH concurred, voicing his profound disapproval of the use of philosophical and pseudoscientific ideas for political purposes, whether by fascists or Marxists. And indeed this became one of the most consistently reiterated themes throughout his later work.

Given the subtle and changing character of the empiricist literature of the 1930s it is no easy task to "place" TWH exactly in relation to contemporary philosophical currents. He was primarily concerned with the methodology of economics, not with philosophy as such, and when Knight demanded that he should reveal his "philosophical position" he reluctantly complied, while insisting that whatever it might be, it was "quite independent of the validity or invalidity of the main propositions about the basic postulates of economics" expounded in his book.[21] And, at the same time, with devastating polemical effect, he turned the tables on Knight, by citing the latter's explicit disclaimer in his *Risk, Uncertainty and Profit* (1921).[22] TWH declared that he was not "concerned to establish any proposition about the 'existence' or 'non-existence' of something, but merely to analyse language and definitions and to uphold the Scientific Principle of Testability,"[23] and this passage combines the logical positivists' distaste for metaphysics with their concern for linguistic precision. His central distinction between tautologies (or "analytic" propositions) and empirical (or "synthetic") propositions is basically Kantian and can be found, among many other sources, in Felix Kaufmann's *Methodenlehre der Sozialwissenschaften* (1936), which TWH cited in his 1938 book.[24] Of far greater interest to present-day readers, however, are his citations from Karl Popper's *Logik der Forschung* (1934),[25] a work then virtually unknown in England. Of course, Popper has subsequently become perhaps the most influential and frequently quoted philosopher of science in the mid- and late-twentieth century, and it is of interest that TWH was one of the first to cite him in an English language book.

TWH's first published reference to Popper's central conception of the "demarcation criterion," now generally recognized as a basic convention or procedural rule for differentiating scientific from nonscientific propositions, occurs in the second edition of his 1938 book,[26] by which time he had spent several years as Popper's colleague at LSE. However, something closely akin to that concept was implied at several points in his 1938 volume, and in view of the importance Popper attached to his disagreement with the Vienna Circle it is worth noting TWH's expressed preference for the distinction between "science" and "non-science," rather than "sense" and "nonsense" which, he added, "used to be employed by writers of the former Vienna Circle."[27] Popper had insisted that to identify the distinction between science and nonscience with that between sense and nonsense was to make an arbitrary verbal stipulation which ignored the difficulties of the demarcation criterion. Pseudoscience could, for example, develop into science proper: indeed, the general progress of human knowledge could be regarded as the transformation of myth, or pseudoscience, into science proper by the process of critical examination. This process was central to Popper's basic conception of scientific knowledge[28] and entirely compatible with TWH's main objective in *The Significance and Basic Postulates of Economic Theory*. In that volume, he declared, his intention was to

> help in elucidating that body of 'pure theory' the possession of which distinguishes Economics from the other social sciences... to arrive at a clear definition of 'pure theory' enabling one to mark off clearly propositions which belong to 'pure theory' from those that do not, to investigate the source of the validity of those propositions, to clarify their relation to the assumptions or postulates on which they rest, including, in particular, the 'ceteris paribus' assumption, and finally to clarify those assumptions themselves by analysing the main concepts... which they contain.[29]

However, before examining how he proposed to carry out this deceptively modest programme it is worth noting one further parallel between TWH and Popper. Whereas Popper's famous "falsificationist" doctrine had originated as a critique of Marxism, of which he had once been an adherent, TWH began as a mild socialist but, by 1938, was focussing his attack on different forms of pseudoscience, namely, von Mises's extreme libertarianism and the fascist totalitarianism by which he was surrounded in Germany. But while their targets were different, their aims were similar: to demarcate genuine scientific knowledge from "other bodies of assertions that might be confused with it," including astrology, phrenology, Freudian psychoanalysis, the Marxist theory of history, or other extremist political creeds. The significance of this problem is abundantly clear in TWH's later writings when, under different postwar circumstances, he came to share Popper's view that Marxism, especially the Stalinist variant, was the most serious threat to liberty and democracy.

IV

Although TWH's above-quoted 1938 statement of intentions appears modest enough, the tone of the volume was sterner, more confident, at times even polemical. While granting that his approach reflected his "personal intellectual tastes" rather than any absolute standard, he refused to enter into debate with those unwilling to accept the rules of his game, or his proposed "enforcement of certain criteria for the scientific investigation of any field."[30] Drawing a clear-cut distinction between science and philosophy, TWH maintained that scientists have "definite, agreed, and relatively conclusive criteria for the testing of propositions, solutions, and theories which 'philosophers' do not accept," and this agreement is the source of science's "cumulative, international, impersonal, and 'coral-reef-like' growth" (p. 7). Rather than beginning with problems that logically come first, scientists

> start at a 'common-sense' level and have to build *upwards* their structure of laws and relations, and *downwards* their foundations – the latter task being by

> criticism and analysis to test and make precise the common-sense notions they start with, and to assume a logically firm and secure base for the superstructure (p. 16; italics in original).

Contrary to those who claimed that concern with foundations was necessarily "philosophical" or "methodological," TWH insisted that if such work was to be "of use to the scientist as such" the methodologist or philosopher "must accept and discipline himself to exactly the same criteria" as the scientist working on the superstructure. Thus, in a sense, the scientific criteria were immanent and empirical, deriving from scientific practice and justifiable on their own terms, since "the discussion of 'methodological' questions – for the scientist at any rate – only has sense in connection with the practical problems of science" (p. 17). The notion that metaphysical assumptions underlie all science and should be examined and formulated by the serious and self-conscious scientific practitioner was "completely misconceived"; and, even if accepted, the discussion of such matters "should be kept strictly separate from the scientific, which should be pushed back as far as it could according to its own methods and criteria" (p. 17). Of course, TWH did not try to specify the precise extent of that territory; nor did he favor "the objection of a rather Anglo-Saxon type'' that "sound instinct and common-sense" could afford a reliable guide (p. 18). On the contrary,

> it is precisely the task of science to supersede crude common-sense notions by critical analysis, and further that *it is the unsatisfactory state of the foundations beneath the common-sense surface which is the most serious and crippling deficiency of contemporary economic science,* since other deficiencies lie rather in the nature of the subject matter as compared with that of the natural sciences and may never be thoroughly overcome in the same way (p. 18; italics supplied).

In an effort to secure the foundations of economic science and to bring its practices up to the standards prevailing in other sciences TWH proposed an "exhaustive two-fold classification of all propositions which have 'scientific' sense" according to whether they are "conceivably falsifiable by empirical observation" (p. 26). Whereas "an empirical proposition must, by definition, be conceivably falsifiable, that is, if true, *exclude* some conceivable possibility," a purely theoretical or analytical proposition "cannot exclude any conceivable occurrence" and is therefore "devoid of empirical content" (p. 27; italics in original). These statements constitute a sizeable step forward from his 1935 "Tautologies" article toward Popper's concept of falsification, which has figured so prominently in postwar methodological literature. Yet while TWH and Popper were, in more than one sense, allies, there were significant differences between their respective positions in the 1930s – differences which still persist, though they have narrowed somewhat.

For example, given TWH's distaste for metaphysics in the 1930s, it seems highly unlikely that he would have approved of Popper's admission that his "demarcation criterion" by which to differentiate scientific from nonscientific propositions was simply

> a proposal for an agreement or convention... [which is] ultimately a matter of decision, going beyond rational argument.... I freely admit that in arriving at my proposals I have been guided, in the last analysis, by value judgments and predilections.... And looking at the thing from a psychological angle, I am inclined to think that scientific discovery is impossible without faith in ideas which are of a purely speculative kind, and sometimes quite hazy, a faith which is comparatively unwarranted from the point of view of science, and which, to that extent, is 'metaphysical.'[31]

Although Popper did not, of course, refer directly to TWH, it is clear that the latter was vulnerable to his criticism of the positivists' "naturalistic" approach, according to which

> only two kinds of statements exist for them: logical tautologies and empirical statements. If methodology is not logic, then, they will conclude, it must be a branch of some empirical science – the science, say, of the behavior of scientists at work.... [This view] is uncritical. Its upholders fail to notice that whenever they believe themselves to have discovered a fact they have only proposed a convention. Hence the convention is liable to turn into a dogma.... What is to be called a 'science' and who is to be called a 'scientist' must always remain a matter of convention or decision.[32]

Popper's views have been quoted at length not only because of his undoubted importance but also because they lead us directly to several of the most fundamental issues in the methodological controversies which have taken place in economics since TWH published his *Significance and Basic Postulates*. There is, of course, an obvious surface resemblance between Popper's concept of falsification and TWH's "Scientific Principle of Testability," but this should not be allowed to obscure the basic differences between TWH's empiricism and Popper's rejection of inductivism, for which he has been criticized by a number of philosophers.[33] Another major difference is that although TWH has subsequently conceded that his 1938 book was excessively "naturalistic," a characteristic he has attributed partly to youthful enthusiasm,[34] and has acknowledged that he had somewhat understated the differences between the natural and the social sciences (a point to be considered later), he has continued to defend staunchly his twofold classification of propositions against a number of serious critics (also discussed later). More generally, however, Popper's remarks also draw attention to the still unresolved but fundamental issue of the source(s), nature, and epistemological status of the methodological criteria or procedural rules appropriate to science.[35] Is it sufficient, as TWH implied, simply to observe what scientists do and to base methodological principles on what might be called "best" or "approved" scientific practice? This, some critics would say, simply amounts to crude inductivism.[36]

But, if not, is some more formal epistemological justification required; and, if so, what? What is meant by Popper's admission that his "demarcation criterion" is merely "a proposal for an agreement or convention... ultimately a matter of decision, going beyond rational argument... guided, in the last analysis, by value judgments and predilections"?[37] Is this a sufficiently secure basis for science, or does it reduce the foundations of the scientific edifice to a matter of personal taste or perhaps intersubjective consensus among those who constitute, albeit only temporarily, the ruling group in any given discipline or subdiscipline?

Issues of this kind have become increasingly prominent in the philosophy of science literature during the past two decades or so, in the works of Stephen Toulmin, Michael Polanyi, Thomas Kuhn, Imre Lakatos, Paul Feyerabend, David Bloor, and others.[38] To explore this literature would, of course, take us too far from our central theme. Nevertheless it is appropriate to recognize that the issues raised by TWH's 1938 book form part of a much wider ongoing debate.

TWH's twofold classification of propositions was designed to expose and counteract the practice of blurring the distinction between causal and definitional relationships, which was especially prevalent in economics with the use of the ceteris paribus clause. His aim was to establish a rule whereby "either a proposition which has sense is conceivably falsifiable by empirical observation or it is not" (p. 26), thereby forbidding the state of affairs in which some authors treat a given proposition as analytical, some treat it as empirical, while others treat it as either or both simultaneously, so that it was "thus 'synthetised' into one proposition" (p. 63). He was not dogmatic, for he conceded that there might be some other conceivable type or types of propositions, adding that

> in the natural sciences certain fundamental propositions can be taken either to be analytical-tautological or to be empirical generalisations, exactly as the ceteris paribus propositions may be so taken.... From the mere wording and form of the proposition one cannot say whether it is the one or the other. One can only find out by a test case when scientists are forced to choose one alternative or the other (pp. 43–44).

But he recognized, as many subsequent writers have done, that any such tests are more difficult to construct, and in fact much more rarely constructed and followed through rigorously, in economics than in other sciences.[39] However, after a lengthy analysis he concluded that

> the ceteris paribus assumption can only be safely and significantly used in conjunction with an empirical generalisation verified as true in a large percentage of cases but occasionally liable to exceptions of a clearly describable type (p. 46).

TWH's twofold classification of propositions has been criticized on a number of occasions by methodologists and philosophers – for example, by Fritz Machlup, in 1955;[40] by Kurt Klappholz and Joseph Agassi, two of his LSE colleagues, in

1958/9;[41] and more recently by Alexander Rosenberg.[42] In the present context it is sufficient to note his concession, in the preface to the 1960 edition of his book, that

> Perhaps I concentrated too exclusively on fitting economic statements into one or other of these two categories, because of what seemed to me the dogmatic and extreme *a priorism* of Professor Mises, which was much more influential in the thirties (p. xxi; italics in original).

Nevertheless, his response fell far short of unconditional surrender, for he maintained that despite various attempts to identify

> a range of important statements used in economics which could not be regarded as either empirical, testable or falsifiable on the one hand or tautological on the other.... [T]hose upholding the importance of a third type of statement disagree completely as to the nature of this third type, and perhaps, or even probably, would reject one another's examples.... My one request is for a number of clear examples [i.e., from economics] (pp. xvi, xx-xxi).

TWH was perfectly correct in this contention, for as Machlup had noted, the third or intermediate class of propositions had been variously interpreted as "procedural rules" (Kaufmann), "complex-analytic propositions" (Montagu), or "constitutive non-epistemic propositions" (Margenau).[43] Nevertheless, Machlup too, was correct in maintaining that all theoretical systems incorporate propositions of this type, such as the heuristic postulates and idealized assumptions employed in abstract models of interdependent constructs which are useful in explaining and predicting observable phenomena. These hypotheses can be of very different levels of generality, some being fundamental (heuristic) and not independently testable (like the so-called hard core assumptions in the methodology of scientific research programmes developed by Imre Lakatos[44]), whereas others are specific (factual) and supposed to correspond to observed facts and conditions. The really important consideration here, however, is not the analysis and classification of propositions as such, but questions such as: What is the nature and role of testing, verification, or falsification in science (or in economics)? What is to be tested, and how are tests to be conducted? One of the greatest virtues of TWH's 1938 book is that he initiated serious discussion of this problem, one that economists had not previously faced squarely. This was, in fact, to become a very fashionable issue in the first two postwar decades.

Curiously enough in the 1940s and 1950s, when economists as a profession were becoming more empirically minded and positivistic, physicists – to whom economists have so often looked for their methodological standards – were becoming more conscious of the role of abstract entities at the foundations of their discipline. This trend has directly affected the views of philosophers of science concerning the relationships between theoretical terms and observation statements, and the role of particular propositions or statements within any theoretical or scientific system. After several decades of intensive and at times highly technical debate among logicians, epistemologists, and philosophers of science, the logical positivists' campaign to dissociate science from metaphysics has failed, and their practice of analyzing individual statements in order to determine whether they are clear and unambiguous and to clarify them as sense or nonsense, scientific or nonscientific, has generally been abandoned. According to Willard Quine, one of the most effective critics of earlier forms of positivism,

> for all its a priori reasonableness, a boundary between analytic and synthetic statements has not been drawn. That there is such a distinction to be drawn at all is an unempirical dogma of empiricists, a metaphysical article of faith,[45]

while Hilary Putnam adopted a somewhat less extreme position, arguing that

> if one wants to have a model of language, it is far better to proceed on the idea that statements fall into three kinds – analytic, synthetic, and lots-of-other-things – than to proceed on the idea that, except for borderline fuzziness, every statement is either analytic or synthetic.[46]

In rejecting Quine's denial that there is any analytic–synthetic distinction, Putnam nevertheless concurred in stressing

> the monolithic character of our conceptual system, the idea of our conceptual system as a massive alliance of beliefs which face the tribunal of experience collectively and not independently, the idea that 'when trouble strikes' revisions can, with a very few exceptions, come anywhere.[47]

This type of approach, which has been gaining support among writers on the methodology of economics in the past decade or so, creates serious problems for those seeking empirical verification or confirmation of economic theories, as it does also for the advocates of falsificationism. It has undermined the proponents of "operationalism," a doctrine originated by the physicist Percy Bridgman and favored by some economists in the early postwar period. According to Bridgman, "the proper definition of a concept is not in terms of its properties but in terms of its actual operations... [that is,] the concept is synonymous with the corresponding set of operations"[48] – an approach bearing a strong family resemblance to Wittgenstein's dictum that "the meaning of a proposition is the method of its verification."[49]

The most effective methodological critic of operationalism in economics is Fritz Machlup, who attacked TWH's position in his important 1955 article on "The Problem of Verification in Economics," referred to earlier. The central issue he posed, in relation to TWH, was "the difference between demands for direct tests of fundamental assumptions, or postulates, and for merely indirect tests through checking the correspondence of deduced consequences with observed sequence of events." After constructing "a graphic 'model' of the use of an analytical apparatus" for heuristic purposes, he concluded that the model could "be tested only by its performance, that is, by yielding conclusions more consistently corresponding with observed changes than alternative machines [or models] can do."[50]

Unfortunately, as is so often the case in academic controversy, the Machlup-TWH exchange was marred by some overstatement and mutual misunderstanding, for Machlup uncharacteristically had deliberately focussed on extreme positions in the interests of clear exposition. As a result he classified TWH as an "ultra-empiricist," that is, one who refused "to recognise the legitimacy of employing at any level of analysis propositions not independently verifiable."[51] He accused TWH of maintaining the need to begin with facts rather than assumptions, quoting his statement that "if one wants to get beyond a certain high level of abstraction one has to begin *more or less* from the beginning with empirical investigation" (1938, p. 166; italics added). This, according to Machlup, meant that TWH regarded statistical investigations and other empirical studies as "the only possible scientific method open" to the economist.[52]

In his rejoinder, Machlup acknowledged that TWH had hedged his position in stating at the beginning of his book that the propositions of economic science "must *conceivably* be capable of empirical testing *or be reducible to such* propositions by logical deduction," but he nevertheless insisted that the general tenor of TWH's work justified the label *ultra-empiricist*.[53] To debate this issue further here would take too much space, for there are grounds for the view that both protagonists' positions were somewhat ambiguous.[54] The important points are that in their exchange the question of "testing" (verification, or confirmation) in economics was brought to the fore and that TWH's empiricism was far removed from Machlup's "conventionalism," which has been gaining support in recent years. In his latest collection of methodological essays Machlup, the arch-antioperationalist, has accepted the label *conventionalist* as a description of his own work, defining that position as: "one who accepts as meaningful and useful, basic propositions that make no assertions but are conventions (resolutions, postulates) with regard to analytic procedure."[55]

Whether it is true, as a very recent commentator has observed, that "conventionalism forms the foundation for most methodological discussions in economics today,"[56] it is undoubtedly the case that both TWH and Popper were opposed to such a position in the 1930s. In his *Logik der Forschung,* Popper acknowledged that conventionalism was a consistent "self-contained and defensible system" but rejected it as a doctrine since it enabled the advocates of any theory to defend it by explaining away potential falsifications. Hence he argued that:

> The only way to avoid conventionalism is by taking a *decision:* the decision not to apply its methods. We decide that, in the case of threat to our system, we will not save it by any kind of *conventionalist strategem,*

such as the introduction of ad hoc hypotheses, adopting

> a sceptical attitude as to the reliability of the experimenter whose observations... we may exclude from science on the ground that they are insufficiently supported, unscientific, or not objective, or even on the ground that the experimenter was a liar.[57]

That such devices could be used to defend any kind of pseudoscience made conventionalism anathema to Popper and, by extension, to TWH.[58] Whether the latter would go further with Popper and accept that methodological rules, including the crucial "demarcation criterion," are also conventions, and that axioms could be regarded either as conventions (implicit definitions) or as empirical or scientific hypotheses, is another question.[59]

In recent years there has been a marked swing of the pendulum of methodological opinion away from the narrower and more rigorous forms of empiricism and logical positivism which were in vogue in the 1930s. Popper's rejection of the principle of induction has been attacked;[60] his conception of falsification has been (wrongly) treated as "naive," and his successor at the LSE, Imre Lakatos, has substituted his own "sophisticated" version of falsificationalism;[61] and Popper's strenuous resistance to efforts to classify him as a conventionalist, even as a "modified" adherent to that doctrine, has necessarily left some observers in a state of bewilderment. The implications of this unfortunate situation will be considered later, in the concluding paragraphs of this essay.

V

Although TWH's *Significance and Basic Postulates* has been generally recognised as a landmark in the literature of economic methodology, it has been the subject of considerable controversy. The earliest reviewers' response was distinctly mixed, combining genuine praise of the author's command of economic theory, philosophy, and logic with reservations about his polemical vigor and controversial style.

The reactions in the two leading English language economic journals were fairly characteristic. Edmund Whittaker commended the book as "useful on the negative side" for most economists since they "have made no special study of logic and are apt to reason loosely at times," but added that "constructively Mr. Hutchison has less to offer."[62] Likewise, Alfred Stonier dismissed TWH's logical positivism as of limited value, regarded his "verifiability criterion" for legitimizing a "synthetic assertion" as "ambiguous," and questioned whether TWH was "in general making assertions,... analysing concepts, or... [merely?] playing a game with words."[63] J. G. Shearer, in *The Economic Record,* reacted more favorably, referring to the broad parallels between TWH's conclusions and the iconoclastic attack on the discipline in Barbara Wootton's *Lament for Economics* (1938). Unlike Whittaker and Stonier, Shearer recognised the central importance of TWH's emphasis on uncertainty and expectations (a point of major interest to economists in the 1970s and 1980s), as well as his desire to make economic theory "more susceptible to the test of empirical verification."[64] But he shared their reservations about TWH's confidence in the possibilities of testing economic theory by statistics. As Stonier observed, TWH

> does seem to be arguing that all economic theory is testable by statistics, and that statistics are descriptions wholly from 'outside' of purely physical facts. This is not satisfactory since all economic statistics imply some economic

> theory, and, on the other hand, some theory is subject only to introspective or interpersonal tests.[65]

These reviewers found it difficult to "place" TWH in relation to other economists – Shearer concluding that despite his severe strictures, TWH was "not unsympathetic to pure theory," while Whittaker regarded his approach as "characteristic" of the "neo-classical" economists.[66] To Maurice Dobb, a Marxist, much of TWH's critique was comparable "to what American institutionalists were saying two decades ago," albeit more weighty, deep, and "radical."

> This wholehearted attack on time-worn dogmas, this snouting out of scholasticism... and the plea for concrete study of actual data... for a vigorous extension of statistical research in the social field – as well as for a widening of the boundaries of what is regarded as the 'economic field' – cannot be too heartily applauded,[67]

and he concluded by demanding a substantial increase in the funding of research into concrete economic and social problems, the neglect of which, "in England at least, borders on a scandal."[68] Nevertheless, he disapproved of TWH's "agnosticism," which implied "a skeptical attitude towards any activity based on a general theory," and did not endorse TWH's call for "a revolution in economic method... and a wiping of the slate clean of the metaphysical notions of which the subject is at present full."[69] Like some later commentators,[70] he rejected TWH's unduly rigid classification of propositions into "verbal definitions and empirical statements," emphasizing the crucial role of a "third type of composite propositions," arguing that such propositions did not merely consist in an expansion of the original definition given to words, for

> If there is a correspondence between the words we use and the contours of the real world, there seems to be no sense in saying that our deductions have nothing to do with facts, but only 'with the way we talk about the facts.'... Since language is the vehicle of thought, reasoning about actual relationships assumes the guise of a discussion about the meaning of words.[71]

Clearly Dobb was reacting against the excesses of linguistic philosophy, then in full flood in Cambridge. His main quarrel was not with orthodox economic method as such,

> but with a false use of that method, creating a distorted picture of contemporary society.... [C]ontroversy in economics is never simply a dispute about words (as has been maintained), but a dispute between different interpretations of capitalism.[72]

In subsequent years TWH has had a distinctly ambivalent attitude toward this review. While appreciating Dobb's endorsement of his attack on the misuse of economics, he felt obliged to express his profound distaste for Dobb's persistent and uncritical endorsement of the Stalinist regime in Russia. Here, as elsewhere, methodology could not be entirely divorced from political implications.[73]

By far the longest and most outspokenly hostile review of TWH's book was the 32-page diatribe in the *Journal of Political Economy* by the eminent and idiosyncratic Chicago economist Frank H. Knight. Describing the volume as "particularly irritating to the reviewer" and "pernicious and dangerous to the young," owing to the "specious plausibility" and "strong intellectual appeal" of the author's conception of science, Knight deplored its "superficiality and dogmatic over-simplification," the positivistic treatment of human beings as natural objects, and the contrast it depicted between "glorified science and a caricature of philosophy." Yet, somewhat inconsistently, he conceded that it was a "very 'learned' work... and hence... valuable as an introduction to the literature of the field. Its fallacies are rather those of omission – what it excludes rather than what it contains." Moreover, such volumes probably did little damage, being "more interesting... to their authors... than to any considerable number of readers," and only "likely to be read and taken seriously by the young."[74]

It is unnecessary to consider all the issues raised in Knight's violent, wide-ranging, but penetrating antipositivist polemic, for TWH's devastatingly effective reply exposed numerous irrelevancies, obscurities, and misrepresentations of his position which it would be tedious to rehearse.[75] Nevertheless, as Knight remarked in a subsequent rejoinder, he was commentating on an entire school of thought (i.e., positivism), rather than a single volume, and his comments on testing and the nature of our knowledge of human conduct – which, he maintained, TWH had ignored in his preoccupation with knowledge of the external world and the truths of logic and mathematics – are of direct interest in relation to subsequent methodological discussion.

Knight attacked the "conventional" element in TWH's account of testing and the element of choice in the definition of propositions and concepts, maintaining that: "Here truth is merely a game in which the players are free to make any rules they please."[76] He put his finger on a weak point in TWH's "matter-of-fact" reference to what is "conceivable" in his central requirement of conceivable testability, and also complained of the failure "to make clear what sort of propositions do and what sort of propositions do not need testing and what tests are accepted as valid and not in themselves in need of testing."[77] Like more recent antipositivists, Knight stressed the limits of testability in the physical sciences, adding (correctly) that those disciplines included "many propositions and terms expressing concepts of a purely interpretative character which are not data of sense observation and do not have 'reality' of that empirical kind."[78] His assertion that "all discussion ultimately rests upon statements of fact and principle which are assumed to be accepted as true and which cannot be defended by argument if they are denied or questioned"[79] sounded suspiciously like dogmatism of the kind TWH was especially concerned to expose; and yet recent philosophers of science have more readily acknowledged (too readily, TWH would still contend) the need for a "hard core" of such statements in any theory or research programme.[80] In the 1930s, such a view was liable to be dismissed by positivists as a species of metaphysics totally irrelevant to the logic and methodology of science. Admittedly, few present-day writers would endorse Knight's terminology when he claimed that "concrete and positive answers to questions in the field of economic *science or policy"* were dependent on "judgments of value and procedure, based on broad, general education in the cultural sense, and on 'insight' into broad human nature and social values, rather than on the findings of possible positive science."[81] But while rejecting Knight's advocacy of "verstehende wissenschaft," TWH recognized the need to go beyond economics "proper" in considering policy questions; and in his more recent writings he has repeatedly emphasized the limitations of the economist's knowledge, and the need to exercise "judgment in its utilization."[82]

With respect to knowledge of human conduct Knight was closer to von Mises than to Robbins, who had emphasized the experiential basis of the fundamental assumptions of orthodox economics.[83] Knight deplored TWH's "ridicule" of the use of introspection, insisting that the truth of the basic propositions of economics is known "more confidently and certainly" than that of "any concrete physical fact or event" or "the truth of any axiom of mathematics or logic." Indeed, "it is not conceivably possible to 'verify' any proposition about 'economic' behaviour by any 'empirical' procedure." Human conduct "cannot be interpreted in terms of positive categories," for knowledge based on observation of behavior is "intuitive in a special sense as compared with any knowledge of nature." Like other positivists, TWH had ignored the problem-solving, purposive character of conduct and the role of individual interests, which are "regularly and properly taken as factual data."[84]

In his reply, TWH referred to the wide gap between his own language and Knight's and dissociated himself from positivism in the latter's sense of the term. Stressing his concern with "the classification of propositions" rather than "types or fields of knowledge," he reiterated his belief that "a proposition simply needs testing in regard to what, if anything, is claimed for it by the person who puts it forward."[85] The validity of any test must necessarily be relative and must involve "the acceptance of certain rules for carrying out tests and also the acceptance of the results of the tests thus carried out," for science would be impossible if the scientists were charlatans or liars or if they were "unable or unwilling to agree to accept the results of the testing of their propositions." Undeniably there were difficulties in devising and conducting tests in economics. But in emphasizing the existence of conventions, TWH maintained that he merely referred to what Knight called "consensus" when Knight asserted that "A conscious critical social consensus is the essence of the idea of objectivity or truth." Far from being dogmatic or simplistic, TWH claimed, his standard was less rigorous than that proposed by Knight, who had stated that a concept "which cannot be measured with any high degree of accuracy" should be avoided "in work pretending to a scientific character."[86] The issue here is the relationship between the nature and effectiveness of tests in economics (and, indeed, in any discipline with pretensions to scientific status) and the prevailing conventions or rules of the scientific community according to which propositions or theories are accepted or rejected as part of the agreed corpus of scientific knowledge. At the time of the Hutchison – Knight exchange it was still usual to regard questions of the validity or truth-value of propositions as a matter for the logician or philosopher of science, whereas more recently, largely as a result of the writings of Polanyi, Kuhn, Toulmin, Lakatos, and others, these issues have become combined with discussions of the sociology and history of science. It will be convenient to postpone discussion of these matters at this point, except to say that there is a crucial distinction to be maintained between "conventionalism" as an epistemological or methodological doctrine and the existence of conventions or the need for "consensus" within the scientific community. It is of course trivially true that science, like any other organized social activity, is necessarily dependent on the acceptance by the majority of its practitioners of a number of recognized and agreed norms, practices, procedures, and rules; otherwise it would break down. But the epistemological status and sources of those conventions, such as Popper's demarcation criterion, has become a subject of considerable interest to postwar students of methodology in economics and the social sciences.

Before turning to the postwar period, two further reactions to the Knight–Hutchison exchange deserve consideration. Felix Kaufmann, a member of the Vienna Circle specializing in social science methodology, rejected Knight's effort to justify his position on ultimate grounds, and his appeal to the "absolute certainty of introspection," but considered that TWH had obliterated the borderline between natural and social science "in accordance with the doctrines of radical behaviourism or physicalism." Kaufmann emphasized how frequently "methodological issues supposed to be specific to a particular empirical science are at bottom problems of the logic of empirical science in general," and contended that TWH's arguments were of this generality. He had rightly stressed the distinction between analytic and empirical propositions, but had not succeeded in completely clarifying the significance of pure theory. The economists' practice of incorporating an indefinite number of undetermined factors in the ceteris paribus pound was, indeed, objectionable, as TWH had maintained; yet that clause was useful as "a way of formulating a *heuristic postulate,* a methodological program." It was essential to distinguish between "disturbing factors" already discovered and those still unknown (for example, when making forecasts based exclusively on price movements without reference to other relevant economic or noneconomic data). All empirical sciences employ the method of

> isolating a small number of factors, analysing the relations between them and making these relations the backbone of a theoretical construction; but the method of isolation also needs a method of synthesis as its counterpart and it is essential to distinguish between heuristic postulates and empirical laws.

A heuristic postulate is a convention, not a proposition belonging to the corpus of science; it

> may have to be replaced by another if it does not lead to the desired results, and accordingly it may be affected by the negative outcome of an empirical test. But it cannot be directly falsified by it.

In practice, the principles of economics are "almost always to be understood as heuristic postulates," not as empirical laws.[87]

These views were constructive and could have served as a basis for a resolution of at least part of the later disagreement between Machlup and Hutchison, for Kaufmann's "heuristic postulates" can be interpreted in instrumentalist (rather than strict positivist) terms as a "third type" of proposition, an essential component of the agreed corpus of methodological or procedural rules required by any scientific community. But, as Adolph Lowe pointed out, in his contribution to what he described as "another *Methodenstreit,*" to treat economic laws merely as "heuristic postulates" would simply enable the economist to avoid the implications of empirical tests, by modifying his postulates.[88] The dangers of such "conventionalist stratagems," as Popper termed them, were to figure prominently in postwar methodological discussion.[89] Like TWH and Kaufmann, Lowe wished to preserve the empirical status of economic laws, arguing that the ceteris paribus clause need not be interpreted in a comprehensive and unrestricted sense: "If we exclude only some 'disturbing elements,' and clearly define them, we are left with sufficient factual substance to raise our hypothesis to the level of a synthetic [i.e., empirical] proposition." Economists from Smith to Marshall had, in fact, interpreted economic laws in this manner, Lowe maintained, thereby justifying the familiar analogy between such laws and the laws of physics. Beyond this, the laws of supply and demand could always be interpreted as a code or line of behavior, "which brings the independent actions of innumerable individuals into agreement, and thus contains an *imperative*, rather than a description of empirical facts." To Lowe, the "laws of the market" did not imply any causal necessity or even statistical probability, for within the framework of economic theory they merely expressed "the conditions for stability and autonomy of the market process as a whole."[90]

Lowe's article marks the end of the first phase of discussion provoked by TWH's book and his exchange with Knight. It would be comforting to be able to report that the outcome was conclusive, whereas in fact it was merely the opening of a campaign which has lasted in certain respects up to the present. One criterion of scientific importance is "fruitfulness," and TWH certainly opened up a range of fundamental issues which have proved irresistible to many of his postwar contemporaries and successors, especially: the nature of economic "laws"; the epistemological status and methodological functions of "assumptions" in economics; and the use of the ceteris paribus clause. Unfortunately, as is so often the case, much of the ensuing discussion has been marred by terminological disagreements and failure to recognize the influence of philosophical differences which most economists (and, less creditably, some economic methodologists too) have had neither the desire nor perhaps the ability to comprehend.

No attempt will be made here to survey the postwar literature on these questions in any detail.[91] The remaining sections will be concerned only with those issues in which TWH was directly involved[92] or with related matters with a general bearing on the state of economic methodology. The concluding section will attempt to survey the current state of play, give some indications of major trends in economic methodology since the 1930s, and provide an assessment of TWH's contribution to the subject.

VI

Since World War II, TWH has devoted much more of his intellectual energies to the history of economic thought than to methodology per se, although the two have rarely been entirely divorced in his writings. His most comprehensive historical study, *A Review of Economic Doctrines 1870–1939*, published in 1953, was followed by a series of articles dealing with individual economists, episodes, or doctrinal schools; and since the mid-1960s he has increasingly focused his attention on contemporary ideas and trends in the discipline. Beginning with *Postive Economics and Policy Objectives* (1964), a systematic historical survey and assessment of the role of value judgments in British economics – a topic he had regarded as largely "played out" in 1938 – his major themes have included: the historiography of economics; the limitations of the economist's knowledge; the relationships between economic ideas and policy; and the professional economist's ethical and public responsibilities. During the past six years he has returned to some of his earlier general methodological concerns in *Knowledge and Ignorance in Economics* (1977); *On Revolutions and Progress in Economics* (1978); and in his latest collection of essays, *The Politics and Philosophy of Economics: Marxists, Keynesians and Austrians (*1981). While retaining his interest in most of the central topics of his *Significance and Basic Postulates* he has both moved with the times and been a leader of methodological opinion, a scholar whose work cannot be dismissed as irrelevant or insignificant even by those who disagree with it.

During the past three decades by far the most prominent and consistantly controversial topic in economic methodology has been the role of "assumptions" in economic theory, which became a major debating point after the appearance of Milton Friedman's notorious essay on *The Methodology of Positive Economics* in 1953. As Mark Blaug has recently observed of this

> centerpiece of postwar economic methodology, the one essay on methodological questions that virtually every economist has read at some stage in his or her career... so subtle is Friedman's argument that even now it is difficult to find two economists who will agree precisely what it was that Friedman said.[92]

It is unnecessary to add yet another review of the assumptions debate. Perhaps the most revealing single feature is, as Lawrence Boland has remarked, the fact that Friedman's essay has been so widely approved by practising economists, notwithstanding the obscurities, inconsistencies, and potentially dangerous professional implications of his argument which have repeatedly been exposed by competent methodologists.[93] The entire subject may perhaps serve as a warning to methodologists tempted to overrate their influence on the profession, a temptation TWH has consistently resisted.

Although TWH frequently referred to Friedman en passant in his later writings, his only extended comment on the "irrelevance of assumptions" argument occurred in the penetrating introduction to the second edition of his *Significance and Basic Postulates* (1960). This restraint is not surprising, for he had made his views known in the first edition and in his exchange with Machlup. In response to Friedman, he denied that the fundamental assumption of maximizing conduct should be accorded privileged epistemological status and complained of the "hopeless ambiguity" resulting from the failure to specify whether it was a tautology, a fact of immediate experience, or a typical behavior pattern. Evidence should be brought to bear in economics wherever possible, he maintained, and as Machlup had conceded that the profit maximization hypothesis could in practice be tested, it would be "methodologically unwise" or "complacently uncritical" to refrain from discovering whether it was true or false.[94] Indeed, he obviously approved of Spiro Latsis's later contention that most of the obscurities in the "assumptions controversy" would disappear if it was regarded, as in Machlup's case, essentially as a conventionalist defence against falsificationism.[95]

For TWH, as for many economists, the debate initiated by Friedman was directly connected with the more immediate and pressing problem of empirical testing, which (as noted earlier) TWH had been the first to introduce into economic literature.[96] This issue assumed increasing importance in the postwar wave of enthusiasm for natural science methods in the social sciences, especially in the context of advanced statistics and econometrics, which were rapidly gaining in professional resources and prestige, and, more broadly, in explorations of the applicability of Karl Popper's doctrine of falsification to the social sciences. In a confident era, when economics was widely regarded – especially by the economists themselves – as the most "scientific" among this group of disciplines, the notion that predictions derived from economic theories or hypotheses could and should be empirically falsifiable proved well-nigh irresistible. But with the passage of time there was a growing appreciation of the practical and theoretical difficulties of devising effective tests. As economic methodologists became more familiar with contemporary philosophy of science, a process that accelerated rapidly after the publication of Thomas S. Kuhn's immensely influential book *The Structure of Scientific Revolutions* (1962), it was increasingly recognized that even in physics, so long held up as the true exemplar of scientific method, testing was often difficult, seldom if ever immediately conclusive, and frequently the subject of protracted controversy.[97] Subsequently, under the influence of Imre Lakatos, the notion of "naive falsificationism" – sometimes wrongly attributed to Popper – gave way to "sophisticated falsification," according to which even after numerous tests scientific theories could, and even should be allowed to, survive, given the difficulty of demonstrating the clear superiority of one theory over another.[98] Moreover, to this should be added the views cited earlier from Quine and Putnam, emphasizing the holistic character of scientific theories[99] and suggesting that the obstacles to effective empirical falsification may indeed be insurmountable.

Among many manifestations of this trend in economic literature, which reflects a growing disenchantment with Friedman's "positive" economics in particular and "positivism" in general, it is sufficient to cite Alan Coddington, who argued that the preconditions for effective testing included the following conditions:

(i) the theory must be coherent and well-defined;
(ii) the empirical materials must be reliable and must be satisfactory empirical counterparts of the concepts of the theory;
(iii) the assumptions made in designating the test must be of very low substantive content compared with the theory, or must be established independently of the test.[100]

Of course many other formulations of this problem have been proposed. The important point, as Coddington and others have acknowledged, is that

> only on very rare occasions will the conditions for consequential testing be fulfilled so manifestly that the issue is beyond dispute.... More realistically, the question is a matter of degree in which the line must be drawn somewhere to delimit situations in which testing is to be regarded as sufficiently consequential to merit the effort involved.... At the present stage of development of economics, there is an enormous potential for pseudo-testing, i.e. ostensible testing which is, in reality, wholly inconsequential.[101]

Needless to say, when faced with this problem, contemporary economists have reacted in a variety of ways which reflect the current state of confusion and dissension within the discipline. To the advocates of economic heterodoxy, which includes a miscellaneous band of institutionalists (though not all of these), Marxists, and antipositivist rationalists,[102] the effort to devise effective empirical tests is inherently futile. To Blaug, who has exposed with unflinching honesty the persistent gap between orthodox methodological preaching and practice, the remedy is to try harder to devise genuinely falsifiable theories and subject them to a series of stringent tests.[103] Yet another view is expressed by Thomas Mayer, who, without advocating (as do some "Austrian" economists) the abandonment of econometrics, argues that the effort to make economics into a "hard" science has in some respects been actively damaging. It has encouraged the choice of "wrong" hypotheses, simply because they "fit the data"; it has distracted attention from the search for "scientific" evidence and from the essential but unglamorous task of data gathering; and it has fostered the preoccupation with advanced mathematical tools. The net result is that

> Much of the published research consists of taking a new technique out for a walk rather than of really trying to solve a problem. And also, economics has become much too isolated from other social sciences, since being hard scientists we do not want to use either the results or tools of those who cannot claim our exalted status.[104]

Recognizing these difficulties TWH has, during the postwar period, substantially moderated his youthful enthusiasm, though without in any sense renouncing his original credo. As a result, some sympathetic critics consider that his methodological views have become more agnostic, even ambiguous, and to the extent that this is so his position fairly accurately reflects some of the uncertainties and disagreements currently expressed by methodologists and philosophers of science.

This applies, for example, to his treatment of testing in economics. In response to Knight's unabashed antipositivist intuitionism, TWH confidently retorted: "Science is impossible in a field where there is no general acceptance... as to intersubjective tests";[105] yet his latest, far more cautious and qualified discussion of this issue, gives little assurance that such acceptance will be forthcoming. He derides as "preposterous" the contention that

> because there are so often immense difficulties in the way of anything resembling decisive tests, therefore the desirability and obligation, so far as practicable, of testing and providing testable formulations, should be dismissed as naive;[106]

but whether statements of good intentions can achieve much is doubtful. It is precisely this acknowledgment of the "immense difficulties" that has encouraged the shift of attention from Popper's falsificationism (which TWH still endorses) to Lakatos's "sophisticated falsificationism" and ultimately to Feyerabend's doctrine of "anything goes," which TWH regards – no doubt justifiably – with such suspicion.[107] The attractions of anarchism, whether methodological or otherwise, are not uncommonly enhanced in periods of doubt and uncertainty about fundamentals.

A related issue, where similar tendencies are apparent, is the much-debated question of the differences between the natural and the social sciences which, TWH acknowledged in 1960, seemed more "important and ineluctable" than he had supposed in 1938.[108] Although he denied that there was any fundamental epistemological distinction between the two groups of disciplines, he has increasingly emphasized the significant differences of "degree" involved. In particular, in his later writings he has focussed attention on the differences of substance or materials rather than methods per se, a position hitherto adopted by methodological holists, intuitionists, subjectivists, and those concerned with the role of "*Verstehen*" (understanding) in human affairs:

> Difficulties in quantifiability, heterogeneity, the absence of 'constants,' the 'openness' or 'complexity' of the material of social and economic systems, or what might be called the historical and institutional dimension (which implies the existence only of trends and not laws), these are all different aspects, or ways of describing the different characteristics of the material of the social as contrasted with the natural sciences. The differences may only be in degree, but amount to such a considerable degree as to constitute a profound contrast.[109]

Here, as elsewhere, TWH reveals himself as more of a methodological pluralist than he was in 1938. While continuing to endorse Popper's falsificationism he is far more conscious of the difficulty, even the impossibility, of eliminating "'historicism,' 'essentialism,' verbalism,' 'fashion,' 'uncontrollable dogmas,' and all the other methodological monstrosities, discerned by Sir Karl in the social sciences,"[110] and the related danger that the methodological principles which have been so effective in physics "may be too exclusivist for a subject with a fundamental historical aspect, like economics." He continues: "It is not good advice to condemn induction if the nature of the material restricts the genuine scope for the hypothetico-deductive method."[111] On this matter the gap between TWH's and Popper's views has widened considerably, partly as a result of the marked growth of advanced mathematical and quantitative economics, about which TWH has become increasingly concerned, largely because it has been accompanied by an exaggerated professional self-confidence among economists. Contrary to Popper's belief that economics has already experienced its "Newtonian Revolution," TWH has dissected the "Crisis of Abstraction" in the 1970s and has identified the James Mill–Ricardo "methodological revolution" as a primary source of the discipline's present discontents.[112]

The collective hubris among his professional colleagues in the postwar period largely explains TWH's repeated insistence on the limitations of the economist's knowledge in his recent works.[113] His treatment of this theme illustrates the conjunction of methodology, history, philosophy, social and political importance, and – by implication – professional responsibility, which is so characteristic of his later writings. In 1960, contrary to his 1938 position, he repudiated efforts to separate metaphysics from science, and subsequently endorsed Popper's view that

> Our often unconscious views on the theory of knowledge and its central problems ('What do we know? How certain is our knowledge?') are decisive for our attitudes towards ourselves and towards politics.[114]

Like Popper, he asserted his faith in the possibility of the growth of knowledge irrespective of the difficulties encountered by scientists and scholars. He held that "there can be no authority for any claim to authority," yet he insisted that "a belief in the authority of scientific truth is indispensable for a free society based on mutual respect."[115] The most fundamental principle of his methodological creed, as expressed in his latest essay on the subject, is the need for

> constant criticism, and the constant pressing of critical distinctions and demarcations as far as they will go, in the first instance in the interests of clarity, and beyond that in the interests of rational public policy debate in a democracy.[116]

VII

Given TWH's warnings about the limitations of the economist's knowledge, it would be foolish to conclude this essay with a confident assessment of the current state and prospects of economic methodology. Indeed, the sheer scale, variety, and complexity of the discipline is enough to discourage any such attempt. Nevertheless, if we may judge by the continuing expressions of dissatisfaction by prominent economists, the reservations and uncertainties offered by contemporary textbook writers, the well-publicized professional disagreements on theoretical and policy issues, and the current spate of methodological writings, there is little reason to believe that economics has yet emerged from the "crisis" that was so widely reported a decade ago. Whether there has been any "progress" in economic methodology as a result of the controversies of the past half century is a much more difficult question, for the answer directly depends on the criteria adopted and, as indicated in previous sections of this essay, on this matter there remains a notable lack of intellectual consensus.

Such a consensus is not, of course, an end in itself, for it could be the result of intellectual stagnation or authoritarian controls. Fortunately at present there seems little danger of either in economics though, as TWH appreciates, there is some risk of going to the other extreme and adopting the principle of "anything goes." The doubts and uncertainties evident in current economic methodology literature can no longer be resolved merely by citing the standards and practices prevailing in the natural sciences. In stark contrast to the overconfident simplifications of the 1930s, the weaknesses of positivism and intuitionism have now been effectively exposed and the balance of trade between the natural and the social sciences has shifted markedly. According to one contemporary philosopher "the social sciences are central to current debates in the history and philosophy of science,"[117] while another, advocating a naturalistic "post-empiricist" philosophy of social science, has even suggested that "setting out modern philosophy of science's implications for social science helps us to see that modern philosophy of science is itself ultimately untenable."[118]

It is obviously impossible to review all the difficulties and dilemmas faced by contemporary social science methodologists. Several have already been revealed in earlier sections of this essay, such as: the problems of empirical testing or falsification; the sources and status of methodological rules, heuristic principles, or basic scientific "conventions"; the relationships between theoretical and observation statements; and the choice of an appropriate scientific language. But what differentiates current from past methodological controversies (e.g., the attacks on economic orthodoxy by historicists and institutionalists) is the sense that traditional beliefs and practices are being undermined from within, that the attack on the cruder forms of positivism has given way to a series of concessions that point the way to subjectivism or relativism.

Exposure of the problems of empirical testing in economics constitutes a prime example, since such testing has been widely regarded as the hallmark of science, especially since TWH's 1938 book. But the admission that empirical testing is often impossible or very difficult, and usually inconclusive, and that economists preach falsification but rarely practice it seriously – a situation presented in forthright terms in Mark Blaug's recent survey[119] – readily leads to the conclusion that the injunction "Go forth and falsify!" is little more than an empty slogan. While it is easy to agree with TWH that we should endeavor to be as scientific as we can, there is a real danger that all confidence in Popperian falsification, which Blaug advocates, will soon fade away. Whether salvation can be found in more historical methods, such as "pattern modeling" or "storytelling,"[120] used either as a substitute or a supplement to Popperian methods, is a matter that cannot be explored here.

The work of T. S. Kuhn has played a major role in undermining confidence in traditional philosophy of science, for it compelled a fundamental reexamination of the relationships between ideas, men, and society by "re-emphasizing the close connections between the socio-historical development of scientific schools, professions and institutions, and the intellectual development of scientific theories themselves."[121] Once it is appreciated that methodological rules, heuristic principles, or basic scientific "conventions" have no absolute validity, science can be regarded as a kind of "game" and attention is inevitably focussed on the origins and status of rules. Although Lakatos dismissed Kuhn's emphasis on the judgments of the scientific community as "mob psychology," he reinforced Kuhn's position by pointing out that Popper had failed to offer a theory of the rational critique of scientific conventions or to ask under what circumstances, if any, should a demarcation criterion be abandoned.[122] Moreover, Lakatos himself adopted a sociological criterion in arguing that "if a demarcation criterion is inconsistent with the basic appraisals of the scientific elite it should be rejected."[123]

Reference to the scientific elite brings us immediately to the problem of the resolution of disagreements within the scientific community – a matter of considerable difficulty in view of recent recognition of the problem of scientific language. As we have seen, TWH consistently emphasized the importance of clarity and still clings to the positivist notion that there is such a thing as "the language of strict science,"[124] whereas contemporary philosophers of science, reacting against positivism, emphasize the element of choice in the classification of terms and propositions and the theory-dependence of both language and observations. As Thomas argues, to cite but one of many examples,

> Post-empiricism holds that the meaning of a term – and, therefore, to an extent the truth-status of statements in which the term appears – is in part determined by its relationship with other terms in its home theory...

and this mutual dependence poses the problems of relativism, commensurability, and cross-theoretical comparison.[125] The implications of this position are alarming to those hostile to intellectual anarchism, for it is tempting to proceed through Kuhn's conception of the incommensurability of paradigms and the sociologist's recognition of the conventional character of language to the ethnomethodologist's extreme relativism, according to which there are no objective and unambiguous procedures for applying social rules since the meanings of particular actions are indexical, or context dependent, rather than dependent on any invariant general principles.[126]

How far considerations of this kind do, in fact, or should enter into the methodology of economics is still uncertain. But it is clear that the difficulties of attaining intersubjective agreement about the meaning of terms, the appropriateness of different intellectual frameworks, and the validity of empirical tests underlie persistent controversies of the Keynesian vs. monetarist type.[127] As Thomas observes,

> Even though social science has generally been characterized by intra-theoretical debate and development, we cannot rest content with an intra-theoretical conception of meaning and truth. A Feyerabendian licence to hold any theory we want precludes the possibility of rational debate between theories. But we *know* that there has been rational debate between theories. Any serious attempt to convince us otherwise ought to be rejected with as much scorn as any attempt to convince us that we do not know other people, material objects, and time to be real.[128]

Issues of this kind are inescapable in the discussion of theory choice in economics, a topic that is figuring more prominently in current methodological literature. Questions as to whether there are any objective criteria for assessing the cognitive value of different theories and, if so, what is the epistemological status of such criteria, will inevitably come to the fore when there is a plethora of rival theories contending for mastery. In a valuable attempt to tackle this problem directly, Vincent Tarascio and Bruce Caldwell have distinguished between empirical criteria of theory choice (e.g., testability of assumptions; realism; predictive adequacy) and nonempirical criteria (e.g., logical consistency; simplicity; elegance; generality; theoretical support).[129] Even this incomplete listing suffices to show the complexity of the problem, especially in view of the so-called Duhem–Quine contention that theories must be accepted or rejected as wholes because it is impossible to falsify a whole theory merely by demonstrating the falsity of a single hypothesis.[131]

As yet TWH has not commented in detail on these issues, but his profound hostility to the more nihilistic forms of antipositivism and antiempiricism is abundantly clear in his latest methodological essay, where he reasserts his faith in the value of

> constant criticism, and the constant pressing of crucial distinctions and demarcations as far as they will go, in the first instance in the interests of clarity, and beyond that in the interests of rational public policy debate in a democracy, that is, if one accepts Sir Karl Popper's prescription: 'Aiming at simplicity and lucidity is a moral duty of all intellectuals: lack of clarity is a sin!'[130]

He is still acutely aware of the dangers of bias and ideology in an "immature" science like economics, many of whose practitioners are deeply involved in controversial public policy issues, a state of affairs that accentuates rather than diminishes the importance of adherence to what he terms the "square," "old-fashioned" academic and scientific virtues. Recognition of the limitations of his earlier youthful naturalistic enthusiasm has led him to a more qualified but still stout defense of empiricism; and he fears the potential excesses of destructive methodological criticism or excessively rigid scientific standards much less than the opposite danger of excessive tolerance or laxity.[132] While acknowledging the absence of any definitive meta-methodological rules, he defends the practice of issuing methodological prescriptions for academics, arguing that if this leads to agnosticism his direct retort is simply that "in economics and the social sciences there is a tremendous lot to withhold judgment and to be agnostic about."[133]

With respect to fashionable large-scale theories about the "growth of knowledge" and the existence of scientific "revolutions," he is once again characteristically cautious, though here too he makes a concession to the opposition in acknowledging that "changes in testable refutable, empirical content" have played a relatively limited role in the history of economics, as compared with the influence of: new policy objectives; changes in interest, research priorities, or attention; and the emergence of a new terminology or intellectual framework – with mathematization as a special case.[134] Unlike Lakatos, he does not consider that "internal" developments within the discipline should necessarily be regarded as predominant; and in contrast with the views of historians of the natural sciences, he suggests that "the steady growth of historical and statistical material might well be regarded as the most solid basis for a belief in the progress of economic knowledge"[135] – a view entirely in harmony with the conclusions of his 1938 book.

TWH would not, of course, make strong claims with respect to the "progress" of economic methodology as reflected in his own writings; nor would it be appropriate to make such claims on his behalf, for as Keith Rivett has argued, the debate over economic methodology represents "one of the great speculative discussions of this and the previous century."[136] Hence a conclusive outcome is hardly likely to be achieved. But if consistent advocacy of high standards can achieve anything, TWH's consistently constructive contributions deserve to be generously acknowledged.

Notes

1 Robbins, Lionel, *An Essay on the Nature and Significance of Economic Science* (London: Macmillan, 1932) pp. 1, 72. The same statements appear in the second edition, of 1935.

2 T.W.H., "Tautologies and the Nature of Economic Theory," *Review of Economic Studies* Vol. 2 (February, 1935) pp. 159–61.

3 Introduction to T.W.H., *The Limitations of General Theories in Macroeconomics* (Washington, D.C.: American Enterprise Institute, 1980). A revised version of this essay is reprinted in T.W.H., *The Philosophy and Politics of Economics. Marxists, Keynesians and Austrians* (Oxford: Basil Blackwell, 1981) pp. 46–107. For a general assessment of T.W.H.'s work as an historian of economics see my forthcoming essay in Warren Samuels, ed., *The Craft of the Historian of Economics. Research in the History of Economic Thought and Methodology* Vol. 1.

4 T.W.H., *Knowledge and Ignorance in Economics* (Oxford: Basil Blackwell, 1977) p. 5. Italics in original.

5 For a general account see my article "The L.S.E. Ethos in the Inter-war Years," *Atlantic Economic Journal* Vol. 10 (March, 1982) pp. 18–30.
6 *Economics Is a Serious Subject* (Cambridge: Heffer and Sons, 1932) pp. 8–9.
7 Ibid. For T.W.H.'s essentially compatible assessment of Marshall's influence see his *A Review of Economic Doctrines 1870–1929* (Oxford: Clarendon Press, 1953), Chap. 4, especially p. 62; also *Philosophy and Politics of Economics,* op. cit., pp. 46–62.
8 Robinson, op. cit., p. 9.
9 T.W.H., "Insularity and Cosmopolitanism in Economic Ideas, 1870–1914," *American Economic Review* Vol. 45 (May, 1955) pp. 1–16. See especially the telling quotation from Dennis Robertson on p. 12.
10 See his two small booklets, *Economics and Human Behavior: A Rejoinder to Social Psychologists* (London: Kegan Paul, Trench, Trubner and Co., 1927), and *Uplift in Economics: A Plea for the Exclusion of Moral Implications from Economics and the Political Sciences* (London: Kegan Paul, Trench, Trubner and Co., 1929).
11 Cf. W. Leontief, "Implicit Theorizing: A Methodological Criticism of the Neo-Cambridge School," *Quarterly Journal of Economics* Vol. 51 (February, 1937) pp. 337–51; T. C. Koopmans, "The Construction of Economic Knowledge," in his *Three Essays on the State of Economic Science* (New York: McGraw-Hill, 1957) especially pp. 130–1, where he specifically refers to parallels between his own and T.W.H.'s ideas. Although both were probably referring mainly to post 1930 Cambridge economics, their remarks broadly apply mutatis mutandis to the earlier period.
12 *The Significance and Basic Postulates of Economic Theory* (London: Macmillan, 1938). All subsequent references will be to the 2nd edition: Augustus M. Kelley. New York, 1960, which has a new Preface. The passage quoted appears on p. xxvi.
13 "Tautologies," op. cit., p. 161, citing Robbins, op. cit. (1932) p. 111 [the same remarks appear in Robbins, op. cit. (1935) p. 122].
14 Ibid.
15 Parts of this debate are considered later in this essay.
16 Robbins, op. cit. (1935) pp. xiii, xi. The Preface gives some idea of the critics' objections. See also R. W. Souter, *Prolegomena to Relativity Economics* (New York: Columbia University Press, 1933); Linley Fraser, "How Do We Want Economists to Behave?" *Economic Journal* Vol. 42 (December, 1932) pp. 193–202; and Frank H. Knight, "Economic Science in Recent Discussion," *American Economic Review* Vol. 24 (June, 1934) pp. 225–38.
17 Cf. "The Problem of Verification in Economics," originally published in the *Southern Economic Journal* (1955) and reprinted in his *Methodology of Economics and Other Social Sciences* (New York: Academic Press, 1978) especially pp. 141–3.
18 Robbins, op. cit. (1935) p. 78.
19 Ibid. (1932) pp. 118–9.
20 T.W.H., "A Reply to Professor Knight," *Journal of Political Economy* Vol. 49 (October, 1941) p. 735.
21 Ibid.
22 Knight had stated, "The text must not be taken as expressing any view whatever as to the ultimate nature of reality or any other philosophical position. The writer is in fact a radical empiricist in logic, which is to say, as far as theoretical reasoning is concerned, an agnostic on all questions beyond fairly immediate facts of experience." *Risk, Uncertainty and Profit* (Boston: Houghton Mifflin, 1921) pp. 200–1. Ironically, in view of his support for Knight, when Machlup attacked T.W.H. as an "ultra-empiricist" he cited William James's radical empiricism as an example of the extreme views to which he took exception. Cf. "The Problem of Verification," op. cit., p. 143.
23 *Significance and Basic Postulates,* op. cit., p. 143.
24 Kaufmann's book was subsequently revised and translated as *Methodology of the Social Sciences* (New York: Oxford University Press, 1944). Kaufmann wrote several articles in the *Review of Economic Studies* and *Economica* before T.W.H. published his

1938 book. Of especial relevance here are the following: "On the Subject-Matter and Method of Economic Science," *Economica* Vol. 13 (November, 1933) pp. 381–401; and "Do Synthetic Propositions A Priori Exist in Economics? A Reply to Dr. Bernadelli," *loc. cit.,* Vol. 4 (August, 1937) pp. 337–42. Cf. the review article by Harro Bernadelli, "What has Philosophy to Contribute to the Social Sciences, and to Economics in Particular?" *loc. cit..* Vol. 3 (November, 1936) pp. 443–54.

25 Published in English as *The Logic of Scientific Discovery* (London: Hutchinson, 1959).

26 *Significance and Basic Postulates*, op. cit., p. vii.

27 Ibid., p. 19.

28 Cf. Popper, op. cit., especially pp. 34 ff. See also Popper's "Autobiography" and "Replies to My Critics" in Paul Arthur Schilpp (ed.), *The Philosophy of Karl Popper* (La Salle, Ill., 1974) Book I p. 3 ff; Book II, p. 961 ff.

29 Op. cit., p. 3.

30 From this point page references to the 1938 book, which has the same pagination in both editions, will be inserted in the text.

31 Popper, *Logic of Scientific Discovery*, pp. 37–8

32 Ibid., pp. 52–3. Sentence order reversed in part. In a footnote to the 1959 edition he noted that the Vienna Circle had criticized his ideas on the grounds that a theory of method which is neither an empirical science nor pure logic is impossible, since what lies outside these two fields must be sheer nonsense. Wittgenstein still held this view as late as 1948. Ibid., p. 51, n.1. Cf. the reference to the emerging "science of science" in T.W.H. (1938) p. 53.

33 Cf. Hilary Putnam, "On Corroboration of Theories," and W. V. Quine, "On Popper's Negative Methodology," Schilpp, op. cit., pp. 221–40 and 218–20; Adolf Grünbaum, "Is Falsifiability the Touchstone of Scientific Rationality? Karl Popper versus Inductivism," in R. S. Cohen, P. K. Feyerabend, and M. W. Wartofsky, *Essays in Memory of Imre Lakatos, Boston Studies in the Philosophy of Science* (Boston: D. Reidel Publishing Co., 1976) pp. 213–52.

34 In his *Knowledge and Ignorance in Economics* op. cit., p. 151, T.W.H. remarked, "though this early essay could be claimed to have been, in many ways, a sceptical work by the standards of 1938, its optimistic 'naturalism' seems now indefensible: that is, its suggestions that the 'social sciences' could and would develop in the same manner as physics and the natural sciences." See also, *Significance and Basic Postulates*, op. cit., pp. xi – xii; and *Politics and Philosophy of Economics,* op. cit., pp. 300–1, and p. 303: "The author of Hutchison, 1938, was a kind of falsificationist, and, as a 25-year-old intellectual was probably, *ipso facto* naive. But there does not seem to be much telling documentary evidence that he was a naive falsificationist in the technical sense introduced by Lakatos."

35 For revealing comments on this matter see Mark Blaug, *The Methodology of Economics, or How Economists Explain* (Cambridge: Cambridge University Press, 1980) pp. 18–20, where he notes the circularity and normative character of Popper's argument, remarking that "the pursuit of science can be justified only in non-scientific terms."

36 Popper, op. cit., p. 52; cf. Blaug, op. cit., pp. 14–16.

37 Cf. supra., pp. 37–8.

38 For example, Stephen Toulmin, *Human Understanding* (Oxford: Clarendon Press, 1972); Michael Polanyi, *Personal Knowledge. Towards a Post-Critical Philosophy* (London: Routledge and Kegan Paul, 1958); Thomas S. Kuhn, *The Structure of Scientific Revolutions* (Chicago: University of Chicago Press, 2nd ed., 1970); Imre Lakatos, in J. Worrall and G. Currie (eds.), *The Methodology of Scientific Research Programmes: Philosophical Papers* (Cambridge: Cambridge University Press, 1978); Paul Feyerabend, *Against Method. Outline of an Anarchistic Theory of Knowledge* (London: Verso, 1978); David Bloor, *Knowledge and Social Imagery* (London: Routledge and Kegan Paul, 1976).

39 This is, indeed, the central theme of Blaug's book, referred to earlier.

40 Cf. "The Problem of Verification," op. cit.

41 Klappholz and Agassi, "Methodological Prescriptions in Economics," *Economica* N.S. Vol. 26 (February, 1959) pp. 60–74; T.W.H.'s "Methodological Prescriptions: A Reply", *loc. cit.,* Vol. 27 (May, 1960) pp. 158–60; Klappholz and Agassi, "A Rejoinder," Ibid., pp. 160–1; T.W.H's *Significance and Basic Postulates,* op. cit., p. xvii–vxiii; and *Philosophy and Politics of Economics,* op. cit., p. 302. Cf. Blaug, op. cit., p. 95 for the view that economic propositions with unspecified ceteris paribus clauses are in fact untestable empirical assertions about the real world: "if a statement is in principle falsifiable, it does forbid some conceivable event or set of events. But the obverse does not hold."

42 Alexander Rosenberg, *Microeconomic Laws, A Philosophical Analysis* (Pittsburgh: University of Pittsburgh Press, 1976).

43 Machlup, "Terence Hutchison's Reluctant Ultra Empiricism," in his *Methodology of Economics,* op. cit., p. 496; originally published as "Rejoinder to a Reluctant Ultra Empiricist," *Southern Economic Journal* Vol. 22 (April, 1956).

44 Lakatos, op. cit., *passim.*

45 Quine, W. V., "Two Dogmas of Empiricism" (1953), reprinted in his *From a Logical Point of View* (New York, 1963) p. 37. For T.W.H.'s dissent from this view see his *Politics and Philosophy of Economics,* op. cit., pp. 301–2. There have been complex debates among philosophers about the concepts of analyticity, synonymy, etc. See, for example, the series of articles by F. Waissman on "Analyticity," in *Analysis* Vol. 10 (December, 1949) to Vol. 13 (March, 1953); also Morton G. White, *Toward Reunion in Philosophy* (Cambridge, Mass.: Harvard University Press, 1956).

46 Putnam, Hilary, "The Analytic and the Synthetic" (1962), reprinted in his *Mind Language and Reality: Philosophical Papers* Vol. 2 (Cambridge: Cambridge University Press, 1975) p. 39.

47 Putnam, op. cit., pp. 42, 40. According to Quine, "Taken collectively, science has a double dependence on language and experience; but this duality is not significantly traceable into statements of science taken one by one.... The unit of empirical significance is the whole of science.... [T]otal science is like a field of force whose boundary conditions are experience. A conflict with experience at the periphery occasions adjustments in the interior of the field.... But the total field is so underdetermined by its boundary conditions, experience, that there is much latitude of choice as to what statements to re-evaluate in the light of any single contrary experience. No particular experiences are linked with any particular statements in the interior of the field, except indirectly through conditions affecting the field as a whole." Op. cit., pp. 42–3. Cf. Morton H. White, "American Philosophy," in Robert E. Spiller and Eric Larrabee (eds.), *American Perspectives* (Cambridge, Mass.: Harvard University Press, 1961) p. 21.

48 Bridgman, *The Logic of Modern Physics* (New York: Macmillan. 1927) pp. 6, 5.

49 *Tractatus Logico-philosophicus,* quoted by Machlup, op. cit., p. 165. Among the numerous critics of this view see, for example, Richard von Mises, *Positivism* (Cambridge: Harvard University Press, 1951).

50 Machlup, op. cit., pp. 133–4. See also his "Operational Concepts and Mental Concepts in Model and Theory Formation" (1960) and "Operationalism and Pure Theory in Economics" (1966) ibid., pp. 159–88, 189–203.

51 Ibid., pp. 141, 143.

52 Ibid., p. 144. Machlup added: "I could have quoted from dozens of critics of economic theory, from adherents of the historical, institutional, quantitative schools, and these quotations might be even more aggressive. I have selected Hutchison because he is the critic best informed about logic and scientific method."

53 Machlup, *Methodology of Economics,* op. cit., p. 493 ff. The quotation, from *Significance and Basic Postulates,* p. 9, continues as follows: "They need not, that is, actually be tested or even be *practically* capable of testing under present or future technical

conditions or conditions of statistical investigation, nor is there any sense in talking of some kind of 'absolute' test which will 'finally' decide whether a proposition is 'absolutely' true or false. But it must be possible to indicate intersubjectively what is the case if they are true or false; their truth or falsity, that is, must make some conceivable empirically noticeable difference, or some such difference must be directly deducible therefrom." (Italics in original.)

54 This is the view taken by Bruce Caldwell, in his now published book, *Beyond Positivism: Economic Methodology in the Twentieth Century* (London: Allen and Unwin, 1982), Chap. 7: "Hutchison versus Machlup – On Indirect Testing and the Rationality Postulate." I am most grateful to the author for allowing me to see this prior to its publication.

55 Machlup, *Methodology of Economics*, op. cit., p. 460.

56 Boland, Lawrence A., "A Critique of Friedman's Critics," *Journal of Economic Literature* Vol. 17 (June, 1979) p. 508. He defines conventionalism as the doctrine that "truth" is essentially a matter of convention: theories are merely "convenient categories or 'filing systems' for positive reports to be judged or compared only by criteria of convenience such as simplicity or degrees of approximation or closeness of 'fit,'' etc.... [Conventionalism] is also the primary source of methodological problems because its application is based on a fundamental contradiction. Conventionalists presume that it is possible to discuss logical validity without reference to truth or falsity.... [It] does not offer a solution to the problem of induction,... only... a way of discussing philosophical obstacles." Ibid.

57 *Logic of Scientific Discovery,* pp. 80, 82, 81.

58 In commenting on Spiro Latsis's recent critique of Machlup's conventionalism, T.W.H. described it as "an admirably perceptive, precise, and penetrating criticism (and quite as 'destructive' as any bloodthirsty 'falsificationalist' would want it to be), *Knowledge and Ignorance,* op. cit., p. 53, citing Latsis's "Situational Determination in Economics." *British Journal for the Philosophy of Science* Vol. 23 (1972) pp. 207–45, and "A Research Programme in Economics," in Spiro Latsis (ed.), *Method and Appraisal in Economics* (Cambridge: Cambridge University Press, 1976) pp. 9–14. T.W.H.'s remarks also appear here on p. 196. For Machlup's response to Latsis see *Methodology of Economics,* op. cit., Chap. 26, pp. 521–34.

59 Popper, op. cit., pp. 52, 53, 72, 80.

60 Cf. Putnam, H., and Quine, W., in Schilpp, op. cit., pp. 221–40 and 218–20.

61 Lakatos, op. cit.

62 Whittaker, Edmund, *American Economic Review* Vol. 30 (March, 1940), p. 128.

63 Stonier, Alfred W., *Economic Journal* Vol. 49 (March, 1939), p. 115.

64 Shearer, J. G., *The Economic Record* Vol. 15 (June, 1939), p. 136.

65 Stonier, op. cit., p. 115. According to Shearer, T.W.H. had not "given careful and prolonged attention to the difficulties and problems of verification in such a science as economics. What serves as verification to one economist is often denied that status by another. Little is said on this subject and the illustrations that are given are distressingly simplified" (op. cit., p. 138). For further discussion of this matter see *supra*, pp. 13–15, and *infra*, pp. 20–21, 25–27.

66 Shearer, op. cit., p. 138; Whittaker, op. cit., p. 128.

67 Dobb, Maurice H., "Scientific Method and the Criticism of Economics," *Science and Society* Vol. 3 (1942), p. 391.

68 Ibid., p. 397.

69 Ibid., pp. 392, 390.

70 *Supra*, pp. 11–14.

71 Dobb, op. cit., p. 395.

72 Ibid., pp. 395, 394.

73 Cf. T.W.H.'s references to Dobb and Cambridge in *On Revolutions and Progress,* and in *The Politics and Philosophy of Economics,* especially Chap. 3.

74 Knight, Frank H., "What is 'Truth' in Economics?" *Journal of Political Economy* Vol. 48 (February, 1940); reprinted in his *On the History and Method of Economics, Selected Essays* (Chicago, 1956) pp. 151–78. The quotations are from pp. 151, 152, and 177 in the 1956 edition, which is used here throughout.
75 Professor William D. Grampp, who was a graduate student at the University of Chicago when Knight published his review, recalls that he and a number of his contemporaries considered it extreme and unfair to Hutchison.
76 Knight, op. cit., p. 154. He was referring to T.W.H.'s statement of intentions and "personal intellectual tastes." Cf. note 30, *supra.*
77 Ibid., p. 155.
78 Knight, "Rejoinder," *Journal of Political Economy* Vol. 49 (October, 1941) pp. 751–2.
79 Knight, "What is 'Truth' in Economics?" op. cit., p. 155.
80 For example, this is a key element in Imre Lakatos's methodology of scientific research programmes.
81 Ibid., p. 177. Italics supplied.
82 Cf. *Economists and Economic Policy,* op. cit., p. 261; *Knowledge and Ignorance in Economics*, op. cit., pp. 19, 27, 33; *Politics and Philosophy of Economics,* op. cit., pp. 194, 198, 273.
83 This was discussed earlier.
84 "What is 'Truth' in Economics?" op. cit., pp. 164, 163, 168n, 163, 169.
85 T.W.H., "Reply to Professor Knight," *Journal of Political Economy* Vol. 49 (October, 1941) p. 736.
86 Ibid., pp. 740, 741.
87 Kaufmann, Felix, "On the Postulates of Economic Theory," *Social Research* Vol. 9 (September, 1942), pp. 395, 383, 380, 388, 390. See also note 24, *supra,* for references to Kaufmann's earlier works.
88 Lowe, Adolph, "A Reconsideration of the Law of Supply and Demand," *Social Research* Vol. 9 (November, 1942) p. 434.
89 Cf. *infra*, p. 31.
90 Lowe, op. cit., p. 434. For a useful discussion of his methodological views, see Fritz Machlup, "Adolph Lowe's Instrumental Analysis," in Robert L. Heilbroner (ed.), *Economic Means and Social Ends: Essays in Political Economics* (Englewood Cliffs, N.J.: Prentice-Hall, 1969), reprinted in Machlup's *Methodology of Economics*, op. cit., pp. 505–511.
91 On the question of economic "laws" see, for example, Blaug, *Methodology of Economics,* op. cit., especially pp. 161–3; also Rosenberg, *Microeconomic Laws,* op. cit., passim. The nature and testing of assumptions is considered *supra,* pp. 13 and *infra,* pp. 24ff especially in connection with Milton Friedman. The ceteris paribus issue is also referred to *supra,* pp. 22.
92 The exchange with Machlup in the mid 1950s has been discussed earlier. The exchange with Klappholz and Agassi (referred to in note 41) will not be examined here as it is primarily focused on the classification of propositions, discussed earlier. For additional criticism of T.W.H.'s position on this matter see also Rosenberg, op. cit., pp. 134–37, 152–55.
93 Cf. Boland, op. cit., p. 503. An attractive but mildly subversive explanation of this state of affairs is the need to provide a persuasive rationalization for "how we do things in economics." Cf. Homa Katouzian, *Ideology and Method in Economics* (London: Macmillan, 1980), p. 46. In addition to the useful bibliography on Friedman's essay in Blaug, op. cit., see also: Caldwell, op. cit., Chap. 12; *idem.,* "A Critique of Friedman's Methodological Instrumentalism," *Southern Economic Journal* Vol. 47, No. 2 (October, 1980), pp. 366–74; and Alan Musgrave, "'Unreal Assumptions' in Economic Theory: The F-Twist Untwisted," *Kyklos* Vol. 34 (1981) pp. 377–87, where he makes the constructive distinction between "Negligibility," "Domain," and

"Heuristic" assumptions. For T.W.H.'s favourable response to this paper see *Philosophy and Politics of Economics,* op. cit., pp. 289–91. There is a valuable background article by Abraham Hirsch, "The 'Assumptions'Controversy in Historical Perspective," *Journal of Economic Issues* Vol. XIV (March, 1980) pp. 99–118. Hirsch places T.W.H. midway between nineteenth century methodological verificationism and the new view of assumptions expressed in different terms by Knight, Machlup, and Friedman. (Cf. his unpublished comments on T.W.H. at the 1981 East Lansing meeting of the History of Economics Society.)

94 *Significance and Basic Postulates,* op. cit., p. xx.

95 Cf. *Knowledge and Ignorance in Economics*, op. cit., pp. 51–3.

96 *Supra.,* p. 13–15.

97 In particular Kuhn emphasized the tenacity with which most scientists cling to their basic intellectual framework, or "paradigm," both in "normal" and in "revolutionary" periods.

98 Lakatos, op. cit. To his critics, including T.W.H., Lakatos allowed too much scope for ad hoc adjustments and defensive stratagems by which a research programme could be protected from falsification. He argued that even in the "degenerative" phase of a research programme the case for abandoning it could, under certain circumstances, be defended. T.W.H. considered this doctrine far too lax to be appropriate for economics. Cf. *Knowledge and Ignorance in Economics,* op. cit., pp. 56–7. But he has stoutly defended Kuhn and Lakatos against the charge that they advocated "anything goes." Cf. *Politics and Philosophy of Economics,* op. cit., p. 301.

99 Supra, p. 14. For further discussion of this point see *infra*, p. 30–32.

100 Coddington, Alan, "Positive Economics," *The Canadian Journal of Economics,* Vol. 5 (February, 1972), p. 11. Among other constructive treatments of this problem see Evan Jones, "Positive Economics or What?" *The Economic Record,* Vol. 53 (1977), p. 355 ff.; and Bruce Caldwell, "Positivist Philosophy of Science and the Methodology of Economics," *Journal of Economic Issues* Vol. 14 (March, 1980), p. 64 ff. Caldwell further develops his critique of falsification in economics in his *Beyond Positivism,* op. cit. For a defence of falsification from a philosophical standpoint, without explicit reference to economics, see Alan Musgrave, "Falsification and its Critics," in P. Suppes (ed.), *Logic Methodology and Philosophy of Science, Boston Studies in the Philosophy of Science*, Vol. 4 (Boston, 1973), pp. 393–406.

101 Coddington, op. cit., pp. 11–12. For a discussion of the same problem from an institutionalist standpoint, see Charles K. Wilbur, "Empirical Verification and Theory Selection: The Keynesian-Monetarist Debate," *Journal of Economic Issues* Vol. 13 (December, 1979), pp. 973–82.

102 For a recent defence of this position, see Martin Hollis and Edward Nell, *Rational Economic Man: A Philosophical Critique of Neo-Classical Economics* (Cambridge: Cambridge University Press, 1975); also the excellent critical review by Kenneth Rivett in *The Economic Record* Vol. 53 (June, 1977), pp. 239–61.

103 Blaug, op. cit., Chap. 15.

104 Mayer, Thomas, "Economics as a Hard Science: Realistic Goal or Wishful Thinking?" *Economic Inquiry* Vol. 18 (April, 1980), pp. 165–78.

105 "Reply to Professor Knight," op. cit., pp. 738–9.

106 *Politics and Philosophy of Economics,* op. cit., p. 284. (Italics in original.)

107 The reference here is to the works cited in note 38, *supra.*

108 *Significance and Basic Postulates*, op. cit., p. viii.

109 *Politics and Philosophy of Economics,* op. cit., p. 276. T.W.H. has quoted approvingly Ravetz's distinction between the "immature" (including social) and "mature" science with the proviso that there is no guarantee that the former will eventually grow up to maturity. He has also emphasized the differences in aims and criteria of different sciences and the need for differing methodological prescriptions. Cf. Ibid., pp. 273–75; *Knowledge and Ignorance in Economics,* op. cit., pp. 35–8, and 46–9;

and J. R. Ravetz, *Scientific Knowledge and Its Social Problems* (Oxford: Clarendon, 1971). Of course Ravetz regards economics as "immature," as does T.W.H. See also his comments on Hayek's recent change of opinion with regard to the differences between the natural and the social sciences. *Politics and Philosophy of Economics,* op. cit., pp. 217–19; and his quotation from Menger, Ibid., p. 187.

110 *Knowledge and Ignorance in Economics,* op. cit., p. 41.

111 Ibid., p. 43.

112 Ibid., Chap. 4; *On Revolutions and Progress in Economics,* op. cit.. Chap. 2.

113 Cf. the quotation on p. 3, *supra.*

114 *Knowledge and Ignorance in Economics,* op. cit., p. 61, where he remarks that "noone has insisted or explained more clearly than Sir Karl that any methodological prescriptions for scientific investments and decisions must inevitably be based on certain ethical or political choices." It is difficult to believe that T.W.H. would have endorsed that view in 1938, notwithstanding his Appendix on "Some Postulates of Economic Liberalism."

115 Quoted from Popper by T.W.H. in his review of *Conjectures and Refutations* in *Economica* Vol. 31 (May, 1964), p. 217.

116 *Politics and Philosophy of Economics,* op. cit., p. 270. For an earlier appeal to democratic values see the concluding chapter of his *'Positive' Economics and Policy Objectives,* op. cit., especially pp. 189–97. It is noteworthy that he did not consider the subject of value judgments worth pursuing in 1938. Cf. *Significance and Basic Postulates*, op. cit., pp. xxii, 154. And notwithstanding his approval of the Austrians' political principles, he continues to be a severe critic of their methodology. Cf. *Politics and Philosophy of Economics*, op. cit., p. 224.

117 Jarvie, I. C., "Laudan's Problematic Progress and the Social Sciences," *Philosophy of the Social Sciences* Vol. 9 (1979) p. 496.

118 Thomas, David, *Naturalism and Social Science. A Post-Empiricist Philosophy of Social Science* (Cambridge: Cambridge University Press, 1979) p. 8. Even more forceful advocacy of the relative importance of social science methodology is expressed by proponents of the so-called strong programme in the sociology of knowledge. See, for example, the articles in *Philosophy of the Social Sciences* Vol. 11 (1981) by David Bloor, "The Strengths of the Strong Programme," pp. 199–213; Barry Barnes, "On the Conventional Character of Knowledge and Cognition," pp. 303–33; and Karin D. Knorr-Cetina, "Society and Scientific Method, or What Do We make of the Distinction Between the Natural and the Social Sciences," pp. 335–59. Thomas's objective, in the work cited, is to acknowledge the difficulties identified by subjectivists and sociologists without abandoning empiricism. See also David Papineau, *For Science in the Social Sciences* (London: Macmillan, 1978). By contrast, Gerard Radnitzky claims that in contemporary philosophy of science psychologism or sociologism has retained, or more correctly regained its dominant position. Cf. his "Popperian Philosophy of Science as an Antidote Against Relativism," in R. S. Cohen, P. K. Feyerabend, and M. W. Wartofsky, (eds.), *Essays in Memory of Imre Lakatos* (Dordrecht, Holland: D. Reidel, 1976), p. 505.

119 Blaug, *Methodology of Economics,* especially pp. 46–52 and 253–64.

120 See, for example, Wilbur, C. K., and Harrison, R. S., "The Methodological Basis of Institutional Economics: Pattern Model, Storytelling and Holism," *Journal of Economic Issues* Vol. 12 (March, 1978) pp. 61–89; Benjamin Ward, *What's Wrong With Economics* (London: Macmillan, 1972) Chap. 12; A. W. Coats, "The Methodology of Economics: Some Recent Contributions," in *Kyklos* Vol. 35 (1982) pp. 310–21; and the powerful review of Blaug by Daniel R. Fusfeld in *History of Political Economy* Vol. 14 (Summer, 1982) pp. 284–86.

121 Toulmin, Stephen, *Human Understanding* Vol. 1 (Oxford: Clarendon Press, 1972), p. 116. The whole section from p. 98ff., while sympathetic to Kuhn's general standpoint, is highly critical of his approach.

122 Lakatos, Imre, "Popper on Demarcation and Induction," in Schilpp (ed.), *The Philosophy of Karl Popper,* op. cit., p. 245. In reply Popper denied that there was any element of arbitrariness in his system or that he was a modified conventionalist. Ibid., pp. 248, 265, 492, 693, 750, 752, 1070, 1114, 1121. See also Husain Sakar, "Imre Lakatos's 'Meta-Methodology': An Appraisal," *Philosophy of the Social Sciences* Vol. 10 (1980) pp. 397–416.

123 Sakar, op. cit., p. 402.

124 T.W.H., *Politics and Philosophy of Economics,* op. cit., pp. 64–5. Cf. Abraham Kaplan, "Positivism," in the *International Encyclopedia of the Social Sciences* Vol. 12 (New York: Collier Macmillan, 1968) p. 391: "Whether a certain language is judged to be 'adequate' for the purposes of science depends on one's convictions as to what there is to be said. On this score, the issues dividing positivism from its critics remained unresolved and, indeed, largely unformulated." As suggested below, *infra.,* p. 31, recent attempts at formulation have been very disturbing to empiricists.

125 Thomas, op. cit., p. 196.

126 Papineau, op. cit., p. 96.

127 Cf., for example, Charles K. Wilbur, "Empirical Verification and Theory Selection: The Keynesian – Monetarist Debate," *Journal of Economic Issues* Vol. 13 (December, 1979) pp. 973–82.

128 Thomas, op. cit., p. 198.

129 Tarascio, Vincent J. and Caldwell, Bruce, "Theory Choice in Economics: Philosophy and Practice," *Journal of Economic Issues* Vol. 13 (December, 1979) pp. 983–1006.

130 Cf. Rod Cross, "The Duhem – Quine Thesis: Lakatos and the Appraisal of Theories in Macroeconomics," *Economic Journal* Vol. 92 (June, 1982) pp. 320–40. On the general issue, see Blaug, *Methodology of Economics,* op. cit., pp. 17–18; and *supra* p. 14.

131 T.W.H., *Politics and Philosophy of Economics,* op. cit., p. 270.

132 For a penetrating and constructive case for avoiding the twin extremes of methodological monism and methodological pluralism by means of rational criticism, see Bruce Caldwell, "On the Critique of Alternative Methodologies: The Austrian Case," unpublished paper delivered at the History of Economics Conference, Duke University May, 1982.

133 T.W.H., *Politics and Philosophy of Economics,* op. cit., p. 298.

134 T.W.H., *On Revolutions and Progress in Economics,* op. cit., Chap. 11, *passim.*

135 Ibid., p. 318.

136 Rivett, Keith, "Hollis and Nell on Methodology," *Economic Record* Vol. 53 (June, 1977) p. 239.

5 What Mirowski's history leaves out

> Economics is more metaphor than science, a way of imposing interpretative order on the buzz of transactions that make up a modern economy. Forecasting, in particular, is a narrative art form; there's no black box to grind up the numbers and produce a reliable prediction.
>
> Charles R. Morris, *New York Times Magazine,* 27 January 1991

My brief is very broad – indeed, almost limitless – and I have no intention of taking it literally. I did not in fact choose my title; but in a sense I asked for it toward the end of my review (1991) of *More Heat than Light,* and our organizer was quick to hoist me with my own petard. On the face of it my task is easy enough, if interpreted loosely. All historical accounts are necessarily incomplete. Selection is unavoidable,[1] and as a historian of economics of uncertain vintage I am hardly likely to be completely taken in by Philip Mirowski's bold, brilliant, fascinating, and at times exasperating and outrageous attempt to wrap up my discipline in his slender Ariadne's thread.[2]

Unlike our author, who confidently straddles a vast domain, I am constrained by the limitations of my knowledge to concentrate on his treatment of "economics as social physics," leaving to others the task of unraveling the story of "physics as nature's economics." Even so, both facets of *More Heat* must be taken into account in considering Mirowski's calculated omissions. With respect to "physics as nature's economics" he deliberately excludes certain "rather tired and worn themes" such as "the prosaic fact that technological innovations may have provided inspiration for certain physical theories ... the old Weberian chestnut about capitalist rationality writ large ... [and] the perennial whipping boy of the history of science literature, the Marxist-inspired Hessen thesis" (*MHL*, 100; cf. 106). Further exclusions are enumerated in the concluding chapter, where he deftly deflects the charge that his account reduces to the historically unworthy portrayal of economics as merely the tail wagged by the physics dog. A more complete account, we are assured, to be incorporated in a future volume entitled *The Realms of the Natural,* will address "any number of other intellectual concerns" which have inspired "many concepts in the history of economic thought." There have, indeed, been

> entire schools of economic thought [which] have denounced and resisted the siren song of a social physics: the German Historicist school for one, and the first two generations of the American Institutionalists for another (Mirowski 1988). Nevertheless, I do assert that within the ambit of the dominant schools of Western economic thought – classical political economy, neoclassical economics, and Marxian economics – the theory of value, the very core of the explanatory structure, has been *dictated* by the evolution of physical theory. Indeed, this has necessarily been the case for the dominant schools in Western culture, for their dominance is due to their emulation of physical explanation, and their resonance with the primal metaphors of body/motion/value.[3]
>
> (396, emphasis added)

As my opening epigraph suggests, the concept of economics as metaphor now has wide currency; but for the present purpose it is vital to distinguish between literary and scientific metaphors. By contrast with literary metaphors, which often serve only ornamental purposes, according to Mirowski,

> much of normal scientific activity can be interpreted as an attempt to render unseemly aspects of metaphors intelligible and pedestrian. A hallmark of scientific metaphors is the fact that they are deemed failures if they can muster only temporary impact and do not manage to become the object of pedantic explication and elaboration.... Scientific metaphors should set in motion research programs ... [because] they provide guidance and structure in the process of inquiry, which might otherwise be even more rife with rampant individualism and random research than is already the case.
>
> (278–79)

The basic similarity between Mirowski's scientific metaphors and Kuhn's paradigms is immediately obvious (cf. *MHL*, 301), at least for periods of "normal science"; yet there are also disquieting differences. For example, Mirowski claims that there is "free play inherent in metaphorical reasoning," as exemplified by the manner in which Adam Smith and J. B. Say developed "disparate theories" based on "essentially the same structural metaphors" (170), while the Cambridge Capital Controversies demonstrate that conflicting scientific metaphors can coexist within the same disciplinary matrix (338ff.). There is no unique way of interpreting a metaphor (or a paradigm?). Thus "the conservation of energy kept undergoing the figure-ground reversal central to Gestalt psychology: depending upon how you looked at it, it was either the most obvious and most important principle in science, or simultaneously the most metaphysical, convoluted, and implausible doctrine to have come down the pike in a long time" (58). How can such a metaphor provide the stability required for a coherent and ongoing program of scientific research?

Unstable, and difficult to interpret though they may be – according to Mirowski – metaphors can have extraordinary staying power and disturbing, unforeseen implications, both intellectual and sociological – although he considers the latter aspect only in passing. For instance, the "effort to reduce economic value to a conserved substance in motion" *dominated* economic thinking "from the mercantilists to the mid-nineteenth century" (185–86); but the explanation of this longevity is apparently sociological rather than purely intellectual, namely, the persistence of the desire "to elevate moral philosophy and political economy to the status of a natural science" (186). Sometimes a metaphor can take over, for once a research strategy has been adopted, a "powerful inertial guidance system" comes into operation (279); and the well-known "principle of tenacity" discourages the abandonment of a budding research program as soon as it encounters unexplained anomalies or seemingly disconfirmatory evidence. At a later stage, as the sorcerer's apprentice discovered, it may be too late to break away. On the other hand a metaphor can be a necessary "fiction" (137),[4] or a "lifeline" (162); and "the trick to metaphorical evaluation is an ability to sense when one has finally ventured beyond the pale, so that the coherence of the metaphor is strained to the point of dismemberment" (314).[5]

According to Mirowski, the economists' subservience to physics metaphors has been a sorry tale of ignorance, error, misappropriation, self-delusion, and resistance to change. In general, "economists have consistently lagged behind physicists in developing and elaborating metaphors; they have freeloaded off physicists for their inspiration, and appropriated it in a shoddy and slipshod manner" (108). Classical economics (note that Mirowski constantly reifies particular schools and phases in economic thought) backed the wrong horse, becoming "inextricably identified with the paradigm of substance theories in physics, and therefore its days were numbered" (201). The conventional triumvirate of marginalist revolutionaries neither understood the energy concept nor grasped its full implications (222), and when physics subsequently underwent fundamental changes

> the neoclassical research program was *forced* to regulate and prohibit the further substantive importation of novel physics metaphors, just as it had to discourage any other conception of value. Consequently, by the 1960s the neoclassical research program became helplessly *locked into* the physics of circa 1860, and persists in this predicament to the very present.
>
> (393–94, emphasis added)

Here we see little evidence of "the freeplay inherent in metaphorical reasoning" (170), scope for divergent and even incompatible interpretations, or opportunity to play the "trick" of "metaphorical evaluation" (cf. 314). Once harnessed to the obsolete physics metaphor, the neoclassical research program's fate was sealed. Coyness and ambivalence was of no avail. The physics metaphor

> cannot seriously be repudiated or relinquished, because *there is nothing else that can hold the neoclassical research program together.* In the absence of the metaphor of utility as nineteenth-century potential energy, there is no alternative theory of value, no heuristic guide to research, no principle upon which to base mathematical formalism, no causal invariant in the Meyersonian

> sense, and most threatening, no basis for the claim that economics has finally become scientific.
>
> (368, emphasis his)

So although the essential problems of neoclassical economics are intellectual – ontological, epistemological, and theoretical – the greatest threat is sociological, that is, the loss of scientific status. No wonder that when competent physicists pronounced the upstart proto-energetics wanting, the early neoclassical economists responded to their "slings and arrows ... with hurt incomprehension, bluster, farrago, protests that the physics was irrelevant, and finally, a feeling of betrayal" (241). There were, of course, challenges from the underworld of economic theory, but they were uniformly unsuccessful, although their history has yet to be written.

How is the critic to respond to Mirowski's argument, after recovering from the initial shock of his breathtaking sweep and the boldness of his claims? Is it sufficient to concentrate on the level of "universal history," the handful of primal metaphors and the "higher plane of synthesis... that uncovers the unity of discourse behind the quotidian barriers of fields or disciplines, or indeed, between the social and the natural" (107)? To raise minor objections about specifics would surely be pedantic and petty-minded. (Nevertheless I touch on a few of his more striking deviations from conventionally accepted versions of the history of economics below.)

To judge by his breezy, witty, often throwaway style, a good deal of Mirowski's text needs to be taken figuratively rather than literally. He too is presumably entitled to a "metaphoric license" that permits him "to slide effortlessly from economic connotations to those of quantitative measurement to those of general worth or virtue" (141). No wonder it is difficult to pin him down! Nevertheless, after his unqualified assertion of the physics metaphor's indispensability to the neoclassical program (quoted above), he adds, somewhat unexpectedly, that "the only proof of this statement can be historical, irredeemably inductive" (368). Unfortunately he makes little effort to provide the evidence required for such a proof.[6]

In his brief concluding chapter Mirowski explains that his critique of neoclassical economics – unquestionably the project's main driving force – proceeds simultaneously on three distinct levels which may, for convenience, be respectively described as internalist, polemical, and conceptual/sociological (or cultural) (398–401). None of this is intrinsically historical or inductive, and this is somewhat surprising, given his earlier work in economic history. In his first book, *The Birth of the Business Cycle*, Mirowski made a systematic effort to integrate the history of economic ideas on his topic with concurrent or earlier developments in economic history; but there is hardly a trace of this effort in *More Heat than Light.* Of course the two projects are very different. *Business Cycle* is not designed as "universal history," and the theory of value, one of the central strands in *More Heat*, is obviously less likely to be closely linked with the historical context than the theory of business cycles, whether as cause or effect. Indeed, in *Business Cycle* Mirowski describes value theory as "the underlying metaphysics of economics," adding that "because of this, it *rules* economic epistemology" (90, emphasis added). In support of this contention, he cites J. S. Mill (via Gunnar

Myrdal) to the effect that "the smallest error on the subject infects with corresponding error all our conclusions; and anything vague or misty in our conception of it creates confusion and uncertainty in everything else" (90). This much, at least, is common to both projects. Whereas *Business Cycle* is a blend of conventional *Dogmengeschichte* and economic history, *More Heat* is essentially metaphysical history, if that is not a contradiction in terms.

Oddly enough, by contrast with several of Mirowski's earlier publications, in *More Heat* it is the history of physics rather than economics that inspires his most intriguing, if somewhat offhand, references to the relationships between ideas and the historical context. For instance, after declaring that "an authentic genetic account of the energy concept must expand to encompass social and economic history" (108), he proceeds to examine Kula's suggestive theory of the various stages in "metrology," adding, a few pages later, that the "lineamentric" and "syndectic" stages in the history of physics "roughly coincide with, respectively, the rise of the world mercantile economy and the institution of the world industrial economy" (119).

How the connections between intellectual innovations and these extremely broad and ill-specified historical processes are to be established is not clear, although we are told that to do so "would demand an entire volume, and would be an immense undertaking in the history of science" (119) – if, one must add, it is possible at all. Still, nothing daunted, our author confidently refers to the "striking" hypothesis that "the major innovations in the theory of motion follow the changing center of gravity of the major trading axis of early modern Europe, stretching from northern Italy through the low countries and terminating in southeastern Britain" (119–20ff.). Most conventional economic historians would surely be reluctant to accept this as more than intriguing speculation; and much the same applies to his claim that "the dematerialization" (or "denaturalization") of the value concept was directly associated with the evolution of the economy, in which "Britain was being surpassed as a manufacturing power and moving towards an economy based on finance and trade ... as manufacture gave way to finance, seeing conservation principles in nature gave way to seeing them more as contingencies, imposed by our accountants in order to keep confusion at bay" (134–35). (What about other countries?) By this time, unfortunately, it is difficult to repress the suspicion that it is Mirowski who "sees" the ubiquitous conservation principles, not his historical subjects. How could a historian go about checking (let alone testing) the evidence for such a claim? Is it a matter of chance correlation, or causation? Or is it, perhaps, not to be taken that seriously?

I can sympathize with Mirowski's impatience with the crudely materialistic idea that "the base controls the superstructure" on the grounds that "experience with evolving economic structures altered perceptions of the metaphor of value, and that in turn set off resonances with the attendant theory of motion" (119). But this, surely, is simply to accept a modified version of the materialist explanation, as it were, at one remove.

Perhaps my objections simply boil down to dissatisfaction with the task of bringing Mirowski's "higher plane of synthesis" down to the historian's mundane level. At least as far as the history of economics is concerned, he does not live up to his slogan that "the best way to talk about science is to examine how people have done it" (8). If economics is "what economists do," as the saying goes, then most of what economists do and have done is missing from *More Heat.* Economic theory in general, and the theory of value in particular, comprise only a part – albeit a fundamental part – of economics, which is, after all, primarily a policy science (8).[7] To study the development of the metaphysical underpinnings, or what Veblen called "the preconceptions of economic science," is a perfectly legitimate undertaking, one that can indeed be revealing; but it is certainly not the whole story – perhaps just the beginning of a new one.

Whatever may be said of Mirowski's universal history, his wide-ranging account of the history of economic thought is frequently defective. Three severely abbreviated examples must suffice for the present purpose. More could of course be cited.

(1) Mirowski correctly notes that "the essence of mercantilism is extremely elusive" (147). Nevertheless he confidently proceeds to subdivide the literature into two discrete categories: "the balance of trade school" and "the free trade school," each identified with a specific period (early to mid-seventeenth century, and 1660–1700). "The first appearance of a conservation principle in Western economic thought" supposedly occurred in the earlier phase, though he concedes that this is "not terribly explicit" (148).

   Apart from the fact that Mirowski completely ignores the substantial peculiarities of British mercantilism, as compared with its counterparts elsewhere, there were no genuine "schools" of economic thought in that period, and his categorization and periodization grossly oversimplify a complex story.[8] In general his brief account exemplifies the dangers of "reading into" seventeenth- and eighteenth-century economic thought sophisticated twentieth-century ideas that were only dimly perceived, if at all, two or three centuries earlier.[9] The mercantilist conceptions of value, money, trade, employment, etc., were embedded in a large, complex, highly uneven literature that was neither wholly systematic nor yet incoherent or entirely preanalytic. Schumpeter's apt term "quasi-system" (1954, 194) draws attention to the evolution of mercantilist theory and policy recommendations in association with changing economic conditions; and Mirowski's practice of extracting out of the context bits and pieces designed to support his preconceived thesis does indeed "overly distort the pamphlet record" (147).

(2) Mirowski's discussion of Adam Smith, a notoriously difficult writer to interpret both consistently and sympathetically, contains a serious error in his analysis of the physiocratic influences on Smith's economics. Far from expressing "disdain for the country peasant and the agricultural economy" (165), Smith went to inordinate lengths in praising the rural husbandman by contrast with the stupid and ignorant factory worker. Moreover, he flatly

asserted the priority of agriculture over manufacture, domestic trade, and foreign trade, with respect to the amount of employment generated by the investment of a given sum of money (Smith [1776] 1976, 360ff., 782–83), a contention that almost gave McCulloch apoplexy. Neither of these views can be even remotely characterized as disdainful, or evidence of Smith's "wariness of the body," whatever that means!

(3) Mirowski's treatment of Marshall (Mirowski 1990b), at least in part, is willfully perverse. To describe that dedicated, careful, painstakingly overcautious and defensive man as "slapdash" (*MHL*, 300, 301) is outrageous, and so is the effort to reduce him to the status of a mere popularizer (262) on a par with Jane Marcet, Harriet Martineau, and Henry Fawcett (83). This may be entertaining, knockabout stuff; but it is hardly serious doctrinal history, for it grossly undervalues Marshall's contribution as a major synthesizer and founder of a doctrinal tradition that dominated academic economics in the leading country of the time for several decades. As Marshall, like Menger, does not fit into Mirowski's general scheme, he is denied the status of a "major protagonist" in the emergence of neoclassical economics (194), although it was largely from his work that neoclassical economics derived its name. Second Wrangler though he was, Marshall was not, unlike Jevons and Walras, a mathematical theorist "first and foremost" (195), and Mirowski, like some earlier commentators, is irritated by Marshall's lack of interest in mathematical consistency (372). This was deliberate, however, stemming from Marshall's low personal and professional valuation of pure theorizing, rather than from any intellectual deficiency. In this sense Marshall's case illustrates the misrepresentation involved in characterizing neoclassical economics as "reprocessed physics" (251). Marshall's goals were primarily social (including professional) and ethical. Admittedly there are legitimate questions as to the precise nature and extent of Marshall's originality, doubts fostered by his uneven and sometimes ungenerous acknowledgment of his debts to his predecessors. But Mirowski is unwilling to grant Marshall any credit whatsoever on this account, and he also fails to acknowledge the work of another major independent founder of modern marginalism, John Bates Clark, who was certainly no physicist manqué.

These remarks have been distinctly more skeptical and critical of *More Heat than Light* than my review cited at the outset, partly because the latter was largely devoted to exposition, but also because a different overall judgment has emerged from a closer rereading with greater attention to specifics. Even now, the most general issue – whether *More Heat* is reliable and accurate, as well as brilliantly stimulating and insightful history – has not yet been squarely addressed.

Without an adequate knowledge of the history of physics, which I lack, it is impossible to justify my strong impression that the focus on metaphors and analogies employed in two such disparate disciplines as physics and economics does not constitute sufficient evidence of similarities and linkages between them.[10] So much of economics, in particular, is omitted from Mirowski's account that it remains highly suggestive, rather than persuasive. Perhaps this is an inescapable consequence of so-called universal history.

It may be appropriate to conclude with the dictum that historians complain if a work is underresearched, not that it is underanalyzed, whereas among economists almost exactly the reverse applies. In this sense my comments here represent a historian's still somewhat baffled reaction to *More Heat than Light.*

Notes

1 "There is no neutrally objective history of economic thought. There must always be some organizational principles of selection, since no work can adequately summarize all thought even within a narrow range of issues and controversies" (Mirowski 1985, 1). But cf. note 4 below.

2 "The adoption of the proto-energetics metaphor and framework of mid-nineteenth-century physics is the birthmark of neoclassical economics, the Ariadne's thread that binds the protagonists, and that can lead us to the fundamental meaning of the neoclassical research program" (*MHL*, 222). Whether there is in fact a single fundamental meaning to that program is, indeed, one of the "fundamental" points at issue.

3 Presumably Mirowski's forthcoming study will identify the intellectual earplugs that enabled members of those schools to resist the "siren song." Why did they not succumb to the dominant influence of "physical explanation?"

It should be noted that Mirowski also excludes two other approaches in addition to the physics-dominated view: "the full-scale denial of value" associated with Barbon, Turgot, and Bailey (cf. 151, 163, 187–91, 399–400), and the "social theory of value" (400), a concept he does not explicate. (But see Mirowski 1990a.) The concept of "social value" has a long and intriguing career in economic writings, one that has not yet found its historian. See Lutz 1990, esp. the chapters by Thomas O. Nitsch and William R. Walters. (Perhaps Mirowski intends to fill this gap.) In general, *More Heat* has the curiously old-fashioned effect of restoring the theory of value to the central place it once occupied in the historiography of economics.

4 Earlier, in discussing the central metaphors of body, motion, and value, he emphasizes that "the central syndectic principle at the heart of each [vertex] is purely conventional and thus, ... simply false" (116; cf. 397). This is course implies that there must be something "true" with which such principles can be compared.

5 "One of the most attractive aspects of analogical reasoning is the prefabricated nature of an interlocking set of explanatory structures and constructs, allowing quickened evaluation of logical coherence" (272). This suggests that the criterion by which the success or failure (truth or falsity?) of a research program must be judged is internal coherence, rather than, say, the capacity to survive thorough and repeated efforts at falsification.

6 However, there is substantial warrant for his complaints that "economics has been the most rigidly doctrinaire of all the social sciences" and that whenever intellectual challenges have appeared, defenders of the mainstream have been remarkably successful in "either co-opting the rival metaphor or else amputating the new offending doctrines as unsound and unscientific" (368). One hopes he will elaborate this historical claim in one of his forthcoming works.

7 One does not need to go as far as Leo Rogin, who focused too narrowly on the "uses" to which economic ideas have been put and the social issues that have invested them with "a public, hence objective character" (1956, 10). A distinguished economist's attempt to interpret the history of his discipline in Deweyite instrumentalist terms is Mitchell's (1967, 1: ch. 1). At the other extreme of the ideas–environment spectrum is Pribram (1983), who is concerned with "the conflicting currents of thought which have

determined the development of methods of reasoning in *all* fields of intellectual, social, political and moral activities" (xlix, emphasis added). The collection of essays edited by Warren Samuels (1983) provides a useful introduction to the range of possible approaches to the subject.

Mirowski does not, in *More Heat,* follow his own earlier injunction that one way to introduce the requisite "principles of selection and organization" is "to first examine the parallel principles of other authors who have sought to outline the history of thought" (*Business Cycle* [1985], 1).

8 For example, balance of trade ideas persisted throughout the pre-1776 period and beyond, thought the evolution of doctrine and changing economic conditions led to an increasing emphasis on the balance of employment rather than, or in addition to, foreign trade in the narrower sense. Mirowski's quartet of free traders (150) – though Petty does not really belong in that company – constituted an intellectually interesting but wholly unrepresentative and un-influential minority writing at a time when protectionist ideas were in the ascendant. These writers were largely forgotten, and disinterred by nineteenth-centuary free-trade enthusiasts, writing in an entirely different "liberal" intellectual context.

9 For an elaboration of this contention see Coats 1973, 485–95.

10 This point has been made effectively by M. Norton Wise and Crosbie Smith (1989, 291, 193): "The *practice* of political economists was not the practice of natural philosophers, for they employed different conceptual and analytic tools even where they employed the same terms to describe natural systems.... There is no reason to suppose that political economists should have developed a conservation principle for economic value from their analogies with physical systems, where it had very limited utility" (emphasis added).

References

Coats, A. W. 1973. The Interpretation of Mercantilist Economics: Some Historiographical Problems. *HOPE* 5:485–95.

_____. 1991. Review of *More Heat than Light,* by Philip Mirowski. *Kyklos* 44.1:131–35.

Lutz, Mark A., ed. 1990. *Social Economics: Retrospect and Prospect.* Boston: Kluwer.

Mirowski, Philip. 1985. *The Birth of the Business Cycle*. New York and London: Garland.

_____. 1988. *Against Mechanism*. Totowa, N.J.: Rowman & Littlefield.

_____. 1989. *More Heat than Light: Economics as Social Physics, Physics as Nature's Economics*. Cambridge: Cambridge University Press. [Citations are abbreviated *MHL*.]

_____. 1990a. Learning the Meaning of a Dollar: Conservation Principles and the Social Theory of Value in Economic Theory. *Social Research* 57:689–717.

_____. 1990b. Smooth Operator: How Marshall's Demand and Supply Curves Made Neoclassicism Safe for Public Consumption but Unfit for Science. In *Alfred Marshall in Retrospect*, edited by Rita McWilliams Tullberg. Aldershot: Edward Elgar.

Mitchell, Wesley. 1967. *Types of Economic Theory: From Mercantilism to Institutionalism.* Vol. 1. Edited by Joseph Dorfman. New York: Kelley.

Pribram, Karl. 1983. *A History of Economic Reasoning.* Baltimore: The Johns Hopkins University Press.

Rogin, Leo. 1956. *The Meaning and Validity of Economic Theory.* New York: Harper.

Samuels, Warren. 1983. *The Craft of the Historian of Economic Thought: Research in the History of Economic Thought and Methodology.* Vol. 1. Greenwich. Conn.: JAI Press.

Schumpeter, Joseph A. 1954. *History of Economic Analysis*. New York: Oxford University Press.

Smith, Adam. [1776] 1976. *An Inquiry into the Nature and Causes of the Wealth of Nations*. Edited by Andrew Skinner and Roy Campbell. Oxford: Oxford University Press.

Wise, M. Norton, with the collaboration of Crosbie Smith. 1989. Work and Waste: Political Economy and Natural Philosophy in Nineteenth-Century Britain. [Part 1.] *History of Science* 27:263–301, 391–449.

6 Review essay: The pillars of economic understanding

A new magisterial history of economic thought?

Fifteen years ago Mark Perlman delivered his Presidential address to the History of Economics Society on: "Perceptions of our Discipline: Three Magisterial Treatments of the Evolution of Economic Thought."[1] Now, after decades of work on the project "in embryo," he has completed (in cooperation with Charles R. McCann, Jr.) the first installment of his own potentially magisterial opus: *The Pillars of Economic Understanding: Ideas and Traditions.*[2] The question whether this work in fact achieves magisterial status must, however, be deferred, for an additional "companion" volume, subtitled *Factors and Markets,*[3] has yet to appear.

Given the absence of the companion volume it would be both premature and misleading to compare in detail the content or structure of *Ideas and Traditions* (text of 580 pages) with that of any member of Perlman's magisterial trio – the studies by Wesley C. Mitchell, Joseph Alois Schumpeter, and Karl Pribram, which weigh in at 839, 1184, and 633 pages respectively.[4] However, it is legitimate to note that whereas Mitchell chose Adam Smith as his starting point, believing that the earlier historical background was "unnecessary clutter" (p. 29), Schumpeter and Pribram, like Perlman and McCann, began their historical surveys with lengthy accounts of pre-Smithian economic thought. While Mitchell focused on the prevailing social, economic, and political environments of the theoretical constructs he studied (p. 30), Pribram concentrated on ideas rather than people or events, for he was especially concerned with "the continual tensions in the philosophical approaches" to the subject (p. 27). Schumpeter's central theme was the development of economic analysis (i.e., theory or "science"), and he emphasized "the filiation of scientific ideas" – that is, "the process by which men's efforts to understand economic phenomena produce, improve, and pull down analytical structures in an unending sequence" (p. 31; cf. Schumpeter 1954, p. 6). Yet he also devoted considerable space to what he termed "the intellectual scenery" (Schumpeter 1954, Part III, chapter 3), in an effort "to broaden the scope and method of economic discourse" (p. 32) by exploring the relationships between economics and law, sociology, history, psychology, and literature. Some critics argued that the combination of analysis and intellectual history gave Schumpeter's *magnum opus* a distinctly schizophrenic quality. As will appear later, Perlman and McCann's book is closer in style and content to

Schumpeter and Pribram than to Mitchell, though it has features in common with all three earlier treatises.

One distinctive feature of *Ideas and Traditions* is that the authors have deliberately "dampened" the conventional chronological watersheds in the history of economic thought – such as that between pre- and post-classical political economy, or the marginal revolution episode – because of their "interest in offering a balanced treatment of various topics, or intellectual *gestalten*, and the 'problem environments' in which they developed" (p. xix). A conspicuous example of what might lightly be termed chronological deviationism is chapter 5, on "Data Collection, Statistical Analysis and Econometrics," which ranges from seventeenth century contributions to the founding of the Econometric Society in 1930. Likewise, chapter 9, on "The German and Austrian Traditions," runs from Adam Muller (1779–1829) through to Fredrich von Hayek and Lionel Robbins in the twentieth century.

A central theme and organizing principle in Perlman and McCann is the role of "patristic legacies," a concept I have not previously encountered in English language general studies of the history of economic thought. The authors' claim that their approach is "quite apart" from traditional views of the economics discipline since it embodies "a deeper appreciation of the influence of patristic thinking" (p. 2). Patristic legacies are "a series of frameworks" or "sets of ideas" which represent "ways of perceiving the evolution of economics" (pp. 29, xix). They provide us with "nodes from which all of the ideas within the confines of the discipline radiate," thereby constituting "a general method of historical appraisal." The influence of patristic legacies is not, however, limited to their effect on a single discipline, for they are essentially cultural traditions that are not merely important, but also ubiquitous.[5]

> The complex of patristic legacies sets the stage for our civilization, in the sense that it establishes a tradition that serves to guide us intellectually, socially, morally, and spiritually, in all aspects of life ... All civilizations have at their heart sets of categorical imperatives (authorities or law codes, if you prefer) derived from appeals to preexisting patristic beliefs. These codifications of acceptable behavior define the boundaries within which individuals in a civilized society must function if the civilization is to endure (pp. 4–5)

The breadth and complexity of Perlman and McCann's conception of their task must by now be obvious. As noted below, patristic legacies can be associated with a country, a theology, or even a single individual: e.g., the Hobbes Patristic Legacy which, "seen both in the positive and negative senses, is almost without parallel as an influence in the development of economic thought in the English-speaking world ... [for it] incarnated the foundations of scientific empiricism" (p. 133). Patristic legacies are authoritative (and exclusively masculine?). They are not a dominant influence, but rather "a guiding factor" (p. 3 n.1). The sources of authority in any culture are various, including: religious revelation, cultural norms, custom, and the intellectual environment or baggage, "for no society can function without a legal, moral, ethical and social structure" (p. 5).

Curiously enough, references to "patristic legacies" in *Ideas and Traditions* are almost entirely confined to the first quarter of the book and the concluding chapter: "What Do We Make Of It All?" Chapter 1 on "The Patristic Traditions in Economics: The Foundations of Our Study" reviews briefly The Classical Greek Patristic Legacy, The Judeo-Christian Legacies, and The Patristic Tradition through the Middle Ages. Chapter 2, "The British Patristic Legacy: Understanding the Hobbes Challenge," ranges from the seventeenth century through to Adam Smith. In the ensuing nine chapter titles (and subtitles) the term "patristic" is absent, sometimes being replaced by "tradition." Presumably there is nothing patristic about "Mercantilism and the Nation State" (chapter 3) or the next chapter on "The Measurement of Economic Magnitudes" (chapter 4). This, like chapters 5 and 9 mentioned earlier, covers a wide chronological span. Chapters 6 to 8 deal, respectively, with: "British Classical Political Economy: Individualism, Utilitarianism, and Property Rights"; "Utilitarianism as the Basis for 'Scientific' Economics: The Emergence of Neoclassicism"; and "The British Historical School and the Post-Marshallian Cambridge Tradition: a Reinterpretation of Utilitarianism." This somewhat miscellaneous chapter (8) includes a brief account of the founding of The London School of Economics, and ends with Keynes and Joan Robinson.

After chapter 9 on "The German and Austrian Traditions," there are two chapters on "The Triumph of Cartesian Rationalism: The French Tradition" (chapter 10, which runs from Say to Bourbaki, and includes Pareto), and "An American Tradition: Institutionalism" (chapter 11). In the final chapter Perlman and McCann review briefly "Some Patristic Traditions Affecting Economics," including: The Legacies of Communitarianism and Individualism; The Methodological Legacies of Descartes' Scientific Truth and Bacon's Scientific Process: Rationality versus Reason; The Patristic Legacy of the Right to Private Property; The Centrality of Work: The Labor Factor versus Marginal Analysis; and The Preferred Way of Life. Short passages on The Role of Rhetoric (to be considered below) and Why Study the History of Economic Thought? conclude the volume.

One of the more conspicuous and idiosyncratic features of Perlman and McCann's treatise is the weight they attach to rhetoric, both as "a form of presentation" and as "a *method of expression* of economic doctrines, [which is] at least as important as the *substance* of those arguments" (Preface, p. xviii; emphasis in original). Nowadays the rhetoric of economics is usually identified with methods of persuasion, and is most widely known through D. McCloskey's many writings. However, it is worth noting that some years before McCloskey entered the lists, Perlman published an article drawing attention to the various forms of persuasion in economic methodology, including "critical (i.e., self-conscious) persuasion."[6] In *Ideas and Traditions* rhetoric appears in many guises and in a variety of historical contexts, so that it becomes a virtually all-purpose concept. The many species of rhetoric include: literary, numerical, mathematical, analytical, descriptive, abstract, ethical, moralistic, Euclidean, scientific, and pseudoscientific forms. To cite some illustrative individual cases, Cantillon's rhetoric is termed "uniquely economic" in its reliance on abstraction (pp. 157, 162), while Hume's is termed "relational" (p. 238). Ricardo's rhetoric is "amazing" because of his "abstract statements designed for ready application and implementation" (p. 267), whereas Jevons's rhetoric is too limited and "incapable of incorporating anything as broad and encompassing" as John Stuart Mill's presentation (p. 319). Perlman and McCann refer to "the rhetorical basis of the economics discipline" (p. 30), and "the rhetorical structures of economic theories" (p. 70), adding that an argument can be changed "by reorienting the rhetoric" (p. 191).

Yet it is not clear whether rhetoric is seen as an autonomous causal factor or merely an integral part of a broader intellectual or cultural process. For example, "although the advent of Political Arithmetic was a revolutionary change ... in the constitution of the language and subject matter of economics ... [and was, indeed,] among the most profound, and seemingly *inevitable*, developments in the entire history of the discipline" (p. 192, emphasis supplied), it did not entail a change of rhetoric, for "the rhetoric used was still that of the literary economists adapted to the new 'numerical order'" (p. 192). In this instance the relationship between form and substance is by no means clear.[7]

I must confess that on first encountering *The Pillars of Economic Understanding* my response was skeptical. Who is likely to read, let alone purchase this tome given the severe decline in the number of history of economic thought courses in American colleges and universities, which might otherwise have constituted the largest potential market for such a work? Admittedly the subject is still taught in many institutions of higher education in other countries where it is even now sometimes regarded as an essential part of the educated economist's knowledge. Beyond this, research in the history of economic thought, or economics, is flourishing and apparently expanding in the USA and in a number of other countries across the globe; and there are many potential readers among professional and business persons, journalists, civil servants, and even politicians who are interested in "policy debates and general societal questions of ethics and social welfare" (p. xx).

Perlman and McCann are quite clear about the potential audience for their work. They specifically target "the serious, college-trained (or otherwise well read, for the two are not necessarily the same) person who seeks to make sense of the current divisions within what had once been a loosely united fraternity" (p. xix). Such persons are unwilling:

> to accept the pseudo-intellectual clamorings of those with a political agenda who mask their cause in economic terms in an effort to lend it an air of respectability. The serious-minded reader wishes to know and understand 1) the rationale behind this endless clamor, 2) what an exploration of the subject will reveal about the cycle of discussion, the sense of optimism and then of failure regarding socio-economic reform, and 3) how all this relates to the topic of general human knowledge. In short, the reader seeks to comprehend the contribution of economics to the overall social conversation (p. xx).

These are ambitious objectives, and the authors are largely justified in claiming that they have been generally ignored in history of economic thought texts, especially those focused mainly or exclusively on the evolution of economic theory.

It would, of course, be premature to judge the wisdom and practicability of the division of subject matter between *Ideas and Traditions* and its forthcoming companion volume. Nevertheless, it seems likely that the two will overlap to a considerable extent. To cite one prominent example, the reader is told that the forthcoming volume will consider the question of "the scientific nature of economics," yet this topic is also repeatedly considered in Volume I – for instance, in connection with the writings of Schumpeter (p. 32), Jevons and Marshall (pp. 199–202), Pigou (pp. 376–79), von Mises (pp. 444–48), Walras (pp. 493–96), and Pareto (p. 502ff). Perlman and McCann refer to the ongoing conflict "between the Platonic/Cartesian economists" who view economics as a "pure science" based on deductive reasoning and logical analysis" and the Aristotelians, who favor "a blend of inductive and deductive reasoning" (p. xix).

One of the most valuable features of Perlman and McCann is their emphasis on the development of economics as an empirical and inductive science. This is a central theme in two key chapters (4 and 5) which have, I believe, no parallel in other English language general histories of economics, too many of which are focused mainly – and to my mind unduly – on the evolution of economic theory (or analysis). *Ideas and Traditions* gives welcome prominence to the work of such individuals as Tooke, Newmarch,[8] Quetelet, and Galton who were neglected by economists in their own day, and by historians of the discipline subsequently. Schumpeter is, at least in part, an honorable exception. The volume also contains a distinctly more empirical portrayal of the Physiocrats than is customary, for they are credited with having given:

> real impetus … to the development of a national accounting *network* [by tailoring] their statements of economic nationalism … to numerical presentation. This form of rhetoric allowed a place for economic planning and for the employment of sophisticated accounting techniques (p. 138).

There are, however, at least two significant interpretative problems in this part of the volume (I also include chapter 3): its distinctly Whiggish tone, and the repeated use of the terms "collectivization" and "planning" which, given their controversial modern connotations,[9] are both anachronistic and potentially misleading when applied to the seventeenth, eighteenth, and nineteenth century literature.

For example, the mercantilist "emphasis on national planning" is said to have "ushered in an era characterized by reliance on data collection and statistical analysis … [indeed] mercantilist doctrines … may be said to have made national income accounting … an *inevitability* (p. 138, emphasis supplied; cf. p. 192). Whereas the British writers started from observation, in a Baconian manner, the French "started from a Cartesian preference for initial logical connection." Happily, the two approaches can be seen as complementary, for the Physiocrats' contribution (including the circular flow diagram) "established the frameworks upon which the later empirical studies would build … [when] linked to the more empirically grounded national accounting framework" they amounted to "something akin to a system of national accounts" (p. 139).

Given Perlman and McCann's desire to reach well-read but non-specialist members of their potential audience, it must be said that readers new to the subject may well ask why the effective empirical development of macroeconomics and the first successful attempts to develop a system of national or social accounts were delayed until this century. Many readers may, of course, be more interested in the outcomes of earlier intellectual investigatory efforts than in the long sequence of failures, blind alleys, or missed opportunities, which have so often occurred in the pursuit of knowledge. Nevertheless the problem should have been addressed more directly and more fully.

Perlman and McCann devote almost one third of their volume to the British patristic legacy and the role of utilitarianism in the evolution of ideas.[10] They regard Hobbes's *Leviathan* (published in 1651) as "one of the great seminal treatises of Western civilization," marking a watershed in seventeenth and eighteenth century British political theory. "The Hobbes Challenge," so-called, centered on the conflict between cognition and faith – the appeal to governmental prescriptions (i.e., legal codes) rather than moral and ethical strictures. Hobbes's conception of security as the basis for the social contract was a utilitarian objective, replacing the Scholastic philosophers' *moral* objective of the pursuit of the greatest good. The crucial problem was how to reconcile individual motives and desires with the need for political and social order – a problem to which Locke gave a political answer. By contrast, Adam Smith's answer to Locke's challenge was that man's love of plenty could provide a sufficient inspiration for cooperation among individuals, so that government was unnecessary, or at least of minimal importance (p. 39). *The Theory of Moral Sentiments*, the importance of which "cannot be overestimated," was a more profound work than the *Wealth of Nations* since it provided answers to Hobbes's theory of the brutish nature of man, and his incomplete understanding of the roles of greed and self-determination in society (pp. 58–59, 70).

Ideas and Traditions is written in a lucid and urbane style and contains many user-friendly passages of summary, assessment, and conclusions. The authors provide generally balanced, albeit necessarily brief, accounts of controversial topics – such as the nature of mercantilism, or Keynes's work and influence, and there are numerous apt and telling quotations from a wide range of primary and secondary sources. The twenty-nine page bibliography, and the two indexes, are very useful.

Of course, no scholarly work on this scale is likely to be flawless, but there are comparatively few obvious errors. For example, Schumpeter's important concept of "the filiation of scientific ideas" is presented as "the filiation of economic ideas"; the first principal of the London School of Economics, the economic historian W. A. S. Hewins, appears as Newins; and Neo-institutionalism (a later phase of "old" institutionalism) is erroneously identified with the New Institutional Economics, while the American Economic Association's original cautious statement of Principles can hardly be said "to promote socialism with a very nationalistic flavor" (p. 538), even though some of the founder members were directly influenced by the example of the *Verein für Sozialpolitik*.

A more sensitive issue is the treatment of Austrian Economics which, particularly in its later forms, strikes this reviewer as unduly favorable. Uninformed readers of the careful and interesting account of von Mises's idiosyncratic methodology might be surprised to learn that his advocacy of praxeology has been an embarrassment to some members of the more recent, vigorous neo-Austrian movement. On a rather different issue, Hayek's *The Road to Serfdom* (1944) "which argued that socialism and all other rationalist communitarianism would eventually lead to totalitarian dictatorship" and "tyranny" (pp. 452, 453) is hardly borne out by subsequent evidence, and deserves to be rejected as a polemic unworthy of its deservedly eminent author.

The final question for this reviewer – can the Perlman/McCann enterprise be deemed magisterial, even in its present incomplete form? Obviously this is partly, perhaps mainly, a matter of definition. Magisterial treatments, we are told, "create frameworks that serve to link together interpretations over time and across other boundaries as well … they are no more than intellectual mappings, or intellectual handles useful to grasp massive amounts of material" (pp. 32–33).

In general these interpretations are "illustrative rather than analytical ... To be magisterial is to give a strong interpretation; it is not to be authoritative" (p. 32). Perlman and McCann modestly "dare to offer" their own interpretation of the development of economic understanding which, they say, at best builds on and complements the Mitchell, Pribram, and Schumpeter treatises (p. 569). And, at least as an interim judgment, they have undoubtedly succeeded.

Notes

1 The address was published in the *History of Economics Society Bulletin* Winter 1986, pp. 9–28.

2 The volume is Mark Perlman and Charles R. McCann, Jr., *The Pillars of Economic Understanding: Ideas and Traditions* (Ann Arbor: The University of Michgan Press, 1998) pp. xx, 639, $79.50. ISBN: 0-472-10907-3. It gives no indication of the precise division of labor between the two authors. In the following account, Perlman's name will occasionally be used alone (hopefully without injustice to McCann) since he is evidently the senior partner. Unless otherwise stated, page numbers in brackets refer to the 1998 volume, which will be cited as *Ideas and Traditions*.

3 I have been privileged to see a detailed Table of Contents of the companion volume, plus a draft introductory chapter entitled "The Economics of Production Factors," but I shall not consider these items in this review essay. Although the publisher has informally requested that the term "companion" rather than "second" be used to describe the concluding installment, the Table of Contents in the 1998 volume is headed: Volume I.

4 The studies are: Mitchell (1967, 1969), Schumpeter (1954), and Pribram (1983). All three were published posthumously.

5 Perlman and McCann define "tradition" conventionally, as "the accumulated wisdom of the ages which has been refined and reconstituted over time by the admixture of the experiences of a multitude of different individuals. This is the patristic influence" (p. 9). As an erstwhile student of Fritz Machlup, I find the relationship between patristic legacies and disciplinary or cultural traditions somewhat confusing. Given the growing contemporary attention to feminist influences, one is tempted to ask: what about matristic influences or legacies?

6 Perlman (1978). The term rhetoric does not appear in this article. The only reference to McCloskey in *Ideas and Traditions* is the comment that she has made "a recent career" of highlighting the role in economics of "epistemic assumptions, [and] anecdotal evidence in the form of fables, parables, or stories from history," and "successfully showing how and when this type of persuasion can be employed" (pp. 578–79).

7 Rhetoric is an essential tool "for the promulgation and continuation" of a society's "structural norms"; and the pattern of society's "evolutionary legal, moral, ethical and social structure ...goes to the very heart of the process of social dynamics" (p. 5).

8 Newmarch, for instance, was a leading figure in a "statistical revolution" who conceived of "the development of a statistical basis for both testing and theorizing within economics" (pp. 196, 199). Perlman and McCann add: "It is with the development of statistical methods and their use in attempting a better understanding of economic relationships at a formal level that modern economics can be said to have arisen" (p. 199).

9 These connotations have ideological and policy, as well as purely semantic, significance. The usual view is that Steuart came closer to advocating a form of national planning than any other pre-Smithian economist, with the possible exception of some cameralists (p. 133; cf. pp. 120–28). Perlman and McCann frequently and effectively employ the term communitarian, which is markedly preferable to collectivist.

10 Schumpeter, who carefully qualified his sweeping assertion that economic *analysis* [sic] "has not been shaped at any time by the philosophical opinions that economists happened to have" was concerned that the historian's interest in philosophy might "obliterate the filiation of scientific ideas." (Cf. 1954, pp. 31, 32; also p. 133). He dismissed utilitarianism as "no philosophy at all in the technical sense, [and] unsurpassedly shallow as a 'philosophy of life' " (p. 407).

References

Mitchell, Wesley C. 1967. *Types of Economic Theory From Mercantilism to Institutionalism,* 2 vols. New York: Augustus Kelley, 1969.

Perlman, Mark. 1978. "Reflections on Methodology." In Jacob S. Dreyer, ed., *Breadth and Depth in Economics: Fritz Machlup – The Man and His Ideas.* Lexington, MA: DC Heath and Co.

Pribram, Karl. 1983. *A History of Economic Reasoning.* Baltimore and London: Johns Hopkins.

Schumpeter, Joseph A. 1954. *A History of Economic Analysis.* New York: Oxford University Press.

7 Review essay: History of political economy

The AEA and the history of economics

To commemorate its centennial in 1985 the AEA undertook and/or sponsored a variety of activities. From the historian of economics' standpoint by far the most interesting of these, both for its symbolic and its actual value, was the Executive Committee's decision to commission five articles "concerning the history of economics in the United States." The authors were selected by a distinguished panel of economists: George J. Stigler; Moses Abramovitz; and Charles Kindelberger, all ex-Presidents, and the results were duly published in December 1985 as part of a special *Supplement to the AEA,* which also contained the latest *Directory of Members.*[1]

For readers of this journal, and, more particularly, from the standpoint of the specialist historian of economics, it is natural to ask why, of the five authors selected for this undertaking only one, Martin Bronfenbrenner, a past President of the History of Economics Society, can be described as a recognized practitioner and expert in the subject?[2] Surely it was incumbent of the Association, through its customary sub-committee procedure, to go to the experts, as one would expect it to do in commissioning essays on specialist topics? Perhaps these are unnecessary, even improper questions, prompted by sour grapes and reflecting a typical trade union demarcationist mentality. After all, most historians of economics are humble, modest toilers in the scholarly vineyard, and unfriendly critics might add – they have plenty to be modest about!

More seriously, however, this group of essays symbolizes the current status of the history of economics in the U.S., and, no doubt, the widespread ignorance of the excellent and wide ranging research activity now in progress (the word is used deliberately). Despite the number of publications in the field, the existence of specialist societies in a number of countries, and the presentation of one hundred forty papers at the latest History of Economics Society meeting, it is still possible for a distinguished and usually well-informed scholar like William Parker to say in print that "the history of economic thought ... [which] once formed a part of the basic culture of every economist, is now almost completely defunct."[3] Ironically this is part of his introductory "history of economics in a nutshell," as described and warmly praised by James Tobin, one of the authors of the five AEA essays reviewed here.

Given this background, my response to the AEA articles is unequivocally ambivalent, if the expression is permissible. On the one hand it is always a pleasure (or almost always!) to see leading economists taking a genuine interest in their discipline's history as – let it be said – all good economists should. On the other hand, one has the right to expect that ventures into this area should be taken seriously, and not in the "idiosyncratic" (i.e., casual, cf p. 11) manner demonstrated by William J. Baumol, in this paper, "On Method in U.S. Economics a Century Earlier," which will be considered more fully below. Bronfenbrenner's provocative paper "Early American Leaders – Institutional and Critical Traditions" is also characteristically idiosyncratic, and much space could fruitfully be occupied in debating his choice of exemplars and his particular interpretations. But while his manner lacks the solemnity one so often encounters among historians of economics he cannot fairly be charged with failure to take his task seriously. Moreover, incidentally, he alone among the five essayists provides any reference to work published in *History of Political Economy,* the recognized leading periodical in the field. This omission helps to account for certain deficiencies in some of the other essays.

The history of economics is a vast subject, and the specialist practitioner in the field cannot expect (or be expected) to be equally well versed in all the content, technicalities, and esoterica of all the many compartments into which it is now subdivided. Hence the well-educated specialist economist interested in the development of his sub-discipline has much to contribute. This comparative advantage is splendidly exemplified in Carl Christ's "Early Progress in Estimating Quantitative Economic Relationships in America," an absolutely central theme in the evolution of "scientific" economics in the United States, one that has, quite understandably, been sorely neglected by most historians. Incidentally, the new interest in the history of econometrics – exemplified by the excellent History of Economics Society session organized by Neil De Marchi at the December, 1985 AEA meeting – is one of the most exciting current developments in the subject, for it promises not only to enhance our knowledge and understanding but also to widen the professional audience and support for the history of economics.

James Tobin's paper on "Neo-Classical Theory in America: J.B. Clark and Fisher" is a second example of the specialist's comparative advantage. His account of Irving Fisher's work is both authoritative and penetrating – indeed to say that it should be required reading for every American graduate economics student is only a slight hyperbole. However, his treatment of Clark is less satisfactory and would have benefited from a more thorough knowledge of (or at least reference to) the relevant literature. The relationship between Clark's earlier work in *The Philosophy of Wealth* (1886) and his masterpiece, *The Distribution of Wealth* (1889), has been extensively debated, including an important essay by his distinguished son, John Maurice. Tobin apparently relies heavily on Paul Homan's perceptive and intelligent *Contemporary Economic Thought* (1928), and one wonders whether he would be satisfied by an historian who drew primarily on a fifty year old source on monetary economics, however respectable? The claim that Clark's later work involved a "conversion" which "completely reversed"

(Tobin p. 29) his earlier position is at best a half truth. So too, is his sub-heading depicting the founding of the AEA as a "Failed Rebellion." This is or is not justifiable according to one's interpretation of the founders' aims. While possibly true of Ely, at least in part, the same cannot be said of the founder member economists, including Clark himself. Even Ely said – among other things, not all of them consistent – that they were struggling "for the right to exist professionally," and in that campaign they were successful. But this is a minor blemish on Tobin's contribution, and we have reason to be grateful for his excellent assessment of Fisher's work.

Of the five essays one is not in any strict sense historical – Jack Hirschleifer's expedition into the "Expanding Domain of Economics." As an amateur on most of the topics he surveys I would suggest that his paper had more educational value for the contemporary economist than any of the others, including Christ's, for he indicates both the possibilities and the severe difficulties facing the current enthusiastic intellectual "imperialists." In one memorable passage on the ever-controversial topic of the postulate of self-interest he comments:

> But the analytically uncomfortable (though humanly gratifying) fact remains: from the most primitive to the most advanced societies, a higher degree of cooperation takes place than can be explained as a merely pragmatic strategy for egoistic man (p. 55).

Shades of *The Theory of Moral Sentiments,* which Hirschleifer cites earlier in his essay. Would that this were included as one of the great books in every prospective professional economist's training.

Baumol's paper is the one most calculated to arouse the doctrinal historian's professional (sic) hackles, and some of the following reactions may seem unduly severe. However, they are designed to emphasize a general principle – the need for rigorous scholarly standards in the history of economics, as in other fields – not to "denigrate" one of the profession's more able, lively, prolific, and well-educated members, from whom we have a right to expect high standards. The verb is chosen advisedly, for Baumol is careful to explain that "nothing here has been intended to denigrate the contributions of earlier American economists" (p. 11), and that he is "not implying even obliquely that there is any reason to feel embarrassment about the work of our predecessors, as a sort of bar sinister in our intellectual family tree" (p. 1). Accepting that these remarks are sincere, the question remains: Why is such a disclaimer necessary? Surely it is possible to demonstrate earlier writers' shortcomings without denigrating them? After all, it is a commonplace among historians of ideas, including scientific ideas, that we stand on the shoulders of giants, and can therefore be expected to see further and (perhaps) more clearly.

The principal shortcomings of Baumol's essay stem from his failure to treat his predecessors with the scholarly care and respect to which they are entitled. This criticism is warranted on the basis of his methods, even if one accepts his general conclusions about the work in the early American economic journals: namely, that it lacked formal mathematics and contained "virtually no systematic use of history, that statistics were cited infrequently, and haphazardly and with little that even approximates rigorous analysis" (p. 1). Curiously enough, Baumol imagines these findings will surprise many of his readers. My own hunch is that this supposition unintentionally flatters them. The great majority of present day economists, I suspect, have insufficient interest or knowledge on which to base any clear expectations on the matter!

It is not my intention to challenge Baumol's conclusions which are of course debatable, or to produce the usual quibbles available to any informed and pedantic historian. There are more serious issues at stake. For instance, consider especially his scope and his method of selecting material. Although his title refers to "a century earlier" (i.e., 1885) he aims to cover the whole period from 1870 to 1914, an era of very substantial developments in American economics, as in professional scholarship generally. (Incidentally, half the authors who form his subjects did not start their careers until some years after the founding of the AEA.) To this end he selects, apparently ''haphazardly,'' a variety of quotations extending from Walker (1888) to Ely (1919) in order to display certain common and presumably enduring features of the literature of the period. As a method of obscuring changes in the discipline it could hardly be improved upon. Even if the writers could be treated as homogeneous units – hardly a reliable assumption, some (e.g., Ely) changed their style and outlook markedly over the period – have we any assurance that the citations we are offered are in any sense representative?

There is, of course, no easy and reliable method of sampling past economic literature; in this matter the reader must perforce rely on the historian's judgment and insight, derived from his intimate knowledge and understanding of the subject and its context. One cannot expect this from a non-specialist. Yet on one topic, a topic on which systematic data is available, Baumol conspicuously fails to fulfill reasonable expectations. In his penultimate "Digression: On Earlier Writings by Women" he offers only a list of half a dozen articles from a scattering of journals and a platitudinous comment that "before World War I, as today, a (distressingly) few women were contributing to the literature" (p. 11). A careful analysis would have provided a firm basis for the quantitative assessment and could be set against Barbara Libby's claim, based on systematic quantitative research, that in fact women figured *more* prominently in the American economics profession before 1920 than during the interwar years.[4] Quantitative studies in the history of economics are unusually difficult. Nevertheless, they can be revealing, as in the present instance. There has been much work of this kind since George Stigler's pioneering efforts, more than twenty years ago, and it deserves to be taken seriously.

Baumals' ostensible subject is "method in early American economic writings" but unfortunately he slips uneasily back and forth between method (in the sense of techniques), the discussion of method, and "methodological orientation" – notwithstanding the very severe strictures on this loose and misleading practice by his former Princeton colleague, Fritz Machlup. At one point he even refers to the "virtual absence" of method (p. 1), which is either incomprehensible, or involves yet another use of the term as, say, equivalent to methodical or systematic. As noted earlier, he is doubtless fully justified in his criticisms of loosely organized exposition, looser standards of evidence (than nowadays), neglect of the quality of evidence, authors' conjectures "that if data were available they would no doubt support their contentions" (p. 3 - i.e., "guesstimates"), anecdotal material, and *obiter dicta.* All of these matters, needless to say, are the subject of repeated complaints by present day commentators on the state of economics, not the least being the lack of concern for the quality of data, a matter emphasized so strongly by another outstanding Princeton economist, Oskar Morgenstern.[5] In the period under Baumol's scrutiny there was a very limited readership for sophisticated economic theory or.systematic statistical presentations, even in the case of the scholarly journals. Neither a *Journal of Economic Theory* nor an *Econometrica,* if available, could have survived, and it is crucial to distinguish between the audience for Irving Fisher's pathbreaking (and quite unusual) doctoral dissertation and that for a representative textbook. With respect to empirical work, a present day reader would get from Baumol no idea of the great strides made, for example, in economic statistics, by Henry Carter Adams (on behalf of the ICC), Frank W. Taussig (on behalf of the Tariff Commission), or Francis À. Walker and a host of other economists (on behalf of the U.S. Census). And while he is correct in drawing attention to the breakthrough in empirical research that occurred during and after World War I, is it good enough to refer to Wesley Mitchell's *Business Cycles* (1913), perhaps his most outstanding achievement, as "just published"?

Turning very briefly to the paper by Martin Bronfenbrenner, the one recognized historian in the authorial quintet, we encounter a very different species of idiosyncracy. Although he provides a densely packed sketch of the historical context, much of it – albeit full of brilliantly provocative original insights that represent caviar to the specialist – is surely too allusive and impressionistic to be fully comprehended by the average graduate student or the representative (and historically 'uneducated') professional reader. Moreover, his casual and unsystematic references to sources will put unnecessary obstacles in the way of those inclined to follow his many stimulating leads. (For example, Joseph Dorfman's "definitive" biography of Thorstein Veblen is seriously out of date, although still valuable.) One small example will suffice to show the need to interpret Bronfenbrenner carefully. He cites John R. Commons and Wesley Mitchell as two institutionalists elected to a one year term as President of the AEA, as though this were a special reduced form of honor reserved for distinguished dissidents. In reality, of course, the practice of two year terms had been abandoned many years earlier! Mitchell was, incidentally, much less "apologetic" about quantitative, empirical economics in his "Presidential Address" (1925)[6] than Bronfenbrenner suggests (on p. 26). Among other shortcomings is an incorrect identification of the editor of the *Journal of Economic Issues* and, more regrettably, the failure to even mention his own important articles on Marxist economics in the United States. Nevertheless, the essay is a gem: vastly entertaining, full of literary references and inventive terminology, and yet careful in the author's initial statement of his brief. Especially welcome to this reviewer are his early remarks on professional issues and influences on American economics. Bronfenrenner abundantly demonstrates that historical scholarship can be serious without being solemn.

In their different ways the two essays by Baumol and Christ exemplify one of the intellectual historian's principal tools, and his problems: hindsight. Baumol's contrast between American economics 'then' and 'now' is essentially static in its failure to appreciate fully the problems his authors faced and how they tried to overcome them. His subjects are treated more as curious relics than living, active, and fallible seekers after enlightenment. Christ, too, fails in some degree to adopt the *ex ante* perspective required to demonstrate how his subjects perceived their problems and how, if ever, they overcame them. Yet his is a relatively definable field in which 'progress' may be, at least in retrospect, demonstrable; hence the 'absolutist' perspective is both more appropriate and defensible than in some other intellectual fields – e.g., economic policy. At the outset he clearly emphasizes some of the discontinuities, blind alleys, and false trails in his story, which, he says, is "full of flashes of insights and moments of blindness, forward steps and false starts" (p. 39). Such is the stuff of which history is made. One longs to know, for example, why two well qualified men working in roughly the same field in a single university were not in closer touch with each other's contributions (p. 46). Language difficulties, the unavailability of modern information retrieval methods, or perhaps a plain ornery human unwillingness to cooperate or personal dislike, all have at times been impediments to the progress of knowledge.

Notes

1 William J. Baumol, '"On Method in U.S. Economics a Century Earlier," pp. 1–12; Martin Brohenbrenner, "Early American Leaders – Institutional and Critical Traditions," pp. 13–27; James Tobin, "Neoclassical Theory in American: J.B. Clark and Fisher," pp. 28–38; Carl F. Christ, "Early Progress in Estimating Quantitative Relationships in America," pp, 39–52; Jack Hirschleifer, "The Expanding Domain of Economics," pp. 53–68. All in *American Economic Review,* Vol. 75 (December, 1985).
2 William J. Baumol is a marginal case. While not, perhaps, a recognized historian of economics he has published a number of valuable historical articles and a section on the history of economics in his latest textbook, *Microtheory: Applications and Origins* (Boston: MIT Press, 1986). (I owe this reference to the editor of the *Bulletin.*)
3 William R. Parker (ed.), *Economic History and the Modern Economist* (Oxford: Blackwell, 1985) p. 8.
4 Cf. her article in James Soltow (ed.), *Essays in Economic and Business History*, Vol. III, 1984.
5 See, for example, the excellent small book by Andrew Kamarck, *Economics and the Real World* (Philadelphia: University of Pennsylvania Press, 1983).
6 "Quantitative Analysis in Economic Theory," *American Economic Review* Vol. XV (March, 1925, pp. 1–12), reprinted in his *The Backward Art of Spending Money and other Essays* (New York: McGraw Hill, 1937). See also Jacob Viner and others, "The Present Status and Future Prospects of Quantitative Economics: Discussion," *American Economic Review,* Supplement Vol. 18 (March, 1928), pp. 28–45.

8 Explanations in history and economics

The concept of explanation is too complex and elusive, and the modes of explanation in different disciplines are too diverse, to permit a thoroughgoing treatment of this subject in a paper of moderate compass. The object here is therefore more modest, namely, to convey some broad impressions of recent changes in the discussion of problems of explanation in economics and history influenced by the reaction against "positivist" philosophy.[1] This reaction has had a greater potential significance for economics than for history given the economists' long-standing desire to be regarded as scientists, whatever that may mean, an aspiration that has had comparatively little appeal to historians. Thus if, as will be argued here, there is a convergence of interests and views between economists and historians concerned with their disciplines' methodologies and practices, this is more likely to be attributable to movements among the former than among the latter. And, indeed, without underestimating the force of professional inertia, this movement is by no means confined to specialist writers on economic methodology.

To state the central motif of this paper briefly and too baldly, during the past decade or two the literature of economic methodology has become more tolerant, more eclectic, more pluralist, less self-confident, and also – as some critics would aver – looser and less "scientific." By contrast, among writers on the nature and methods of history there has been a discernible trend toward more analytical, rigorous, and systematic interpretations of the individuating features of history as an academic discipline, inspired in part by recent methodological developments and discussions in economic and social history. Underlying these changes of focus and interest in economics and history, and in harmony with broader contemporary philosophical trends, there has been a shift away from abstract discussions of general methodological and epistemological questions toward more specific and detailed investigations of the distinctive characteristics, objectives, substance, and problems of particular disciplines, subdisciplines, or intellectual fields.[2] Thus, for example, the perennial debate about the general differences between the natural sciences and the social sciences has lost its appeal as the intellectual returns from that exercise have approached zero. Not that the fundamental issues involved have been definitively settled; on the contrary, they still lurk in the background of current writings;[3] and, in a sense, they are inescapable, unless they are simply defined away as, for example, in the present instance, by viewing history exclusively as a social science.[4] To consider this point further would take us into those very questions of categorization and taxonomy that now seem so unfruitful. Instead, in line with current thinking, if there is indeed a methodological convergence or a partial overlap between economics and history, it is to be sought in the specific characteristics of these disciplines rather than in more abstract methodological and epistemological terms.

A leading economic methodologist has recently referred *en passant* to "the famous question of the nature of historical explanation and, in particular, on how historical explanations differ from the explanations offered by economic models,"[5] and the vast sprawling literature on these matters cannot be adequately summarized here. A comprehensive treatment of the subject would have to cover at least the following issues, all of which have surfaced in recent discussion of methodology in economics and history:

(a) The fundamental nature of explanation (including the problems associated with the nature and types of causality; in fact, all the key terms involved, such as cause, theory, law, model, hypothesis, etc., are debatable and in part problematic)
(b) Whether all, or even parts of a science or discipline need be explanatory (i.e., the respective roles of explanation, heuristic models, "understanding," hermeneutic interpretation, "storytelling," etc.)
(c) The various species of explanation (e.g., in the social and historical disciplines: intentionalism, functionalism, statistical probabilism, behaviorism, realism; systems theorists, whose ideas are beginning to permeate the social sciences, identify many other species)
(d) Which types of explanation are appropriate to the social sciences and humanities, as against the natural sciences (a point referred to in the preceding paragraph)
(e) The various levels of explanation and their interrelations (e.g., macro vs. micro; individualistic vs. holistic; intermediate levels or structures)

Broadly speaking the term "explanation" has three distinct but related meanings: (a) to remove a perplexity or solve a mystery; (b) to change the unknown into the known; and (c) to give the causes of the phenomenon to be explained (the explanadum).[6] Of these, the first two are expressed in psychological terms, and are regarded by most philosophers and social scientists as too relativistic and subjective. They do not stipulate the logical requirements to be fulfilled, and they fail to indicate that the explanation of a phenomenon involves the attempt to relate it to others like it and to give a systematic account of phenomena which reveals their interrelationships. The third type is inadequate: it may partially account for the explanation of events but not of regularities, dispositions, and other types of phenomena. If by "cause" we mean lawlike regularities of the kind that "Events like *A* regularly precede and are contiguous with events like *B*," then this type of explanation is compatible with the well-known nomological-deductive (DN) model of explanation. In the following account attention will be focused initially on the DN model because of its centrality in positivist economics and its prominence in neoclassical textbooks.[7] Other types of explanation will be considered later.

In a famous paper on "The Functions of General Laws in History" (1942), Carl Hempel argued that the same basic "nomological hypothetico-deductive" (i.e., DN) model of explanation applies in history as in the natural sciences, and this claim inspired a protracted and fruitful debate among philosophers, logicians, historians, and other social scientists. According to Hempel, whose views were endorsed by Braithwaite, Nagel, Popper, and others, particular facts are explained by subsuming them under true general laws, while general regularities are explained by subsumption under still broader true laws. One can legitimately ask for an explanation of the general law that figures in the initial explanation, but an explanation of the general law itself would be a different and additional explanation, not an essential part of the original explanation of the particular fact. Much of the subsequent debate among historians and philosophers of history turned on the question of the nature and necessity of the general regularities or universal, scientific, so-called "covering" laws. While the details of this controversy need not concern us, it is essential to note that in a subsequent paper of 1948 Hempel conceded that in historical explanations universal "laws" would have a much more limited role, so that the best to be hoped for is a looser kind of "explanation sketch" than the standard scientific DN model.[8] The significance of this concession is obvious when it is viewed in relation to the discussion of testability or falsifiability in economics during the past two or three decades.

Explanations in economics

Among the philosophers featured in recent economic methodology the central figure is Karl Popper, who regarded explanation as the major goal of science and developed his doctrine of falsification as a reaction against the verifiability principle enunciated, and much modified over time, by the logical positivists. According to Popper's fallibilist doctrine, verification or proof of scientific theories or statements is unattainable owing to the insoluble problem of induction; consequently the best we can hope for is a series of "conjectures and refutations."[9] As all scientific theories, hypotheses, and statements must be conceivably falsifiable, our confidence in them will be directly related to their capacity to withstand sustained attempts to test and falsify (or refute) them. The concept of empirical testing was widely discussed, in relation to both the theory and practice of economics, during the post-World War II decades, though not usually in explicitly Popperian terms. However, as Mark Blaug clearly demonstrated in his provocative book, *The Methodology of Economics,* professional economists have generally failed to practice the Popperian ideal even when they preached it. That is, they have neither tried hard enough to formulate empirically testable theories nor made serious efforts to falsify them. In effect, he concluded, in a memorable phrase, they have been engaged in "playing tennis with the net down."[10]

Curiously enough, although Blaug's findings were fully compatible with methodological and sociological studies of the behavior of natural scientists – for it is clear that few if any new scientific theories or budding research programs (to use Lakatosian terminology) would survive if Popperian procedures were followed rigorously – this did not induce him to abandon falsification as the most suitable methodology for economics. However, during the past decade or so other economic methodologists have become increasingly disenchanted with falsificationism, which now appears as neither the sole nor, for some, even a useful methodological approach.[11] On the other hand, there is general support for Popper's advocacy of the critical examination and, where possible, also the testing of economic theories.

From the present standpoint, a significant step in the disintegration of falsificationism was taken by another committed Popperian, Johannes Klant, in his illuminating study *The Rules of the Game*. Klant concluded, among other things, that while

> empirical scientists should *strive* to achieve falsifiable theories... in economics proof must usually be furnished in rational discussions of the *plausibility* of hypotheses.... A logical analysis of the relations between general and specific theories does not give grounds for assuming that the objective, namely, falsifiable general economic theories, cannot be reached. The rapid historical changeability in the domain of research and the instability of many human behavioral patterns lead one to suspect, however, that we shall never succeed and that numerical constants will never be discovered. As a rule, economic theories are therefore more in the nature of explanation sketches.[12]

Klant's reference to explanation sketches is significant not only because it recalls Hempel's distinction between the genuine natural-science species of DN explanations and the looser types of explanations used by historians (to be considered below), but also because it reflects the loosening of the positivists' hold over recent economic methodology writing. Among other moves in this direction we may include Caldwell's careful, flexible, and open-minded advocacy of "methodological pluralism"; Bart Nooteboom's extended examination of the role of "plausibility" in economics, a point mentioned earlier by Klant; and even Donald McCloskey's extreme near-Feyerabendian claim that all scientific argument is reducible to "rhetoric" or "persuasion," a view that has yet to gain significant support from economic methodologists.[13] Recent research by Wade Hands has demonstrated that Popper's account of economics is not only different from but inconsistent with his treatment of natural science,[14] while Klant and Caldwell have shown that in his later years Popper retreated from his original clear-cut falsificationist doctrine. For example, contrary to his original 1934 position, which required that statements of empirical science must be "conclusively decidable," that is, refutable by experience, in his later "criticistic" account he argued that irrefutable philosophical theories could also be subject to the same process of critical examination for

> every *rational* theory, no matter whether scientific or philosophical, is rational in so far as it tries to *solve certain problems*.... Now if we look upon a

> theory as a proposed solution to a set of problems, then the theory immediately lends itself to critical discussion – even if it is non-empirical and irrefutable. For we can now ask such questions as, Does it solve the problem? Does it solve it better than other theories? Has it perhaps merely shifted the problem? Is the solution simple? Is it fruitful? Does it perhaps contradict other philosophical theories needed for solving other problems?[15]

In this sense, even a metaphysical theory is

> similar to a scientific one. It is vaguer, no doubt, and inferior in many respects; and its irrefutability or lack of testability is its greatest vice. But, as long as a metaphysical theory can be rationally criticized, I should be inclined to take seriously its implicit claim to be considered tentatively, as true.[16]

This approach, which Caldwell terms "criticizability," substantially weakens Popper's famous demarcation criterion by which science is differentiated from nonscience, which was a central element in Popper's falsificationism. As Klant observes, it means that the acceptance or rejection of an irrefutable theory

> cannot be based exclusively on empirical scientific values. If the logical conditions of falsifiability... should not be satisfied, economics must be regarded as a form of philosophy, with the then inevitable schools of thought. Their adherents try to convince others of the plausibility of their point of view.... If only logic and not, at the same time, empirical testing forces mutual criticism in the direction of a consensus, a gap is left for extrascientific values that may lead in various directions.[17]

This, of course, is precisely what innumerable critics of neoclassical economics have been saying for decades: economics is not a value-free social science; there are, indeed, contending schools of thought with legitimate scientific claims. Consequently, as Klant succinctly puts it: "The difference between physics and the social sciences seems to be only one of degree, namely, very large."[18] Historians, too, are likely to find the doctrine of criticizability congenial, for they have never been attracted by the more stringent concepts of falsifiability or empirical testing. However, this does not mean there are no differences between explanations in economics and their counterparts in history. Caldwell endorses Popper's view that economists approach the problem of explanation in terms of the logic of the situation, according to which typical rather than actual initial conditions are invoked to explain a certain kind or type of event.[19] This obviously differentiates history from economics, for historians are concerned with conceptual rather than typical initial conditions and are generally (some would say invariably) concerned with singular rather than (or as well as) typical events; and no model is required to explain a singular event. Even this is an inaccurate and misleading view of historical work, which, like theories in economics, runs the entire gamut from very general to highly specific problems and explanations.

Moreover, in both fields any event or sequence of events has to be located within a specific historical context unless, of course, it is purely formal and abstract (as is unfortunately the case with much high theory in economics).

Another distinctive feature of situational analysis in neoclassical economics, according to Caldwell, is that it always starts out from the rationality principle. This is known to be descriptively false, but it is accompanied by variable conditions designed to enhance its usefulness and relevance when it is applied to actual situations. "The changes in theory that emerge are still criticizable: certain variations in initial conditions are better than others, for any number of reasons (some make better sense of the empirical basis, some are more elegant, some are more general, and so forth). They can be compared and criticized, which is the key."[20] The same is broadly true of historical explanations, for although the initial conditions are actual, they are selected by the historian from a potentially infinite stock, and for a combination of empirical and theoretical reasons – although the theory is more often implicit than explicit. However, historians have a wider range of theory choice than neoclassical economists, for they are not bound by the rationality principle or, indeed, by any other single basic postulate.

Closely related to, but logically independent of, the rationality principle is the doctrine of methodological individualism, according to which explanations of economic, social, or political phenomena must be expressed in terms of the beliefs, attitudes, and decisions of individuals. This idea has a long history, and takes many forms in economics.[21] In an extreme version, associated with one strand in the Austrian tradition, it is trivially true: all actions are performed by individuals; and the broader interpretation of its significance is complicated by its frequent association with political individualism, which is logically and methodologically distinct. In general, however, methodological individualism is fundamental to mainstream neoclassical economics, directly influencing the theory of consumers' behavior, for example, and underlying the search for the microfoundations of macroeconomics (and excluding approaches that work in the opposite direction).[22] Methodological individualism is important in the present context for, if adopted, it significantly narrows the range of acceptable explanations in economics, most notably by excluding its antithesis – methodological holism, the approach that accepts explanations of the nature and significance of social wholes, groups, or entities that are nor reducible to individual terms. As is unfortunately so often the case in methodological controversy, the individualist-versus-holist issue is usually couched in extreme terms – the one supposedly reductionist, the other antireductionist. Nevertheless, the orthodox approach is basically restrictive, in that it takes individual preferences and purposes as given (or exogenous, like technological change), regarding any inquiry into the origins and nature of individual preferences and purposes as beyond the "proper" scope of economics.[23] To its defenders this limitation appears simply as an argument for a sensible division of academic labor; to its critics, it appears as a willful adherence to a narrowly blinkered approach to economic and social life, one that is partially (perhaps even primarily) motivated by the desire to protect the orthodox paradigm from serious encroachments that would undermine its intellectual hegemony.

The relevance of this issue to the problem of explanation in economics was admirably demonstrated in Paul A. Samuelson's classic *Foundations of Economic Analysis* (1947), in which he distinguished between endogenous economic variables, which are causal in nature, and exogenous variables that are purely "historical" in character.[24] Not all economic writers have been so frank in acknowledging the self-imposed limits of their explanatory schema.

Samuelson's position is of special interest given his great influence on the subsequent mathematization of economics which, together with the pressure toward quantification, has profoundly influenced the discipline's postwar history. From the present standpoint the most significant effect has been the pressure toward formalism, the effort to make economics what Nicholas Georgescu-Roegen has termed an "arithmomorphic" science, one that seeks to reduce its subject matter to readily manipulable homogeneous units which can be handled conveniently in restricted formal models that seek logical closure.[25] This tendency is not, of course, new; the economists' long-standing desire to model their science on physics, that "icon of scientificity," has inevitably predisposed them to favor mechanistic explanations of a precise, rigorous, general, and systematic character.[26] (As will be seen later, no such methodological value system applies in the case of history.) All but the most prejudiced critics of neoclassical economics will admit the logical power and effectiveness of mathematical economics in handling complex problems involving a multiplicity of variables; but there are also costs involved, in terms of explanatory breadth. It appears that these costs have been increasingly emphasized in recent years, and not only by heterodox critics.[27]

Explanations in history

Strictly speaking, there is nothing in the literature on the methodology and philosophy of history to compare with the positivist-falsificationist theme in economic methodology. The majority of historians pride themselves on being practitioners, diligent workers in the archives rather than theorists (an almost exact reversal of the professional pecking order from that in economics). In the training and socialization of neophytes, learning by doing – often depicted as an arcane mystery, in the correct medieval sense of that term – usually takes precedence over an explicit introduction to methodological issues; and the general distaste for such issues is, if possible, even deeper and more widespread among historians than among economists. One major difference, however, is that many economists feel they have no choice: much as they would like to avoid methodological controversy there are divisions within their ranks that cannot be denied. For, unlike history, economics is a policy science (however much some theorists would seemingly like to treat it purely as a good game); consequently economists cannot be indifferent to questions about their scientific status, the validity of their claims to expertise, and the policy relevance of their conclusions. Even discussions of such seemingly esoteric matters as the role of mathematical formalism include references to issues of social and professional status and ideology, curiously enough often pulling simultaneously in two different directions: on the one hand the desire to restrain open professional dissensus, which might cast doubt on the reliability and validity of their knowledge; on the other, the desire to correct and censure those whose work falls below acceptable standards.[28]

Broadly speaking, economists and historians approach the problem of explanation from radically different, if not incompatible, standpoints. As already indicated, the prestige system in economics elevates general theorizing, preferably supplemented by rigorous measurements, to the top of the pecking order, while the more historically oriented topics – such as economic development, comparative economic systems, economic history and the history of economic thought – occupy the lower levels. Whereas economists highly value simplicity, elegance, precision, rigor, and system, historians are more concerned with accuracy and, if possible, completeness in the discovery, presentation, and interpretation of evidence – matters on which many economists are notoriously lax. As one student of historical explanations has observed, among historians "under-*researching* is frowned upon, under-explaining is not";[29] and it is tempting to argue that exactly the reverse is true in economics – even if both sides have been shifting their positions somewhat of late.

In considering historical explanations, Hempel's account of the nature and necessity of general regularities or "covering laws" is a convenient starting point, for it became the focus of debate among philosophers of history and methodologists for several decades. In the process a number of general arguments were advanced, which can be summarized as follows:[30]

(a) The distinction between highly confirmed generalizations and lawlike ones is artificial; and the distance between explanations that contain causal laws and those that merely appeal to the notion of cause can perhaps never be eliminated.
(b) Both social scientists and historians tacitly employ many "laws" or "truisms" that are so well known that no special reference to them is required; and the "new" or "cliometric" historians and social scientists insist that these tacit laws must be explicated, so as to make them "criticizable."[31]
(c) Historical events are too complex to be explained by the covering law model: it is impossible to produce complete generalizations; moreover this is unnecessary. Every event is an event *under a given description of a certain type or class,* for if it were literally unique, it would be undescribable. It is necessary to specify what aspect or aspects need to be explained, and if this is done, an adequate or satisfactory explanation is in principle attainable.
(d) Instead of explanations involving deducibility from general laws, it is possible, and maybe necessary, to employ generalizations representing imprecise correlations using loose terms – i.e., assessments of judgments. Thus, in behavioral explanations the motives must be *relevant* to the situation; there must be *evidence* in support of the argument that they are relevant, and there must be *grounds* for believing that these motives were causally efficacious in the instance.

(e) Explanations of human behavior in terms of motivations or dispositions are not lawlike in the strict sense, for it is not a general law that humans will always react the same way under given circumstances: superficially similar behavior may be attributable to a variety of motivations and purposes. The argument that insofar as people are rational they will try to maximize utility is simply a tautology, or a definition, not an explanation.[32] Whether individual purposes, dispositions, motives, and reasons constitute a necessary and/or sufficient basis for the explanation of human action has been the subject of considerable controversy. Some historians and social scientists emphasize the role of social and institutional influences on human behavior, while reference to psychological, biological, and even physical levels of explanation raises the problems of reductionism, determinism, and infinite regress.

(f) There are differing, and in principle equally valid levels and types of explanation depending on the purpose of the exercise. In some instances "cookery book knowledge" is sufficient (i.e., one can make a cake without knowing the laws of thermodynamics). The analogy with maps is useful here: a small-scale map is appropriate for a pilot on a long-distance plane journey, and a large-scale map for a person looking for a city street. If the level of explanation is too broad, it will be empty; if too narrow, it will be too specific and detailed.

(g) In order to avoid excessive or insufficient generality the event or situation to be explained can be analyzed into its component parts, to some of which genuine statistical (though not universal) laws are applicable. Thus the explanation of an historical event may be a conjunction of explanations of the component event constituting the explanandum.

(h) More generally, historical accounts may employ sufficient rather than necessary explanations – i.e., the explanation indicates conditions temporally prior to or simultaneous with the event to be explained, which are jointly sufficient but not independently necessary for the occurrence of the event. In other words, the event "falls into place" as the outcome of a sequence – the logical relationship is not implicative but conjunctive. The structure is one of coherent narrative (see below), not hypothetico-deductive logic.

(i) An example of this looser type of model employed by historians is W. B. Gallie's "characteristically genetic explanations"[33] which involves: (i) a number of temporally prior conditions, (ii) identification of the event or action as one of a kind that requires for its occurrence some disjunction of describable conditions, (iii) the production of evidence that such a necessary condition did in fact exist with the occurrence in question. If a more complete explanation is required, then different or additional necessary conditions can be specified.

(j) The positivistic distinction between the science and the art of historical writing is false. Getting the "facts" involves prior assumptions and criteria of selection as well as technical knowledge (e.g., palaeography and esoteric skills). The construction of historical narratives is not simply a literary art: *it involves analysis* – indeed, narrative may be a unique form of explanation required in reconstructing the past. It involves more than simply a chain of causation. To Philip Roth, narrative forms function as methodological paradigms in history which can be judged relative to their fruitfulness in guiding research and solving problems.[34] They are underdetermined by their evidence, for agreement on the evidence still allows for the constitution of incompatible histories. Thus explanations are historically contingent phenomena which involve pattern finding and problem solving.

According to the historical sociologist Philip Abrams, there has lately been

> a great increase in the interpretative ambition, scope, and self-consciousness with which narrative and formal modes of explanation are counterpointed... [a distinct tendency to] move not so much beyond narrative as towards a much more theoretically deliberate use of narrative as part of a type of explanation which plainly seeks more than plausibility in depth. ... [The] continuous confrontation and interweaving of narrative and theoretical matter... [involves] breaking of the bounds of conventional distinctions between types of explanation.

There seems to have been a

> cumulative movement on both sides toward a sensible intellectual pluralism in which theory and narrative cease to stand over against one another as principled alternatives and are instead locked together in a unified project of explanation.[35]

Needless to say, the foregoing account of historical explanation is neither complete nor definitive. It is merely designed to give an indication of the general trend of discussion, for there is no consensus among historians. Many, indeed, regard such matters as too abstract to be of interest.[36]

As the eminent philosopher of history William Dray has observed, "the explanations found in history books are a logically miscellaneous lot"[37] and in weighing the arguments for and against a specific conclusion or interpretation historians follow "the logic of practical choices instead of that of scientific deduction."[38] As the historian has a wider choice of statements to process than the economist, historical explanations are accordingly more complex and elusive than their counterparts in economics. "To explain what happens and to describe what happens coincide... [and] a narrative that fails to explain is less than a narrative."[39] Unlike an argument, a story does not require a predictable but merely an acceptable outcome, analogous to the outcome of a well-constructed play (a favorite analogy among historical methodologists). Michael Scriven argues that the objective should be to attain "plausibility in depth."[40] In retrospect the sequential logic is recognizable because of the teleologically oriented movement of our expectations when we were following the story.

> Every historical narrative is looking for an explanation to incorporate into itself, because it has failed to explain itself. It needs to be put back on track again.

> Hence the criterion of a good explanation is a pragmatic one. Its function is an eminently corrective one.[41]

Of course, a critical feature of historical explanations is their concern with processes over time, so that the distinctive features are associated with sequential analysis, "temporarily overlapping" descriptions, or the "processive" explanations referred to by Dray.[42] As the economists become more interested in the problems of "historical" as against "logical" time – a point mentioned later – such explanations will acquire added interest to them.

A convergence between economics and history?

As is well known, by comparison with the early post-World War II decades, the era of the Keynesian hegemony, the economics profession has subsequently experienced both a loss of professional and scientific confidence and a significant decline in public influence and esteem. The reasons for this sea change are various, and by no means confined to economics. Of special relevance here has been the exposure of serious defects in the positivist view of science and the concurrent decline in the economists' capacity to manage the economy and predict its future course. While the so-called mathematical-quantitative revolution has by no means entirely lost its momentum – academic inertia alone would preclude such an outcome – there has been a proliferation of methodological viewpoints (as noted earlier) and rival doctrinal schools (all of them still in the minority) to challenge the ruling neoclassical orthodoxy.

One aspect of this challenge has been the increasing advocacy of configurational models of explanation either to supplement or replace the conventional DN type.[43] These models have various forms and names, including "pattern modeling" (Wilber and Harrison); "storytelling" (Ward: this term has become part of common professional usage in economics); "pattern predictions" or "orientation theories" (Hayek); "holism" (Gruchy); "appreciative theory" (Nelson and Winter); and "process" theories and path-dependency analysis (Langlois).[44] There is no precise uniformity in these conceptions; nor is this to be expected. Nevertheless the family resemblances are unmistakable.

The application of configurational theories to economic data requires qualities of theoretical judgment and sensitivity to the nature and limitations of evidence more familiar to historians than to economists, whose training nowadays heavily emphasizes the command of techniques. According to Hayek, for example:

> when we deal with very complex phenomena the *recognition* of the conditions to which the theory applies may often require the ready perception of patterns or configurations which demand a special skill which few acquire. The selection and application of the appropriate scheme thus becomes something of an art where success or failure cannot be ascertained by any mechanical test... [and] this distinction constitutes no more than a distinction of degree from the physical sciences.[45]

According to Nelson and Winter, appreciative theory is "more intuitive and modified by common sense" than formal theory.[46] Like storytelling and pattern modeling, it focuses on certain variables, certain mechanisms, certain connections rather than others, and is more tailored to the particulars, a point repeatedly emphasized by Herbert Simon, who has long criticized economists for their refusal to seriously examine the validity and accuracy of the ancillary assumptions required in applying general economic theory to practical problems.

This requirement has long been familiar to economic historians, the indigenous occupants of the territory linking economics and history. As M. M. Postan noted half a century ago:

> This residuum of social life fills the background of economic theories as a kind of invisible presence: mentioned frequently and always reverentially, but seldom studied, never analysed. Sometimes it makes a fleeting entry into an economic theorem in the famous disguise of "other things being equal," only to pass out of discussion with its incognito intact. Even though the one thing we know for certain about the "other conditions" is that they cannot possibly be equal, little is done to establish their true identity, to go behind their variety and flux, and to understand the intricacies of their pattern.[47]

Of course, there is justification for Blaug's demurrer that:

> In able hands it [i.e., storytelling and pattern modeling] can be extremely persuasive... yet it is never easy to explain afterwards why it has persuaded.... because storytelling lacks rigor, lacks a definite logical structure, it is all too easy and virtually impossible to falsify. It is or can be persuasive precisely because it never runs the risk of being wrong.

Yet he is honest enough to concede that: "Perhaps economic problems are so intractable that this is the best we can do."[48]

Nooteboom's attempt to explicate the nature of "plausibility" in economics is useful at this point, a concept he defines as "coherence in the wider totality of knowledge and experience."[49] Limitations of space preclude a detailed review and critique of his analysis, which includes the role of assumptions (including social conditions and institutions), background knowledge, rules of syntax, assessment of the stability of causal relationships, and procedures for dealing with empirical anomalies. Some, though not all, of these elements also enter into the assessment of historical accounts.

Econometrics is a major field or approach in economics where intractable problems of explanation arise – although it has been unduly neglected by economic methodologists. As noted by Laurence Klein, a Nobel Prize-winning econometrician, some thirty years ago,

> econometrics is a way of studying history – a very systematic way.... The econometrician tries to piece together the fundamental aspects of economic

> behavior by looking at the interrelationships of the quantitative magnitudes generated historically, and then tries to extrapolate past behavior into an unknown future.... A sensible method of extrapolation is not naive or mechanical, and the econometrician is no less flexible than any other historian who tries to evaluate the future on the basis of the past.[50]

Some severe critics have argued that econometricians have been prone to unreflective, mechanistic treatments of the theory/measurement problems they encounter, for example in Nobel Prize-winning Ragnar Frisch's derogatory reference to "playometrics" and Norbert Wiener's earlier complaint that

> An econometrician will develop an ingenious theory of demand and supply, inventories and employment, and the like, with a relative or total indifference to... methods by which these elusive qualities are observed and measured. Their quantitative theories are treated with the unquestioning respect with which the physicists of a less sophisticated age treated the concepts of the Newtonian physics. Very few econometricians are aware that if they are to imitate the procedure of modern physics and not its mere appearances, a mathematical economics must begin with a critical account of these qualitative notions and the means adopted for collecting and measuring them.[51]

Recent econometric work by such critical practitioners as D. Henry, E. Learner, C. Sims, and T. Mayer is beginning to remedy this situation.

According to Mary Morgan, a leading historian of the subject:

> Econometrics seems to me not so much an art as a craft skill. It requires lots of judgment as well as some artistic skills and luck. A good econometrician, like a good historian, will take account of all the problems and will not throw away any of the inconvenient things encountered.
>
> Finding an empirical model to match the theory involves:
>
> a) Translating the verbal theory into mathematical form, and deciding in what form variables should be used and on the functional form for each theory;
> b) Finding ways of dealing with the *ceteris paribus* clauses under which the theory is assumed to hold (for example, choosing homogeneous periods);
> c) Finding the correct model for time and space: specifying the time adjustment/dynamic processes for each theory and taking into account local specific factors (e.g., institutional features such as price-setting mechanisms).[52]

Obviously, the majority of historians do not face the problem of translating a verbal theory into mathematical form, or choosing homogeneous time periods, however defined. But they are implicitly or explicitly concerned, in their own way, with *ceteris paribus* conditions, i.e., in deciding what should be treated as a given for the purpose of the explanation required. Like econometricians, they are concerned with finding "satisfactory" (i.e., plausible) empirical explanatory models, rather than with demonstrating the truth or otherwise of fundamental theories. What is or is not satisfactory depends on the purpose of the exercise, both for historians and econometricians, and while the latter are of course much more preoccupied with quantitative data, both groups seek to bring theory (explicit or implicit) into closer contact with data. Moreover, as Morgan observes, the "correct" model for an econometrician is necessarily economy- and time-specific rather than general and atemporal.

It was in the "new" or cliometric history that the problems of applying economic theory to the past generated the most thorough and penetrating discussion, from the late 1950s onward, partly because some of the cliometricians aggressively insisted on their superiority over traditional or "old" economic history. Now that the dust has settled, it is clear that they overstated their case, and many critics have questioned the excessive reliance on static neoclassical price theory, which, as the previous account suggests, entailed an unwarranted restriction in the range of usable explanatory models. As one astute commentator noted, the difficulties involved in cliometric or econometric history included:

> the imperfections in surviving data; the needling question (usually unresolved) of how well the sample of surviving evidence delineates the larger universe from which it comes; the uncertain operation of relevant, non-operational causal factors; the unknown degree of imperfection in any theoretical model resulting from its neglect of non-operational factors and its assumptions which distort reality – an unknown which remains immutable for want of an operational way of testing how much that neglect and distortion affects the ultimate explanatory power of the model.[53]

After making due allowance for the quasi-positivist language in this passage, which is rarely found among current philosophers and methodologists of history, there are obvious parallels between the two disciplines. Historians, economic historians, and economists share a number of common problems, for example: (1) How far back in time to begin the exercise? (2) What background knowledge is required? (3) What data is available? How reliable is it? (4) What explanatory variables are to be included? (5) What parameters are to be taken as given? (6) What time lags are involved in the model?

Conclusions

As noted at the outset, this account is broad and impressionistic: it is an (incomplete) literature survey, not an attempt to prescribe methodological principles or procedural rules. It is not designed to suggest that the basic problems of economics and history are identical, or that there is a prospective merger of the two disciplines. The pressures toward the subdivision, specialization, and compartmentalization of knowledge suffice to preclude such an outcome. Nevertheless, there are certain trends in economic research over the past two decades or so that are requiring economists to confront intellectual problems not dissimilar to those long encountered by historians – in particular, problems of expectations, uncertainty, imperfect information, the role of institutions, and processes in "real" or historical time. These are issues of profound significance, some of them of baffling complexity so far proving beyond the range and capacity of conventional mathematical methods of analyzing economic dynamics. Up to a point, the accompanying shift of emphasis from the traditional economist's concern with outcomes toward various forms of "process" analysis represents a shift in the historian's direction, for historical outcomes are usually known in advance of investigation and are therefore of comparatively limited interest. When the economist turns to processes, however, the focus differs from that of the historian since he (or she) usually wishes to go beyond the past and the present to the future consequences – which adds an additional intractable dimension.

Only the barest indications of the nature and implications of these research interests can be given here. For example, the economists' growing concern with the problem of "real" or "historical" time,[54] and the concomitant long-standing dissatisfaction with the concept of equilibrium, has been expressed by a variety of distinguished authors – such as Joan Robinson, John Hicks, Nicholas Kaldor, Nicholas Georgescu-Roegen, George Shackle, and Ludwig Lachmann, who are members of no single doctrinal school. Their interest is paralleled in the natural sciences by students of the "irreversibility" of time, such as Ilya Prigogine and Stephen Jay Gould. A closely related issue, one that has long exercised the heterodox critics of neoclassical economics, is the problem of institutional change and the pervasive influence of institutions on economic behavior. Here there are various efforts to break away from the conventional neoclassical methodological individualism without going to the other extreme and embracing methodological holism. Related to this is the emergence of the so-called "new" institutional economics, currently engaged in a vigorous turf battle with spokesmen for the older version, which is now enjoying a revival, together with various species of evolutionary economics (pace Thorstein Veblen).[55] Finally, interest in problems of uncertainty, expectations and imperfect information is drawing economists willy-nilly (or sometime even kicking and screaming) toward decision theories and psychology. Indeed, the annulment of the earlier divorce of economics and psychology and the many contemporary attempts to effect a reconciliation and promote cooperation between the two are yet other exciting research developments now under way.[56]

Of course, to repeat, this is merely to suggest that economists and historians are likely to benefit increasingly in the future from learning about research procedures, problem-solving methods, and basic methodological principles from studying each other's work. As economics becomes broader in content and more flexible in methods it will seem less arcane and remote to historians. As history becomes more self-consciously theoretical and methodologically more sophisticated, economists should find it a more attractive and fruitful field of study. And this will be part of the wider process that the anthropologist Clifford Geertz terms the refiguration of social thought.[57]

Notes

1 The term "positivist" is used here to describe the view that science is and should aim to be a body of objective, empirically verified or tested propositions or laws designed for the purposes of prediction and control. In recent economic literature it usually refers to the logical positivist and/or logical empiricist philosophies of natural science developed in the interwar years, and reaching a peak in the 1940s and 1950s. For an authoritative account by a leading economic methodologist, see Bruce J. Caldwell, *Beyond Positivism: Economic Methodology in the Twentieth Century* (London: George Allen and Unwin, 1982), esp. chs. 2 and 3. See also the introduction to Daniel M. Hausman, *The Philosophy of Economics: An Anthology* (Cambridge: Cambridge University Press, 1984), esp. pp. 40–42; the balanced account in Geoffrey M. Hodgson, *Economics and Institutions: A Manifesto for a Modern Institutionalist Economics* (Cambridge, Oxford: Polity Press, 1988), chs. 2 and 3; and Lawrence A. Boland, "Methodology," in *The New Palgrave: A Dictionary of Economics,* ed. John Eatwell, Murray Milgate, Peter Newman (London: Macmillan, 1987), 3: 455–458.

There are excellent bibliographies of recent economic methodology literature in Hausman, *Philosophy of Economics,* Caldwell, *Beyond Positivism* and idem, *Appraisal and Criticism in Economics: A Book of Readings* (London: George Allen & Unwin, 1984).

2 In advocating the study of "local methodology," the philosopher Hilary Putnam has remarked: "We learn better how to do history by doing history, not by doing anything else. I suspect the same is true of philosophy, or economics, or sociology" ("Zur lage der sozialwissenschaften" [On the Status of the Social Sciences], in *I. W. K. Mitteilungen des Institute für Wissenschaften und Kunst,* no. 4, 1984, p. 91). This accurately conveys the general contemporary urge to bring theory, methodology, and practice closer together.

3 And not always in the background, as for example in the recent study by Patrick J. O'Sullivan, *Economic Methodology and Freedom to Choose* (London: Allen & Unwin, 1987).

4 To a positivist, the central issue of this paper would be the demarcation criterion by which to differentiate scientific from nonscientific explanations, and whether history should be viewed as a science or simply as one of the humanities. The former issue will be referred to below; the second will not.

5 Mark Blaug, "John Hicks and the Methodology of Economics," in Neil De Marchi, ed., *The Popperian Legacy in Economics: Papers Presented at a Symposium in Amsterdam, December 1985* (Cambridge: Cambridge University Press, 1988), p. 189.

6 Cf. Sidney Morgenbesser, "Scientific Explanation," in David L. Sills, ed., *International Encyclopedia of the Social Sciences* (New York: Macmillan, 1968), 14: 117–123.

7 This account draws on Caldwell, *Beyond Positivism*, esp. pp. 53–60; Hausman, *Philosophy of Economics,* pp. 6–9.

8 Carl Hempel, "The Function of General Laws in History," *Journal of Philosophy* 39 (1942): 35–48; and idem (with P. Oppenheim), "Studies in the Logic of Explanation," *Philosophy of Science* 15 (1948): 135–175.

9 Karl Popper's major works are *Logik der Forschung* (1934), translated as *The Logic of Scientific Discovery* (New York: Basic Books, 1959); *Conjectures and Refutations: The Growth of Scientific Knowledge*, 2nd ed. (New York: Basic Books, 1965); and *Objective Knowledge: An Evolutionary Approach* (Oxford: Clarendon Press, 1972).

10 Mark Blaug, *The Methodology of Economics: or How Economists Explain* (Cambridge: Cambridge University Press, 1980), p. 256. E. R. Canterbery and R. J. Burkhardt examined 542 empirical articles in four major economics journals covering the 1973–78 period and found that only in three cases were attempts made to falsify the hypothesis. Cf. "What Do We Mean by Asking Whether Economics Is a Science?," in A. S. Eichner, ed., *Why Economics Is Not Yet a Science* (London: Macmillan, 1983), pp. 15–40.

11 For an unusually harsh judgment, see Daniel M. Hausman, "An Appraisal of Popperian Methodology," in De Marchi, *Popperian Legacy*, p. 65. He maintains that: "nontrivial questions about the testability of economics cannot be asked within the confines of Popper's falsificationism.... the notion of falsification as a purely logical relation between theories and basic statements or observation reports, which Popper has stressed again and again throughout his long career, is irrelevant to any important questions concerning science. On the other hand, Popper's relevant views concerning falsificationism as a methodology or a policy are unfounded and unacceptable." See also Bruce J. Caldwell, "Some Problems with Falsificationism in Economics," *Philosophy of the Social Sciences* 14 (1984): 489–495; and Andrea Salanti, "Falsification and Fallibilism as Epistemic Foundations of Economics: A Critical View," *Kyklos* 40 (1987): 368–391.

For a recent defense of falsificationism see, for example, Terence Hutchison, "The Case for Falsification," in De Marchi, *Popperian Legacy*, pp. 169–181. Hutchison introduced Popper's name, and the concept of conceivable empirical testability, into economic literature in his classic study, *The Significance and Basic Postulates of Economic Theory* (London: Macmillan, 1938; 2nd ed., with a new preface, New York: Augustus Kelley, 1960). For a general review of his later work, see my "Half a Century of Methodological Controversy in Economics: As Reflected in the Writings of T. W. Hutchison," in A. W. Coats, ed., *Methodological Controversy in Economics: Historical Essays in Honor of T. W. Hutchison* (Greenwich, Conn.: JAI Press Inc., 1983), pp. 1–42.

12 Johannes Klant, *The Rules of the Game: The Logical Structure of Economic Theories* (Cambridge: Cambridge University Press, 1984), pp. 184–186; italics in original. The original Dutch version was published in 1973 and 1979. See also his essay "The Natural Order" in De Marchi, *Popperian Legacy,* esp. pp. 111–114.

13 See Caldwell, *Beyond Positivism,* esp. ch. 13, and his "The Case for Pluralism," in De Marchi, *Popperian Legacy,* pp. 231–244; Bart Nooteboom, "Plausibility in Economics," *Economics and Philosophy* 2 (October 1986): 197–224; and Donald N. McCloskey, *The Rhetoric of Economics* (Madison, Wis.: University of Wisconsin Press, 1985). For criticism of McCloskey's position, see, for example, Bruce J. Caldwell and A. W. Coats, "The Rhetoric of Economists: A Comment on McCloskey," *Journal of Economic Literature* 22 (June 1984): 375–378 and McCloskey's "Reply to Caldwell and Coats," ibid., pp. 359–380; also the symposium in *Economics and Philosophy* 4 (April 1988): 89–175, with contributions by Uskali Mäki, Steven Rappaport, Alexander Rosenberg, and McCloskey.

14 Wade Hands, "Karl Popper and Economic Methodology," *Economics and Philosophy* 1 (1985): 83–100; also idem, "Ad Hocness in Economics and the Popperian Tradition," in De Marchi, *Popperian Legacy,* pp. 121–137.

15 Quoted by Caldwell in an unpublished paper, "Clarifying Popper," Department of Economics, University of North Carolina at Greensboro, p. 26 from Popper, *Conjectures and Refutations,* p. 199. See also Klant, in De Marchi, *Popperian Legacy,* p. 108. In his "Appraisal of Popperian Methodology," p. 81, Hausman concludes that Popper seemed to view economic theory as "an unfalsifiable metaphysical theory that might be of use in the development of empirical theories." He adds that "the costs of such an interpretation are considerable."

16 Caldwell, "Clarifying Popper," p. 27.

17 Klant, "Natural Order," p. 108.

18 Ibid., p. 110.

19 Caldwell, *Beyond Positivism*, pp. 13 ff. According to Popper, situational analysis involves "constructing *a model of the social situation,* including especially the institutional situation, in which an agent is acting, in such a manner as to explain the rationality (the zero character) of his action. Such models, then, are the testable hypotheses of the social sciences": cited by Blaug, *Methodology,* p. 51; italics in original. See also the valuable discussion in Hands, "Karl Popper and Economic Methodology."

20 Caldwell, *Beyond Positivism,* p. 29.

21 Hodgson, *Economics and Institutions,* ch. 3, provides a thoughtful critique of methodological individualism in economics. For a wider and penetrating survey of the subject, see Christopher Lloyd, *Explanation in Social History* (Oxford: Basil Blackwell, 1986), esp. ch. 8; also Blaug, *Methodology,* pp. 46 ff.

22 For an interesting but unsatisfactory attempt to work downward from macro to micro, see John Foster, *Evolutionary Macroeconomics* (London: Allen & Unwin, 1987). Generally speaking, attempts to develop an evolutionary economics clash with or seek to drastically modify the conventional individualist approach.

23 Cf. Hodgson, *Economics and Institutions*, for extended critique of this practice, one of many recently published. This issue raises the general question of the relations between economics and psychology, to which reference is made below.

24 I owe this reference to Kurt Dopfer, "The Histonomic Approach to Economics: Beyond Pure Theory and Pure Experience," *Journal of Economic Issues* 20 (December 1986): 994.

25 Cf. his *The Entropy Law and the Economic Process* (Cambridge: Harvard University Press, 1971). An original and telling analysis of the consequences of this tendency is presented in Henry K. H. Woo, *What's Wrong with Formalization in Economics? An Epistemological Critique* (Newark, Calif.: Victoria Press, 1986).

26 For a powerful critique, see Philip Mirowski, *Against Mechanism: Protecting Economics from Science* (Totowa, N.J.: Rowman & Littlefield, 1988).

27 See, for example, the brilliant analysis in Philip Mirowski's "Mathematical Formalism and Economic Explanation," in Mirowski, ed., *The Reconstruction of Economic Theory* (Boston: Kluwer-Nijhoff, 1986), pp. 179–204. Also, in the same volume, Donald W. Katzner, "The Role of Formalism in Economic Thought, with Illustrations Drawn from the Analysis of Social Interaction in the Firm," pp. 137–177. Other recent general critical analyses by competent mathematical economists include Michio Morishima, "The Good and Bad Uses of Mathematics," in Peter Wiles and Guy Routh, *Economics in Disarray* (Oxford: Basil Blackwell, 1984), pp. 51–73; and John Blatt, "How Economists Misuse Mathematics," in Eichner, *Why Economics Is Not Yet a Science*, pp. 166–186.

A particularly effective feature of Mirowski's account is his reply to two major defenses of the mathematical approach to economics, namely: (i) that the subject matter presents itself in quantitative form," i.e., that economics is "naturally quantitative"; and (ii) that mathematics is either "just another language" imposing "logical rigor upon the loose and imprecise common discussion of economic phenomena," or even that "mathematical formalism *is* logic": "Mathematical Formalism," pp. 181–182; italics in original. It should be noted that few if any of the critics argue that either formalism or mathematics should be abandoned. Mirowski, in particular, argues that for historical reasons economists are mainly using the wrong kind of mathematics.

That the use of "loose concepts" is necessary and indeed unavoidable in economics, see Andrew Kamarck, *Economics and the Real World* (Philadelphia: University of Pennsylvania Press, 1983), esp. p. 27. Kamarck is an experienced professional practitioner.

28 However, there is no explicit code of professional ethics for economists and no procedure for establishing or enforcing acceptable standards. Even the academic process has only limited influence on entry into the profession.

29 Gene Wise, *American Historical Explanations: A Strategy for Grounded Inquiry,* 2nd ed. (Minneapolis: University of Minnesota Press, 1980), p. viii; italics in original.

This volume is one of a number of recent efforts to distill general principles of theorizing and explanation from historians' practices. See also Dale H. Porter, *The Emergence of the Past: A Theory of Historical Explanation* (Chicago: University of Chicago Press, 1981).

30 The following account is based on a variety of sources, and no detailed citations will be provided. See, for example, Rudolph H. Weingartner, "Historical Explanation," *Encyclopedia of Philosophy,* ed. Paul Edwards (New York: Macmillan, 1967), 4: 159–163. There is a valuable survey of the literature in Lloyd, *Explanation in Social History,* to which I am considerably indebted. See also later footnotes in this section.

31 P. D. McClelland, *Causal Explanation and Model Building in History, Economics, and the New Economic History* (Ithaca: Cornell University Press, 1975) contains a valuable review of its subject.

32 Cf. Alexander Rosenberg, "Can Economics Explain Everything?," *Philosophy of the Social Sciences* 9 (1979): 509–529. The contention that "all agents act purposefully" is lawlike, but also empty, and trivially true.

33 W. B. Gallie, "Explanations in History and the Genetic Sciences," in B. Brody, ed., *Readings in the Philosophy of Science* (Englewood Cliffs, N.J.: Prentice-Hall, 1970), pp. 150–166.

34 Philip Roth, "Narrative Explanations: The Case of History," *History and Theory* 27 (1988): 1–13. This is but one example from a very large literature. *History and Theory* is a rich source of debate on historical methodology.

35 Philip Abrams, "History, Sociology, Historical Sociology," *Past and Present* no. 87 (May 1980): 10, 11.

36 A common attitude is described by Eric Jones as "confusionist," according to which "... everything influences and nothing determines everything else.... The disdain for model building expressed by most general historians of my acquaintance seems to rely on easy shots at the more exaggerated claims of social science; on a failure to understand that the point of a theoretical construct is to get something just wrong enough to help comprehend which parts are just right; and on an equivalent failure to accept that we are all building models anyway." By contrast, the typical neoclassical economist is a "Rigidifier" who "thinks that we already possess adequate economic theory and that the economic historian's role is to show how past experience bears it out.... On the Rigidifier's standard view, history is a storehouse in which the bits that do not fit may be left to rot...": "Very Long-Term Economic Development as the History Survey," Economics Discussion Papers no. 2, La Trobe University School of Economics, 1985, pp. 5–8.

37 William Dray, *Laws and Explanation in History* (London: Oxford University Press, 1957), p. 85.

38 Paul Ricoeur, *Time and Narrative,* vol. 1 (Chicago: University of Chicago Press, 1984), p. 125.

39 Ibid., p. 148.

40 Cf. Michael Scriven, "Truisms as Grounds for Historical Explanation," in Patrick Gardiner, ed., *Theories of History: Readings in Classical and Contemporary Sources* (Glencoe, I11.: Free Press, 1959), pp. 443–475. This concept resembles the nation of "thick description" associated with the anthropologist Clifford Geertz, and initiated by the philosopher G. Ryle, "Thinking and Reflecting," in G. Veysey, ed., *The Human Agent* (London: Macmillan, 1968), p. 221. For Geertz, see his "Thick Description: Toward an Interpretation Theory of Culture," in *The Interpretation of Cultures: Selected Essays* (New York: Basic Books, 1973), pp. 3–30.

41 Ricoeur, *Time and Narrative,* p. 155.

42 William Dray, "Narrative versus Analysis in History," *Philosophy of the Social Sciences* 15 (1985): 127. This article contains a very clear review of various historians' views on this subject.

43 In addition to the "theoretical" mode, Louis Mink identified the "categorical" and "configurational" modes of explanation. Cf. "History and Fiction as Modes of

Comprehension," *New Literary History* 1 (1970): 541–558. Categorical refers to the identification of an event as one of a given species, whereas configurational refers to placing an event in a historical context. Cf. Blaug, *Methodology of Economics*, pp. 127, 261, on the closely similar concepts of "storytelling" and "colligation," i.e., "the binding together of facts, low level generalisations, high level theories, and value judgments in a coherent narrative." This is inadequate, however persuasive, because "the demands of policymakers will nevertheless drive us back to the use of econometrics, which alone can provide a quantitative as well as a qualitative calculus."

44 C. K. Wilber and R. S. Harrison, "The Methodological Basis of Institutional Economics: Pattern Model, Storytelling, and Holism," *Journal of Economic Issues* 12 (1978): 61–89; B. Ward, *What's Wrong with Economics?* (London: Macmillan, 1971); F. A. Hayek, "Degrees of Explanation" and "The Theory of Complex Phenomena," in his *Studies in Philosophy, Politics and Economics* (Chicago: University of Chicago Press, 1967), pp. 3–21, 22–42; A. Gruchy, *Contemporary Economic Thought: The Contributions of Neo-Institutional Economics* (Clifton, N.J.: Augustus Kelley, 1972); R. Nelson and S. Winter, *An Evolutionary Theory of Economic Change* (Cambridge, Mass: Belknap Press, 1982); R. Langlois, *Economics as a Process: Essays in the New Institutional Economics* (Cambridge: Cambridge University Press, 1986).

45 Hayek, "Degrees of Explanation," p. 18. The significance of tacit knowledge has been emphasized by Michael Polanyi, in his *Personal Knowledge: Towards a Post-Critical Philosophy* (London: Routledge & Kegan Paul, 1957) and *The Tacit Dimension* (London: Routledge & Kegan Paul, 1967), and the role of pattern recognition by the eminent physicist John Ziman, *Reliable Knowledge: An Exploration of the Grounds for the Belief in Science* (Cambridge: Cambridge University Press, 1978).

46 Nelson and Winter, *Evolutionary Theory,* pp. 4, 14.

47 M. M. Postan, "The Historical Method in Social Science," in N. B. Harte, ed., *The Study of Economic History* (London: Frank Cass, 1971), p. 134.

48 Blaug, *Methodology of Economics,* p. 127. There is a much fuller and more sympathetic treatment in Caldwell, *Beyond Positivism,* pp. 200–203: "the Institutionalist methodological research agenda... is a grand and ambitious vision," but it "faces far more difficulties in its application than any we have yet examined." This is partly because Caldwell is seeking more stringent standards than are attainable in practice. Cf. his more recent criterion of criticizability referred to earlier.

49 Nooteboom, "Plausibility in Economics." His approach does not involve the abandonment of falsification, but it reveals the complexity and subtlety of the elements involved in the process of testing economic models. Discovery and justification of theories goes hand in hand, contrary to the logical positivist's view.

50 Laurence Klein, *A Textbook of Econometrics* (Evanston, I11.: Row Peterson, 1953), p. 2.

51 Norbert Wiener, *God and Golem* (1964), cited in Joan Robinson, "Thinking about Thinking," *Collected Economic Papers*, vol. 5 (Cambridge, Mass.: MIT Press, 1980), p. 4.

52 Mary Morgan, "Finding a Satisfactory Empirical Model," in De Marchi, *Popperian Legacy,* p. 201 (and p. 44, where she notes that econometricians usually do not compare empirical models but deal with them only one at a time).

53 McClelland, *Causal Explanation,* p. 226. For a confident recent review of the cliometricians' achievements see Donald N. McCloskey, *Econometric History* (London: Macmillan Education, 1987). The author favors a broad and loose definition of the field as "historical economics" which would, taken literally, include much earlier work in the field since the late nineteenth century.

54 Two useful pioneering efforts are Gordon Winston, *The Timing of Economic Activities: Firms, Households and Markets in Time-Specific Activities,* 2nd ed. (Minneapolis: University of Minnesota Press, 1980), and Randall Bausor, "Time and the Structure

of Economic Analysis," *Journal of Post-Keynesian Economics* 5 (1982–3): 163–179. (This is one of a series of stimulating articles by this author.)

55 On the "new" and refurbished version of the "old" institutionalism, see Langlois, *Economics as a Process,* and Hodgson, *Economics and Institutions.* Hodgson and Lloyd, *Explanation in Social History,* discuss both the relationship between individualism and holism and the need for a *via media.*

56 See, for example, the essays in Robin Hogarth and Melvin Reder, eds., *Rational Choice: The Contrast between Economics and Psychology* (Chicago: University of Chicago Press, 1986, 1987) and Peter Earl, *Psychological Economics* (Boston: Kluwer, 1987).

57 Clifford Geertz, "Blurred Genres: The Refiguration of Social Thought," in his *Local Knowledge: Further Essays in Interpretative Anthropology* (New York: Basic Books, 1983), pp. 19–35. For a relevant example, see Dopfer, "The Histonomic Approach to Economics."

9 Comments on Schabas

The nature and significance of the "New" economic history: A response to "Parmenides and the Cliometricians"

My reactions to Margaret Schabas's stimulating and provocative chapter are disturbingly mixed. While I agree with a good many of her specific observations and assertions, and have some sympathy with the general thrust of her argument, the choice of cliometrics to exemplify certain general methodological and philosophical issues strikes me as doubly unfortunate – because cliometrics was a unique and essentially transitory episode in the development of economic history as an academic discipline and because Schabas's account of it is misleadingly selective.

Of course I appreciate that Schabas is primarily concerned with using cliometrics as a convenient peg on which to hang her general case. But there is a real danger that the peg may in fact be a straw man – to use an excruciatingly mixed metaphor.

Contrary to Schabas's claim, although cliometrics may have "overshadowed traditional economic history within a decade or two of its formation," this is true only of the United States. It is certainly not true that its exponents have constituted "the dominant group of economic historians in the English-speaking world since the 1960s." Without quibbling about the precise meaning of "dominant," I fear that Schabas has been taken in by the cliometricians' loud, sometimes belligerent, and oft-repeated propaganda.[1] Intellectual revolutions rarely spread so swiftly. As an economic historian with a strong professional interest in economic methodology, I was teaching in an English university both before and after cliometrics burst upon the transatlantic scene in the late 1950s, and I can testify that the vast majority of my professional peers were equipped neither intellectually nor technically to take effective advantage of the new wave, even had they been inclined to do so. On the contrary, most of them viewed the new economic history with a combination of bewilderment, scepticism, and even hostility.[2] None of these sentiments was entirely commendable; but they were understandable, given the cliometricians' vigorous initial overselling of their claims. Even now, any suggestion that economic history in Britain is dominated by cliometrics can be dispelled quickly by perusing the *Economic History Review,* one of the leading scholarly periodicals in the discipline. And, I believe, much the same is true of the Commonwealth and the Scandinavian countries, which have long been distinguished centers of economic history research.

The situation was, however, very different in the United States where, for a time, the cliometricians swept all before them, for reasons I have discussed elsewhere (Coats, 1980, 1990).[3] Even so, it is crucial to recognize that as a group the "new" economic historians were not homogeneous, and the early phase of missionary overenthusiasm and exaggeration soon gave way to a more sober and balanced outlook. Schabas distorts the record by focusing so heavily on the work of Robert Fogel, the new economic history's most spectacular, energetic, and untypical practitioner, and on *Time on the Cross*, by Fogel and Stanley Engerman (1974), the movement's most spectacular, but unique, literary product.[4] Fogel far outreached other cliometricians in his deployment of large-scale counterfactual models – the least plausible of that controversial species. Hence it is no surprise that one critic spoke of his "daredevil impulse." *Time on the Cross,* unquestionably the most controversial economic history book ever published, made extraordinarily bold and, as it transpired, significantly overstated claims for the novelty, objectivity, and scientific validity of its authors' findings. These claims were quickly challenged, and on many points rejected, by a variety of competent critics.[5] It was at this time, the mid-1970s, that the new economic history can be said to have come of age. In the early years too much energy had been expended in overemphasizing the supposedly revolutionary break with the past and denigrating the achievements of earlier economic historians. *Time on the Cross* inaugurated a brief phase of bitter internecine warfare;[6] but in due course the cliometricians returned to the constructive work of developing their subject in accordance with the long-standing theoretical-quantitative tradition in American economics – especially that associated with Simon Kuznets, the National Bureau of Economic Research, and the Conference on Income and Wealth.

Schabas contends that the cliometricians "established a general all-purpose theory" that "eliminated the possibility of a changing world,"[7] and that "they had a deep-seated commitment to universal rationality." Yet this theory, and this commitment, were firmly "established" in economics long before cliometrics was even heard of. Historians of economics, including Schabas, are well aware of the long-standing objections to these features of mainstream classical and neoclassical economics. For example, leaders of the nineteenth-century German historical school accused the classical economists of "cosmopolitanism" and "perpetualism" – that is, the presumption that their theories were true of all times and all places. Several decades later the aggressive British economic historian, William Cunningham, made essentially the same point – albeit in less sweeping terms--in attacking his outstanding Cambridge colleague, Alfred Marshall; and Thorstein Veblen's oft-quoted American caricature of the hedonistic psychology presupposed in conventional economic analysis was specifically designed to ridicule and undermine the orthodox economists' "commitment to universal rationality," in what he saw as a post-Darwinian "world in flux."[8]

So what, then, differentiated cliometrics from "good old economic history," to cite Max Hartwell's apt description? Was it simply the clarity, force, and occasional extremism of the cliometricians' claims, or the fact that they were, for the most part, economist historians, rather than historians concerned with the economic past? Schabas correctly observes that with respect to numerical analysis the two species of economic history differed only in degree rather than in kind. Even so, the difference was striking. The cliometricians believed, and rightly, that there were vast, largely untapped statistical sources directly bearing on the history of the American economy; and they were eager to use state-of-the-art methods of processing and analyzing this data, methods unknown to most of the earlier economic historians. In this respect American economic history was largely catching up with American economics. Yet contrary to Schabas's account, the problem of data quantity often proved less serious than the problem of data quality; and for some cliometricians the urge to be quantitative (and therefore "scientific") led – as in economics – to an uncritical use of these source materials. This was especially obvious in some parts of *Time on the Cross* because the authors were so determined to push their enquiries, often ingeniously, into topics hitherto regarded as beyond the conventional boundaries of economics.

Schabas is on shaky ground in asserting that the new economic historians sought "photographic realism," or that "they let the facts speak for themselves" – whatever that means (McCloskey, 1981: xvii, 4–5; 1987: 11). In some instances, of course, the discovery, compilation, and interpretation of quantitative data took precedence over theorizing, for as Fogel once observed, the aim of the new economic history was to put American economic history on a "sound quantitative foundation." But this did not entail any abandonment of theory. Indeed, one of the basic differences between the "good old" and the "new" economic history was the latter's *explicit* use of economic theory – as against the looser tacit or implicit theorizing often to be found in the earlier economic history literature (Fogel, 1983: 6, 9).[10] And it is difficult to think of an American cliometrician of the past thirty years or so who was not, in one way or another, aware of and reliant on static neoclassical price theory as the appropriate analytical starting point.

There is room for debate as to whether the cliometricians could or should have developed their own theory, especially if, as Conrad and Meyer suggested, they hoped and expected to "influence the development of economics."[11] But on the whole they were net borrowers from contemporary economics and eager to be viewed as the economists' scientific and professional equals. (The fact that British economic history had for so long developed in quasi-independence from economics helps to explain the slow and reluctant acceptance of cliometrics in that region.)

In my view the "heart" of the econometrics movement was not "the implicit assumption that human rationality has remained the same over the centuries," but a particular conception of how economic history, and perhaps history in general, could be made "scientific." It was this, as much as explicit theory, techniques, and a naive belief in the statistical testing of hypotheses, that differentiated the new from the old economic history.

By far the most original and stimulating part of Schabas's essay is the section wherein she compares two "worlds," as known to and perceived by natural scientists and economists respectively. This raises fundamental epistemological and ontological questions that extend far beyond the cliometricians' world, questions that cannot be discussed briefly here. Hacking's observations about laboratory life and the consequences of the advanced technology available to natural scientists have no counterpart in late twentieth-century economics, which is only just beginning to develop a limited body of interesting and reasonably well-established experimental data.[12] In economics these days, methodological fashions rise and fall so readily that it is hazardous to generalize about the current state of knowledge. Even if economics has more "constants" than natural science – a point I feel Schabas somewhat overstates[13] – its relatively primitive gropings with more time-sensitive species of analysis (such as nonlinear, path-dependent, and irreversible processes; uncertainty; imperfect information; and the like) reveal that the discipline already has more "flux" than it can handle. Of quite a different order, however, is the possibility that if Schabas is correct, economists have yet another reason why they should abandon their long-standing urge to emulate physics, the "icon of scientificity." As recently suggested by Philip Mirowski (1989), in his provocative study *More Heat Than Light*,[14] economists have in any case been aping an outmoded nineteenth century conception of physics. If they attempted to take late twentieth-century physics as their model, they would be in even deeper trouble.

Notes

1 This is obviously a matter of judgment, depending in part on whether a broad or narrow definition of cliometrics is employed. One can acknowledge that cliometric conceptions and methods have made valuable and permanent contributions to economic history, without accepting either the movement's initial inflated claims or the view that it has dominated or completely transformed the subject, even in the United States. However, in developing her case, Schabas focuses on its more extreme and untypical manifestations.

In the following account *cliometrics* and *new economic history* will be treated as synonymous.

2 See, for example, the papers on "The Future of the New Economic History in Britain" by Jonathan R. T. Hughes, R. M. Hartwell, Barry Supple, and R. C. O. Matthews, in McCloskey (1971: 401–433). See also the editor's introduction (1971: 3). For a later assessment see Coleman (1987: especially 122–126).

Unlike the United States, there was no open intergenerational conflict over cliometrics among British economic historians.

3 On the "cultural warfare" among American economic historians resulting from the cliometricians' efforts to tear the fabric of traditional history to shreds, see Fogel (1983: 65). One traditional historian interpreted the cliometricians' message as: "Retool, rethink, conform, or be plowed under" (Fogel, 1983: 65). In this balanced essay, Fogel acknowledges the cliometricians' dependence on traditional methods, adding that overreliance on "mathematical wizardry or computer magic" sometimes led to embarrassing failures. He confirms that "The anticipated rout of traditional historians has not materialized and history has not been transformed into a science" (Fogel, 1983: 67). But the effect of cliometrics on economic history has, however, been considerable.

4 Schabas ignores the important fact that at the memorable Williamstown meeting in 1957, A. H. Conrad and J. R. Meyer produced two papers – the one she mentions on "The Economics of Slavery in the Ante-bellum South" and another, more general treatment of "Economic Theory, Statistical Inference and Economic History." It is arguable that the latter was the more significant of the two, given the subsequent development of cliometrics. Both were reprinted in their collection of essays (Conrad and Meyer, 1964). Note the word econometric in their title. Cf. Donald McCloskey's recent survey (1987). This title implies, incorrectly, that all economic history is now econometric.

5 In addition to a long series of reviews, at least one of book length, the most accessible source is a collection of papers by Paul A. David et al. (1976). Many of the serious criticisms of *Time on the Cross* have never been directly answered by its authors. Moreover, the passage Schabas cites on p. 190, supposedly a discovery of *Time on the Cross,* simply summarizes the main conclusion of Conrad and Meyer's article published seventeen years earlier. Incidentially, Fogel and Engerman (1974: vol. 2, 160–160) did in fact refer to a shadow price for freedom.

6 Donald McCloskey has commented amusingly, that "The violence surrounding *Time on the Cross* is only the latest and largest in a series of intellectual muggings," adding that "In common with street crime, political purges and scholarly controversy in other fields, the violence is greatest among the closest neighbors." Cf. McCloskey (1981: 11–12). In the foreword to this volume Barry Supple wisely observes that controversy among the new economic historians has been due both to their felt "need to proselytize" and to their striving "with fierce enthusiasm to satisfy two sets of scholarly standards – those of economic theory and of historical evidence" (McCloskey, 1981: ix). The desire to achieve academic recognition and status by participating actively in the contemporary so-called quantitative-scientific revolution in economics was a major influence. Generally speaking, cliometrics has become much less controversial in the past decade or so.

7 The meaning of the second half of this statement is unclear to me. It confuses three possibilities: the practical usefulness of the cliometricians' models, intellectual discussions about how the economic world really is and how it should be represented in models, and methodological arguments about the way to find out about the world using those models (adapted from Morgan 1991: 244).

Most, but not all, of the cliometricians seem to have been epistemologically innocent. They were, as Schabas recognizes, essentially positivists (if that term still means anything), drawing on contemporary static neoclassical price theory. For a characteristically illuminating comment see Parker (1973: 13): "The new work justified the ways of the price system to men. And rightly so. If a model of an economy with flexible prices does not test out in early nineteenth century America, where, one wonders, is it to be used? The great constructive contribution of their work lay... in its shadowy adumbration of the machinery of a growing competitive economy. A sympathetic imagination can pick up the noise of growth behind these essentially static tableaux." But, as Schabas observes, the cliometricians too often seemed satisfied with models "by definition too stylized to correspond to the world as it actually is." They made little or no use of nonlinear models and took no interest in what is nowadays sometimes referred to as "real" historical time. Unfortunately, despite a tremendous investment of intellectual resources, the economists of the period were unable to develop a satisfactory theory of economic growth. See, for example, the magisterial survey article by Hahn and Matthews (1964: 779–902).

8 Schabas's concluding quotation from Jevons demonstrates that the commitment to rationality was no new phenomenon. However, she correctly emphasizes the cliometricians' unusually clear, explicit, and far-reaching use of that concept.

9 McCloskey implies that prior to 1957 economic historians made virtually no use of economic theory. This is wrong.

10 To quote McCloskey (1981: 14), a leading spokesman for cliometrics: "'Theory tells us' is as foolish in its own way as 'the facts say.'" I doubt that the new economic historians were as naive as Schabas implies.
11 Whether the economic historians' "limited" generalizations are liable, even able, to influence the development of economics is at least debatable.
12 However, some of the cliometricians' significant contributions to economic history were directly dependent on the availability of high-speed computers.
13 Her "admittedly undersubstantiated" discussion turns partly, if not largely, on matters of definition. Constancy in the economist's subject matter needs to be considered in relation to the problems addressed, rather than in quasi-absolute terms.
14 The subtitle is *Economics as Social Physics, Physics as Nature's Economics.*

References

Coats, A. W. (1980). "The Historical Context of the 'New' Economic History." *Journal of European Economic History* 9(1) (Spring), 185–207.

____. (1990). "Disciplinary Self-Examination, Departments and Research Traditions in Economic History: The Anglo-American Story." *Scandinanvian Economic History Review* 38(1), 3–18.

Coleman, D. C. (1987). *History and the Economic Past: An Account of the Rise and Decline of Economic History in Britain.* Oxford: Clarendon Press.

Conrad, A. H., and J. R. Meyer. (1964). *The Economics of Slavery and Other Studies in Econometric History.* Chicago: University of Chicago Press.

David, Paul A., et al. (1976). *Reckoning with Slavery: A Critical Study in the Quantitative History of American Negro Slavery.* New York: Oxford University Press.

Fogel, Robert W. (1983). "'Scientific' and Traditional History." In Robert William Fogel and G. R. Elton, *Which Road to the Past? Two Views of History.* New Haven: Yale University Press.

Fogel, Robert W., and Stanley L. Engerman. (1974). *Time on the Cross.* Boston: Little, Brown.

Hahn, F. H., and R. C. O. Matthews. (1964). "The Theory of Economic Growth: A Survey." *Economic Journal* 74 (December), 779–902.

McCloskey, Donald W. (ed.). (1971). *Essays on a Mature Economy: Britain After 1840.* Princeton, NJ: Princeton University Press.

____. (1981). *Enterprise and Trade in Victorian Britain: Essays in Historical Economics.* London: George Allen and Unwin.

____. (1987). *Econometric History.* Basingstoke, Hants.: Macmillan.

Mirowski, Philip. (1989). *More Heat Than Light: Economics as Social Physics, Physics as Nature's Economics.* Cambridge: Cambridge University Press.

Morgan, Mary. (1991). "The Stamping Out of Process Analysis in Econometrics." In Neil De Marchi and Mark Blaug (eds.), *Appraising Economic Theories: Studies in the Methodology of Research Programs.* Aldershot, Hants.: Edward Elgar.

Parker, William N. (1973). "Through Growth and Beyond: Three Decades in Economic and Business History." In Louis P. Cain and Paul J. Uselding (eds.), *Business Enterprise and Economic Change: Essays in Honor of Harold J. Williamson.* Kent, Ohio: Kent State University Press.

10 What is American about American economics?

Introduction

The organizer of this symposium deliberately posed a sweeping, over ambitious open-ended question to which there is obviously no single answer. As the first contributor I am privileged, for I am not constrained by the fear of duplicating what my fellow symposiasts are going to say. The duplication, in any case, is unlikely to be great given my somewhat idiosyncratic approach, which focuses on the general intellectual and social context of economic thought, rather than on the development of economic analysis. There is, of course, ample scope for both, and indeed other, interpretative standpoints.

Are Americans and their experiences exceptional?

One obvious answer to the question "What is American about American economics?" is that it is a species of economics produced by Americans. Or, to adapt Jacob Viner's oft-quoted quip: " American economics is what American economists do (or have done)." This response is evasive; and it may seem trivial. Yet it raises a prior question: "What is an American?" – a question that has often formed the starting point of American Studies courses, and provoked endless debate. Much of this debate arises directly or indirectly from efforts to assess the impact and role in American history of the immense, irregular flow of immigrants over several centuries. In his late eighteenth-century *Letter from an American Farmer* St. John Crevecourt confidently asserted that "The American is a new man who acts on new principles" (Crevecourt [1782] 1981). If this is true, and applied to economics, it means the subject is culture-bound and not a universal science, as many economists want to believe.

Far greater thinkers than Crevecourt – such as Alexis de Tocqueville, James Bryce, and Frederick Jackson Turner – have tackled Crevecourt's question "What then is this new man?" This is not the place to review the endless litany of attempts to define "*the* American character," or to provide a comprehensive and definite list of distinctive American "traits." But before abandoning these very abstract and general issues, let me warn you against one familiar and superficially attractive idea – the notion of American "exceptionalism." Like "the American character," and "American traits," this concept can be formulated in a variety of ways designed to pinpoint America's uniqueness. But it can be a snare and a delusion. A recent extreme example of this is Dorothy Ross's *The Origins of American Social Science* (Ross 1991), in many other respects an admirably scholarly volume, in which "exceptionalism" runs riot. Ross refers to it roughly a hundred times in just over 500 pages, and in a mind-boggling variety of definitions and characterizations which I shall not try to enumerate here.[1] One is tempted to adapt George Orwell, by saying that all countries are exceptional, but some are more exceptional than others! The pursuit of exceptionalism will not help us here.

The question "Who is an American?" is relevant to the history of American economic thought as soon as we differentiate between those economic writers who were born, bred, and trained (if at all) and lived in the colonies or the United States, and those who were born and educated (though not necessarily trained) abroad before arriving in this country – usually, but not invariably, from across the Atlantic. According to Joseph Dorfman's encyclopedic five-volume survey, *The Economic Mind in American Civilization* (Dorfman 1947–59), there were more noteworthy foreign-born economic writers in the pre-Civil War era than in the 1895–1918 period covered in his third volume. This is surprising, given the vast increase in the flood of immigrants into the United States around the turn of the century (although the pre-Civil War period was, of course, much longer). In the twentieth century, especially during and after the 1930s, a considerable number of so-called illustrious immigrants came to the United States from Europe. Several became president of the American Economic Association (AEA), and the list of American economist Nobel prizewinners includes a number who cannot be classified as pure Americans – for example, Coase, Debreu, Harsanyi, Koopmans, Leontief, Lewis, Modigliani, and perhaps Hayek. Some, but not all, did their prizewinning work before they were permanently domiciled in the United States. And an earlier example is Schumpeter, who was a well-established professor in Europe before he migrated to America in the early 1930s, becoming president of the AEA in 1947.

Even in a large and rapidly growing professional community of economists this small band of outstanding immigrants (together with others – for example, Kenneth Boulding, J.K. Galbraith), located in strategic institutions, doubtless made a disproportionate impact on research, and probably also on teaching. But it would take a historian of Bob Fogel's boldness and ingenuity to demonstrate counterfactually what the state of American economics would now be were it not for the immigrants' contributions.

Some hypotheses

A number of competing, conflicting, complementary, or overlapping hypotheses have been advanced to account for the distinctive qualities and features of American intellectual history, some of which apply to American economic thought. The following examples are not necessarily listed in order of importance, nor should the amount of space devoted to each be taken as an index of its significance.

1 Among the general characteristics of American ideas and intellectual life identified by American historians are: distaste for "pure" theory and speculative ideas; preference for "practical" or "applied" ideas; lack of interest in and ability at construction of elaborate intellectual or doctrinal systems; lack of originality, especially with respect to fundamentals; prevalent broad sociopolitical consensus.

2 The United States made no progress in the development of the theory of political economy prior to 1876 mainly because Americans were too preoccupied with the urgent needs of a new society to devote themselves to original thought (Dunbar 1886).

3 However, it has been argued that a new environment stimulates novel ideas appropriate to the circumstance, and there is abundant evidence of this in the early economic literature (Fetter 1943; Conkin 1980). Indeed, there was probably an excess of originality, flexibility, and ingenuity, especially on policy issues. American economic writers were eager to break free from inherited European economic ideas, or to adapt them to indigenous needs and interests.

4 Overreadiness to modify or scrap existing ideas in response to some new intellectual impulses or the pressure of current concerns helps to explain the inability or reluctance to undertake sustained analysis. In the crucial formative phase of professionalization in the social sciences during the late nineteenth and early twentieth centuries, there was excessive product differentiation among American economics textbook writers that reflected the intensity of personal and institutional competition. Numerous commentators have noted the prevalence of hypercriticism or "super individualism" in economics (Laughlin 1906; Clark 1927; Norton 1969).

5 "Plus ça change, plus c'est la même chose." In a recent symposium on the question "Is there a European Economics?" (Frey and Frey 1995), a number of distinguished economists argue that American economists are more susceptible to intellectual fashions; more introverted, more academically oriented, more narrowly specialized (see below, item 6), and less tolerant intellectually than their European counterparts. (This is not based on a systematic opinion poll, but it has some echoes of earlier characteristics.)

6 The weakness and delayed development of theory is by no means peculiar to American economic thought. The American distaste for abstract and speculative inquiry, whether in philosophy, politics, or natural science, is a historiographical commonplace. (Religion, especially in the colonial period, may be an exception.) According to Daniel Boorstin: "this kind of knowledge which life in America made possible, precisely because it was factual and miscellaneous, required no preliminary training.... All knowledge seemed to come in small miscellaneous parcels" (Boorstin 1958: 162, 168). Curiously enough, when the late nineteenth-century revolution in American higher education occurred, the rapid expansion of university departments facilitated a high degree of specialization and compartmentalization of academic labor. This was not, of course, a uniquely American movement, but it seems to have

started earlier, and proceeded more rapidly and with greater enthusiasm than elsewhere. The combined impact of secularization, late industrialism (by comparison with Europe), urbanization, and modernization accorded with the desire to make knowledge serviceable (knowledge as technology, that is, ideas that "work").

7 The conspicuous early American intellectual achievements in empirical studies were directly dependent on keen observation and assiduous data collection. In producing works of travel or natural history, or in undertaking investigations in geology rather than, say, physics, American authors were less constrained by the European heritage, which was a source of strength in elementary work, but inhibiting to advanced thinking or research in more theoretical fields. This bias against so-called pure theory persisted long after the late nineteenth- and early twentieth-century expansion of the academic profession. Caustic critics have argued that when a sophisticated indigenous intellectual system eventually emerged – that is, pragmatist philosophy – it was little more than an elaborate rationalization of deep-rooted and widely held beliefs and values. Pragmatism, it has been said, has rested glacier-like "on miles of submerged conviction ... the American deals with concrete cases because he never doubts his general principles" (Hartz 1955: 59).

8 In the 1950s American historians emphasized the continuities and consensus features of their past. According to Hartz, the great majority of Americans have been liberals of one species or another. America never had a feudal aristocracy, and therefore did not need to develop a radical or socialist counterweight. The conflicts between American reformers and conservatives have lacked depth, "forever dissolving into common agreements," while Hartz's student, the brilliant British political scientist Bernard Crick, argued that this explained why American political scientists had consistently failed to engage in fundamental thinking about the nature of politics (Crick 1959). (Needless to say, this thesis was not welcomed by American political scientists!) Have American economists, likewise, failed to examine the fundamental nature of an economic system, relying instead on European authors (e.g., Smith, Walras, Hayek)? Does the liberal predominance help to explain the weakness of radical and Marxist economics in the United States? (Ward 1979). Hartz has said of pragmatism, "it is only when you take your ethics [or politics, or economics?] for granted that all problems appear as problems of technique" (Hartz 1955: 10). Does this shed any light on the unusual strength of formalism and technical skill in contemporary academic economics? (Some symposiasts in Frey and Frey (1995) argued that European economists were concerned with deeper issues!) (N.B. the term "formalism" is used quite differently in Morton White's (1976) stimulating, pragmatist-flavored account of American turn-of-the-century intellectual development.)

9 Daniel Boorstin claimed that in the colonial period, "American life quickly proved uncongenial to any special class of knowers" (Boorstin 1958), while Richard Hofstadter maintained that anti-intellectualism has been both powerful and endemic throughout the nation's history (Hofstadter 1964). Deference

and respect for intellectual, social, and political authority have been limited; and in a democratic and egalitarian society, "anti-establishment" sentiments have generally commanded widespread support.

In his influential education tract, The School and Society (Dewey 1900), John Dewey contrasted the impulse to create and produce with mere intellectual virtues. Separation of "theory" from "practice" threatened to perpetuate the division between "cultured" persons and ordinary workers. (This may underlie the distaste for "grand theory" which gives its originators undue influence and a sense of superiority to its followers.) In his Reconstruction in Philosophy (Dewey 1920), he made a comprehensive attack on "traditional" philosophy. The parallel with Richard Rorty's (1980) influential Philosophy and the Mirror of Nature is intriguing. (But this is no place to embark on a comparison between early and late twentieth-century American pragmatism, or its relationship to the philosophy and methodology of economics.)

10 Anti-establishment sentiments have long been sustained by geographical diversity and the persistence of regional rivalries (the Civil War being the most extreme example). In intellectual and cultural affairs there has been lasting suspicion, even hostility, between "east" and "west" (both geographically shifting concepts). The older eastern universities and prestigious liberal arts colleges have been seen as institutional representations of an elitist "genteel" tradition. By contrast, it has been said that in the newer state universities the main standards were quantitative, their main concerns were materialistic, their education bias utilitarian, and their outlook optimistic (Foerster 1937). Is it a coincidence that the founding triumvirate of the principal anti-establishment movement in economics – Veblen, Commons, and Mitchell – were all born in the middle west?[2] On the other hand, the growing size and representativeness of the AEA has operated as a unifying force – and also as a forum wherein intra-professional and doctrinal divisions can be aired.

11 It has been argued that the decentralization and competitiveness of American academic life has been a positive stimulus to the growth of scientific knowledge (David 1991). On the other hand, the number, geographical dispersion, and heterogeneity of American academic institutions has facilitated the formation and survival of minority and/or heterodox intellectual interests and schools of thought. In his History of Economic Analysis, Schumpeter (1954) remarked that the rapid growth of American higher education between 1870 and 1920 meant that employment opportunities in academia outstripped the growth of "fully competent personnel." Many of the new entrants were "practically untrained"; sharply divergent educational backgrounds and levels coexisted; and "for a considerable period of time there were no professional standards, and competent teaching was not always guaranteed" (Schumpeter 1954: 864). However, in the past half-century, circumstances have changed markedly. The recent report of the AEA's Commission on Graduate Education in Economics (Krueger et al. 1991) reveals the remarkable homogeneity and uniformity of graduate training in the discipline. This has been facilitated by

the expansion and increased efficiency of communication. The AEA has contributed to this general process.

12 Throughout American history (with the possible exception of the past two decades or so) the American intellectual and academic communities have been comparatively weak by European standards. This is in large part a by-product of the "practical" bias in American life, and the lack of respect for thinking rather than doing. Prior to the Civil War, and for a limited period thereafter, attacks on professors were usually based on charges of religious heresy. However, during the early phase of rapid university expansion (1870–1920), the social scientists, and especially the economists, were the primary targets of serious and well-publicized efforts to curtail academic freedom (Hofstadter and Metzger 1955). This generated what Mary Furner (1975) has called, in her classic study, the crisis of advocacy versus objectivity. Economists and other social scientists, in varying degrees, felt the need to be useful to society, while simultaneously seeking recognition as impartial scholars and/or objective scientists. For economists this often meant studying pressing contemporary problems and making constructive policy recommendations, which thrust them into the arena of public controversy. The extra-mural threats to freedom of expression and job security led to the development of a consensus about the limits of acceptable academic behavior. This necessarily involved the discouragement or repression of radical views, and, according to some observers, a surrender to the growing power of the corporate business interests. Comparisons between expanding universities and expanding business organizations have become commonplace (Veblen [1918] 1954; Barrow 1990).

13 This, however, was an unstable accommodation, which provided little protection for intellectual freedom during the two World Wars and after 1945 (Gruber 1975; Schrecker 1986). To a European, it seems curious, to say the least, that in a country where professors and intellectuals have so often been viewed as weak and ineffectual, they should also be seen at times as a powerful subversive force, against which brutal and organized suppression was justified. Extended pressures on the academic community in the post-1945 period led to widespread self-imposed restraints on freedom of expression, and may well have contributed, in economics as elsewhere, to the shift toward politically safer quantitative and technical work (Schrecker 1986; Lazarsfeld and Thielens 1958).[3]

Afterthoughts

In the preceding section I have deliberately concentrated on very general issues, in the hope of provoking discussion. The list of items is not, of course, exhaustive, and I have made no specific references to the history of American economic thought as such – in particular the hoary old question whether institutionalism is a uniquely American phenomenon. Other panellists may wish to take up this and related issues. (However, I cannot resist the comment that despite numerous earlier reports of its demise, institutional economics, both in its old and new forms, is nowadays enjoying a vigorous new lease of life – with exciting future prospects. Perhaps this is, after all, an example of American exceptionalism?)

Given the nature of this inquiry the foregoing account is necessarily somewhat sweeping and simplistic. Many qualifications are required, for example the distinction between academics and intellectuals. The organization of large-scale twentieth-century universities has, in many respects, been inimical to intellectual activity.

Notes

1 See my review of Ross (Coats 1992). The most recent contribution to this literature is Seymour Martin Lipset's *American Exceptionalism: A Double-Edged Sword* (Lipset 1996).

2 The idiosyncratic Texas-trained, Colorado-based institutionalist, J. Fagg Foster, viewed institutional economics as a direct by-product of the American frontier experience (Miller 1994: 257).

3 It is tempting to suggest that European academics have, generally speaking, enjoyed greater intellectual, political, and social freedom and security than their American counterparts. However, I know of no systematic comparative study of these matters, and Nazi- and Communist-dominated eras obviously constitute major exceptions to any such generalization.

References

Barrow, C. (1990). *Universities and the Capitalist State: Corporate Liberalism and the Reconstruction of American Higher Education, 1894–1928*, Madison: University of Wisconsin Press.

Boorstin, D. (1958). *The Americans: The Colonial Experience,* New York: Random House.

Clark, J. M. (1927). "Recent Developments in Economics," in Edward C. Hayes (ed.), *Recent Developments in the Social Sciences,* Philadelphia: Lippincott.

Coats, A. W. (1992). "Review of *The Origins of American Social Science* by Dorothy Ross," *Academe* 78(January–February): 43–44.

Conkin, P. (1980). *Prophets of American Prosperity: America's First Political Economists*, Bloomington, Ind.: Indiana University Press.

Crevecourt, St. J. ([1782] 1981). *Letters from an American Farmer*, Harmondsworth: Penguin.

Crick, B. (1959). *The American Science of Politics,* London: Routledge & Kegan Paul.

David, J. B. (1991). *Scientific Growth: Essays on the Social Organization and Ethos of Science*, Berkeley: University of California Press.

Dewey, J. (1900). *The School and Society*, New York: McClure, Phillips.

____. (1920). *Reconstruction in Philosophy*, New York: Holt.

Dorfman, J. (1947–59). *The Economic Mind in American Civilization,* 5 vols, New York: Viking.

Dunbar, C. (1886). "Economic Science in America, 1776–1886," *North American Review* 122(January): 124–154.

Fetter, F. (1943). "The Early History of Political Economy in the United States," *Proceedings of the American Philosophical Society* 87(July): 51–60.

Foerster, N. (1937). *The American State University: Its Relation to Democracy*, Chapel Hill, NC: University of North Carolina Press.

Frey, R.L. and B. Frey (eds) (1995). "Is there a European Economics?," *Kyklos*. 48 (2): 185–311.

Furner, M.O. (1975). *Advocacy versus Objectivity: A Crisis in the Professionalization of American Social Science 1865–1905*, Lexington, Ky.: University of Kentucky Press.

Gruber, C.S. (1975). *Mars and Minerva: World War I and the Uses of Higher Learning in America,* Baton Rouge, La.: Louisiana State University Press.

Hartz, L. (1955). *The Liberal Tradition in America*, New York: Harcourt Brace.

Hofstadter, R. (1964). *Anti-intellectualism in American Life,* New York: Oxford University Press.

Hofstadter, R. and W.R Metzger (1955). *The Development of Academic Freedom in the United States*, New York: Columbia University Press.

Krueger, A.O. et al. (1991). "Report of the Commission on Graduate Education in Economics," *Journal of Economic Literature*. 29(September): 1035–1053.

Laughlin, J.L. (1906). *Industrial America,* New York: Scribners.

Lazarsfeld, P. and W. Thielens, Jr. (1958). *The Academic Mind*, Glencoe, I11.: The Free Press.

Lipset, S.M. (1996). *American Exceptionalism: A Double-Edged Sword*, New York: Norton.

Miller, E.S. (1994). "J. Fagg Foster," in Geoffrey Hodgson, Warren Samuels, and Marc Tool (eds), *The Elgar Companion to Institutional and Evolutionary Economics,* vol. 1, Cheltenham: Edward Elgar.

Norton, H.S. (1969). *The Role of the Economist in Government: A Study of Economic Advice Since 1920,* Berkeley: McCutchan.

Rorty, R. (1980). *Philosophy and the Mirror of Nature*, Oxford: Blackwell.

Ross, D. (1991). *The Origins of American Social Science*, Cambridge: Cambridge University Press.

Schrecker, E.W. (1986). *No Ivory Tower: McCarthyism and the Universities*, New York: Oxford University Press.

Schumpeter, J.A. (1954). *A History of Economic Analysis,* New York: Oxford University Press.

Veblen, T. ([1918] 1954). *The Higher Learning in America: A Memorandum on the Conduct of Universities by Businessmen*, Stanford, Calif.: Stanford University Press.

Ward, B. (1979). *The Ideal Worlds of Economics: Liberal, Radical and Conservative World Views,* London: Macmillan.

White, M.D. (1976). *Social Thought in America: The Revolt Against Formalism*, New York: Oxford University Press.

11 Research priorities in the history of economics

The history of economic ideas occupies an uncomfortable position in the academic spectrum, in the interstices between the vigorously-expanding and rapidly changing disciplines of economics and economic history, and its present condition exhibits both ambivalent and contradictory features. While its pedagogical importance has unquestionably declined in recent decades, there has been a concomitant growth of research and publication; and, before considering the needs of the future, it seems advisable to indicate the main reasons for this curiously mixed state of affairs.

Most present-day economists are still guilty of that "provincialism in time" of which Lord Robbins complained so eloquently some years ago, notwithstanding their continued preoccupation with long-run economic growth.[1] The explosion of research and publication, and the economists' increasing involvement in business and governmental affairs, have combined to put such pressure on the curriculum that academic economists nowadays regard the history of their discipline either as an unnecessary luxury or, more frequently, as a wasteful diversion of time and energy from more immediately productive pursuits. The decline in the number of courses in the history of economics in the United States, recently noted by Donald Gordon,[2] has been paralleled elsewhere,[3] and only a bold prophet would forecast a reversal of this trend in the foreseeable future. Nor have the economic historians stepped into the breach, for they still generally prefer to explain their problems in terms of the "arsenic of practical motives" rather than the "spells and incantations" of economic thinkers.[4]

However, the state of research in the history of economic thought is much more encouraging than the teaching situation. The sheer volume of current and prospective publications is surprising, considering how unfashionable the subject is,[5] and in many instances the quality is high. The number of published articles in the field rose from around 30 per annum in the early 1940s to 45 per annum in the early 1950s and 60 per annum a decade later,[6] and there is a flourishing market in reprints and new editions of economic classics – an activity in which Augustus Kelley's entrepreneurship has been outstanding. Even more striking is the flow of recent and prospective editions of the works of outstanding economic thinkers, many of which are being sponsored by leading organizations of economists, as though they were trying to make amends for the deplorable deficiencies in their current teaching.[7] Yet studies of this kind, however distinguished, provide no grounds for complacency: they are not novel,[8] nor do they represent any new departure in the historiography of economics. On the contrary, they may be interpreted as evidence of the proclivity to ancestor worship which was once an occupational disease among economists. Too often, instead of providing corrective therapy, historians of economics have exacerbated the complaint either by ransacking the past for evidence of the antecedents of contemporary verities or by concentrating unduly on the immanent development of economic ideas as an autonomous body of theoretical knowledge. They have, moreover, tended to neglect the historical context and, more especially, the *uses* to which economic ideas have been put. The history of the economist's techniques (apart from statistics) has been almost wholly ignored, and one of the most distinguished scholars in the field has asserted, apparently without arousing serious opposition, that

> there is no objective meaning to the term progress in matters of economic or any other policy because there is no valid standard for interpersonal comparisons … and the same thing applies of course to all systems of political economy if we exclude from them technical excellencies or deficiencies.[9]

For the present writer this contention is altogether too nihilistic; indeed, there are clear indications that future historians of economics can perform a much more constructive intellectual function than their predecessors. Our conception of the subject must be revised in conformity with the economist's changing role in the modern world. Some of the traditional functions of courses and textbooks in the history of economics are now either obsolete or irrelevant, for as economists have become more confident of their scientific and public importance, the value of history as a device for transmitting to apprentices the beliefs and values of the scientific establishment has correspondingly diminished.[10] And as protracted disputes about fundamental issues of methodology, social philosophy, or ideology are less frequent and disruptive, the need to strengthen disciplinary loyalties by inculcating respect for one's elders and betters has also become less urgent. Admittedly, the history of economics can still provide striking examples of the limitations of the economist's knowledge and a valuable perspective on the current situation. But there are other, possibly more effective, ways of performing these functions; and it is arguable that the specialist (in, say, international or monetary economics) may be better equipped to introduce his advanced students to the doctrinal history of his topic than the general historian of economics, who has a wider and more important task.[11]

In the past far too much effort has been devoted to *Dogmengeschichte*, to the writing of histories of economics for economists, and the task of identifying the sources and tracing the changing interpretations of individual concepts or theories. Moreover, this work has frequently been undertaken either by graduate students seeking a safe thesis topic, established economists in quest of a respectable lineage for their pet ideas, or senior members of the profession hoping to find some diversion in their leisure hours or their retirement.

Research of this kind easily degenerates into antiquarianism owing to the failure to ask: *What* are the significant ideas, and *why* are they significant? And whenever such questions are posed, the answers are usually expressed in terms of *theoretical* significance, while references to the "influence" of men or ideas are rarely based on close or systematic study of the relevant period. Most historians of economics have lacked a sufficiently broad or explicit intellectual framework, and have consequently tended to treat their subject in a vacuum. They have been reluctant to study the emergence of economics as an intellectual specialism,[12] and its relations with philosophy, theology, ethics, politics, and the natural sciences, and have concentrated instead on the succession of particular theorems, theories, or individuals.

Biographers of great economists have rarely succeeded in placing their subjects squarely within the contemporary intellectual environment; but those who contemplate such a task must not underestimate its scope and complexity. As Wesley Mitchell remarked, the historian who studies a particular thinker must examine

> the type of problems the man attacks, his way of formulating them, what materials he had to work with, the general method he employed, the things he took for granted without enquiry, the grounds for the confidence he felt in his results, what use he put these results to, their acceptance or rejection by his contemporaries and the reaction of his scientific work upon social processes.[13]

Research of this kind demands a measure of commitment to the past which comparatively few historians of economics have been prepared to make; and when one moves from the individual case to a general interpretation of the development of economic ideas, the problem of perspective becomes crucial. Schumpeter, for instance, exemplifies one kind of distortion, for his positivistic ideal of an "objective" history of economic analysis was incompatible with his comprehensive interest in the "intellectual scenery" to which he devoted so much of his *magnum opus;*[14] and the outcome was almost schizophrenic. At the other extreme, a rigid and simplistic instrumentalist conception of the relationship between ideas and events vitiated Leo Rogin's attempt to identify and appraise the central policy orientation of the theories propounded by the great economists.[15] And yet his collateral aim of assessing the "validity" of their work in terms of the issues confronting them was a useful pioneering foray into virtually uncharted territory.

The time is not yet ripe for a comprehensive reinterpretation of the history of economics: too much of the groundwork has still to be laid. We must study the development of "applied" economics, the evolution of data, techniques, and tools, in order to trace the growth of the economist's knowledge (rather than simply his theory), before proceeding to examine the uses to which this knowledge has been put. When, if ever, have critical breakthroughs occurred, and what has been their impact? The Keynesian Revolution is an obvious case in point; but have there been earlier examples, and if not, why not?[16] There have been no crucial experiments in economics as in the natural sciences, but this does not mean that the only significant turning points have been purely theoretical ones. The interaction of ideas and events, of individual genius and environmental conditions, has been unusually complex in the history of economics, and studies of these matters offer an exciting challenge to scholarship; but they will be difficult and controversial, especially with recent periods.

For the present generation of scholars the most fruitful research topics are the relationship of economic thought to policy and the sociology of economics. In the past few historians have *systematically* investigated the ideas of even the greatest economists, let alone the supporting players and popularizers, partly because such studies are too time-consuming and too demanding intellectually. The propagation of economic ideas has been grossly neglected,[17] and there is an urgent need for careful research into the rise, dissemination, and impact of popular economic ideas – popular fallacies – and their relationship to the ruling "scientific" conceptions of the time. Systematic investigation of these problems would shed valuable light on those intellectual lags by which, according to Keynes, the ideas of defunct authorities have come to rule the world. And in addition to the process of communication between the scientific *cognoscenti* and the lay public,[18] we need systematic studies of the interregional and international diffusion of economic ideas.[19]

To the study of economic thought and policy, and the propagation and diffusion of economic ideas, the serious historian of economics can bring precise knowledge and understanding of the relevant economic ideas and a systematic interest in their development, matters on which general intellectual historians tend to be either superficial or downright incompetent. Studies of recent economic thought and policy are especially important because the economist's direct influence has latterly been much greater than in most earlier times. Fortunately there is some progress in this area, facilitated by the growing literature of memoirs and biographies by former economic advisers.[20] Yet, we urgently need more research into these questions, if only to advance the education of historians, whose notions of the nature and influence of economic ideas are lamentably deficient. Initially the most fruitful work will probably be done in detail, by starting from specific policy measures – edicts, executive decisions, legislative enactments, etc. – and attempting to trace their antecedents. Studies of this kind call for detailed knowledge of constitutional forms and procedures, channels of communication, and the activities of individuals and pressure groups. The results may be inconclusive, for the influence of ideas is diffuse and exceedingly difficult to identify, especially in a democracy (in a monarchy or dictatorship a thinker who commands the ear of the ruler or his mistress may exert a direct and immediate impact). At times it may transpire that economists have often been not only wrong but also unimportant and sometimes ridiculous.[21] Yet even here, knowledge is preferable to ignorance, although it will probably lead to the destruction of some charming myths, such as the story that the Eden Treaty of 1786 was the by-product of conversations between Adam Smith and Lord Shelburne during a coach journey from Glasgow to London.[22] We should not confine our attention to success stories, for abortive movements may also repay investigation, as, for instance, late-nineteenth-century bimetallism, an issue of international scope which posed fundamental questions of theory and policy and brought many of the leading contemporary economists into conflict both with their professional colleagues and with members of the public. However, a subject of this kind cannot be undertaken lightheartedly, for in addition to an investigation of contemporary monetary theory and the intricacies of a protracted and highly technical debate, it would require a thorough knowledge of monetary arrangements in a series of leading countries and an estimate of the probable consequences of any policy changes. Hence it would extend well beyond the conventional boundaries of the history of economics and would incorporate a significant proportion of the economic and social history of the period.[23]

In conjunction with studies of economic thought and policy, there is also an urgent need for research into the sociology of economics, a broad area ranging from the murky depths of methodology to the simple but tedious compilation of data on such matters as the changing content and functions of the academic curriculum or the employment of economists. Historians have displayed comparatively little interest in the nature and development of economics as an intellectual discipline, and those seeking fruitful hypotheses will find a rich mine in the early pages of Mitchell's *Lectures* and Schumpeter's *History*. At the more philosophical end of the spectrum we need to collate existing studies of the methodology of economics and the changing focus and significance of methodological controversy, with the aim of tracing the progress of economics as a science by comparison with the social and natural sciences and other intellectual disciplines with which it has traditionally been linked. Research on these lines is already under way on both sides of the Atlantic, but there is a real danger that it will be left to sociologists or intellectual historians, few of whom understand the economist's intellectual equipment and distinctive point of view. Work of this kind will enhance our understanding of the general historical significance of economics – its debts to theology and moral philosophy and its protracted (and largely unheeded) obeisances to the natural sciences. And indeed, on closer scrutiny, it may transpire that economists *qua* economists have made significant contributions to other disciplines, so that the balance of intellectual accounts is more favorable than we usually suppose.

Beyond this, we need more systematic analysis of the emergence of economics as an intellectual specialism – a "discipline" or "profession" – in relation both to the academic world and the public. Who were the "economists," and when did they become an identifiable body of experts?[24] What was their social background and education,[25] and how did this influence their work? How have their social activities changed – their clubs, associations and informal channels of communication – and when, if ever, have they constituted an "intellectual community," and with what effect?[26] What have been the qualifications for entry into the "profession" – if, indeed, there is one; and how have these requirements varied over time, and differed from those applicable to other disciplines and learned professions? Information on these matters would be directly relevant to studies of economic thought and policy by helping to clarify the nature of the economists' activities and their influence. It will also, indirectly, shed new light on the philosophy and methodology of economics, revealing the economist's distinctive intellectual equipment and the preconceptions[27] and patterns of authority[28] within the field. Research of this kind should be comparative in space as well as in time, and the possibilities are virtually endless.

The foregoing list of topics is by no means exhaustive; but it is sufficient to indicate that conventional editions of standard works, biographies, and histories of economic theory constitute but a small part of the task ahead. And as historians of economics venture more boldly into uncharted territory, we shall need to reexamine not only our methodology, historiography, and choice of relevant questions, but also our sources. After considerable experience on both sides of the Atlantic, the present writer believes that historians of economics should be thoroughly ashamed of the current archival situation, especially in Britain.[29] No serious effort has been made to preserve, catalogue, and disseminate information about the correspondence and manuscripts of even the greatest economists; and the situation is even worse if one seeks the minor figures – the also-rans, the near-economists, quacks, and popularizers.[30] A comprehensive effort to rectify this situation would be an enormous undertaking, and the preliminary task of defining the field would not be easy. Nevertheless a start must be made. Historians of economics should pool their knowledge and mobilize their collective influence to obtain financial aid for the establishment of registers of archives in their field. Bibliographical and reference services should be established to extend the valuable work initiated by Higgs, Hanson, and Black;[31] and more urgently still, we should initiate a crash program to trace and preserve surviving papers, including those of senior members of the profession. Let us hope that the inauguration of *History of Political Economy* marks the beginning of a new era in the history of economics.[32]

Notes

1 Lionel Robbins, *The Theory of Economic Policy in English Classical Political Economy* (London, 1952), p. 2.
2 Donald Gordon, "The Role of the History of Economic Thought in the Understanding of Modern Theory," *American Economic Review* 55 supplement (May 1965): 119–127.
3 For example in Britain. Among forty-one British degree courses in economics, the history of economic thought is now compulsory in only two, and optional in eight more. Cf. "Report of the Careers Advisory Research Centre," May 1968.
4 George Unwin, *Studies in Economic History* : *The Collected Papers of George Unwin*, ed. R. H. Tawney (London, 1927), p. 158: "It is an undoubted fact, says Voltaire somewhere, that spells and incantations are capable of destroying whole flocks of sheep, if accompanied by sufficient quantities of arsenic. This saying has always appeared to me to afford a suggestive introduction to the study of the influence of ideas, of theory, upon economic development. Not that the parallelism is altogether sound or complete; but it furnishes a useful corrective to a tendency which is as misleading as it is all but universal – the tendency to overestimate the active part which wise forethought and the deliberate pursuit of clear ideas has played in the economic history of nations. In the sixteenth century it is especially necessary to look behind the spells and incantations of theory for the arsenic of practical motives."
5 For a preliminary, and certainly incomplete, list of research in progress and forthcoming publications, mainly in British universities, see the *History of Economic Thought*

Newsletter, no. 1 (Nov. 1968), obtainable free of charge from A. W. Coats, Department of Economic and Social History, University of Nottingham, England.

6 The data are derived from the American Economic Association, *Index of Economic Journals*, vols. 3–5. These figures probably represent a declining proportion of the total number of articles printed.

7 Among the most important are the definitive editions of Walter Bagebot *(The Economist*, London), Jeremy Bentham (University of London), John Stuart Mill (University of Toronto), and the projected bicentenary edition of Adam Smith (University of Glasgow). The Royal Economic Society is sponsoring editions of William Stanley Jevons, John Maynard Keynes, Alfred Marshall, and Lord Overstone; the Scottish Economic Society's series of Economic Classics includes James Mill and Sir James Steuart (already published) and James Anderson, Thomas Chalmers, John Law, James Lauderdale, Dugald Stewart, and Robert Wallace; and the American Economic Association has supported a number of similar ventures.

8 The British Economic Association was originally conceived as a reprint society. Cf. A. W. Coats, "The Origins and Early Development of the Royal Economic Society," *Economic Journal* 78 (June 1968): 349–71. The distinguished ten-volume edition of *The Works and Correspondence of David Ricardo,* ed. P. Sraffa and M. H. Dobb, was initiated by the Royal Economic Society in the mid-1920s, and William Jaffé's monumental study of Léon Walras was under active consideration by 1930.

9 Joseph A. Schumpeter, *History of Economic Analysis* (New York, 1954), p.40.

10 There are some penetrating comments on the use and abuse of history in natural science textbooks in Thomas S. Kuhn, *The Structure of Scientific Revolutions* (Chicago, 1962), chap. 11.

11 What is the proper role of the history of economic thought in the training of economists? Readers of this journal might well answer, if they can, Donald Gordon's contention ("Role of the History of Economic Thought") that a graduate student faced with a choice between a course in the history of economics and an additional course in theory, technique, or applied economics, would be justified in rejecting the history course.

12 At first sight William Letwin's *The Origins of Scientific Economics: English Economic Thought, 1660–1776* (London, 1963) seems to be an exception to this generalization, for the author endeavors to show that "scientific" economics emerged at a particular moment of time. Yet by concentrating on the formulation of certain theoretical ideas, he not only wrenches them from their historical context but also neglects the relationship between theory and practice and between economic and noneconomic ideas.

13 Wesley C. Mitchell, *Types of Economic Theory from Mercantilism to Institutionalism*, ed. Joseph Dorfman (New York, 1967), pp. 6–7. Cf. William Jaffé, "Biography and Economic Analysis," *Western Economic Journal* 3 (1965): 223–32.

14 Schumpeter, *History*, especially pt. 1.

15 Leo Rogin, *The Meaning and Validity of Economic Theory. A Historical Approach* (New York, 1956). Intellectual biases of the kind displayed in the Schumpeter and Rogin volumes are not inevitable, and recently a more detached approach has been apparent. See, for example, Joseph J. Spengler, "Economics: Its History, Themes, Approaches," *Journal of Economic Issues* 2 (1968): 5–30. For a series of essays written from a sociology of knowledge viewpoint, see R. V. Eagly, ed., *Events, Ideology and Economic Theory: The Determinants of Progress in the Development of Economic Analysis* (Detroit, 1968). Unfortunately, I have been unable to obtain a copy of this volume before going to press.

16 Kuhn, *Structure of Scientific Revolutions*, is a fruitful source of hypotheses on these matters. Cf. the comments on Kuhn in Gordon, "Role of the History of Economic Thought," pp. 122–125, and A. W. Coats, "Is There a 'Structure of Scientific Revolutions' in Economics?" *Kyklos*, forthcoming.

17 There are, of course, some exceptions to this generalization. For example, studies of the "influence" of classical economists, such as S. G. Checkland, "The Propagation of

Ricardian Economics in England," *Economica*, n.s. 16 (1949): 40–52; Mark Blaug, *Ricardian Economics: A Historical Study* (London, 1958), chap. 7; and R. K. Webb, *The British Working Class Reader, 1790–1848* (London, 1955).

18 F. W. Fetter's *Development of British Monetary Orthodoxy, 1797–1875* (Cambridge, Mass., 1965) is a masterly example in this genre.

19 This subject has been seriously neglected by the insular British, but most fruitfully examined by Craufurd Goodwin and others. See, for example, Goodwin's *Canadian Economic Thought* (Durham, N.C., 1961) and *Economic Enquiry in Australia* (Durham, N.C., 1966). Also Craufurd Goodwin and I. B. Holley, *The Transfer of Ideas: Historical Essays* (Durham, N.C., 1968).

20 Two important American studies by participants in the policy-making process are Walter Heller, *New Dimensions of Political Economy* (Cambridge, Mass., 1966) and James Tobin, *National Economic Policy* (New Haven, 1966). Among studies of recent British economic thought and policy, two are of special interest: T. W. Hutchison's *Economists and Economic Policy in Britain, 1946–66: Some Aspects of Their Interrelations* (London, 1968); and Donald Winch's forthcoming "Economic Thought and Policy, 1900–1960" (provisional title). I have had the privilege of reading this book in manuscript. Another study of a different kind covering roughly this same period is Eric Roll, *The World After Keynes: An Examination of the Economic Order* (London, 1968).

21 See, for example, A. W. Coats, "Political Economy and the Tariff Reform Campaign of 1903," *Journal of Law and Economics* 2 (1968): 181–229.

22 Jacob Viner, *Guide to John Rae's Life of Adam Smith* (New York, 1965), p. 153. Cf. Simon Foley, "The Anglo-French Commercial Treaty of 1786" (B.A. diss., University of Nottingham 1966); also Bernard Semmel, "The Hume-Tucker Debate and Pitt's Trade Proposals," *Economic Journal* 75 (1965): 759–70.

23 R. D. Collison Black's *Economic Thought and the Irish Question, 1817–70* (Cambridge, 1960) is an outstanding example of this species. It was the product of nearly ten years' hard labor!

24 A start has been made by George J. Stigler, "Statistical Studies in the History of Economic Thought," *Essays in the History of Economics* (Chicago, 1965), pp. 31–50; also John B. Parrish, "Rise of Economics as an Academic Discipline: The Formative Years to 1900," *Southern Economic Journal* 34 (1967): 1–16.

25 See for example, A. W. and S. E. Coats, "The Social Composition of the Royal Economic Society and the Beginnings of the British Economics 'Profession,' 1890–1915," *British Journal of Sociology*, forthcoming.

26 For suggestive comparisons, see Warren O. Hagstrom, *The Scientific Community* (New York, 1965).

27 Much has been written on this theme ever since Thorstein Veblen's famous essays, "The Preconceptions of Economic Science," *Quarterly Journal of Economics* 13–14 (1899–1900): 121–50, 396–426, 240–69.

28 This subject can be approached in various ways. On a general level, see, for example, A. W. Coats, "The Role of Authority in the Development of British Economics," *Journal of Law and Economics* 7 (1964): 85–106. On the influence of editors, see the suggestive essay by Diana Crane, "The Gatekeepers of Science: Some Factors Affecting the Selection of Articles for Economic Journals," *American Sociologist* 2 (Nov. 1967): 195–201. On the influence of foundations, see G. J. Stigler, "The Foundations and Economics" in Warren Weaver, ed., *U.S. Philanthropic Foundations, Their History, Structure, Management, and Record* (New York, 1967), pp. 276–86.

29 This remark may appear ungrateful, for the writer has received invaluable assistance from various librarians, archivists, and private persons. However, the blame lies mainly on the scholars who have allowed the situation to persist. I have no experience of the European continent, but the situation in the United States is far better than in Britain, where there are no counterparts of the outstanding collections like the Ely papers in

Wisconsin, the H. C. Adams papers in Michigan, and the Seligman papers at Columbia; and the American Economic Association's records are accessible and well housed, though uncatalogued. By contrast, despite the existence of a library constructed to house Marshall's books, there are significant Marshall letters in Cambridge unrecorded in the Marshall Library, letters which a research worker can find only by chance. And the fact that some of Marshall's important early manuscripts have recently come to light after lying unnoticed for years requires no comment. See the Report by J. K. Whitaker in the *History of Economic Thought Newsletter* (1968), pp. 7–9.

30 After extensive discussions with historians of economics, and various bizarre personal experiences, I conclude that we live in an unreal world wherein the principal obstacle to research is not wilful destruction, but human irrationality. Precious historical documents survive the hazards of casual use as shopping lists or stuffing for carpet slippers only by accident or oversight. And yet, *mirabile dictu*, they do survive, and valuable caches are continually being uncovered.

31 Henry Higgs, *Bibliography of Economics, 1751–1775* (Cambridge, 1935); Laurence William Hanson, *Contemporary Printed Sources for British and Irish Economic History, 1701–1750* (Cambridge, 1963); R. D. Collison Black, *A Catalogue of Economic Pamphlets Published Between 1750 and 1900 and Now Housed in Irish Libraries* (New York: Augustus Kelley) forthcoming. Acknowledgment should also be made to the American Economic Association for its *Index of Economic Journals* and the prospective bibliography of economic essays in Festschriften and collective volumes.

32 The foregoing article is a substantially rewritten version of a paper presented at a conference on the History of Economic Thought held at the University of Sussex, England, in January 1968.

12 The first decade of *HOPE* (1968–79)

I

Any attempt to review the recent development, condition, and prospects of an academic discipline is an inherently hazardous, if not foolhardy enterprise. But as the flood of academic publications rises inexorably the need for survey articles also increases, notwithstanding their obvious limitations. The present exercise is, admittedly, personal and impressionistic rather than authoritative or exhaustive. Indeed, any effort to select seminal contributions or peak performances would be highly presumptuous; moreover it would expose the limitations of my knowledge and judgment and arouse the lasting animosities of those who consider their achievements have been undervalued! Nevertheless, in view of the encouraging revival of interest in the history of economics during the past decade or so, not only in the U.S.A. and Britain, it seems worth recording for posterity some features of the subject's organisation, content, and teaching, against the background of my somewhat injudicious programmatic observations in the first issue of this journal.[1]

II

Wise historians avoid the term 'origins' when describing intellectual movements, for genuine novelties are rare in the history of ideas, and seldom worth investigating in detail. However the risks are less daunting when considering a revivalist upsurge rather than a supposedly new departure.

During the 1950s teaching in the history of economics was manifestly declining on both sides of the Atlantic, and although there was a continuing, even increasing output of high-quality editorial and research publications, individual enterprise alone could not have reversed the trend. A scholarly movement is a collective phenomenon requiring leaders and followers as well as ideas. It needs an institutional base (or bases) and an 'invisible college' or communications network. Research provision is also essential, although where capital intensity and entry costs are low, as in the history of economics, the financial burdens constitute no significant barrier. But above all, it requires scholarly publication outlets and an organisational core, usually in the form of conferences and/or a learned society. In the present instance British and American contributions were complementary and mutually reinforcing – the British organised the first series of meetings specifically devoted to the subject and produced a *Newsletter*, while the Americans launched the first major periodical and provided the majority of personnel, both entrepreneurs and adherents. However, questions of priority are less interesting than the national differences of approach and response, which should be noted by students of the international diffusion of ideas.

In the British case the principal turning point was the conference organised by Donald Winch at the University of Sussex, in January 1968.[2] While the idea had evidently been germinating for several years, it was first seriously discussed at the University of Kent in mid-1966 during a Social Science Research Council gathering designed to explore that infant body's potential range of activities. Winch's main collaborator was R. D. Collison Black, and Lord Robbins functioned as a benevolent angel by consenting to chair the meetings. To those who had laboured for years in the vineyard in comparative isolation, the news seemed almost providential. Moreover, as it transpired, the Sussex conference exceeded the most optimistic expectations in terms of intellectual stimulus, colleagueship, and – rarer still – constructive ideas and effective action. An especially promising feature of the small, distinguished, and enthusiastic band of participants was the wide range of age and experience, which boded well for the future.[3] The most valuable fruits were three productive decisions: to hold another conference (which proved to be the second in a continuing annual series); to launch the *History of Economic Thought Newsletter* (the 30th issue of which has just recently appeared); and to undertake an ambitious Guide to Archive Sources.[4]

To readers of *HOPE*, the most significant incident at the Sussex meeting was the announcement that Duke University proposed to publish a new specialist history of economics periodical, a scheme which had been conceived several years earlier.[5] To some of those present this seemed a typically rash, over-optimistic American venture, especially when it became known that a similar plan had been abandoned a year or two earlier in Britain. Its initiators, Bernard Corry and Mark Blaug, had obtained the necessary assurance of financial support from a reputable publisher and had sounded out a number of eminent scholarly statesmen and journal editors, but with discouraging results. Some respondents were opposed in principle to the segregation of history of economics articles in a specialist publication on the grounds that they would be ignored by the majority of practising economists, thereby exacerbating the 'provincialism in time' already so serious a blight on the profession. Some journal editors also expressed misgivings, conceivably prompted by the prospect of additional competition for subscribers, arguing that they were always pleased to publish historical articles of sufficiently high quality. More important, however, was the unsatisfactory response, in terms both of quality and quantity, to Corry and Blaug's efforts to solicit papers for their proposed new periodical, which persuaded them that its long-term prospects were poor.

Against this background the Duke proposal encountered mild but understandable scepticism – albeit accompanied by sincere expressions of goodwill and promises of support. It was amusing to witness the successive British reactions, knowing but deflating. Initially there were counsels of caution and delay, followed by the suggestion that if the die was indeed cast then the editors should certainly confine themselves to one issue a year until the market could be tested – a recommendation countered by the information that Duke University Press stipulated a minimum of two issues a year as a condition of publication! However at this distance in time, and with the benefit of hindsight, it is an unqualified pleasure to congratulate the editor and his collaborators on the fruits of their initiative, and to give thanks for those who are willing to take scholarly risks against sound advice.

Since those heady early days the history of economic thought revival has gone from strength to strength. Progress has, admittedly, been modest in scale by comparison with some academic sub-disciplines, but it has been solid in substance and impressive in range and quality. The success of *HOPE*, and the rapid expansion of the History of Economics Society founded at Duke in 1974, have been partly attributable to the sheer size and resources of the American academic community, which make it relatively easy to enlist the critical minimum of effort and support required by new scholarly ventures. Subsequent developments in the U.S.A. reveal the differences between the piecemeal pragmatism and relaxed informality of the British history of economics gatherings and the scale, structure, and more competitive atmosphere of the American conferences.[6] On the British side there is still no formal organisation,[7] and there are no officers or recognised procedures for selecting speakers or meeting places. Nevertheless, to judge by the quality of the participants and the papers delivered, the results have been successful. With smaller numbers and careful selection of speakers the standards have probably been consistently higher than at the American meetings, and the programmes have been arranged with fewer papers and no assigned discussants so as to allow the maximum amount of time for informal comment and debate. One of the most striking features of the British gatherings has been their cosmopolitanism, for among an annual average of around thirty to forty participants there have often been scholars from at least eight or nine different overseas countries, a characteristic that may well be a testimony to the *Newsletter*'s effectiveness in making contacts and attracting support from widely scattered locations.[8] Members of the *Newsletter* 's editorial board, who meet as a group only at conferences, took the initiative with the Guide to Archive Sources project, and decisions whether, where, and when to hold future meetings are still taken in an *ad hoc* manner, the conference organiser merely being a volunteer who is prepared to make the necessary arrangements at his home institution.

It is easier to explain the momentum of the history of economics revival, once it got under way, than its timing. Correspondence and enquiries preparatory to the Sussex conference disclosed the existence of wider, more influential, and more enthusiastic support than had initially been anticipated.[9] There was direct and significant encouragement from the otherwise often inactive Royal Economic Society (R.E.S.), whose Publications Secretary, Austin Robinson, had long and vigorously supported scholarly editions of such major economists as Ricardo, Marshall, Keynes, and Quesnay. The unearthing of substantial caches of Jevons papers by Black, and Overstone papers by Denis O'Brien, had stirred the imaginations of other would-be treasure seekers; and it is fitting at this point to acknowledge the R.E.S.'s prompt and tangible support both for the *Newsletter* and the Guide to Archive Sources. Other motives underlying the enthusiastic response to the new initiative are revealed in the pre-conference suggestions designed to promote the cause, such as: the compilation of bibliographies, and a register of research in progress; the publication of documents and reprints; a review of teaching activities and prospects; and the exchange of other information of interest. There was, in fact, a marked contrast between the generally favourable impression of the quality, and even the volume, of research in progress, and the almost universally gloomy view of the likelihood of a revival in teaching.[10]

The precise timing of the renaissance is at least partly attributable to chance, although it has obviously been but one manifestation of a widespread, deeply held, and growing belief since the late 1950s and early 1960s that theoretical refinements, technical sophistication, mathematisation, and quantification in economics were being treated as ends in themselves. A revival of interest in historical, institutional, and other qualitative approaches both in the training of apprentices and in professional practice, represented a natural and healthy reaction.[11] Economic development was one fashionable postwar sub-discipline in which these dimensions had to be rediscovered after the failure of naive early postwar attempts to apply the latest theoretical models and techniques to the problems of backward economies without due regard to their political and cultural context. On a more philosophical plane, there was a parallel reaction against the vogue of scientism and positivist methodology which, like mathematical modelbuilding, had been oversold by some of its proponents. Well before the widespread public and professional concern at the apparent failure of Keynesian-type policies, which directly contributed to the recent so-called crisis in economics,[12] there was a burst of enthusiasm among older and middle-aged economists for the central message of Thomas S. Kuhn's enormously influential *Structure of scientific revolutions* (1962). Kuhn not only exposed the philosophical and methodological weaknesses of "naive falsification" (to use Imre Lakatos's expressive term) then being advocated by some narrow-minded young economists, but also revealed some of the limitations of scientific methods in the natural sciences, towards which generations of economists had been unduly deferential. His persuasive blend of philosophy, history, and sociology of science struck a responsive chord among leaders of the history of economics revival.[13] And if it was in fact a revolution rather than a revival – which seems highly doubtful – it was certainly an untypical one, since the initiative came largely from the middle-aged and older generations who were reacting against the excesses of the young. It was, in effect, a generation conflict in reverse.

III

How far, and in what directions, has the history of economics progressed since the inauguration of this journal in 1969? Has recent experience fulfilled the hope, expressed on that occasion, that a new era was dawning in our subject?

Opinions on this point will doubtless differ, and unfortunately there is as yet insufficient evidence on which to base a judgment. Those of us most closely involved can too easily be blinded by our personal and professional commitments, the flurry of activity around us, our manifest inability to keep abreast of the flow of new and forthcoming publications, and the well-nigh irresistible urge to self-congratulation. As in 1969, the healthy state of research and publication is obvious enough, and there does seem to be some evidence of the reversal of the decline of teaching in the history of economics which was so marked in the 1950s and 1960s. But the extent of that reversal is difficult to gauge,[14] and dedicated scholars sometimes regard the revival of interest in the subject as a mixed blessing.

As is well known, the much publicised 'crisis' in economic theory and policy since the late 1960s has encouraged proponents of a variety of un- or anti-orthodox doctrines and approaches, many of whom have uninhibitedly ransacked the past in search of authoritative pedigrees. The inevitable consequence, as Mark Blaug noted recently (in uncharacteristically circumspect terms), is that the history of economics "seems to be becoming the arena in which some of these controversial questions may be fought out."[15] Unlike animals, human beings exist in an 'extended present': our future is largely unknown, and when confusion reigns in the immediate present we frequently turn to the past for solace, reorientation, and even guidance. By drawing on the legacy of the past and 'standing on the shoulders of giants' we are supposedly enabled to see farther and more clearly. The effort to do so is a much more common practice among social than among natural scientists, of which Alfred North Whitehead once observed: "A science which hesitates to forget its founders is lost." But whether we approve or not, such forgetfulness is unusual among economists partly because – as students of methodology know only too well – there is no agreed and effective procedure for eliminating false or misleading theories.[16] Yet to use the past primarily as a source of solutions to present difficulties and discontents necessarily involves a selective and short-sighted procedure, which provides a weak and distorted foundation for historical research.

In this situation competent and broad-minded historians of economics can make a valuable contribution as guardians of the discipline's traditions, values, and standards.[17] Of course they do not always agree among themselves, nor are there any generally recognised criteria for accepting or rejecting conflicting interpretations of the history of economics or assessments of the great figures of the past.[18] Nevertheless, historians are often in a better position to make broadly balanced judgments about the current state, problems, and prospects of economics than busy professional practitioners, many of whom are myopically focusing on a narrow segment of the terrain. On some issues and at some times professional opinion is too rigid; at others it fluctuates erratically. With respect to the past, it can range from uncritical ancestor worship through studied neglect to the iconoclastic dismissal of past performances as irrelevant or even harmful distractions from more pressing current concerns. Hence in periods of storm and stress such as the 1970s, the historian (like the methodologist) may perform a valuable function as a kind of professional compass or gyroscope.

The opportunities to perform this service have undoubtedly expanded significantly in the past decade or so, even if it is admitted that the number of new courses in the history of economics has grown only modestly. There have, for example, been many more academic gatherings at which historians of economics have been able to display their wares – most notably, of course, the innumerable lectures, conferences, symposia, etc., directly or indirectly inspired by the Adam Smith bicentennial.[19] Many non-specialists have attended these meetings; and they are also to be found at the increasing number of specialist history of economics conferences, and in attendance at the historical sections which now appear more frequently on the programmes of national or international scholarly organisations.[20] One of the inherent characteristics of our field is its openness: there need be no insuperable intellectual barriers between the cognoscenti and the laity, hence there is ample scope for historians of economics to undertake missionary work. There is, of course, a concomitant disadvantage: our subject suffers from the defects of its virtues. While we can benefit from our broad and diffuse links with neighbouring disciplines, such as economic and social history, intellectual history, the history and philosophy of science, the sociology of the social sciences, and – through economic thought and policy – with public administration and politics, we necessarily suffer from the fact that too few of our practitioners are specialists. The subject is still too often regarded by students as boring, or a soft option; while too many regard it as a suitable twilight diversion for senior citizens. The field is neither substantial nor prestigious enough in the U.S.A. and Britain to attract and hold more than a few outstanding full-time contributors,[21] while the ease of entry makes it correspondingly more difficult to establish and maintain consistently high professional standards. The need to define and propagate such standards may well be the most urgent task facing us in the next decade or so, especially if there is a continuing urge to examine the historical antecedents of current debates or to apply the 'lessons of the past' to the problems of the present.

It is here that *HOPE*'s role is proving to be especially constructive. There is no evidence to support the pessimists' initial predictions that its advent would eliminate history of economics articles from the general economic journals.[22] On the contrary, it is well known that a new specialist periodical (and for that matter a new scholarly association) usually stimulates activity in its field by providing an added incentive for prospective contributors, a common focus of attention for interested parties, and a medium of communication between them. *HOPE* has already become an integral component of the expanding cumulative literature on the history of economics, and its pages must be studied closely by any scholar who proposes to discover, evaluate, and build upon established knowledge of the subject.[23] Moreover, as the quality of its articles has clearly exceeded the initial modest expectations, it seems legitimate to claim that it has helped to raise both the standards and the expectations of performance in the field. The fact that its contributors have included some of the world's leading economists has also done its reputation no harm.

Turning to more specific matters, there has certainly been no major conceptual or historiographical breakthrough in our subject since *HOPE* began – hence the editor's recent plea for more 'theory,' and his suggestive, but unduly neglected study of the scope for 'process analysis.'[24] Some of the intellectual energy which might otherwise have been devoted to these purposes has undoubtedly been absorbed by efforts to apply philosophy of science frameworks (i.e., Kuhn, Lakatos, and to a lesser extent Foucault) to economics, both to specific episodes and to the formulation of development patterns in economic ideas since the mid-eighteenth century. Estimates of the value of these fashionable exercises will necessarily differ, for some will maintain that historians of economics are better employed on other matters, such as: intensive studies of individual thinkers, both great and small; the refinement or reinterpretation of old or unfamiliar theories and the tracing of their influence; or the scrutiny and editing of hitherto neglected or recently discovered texts and documents.

Yet there is surely something to be said for bold experiments even if they do not lead to paradigm breakthroughs or the emergence of a new 'magnificent dynamics' for our discipline. A good case can be made for the claim that Lakatos's methodology of scientific research programmes has already proved fruitful in elucidating 'progressive' and 'degenerating' phases in the development of economic ideas.[25] Lakatos's approach is less vague yet more flexible than Kuhn's; and while his terminology and conceptual apparatus have been perceptively utilised by authors who would not regard themselves as *bona fide* historians of economics, there is also the genuine promise displayed in Joseph Remenyi's brilliant reformulation of Lakatos in terms of sub-disciplines, cores, and demi-cores.[26]

It is too early to assess the fruitfulness of Remenyi's bold new framework; but there is no denying the validity of his starting-point – the need to find some alternative to the conventional 'great man,' 'great theory,' or 'great school' approach when dealing with mid- and late-twentieth-century economic literature. The sheer volume and compartmentalization of this work makes it difficult, if not impossible, to present a balanced and comprehensive *tour d'horizon*. Further historians will, no doubt, draw thankfully on the growing number of surveys of contemporary economic thought; collections of major articles selected by committees; the invaluable review essays in such periodicals as the *Journal of Economic Literature*; and the occasional collaborative survey volume.[27] They will also be able to use the stimulating series of current intellectual biographies of contemporary 'great economists' – the Nobel prizewinners in the *Swedish Economic Journal*.[28] Nevertheless, without an adequate conceptual framework, there will be no method of identifying 'significant' contributions, and the links between the past and the present will be lost amid a welter of contemporary disputes and structureless description.

One obvious method of coping with the increasing flood of economic literature is by statistical methods, in which George Stigler has been the pioneer.[29] Many others have followed his lead, concentrating almost exclusively on the last two or three decades, and most of this work has provided links between the recent development of economics and more systematic research on the scientific communications network, the academic reward system, and related aspects of professional organisation and structure. Comparatively little of this research has yet surfaced in *HOPE* [30] but it seems certain to be of increasing interest to future historians of economics.

Two other recent innovations in our subject deserve special mention, one technical, the other historiographical. The first of these is the application of precise statistical methods to authorship attribution problems in economics, an approach initiated by D. P. O'Brien and A. C. Darnell.[31] While the scope for research of this kind is doubtless limited, there is no denying the fascination of the combination of literary detection and analytical sophistication involved. Indeed, it presents unusual opportunities for useful labour on early economic texts for economists who might otherwise be engaged in constructing oversimplified mathematical models of great economists' ideas.

The second species of innovation, historiography, illustrates the reasons why contemporary bibliographers often bracket the history of economics with methodology. Two current scholarly enterprises linking the two, and yielding valuable new insights and interpretations, are the studies of "The craft of the historian of economics" initiated by Warren Samuels at the East Lansing History of Economics Society meeting, in 1980,[32] and T. W. Hutchison's essays on various 'versions' of the history of economics.[33] From the former it is already clear that a systematic examination of a leading historian's work can not only reveal his underlying 'vision,'[34] but can also suggest methods and principles by which to organise the vast amount of relevant material, a problem that has severely taxed many thoughtful teachers of our subject. Ordinary mortals cannot be expected to emulate a Cannan, Mitchell, Robbins, or Schumpeter, nor perhaps should we aim to do so, but we can certainly learn from their example. Hutchison's work is potentially even more important, both to the cognoscenti and the economics profession at large. Despite the polemical overtones, which may deter some austere readers, his learned and penetrating historiographical exercises reveal abuses too numerous to relate, and provide abundant support for his contention that "the standards generally maintained in writing the history of economics, including contemporary history, may be taken as a reflection, or indicator, of how far economics is being pursued as a serious subject."[35] Thus the maintenance and enhancement of standards in our field, one of *HOPE*'s primary purposes, may indeed not merely discourage future wilful or unintentional distortions of the past: it may also help to raise the quality and moderate the excess of ongoing controversies about current issues.

IV

As noted earlier, the revival of interest in the history of economics has been a mixed blessing. Serious scholarship has been virtually swamped by promiscuous citations from past literature in support of arguments and prescriptions designed to shape current and future methodology, doctrine, and policy recommendations. Against this background, readers of *HOPE* will assuredly endorse Hutchison's appeal for "genuine scientific research," even if they do not fully share his profound concern about "the bad conscience and the evil apologetic" displayed by some "hired prizefighters engaged in contemporary controversies."[36] Few specialists would deny that the discussions of the past decade or two have generated some valuable new light, as well as an abundance of unnecessary heat; but they may find it difficult to agree on the nature and balance of the gains and losses. In compiling my own personal shortlist, the deficits would include: the unproductive quibbling about the exact definition and merits of various species of Keynesianism; the intense and protracted squabble among and between Marxians and Sraffians; and the interminable disputes about the interpretation of Ricardo's ideas and influence. On the credit side there is: the rediscovery of neglected earlier work on uncertainty, expectations, information, and the coordination problem; the more accurate and precise interpretation of Walras's general equilibrium theory; the re-examination of the antecedents and consequents of Keynes's ideas, including pre-1936 monetary economics; the reawakening of serious interest in subjectivism, consumers' and businessmen's motivations and behaviour, and Austrian economics; and the renewed appreciation of the need to incorporate historical time, technology, and institutional change into the main corpus of economic theory. On all these matters historians of economics have had, actually or potentially, constructive contributions to offer their professional colleagues. But alas, too often they have stood aloof, despite the plethora of historical references in recent controversial literature.

In concluding this selective review it is appropriate to reconsider some of the 'research priorities' mentioned in the inaugural issue of *HOPE* (which did not, of course, represent approved editorial policy). At first glance the findings of the De Marchi/Lodewijks investigation seem discouraging, for the pattern of submissions to this journal has remained obstinately conventional.[37] There has been no marked shift towards studies of the development of 'applied' economics or the evolution of the economist's techniques, tools, and data. Nor has there been any clear relative expansion of contributions on the relationships between economic thought and policy or the sociology of economics. There has, however, been much valuable research on some of these matters and the potentialities for future work are now much clearer and more promising than in the late sixties.

No attempt will be made here to review all these potentialities. But economic thought and policy deserves special attention because its range is so broad and fascinating and it is a field of continuing academic and public importance in which historians of economics have clear comparative advantages over other scholars.[38] The role of economists in government, to which an entire issue of *HOPE* was recently devoted,[39] is only one part of this territory – albeit an especially stimulating and significant part; and research on economic policy-making decisions, processes, and influences need not be restricted either chronologically or geographically. There is, for example, scope for *systematic* studies of mercantilist writers' contributions to policy in their varying capacities as intellectuals, propagandists, legislators, advisers, and public officials. More generally, it is time to shift the spotlight away from the 'great men,' who continue to feature so prominently in submissions to *HOPE*, towards some of the supporting players and popularisers, whose theoretical originality is limited by comparison with their practical impact. In an age such as ours, when the majority of professional economists are engaged in non-academic employment, it is appropriate to devote more attention to the uses to which economic ideas are put – to the propagation of economic ideas; the rise, dissemination, and influence of popular economic ideas (including fallacies), and their relationship to the prevailing 'scientific' conceptions at any time. This will, of course, necessarily entail a substantial broadening of the scope of our discipline, as conventionally interpreted. And so much the better, for it will bring historians of economics into closer contact with scholars in cognate disciplines, such as philosophy, theology, ethics, politics, sociology, and perhaps even the natural sciences.[40] It will, moreover, serve to emphasise the central position which economic ideas should, but as yet do not, occupy in intellectual history.[41]

Such a move need not entail any abandonment of perennial fundamental issues in economics, such as: the nature and limitations of the economist's knowledge and skills at any given time;[42] the linkages between economic theory (science?) and its practical applications; the extent of contact, interchange, collaboration, or conflict between academic (scientific or professional) economists and their professional counterparts in the real world, and with other intellectuals, businessmen, politicians, etc.[43] To advocate an anti-chronological approach in a journal devoted to the history of ideas may seem anomalous, but there is so much to be learnt from the lessons of the present, or recent past. Studies of economists' advisory, administrative, technocratic, and intelligence functions in modern large-scale bureaucracies – private and public, local, national, and international – are likely to be much more revealing of the past, current, and perhaps even prospective state of our discipline than many contemporary academic disputes. Recent experience has raised important questions about: the appropriateness or otherwise of conventional academic training in economics for those destined to spend all or most of their careers in nonacademic employment; problems of professional ethics and standards arising both within academia and beyond;[44] and the larger issue of the nature and extent of 'progress' in economic knowledge. There is scope for modest studies of the economists' changing attitudes towards themselves, their intellectual and professional peers, and the public at large; and for those with a taste for sweeping speculation, there is the question of the economists' place in the 'new class' which is said to be re-shaping present and future society.[45]

Reference to these multifarious and bewildering possibilities need not imply any denigration of traditional research in the history of economics. Indeed, a case can be made for further consolidation of existing territory, including the areas mentioned above, rather than a restless searching for even more ambitious innovations, for we are a relatively small community and we must not disperse our energies too prodigally. Parallels, extensions, or adaptations of projects cited earlier can provide full employment for readers of this journal for the foreseeable future, and this is a privileged prospect nowadays. There is every reason to expect in the years to come a continuing growth of interest and activity in our field, a sustained and hopefully rising quality of performance, and active colonising of the new territories recently opened up. This does not, of course, imply that there are no new fields to conquer. Indeed, to end on such a note would be to conclude a decade of *HOPE* with a counsel of despair.

Notes

In preparing this article I have had considerable help and advice from the following: P. Barucci, R. D. C. Black, M. Blaug, W. Samuels, K. I. Vaughn, and especially D. Winch and the editors of *HOPE*.

1 'Research priorities in the History of Economics,' *HOPE* 1 (Spring 1969): 9–18. It is perhaps appropriate to apologise for the predominantly Anglo-American bias in the present article, and to invite comments and supplementary contributions from other countries.

2 Six years earlier Winch had published a suggestive article, 'What price the history of economic thought?' *Scottish Journal of Political Economy* 9 (Nov. 1962): 193–204.

3 The participants included Winch, Black, L. Robbins, W. Barber, M. Blaug, M. Bowley, S. G. Checkland, A. W. Coats, D. Collard, B. A. Corry, H. D. Dickinson, C. D. Goodwin, J. R. Hicks, R. L. Meek, D. P. O'Brien, R. S. Sayers, G. L. S. Shackle, and A. S. Skinner.

4 This eventually materialised as R. P. Sturges, ed., *Economists' papers 1750–1950* (London, 1975). Plans for an updating are now under discussion. This is an appropriate point to ask: Why is there no comparable American compilation? Is this a reflection of the continuing undervaluation of American economic thought? Copies of the *History of Economic Thought Newsletter* can be obtained from the editor, Mrs. Jackie Wright, Department of Economics, Queen's University, Belfast.

5 The editor traces the antecedents back to the 1930s and emphasises the personal influence of Joe Spengler at Duke. A firm decision to proceed with the publication was made in 1967.

6 It should be noted that some readers of earlier drafts (who have not attended the meetings on both sides of the Atlantic!) have taken mild exception to this impressionistic judgment. It is appropriate to mention here the American counterpart to the *Newsletter*, the History of Economics Society's *HES Bulletin* edited by K. I. Vaughn at George Mason University, Fairfax, Va. It is in its fourth year in 1983.

7 As evidence of open-mindedness and adaptability it should be noted that we designated ourselves an "international organization" with alacrity once we were informed that this step would facilitate the attendance of Japanese scholars at our meetings!

8 Conference reports have appeared in successive issues of the *Newsletter*. The first ten volumes of *HOPE* contained nine articles originally delivered at the British meetings. Four more appeared in a special Jevons number of the *Manchester School* 40 (March 1972), and several papers from the Loughborough conference (1978) have appeared in D. P. O'Brien and J. Presley, *Pioneers of modern economics* (London, 1979). Among the many scholarly contacts established through the *Newsletter*, Piero Barucci of the University of Florence deserves special mention, for he has subsequently played a major role in initiating international exchanges of scholars and students, organising conferences, research projects, and publications, and editing the periodical *Bolletino di Informazione, Storia del Pensiero Economico*, issued from the University of Florence. Another energetic and successful Mediterranean entrepreneur in the History of Economic Thought is Professor Lazaros Houmanides of the Piraeus Graduate School of Industrial Studies.

9 In part this reflected the growing dissatisfaction with the existing state of economics which came to a head in the early 1970s. For a review of this episode see my article 'The current "crisis" in economics in historical perspective,' *Nebraska Journal of Economics and Business* 16 (Summer 1977): 3–16. For evidence of continuing concern and fragmentation of the discipline see the essays in Daniel Bell and Irving Kristol, *The crisis in economic theory* (New York, 1981).

10 The predominance of positivistic approaches to economics and the increasing emphasis on sophisticated mathematical theory and econometric measurements seemed, inevitably, to push the history of economics out of the curriculum, or at least into a very

subordinate place. For discussions of teaching in *HOPE* see Pedro Schwartz, 'Teaching the history of economic thought: report of a symposium at Bristol, 1973,' in *HOPE* 7 (Spring 1975): 112 ff, with an Appendix by Samuel Hollander; Vladimir G. Treml and Dimitri M. Gallik, 'Teaching the history of economic thought in the USSR,' *HOPE* 5 (Spring 1973): 215 ff. A systematic survey of the changing content of teaching in the history of economics during the past decade or so would be of considerable interest. See also note 14 below, and Vincent J. Tarascio's article in *HOPE* 3 (Fall 1971).

11 For a powerful defence of the role of economic history in the training of economists see Donald J. McCloskey, 'Does the past have useful economics?' *Journal of Economic Literature* 14 (June 1976): 434–61. For an attempt to apply a parallel argument to our subject see my 'Reflections on the role of the history of economics in the training of economists,' in *Studi in memoria di Federigo Melis*, vol. 5 (Rome, 1978). Unfortunately this has not yet had much discernible effect on the profession's structure and practice, notwithstanding the numerous comments by eminent economists on the desirability of more historical inputs in the training of economics students. Professional inertia and prejudice are not so easily overcome.

12 Cf. note 9 above for references.

13 Among the numerous attempts to discuss the relevance of Kuhn's approach to the history of economics in this journal see Bronfenbrenner (vol. 3); Kunin and Weaver (vol. 3); Karsten (vol. 5); Ben-David (vol. 7); Blaug (vol. 7); and Goodwin (vol. 12). For a comprehensive review of the issues see T. W. Hutchison, *On revolutions and progress in economic knowledge* (Cambridge, 1978), esp. ch. 11.

14 For evidence of recent changes in the number of history of economic thought books and articles published see Neil De Marchi and John Lodewijks, '*HOPE* and the journal literature in the history of economic thought,' below in this issue.

There is some evidence of an increase in the number of courses offered in the subject in the U.S.A. Cf. De Marchi and Lodewijks, ibid., citing John J. Siegfried and James T. Wilkinson. In the UK the number of courses rose from 2 (compulsory) and 8 (optional) out of 41 economics degree programs in 1968 to 7 (compulsory) and 30 (optional) out of 71 degree programs in 1978/9. Cf. Reports of the Careers Advisory Research Centre for those years. More recently Gavin Kennedy found that the history of economics was optional in 11 out of the 19 universities responding to his enquiry. More surprisingly, the subject ranked eighth in popularity out of 22 specialist options, above Monetary and Mathematical Economics! Cf. his 'Students numbers and choices in economics at UK universities, 1981–2 session,' available from the Department of Economics at the University of Strathclyde. The data are, of course, too slender to support any general speculations about cultural differences. A list of the countries – no doubt incomplete – in which there is evidence of a lively interest in the subject must include East Germany, Greece, Italy, Japan, Spain, Yugoslavia, and Australia, where a new History of Economic Thought Society (HETSA) has recently started its own *Newsletter* (copies obtainable from John Wood, School of Economics and Finance, Western Australian Institute of Technology, South Bentley, W.A.).

15 Cf. Mark Blaug, *Economic theory in retrospect* (Cambridge, 1978), p. xiii and also p. xii.

16 If evidence for this statement is needed, it is provided in Mark Blaug's *The methodology of economics; or how economists explain* (Cambridge, 1980), Part III.

17 This is clearly indicated in Hutchison, *On revolutions*, esp. chs. 8, 9, and 11, and, less directly, in Craufurd D. Goodwin's Presidential Address to the History of Economics Society, 'Toward a theory of the history of economics,' *HOPE* 12 (Winter 1980), esp. p. 618. See also Coats, 'Reflections on the role of the history of economics,' passim.

18 Of course in part these conflicts reflect the major contending approaches to economics, such as neoclassical, Marxist-institutionalist, etc. But in some cases they involve more general methodological criteria. See, for example, the fundamental disagreement in the following exchanges: D. P. O'Brien, 'Ricardian economics and the economics of David Ricardo,' *Oxford Economic Papers* 33 (Nov. 1981): 352–86; Samuel Hollander,

'The economics of David Ricardo: a response to Professor O'Brien,' ibid. 34: 1–22; and O'Brien, 'Ricardian Economics,' ibid. 247–52. Both these historians of economics would, I suspect, accept the designation 'neo-classical.'

19 There are valuable surveys of the vast literary output in Horst Recktenwald, 'An Adam Smith renaissance *anno* 1976? The bicentenary output,' *Journal of Economic Literature* 16 (March 1976): 56–83; and E. G. West, 'Scotland's resurgent economist: a survey of the new literature on Adam Smith,' *Southern Economic Journal* 45 (Oct. 1978): 343–69. Another major international occasion was the conference, 'Malthus hier et aujourd'hui' organised by Unesco and the Société de Démographie Historique, in Paris, May 1980. The mind boggles at the array of scholarly orgies to be held in honour of J. M. Keynes and K. Marx in 1983!

20 Among national organisations the American Economic Association has had history of economics sessions at several of its recent annual meetings. The sessions on Economic Thought and Policy at the quadrennial congresses of the International Economic History Association at Leningrad (1970), Copenhagen (1974), Edinburgh (1978), and Budapest (1982) are also of interest both as a sign of recognition and as opportunities for historians of economics to perform as *révélateurs*. Five papers from the Copenhagen meetings subsequently appeared in *HOPE* – four in vol. 9 (Spring 1977) and one in vol. 10 (Summer 1978).

21 However the numbers 'interested' are by no means insignificant. The History of Economics Society now has about 570 members; the *Newsletter* about 370 subscribers; and in the A.E.A.'s 1978 Handbook 310 members listed the history of economics as one of their sub-fields. (The comparable number in 1964 was 300.) The subject is taught in one form or another in about 50 Italian universities, where there are specialist chairs. See also the report on the thirtieth anniversary of the Society for the History of Economic Thought (Japan), with its 700 members in about 180 colleges and universities, in the *HES Bulletin* 3 (Winter 1982) : 23–26.

22 Cf. De Marchi and Lodewijks' article below in this issue for relevant data.

23 Although the *Journal of Economic Literature*, the AEA *Index*, and the occasional lists of recent publications in the *Newsletter* provide some coverage, there is a need for a more regular and systematic international bibliographical service for historians of economics. There is a valuable bibliographical essay on the History of Economic Thought by R. D. Collison Black in John Fletcher, ed., *The use of economic literature* (London, 1971). A revised version will appear in Fletcher, ed., *Information sources in economics* (London, 1983).

24 See note 17 above, and his 'Economic theory and society: a plea for process analysis,' *American Economic Review* 2 (May 1972): 409–15. Two broadly suggestive background articles are Warren J. Samuels, 'The history of economic thought as intellectual history,' *HOPE* 6 (Fall 1974): 305–23, and Vincent J. Tarascio, 'Intellectual history and the social sciences: the problem of methodological pluralism,' *Social Science Quarterly* 56 (June 1975): 37–54.

25 Cf. the initial attempts to apply Lakatos's approach in Spiro Latsis, ed., *Method and appraisal in economics* (Cambridge, 1974). For very mixed reactions see Lord Robbins's 'Review essay,' *Journal of Economic Literature* 17 (Sept. 1979): 996–1004; and the 'Review symposium' by Douglas W. Hands, G. C. Archibald, and Joseph Agassi in *Philosophy of the Social Sciences* 9 (1979): 293–303.

26 'Core demi-core interaction: toward a general theory of disciplinary and subdisciplinary growth,' *HOPE* 11 (Spring 1979): 30–63.

27 For example, Sidney Weintraub, ed., *Modern economic thought* (Philadelphia, 1977). The two-volume *Surveys of Contemporary Economics* published under the auspices of the AEA in 1948 and 1952 are now of considerable historical value, as are the *Survey of Economic Theory* and *Survey of Applied Economics* sponsored jointly by the AEA and RES in the 1960s and 70s.

28. These are to be reprinted, together with other biographical essays on recent economists, by Warren Samuels and H. W. Spiegel, as a sequel to H. W. Spiegel's well-known collection *The development of economic thought* (New York, 1964).

29 See 'Statistical studies in the history of economic thought' in his *Essays in the history of economics* (Chicago, 1965), pp. 31–50; 'The citation practices of doctorates in economics,' *Journal of Political Economy* 83 (1975): 477–507 (with Claire Friedland); and 'The literature of economics: the case of the kinked oligopoly demand curve,' *Economic Inquiry* 16 (April 1978): 185–204; reprinted in his *The economist as preacher* (Chicago, 1982). See also note 30 below.

30 Cf. Robert V. Eagly, 'Contemporary profile of conventional economists,' *HOPE* 6 (Spring 1974): 76–91; Michael David Bordo and Daniel Landau, 'The pattern of citations in economic theory, 1945–68: an exploration towards a quantitative history of thought,' *HOPE* 11 (Summer 1979): 240–53; George J. Stigler and Claire Friedland, 'The pattern of citation practices in economics,' *HOPE* 11 (Spring 1979): 1–20. Articles on these subjects have also appeared in the *American Economic Review, Canadian Journal of Economics, Journal of Economic Literature, Journal of Political Economy, Public Choice, Quarterly Review of Economics and Business, Southern Economic Journal*, and the *Western Economic Journal* (now *Economic Inquiry).*

31 See their book, *Authorship puzzles in the history of economics: a statistical approach* (London, 1982), containing studies of Child, Torrens, McCulloch, Bailey and Huskisson and various articles in the nineteenth-century literary reviews; also their exchange with William O. Thweatt in *HOPE* 12 (Fall 1980).

32 A collection of essays under this title, edited by Warren Samuels, will be published by the J.A.I. Press.

33 Hutchison, *On revolutions*, chs. 5, 8, and 9, examines Keynesian, revolutionary, and traditional versions of the history of economics.

34 An instructive example is Spengler, whose 'vision' is difficult to grasp, despite the volume of his writings, partly because he has never produced a general survey or text-book. Jacob Viner is a somewhat similar case.

35 Hutchison, *On revolutions*, p. 276.

36 The words quoted are from Karl Marx, *Capital* vol. 1 (Moscow, 1961), p. 15, cited by Hutchison, *On revolutions*, p. 227.

37 Cf. their Table 4; also their Tables 1 and 2, which reveal the heavy concentrations on English-language, especially British, topics, and familiar themes.

38 Valuable recent works, illustrating the variety of available approaches, include W. Barber, *British economic thought and India, 1600-1858* (Oxford, 1975); S. Ambirajan, *Classical political economy and British policy in India* (Cambridge, 1978); Barry Gordon, *Political economy in Parliament, 1819–1823* (London, 1976); Boyd Hilton, *Corn, cash, commerce: the economic policies of the Tory governments, 1815–1830* (Oxford, 1977); Susan Howson and Donald Winch, *The Economic Advisory Council, 1930–1939: a study in economic advice during depression and recovery* (Cambridge, 1977); Barry Gordon, *Economic doctrine and Tory liberalism, 1824–1830* (London, 1979); and Frank W. Fetter, *The economist in Parliament, 1780–1868* (Durham, N.C., 1980). There is ample scope for parallel studies of other periods and countries.

39 See *HOPE*, vol. 13, which contains useful bibliographies and suggestions for further research. Also Laughlin Currie, *The role of the economic adviser in developing countries* (Westport, Conn., 1981), a volume that is less general than its title suggests.

40 An unusual but fascinating example of collaboration is the American Academy of Arts and Sciences' project on the growth of knowledge. See Alexandra Oleson and Sanborn C. Brown, eds. *The pursuit of knowledge in the early American Republic: American scientific and learned societies from colonial limes to the Civil War* (Baltimore, 1976); and Alexandra Oleson and John Voss, *The organization of knowledge in modern*

America, 1860–1920 (Baltimore, 1979). The latter volume includes a chapter by Dorothy Ross on the social sciences. Economics will be treated separately in the next volume, on the 1920–70 period.

41 See, for example, John Higham and Paul K. Conkin, *New directions in American intellectual history* (Baltimore, 1979); also the valuable review of the issues by Warren Samuels in *HOPE*, vol. 6, referred to in note 24 above.

42 There is, incidentally, no up-to-date general study of the history of economic methodology. See, for example, the brief survey in Blaug, *Methodology of economics*, Part II; also the forthcoming volume of essays in honour of T. W. Hutchison, *Methodological controversy in economics: historical essays*, ed. A. W. Coats (Greenwich, CT, 1983).

43 The public-relations dimensions of economics have never been systematically studied – e.g., the attitudes of businessmen to the economics profession; the growth and influence of economic and financial journalism; and the vital connecting links between academic economics and politics – on which there is, of course, a considerable volume of particularised and anecdotal material. There is growing literature on the professionalisation of economics and the social sciences, much of which is of direct interest to historians of economics. For example, Burton Bledstein, *The culture of professionalism: the middle class and the developments of higher education in America* (New York, 1976); Mary O. Furner, *Advocacy and objectivity: a crisis in the professionalization of American social science* (Lexington, Ky., 1975); Thomas L. Haskell, *The emergence of professional social science: the American Social Science Association and the nineteenth-century crisis of authority* (Urbana, III., 1977); and a suggestive comparative Anglo-American study, Magali Sarfatti Larson, *The rise of professionalism: a sociological analysis* (Berkeley and Los Angeles, 1977). In comparison with the literature on the development of sociology, there is little on the economics profession. See, however, my essays, 'The development of the economics profession in England: a preliminary review' in L. Houmanidis, ed., *International Congress of Economic History and History of Economic Theories* (Piraeus, 1975), pp. 277–290; 'Methodology and professionalism in economics: a subordinate theme in Machlup's writings,' in Jacob S. Dreyer ed., *Breadth and depth in economics: Fritz Machlup – the man and his ideas* (Lexington, Mass., 1978), pp. 23–35; and *Reflections on the professionalisation of economics*, University of Newcastle, N.S.W., Australia, 1980. The late Harry G. Johnson was one of the most vigorous and perceptive recent commentators on the state of the economics profession.

44 Among historians of economics, the most consistently penetrating commentator on these matters during the past two decades has been T. W. Hutchison. See, for example, his *'Positive' economics and policy objectives* (London, 1964); *Economics and economic policy in Britain, 1946–1966: some aspects of their interrelations* (London, 1968); *Keynes versus the 'Keynesians' ... ?* (London, 1977); *Knowledge and ignorance in economics* (Oxford, 1977), esp. chs. 1, 2, and 5; and *The politics and philosophy of economics* (New York, 1981).

45 Cf. Alvin Gouldner, *The future of intellectuals and the rise of the new class* (New York, 1979). This is a familiar theme in the literature of post-industrial societies.

13 Economics, history and HOPE

I. A personal note

Though nominally an economic and social historian for most of my academic career, the history of economics has always been my real intellectual haven, and I cannot refrain from saying how privileged I feel to have been President of this Society – small though we are amid the great national and multinational conglomerates. Moreover, that sentiment is all the more pure and unalloyed now that the arduous task of organizing the annual meeting is well behind me.

Despite the emotional aspect of my present situation, as a committed observer of the sociology of academic life I cannot avoid a sense of detachment, as I view this familiar ritual of the learned community, one that tempers uninhibited opportunity with responsibility.

The nearest equivalent in my experience was the delivery of an inaugural lecture over twenty years ago, a ritual now sadly almost defunct in British universities. It is a strange ceremony, for the lecturer may be either a comparative newcomer, and therefore an object of curiosity to many in his audience or, alternatively, a long standing colleague who has risen through the local non-professional ranks, and whose special preoccupations and prejudices sometimes merit the contempt born of over-familiarity. I leave you to judge whether this hazard is avoided in the present instance.

I began my inaugural by citing my predecessor, J. D. Chambers, a distinguished and entertaining economic historian – a rare example of the breed, as you will appreciate – who had described an inaugural as a privileged occasion when the lecturer should perhaps bait the *cognoscenti* without boring the laity, if necessary throwing his cap over the windmill with the assurance that his chair would not be required to follow.

Since the present audience mostly consists of *congnoscenti*, I feel free both to bait and to bore without discriminating.

But before turning at last to my theme, let me offer another footnote to my inaugural, putting the occasion in an appropriately humble perspective. My lecture was subsequently included in an comprehensive collection of economic history inaugurals delivered in Britain[1] – no great distinction, in that: completeness not quality was the criterion; whereupon a long suffering nonprofessorial reviewer seized his chance eagerly. The moral of this volume, he pronounced, is clear: if you become a professor, don't give an inaugural; if you have to give an inaugural, don't publish it; if you are obliged to publish it, above all don't allow it to be reprinted! The sound of deflating academic egos was clearly audible.

II. The status of HOPE

Turning to more serious matters, how can I bait the *congnoscenti* while preserving whatever scholarly dignity attaches to this occasion? It would be pretentious to claim that the solution was heaven-sent – I prefer the terms contingent and context-dependent, currently fashionable among historians and sociologists of science; and it takes the form of an unfortunate statement by a personal friend, the eminent Yale economic historian, William R. Parker, past President of the Economic History Association and a leading authority on the historiography of American economic history, in the introduction to his newly published collection of essays on *Economic History and the Modern Economist*.[2] The authors include such luminaries as Kenneth Arrow, Robert Solow, Paul David, Peter Temin, Donald McCloskey, Walt Rostow, Gavin Wright, and Charles Kindleberger, in order of appearance. The blurb by James Tobin expressly praises the introductory "history of economics in a nutshell," and I shall not consider whether that evaluation is or is not warranted. The real shock comes with Bill Parker's observation that whereas economic history is "clearly an endangered species in modern economics programs… the history of economic thought…[which] once formed a part of the basic culture of every economist, is now almost completely defunct."[3]

I cite this passage not in order to belittle the author, for whom I have great respect and affection; nor yet as a prelude to citing our private correspondence, after he had generously sent me a pre-publication copy of the page proofs. Our presence here seems to afford about as conclusive a falsification of his empirical hypothesis as we are likely to get in the human sciences. My purpose is, rather, to ask you as directly and forcefully as possible: if an intelligent and usually well-informed observer can make a statement like that, **What the hell have we been doing in this Society the past few years?** I assume, in a spirit of generosity, that none of Parker's co-authors saw his introduction in advance of publication. But Tobin cannot be so exonerated; and there is the additional irony that he was one of the five distinguished authors especially commissioned by the AEA to write on early American economics in last December's centenary celebration issue of the *AER*.[4] Only one of those five, Martin Bronfenbrenner, was a recognized historian of economics (and also a past President of this Society). Why this was the case I leave you to judge.

I recite this sorry tale neither in order to convert this otherwise happy occasion into a wake, nor simply to complain that we are undeservedly neglected and undervalued – though this is certainly the case. We should not be too despondent. One swallow does not make a summer, so they say; and two Yale economists do not make a winter of discontent. The point is: **What are we going to do about it?** To say we have for too long been hiding our intellectual light under a bushel is simply a gross bit of British understatement. We have come a long way since Benjamin Ward placed us on the lowest level of his provisional hierarchy of economic fields fifteen years ago;[5] and we can derive no satisfaction from the current troubled state of economic history, which he placed one level above us. The two fields are interdependent and should be collaborating more actively, although they necessarily compete for scarce time and space in the already overcrowded economics curriculum.

In the brief time your patience may allow I offer a call to arms, rather than a calculated review of the past history, present condition, and future prospects of our subdiscipline – although as I shall try to indicate later, I firmly believe the prevailing intellectual so. Nevertheless I admit that, like the economist who is skilled in explaining tomorrow why what he predicted yesterday did not happen today, I have been waiting some time for the inevitable to occur.

Certainly there are few quick gains to be made: the forces of inertia in the academic community are far too strong. Admittedly in the case of economics there is a potential army of allies (the military metaphor once again) outside the groves of academe, among the innumerable economists working in business, banking, the press, government and international agencies.[6] Many of them share our feeling that economics has become far too narrow, technical and myopic. Nevertheless we must recognize the strength of the opposition, for many of those ivory tower economists in positions to affect key decisions about such matters as: the range of courses offered; departmental requirements; the choice of suitably 'professional' dissertation topics; which departmental vacancies should be filled; promotion and tenure; – received their training before the early 1970's in an era of professional *hubris*, when confidence in positive (or positivist) economics, mathematization, and quantification was riding high. This, incidentally, is a reminder of the generation factor in the development of academic disciplines, an element hitherto unduly neglected by historians.

Facing these odds, which will at times seem overwhelming, I firmly believe we must move actively, even aggressively, and proselytize on behalf of our subject in the academic corridors of power, over coffee and at lunch, in departmental meetings, at general conferences of economists, in the journals, or wherever we might get a sympathetic hearing. We need firm evidence in support of our case, such as the ever burgeoning number of papers at these meetings, the number of publications in our field, specific illustrations of the historical antecedents and counterparts of present professional concerns, etc. As a society we need to compile a comprehensive list of courses currently offered and, obversely, a 'hit list' of institutions where the subject is lacking – though I doubt we can go as far as the AAUP in censuring the delinquents! Some data on these matters have been compiled for Britain and, more recently, for Germany – as shown in Jurgen Backhaus's valuable recent paper in our *Bulletin*.[7] Why have the Americans been so backward, as with the oft-mentioned proposal to record the archives of leading American economists?

One reason why Bill Parker failed to appreciate the gains we have made since this Society was formed, although he is (or was) a member, is that his eyes were probably focused on the handful of so-called elite universities, especially the Ivy League. He is of course correct in noting that the number of required courses in the field dropped considerably from the 1950's, although it has probably recovered more recently. He is also right in saying there are now few full-time positions in the field – at least in Anglo-Saxon countries – and that if the history of economic thought "is to be studied and taught well, [it] requires considerable philosophical depth and is, in fact, a sub-field of intellectual, rather than social history."[8] Yet there are gains as well as losses, for the typical historian of economics now is also a specialist in one or two subfields of economics as well as in doctrinal history, and he (or she) is on the average far better-equipped in theory and technique than his (or her) predecessors of yesteryear, as I can attest from personal experience. And, I would argue on the basis of the papers given at these meetings, the field is now often being treated with much greater methodological sophistication and philosophical depth than was the case a few years ago. This is one of the by-products of the troubled state of economics, of which we have heard so much.

What is gained from closer contact with economists, and by implication, greater opportunities to influence the orthodox curriculum, has been partially offset by the divorce from general intellectual, social, and economic history, a situation far less unavoidable than is generally supposed. To discuss this aspect properly would take me too far into the problem of serving two or more sets of professional collegues. It is enough for the present to concentrate on our role in relation to economists, both aspiring professionals and more general students. However, with respect to the broader issue of intellectual history let me first simply refer to the most ambitious project in the history of economics the world has ever seen, some by-products of which appeared in one session of the 1986 conference.[9] I use this immodest description unashamedly, for I was neither one of the initiators, nor an organizer, but initially a sceptic. Now, as a convert, after a major conference in Italy two months ago involving some 60 persons and 70 papers from 12 countries, I can confidently predict that the five projected volumes from the first stage of this undertaking, organized concurrently from Cambridge (UK), Paris, and Florence, will eventually yield, from a mass of sometimes boring detail, some striking generalizations about the intellectual, social, political, and economic context of the introduction and acceptance of political economy in European, British, American, and Japanese universities.[10] In due course I hope it will lead to further instalments carrying the story into the twentieth century and beyond World War II, and that special attention will be paid to the professionalization of economics both within and outside educational institutions, a process that had hardly begun seriously before the end of the last century, of the terminal date for more of the studies currently under way.

III. HOPE and its neighbors

At this point it would be appropriate to outline some of the arguments historians of economics can use in trying to persuade economists of the importance of our subject in the training of economists, but there is an accessible and probably familiar literature on this subject.[11] Therefore, instead of going over this ground yet again, I shall devote the rest of my time to elaborating and, I trust, justifying my earlier assertion that the prevailing intellectual currents are now more decisively in our favor than at any time in the past two decades. The grounds for this contention are various, and cannot be presented fully here. Moreover I shall not indulge in bibliometrics, though in each instance a sufficient number of supporting illustrations and weighty opinions could be provided to suggest that the matter should be taken seriously.

One of my principal aims is to suggest that historians of economics can draw upon their links with the community of historians in enhancing their role in the economics curriculum.

1) Having criticized part of the introduction to Parker's collection let me commend the volume as a valuable compendium of arguments in favor of a historical input into the economics curriculum, many of which apply with equal force to the history of economics and economic history. Numerous other economists and social scientists have been acknowledging the historicity of economics as a discipline, and the historical character and context of economic ideas and activities, and I shall spare you a catalogue of citations some of which, admittedly, amount to little more than pious platitudes and unsupported *obiter dicta*.

2) On a much broader plane, recent writings on economic methodology and in the now interrelated fields of the history, philosophy, and sociology of science, have demonstrated a marked trend away from the (now largely discredited) positivist (or logical empiricist) view of science towards a much more open, flexible, and historically-oriented conception of the nature and development of scientific knowledge, broadly defined as including the natural, social and human sciences.[12] By far the most influential single text in this movement has, of course, been T.S. Kuhn's *The Structure of Scientific Revolutions*, which compelled a fundamental re-examination of the relationships between the socio-historical development of scientific schools, professions and institutions, and the intellectual development of scientific theories themselves.[13] Although he has been severely criticized, Kuhn has been given a disproportionate share of the credit for subsequent developments; but the fact that such names as N. Hanson, S. Toulmin, M. Polanyi, K. Popper, I. Lakatos, P. Feyerabend, P. Duhem, and W. Quine are now familiar to many in this audience is an indication of the extent to which our interests have broadened and deepened since *HOPE* Vol. 1 appeared, in 1969. Whether we have fully assimilated and applied the lessons and insights of this growth of knowledge movement – apart from the aformentioned shift in economic methodology and various abortive efforts to develop general theories of the evolution of economics – is another matter. Nevertheless these ideas and the controversies surrounding them have permeated into economics, the most tightly insulated of the social science disciplines. And I firmly believe this influence will grow in the future.

3) I shall not submit here yet another plea for a more non-deterministic sociological approach to our subject. Instead, I wish to emphasize the implications of the growth of knowledge movement for our conception of modeling or theorizing in economics, now that the severe limits of the scope for falsification are more

widely acknowledged. Oddly enough, Mark Blaug undermined his own falsificationist case in his *Methodology of Economics: Or How Economists Explain*,[14] by showing how rarely economists practice the falsificationist doctrine they preach. A better example for my purpose, however, is J.J. Klant, who, although basically sympathetic to Popper, has depicted falsification as an ideal unlikely to be attained in practice except within narrow limits and under the most stringent conditions. Owing to "the rapid changeability in the domain of research and the instability of many human behavioral patterns," Klant doubted that any "universal numerical constants" would be found, so that economists would be obliged to use "explanation sketches" and other non-falsifiable "explanatory schemata" to supplement the few limited empirically refutable theories available to them. Consequently, he concluded: "In economics proof must usually be furnished in rational discussions of the *plausibility* of hypotheses."[15]

Klant was not alone in this general conclusion. In 1981 the economic methodologist most closely associated with positivism, Terence Hutchison, who has modified his views somewhat in later years, wrote that

> Difficulties in quantifiability, the absence of constants, the 'openness' or 'complexity' of the material of social and economic systems, or what might be called the historical and institutional dimension (which implies the existence only of trends not laws), these are all different aspects, or ways of describing the different characteristics of the material of the social as contrasted with the natural sciences. The differences may only be in degree, but amount to such a degree as to constitute a profound contrast.[16]

I believe neither Klant nor Hutchison realises how far the recognition of these elements takes us away from positivism or logical empiricism to a more difficult territory *Beyond Objectivism and Relativism: Science, Hermeneutics, Praxis*, to cite the title of a stimulating book by Richard Bernstein.[17] I am personally uneasy how far we should go towards hermeneutics, although there are precedents in the history and philosophy of science and in economics. For example, Marshall remarked that

> The forces of which economics has to take account are more numerous, less definite, less well known, and more diverse in character than those of mechanics; while the material on which they act is more uncertain and less homogeneous,[18] and this helps to explain why looser forms of explanation and 'interpretation' may be more useful than attempts at formal empirical testing.

I am tempted here to digress into a discussion of the relationship between the mechanist and organicist analogies (world hypotheses or root metaphors in Stephen Pepper's terms[19]) which have underlain major disputes between different schools of economics, but I will restrain myself. Marshall's difficulties in trying to bring mechanics and biology together in economics are already familiar; and he never succeeded in fully synthesizing the two 'worlds.'

The relevance of these comments will become clear anon.

4) So, falsification is difficult in economics: some would say well-nigh impossible. Where do we go from here?

My own modest contribution to the debate is to suggest that where falsification is impossible, impossibly difficult, or impracticable, economists should turn more *deliberately, self-consciously, and explicitly* to looser kinds of models of the kind employed by historians and other scholars experienced in dealing with problems that cannot be handled with the formal, mathematical, hypothetico-deductive models that have come to dominate the training of economists. Severe criticism of this training has become increasingly insistent during the past decade or two, much of it emanating from leading economists with impeccable professional credentials. But here, as elsewhere rejection of one kind of procedure without a commitment to an alternative is a recipe for chaos.

5) In practice many economists already employ less rigid models than those taught in the more technocratically demanding graduate courses, but they do so in a casual, implicit, sometimes concealed and half-ashamed fahion resembling their too often casual use of empirical data – another matter on which they have much to learn from historians, who are nothing if not preoccupied with problems of the nature, limitations and interpretation of evidence. These looser models of which I speak have a surprising variety of names, the most familiar to economists being "storytelling," an approach discussed by Benjamin Ward (1967). Other concepts include the "appreciative theory" proposed by Richard Nelson and Sydney Winter (1982); "orientation theories" or "pattern predictions'' suggested by Hayek (1978; 1967); "pattern modeling" (various writers[20]); "holism" (Smuts, 1920: Gruchy, 1947); and the numerous species of "explanation sketches," "explanatory schema" (Klant, 1984) and "configurational understanding, with their "temporally overlapping" descriptions or "processive explanations" used by historians.[21] Recent doubts about the status and value of general theories, and the growing interest in "situational" or context-dependent explanations in economics, are inevitably bringing economists closer to the problems and procedures of the community of historians.

An earlier example, familiar to some of you, which was too readily dismissed by some economist critics as "measurement without theory," is the so-called "analytic description" developed by Wesley Mitchell at the National Bureau in the days when mathematical economics was a comparatively minor element in the discipline.[22] The conjuncture of the terms "analytic" and "description," which are often believed to represent entirely different procedures, would be fully comprehensible to any contemporary student of the relationships between analysis, causal explanation, and narrative in history.

6) Hayek's conception of the "essentially complex" character of economic phenomena forms part of his long lasting critique of "scientism" – i.e., the error of applying uncritically to the social sciences beliefs and methods that

have been applied successfully in the natural sciences. Unlike the latter, the social sciences have "organized complexity," in which, as Herbert Simon has remarked,

> the character of the structures depends not only on the properties of the individual elements of which they are composed, and the relative frequency with which they occur, but also on the manner in which the individual elements are connected with one another,[23]

consequently we need specific information about the individual elements, and can only produce

> mere pattern predictions – predictions of some of the general attributes of the structures that will form themselves, but not containing specific statements about the individual elements of which the structures are made up.[24]

Some years earlier Hayek discussed the problems of dealing with complexity in terms that historians would immediately understand:

> Where we deal with very complex phenomena the *recognition* of the conditions to which the theory applies may often require the ready perception of patterns or configurations which will demand a special skill which few acquire. The selection and application of the appropriate scheme thus becomes something of an art where success or failure cannot be ascertained by any mechanical test. The possession of such a ready-made pattern of significant relationships gives us a sense for the physiogonomy of events which will guide us in our observation of the environment. But even this constitutes no more than a distinction of degree from the physical sciences: the reading of many instruments also requires very special skills and there will be no other test tor its correctness than that the great majority of properly trained observers agree.[25]

7) To my mind, the most promising of these looser types of explanation for economics, is "pattern modeling," effectively presented as analagous to "story-telling" by Wilbur and Harrison.[26] Although it is described as "the" method implicit in institutional economics, Wilber and Harrison explicitly deny any intention of claiming that it is the sole method that should be adopted, and their account is consistent with the view that pattern modeling and conventional theory are not necessarily incompatible. Following Caldwell,[27] I would emphasize the need to avoid any kind of methodological monism, especially now, given the highly contentious condition of contemporary economics.

Like historians, or cultural anthropologists, pattern modelers view their subject matter from the participant observer's perspective, immersing themselves in their data, utilizing relatively concrete concepts that are particularized and close to the reality under investigation. They seek recurrent themes and patterns in the data to serve as a basis for tentative plausible hypotheses, cross-checking different types and sources of evidence in an effort to assess the validity of their initial interpretations. They are seeking 'understanding,' not 'prediction,' and they endeavor to link together validated hypotheses or themes in a pattern of interactive relationships appropriate to the problem being studied. In Kaplan's terminology such theories are concatenated, not hierarchical, like formal theories; the subject-matter takes primacy over the method employed, and both explanandum and explanans are on the same level of generality.[28]

Caldwell provides a more sympathetic account of pattern modeling than Blaug, while fully recognizing the difficulties involved. There is justice in Blaug's comment that

> In able hands, it [i.e., storytelling] can be extremely persuasive...yet it is never easy to explain afterwards why it has persuaded...because storytelling lacks rigor, lacks a definite logical structure, it is all too easy and virtually impossible to falsify. It is or can be persuasive precisely because it never runs the risk of being wrong.

Yet he concedes that: "Perhaps economic problems are so intractable that storytelling is the best we can do."[29]

Caldwell makes an important point when he observes that Wilber and Harrison's strategy faces immense difficulties, not least that of persuading non-institutionalist economists of the promise inherent in their paradigm. The first requirement, he wisely adds, is to develop a pattern model as an exemplar, to demonstrate its practical utility.

8) Nelson and Winter's concept of "appreciative theory" is calculated to appeal to economists not only because of its authors' impeccable professional credentials, but also because they present it as compatible with conventional formal theory. In a way this is surprising, for they begin with an all-out attack on the central 'hard core' of neoclassical economics, claiming that "a major reconstruction of the theoretical foundations of our discipline is a precondition for significant growth in our understanding of economic change," a view frequently expressed by heterodox critics. They aim to dispense with "all the components of the maximization model – the global objective function, the well-defined choice set, and the maximizing choice rationalization of firms' actions."[30]

Appreciative theory, they say, is a species of theory complementary to more conventional formal theorizing. Like storytelling, it focuses on certain variables, certain mechanisms, certain connections rather than others. It is more tailored to the particulars and is less rigorous than formal theory. Starting from a scan of the data it provides a somewhat vague but believable account of what is going on.[31] Appreciative theory, is "more intuitive and modified by judgment and common sense" than formal theory, but at points Nelson and Winter seem undecided as to whether they are simply considering two different theories or two quite different and incompatible modes of theorizing.[32]

As Phillip Mirowski pointed out in a perceptive review, Nelson and Winter seem to want to have their cake and eat it. On the one hand they level an all-out attack on orthodox theory and orthodox training in economics, and on the other they claim that their book "subsumes the orthodox view." Mirowski considers that the disaffected groups in economics are so roundly misrepresented that they will ignore it, whereas orthodox economists will consider it only marginally different from what they have been doing – and this is confirmed by William Baumol's review of the book.[33]

9) A related approach is to be found in Richard Langlois's collection of "new institutionalists" essays.[34] This includes such authors as Stephen Littlechild, Brian Loasby, Ronald Heiner, Andrew Shotter, Richard Nelson, Gerald O'Driscoll Jr., Oliver Williamson, and Axel Leijonhufvud. Despite their several differences they can be viewed as allies of two other current groups who, in different ways, acknowledge the historicity of economics: the Neo-Austrians and the Post-Keynesians. As their views are familiar, I can be brief. The main point is that their dissatisfaction with current neo-classical equilibrium theorizing has led them to emphasize the central importance of human ignorance, the heterogeneity of expectations, uncertainty and the complexity of decision-making. Like the new institutionalists, they focus on processes and the distinction between "logical" and "historical" time, to use Joan Robinson's terminology.[35] Historical or real time is irreversible: in George Shackle's imaginative if extreme terms, the future is not merely unknown but unknowable, and it cannot be captured in models that treat uncertainty in terms of predictable risk, and probability distributions that assume economic agents possess actuarial knowledge of things to come.[36] According to Paul Davidson, a leading Post-Keynesian, three propositions are central in the doctrines of his school: "1) the economy is a historical process; 2) in a world where uncertainty is unavoidable, expectations have an unavoidable and significant effect on economic outcomes; and 3) economic and political institutions play a significant role in shaping events."[37] Taken together, these statements are of such startling banality that any common sense historian would rub his eyes in wonder: how could anyone ever have thought otherwise? Such is the distance some economists have come from the historian's world.

This audience need not be reminded that the role of time, historical change, and expectations were fully appreciated by Alfred Marshall and J.M. Keynes – though inadequately handled in the *General Theory*. Nowadays leading general equilibrium theorists like Frank Hahn acknowledge their failure to deal with what he calls a "sequence economy." As he has observed, *"The assumption that all intertemporal and contingent markets exist has the effect of collapsing the future into the present."* [38]

10) On the subject of economists' profound disrespect for facts emphasized by Michio Morishima, Peter Wiles and others, I recommend a perceptive little book, *Economics and the Real World*, by Andrew Kamarck, who has worked for many years with the World Bank. In certain respects Kamarck's book can be viewed as

an updating and elaboration of Oskar Morgenstern's famous, but unduly neglected exposé of the limitations of economic data: *On the Accuracy of Economic Observations*.[39]

Like many other critics of contemporary economics Kamarck believes that

> Economists have been led astray by the mechanics analogy. Subconsciously, many economists tend to feel that our predicted data, like those of astronomers predicting an eclipse, should be precise, unequivocal and unconditional. But this standard is inherently impossible in economics.[40]

Economists should be more concerned with accuracy and less with the quest for precision, some of which is spurious. All too often, Kamarck argues, economists are obliged to work with "loose concepts" – a term borrowed from the philosopher, Max Black, to describe the inescapable indefiniteness of the individual units and the inexactness of the classes of objects that form much of the economists' subject-matter. Where loose concepts are involved,

> the use of customary methods of logical reasoning forces one to make demarcations in the neutral or borderline cases that are not clear. However one must recognize that these demarcations are arbitrary or judgmental. There are no logical rules that precisely locate the borderlines. As long as one is fully aware of what cases can be considered as clear cut and what cases are borderline, one can reason with loose concepts and reach useful conclusions.[41]

This leads back to another of my main themes. Apprentice economists who are obliged to devote most of their time to the study of complex and abstract mathematical theories, and statistical and econometric methods, are unlikely to develop the qualities of *judgment* required for working with data on "applied" problems. This is yet another consequence of the virtual exclusion of history, sociology, political science, and humanistic elements from the training program. Economists who have spent much or most of their careers dealing with contemporary problems, whether in business, government, or international agencies, are especially concerned about this state of affairs.[42]

11) One theme in contemporary critiques of orthodox economics which strikes at the heart of the professional establishment is the widespread dissatisfaction with econometrics, of which such high hopes were entertained in the early post World War II decades.[43] Yet curiously enough, here too there are links with history, for as Lawrence Klein, Nobel prizewinner, observed thirty years ago:

> econometrics is a way of studying history – a very systematic way... The econometrician tries to piece together the fundamental aspects of economic behavior by looking at the interrelationships of the quantitative magnitudes generated historically, and then tries to extrapolate past behavior into an unknown future... A sensible method of extrapolation is not naive or

> mechanical, and the econometrician is no less flexible than any other historian who tries to evaluate the future on the basis of the past.[44]

As a young historian of econometrics has recently remarked:

> Econometrics seems to me not so much an art as a craft skill. It requires lots of judgment as well as some artistic skills, and luck. A good econometrician, like a good historian, will take account of all the problems and will not throw away any of the inconvenient things encountered.[45]

Earlier, she noted that the history of econometrics "has to an important degree set present practice," most of which consists of "getting together the right sorts of approximations as to make a 'good' empirical model," and the objective is to prove not to refute the model. As with the historian (though Mary Morgan does not make the explicit comparison),

> The problem of finding an empirical model has three parts to it. Firstly, there is the problem of translating a verbal theory into a mathematical form. This involves the functional form of the equation, the form that the individual variables in the equation should have. Secondly, there is the problem of dealing with the ceteris paribus clauses under which the theory is assumed to hold and, under that, choosing homogeneous time periods. Thirdly, there is the problem of finding the correct model, the one that is specifically relevant to that economy, that time, and specifying the dynamic adjustments involved. In practice these three were interwoven. The third aspect continues to occupy econometricians today.[46]

My technical competence is too limited to enable me to build on these observations in pursuing the analogy between econometrics and history, and there is a serious risk of superficiality and establishing false trails. Nevertheless, the use of econometrics in economic history, one of the most 'naturally' quantitative parts of historical studies, is familiar to me, and I believe somewhat similar difficulties apply, *mutatis mutandis*. As one astute commentator has remarked of 'cliometric,' (i.e., econometric history) the general difficulties encountered include:

> the imperfections in surviving data; the needling question (usually unresolved) of how well the sample of surviving evidence delineates the larger universe from which it comes; the uncertain operation of relevant, non-operational causal factors; the unknown degree of imperfection in any theoretical model resulting from its neglect of non-operational factors and its assumptions which distort reality – an unknown which remains immutable for want of an operational way of testing how much that neglect and distortion affects the ultimate explanatory power of the model.[47]

In constructing their theories econometricians and historians have a number of obvious problems in common, for example:

i) how far back in time to begin the exercise?
ii) what background knowledge is required?
iii) what data is available; how reliable is it?
iv) what explanatory variables are to be included?
v) what parameters are to be taken as given?
vi) what time lags are involved in the model?

12) The current commonplace that facts are theory-laden, i.e., that their meaning – like that of a text – is matter of interpretation, does not mean that any interpretation is as good as any other. On this matter such differing scholars as Stanley Fish, Richard Rorty, and Geoffrey Elton – the distinguished and methodologically conservative historian – are in agreement.[48] Facts, like texts, are capable of a variety but not an infinity of interpretations; the constraints are imposed by the historical situation from which they arise, the rules of evidence, and the traditions of the relevant disciplinary community. A number of flowers may bloom, but nowhere near a thousand, to distort a well-known phrase.

Here too we have much to learn from the historian. If you want a model, I recommend Elton's *The Practice of History* written 20 years ago, rather than his more recent, rather anodyne exchange with Robert Fogel in their book, *Which Road to the Past* – wherein, to my mind, Elton got the better of the exchange.[49]

13) As a number of contemporary scholars have remarked, history is by far the best way, possibly indeed the only way, of teaching method – by case studies of what Kuhn has called exemplars. From this we can learn the limits as well as the merits of different ways of *doing* economics.

At this point it would be appropriate here to discuss the interrelationship between genuine history and Laktos's concept of rational reconstructions, but the hour is late.[50]

IV Concluding comments

14) In conclusion, reverting to our educational function, as historians of economics we are familiar with the extraordinary continuity of classical and neo-classical economics over the past two centuries, a continuity that has no counterpart in other social science disciplines or in the humanities – or perhaps, arguably, even in the natural sciences. This is, I believe, a source of weakness as well as strength. Underlying this continuity is a basic paradigm, derived from the metaphysics of Newtonian mechanics,[51] and this underlies the urge for formalization and the unity of economic theory – for example in the unification and mathematization of

late 19th century marginalism, and in what Schumpeter regarded as the subject's peak achievement, Walras's general equilibrium theory.[52]

With two centuries of intellectual tradition behind us I am neither foolish nor bold enough to prophesy a Kuhnian revolution in the forseeable future. But for the present at least I believe it is our duty to emphasize the polyparadigmatic character of contemporary economics, whether in terms of the contending schools of thought, or Benjamin Ward's three "ideal worlds" of Liberal, Radical and Conservative economics[53] – a study that deserves more respectful attention than it has hitherto received. None of these three worlds is homogenous or monolithic. But taken together, this trifurcation or "ideological polysocialization," Ward contends, has a "considerable impact on the nature of professional understanding and counsel," and he considers that "a serious effort at sympathetic understanding of the consequences of *internalizing* opposing world views would seem to be minimal test of scholarly seriousness" in economics.[54] Each of these world views, Ward claims, is persuasive; each contradicts no known facts; each is consistent in its policy implications with reasonable codes of morality; each is coherent, the parts being mutually compatible and usually mutually reinforcing. As the predominant number of American economists is liberal, "our scholarly approach has been transformed into a system of indoctrination in liberal values and how to use such values in dealing with economic policy and the interpretation of society."

Perhaps the most interesting feature of Ward's account is his admission that in studying each of the three worlds he became, in sequence, persuaded by its validity. It was "impossible" to work on any two of the worlds simultaneously or to switch from one to the other until each had been internalized. Yet, "each switch was total, in that the intuitional elements and the emotional tone of my approach to problems switched at the same time." In the end, "Though with views somewhat modified," because there were a few surprises on the way, he emerged "from the process with a primary adherence to the same world view with which I began the project."[55] That he managed to avoid multiple schizophrenia may be explained by his prior training as a specialist in comparative economic systems!

Ward's "worlds" constitute but one way of tackling the current varieties of economics, in direct opposition to the orthodox view that, in the end, all the social sciences will eventually be colonies of economics.[56] In my view this perspective simply reinforces the intellectual narrowness and complacency that is already far too widespread in the profession. By way of antidote I recommend Alexander Rosenberg's penetrating article, directed at the current AEA President, Gary Becker, entitled, "Can Economic Theory Explain Everything?"[57] To my mind the answer to Rosenberg's question is a resounding and unequivocal: No.

Historians of economics are uniquely equipped to understand and explain to their fellow professionals and to other scholars, the nature, sources, and significance of the current polyparadigmatic state of the discipline. As Terence Hutchison has said, the variety of standpoints from which the subject's history and historiography can be viewed demonstrates its epistemologically heterogeneous character; and he argues that possibly "some types of interpretation, or explanation, are valid, adequate, and relevant, regarding some phases (or 'revolutions'), while other types are more applicable in other cases."[58]

It is our task, and our duty, to educate the economists, to make them more aware of the range and limitations of the subject before they do more damage to the profession's reputation and to our society.

Notes

1 Coats (1971).
2 Parker (1986).
3 Ibid., p. 3.
4 Tobin (1985).
5 Ward (1972).
6 For introductions to the work of economists in two of these areas see Coats (1981 and 1986).
7 Backhaus (1986).
8 Private correspondence from W. N. Parker. March 21, 1986.
9 "Aspects of the Institutionalization of Political Economy in American Universities in the Nineteenth Century," including papers by Byrd Jones (on Harvard); William Phillips (on South Carolina); Frank Rozwadowski (on Columbia); and Richard Adelstein (on MIT).
10 The conference on "The Institutionalization of Political Economy; its Introduction and Acceptance into European, North American, and Japanese Universities" was held at San Miniato (Pisa) from 1–4 April 1986. The volumes on the USA (ed. W.J. Barber) and Japan (ed. H. Mizuta and C. Sugiyama) are already in the press. The French papers will appear in Economies et Sociètés, and the British papers will be published by Cambridge University Press.
11 For example Hollander (1975), Corry (1975), Schwartz (1975), Cesareno (1983), Backhaus (1986) and, less accessible, Coats (1978). See also the discussion of related issues in Samuels (1974), Tarascio (1975), and Goodwin (1972).
12 That some distinguished natural scientists are stressing the role of time and the essentially historical character of their disciplines is of special interest. For example, Prigogine and Stengers (1984); Gould (1986).
13 Kuhn (1962); Toulmin (1972) p. 116.
14 Blaug (1980).
15 Klant (1984) especially pp. 185–86, italics in original. For a recent discussion of falsification see Caldwell (1984).
16 Hutchison (1981) p. 276.
17 Bernstein (1983).
18 Marshall (1952) p. 637.
19 Pepper (1942). It would be appropriate to refer here to the large literature on the evolutionary approach to economics, for example in the work of Kenneth Boulding and the many institutionalist writers, but it would take us too far afield. But see the reference to Langlois below, footnote 34.
20 Kaplan (1964), Diesing (1971), Wilber and Harrison (1978).
21 Dray (1985) citing the work of Louis Mink and J. H. Hexter. There is a vast literature on historical explanation. Among recent work I have found Wise (1980) and Porter (1981) especially suggestive. The journal *Theory and History* is a rich source of ideas on this subject.
22 Koopmans (1947); Vining (1949); cf Friedman (1952).
23 Simon (1981) p. 195.
24 Hayek (1978) pp. 26–7.

25 Hayek (1967) p. 18. Italics supplied. The importance of skill in pattern recognition is emphasized by the physicist John Ziman (1978).
26 Wilber and Harrison (1978). This is criticized sympathetically in Caldwell (1982) pp. 200–4.
27 Ibid.
28 Kaplan (1974).
29 Blaug (1980) p. 127.
30 Nelson and Winter (1982) pp. 4, 14.
31 Nelson (1986) p. 136. For the present purpose I assume Winter would accept this account.
32 Nelson and Winter (1982) p. 9.
33 Baumol (1983); Mirowski (1983) p. 766.
34 Langlois (1986). Stretching the definition slightly, Robert Clower could be viewed as a new institutionalist, although his name does not appear in Langlois's index. Cf. the references to conceptual coherence and "storytelling" in (Walker, 1984) especially Part IV and pp. 264, 269, 271–2. For a critical review of Clower's work from an orthodox general equilibrium theorist see Hahn (1986). Clower's review of Friedman and Schwartz, in Walker, pp. 59–77 is especially pertinent in the present context.
35 Robinson (1980); Hicks (1979).
36 Shackle (1961).
37 Davidson (1981).
38 Hahn (1981) p. 132. There are severe criticisms of mathematical economics by Morishima (1984) and Blatt (1983).
39 Morgenstern (1950). Knut Wicksell was an illustrious precursor with a similar complaint: "We economists are essentially only dilettanti in the field of historical research, with the usual faults of all dilettantism: over-hasty conclusions, insufficient criticism of sources, tendentious colouring of facts, and even, on occasion, unconscious fabrication of them." Quoted by Clower in Walker (1984) p. 59.
40 Kamarck (1983) p. 21.
41 Ibid., p. 27.
42 For example. Phelps Brown (1973) and the views of non-academic economists in Coats (1981, 1986).
43 Hendry (1980); Leamer (1983); Mayer (1980); are recent examples of papers highly critical of econometrics. See also Leontief (1971).
44 Klein (1953) p. 2.
45 Morgan (1985) p. 56.
46 Ibid., pp. 45, 46, 49. Italics in original.
47 McClelland (1975) p. 226.
48 Fish (1979) p. 265; Rorty (1982) p. 160; Elton (1969).
49 Elton (1967); Fogel and Elton (1983).
50 Lakatos (1971).
51 Or, perhaps, energetics, as Philip Mirowski has persuasively argued (1984).
52 For an original and incisive critique of formalism in economics see Woo (1986). It is interesting to speculate whether, with the contemporary revival of interest in pragmatism, there may be a return to the concerns of the *fin de siècle* "revolt against formalism." Cf. White (1957).
53 Ward (1979). For recent attempts to provide a polyparadigmatic approach for students see Dow (1985) and Cole, Cameron and Edwards (1983).
54 Ward (1979) p. 462.
55 Ibid., viii, pp. 461–2, 467.
56 Stigler (1984) pp. 301–35.
57 Rosenberg (1979) pp. 509–29.
58 Hutchison (1978) p. 313.

References

Backhaus, Juergen. "History of Economic Thought – What For? Empirical Observations From German Universities," *History of Economics Society Bulletin* Vol. 8 (Winter, 1986) pp. 60–66.

Baumol, William J. "Review of Richard Nelson and Sidney Winter, *An Evolutionary Theory of Economic Change*," *Journal of Economic Literature* Vol. 21 (June, 1983) pp. 280–81.

Bernstein, Richard. *Beyond Objectivism and Relativism: Science, Hermeneutics, Praxis* (Philadelphia: University of Pennsylvania Press, 1983).

Blatt, John. "How Economists Misuse Mathematics," in Eichner, Alfred ed., *Why Economics is Not Yet a Science* (Armonck, N.Y.: M.E. Sharpe, 1983) pp. 166–86.

Blaug, Mark. *The Methodology of Economics, Or How Economists Explain* (Cambridge: Cambridge University Press, 1980).

Caldwell, Bruce J. *Beyond Positivism: Economic Methodology in the Twentieth Century* (London: George Allen and Unwin, 1982).

——. "Some Problems with Falsification in Economics," *Philosophy of the Social Sciences* Vol. 14 (1984) pp. 489–95.

Cesareno, Filippo. "On the Role of the History of Economics," *History of Political Economy* Vol. 15 (Spring, 1983) pp. 63–82.

Clower, Robert. "Monetary History and Positive Economics," in Walker, Donald A. ed., *Money and Markets. Essays by Robert W. Clower* (Cambridge University Press, 1984).

Coats, A.W. "Economic Growth: The Economic and Social Historian's Dilemma," in Harte, N.B. ed., *The Study of Economic History* (London: Frank Cass, 1971) pp. 331–48.

——. "Reflections on the Role of the History of Economics in the Training of Economists," in *Studi in memorial di Federigo Melis* Vol. 5 (Roma: Giannini Editore, 1978) pp. 291–305.

——. *Economists in Gevernment. An International Comparative Study* (Durham, N.C.: Duke University Press, 1981).

——. (ed.) *Economists in International Agencies. An Exploratory Study* (New York: Praeger, 1986).

Cole, Ken; Cameron, John; and Edwards, Chris: *Why Economists Disagree: The Political Economy of Economists* (London: Longmans, 1983).

Corry, Bernard. "Should Economists Abandon Hope?," *History of Political Economy* Vol. 7 (Summer, 1975) pp. 252–60.

Davidson, Paul. "Post-Keynesian Economics," in Bell, Daniel and Kristol, Irving eds., *The Crisis in Economic Theory* (New York: Basic Books, 1981) pp. 158–64.

Diesing, Paul. *Patterns of Discovery in the Social Sciences* (Chicago: Aldine Atherton, 1971).

Dow, Shiela. *Macroeconomic Thought: A Methodological Approach* (Oxford: Basil Blackwell, 1985).

Dray, William. "Narrative versus Analysis in History," *Philosophy of the Social Sciences* Vol. 15 (1985) pp. 125–45.

Elton, Geoffrey R. *The Practice of History* (Glasgow: Collins, Fontain, 1967).

Fogel, Robert William and Elton, Geoffrey R. *Which Road to the Past? Two Views of History* (New Haven: Yale University Press, 1983).

Fish, Stanley. "Normal Circumstances. Literal Language. Direct Speech Acts, the Ordinary, the Everyday, the Obvious, What Goes Without Saying, and Other Special Cases,"

in Rubinow, Paul and Sullivan. William M. *Interpretative Social Science. A Reader* (Berkeley: University of California Press, 1979) pp. 243–65.
Friedman, Milton. "The Economic Theorist," in Burns, Arthur F.. *Wesley Clair Mitchell, The Economic Scientist* (New York: National Bureau of Economic Research, 1952).
Goodwin, Craufurd D. "Economic Theory and Society: A Plea For Process Analysis," *American Economic Review, Papers and Proceedings* Vol. 62 (May, 1972) pp. 409–15.
Gould, Stephen Jay. "Evolution and the Triumph of Homology, or Why History Matters," *American Scientist* Vol. 74 (January – February, 1986) pp. 60–69.
Gruchy, Allen G. *Modern Economic Thought, The American Contribution* (New York: Prentice Hall, 1947).
Hahn, Frank A. "General Equilibrium Theory," in Bell, Daniel and Kristol, Irving, eds. *The Crisis in Economic Theory* (New York: Basic Books, 1981) pp. 123–38.
——. "Review of Walker, Donald A., *Money and Markets Essays by Robert W. Clower*" in *Economica* N.S. Vol. 53 (August, 1986) pp. 404–5.
Hayek, F.A. *Studies in Philosophy, Politics and Economics* (Chicago: University of Chicago Press, 1967).
——. *New Studies in Philosophy, Politics and Economics* (Chicago: University of Chicago Press, 1978).
Hendry, David F. "Econometrics – Alchemy or Science?." *Economica* N.S. Vol. 47 (November, 1980) pp. 387–406.
Hicks. "Some Questions of Time in Economics," in Tang, Anthony M., Westerfield, Fred M., and Worley, James S. eds. *Evolution, Welfare, and Time in Economics* (Lexington, Mass.: D.C. Heath, 1976) pp. 135–51.
——. *Causality in Economics* (New York: Basic Books, 1979).
Hollander, Samuel. "Appendix: Attack the Best Defence," *History of Political Economy* Vol. 7 (Spring, 1975) pp. 115–22.
Hutchison, Terence W. *On Revolutions and Progress in Economic Knowledge* (Cambridge: Cambridge University Press, 1978).
——. *The Politics and Philosophy of Economics: Marxists, Keynesians, and Austrians* (Oxford: Basil Blackwell, 1981).
Kamarck, Andrew. *Economics and the Real World* (Philadelphia: University of Pennsylvania Press, 1983).
Kaplan, Abraham. *The Conduct of Inquiry: Methodology for Behavioral Science* (San Francisco: Chandler Publishing Co., 1964).
Klant, J.J. *The Rules of the Game. The Logical Structure of Economic Theories* (Cambridge: Cambridge University Press, 1984).
Klein, Lawrence. *A Textbook of Econometrics* (Evanston, III.: 1953).
Koopmans, Tjalling. "Measurement Without Theory," *Review of Economics and Statistics* Vol. 29 (August, 1947) pp. 162–72.
Kuhn, Thomas S. *The Structure of Scientific Revolutions* (Chicago: University of Chicago Press, 1962, 1970).
Lakatos, Imre. "History of Science and its Rational Reconstructions," in Buck, Roger C. and Cohen, Robert, *P. S. A. 1970. In Memory of Rudolph Carnap. Boston Studies in the Philosophy of Science* Vol. 8 (Dordrecht: Reidel, 1971) pp. 91–136 and 174–82.
Langlois, Richard N., ed. *Economics as a Process. Essays in the New Institutional Economics* (Cambridge: Cambridge University Press, 1986).
Leamer, Edward. "Let's take the 'con' out of Econometrics," *American Economic Review* Vol. 73 (March, 1983) pp. 31–43.

Leontief, Wassily. "Theoretical Assumptions and Nonobserved Facts," *American Economic Review* Vol. 61 (March, 1971) pp. 1–7.

Marshall, Alfred. *Principles of Economics* 8th ed. (London: Macmillan, 1952).

Mayer, Thomas. "Economics as a Hard Science: Realistic Goal or Wishful Thinking?," *Economic Inquiry* Vol. 18 (April, 1980) pp. 165–78.

McClelland, Peter D. *Causal Explanation and Model Building in Economics and the New Economic History* (Ithaca: Cornell University Press, 1975).

Mirowski, Philip. "An Evolutionary Theory of Economics Change," *Journal of Economic Issues* Vol. 17 (September, 1983) pp. 757–68.

——. "Physics and the 'Marginalist Revolution,'" *Cambridge Journal of Economics* Vol. 8 (1984) pp. 361–79.

Morgan, Mary. "Finding a Satisfactory Empirical Model," in, *The Popperian Legacy in Economics*, De Marchi, Neil ed. (Cambridge: Cambridge University Press) forthcoming.

Morgenstern, Oskar. *On the Accuracy of Economic Observations* 2nd ed. (Princeton: Princeton University Press, 1963).

Morishima, Michio, "The Good and Bad Uses of Mathematics," in Wiles, Peter and Routh, Guy. ed., *Economics in Disarray* (Oxford: Basil Blackwell, 1984) pp. 51–77.

Nelson, Richard R. and Winter, Sidney. *An Evolutionary Theory of Economic Change* (Cambridge, Mass.: Belknap Press of Harvard University Press, 1982).

Nelson, Richard R. "The Tension Between Process Stories and Equilibrium Models: Analyzing the Productivity Growth Slowdown of the 1870's," in Richard Langlois, ed. *Economics as a Process: Essays in the New Institutional Economics* (Cambridge University Press, 1986).

Parker, Willliam N. *Economic History and the Modern Economist* (Oxford: Basil Blackwell, 1983).

Pepper, Stephen. *World Hypotheses. A Study in Evidence* (Berkeley: University of California Press. 1942).

Phelps Brown, Henry. "The Underdevelopment of Economics," *Economic Journal* Vol. 82 (March, 1973) pp. 1–10.

Porter, Dale H. *The Emergence of the Past. A Theory of Historical Explanation* (Chicago: University of Chicago Press, 1981).

Prigogine, Ilya and Stengers, Isabelle. *Order Out of Chaos. Man's New Dialogue With Nature* (Toronto: Bantam Books, 1984).

Robinson, Joan. "History versus Equilibrium," in Robinson, *Collected Economic Papers* Vol. 5 (Oxford: Basil Blackwell, 1980) pp. 48–58.

Rorty, Richard. *The Consequences of Pragmatism. (Essays 1972–80)* (Minneapolis: University of Minnesota Press, 1982).

Rosenberg, Alexander. "Can Economic Theory Explain Everything?," *Philosophy of the Social Sciences* Vol. 9 (December. 1979) pp. 509–29.

Samuels, Warren. "The History of Economic Thought as Intellectual History," *History of Political Economy* Vol. 6 (Fall, 1974) pp. 305–23.

Schwartz, Pedro. "Teaching the History of Economic Thought: Report of a Symposium at Bristol, 1973," *History of Political Economy* Vol. 7 (Spring, 1975) pp. 112–15.

Shackle, G.L.S. *Decision, Order, Time in Human Affairs* (Cambridge: Cambridge University Press, 1961).

Simon, Herbert. "The Architecture of Complexity," in Simon, *The Sciences of the Artificial* (Cambridge, Mass.: MIT Press, 1981).

Suts, Jan Christian. *Holism and Evolution* (New York: Macmillan, 1920).

Stigler, George J. "Economics – The Imperial Science," *Scandinavian Journal of Economics* Vol. 86 (1984) pp. 301–35.

Tarascio, Vincent J. "Intellectual History and the Social Sciences: The Problem of Methodological Pluralism," *Social Science Quarterly* Vol. 56 (June, 1975) pp. 37–54.

Tobin, James. "Neo-classical Theory in America: J.B. Clark and Fisher," *American Economic Review* Vol. 75 (December, 1975) pp. 28–38.

Toulmin, Stephen. *Human Understanding* Vol. 1 (Oxford: Clarendon Press, 1972).

Vining, Rutledge. "Koopmans on the Choice of Variables to be Studied and of Methods of Measurement," *Review of Economics and Statistics* Vol. 31 (May, 1949) pp. 77–94.

Walker, Donald A. ed. *Money and Markets. Essays by Robert Clower.* (Cambridge: Cambridge University Press, 1984).

Ward, Benjamin. *What's Wrong With Economics* (London: Macmillan, 1972).

——. *The Ideal Worlds of Economics. Liberal, Radical and Conservative World Views* (New York: Basic Books, 1979).

White, Morton G. *Social Thought in America: The Revolt Against Formalism* (Boston: Beacon Press, 1957, 1966).

Wilber, Charles K. and Harrison, Robert S. "The Methodological Basis of Institutional Economics: Pattern Model, Storytelling, and Holism," *Journal of Economic Issues* Vol. 12 (March, 1978) pp. 61–89.

Wise, Gene. *American Historical Explanations* (Minneapolis: University of Minnesota, 1980).

Woo, Henry. *What's Wrong With Formalization in Economics? An Epistemological Critique* (Newark: Victoria Press, 1986).

Ziman, John. *Reliable Knowledge. An Exploration of the Grounds for Belief in Science.* (Cambridge: Cambridge University Press, 1978).

14 Situational determinism in economics

The implications of Lastis's argument for the historian of economics

Lastis's paper is an important and constructive contribution to the methodology and history of economics even if one questions his proposition that 'the adoption of antipsychologism as a heuristic canon is not only unnecessary but, by restricting permissible types of explanatory generalisation, may halt progress in microeconomics' (Lastis [1972], p. 229). For, as befits a philosopher of science, his method is more important than his implied historical judgment. By focusing attention on a fairly narrow, long-established, and theoretically sophisticated segment of economic analysis, and providing a more penetrating and methodologically more precise review of its evolution, he has helped to elucidate the nature and significance of scientific 'progress' in economics. In the process he has demonstrated that Lakatos's 'research programme' concept is a more powerful weapon than Kuhn's blunt and multi-faceted 'paradigm' instrument; and, after the initial dust of controversy has settled, he may be seen to have provided a more secure basis for agreement and mutual understanding between economists of differing methodological persuasions.[1]

Within the scientific community, as among members of the general public, economics has long been regarded as the most advanced, prestigious, and scientific of the social sciences. This reputation derives from a familiar combination of features, including the technical complexity and manifest social significance of its subject-matter, and the sophistication of its mathematical and quantitative methods. But most important of all, at least to the community of scholars and scientists, is the remarkable fertility and continuity of its central corpus of theory. Of course, a cynic might ask whether this continuity is evidence of anything other than sheer survival value, a question which fortunately need not be considered here. However it should be noted that at least one distinguished recent philosopher has maintained that the definition of 'science' is ultimately reducible to a matter of 'tradition'.[2] And the contention is relevant, since Lastis's paper provides clear evidence of doctrinal continuity in the orthodox micro-economic theory of the firm. This continuity has been maintained in a number of ways, for example by successive theoretical modifications, refinements, and reinterpretations, and by determined resistance to the numerous critics who have proposed to reformulate the inherited theory drastically, abandon it, or apply it to problems which it was incapable of handling.

In the process, the theory has become more systematic, more rigorous, and more restricted in scope; and those who are disturbed by these developments may be consoled by the suggestion that 'the exact sciences have won some of their earlier successes by avoiding the kind of problems still too difficult for their yet undeveloped powers'.[3] Whether such gains are more than offset by the losses entailed in neglecting the more difficult problems is obviously a matter of historical judgment, one that will depend on the selection of appropriate criteria of scientific, or perhaps social, importance. There is obviously a danger of undue concentration on trivial 'puzzles' while major gaps or anomalies are ignored. Moreover any judgment will necessarily depend on the time perspective adopted, since short run losses may eventually be outweighed by the higher long run returns from scientifically more productive 'roundabout processes', as in Austrian capital theory. Finally, we must not only consider the effects on the theory itself or the segment of the discipline in question, but also the effects on the discipline as a whole, and on related disciplines. Thus even if we convert Lastis's careful conjecture into the counter-factual proposition that 'the adoption of anti-psychologism as a heuristic canon' has in fact halted 'progress in economics', it is at least arguable that the economists' wilful rejection of the more intractable aspects of the theory of the firm may have contributed indirectly to the adoption of alternative strategies by other scholars or by lapsed economists: for example organisation theory, and studies of managerial decision-making and administrative behaviour.

Needless to say, Lastis's account of the evolution of situational determinism in the theory of the firm will not satisfy the historian of economics, since he has deliberately abstracted from the historical context in which it occurred. Nevertheless, his approach is suggestive, as may be indicated by a brief sketch of similar, but earlier, developments in the theory of consumer's behaviour (to which he alludes in a footnote).[4] The protracted controversy surrounding this subject can be traced back through the *Methodenstreit* of the 1880s to the early nineteenth century attacks on classical economics by literary and social reformist critics, who maintained that the economists had grossly overrated the importance of self-interest and thereby presented a debased and one-sided view of human nature and society. The later phase of criticism, which gathered momentum from the 1880s, rested on more secure foundations as the growth of experimental psychology encouraged the repudiation of the hedonistic theory of behaviour, which was presumed to underly the new subjective (or so-called 'psychological') theory of value – especially the marginal utility version propounded by W. S. Jevons. In the ensuing debate among the economists those who contended that economics was vitiated, or at least seriously impaired, by its dependence on unsound psychological foundations looked for support, successively, to the physiological and biological theory of William James, the instinct theory of William MacDougall and the behaviourism of John Broadus Watson. The issue had to be faced squarely for MacDougall, in particular, threw down the gauntlet, by declaring

> it would be a libel, not altogether devoid of truth, to say that classical political economy was a tissue of false conclusions drawn from false psychological

> assumptions.... The great assumption of the classical political economy was that man is a reasonable being who always intelligently seeks his own good and is guided in all his activities by enlightened self-interest, ... [whereas in fact] mankind is only a little bit reasonable and to a great extent very unintelligently moved in quite unreasonable ways.[5]

Among those American economists disposed to plead guilty to MacDougall's accusations were such significant figures as Thorstein Veblen, Wesley Mitchell, Frank A. Fetter, and John Maurice Clark. Individually or collectively they maintained that in its existing condition economic theory was unrealistic, incomplete, and incapable of providing a basis for predictions since it had adopted an unscientific subjective approach, underestimated the importance of irrational impulses and habitual conduct, and neglected societal influences on individual behaviour. It was therefore unable to explain the origin and nature of consumer's wants, individual responses to the availability of new commodities, or the effects of advertising and social emulation. Of course, these admissions did not go unchallenged among the leading defenders of the orthodox tradition, among whom were such powerful spokesmen as Irving Fisher, Arthur T. Hadley, Herbert J. Davenport, and Frank H. Knight, who either denied the relevance of psychology to economics or regarded it as a peripheral modifier rather than a decisive negation of the subjective theory of value.

In terms of Lakatos's methodology of research programmes it is especially interesting to trace, over a period of three or four decades, the gradual emergence of a concensus of opinion that in its central theory of value economics required no psychological theory, but only a fundamental postulate – variously termed the principal of rationality, or the logic of choice. The routes by which this conclusion was reached were necessarily various. Fisher, for example, from his *Mathematical Investigations in the Theory of Value and Prices* (1892) through his *Elementary Principles of Economics* (1912) consistently maintained that psychology was irrelevant to economics. Davenport, after stressing the importance of psychology in the process of valuation in his *Value and Distribution* (1908), subsequently produced a textbook, *The Economics of Enterprise* (1913), which wholly ignored valuations and defined economics as 'the science which treats phenomena from the standpoint of price' (p. 25). Mitchell, after several ambitious programmatic statements of the importance of psychology eventually settled for a Veblenian type of 'pecuniary logic', after a stimulating discussion of the influence of money on individual behaviour.[6] Knight, in characteristically iconoclastic fashion, embraced behaviourism as an adequate foundation not on account of its positive merits, but because it was 'less a psychology, than a dogmatic repudiation of everything properly to be called by that name'.[7] In Knight's hands the separation of economics and psychology became absolute, for science was to him 'the technique of prediction'[8] and

> The basis of a *science* of conduct must be fixed principles of action, enduring and stable motives. It is doubtful, however, whether this is fundamentally the character of human life.[9]

Anyone who interpreted the premises of economics as a literal description of human behaviour was badly mistaken, but the postulate of rationality, like other scientific premises, was not actually true—in other words, it was an 'irrefutable core'. The critics had

> made little headway in bringing forth substitute principles. I do not believe that they ever will. The structures are valid as *limitations* on the familiar reasonings, not as negations. The principles of the established economics are partial statements, but sound as far as they go, and they go about as far as general principles can be carried.[10]

And there, at least as far as the majority of American economists were concerned, the matter rested.[11]

Moderate commentators, like Zenas Clark Dickinson,[12] fully appreciated that there were important problems on the borderlines between economics and related disciplines. But, like the majority of his professional colleagues, he was content to leave them to specialists in other fields. The scope of economics had been redefined, on traditional lines, by discussion and eventual agreement. In the process the basic theory had been explicated, simplified and effectively protected from refutation.

Whether such a process was inevitable or desirable is, of course, quite another matter.

Notes

1 This may occur as the specific strengths and limitations of different 'research programmes' become more widely appreciated. For an earlier constructive effort to expose the fundamental irreconcilability of different approaches to economics see Briefs (1961).

2 Gallie (1957).

3 Deutsch (1958), p. 28.

4 P. 208, footnote 3. The following account will be confined to the American discussion, which was intense and protracted from the early 1890s to the later 1920s. It is based on Chapter 3 of my unpublished Ph.D. thesis, 'Methodological Controversy as an Approach to the History of American Economics, 1885–1930', Johns Hopkins, 1953. However, many of the same issues were raised in Britain albeit less heatedly and persistently, for example by such heterodox writers as J. A. Hobson and P. Sargent Florence.

5 MacDougall (1908), p. 11.

6 Cf. his (1916) and the title essay in his (1937). His main works on business cycles were almost purely quantitative, and owed nothing to psychological theory.

7 Knight (1931), p. 64. See also his (1921a), pp. 203–4, 208.

8 Knight (1924); p. 232.

9 Knight (1921a), p. 53, italics in original.

10 Knight (1921b), p. 145.

11 There has been, of course, much subsequent discussion of ordinal and cardinal utility, indifference curve analysis, revealed preference, etc. But these topics have not entailed any serious questioning of the principle of rationality or the fundamental relationship between economics and psychology. It should, however, be noted that in the period under review there was a considerable effort among American economists to develop

a 'social' approach to value and welfare theory, in opposition to the orthodox tradition of methodological individualism. However, it would be inappropriate to raise these matters here. They are considered, for the pre-1930 period, in my thesis cited above, p. 286, footnote 1.

12 Dickinson (1922). This is still the best published review of the debate up to that point.

References

Briefs, H. W. (1961): *Three Views of Method in Economics.*

Deutsch, K. W. (1958): 'Scientific and Humanistic Knowledge in the Growth of Civilisation', in Harcourt Brown (*ed.*): *Science and Creative Spirit, Essays in Humanistic Aspects of Science.*

Dickinson, Z. C. (1922): *Economic Motives: A Study in the Psychological Foundations of Economic Theory, with some Reference to Other Social Studies.*

Gallie, W. B. (1957): 'What Makes a Subject Scientific?', *British Journal for the Philosophy of Science*, 8, pp. 118–39.

Knight, F. H. (1921a): *Risk, Uncertainty and Profit.*

Knight, F. H. (1921b): 'Traditional Economic Theory: Discussion', *American Economic Review*, 11.

Knight, F. H. (1924): 'The Limitations of Scientific Method in Economics', in R. G. Tugwell (*ed.*): *The Trend of Economics.*

Knight, F. H. (1931): 'The Relation of Utility Theory to Economic Method in the Work of William Stanley Jevons and Others', in Stuart A. Rice (*ed.*): *Methods in Social Science: a Case Book.*

Lastis, S. J. (1972): 'Situational Determinism in Economics', *British Journal for the Philosophy of Science*, 23, pp. 207–245.

MacDougall, W. (1908): *An Introduction to Social Psychology.*

Mitchell, W. C. (1916): 'The Role of Money in Economic Theory', *American Economic Review*, 6.

Mitchell, W. C. (1937): *The Backward Art of Spending Money.*

15 Economics and psychology

The death and resurrection of a research programme

I

Imre Lakatos originally conceived his methodology of scientific research programmes (MSRP) as a procedure for analysing and appraising developments in the natural sciences. Yet he deliberately designed the Nafplion Colloquium as an opportunity to test its applicability to the history of economics, and thereby to encourage an assessment of its wider implications. In so doing he undoubtedly gave hostages to fortune, for there was every likelihood that MSRP would be interpreted too loosely and applied to circumstances to which it is scarcely appropriate. Some members of the Colloquium did not hesitate to suggest that these deficiencies were exemplified in the present case, and in revising my paper for publication I have endeavoured to take account of their legitimate misgivings.[1] While confidently predicting that it will not be long before Imre's spirit cries out, in the manner of its illustrious antagonist: 'Je ne suis pas Lakatosiste!' I have no desire to hasten that evil day, for this essay is designed as a constructive contribution to the collective effort to assess the value of MSRP as a research tool for the historian of economics.

As a rule, historians are notoriously reluctant to commit themselves to any specific theory or interpretative framework, preferring instead to concentrate on small- or medium-scale problems for which, so they imagine, no general theory is required. On those comparatively rare occasions when they feel compelled to venture on to a broader plane of discourse they tend to resort to intuition or implicit theorising, rather than exposing their habitual loose, unsystematic, and possibly subconscious patterns of explanation. Such an evasion of responsibility is profoundly unsatisfactory to the philosopher or historian of science or any intellectual discipline. The quest for an adequate explanation may be doomed to disappointment, but it is a challenge to be faced; and in the present imperfect state of our knowledge MSRP offers the best hope of success for the historian of economics who is seeking to understand the general development of his field. MSRP is assuredly more promising than T. S. Kuhn's suggestive 'structure of scientific revolutions', which was too rigid and monolithic in its original form, and in subsequent versions seriously lacking in precision and specificity, largely owing to the vagueness of such key terms as 'paradigm', 'crisis', 'revolution' and 'normal science'.[2]

As the Nafplion discussions revealed, it is still much too early to pronounce a definitive judgment on the value of MSRP as applied to the natural sciences, let alone economics and her softer sister disciplines. There is still much solid historical research to be done, and the precise nature and interpretation of MSRP is still not yet clear. Yet, paradoxically enough, herein lies much of its promise for the historian of economics, for while MSRP is more precise, specific and subtle than Kuhn's theory, it nevertheless possesses a measure of flexibility that prevents it from hardening into a rigid dogma, even in the hands of its most unimaginative exponents. In one of his last writings, Imre himself described MSRP as 'a new and perhaps a bit too elaborate philosophical framework',[3] for he was fully aware that historical facts are notoriously messy and recalcitrant, and that efforts to pour them into preconceived moulds fashioned by philosophers of science might prove neither intellectually nor aesthetically pleasing. In the present instance it is undeniably difficult to resist the temptation to adapt MSRP to fit the facts while trying to remain tolerably faithful to the author's original conception. The protracted controversy in the USA concerning the relations between economics and psychology, which is the subject of this exercise, falls so far short of the strict requirements of the 'paradigm' case of MSRP, i.e., Newtonian physics, that it hardly constitutes a suitable test. Yet here, as elsewhere, the proof of the pudding must be in the eating. MSRP does not only apply to success stories; it also affords insights into 'budding' or 'emergent' programmes.[4] The attempt to infuse psychology into economics manifestly failed in the period under review; it was premature, as well as abortive – so much so that one may be unduly straining the gynaecological metaphor in suggesting that the subsequent renaissance of interest in these matters constitutes a resurrection. Yet the resulting controversy was serious, intense, protracted, and wide-ranging, and almost all the leading American economists entered the lists. The issues included most of the fundamental questions about economics and psychology which have arisen either before or since; and the discussion formed part of a larger debate encompassing many of the perennial problems of the methodology of the social sciences, such as: the epistemological status and functions of theory; its explanatory and/or predictive value; the realism of assumptions; and the methodological similarities and differences between the social and the natural sciences.[5] The controversy was therefore substantial enough to provide at least a preliminary test of MSRP as a tool for the historian of economics; and an incidental, more practical advantage is the existence of close parallels with the example presented by Latsis,[6] the first serious attempt to apply MSRP to that discipline. Whereas Latsis dealt with the theory of the firm, I am concerned with aspects of the theory of consumer's demand which, Latsis maintained, was based on 'a very similar, if not identical programme'.[7] Yet the two cases were not exactly parallel either with respect to the sequence of events, the details of the controversy, or its outcome. During the period under review, from the early 1880s to the late 1920s, repeated efforts were made to discredit the subjective theory of value which underlay the theory of demand formulated during the so-called 'marginal revolution' of the 1870s.[8] Unlike the theory of the firm, in the present case the principal stimulus to efforts to launch a new research programme came from developments in the neighbour discipline of psychology. The innovators' intentions were clear enough, even though as a group they were generally disunited, unable to define or comprehend the target of their attacks, and quite incapable of formulating an effective rival programme. Yet their efforts did not go unheeded, for the defenders of the received tradition of economics were sensitive to the limitations of the subjective theory of value; and in the process of defending their position they succeeded in refining and strengthening the 'neoclassical' research programme.

In the ensuing pages a brief review of the critical attacks on the 'orthodox' theory of consumer's demand to be found in the American economic literature of the period is followed by an account of the defence and reinterpretation of the received doctrine put forward by its proponents; an assessment of the consequent gains and losses to economic 'science', in the light of recent discussions of these same issues; and some concluding remarks on the value of MSRP as a tool of research for the historian of economics. In the interests of brevity, attention will be concentrated on the bare essentials of the story while endeavouring to minimise the unavoidable oversimplifications involved in this, or indeed any, attempt to 'rationally reconstruct' a complex episode in the history of ideas.

II

The intellectual background to the American discussion of the psychological foundations of economic theory can be depicted very briefly. During the second half of the nineteenth century the development of new ideas and experimental methods in psychology led to the formulation of three major new approaches in the USA, each of which seemed directly applicable to economics: namely, William James's conception of the physiological and biological determinants of human behaviour; William McDougall's instinct theory; and John Broadus Watson's behaviourism.[9] At about the same time, the new 'subjective' theories of value commonly associated with the so-called 'marginal revolution' of the 1870s[10] were being assimilated, not without difficulty, into the central corpus of economic theory. In retrospect it seems hardly surprising that the trend towards objectivism in psychology should clash with an apparently contradictory trend in economics. As the critics of economic orthodoxy never tired of reiterating, economics is a social not a natural science, and must necessarily take account of new knowledge of human behaviour provided by the psychologists and other social scientists.[11] This seemingly obvious commonsense contention was not unduly shaken by the conspicuous disagreements among the psychologists. Admittedly some over-enthusiastic advocates of a marriage, or at least more intimate relations between the two disciplines committed themselves to support of one or other versions of the new psychology only to find it subsequently discredited by even newer ideas or research findings. But they were usually undismayed, presumably concluding that such were the inevitable risks of research in new and hitherto uncharted fields of inquiry.

The variety of responses to the challenges offered by the new psychological ideas makes it difficult to summarise the various and occasionally conflicting positions adopted. A broad distinction between 'critics' and 'defenders' of the received tradition is not seriously misleading, although some of the participants appeared to change sides during the course of the debate,[12] but there is some danger of implying that the received tradition of economics was sufficiently well established and unified to be recognised without difficulty. Indeed, one of the constructive outcomes of the discussion, as will be shown later, was a more precise and systematic formulation of the 'orthodox' position. Nevertheless, it is reasonably safe to subdivide the responses to the new psychology into three broad categories. Some economists flatly denied that any psychology whatsoever was relevant to economics, arguing that economists should concentrate their attention on catallactics, the science of exchanges, in which the only elements of value to be included were exchange values, or prices, without reference to the motives of those entering into exchanges.[13] At the other end of the spectrum were those who held that the recent developments in psychology had so undermined the subjective theory of value that it was necessary to undertake a wholesale reconstruction of the foundations of economic theory.[14] Finally, in an intermediate position, were those who maintained that the new ideas could be assimilated, either wholly or in part, without undue difficulty, so that only minor changes in terminology, shifts in theoretical formulation or interpretation, or modifications in the conclusions of economic theory, were required.[15]

Generally speaking, critics of the subjective theory of value focused their attention on the marginal utility variant which, they contended, presupposed the hedonistic theory of motivation which had been utterly discredited by professional psychologists.[16] In the economic literature, Thorstein Veblen's devastating satirical portrayal of the hedonistic conception of man as responding passively to external stimuli was especially persuasive when juxtaposed against the positive, actively intelligent interpretation of human nature presented in William James's well-known work.[17] Veblen's attempt to formulate an alternative 'evolutionary' research programme for economics failed completely,[18] and his whole-hearted commitment to a pre-McDougall version of the instinct theory of psychology has often been regarded as a particular weakness of his system.[19] Nevertheless, he exerted a considerable influence on the younger *fin de siécle* generation of American economists, spreading doubts about the psychological and methodological foundations of the orthodox doctrines. When the defenders denied – as most did – that marginal utility presupposed hedonism, the critics merely shifted their ground and attacked the 'hard core' of economic theory, in particular the conception of the 'economic man'. Economic theory, it was said, assumed that the individual consumer possessed a stable and consistent scale of preferences, and was able and willing to make the requisite rational calculations of satisfactions depicted in the marginalists' conception of equilibrium – that he possessed, in J. M. Clark's words, an 'irrationally rational passion for dispassionate calculation'.[20] These assumptions were flatly in conflict with the findings of recent psychological research, which demonstrated that human behaviour was seldom rational, and often impulsive, instinctive, inconsistent, and in other respects unstable. By contrast with the economists' static and passive view of human nature, psychologists (and also the pragmatist philosophers Peirce, James and Dewey, who were becoming increasingly influential in the United States) stressed the active, dynamic, and constructive aspects of human behaviour.[21] The economists' theory was not only unrealistic and demonstrably unscientific; it was also too restrictive, since it was incapable of explaining relevant past and contemporary phenomena – for example, how consumers respond to new commodities or situations; how preferences are formed and changed; and how effective are advertisers' efforts to influence sales.

A related, though not wholly consistent set of arguments focused attention on the stabilising, and presumably non-rational influence of habit and the social determinants of behaviour, such as custom and social emulation. Some critics conceded that earlier economists had made passing reference to these factors; but their true significance had been neglected, for the conventional individualistic theories of consumer's behaviour could neither explain the origins nor assess the role or the effects of changes in these social forces.[22] Moreover, they claimed that economic theory was based on discredited subjective and unscientific notions such as introspcction, whereas the new trends in psychology were based on the objective and measurable aspects of human behaviour. In its most extreme form this view presupposed that 'science is measurement', and that the social sciences should be modelled on the methodology of the natural sciences.[23] Not all the critics went this far; but they were generally agreed that if economists would acknowledge the validity and relevance of recent advances in psychology they would not only become more sensitive to the limitations of their theories, but would also discover hypotheses and methods that would enable them to establish their discipline on a more scientific foundation.

Viewed from the perspective of MSRP, this miscellaneous ragbag of assertions and complaints does not amount to much. Apart from some valid and pertinent criticisms of the received economic doctrine about the most one can discern, even on a generous interpretation, are a few elements which might form part of the hard core of an embryonic rival research programme, and some statements constitutive of a positive and a negative heuristic. The proposed new psychology-based theory of consumer's demand was really no more than a preliminary declaration of intent; and regrettably, even its most persistent proponents contributed nothing more constructive than a few well-directed critical articles or passages in elementary textbooks. There was, in other words, no sustained effort to devise or test an alternative economic theory. Moreover, notwithstanding their confident pronouncements about the proper method of developing economic science, none of the leading critics ever undertook any detailed empirical studies of the type required to advance their programme. They preferred the easy path of destructive criticism to the painstaking uphill task of constructive economic research.

Nevertheless, with some stretch of the imagination, it is possible to spell out the ingredients of this abortive rival research programme. The following items are presented schematically, for they can be reformulated or reinterpreted in a variety of ways.

Broadly speaking, the critics' proposals included the following assumptions and procedures:

(i) Employ methods similar or identical to those used in the natural sciences.
(ii) Adopt 'realistic' fundamental assumptions, i.e., assumptions compatible with observed behaviour or consistent with the findings of other scientific disciplines (especially psychology).
(iii) Derive assumptions from the study of psychology (and other disciplines) and empirical research into the actual behaviour and motivations of consumers.
(iv) Abandon efforts to formulate abstract, general theories and concentrate on the development of more specific, low- or middle-level, empirically grounded theories.
(v) Develop empirically testable theories which will serve as a basis for scientific explanation, prediction, and/or control.
(vi) undertake systematic empirical studies (and draw upon any relevant studies undertaken by scholars in related disciplines) as a basis for formulating sound empirical generalisations and for testing and, if necessary, reformulating established theories.
(vii) Wherever possible, replace static theories by empirically grounded dynamic theories (e.g. to take account of changes of income, tastes, new commodities, etc.).
(viii) Broaden the scope of economic theory to take account of the social forces influencing economic behaviour (e.g. habit, custom, social emulation, advertising, etc.).
(ix) Go beyond prices and exchange values to examine the influence of market and non-market forces on economic and social welfare.

As already noted, this 'rational reconstruction' is inevitably somewhat speculative – the more so as the research programme was so ill-formed. Yet it may be suggested that the first three (or perhaps even the first five) propositions constituted the hard core, since they could not have been given up without abandoning the entire programme.[24] Propositions (vi)–(ix), on the other hand, comprised the positive heuristic, i.e., the presciption how to develop the programme both theoretically and empirically. And propositions (viii) and (ix) may be said to illustrate the kind of problem-shift entailed by this novel programme.

III

On the whole, the defenders of the orthodox tradition experienced comparatively little difficulty in dividing, defeating, or simply dismissing the opposition. As might be expected, given the strength and durability of the central corpus or economic theory, they were less disunited than their opponents, and they found it easy to expose the gaps and inconsistencies in the critics' contentions. They dismissed as irrelevant suggestions that the boundaries of economics should be systematically broadened to take account of matters which had been conventionally regarded as belonging to other disciplines and indeed, as with the marginal revolution, the general effect of the controversy was to narrow the accepted interpretation of the scope of economics.[25] But above all, the defenders were able to point to their critics' failure to develop a viable alternative theory.

During the debate two general themes emerged, and despite the considerable area of disagreement there was undoubtedly some convergence towards a consensus of opinion on certain essentials.[26] Firstly, virtually all parties agreed in repudiating hedonism as a valid psychological theory, the defenders adding their denial that it had ever constituted an essential foundation for marginal utility analysis. Secondly, there was a marked, albeit by no means unanimous, shift of opinion in favour of a more 'objective' approach to human behaviour, though the nature and significance of this shift was variously interpreted. Some, especially certain critics, advocated the wholesale adoption of behaviourism as the only appropriate psychological basis for economic theory,[27] whereas others merely regarded objective methods as sources of specific hypotheses, generalisations, and relevant data. Curiously enough, the critics who were most receptive to behaviourism in one form or another eventually found allies among those defenders who argued that psychology, as a discipline, had no relevance to economics, the science of prices (or the logic of choice, as it has subsequently been termed). And yet, at the same time, subjective interpretations of consumer's behaviour continued to figure prominently in the textbooks, sometimes with modified terminology designed to purge them of psychological overtones.

Without entering into the details of the matter it is sufficient to illustrate the formulation of the strict constructionist defence of the orthodox hard core by quoting the views of two leading American economic theorists, Irving Fisher and Frank H. Knight. In his doctoral dissertation, published in 1892, Fisher endeavoured both to delineate the scope of economics and to define the type of explanation appropriate to it, by asserting 'this foisting of Psychology on Economics seems to me inappropriate and vicious … to fix the idea of utility the economist should go no further than is serviceable in explaining *economic* facts. It is not his province to build a theory of psychology.'[28] For the purpose of price theory it was sufficient to adopt the postulate that '*Each individual acts as he desires*,' for questions about the antecedents of desire lay 'completely within the realm of psychology'. Discussions of subjective states of mind should be avoided, for 'while utility has a 'common sense' meaning relating to feelings, when economics attempts to be a positive science, it must seek a definition which connects it with objective and commodity.'[29]

Some thirty years later Knight adopted broadly the same position, but he specified the methodological implications in a much more extreme and detailed manner. He welcomed the economists' tendency to view the psychology of their subject as behaviouristic on the paradoxical grounds that behaviourism was 'less a psychology than a dogmatic repudiation of everything to be called by that name'.[30] Many of the critics' contentions were valid from a psychological standpoint, but they were irrelevant to economics as a science, for '… the basis of a *science* of conduct must be fixed principles of action, enduring and stable motives. It is doubtful, however, if this is fundamentally the character of human life.'[31] Indeed, the essential distinction between the natural and the social sciences was that the latter must take account of 'the facts of consciousness and mental communication. In human behaviour we have a kind of direct knowledge of motives, whereas we only infer the existence of physical forces from observations of the changes specific to each. Hence the irresistible urge to treat motives as real.'[32] It was therefore necessary to recognise the severe limitations of economics as a science and, with, reference to economic theory, to grasp that 'there are no laws regarding the *content* of economic behaviour, but there are laws universally valid as to its *form*'.[33] The critics had failed to offer any constructive proposals and they had 'made little headway in bringing forth substitute principles.' I do not believe that they ever will. The strictures are valid as *limitations* on the familiar reasonings, not as negations. The principles of the established economies are partial statements, but sound as far as they go, and they go about as far as general principles can be carried.'[34]

It would be quite wrong to suggest that Knight's interpretation of the proper relationship between economics and psychology was generally accepted in all its details by defenders of the orthodox tradition, most of whom were far less subtle and less interested in methodological and philosophical issues. Nevertheless, Knight's austerely restrictive conception of the scope of economic science, and his pessimistic view of the potentialities of economic theory pointed the way that subsequent studies of utility and demand analysis were to follow. By the end of the 1920s it was already clear that the more ambitious efforts to infuse psychology into economics, or to reconstruct basic economic theory in terms compatible with the new psychologies, had manifestly failed. And the development of the Slutzky-Hicks-Allen indifference curve analysis a few years later seemed to confirm that psychology had little or nothing to contribute to the theoretical apparatus.[35]

Yet this does not mean that the controversy was futile or unimportant, even from the most severely orthodox standpoint. During the debate the hard core of economic theory was not merely preserved intact; it was also reinforced, as its key terms were more carefully specified. Moreover, the protective belt of auxiliary hypotheses was strengthened by the elimination of unnecessary and suspect propositions. The fundamental assumption, which had earlier been identified with the popular notion of the economic man, was reformulated in less objectionable terms as the abstract concept of rationality,[36] or the logic of choice – what Veblen and his followers had scathingly dismissed as the 'pecuniary logic'. It is important not to underestimate the significance of this development. At the time the general level of methodological sophistication in economics was undeniably low, not only in the USA, and there was insufficient recognition of the nature and limitations of the conventional analysis. Restoration of confidence in the basic theory was an essential prerequisite to its subsequent elaboration, an observation that applies not only to the theory of consumer's demand but also to other related areas of microeconomics.

By the end of the 1920s the essential components of the hard core of orthodox demand analysis had emerged, by implication if not explicitly, in roughly the following form:

(i) Basic economic theory is necessarily abstract, static and general in form.
(ii) The fundamental assumptions must therefore be simple, uniform and constant; they can neither be 'realistic' nor subject to falsification.
(iii) It is assumed that consumers aim to maximise their satisfactions (total utility).
(iv) They have limited incomes.
(v) They have unlimited wants in general, but normally experience eventually diminishing marginal utility from consuming successive units of a given commodity.
(vi) They have full (or perfect) knowledge of relevant market conditions, for example, prices, the range of available goods and services, etc.
(vii) They make rational calculations of alternative uses of their income, especially by adjusting their expenditures at the margin.
(viii) The individual's decisions are independent of those of other individuals.

This list is, of course, necessarily debatable, for assumptions can be specified in a variety of ways and in more or less detail. (For instance, is it necessary in the present case to specify zero costs of information, or to assume that the individual consumer knows in advance that a given commodity or service will fulfil his expectations?) Yet by adding the positive heuristic implied by the orthodox demand analysis we increase its resemblance to a full Lakatosian MSRP – though it still falls far short of that ideal type. If the positive heuristic is defined as a series of suggestions or instructions for improving the theory and testing its implications, it may be said to have included the following:

(i) construct static models;
(ii) reduce the number of postulates to a minimum (including psychological postulates);
(iii) develop general theories;
(iv) concentrate on the analysis of prices or exchange values (ignoring, as far as possible, such questions as the origin and nature of wants and satisfactions, the structure and stability of preferences, processes of valuation, etc.);
(v) reinterpret the theory to take account of discrepancies between the assumptions and the facts (as revealed by casual empiricism).

IV

It is now time to consider the significance of this controversy both from the broader standpoint of the history of economics and, more narrowly, in terms of the applicability of MSRP to the discipline. This is no easy undertaking, given the philosophical, methodological, and substantive problems of interpretation involved.

As already indicated, the victory of the orthodox research programme was virtually complete. Both during and after the debate marginal utility theory continued to dominate the economics textbooks – admittedly often in a supposedly objective, quasi-behaviouristic form – until it was supplemented or displaced by indifference curve analysis and, very recently, by 'revealed preference' theory. In the process the majority of economics students were effectively immunised against contamination by psychologists.[37] Yet whatever the pedagogical advantages of this practice the results were obviously by no means costless in terms of the progress of the subject. As might be expected, interest in the theory of value; economic motivation; the formation, structure, and stability of consumers' preferences, and indeed almost all aspects of economic psychology, declined sharply, as revealed by an analysis of leading economics journals.[38] On the other hand, the slow adoption of utility analysis as a tool of research,[39] and repeated expressions of concern about its theoretical limitations – from respectably orthodox, as well as heterodox economists[40] – are somewhat more unpredictable and disquieting. And the recent resurgence of economists' complaints about the isolation of their subject from other social sciences, including psychology, and the serious neglect of important theoretical and empirical problems in economic psychology,[41] suggests the need for a fresh historical and methodological appraisal of the whole episode.

As is well known, methodological controversy is seldom, if ever, confined to purely methodological issues. But even if space permitted, it would be inappropriate for the present purpose to consider the wider economic and social context of the debate, even the professional academic context. In the Lakatosian MSRP this 'externalist rubbish' (as one Nafplion participant described it) has only a subordinate place, if indeed that. Nor is it necessary to examine the contending philosophical convictions underlying the critics' and defenders' views, although some of the controversialists were certainly sensitive to this level of discourse.[42] We cannot, however, ignore the fact that MSRP embodies criteria for the normative appraisal of scientific theories, and it is accordingly necessary to attempt an exposition of the criteria of 'good' scientific theories to be found, or implied in the literature of economics. Some of these criteria differ from, and may even conflict with MSRP, and they will perhaps seem somewhat bizarre to conventional philosophers of science. But there is no single, universally agreed set of evaluative criteria,[43] and the following list seems not only pertinent to the present case but also to the general history of economics.

The criteria of 'good' theories, as seen by economists past and present, include the following elements:

(a) consistency;
(b) simplicity;
(c) generality;
(d) fruitfulness, i.e. adaptability, extensibility;
(e) manageability, i.e. amenability, in terms of available techniques;
(f) congruence with reality, i.e. capacity to explain part of the available empirical knowledge;

(g) testability, i.e. capacity to generate falsifiable predictions;
(h) relevance to the expectations of the scientific community.

The individual items can, of course, be formulated and interpreted in a variety of ways. Not all the criteria can necessarily be fulfilled simultaneously, and they are unlikely to be valued equally.[44] Indeed, the need for some trade-off between them is one of the most familiar sources of irreconcilable methodological disagreements. In the present case, the critics of the orthodox research programme generally emphasised the importance of criteria (*f*), (*g*) and (*h*); and they construed 'relevance' so as to include not only 'internal' criteria of scientific importance but also, like many other economists, 'external' criteria of relevance to social policy. To this end they were prepared to forgo a considerable measure of generality and simplicity, whereas these criteria, together with (*d*), (*e*), and (*f*), ranked very high among the defenders.

To present-day economists, and advocates of MSRP, the most striking feature of the orthodox programme was the comparatively low valuation its proponents placed on criterion (g), testability. As George Stigler, himself no ardent defender of economic heterodoxy, concluded:

> Had specific tests been made of the implications of theories, the unfruitfulness of the ruling utility theory as a source of hypotheses in demand would soon have become apparent. Had these economists sought to establish true economic theories of economic behavior – that is, to isolate uniformities of economic events that permitted prediction of the effects of given conditions – they would not long have been content with the knowledge that demand curves have negative slopes ... (Whereas in fact) Not only were such specific implications not sought and tested, but there was a tendency, when there appeared to be the threat of an empirical test, to reformulate the theory to make the test ineffective.[45]

When viewed in relation to the long-term progress of economic science, the essential question here is: how much explanatory power and predictive efficiency should be sacrificed for the sake of preserving a theory possessing considerable simplicity, generality, fruitfulness, and manageability? This problem was recognised towards the close of the controversy by another highly respected economist, Jacob Viner, who deplored the

> all-too-prevalent methodological fanaticism which prefers the accurate but superficial to the approximate but fundamental, and which makes adaptability to its special technique of investigation, rather than importance, the standard for the selection of problems and the delimitation of the scope of the inquiry.[46]

Of course the criteria of 'importance' were at the very heart of the dispute, for the contending parties had entirely different conceptions of the fundamental purposes of economic theory (for example, whether its function is purely explanatory and/or predictive and/or a device for solving immediately practical problems) and they could not agree as to the relative importance of the various theoretical and empirical problems requiring solution.

Differences of this kind also underlay the disagreement about the proper scope of economics, a species of demarcation dispute which is all too common among social scientists, and probably much less so among physical scientists.[47] It would be pointless to try to resolve the issue here; but if there is indeed a resurrection of the heterodox research programme which was so roundly defeated before 1930, it is largely due to the resurgence of interest in a set of problems which the orthodox theory of consumers' demand is incapable of handling. And it must be stressed that these include theoretical, as well as empirical problems. As Herbert Simon noted more than a decade ago,

> economics has been moving steadily into newer areas where the power of the (orthodox or, as he terms it, 'classical') model has never been demonstrated and where its adequacy must be considered anew … Classical economics was highly successful in handling small-maze problems without depending on psychology. Labor relations, imperfect competition, uncertainty, and long-run dynamics encase the decision-maker in a much larger maze than those considered in classical short-run static theory. In these areas the economist and the psychologist have numerous common interests in cognitive theory that they have not shared previously.[48]

Much more recently, as the result of persistent, widespread and growing dissatisfaction with the theoretical refinements and empirical limitations of available theories of demand and consumer's behaviour there has been a swelling chorus of demands for new research into a wide range of problems recognised as relevant and important by the critics of half a century ago. Current complaints about the existing theory have an inescapable quality of *déjà vu* to those familiar with the literature reviewed in Section II of this paper, and it is not only the ignorant or the methodological fanatics who voice them. Criticism extends from the fundamental assumptions of maximising behaviour to the economists' failure to examine the process of individual decision-making, the neglect of the relationship between individual and household behaviour, the problems posed by new goods, changes of income and tastes, advertising, social interaction, and so on;[49] and there is considerable evidence of research designed to develop new theories to deal with these unsolved problems and to provide data to fill gaps in existing knowledge. Whether this amounts to a new research programme, rather than a disconnected series of *ad hoc* hypotheses and empirical generalisations it is still too early to say. But if it does, it will surely be legitimate to regard it as the resurrection of a departed spirit of fifty years ago.

What conclusions can the historian of economics draw from this experience? Would it be true to suggest that the successful defence of the orthodox tradition has retarded the development of economics? There is certainly some justification for Latsis' view that 'the adoption of anti-psychologism as a heuristic canon is not only unnecessary but, by restricting permissible types of explanatory generalisation, may halt progress in microeconomics',[50] yet it is very doubtful that any viable alternative course was available in the 1920s. Despite the scientific status of the new empirical findings in psychology, that discipline was still in a highly unsettled state, and the efforts to infuse psychology into economics at that time were over-ambitious, premature, sometimes confused, and generally lacking in persistence and clarity of focus. Moreover, it must be remembered that the methodological foundations of economics were weak, and the discipline was under severe and repeated attacks from those who were hostile to all theory and who favoured either descriptive studies or extensions of scope that threatened to convert economics into encyclopaedic sociology. While the desire to facilitate the application of mathematical and statistical techniques[51] and the preference for analytical convenience over testability and descriptive complexity may be regarded as 'temptations'[52] they were by no means easy to resist.

MSRP is helpful in evaluating this episode for Lakatos fully appreciated the difficulty of deciding whether a research programme is degenerating and if so whether it is likely to recover in the foreseeable future. The orthodox programme was not progressing empirically, and in certain respects it was degenerating theoretically as economists reinterpreted the established theory, and added fresh terminological refinements and *ad hoc* assumptions in an effort to protect it from refutation.[53] As one later commentator remarked, even when economists admitted the importance of psychology they recognised it as a 'theoretical obstacle' and therefore 'it is small wonder that psychology gets such summary treatment in most modern texts on economic theory.'[54] Yet it would surely have been wrong to abandon the degenerating orthodox programme in the absence of a viable alternative; and, as we have seen, the critics manifestly failed to provide one. It is therefore appropriate to credit the pre-1930 defenders of economic orthodoxy for their efforts to preserve the intellectual capital which had been accumulated by several previous generations. It may, indeed, be the right way to protect scientific traditions from disintegration, especially when one recalls the dictum that 'the exact sciences have won some of their earlier successes by avoiding the kind of problems still too difficult for their undeveloped powers'.[55]

V

What light does the foregoing account shed on the value of MSRP to the historian of economics? Obviously no general conclusions can be derived from a single case study, but it is worth recording a few provisional impressions for the benefit of future investigators.

It is seldom easy to reconstruct the principles and processes that scientists actually adopt in developing and testing their theories, and it is surely more difficult to do this in economics than in physics. As some Nafplion participants observed, MSRP is based on the 'paradigm' case of Newtonian physics, and there is no precisely comparable paradigm or exemplar in economics. It is therefore correspondingly more difficult to devise acceptable standards (whether in MSRP or other terms) for judging scientific performance in economics, and this helps to account for much, though by no means all, of the perennial philosophical and methodological disagreements in the discipline. These circumstances may constitute an argument for applying exogenous, rather than endogenous criteria of appraisal; but even if this were conceded it would not necessarily follow that MSRP was an appropriate source of such criteria. It is difficult to find satisfactory examples of theoretical progressiveness (involving new and unexpected predictions) in economics, let alone empirical progressiveness (i e. corroborated predictions) although economists have produced numerous *ad hoc* empirical generalisations. Considerations of this kind have led some critics to conclude that economics is not a science at all – or, at least, not a developmental science;[56] but this view is obviously unacceptable to the present writer since it would render pointless any attempt to apply MSRP to the subject.

Nevertheless, these warnings must be heeded, and MSRP must be applied to economics with due caution. Much depends on how literally it is interpreted. For example, it may be said that the entire history of economics constitutes one massive unitary research programme, and that the methodological disagreements among economists are merely 'family quarrels'.[57] To the present writer this view seems a drastic over-simplification; yet even if it were true, it would not necessarily destroy the value of MSRP as a tool of methodological and historical appraisal. As the foregoing paragraphs show, MSRP is a valuable tool for analysing the methods by which an established research programme or scientific tradition is preserved, and the changes it undergoes in the process at the hands of its proponents. The great difficulty in economics is not so much to decide whether there are many research programmes or only one, but how to decide whether a given programme is degenerating, static, or progressing. For as noted above, clear-cut examples of theoretical and empirical progressiveness are hard to find. Too often, it seems, research programmes in economics are preserved long after they have entered their degenerative phase, while new programmes are too readily adopted, and too casually abandoned. And if this judgment is accepted, it raises the intriguing question: what leads economists, or indeed any scientists, to espouse one research programme rather than another?[58] This is a problem that Lakatosians need to tackle in relation to the history of physics and other natural sciences, as well as the social sciences.

This leads us directly to a further general observation about the applicability of MSRP to economics. Derisory references to 'externalist rubbish' notwithstanding, it is clear that Imre Lakatos acknowledged the presence of psychological, sociological and other extra-scientific influences on the history of science. His aim in developing MSRP was not to ignore these factors but to relegate them to a subordinate place, so that they would not be brought into the account until the internal influences had been fully explored. This approach is even more valuable for the history of economics than for the history of the natural sciences, for although external factors have undoubtedly played a larger part in the former[59] it is all too easy to fall back on them – for example, environmental[60] or ideological influences – as a substitute for detailed historical research. In other words, MSRP represents a sound approach to an explanatory model for the history of economics, even though it will probably take us less far in that field than in physics.

In the end, the value of MSRP to the historian of economics will depend on the correspondence between its component parts (including the logical relationships between them) and the historical facts. The crucial question is: how far is it possible to identify research programmes in the literature of the subject, with their hard cores, protective belts, positive and negative heuristics, progressive and degenerative phases, and so on? To the historian, MSRP is essentially a practical tool which will ultimately be judged by its results. At this early stage of its application it seems to possess considerable promise.

Notes

1 The subject-matter of this paper has undergone several metamorphoses which may be worth recording, for the sake of future devotees of Lakatosiana. It originally formed part of chapter 3, entitled 'Economics and Psychology' of Coats (1953). Twenty years later, after an appearance at Imre's LSE seminar, he persuaded me to produce an abbreviated version, which was published (Coats, 1974). A more extended treatment, prepared for Nafplion, was already obsolete by the time it was presented to the Colloquium in a substantially modified form. The present, and I trust final, version owes much to the ideas and examples encountered during that memorable gathering, and to Mark Blaug's brilliant essay printed elsewhere in this volume. I have also benefited from constructive comments by Spiro Latsis, John Maloney and Ian Stewart.

2 Kuhn (1970). A revealing account of the successive shifts of Kuhn's position is contained in Toulmin (1972) pp. 98–117.

3 Lakatos and Zahar (1973), p. 16.

4 Latsis (1972), pp. 208, 229.

5 Coats (1953).

6 Latsis (1972).

7 Latsis (1972), p. 208n.

8 For a recent review of this episode see Black, Coats and Goodwin (1970).

9 James (1890), McDougall (1908), Watson (1914).

10 Black, Coats and Goodwin (1970).

11 Although, as noted below, some of these critics favoured the adoption of natural science methods in economics.

12 For example, Herbert Davenport, having declared in 1894 that 'we need to reconstruct the psychological basis of our science … no shirking of psychological difficulties will suffice', added in 1908 that 'the next line of advance in economic theory will be distinctly psychological in character, and that further progress awaits its new impulse at the hands of the psychologists'. Yet he subsequently maintained that economics was the 'science that treats phenomena from the standpoint of price', a position implying that psychology was irrelevant. Davenport (1894), pp. 562–3; (1908), p. 312; and (1913), p. 25. In fact the change in his views was less real than apparent. Coats (1953), pp. 240–6.

Wesley C. Mitchell frequently advocated the importance of psychology for economics and repeatedly warned his fellow economists of the danger of relying on false psychological premises. Yet he conceded that 'for many purposes of economic theory it does not matter for what people want their dollars … in many cases little does lie behind the dollars; the symbols have become the real thing'. He drew attention to the influence of the use of money on the growth of rationality in economic affairs, but while stressing the evolution of habits and institutions, in a manner reminiscent of

Thorstein Veblen, he actually devoted his main research efforts to the statistical study of business cycles, a field in which psychology played virtually no part whatsoever. For his earlier views on economics and psychology see, for example, Mitchell (1910) and (1937).

13 For example, Davenport (1913), p. 99; Hadley (1893); Fisher (1892).

14 Veblen (1932), especially pp. 73, 157, 141.

15 Fetter (1915) endeavoured to take account of these new developments. Cf. his earlier text, Fetter (1904). For a careful critical analysis of the attempt see Whittaker (1916).

16 Of the three co-founders of the marginal utility revolution, one, W. S. Jevons, adopted the language of hedonism, thereby revealing his intellectual links with the Benthamite utilitarian tradition. See, for example, Black (1970).

17 Veblen (1932), p. 73; the hedonist conceived man as 'a lightning calculator of pleasures and pains, who oscillates like a homogeneous globule of desire of happiness under the influence of stimuli that shift him about the area, but leave him intact...Self-imposed in elemental space, he spins symmetrically about his own spiritual axis until the parallelogram of forces bears down upon him, whereupon he follows the line of least resistance'.

18 Coats (1954); for a more favourable view see Gruchy (1947).

19 For a different interpretation see Ayres (1958).

20 Clark (1936) considered that this criticism was subsidiary to the main charge that marginal utility analysis assumed a static view of human nature. Whether economic theory actually presupposed the notion of an 'economic man' or rational calculator of pleasures and pains is not the issue here. As will be indicated below, the 'fundamental assumption' underlying demand theory had not yet been fully and unambiguously specified.

21 For a careful effort to take account of these views see Stuart (1986a), (1986b) and (1917).

22 There were at least two distinct motives underlying these efforts – to enhance the realism of economic theory, and to enable economists to take account of welfare considerations. See, for example, the essays in Clark (1936) and his (1946). Other contributions in this vein include: Anderson (1911), Cooley (1913), Fetter (1920) and (1923), Haney (1914), Viner (1925), Wolfe (1924).

23 For example, Tugwell (1922) and (1924), Copeland (1931).

24 As the Nafplion discussions revealed, even with a well-developed programme in physics it is sometimes difficult to decide whether a specific statement should be regarded as part of the hard core or the positive heuristic.

25 Winch (1970).

26 Boucke (1922), Clark (1921), and Parry (1921).

27 For example, Tugwell (1922), p. 332 and, from a very different point of view, Knight, infra. A balanced interpretation of the relevance of behaviourism to economics was presented in Dickinson (1922).

28 Fisher (1892), pp. 5, 11. Italic in original.

29 Fisher (1892), pp. 11, 17. Italic in original.

30 Knight (1931a), p. 64.

31 Knight (1921a).

32 Knight (1931a), p. 67.

33 Knight (1924).

34 Knight (1921b).

It would be inappropriate to discuss here Knight's epistemological views, which involved the assertion that scientific knowledge was ultimately inferior to knowledge derived from intuition, emotion and common sense, for this would take us too far afield. See Knight (1924), (1925a) and (1925b).

35 For example, Robbins (1935) 'It is difficult to overstress its importance. With one slash of Occam's razor it extrudes from economic analysis for ever the last vestiges of psychological hedonism.' This is not in fact the case, for economists still employ the

notion of 'hedonic indexes', though in a somewhat different context. For further comment on the limitations of indifference curve analysis cf. *infra*., p. 55, footnote 40.

It is worth noting that in his outstanding pioneer article of 1915, 'On the Theory of the Budget of the Consumer', E. V. Slutzky had begun by asserting that 'if we wish to place economic science upon a solid basis, we must make it completely independent of psychological assumptions and philosophical hypotheses'. Later, however, he acknowledged the complexities arising from the *factual* interdependence between economics and psychology, leaving 'a more profound investigation' of 'the manifestations of utility in the consciousness of the individual' to 'future studies'. Cf. Ekelund, Furubotn and Gramm (1972), pp. 189, 215, 216–18.

36 For example, as Z. C. Dickinson put it: 'The "rationality" which we do assume is merely some ability to learn connections between present goods or situations ... and future final utilities, which faculty everyone ... has always known to be lamentably imperfect.' Dickinson (1922), p. 86.

37 As Spiro Latsis has said elsewhere in this volume, in the usual treatment by economists the consumer is 'psychologically anonymous' and can therefore be endowed with any traits we wish. See his essay 'A Research Programme in Economics,' pp. 1–41.

38 This is evident from an analysis of articles in the American Economic Association's *Index of Economic Journals*, Coats (1971). In MSRP terms this represents a substantial problem-shift.

39 See Stigler (1970).

40 As Mark Blaug observed, 'the attitude of the utility theorists was that utility theory was merely a matter of systematic common sense', citing Stigler's view that the long labours of many able economists working in this field had merely buttressed the view that all demand curves have negative slopes, which they 'had known all along'. E. J. Mishan has extended the same general criticism to indifference curve and revealed preference analysis, advocating the abandonment of all these theorems since 'there is nothing the practising economist can take away with him to help him come to grips with the complexities of the real world'. Blaug (1968), p. 359; Mishan (1961), especially p. 327. For other criticisms see footnotes 45–49.

41 Infra., pp. 57, 58 and references in footnotes 48 and 49.

42 Knight (1931b).

43 See, for example, the list of 70 criteria ranked in 24 subdivisions by S. C. Dodd, reproduced in Zaltman, Pinson and Angelmar (1973), pp. 92–3. Criteria (*c*), (*e*) and (*f*) were considered by Stigler in a context directly relevant to this essay. Cf. his (1950) reprinted in Stigler (1965).

44 The weight attached to particular criteria will vary according to whether one is evaluating a single theory or an entire research programme. In MSRP Lakatos was essentially concerned with sequences of theories. I owe this point to Mr J. Maloney.

45 Stigler (1965), pp. 155, 153. Blaug concurs, concluding that 'the long and tortuous history of utility theory presents a disheartening picture' (Blaug (1968), p. 359).

46 Viner (1925), p. 212.

47 This is doubtless because natural scientists disagree less markedly about the social purposes and relevance of their work.

48 Simon (1963), pp. 709, 711. A somewhat similar range of problems was mentioned forty years earlier by Dickinson (1922). For further statements of Simon's views see his (1959) and his essay 'From Substantive to Procedural Rationality', in this volume, pp. 129–48.

49 For a comprehensive review of the literature see 'The State of Contemporary Demand Theory' by the editors in Ekelund, Furubotn and Gramm (1972), pp. 57–93. Shubik (1970) is an especially devastating and witty critique of the pretensions of recent demand theory. Two further articles should be noted: Tobin and Dolbear (1963) and Ferber (1973).

50 Latsis (1972), p.229.

51 For a balanced statement of the economists' need to draw on available quantitative work in psychology see Dickinson (1924).
52 Latsis (1972).
53 The slow revival of criticism after the 1920s is surely due in part to the decline of interest in microeconomics. The orthodox explanatory models seemed less unsatisfactory when applied to group or aggregative problems as contrasted with individual behaviour.
54 Hayes (1950), p. 293. This valuable survey article reveals the continuity between the earlier and later critics of economic theory. Cf. his argument that: 'If further psychological assumptions promise to improve prediction and control ... it would be absurd to exclude psychology from economics on the grounds either that it seems *a priori* to be unimportant, or that its inclusion would destroy the distinctiveness of the economic discipline ... The crux of the matter is whether or not psychological data, principles, and research techniques promise to increase substantially our capacity to understand, predict and control economic behavior, and this question can only be answered after the fact, not before it.' (Ibid. p. 303.)
55 Deutsch (1958), pp. 9–10. Also Neumann and Morgenstern (1944), pp. 6–7; Medawar (1967), p. 7. The reluctance to abandon the scientific gains of the past has been dignified as the 'principle of tenacity'.
56 Latsis (1972), p. 207.
57 As some methodologists have noted, theories in economics are as often complementary or overlapping as competitive, a point that helps to explain their survival value.
58 As Kuhn recognized, the allegiance to one paradigm or research programme rather than another – at least in its early stages – is matter of 'promise' or expectations, rather than performance. Kuhn undoubtedly exaggerated the non-rational elements in such attachments, and especially in cases of paradigm-switching. But it is doubtful whether an internalist explanation can provide a satisfactory solution to this problem.
59 For a stimulating discussion of the influence of 'lay images' in the social sciences see Lammers (1974).
60 On environmentalist explanations in economics see Coats (1970).

References

Anderson, B. M. (1911): *Social Value.*

Ayres, C. E. (1958): 'Veblen's Theory of Instincts', in D. F. Dowd (ed.): *Thorstein Veblen: A Critical Reappraisal*, pp. 25–37.

Black, R. D. C. (1970): 'W. S. Jevons and the Foundation of Modern Economics,' in Black, Coats and Goodwin (1970), pp. 98–112.

Black, R. D. C., Coats, A. W. and Goodwin, C. D. W. (eds.) (1970): *The Marginal Revolution in Economics, Interpretation and Evaluation.*

Blaug, M. (1968): *Economic Theory in Retrospect*, 2nd edn.

Blaug, M. (1970): 'Was there a Marginal Revolution?', in Black, Coats and Goodwin (1970), pp. 3–14.

Boucke, O. F. (1922): 'A Unique Situation in Economic Theory', *The American Economic Review*, 11, pp. 598–605.

Clark, J. M. (1921): 'Soundings in Non-Euclidean Economics', *The American Economic Review, Supplement*, 11, pp. 132–43.

Clark, J. M. (1936): *A Preface to Social Economics.*

Clark, J. M. (1946): 'Realism and Relevance in the Theory of Demand', *Journal of Political Economy*, 59, pp. 347–53.

Coats, A. W. (1953): 'Methodological Controversy as an Approach to the History of American Economics, 1885–1930', Unpublished PhD thesis, Johns Hopkins.

Coats, A. W. (1954): 'The Influence of Veblen's Methodology', *Journal of Political Economy*, 62, pp. 529–37.

Coats, A. W. (1970): 'The Economic and Social Context of the Marginal Revolution of the 1870s', in Black, Coats and Goodwin (1970), pp. 37–58.

Coats, A. W. (1971): 'The Role of Scholarly Journals in the History of Economics: An Essay', *Journal of Economic Literature*, 9, pp. 29–44.

Coats, A. W. (1974): 'Situational Determinism in Economics. The Implications of Latsis's Argument for the History of Economics', *The British Journal for the Philosophy of Science*, 25, pp. 285–8.

Cooley C. H. (1913): 'The Institutional Character of Pecuniary Valuation', *American Journal of Sociology*, 18, pp. 543–55.

Copeland, M. A. (1931): 'Economic Theory and the Natural Science Point of View', *The American Economic Review*, 21, pp. 67–79.

Davenport, H. J. (1894): 'The Formula of Sacrifice', *Journal of Political Economy*, 2, pp. 561–73.

Davenport, H. J. (1908): *Value and Distribution: A Critical and Constructive Study*.

Davenport, H. J. (1913): *The Economics of Enterprise*.

Deutsch, K. W. (1958): 'Scientific and Humanistic Knowledge in the Growth of Civilization', in H. Brown (ed.): *Science and the Creative Spirit, Essays in Humanistic Aspects of Science*.

Dickinson, Z. C. (1922): *Economic Motives, A Study in the Psychological Foundations of Economic Theory, with some Reference to other Social Sciences*.

Dickinson, Z. C. (1924): 'Quantitative Methods in Psychological Economics', *The American Economic Review, Supplement*, 14, pp. 117–26.

Ekelund, R. B. Jr., Furubotn, E. G. and Gramm, W. P. (eds.) (1972): *The Evolution of Modern Demand Theory*.

Ferber, R. (1973): 'Consumer Economics', *Journal of Economic Literature*, 11, p. 1332.

Fetter, F. A. (1904): *The Principles of Economics*.

Fetter, F. A. (1915): *Economic Principles*.

Fetter, F. A. (1920): 'Price Economics versus Welfare Economics: Contemporary Opinion', *The American Economic Review*, 10, pp. 719–37.

Fetter, F. A. (1923): 'Value and the Larger Economics, II, Value Giving Way to Welfare', *Journal of Political Economy*, 31, pp. 790–803.

Fisher, I. (1892): 'Mathematical Investigations in the Theory of Value and Prices', *Transactions of the Connecticut Academy*, 9.

Gruchy, A. G. (1947): *Modern Economic Thought: The American Contribution*.

Hadley, A. T. (1893): 'Recent Tendencies in Economic Literature', *Yale Review*, 3, pp. 251–60.

Haney, L. (1914): 'The Social Point of View in Economics, I and II', *Quarterly Journal of Economics*, 28, pp. 115–39, 292–321.

Hayes, S. P. Jr. (1950): 'Some Psychological Problems of Economics', *Psychological Bulletin*, 47, pp. 289–330.

James, W. (1890): *Principles of Psychology*.

Knight, F. A. (1921a): *Risk, Uncertainty and Profit*.

Knight, F. A. (1921b): 'Traditional Economic Theory: Discussion', *The American Economic Review*, Supplement, 11, pp. 143–7.

Knight, F. A. (1924): 'The Limitations of Scientific Method in Economics,' in Tugwell (1924), pp. 229–67.

Knight, F. A. (1925a): 'Economic Psychology and the Value Problem', *Quarterly Journal of Economics*, 39, pp. 372–409.

Knight, F. A. (1925b): 'Fact and Metaphysics in Economic Psychology', *The American Economic Review*, 15, pp. 247–66.

Knight, F. A. (1931a): 'The Relations of Utility Theory to Economic Method in the Work of William Stanley Jevons and Others', in S. A. Rice (ed.): *Methods in Social Science: A Case Book*, pp. 59–69.

Knight, F. A. (1931b): 'Marginal Utility Economics', *Encyclopedia of Social Sciences*, 5, pp. 357–63.

Kuhn, T. S. (1970) : *The Structure of Scientific Revolutions*, 2nd edn.

Koch, S. (ed.) (1963): *Psychology: A Study of a Science*, vol. 6.

Lakatos, I. and Zahar, E. (1976): 'Why did Copernicus's Programme Supercede Ptolemy's?' in R. Westman (ed.): *The Copernican Achievement*.

Lammers, C. J. (1974): 'Mono- and Poly-paradigmatic Developments in Natural and Social Sciences' in R. Whitley (ed.): *Social Processes of Scientific Development*, pp. 123–47.

Latsis, S. J. (1972): 'Situational Determinism in Economics', *The British Journal for the Philosophy of Science*, 23, pp. 207–45.

McDougall, W. (1908): *An Introduction to Social Psychology*.

Medawar, P. (1967): *The Art of the Soluble*.

Mishan, E. J. (1961): 'Theories of Consumer Behavior: A Cynical View', *Economica*, reprinted in Ekelund, Furubotn and Gramm (1972), pp. 327–37.

Mitchell, W. C. (1910): 'The Rationality of Economic Activity', *Journal of Political Economy*, 18, pp. 97–113, 197–216.

Mitchell, W. C. (1937): *The Backward Art of Spending Money and other Essays*.

Neumann, J. von and Morgenstern, O. (1944): *The Theory of Games and Economic Behavior*.

Parry, C. E. (1921): 'A Revaluation of Traditional Economic Theory', *The American Economic Review*, Supplement, 11, pp. 123–31.

Robbins, L. C. (1935): *The Nature and Significance of Economic Science*.

Shubik, M. (1970): 'A Curmudgeon's Guide to Microeconomics', *Journal of Economic Literature*, 8, pp. 405–34.

Simon, H. A. (1963): 'Economics and Psychology', in S. Koch (ed.): *Psychology: A Study of a Science*, vol. 6, pp. 685–723.

Simon, H. A. (1959): 'Theories of Decision-Making in Economics and Behavioral Science', *The American Economic Review*, 49, pp. 253–83.

Slutzky, E. V. (1915): 'On the Theory of the Budget of the Consumer', translation reprinted in Ekelund, Furubotn and Gramm (1972).

Stigler, G. J. (1950): 'The Development of Utility Theory', *Journal of Political Economy*, reprinted in G. J. Stigler (ed.) (1965): *Essays in the History of Economics*, pp. 66–155.

Stigler, G. J. (1970): 'The Adoption of the Marginal Utility Theory', in Black, Coats and Goodwin (1970), pp. 305–20.

Stuart, H. W. (1896a): 'The Hedonistic Interpretation of Subjective Value', *Journal of Political Economy*, 4, pp. 64–84.

Stuart, H. W. (1896b): 'Subjective and Exchange Value', *Journal of Political Economy*, 4, pp. 208–39.

Stuart, H. W. (1917): 'The Phases of the Economic Interest', in *Creative Intelligence: Essays in the Pragmatic Attitude*, pp. 282–353.

Tobin, J. and Dolbear, F. T. Jr. (1963): 'Comments on the Relevance of Psychology to Economic Theory and Research', in S. Koch (ed.): *Psychology: A Study of a Science*, vol. 6, pp. 677–84.

Toulmin, S. (1972): *Human Understanding.*

Tugwell, R. G. (1922): 'Human Nature and Economic Theory', *Journal of Political Economy*, 22, pp. 317–45.

Tugwell, R. G. (1924): 'Experimental Economics', in R.G. Tugwell (ed.): *The Trend of Economics*, pp. 371–42.

Veblen, T. (1932): *The Place of Science in Modern Civilisation and other Essays.*

Viner, J. (1925): 'The Utility Concept in Value Theory and its Critics', I and II, *Journal of Political Economy*, reprinted in his collected essays, *The Long View and The Short*, 1958, pp. 177–212.

Watson, J. B. (1914): *Behavior: An Introduction to Comparative Psychology.*

Whittaker, A. C. (1916): 'Fetter's Principles of Economics', *The Political Science Quarterly*, 31, pp. 430–44.

Winch, D. (1970): 'Marginalism and the Boundaries of Economic Science', in Black, Coats and Goodwin (1970), pp. 59–77.

Wolfe, A. B. (1924): 'Functional Economics', in Tugwell (1924), pp. 452–82.

Zaltman, G., Pinson, C. R. A. and Angelmar, R. (1973): *Metatheory and Consumer Research.*

16 Economics and psychology

A resurrection story

The original debate and its aftermath

Although few historians of economics nowadays view the so-called "marginal revolution" of the 1870s as a complete break with the past, it is still generally seen as an important turning point in the development of the discipline: the beginning of modern professionalized academic economics, and a major paradigm shift which, one recent scholar has persuasively argued, inaugurated a new research program (Fisher, 1986). Central to the achievement of the three major innovators – Jevons, Menger, and Walras – was the formulation and elaboration of a new "subjective" theory of value to supplant the dominant "objective" cost of production theory, which in turn contributed to a fundamental shift of focus from supply-based to demand-based theories of value, production, and distribution (Black, Coats, and Goodwin, 1970). There was, of course, much more to the marginal revolution than this. But for present purposes it will serve as a convenient starting point, for it was followed by a protracted, intense, and complex debate about the relations between economics and psychology which lasted at least until the late 1920s, and which involved many scholars from both disciplines and several different countries.

The controversy was especially vigorous in the United States, where there were strongly marked methodological and doctrinal disagreements. In the course of the discussion three distinct positions emerged: (1) the view that psychology of any kind was irrelevant to economics, since it was exclusively concerned with exchange values or prices irrespective of the motives of those entering into market transactions; (2) the diametrically opposite contention that developments in psychology had so undermined the subjective theory of value that a wholesale reconstruction of the foundations of economics was required; and (3) an intermediate response from those who considered that the new ideas could be assimilated, either wholly or in part, by means of a change in terminology, shifts in theoretical formulation or interpretation, or modifications in theoretical conclusions (Coats, 1976).

In retrospect the most striking feature of this episode is the similarity between the issues in debate at that time and the arguments expressed in the current literature on the relations between economics and psychology, including some of the chapters in this book. Unlike many academic controversies, the earlier debate appeared to be effectively settled by 1930, with victory going to those who rejected all proposals either to abandon the basic "hard core" assumptions of orthodox economic theory or to modify them substantially to take account of psychological theory or research findings. This conclusion accorded both with the post-1870 narrowing of the boundaries of economics (Winch, 1970) and with the broader trend toward the subdivision and compartmentalization of the social sciences. In the process, the central theory of economics was not simply preserved intact: it was reinforced by the more precise specification of its key terms and purged (it was hoped) of subjective psychological residues. (There was also a curious alliance between those who embraced the "objective," and therefore "scientific," behaviorism of J.B. Watson, and Frank H. Knight, who welcomed behaviorism but denied that it was a legitimate psychological theory of human behavior: see Coats, 1976.) The "fundamental assumption," which had so often been identified with the crude and potentially misleading concept of *homo oeconomicus*, was depersonalized and expressed in more abstract terms as the concept of rationality or the logic of choice.

During the next two decades or so this conclusion was strongly reinforced by Robbins' famous and influential (albeit controversial) methodological essay, *The Nature and Significance of Economic Science* (1932/1984) and by major developments in the theory of consumers' demand. The basic postulates of economics, Robbins declared, represented "simple and indisputable facts of experience," which required neither theoretical support nor experimental confirmation. They were givens. Although economic theory included an account of the individual's subjective valuations, the rationality assumption entailed no concession to hedonism or any other psychological doctrine. It merely signified consistency of choice. Other economists – some of them highly critical (for example, Hutchison, 1938) – argued that additional, highly restrictive assumptions were also involved, making the foundations of economic analysis purely theoretical and un-testable; but this contention did not significantly affect the course of mainstream theory in the ensuing decades.

Also in the 1930s a further step away from conventional marginal utility theory was taken in the Hicks-Allen development of indifference curve analysis, which dispensed with the troublesome concept of cardinal utility, and this was shortly followed by Samuelson's formulation of an operationalist type of "revealed preference" theory which, he claimed, eliminated all nonobservables – such as motivations, introspection, states of mind, etc. – including those presupposed in the Hicks-Allen ordinalist interpretation. For Samuelson, as for many others, this effectively completed the divorce of economics from psychology, fields with which it had been intimately associated in varying degrees ever since the eighteenth century. Yet, as Stanley Wong has persuasively argued, this conclusion was false. Samuelson's successive contributions to this subject were not simply inconsistent; his entire program was methodological, not substantive.

> It was launched by Samuelson because ordinal utility theory [Hicks-Allen] was considered methodologically unsatisfactory, not because it was

> inadequate theoretically or empirically; it was not asserted that the Samuelson Theory (revealed preference theory) offered new insights into consumer behavior (Wong, 1978, p. 127).

In the three decades since it was supposed that Houthakker had "completed" Samuelson's research program (Wong, 1978, p. 2) economists have demonstrated no desire to abandon utility theory. On the contrary, there is a voluminous and highly technical literature on the subject, largely concerned with problems arising from uncertainty and expectations, complications either overlooked or deliberately ignored by earlier generations of economists. However, the development of the expected utility (EU) research program has so far failed to produce results commensurate with the considerable investment of intellectual resources it has attracted. According to a major recent survey of the literature,

> ... the EU model does not offer a rich descriptive theory of problem representation [*pace* Cross] and will therefore not easily predict new context effects.... The failure of EU theory as both a descriptive and predictive model stems from an inadequate recognition of various psychological principles of judgment and choice ...

which the author illustrates with a variety of examples drawn from recent research (Schoemaker, 1982, p. 548*ff*.; cf. Arrow, 1982, p. 8). He therefore concludes that while the EU model

> ... has yielded deeper insights and more refined questions, both descriptively and normatively ... its present paradigmatic status (in certain fields) should he questioned.... [A]t the individual level EU maximization is more the exception than the rule, at least for the type of decision tasks examined....

and despite its "mathematical tractability" the model lacks "structural validity at the individual level" (Schoemaker, 1982, pp. 530, 550).

Both the critics and the defenders (for example, Gary Becker) agree that utility maximization models may simply generate a "bundle of empty tautologics" rather than a theoretical foundation for predicting behavioral responses to various changes (cf. Rosenberg. 1979). But while the defenders contend that the theory's generality enables the economist to extend his analysis over an ever-widening domain of human affairs, making it the archetypal imperialistic science (Stigler, 1984), some critics view it as a massive misdirection of intellectual energies. To Tibor Scitovsky, for instance, the concept of utility maximization "set back generations of scientific inquiry into consumer behavior, for it seemed to rule out – as a logical impossibility – any conflict between what man chooses to get and what will best satisfy him" (quoted in Schoemaker, 1982, pp. 539–540).

Although the logic of choice approach gained the ascendancy in the post-1930 period, it by no means achieved a complete hegemony. Textbook presentations of utility theory predominated for at least two decades – often accompanied by strenuous denials of all psychological implications – and for some time thereafter they appeared side by side with indifference curves. Moreover in the influential literature stemming from Cambridge, England, under Marshall's powerful shade, no effort was made to exclude references to psychological factors. Admittedly Marshall's followers did not systematically explore his subtle account of the interactions of "wants" and "activities" which was so penetratingly analyzed by the sociologist, Talcott Parsons (1931, 1932). Nevertheless, Ralph Hawtrey's *The Economic Problem* (1926) contains an account of the differences between passive spectators and active participants in enjoyable activities and introduces a suggestive distinction between defensive and creative products, while his extensive writings on monetary topics display a keen awareness of the part played by psychological factors in economic life. Much the same is true of A.C. Pigou's treatment of waves of optimism and pessimism in business cycles, but by far the most widely known examples of this genre are to be found in J.M. Keynes' works, especially his concepts of "animal spirits" and psychological "propensities," and the so-called psychological "law" underlying the relationship between consumption and income (Keynes, 1936. p. 96). Despite his open break with the past, Keynes was quintessentially Marshallian by upbringing and predilection; whereas Hicks, who had learned his advanced economics at the London School of Economics under Robbins' aegis, was primarily influenced by the works of continental economists, such as Pareto, Walras, and the early Austrians. His attempt to dissociate economics from psychology by means of indifference analysis was fully compatible with the view of the original Austrian marginalists (cf. section 3 of chapter 7).

Defenders of classical and neoclassical economics could legitimately claim that neither Keynes' pseudo-psychological "law" nor the innumerable references in economic literature to the psychological "facts" of everyday life called for a surrender, or even major concessions, to those who sought to combine or integrate the two disciplines. Schumpeter, a great historian of economics and a major creative economist in his own right, possibly overstated the case in asserting that "economists have never allowed their analysis to be influenced by the professional psychologists of their time, but have always framed for themselves such assumptions about psychical processes as they thought it desirable to make." Evidently casual empiricism is applied here as elsewhere. However, Schumpeter distinguished sharply between technical or formal economic analysis and what he called "economic sociology" and was much more positive about the latter. Experimental psychology, he contended, did not, but should, interest economists: "the efforts of psychologists to measure physical quantities is not a matter of indifference to any economist who is not lacking in scientific imagination." Behaviorism was an "ideology" that led to meaningless experimentation. It was also programmatic like psychologism, the methodological position that "psychology is really the basis from which any social science must start and from which all fundamental explanation must run." However, Gestalt psychology held significant promise, and Freudian psychology had "vast possibilities" of application to economics and sociology (Schumpeter, 1954, pp. 1058, 27, 797–798, respectively). Here, as always, Schumpeter was open-minded and methodologically eclectic. No doubt he would have welcomed much of the recent active research linking economics and psychology undertaken in the four decades since his death.

Double standards, prejudice, and talking at cross purposes

Rod Cross' paper (Cross, 1988, chapter 4) is a copybook example of the combination of methodological prejudices, misunderstandings, and unduly exacting demands that has discouraged many mainstream economists from collaborating effectively with psychologists. Of course, he is quite justified in dismissing as useless "highly abstract discussions of what psychology might have to offer" (section 4, Cross' italics; cf. Schumpeter, 1954, p. 797). But he is far too severe in requiring that economists should consider only those infusions from "psychological theories" (*sic.*) which can either explain existing anomalies in a "non ad hoc fashion," predict "novel facts and other forms of insight," and generate "clear refutable content." Curiously enough, it is the economists' own failure to fulfil these Lakatosian expectations that has been a major focus of complaint in the recent flood of methodological literature, including some of Cross' own strictures on econometrics! (see Cross 1984, pp. 93*ff*, 111*ff*). Why should contributions from psychology be required to live up to these standards? While it may be true that contemporary psychology contains "a welter of conflicting explanations," does this necessarily entail that they are all useless, however difficult it may be to sort the wheat from the chaff? Is the would-be collaborator inevitably condemned to what Cross (section 3) characterizes as "the infinite regress of choosing a psychological theory of choice between competing psychological theories of choice, learning and decision-making"?

Witticisms aside, why should not economists, like others, learn by trial and error what psychologists have to offer them? After all, there are innumerable relevant offerings cited in this book and in the other sources listed in the bibliography. Certainly it would be more convenient – and remarkable – if there were an array of ready-made psychological solutions for the economist's difficulties. Were this so they would surely have been discovered and utilized by now, and there would be no need to appeal for collaboration. The fact that earlier generations of economists have missed opportunities to learn from psychology (Cross, 1988, section 1) or to benefit from Shackle's wise insights (section 4; cf. Earl, 1983a, 1986b) need not preclude them from mending their ways in the future. Cross himself welcomes Akerlof's contributions as "piecemeal engineering," implying that Akerlof is not unduly deterred by the fact that interdisciplinary work is still in its early stages and lacking "a set of problems with a natural agenda" (Akerlof, 1984, p. 6, quoted by Cross, 1988, in section 4) – whatever that is.

Cross whole approach – where it is consistent – reflects the typical economist's demand for an "integrating theoretical structure" (Hirshleifer, 1985, pp. 61–62, quoted by Cross, 1988, in section 3), as if it were the sole precondition of useful interactions. In dismissing Bausor's desire for "a richer and more complex characterization of economics than that provided by the Arrow-Debreu general equilibrium model," Cross reflects the economist's preference for generality and simplicity over all other criteria of theory choice (for gentle criticism of the predilection see Hirschman, 1984). But surely the two kinds of approaches can coexist? All that may be required, at least at this stage, is a marginal shift of resources away from theories with "systemwide implications" (Cross' final line) towards more specific "psychological accounts of cognitive process." Indeed this may be unavoidable as economists develop theories about:

> Labor relations, imperfect competition, uncertainty and long-run dynamics [which] encase the decision-maker in a much larger maze than those considered in classical short-run theory. In these areas the economist and the psychologist have numerous common interests in cognitive theory that they have not shared previously (Simon, 1963, p. 709).

Cross demonstrates a curious concern that the infusion of psychology into economics might lead to a loss of "content" – curious, because many observers consider that the discipline already suffers from a lack of substantive content in its more formalized mathematical models (cf. Woo, 1986, Mirowski, 1986), a deficiency that could be remedied by an infusion of empirical content. There is too little prospect of a wave of enthusiasm for interdisciplinary work among economists to warrant the fear that it will radically transform their discipline, undermine its authority, and disturb its present isolation. The principal obstacle to collaborative research is, perhaps, the fundamental difference in style, or even metaphysics, between the two fields. Whereas psychologists tend to look for evidence of behavior and seek to formulate hypotheses to explain it, economists tend to work in the opposite direction, by starting out with formal theory and then considering what modifications might be required to make it applicable to the explanation of specific economic problems (this point was made many years ago: for example, Robinson, 1932, 1933). The very existence of these contrasting approaches suggests that some combination or interaction between the two might prove highly fruitful to both parties. Who knows, it might even encourage "alternative research programs" (Cross, 1988, section 5)!

In their fierce determination to protect their theory from refutation by means of what Popper has termed "defensive strategies," economists have retreated further and further into abstract realms that preserve generality at the expense of substantive content. This is no new phenomenon. As far back as 1925 that respected orthodox economist, Jacob Viner, deplored the

> all-too-prevalent methodological fanaticism which prefers the accurate but superficial to the approximate but fundamental, and which makes adaptability to its special technique of investigation, rather than importance, the standard for the selection of problems and the delimitation of the scope of inquiry (Viner, 1925, p. 659).

In the highly pertinent case of utility theory, for example, George Stigler (himself no radical) remarked, in a classic historical review of the literature, that

> Had specific tests been made of the implications of theories, the unfruitfulness of the ruling utility theory as a source of hypotheses in demand would soon have become apparent.... Not only were such specific implications not sought and tested, but there was a tendency, when they appeared to be a threat of an empirical test, to reformulate the theory to make the test ineffective (1965, pp. 155, 153).

This practice – what Mark Blaug has wittily termed "playing tennis with the net down" – is still widespread, as is clear from his *The Methodology of Economics, or How Economists Explain* (Blaug, 1980).

As A.K. Sen has noted in a recent review of the literature on problems of individual and collective wants and social welfare, the prevalence of purely formal analysis and the willful exclusion of variables that might conceivably provide new information and insights into economic behavior seriously impoverishes economic theory (Sen. 1982, pp. 102–103; cf. Baxter, in this book). According to Tversky and Kahneman, who have done important work in linking economics and psychology, economists have put the hypothesis of rational action "beyond question" so that the burden of proof has been placed "squarely on any alternative analysis of belief and choice. The advantage of the rational model is compounded because no other theory of judgment and decision can ever match it in scope, power and simplicity" (1987, p. 34).

Perhaps the orthodox victory in the earlier phase of debate has proved more inhibiting of the progress of economics than its proponents appreciated.

Coming full circle?

What of the present state of play? Cross, 1988, is fully justified in questioning whether current and future attempts to infuse psychology into economics are more likely to be successful (by what criterion?) than were the pre-1930 efforts. More specifically, "Are either the problems faced by theories in economics more severe, or is what psychology has to offer more compelling?" (section 4) than was the case half a century ago. I shall consider these questions in turn, and in both cases offer a strongly affirmative answer.

To judge by the flood of literature on the parlous state of the discipline, economic theory can hardly have been in a more serious condition before 1930. Sample titles, such as: *What's Wrong with Economics?* (Ward, 1972); *The Crisis in Economic Theory* (Bell and Kristol (eds.), 1981); *Economists at Bay, or Why the Experts Will Never Solve Your Problems* (Lekachman, 1976); *Why Economics is Not Yet a Science* (Eichner (ed.), 1983); *Economics and the Real World* (Kamarck, 1983); *Economics in Disarray* (Wiles and Routh (eds.), 1984), all written by recognized economists, either individually or in groups, do not suggest that complacency prevails. This catalogue could easily be supplemented by other book titles and innumerable articles produced by economists with recognized professional credentials. No doubt the collective "self-flagellation" revealed in these works reflects the combination of professional and public concern following the ending of the Keynesian hegemony (*c.* 1945–1965), and represents a reaction from the collective hubris and exaggerated claims of that era. Moreover, this reaction is partly attributable to recent adverse movements in the economy in a period when economists have given hostages to fortune by playing an increasingly prominent role in public affairs and policymaking.

Many of the pre-1930 criticisms of economic orthodoxy are echoed in recent writings, including the need for: (1) more "realistic" assumptions compatible with observed behavior, and consistent with the findings of other disciplines, including psychology; (2) a shift of focus away from abstract, general theories towards more specific, low- or middle-level empirically grounded theories which should be testable; (3) more systematic empirical research, as a basis for sound empirical generalizations; (4) more dynamic theories, incorporating changes in incomes, tastes, expectations, new commodities, etc.; (5) a broadening of the scope of economic theory, taking account of such influences on economic behavior as habit, custom, social emulation, advertising, etc.; and (6) studies of the influence of market and nonmarket forces on economic and social welfare (cf. Coats, 1976, pp. 49–50).

Doubtless some of these demands are being met, whether by mainstream economists or their critics, and to this extent the discipline may be in better shape than it was 50 years ago. Nevertheless, there are countervailing influences, such as the Friedmanite denial of the relevance of realistic assumptions (which has been widely accepted, notwithstanding severe strictures from numerous methodologists); the undue preoccupation with highly formalistic theory in the training of economists – a sociological as well as an intellectual problem (cf. Earl, 1983c; Woo, 1986); and the dominant influence of general equilibrium models in theoretical economics (Mirowski, 1986). Recent efforts to take account of ignorance and uncertainty in economic life have encountered formidable difficulties. Initial setbacks are only to be expected. Yet, to many qualified observers many economists seem preoccupied with "good games" (Hicks, 1979, p. viii) that have intellectual value but do not enhance their capacity to contribute to the solution of society's pressing problems. Some critics even accuse them of engaging in useless activities equivalent to optimizing the location of deckchairs on the Titanic.

Another prominent feature of recent economics is the tendency to split into warring camps – for example, Keynesians versus Monetarists; or various splinter or dissident groups such as the Austrians, Post Keynesians, New Classicals, Institutionalists (Old and New), Marxists, Sraffians, Radicals, etc. Whether this is a temporary state of affairs is impossible to say. Possibly the current buzzing, blooming confusion is merely the harbinger of a grand new synthesis. As William Baumol observed of the new industrial organization theory of contestable markets: "No uprising by a tiny band of rebels can hope to change an established order and when the time for rebellion is ripe it seems to break out simultaneously and independently in a variety of disconnected centers each offering its own program for the future" (1982, p. 1).

Turning to Cross' second question, "is what psychology has to offer more compelling" than was the case in 1930? – and noting the loaded word "compelling" – one is tempted to respond: can there be any reasonable doubt that 50 years of research into the relations between economics and psychology (including both psychological economics and economic psychology) has added to the corpus of useful theory and empirical result accessible to economists enterprising and open-minded enough to take advantage of it? The substantial bibliography in this book provides a more than adequate starting point. To quote but three examples: 30 years of research in cognitive psychology has immensely enhanced our knowledge of learning and decision-making processes (cf. Simon, 1987); the value of George Katona's even longer series of studies of consumer's attitudes is now much more widely appreciated; and we have recently witness "the behavioral rising in economics" (Gilad, Kaish and Loeb, 1984; see also the two-volume set edited by Gilad and Kaish, 1986). In addition to the inauguration of several new journals concerned with aspects of the relations between economics and psychology, the founding of the Society for the Advancement of Behavioral Economics promises to provide a valuable forum for the exchange of ideas, the coordination of research, the solution of problems of interest to scholars in both fields – possibly in other social sciences also. The proponents of this new movement cite four broad objections to mainstream economic theorizing: (1) a rejection of positivism as the methodological foundation for economic research; (2) a refusal to accept the use of deductive reasoning as a sufficient basis for a (social) science, (3) a marked dislike of static analysis of equilibrium *outcomes* rather than disequilibrium *processes;* and most important of all, (4) a unanimous objection to the *simplistic* economic model of rational agents exhibiting optimizing behavior (Gilad, Kaish, and Loeb, 1984, p. 2, italics in original).

The basic postulates of behavioral economics cited in this manifesto bear a remarkable resemblance to the pre-1930 criticisms of economics cited earlier (Coats, 1976, pp. 49–50; cf. Gilad, Kaish, and Loeb, p. 4). And, exactly like some of the earlier institutionalists, the authors of the new program claim that behavioral economics "is not a field of economics as much as a way of looking at the traditional fields" (Gilad, Kaish, and Loeb, p. 3). Doubtless mainstream economists will dismiss this characterization as an evasion of the responsibility to produce a genuine scientific theory, whereas sympathizers may interpret it as a sensible reluctance to engage in premature generalization.

The revisionists

We live in exciting times. Economics is in a highly unstable and transitional phase, perhaps more so than other social sciences considering that its central structure has so long withstood attack from a motley army of besiegers. No doubt the vast majority of economists adheres to the mainstream theories, but there is a considerable array of contending paradigms and approaches. Revisionists starting from the mainstream are working toward what they call a "new institutional economics" which has certain affinities to and some common sources (such as the work of Herbert Simon) with behavioral economics. According to one spokesman its central themes include the following:

1. Although definitely rational in a true sense, the agent of economic theory is not best conceived as rational in the narrow sense of maximizing within a framework of known alternatives.
2. Economic phenomena are in large measure the result of learning over time by economic agents; economic explanation should thus be a dynamic exercise – dynamic not merely in the sense of dynamic neoclassical models, but in a sense best rendered as evolutionary.
3. The coordination of economic activity is not merely a matter of premediated transactions in markets, but is supported by a wide range of economic and social institutions that are themselves an important topic of theoretical inquiry (Langlois, 1986, pp. 5–6).

As this manifesto suggests, the "new institutionalists" are less critical of the orthodox approach to economic rationality than either the behavioralists or the older generation of American institutionalists – Thorstein Veblen, John R. Commons, Wesley Mitchell, and Clarence Ayres. Nevertheless the differences between the old and new species are less marked than the latter claim, for they have major interests and aims in common, such as: broadening the scope of economics; viewing economic phenomena as processes with a history and a future, rather than as equilibria; emphasizing the interdependence of institutions and economic activity; and making economics a more "evolutionary" discipline, which was Veblen's primary objective. Generally speaking, the new institutionalists attach much less importance to psychology than their pre-1930 precursors. As Simon (1987) has noted, their analyses rely not on rationality assumptions but on "assumptions of informational or other limits on rationality" – that is, on sociological rather than psychological postulates. It is no coincidence that they trace their antecedents, in part, to Menger, who made limited use of psychology in his general theory, while emphasizing the importance of institutions (Runde, in section 3 of chapter 7; Langlois, 1986, pp. 4–5).

What are the prospects?

It may be both unseemly and hazardous for a historian of economics to engage in futurology. Yet some tentative concluding suggestions about the prospective relations between economics and psychology may be in order. At least four distinct scenarios can be envisaged.

1. The optimistic view that a new synthesis or paradigm is on the horizon or already here. Thus Scitovsky (1985, p. 19):

> The occasional bits of psychology to be found scattered in the writings of economists can be added up to yield a new, richer framework for economic

> analysis, capable of explaining many economic problems that are waiting to be explained. All that is needed is an ingenious young economist to collect the bits and pieces and integrate them into a coherent theory.

Shlomo Maital is even more confident, discussing in some detail the requirements a new paradigm must satisfy (1982, chapter 11, especially p. 262*ff.*), while others explore the broader implications of the "revival of subjectivism" (Wiseman, 1983, especially pp. 87–103 by Coats).

2. The pessimistic view that significant change is either impossible or unlikely given the strength of professional inertia and the pressures to conformity. Supporters of this general position differ markedly in their assessments of the status quo, as is hardly surprising, for despite considerable piecemeal evidence and abundant casual gossip there has been no systematic empirical research on the structure and functioning of the economics profession, even for the United States. Thus the pessimists disagree, for example, about the extent of control over resources and access to influential positions exercised by the discipline's power elite; how far new and prospective recruits are effectively socialized into conformity with the prevailing orthodoxy; the degree of uniformity in graduate training both within and outside the leading schools; the influence of textbooks in disseminating and maintaining established views; and the role of exogenous societal pressures in reinforcing the profession's dominant beliefs and practices. There is a large, scattered, and uneven literature on these matters which it would be misleading to cite selectively and inappropriate to list in detail. However, it is important to appreciate that this literature does not emanate exclusively from dissidents or members of the splinter groups mentioned earlier. Indeed, the state of economics is sufficiently distinctive to attract the attention of scholars concerned with comparative analysis of the sciences (Whitley, 1984).

3. The view that, as on many previous occasions, the economists will make moderate, ad hoc revisions to accommodate some of their critics' objections while preserving intact the existing disciplinary structure, hardcore assumptions, and set of problems. According to two recent Austrian commentators

> There is a "sponginess" to neoclassical economics that enables it to absorb divergent elements around it without ever emphasizing their main points. These fringe ideas become footnotes to which theorists can refer as evidence that they have taken the ideas into account (O'Driscoll and Rizzo, 1985, p. 231).

Or, again, from a "new institutionalist" viewpoint

> ... a major reason for heterdoxy's lack of influence is that many complaints and proposals can be accommodated by slight changes of meaning, treated and accommodated as special case models, or absorbed by broadening the theory somewhat, all with very few ripples. *The fact that prevailing theory*

> *defines what are reasonable and sophisticated objections to prevailing theory and what distinguishes appropriate from inappropriate proposals for amendement and reform is another defense.* It is employed primarily when the complaint seems uninteresting and unimportant, but *tends to be used also in cases where the complaint is potentially important but not easily treated by marginal modifications of the theory....*
>
> If the contemporary critics of othodoxy can be accused of not appreciating the importance of a coherent theoretical structure and of underestimating the resiliency and absorptive capacity of prevailing economic orthodoxy, the defenders of orthodoxy can be accused of trying to deny the importance of phenomena with which orthodoxy deals inadequately and at the same time overestimating the potential ability of models within the orthodox framework somehow to encompass these phenomena (Nelson and Winter, 1982, p. 48, italics added).

Of course, neither of these passages is necessarily representative. But taken together they help to suggest why the mainstream classical and neoclassical structure has survived virtually intact for so long, notwithstanding innumerable persuasive and effective attacks, while the second passage contains cogent reasons why the heterodox and orthodox approaches have failed to combine into a synthesis. It is too early to conjecture whether the current revisionist movement from within economics, in response to the behavioral and experimental work in psychology, is likely to change the existing content and structure of economics significantly (Frey, 1986, p. 544). Yet it certainly appears that the resurrection of the movement to bring economists and psychology into close and more fruitful contact is far more promising than its pre-1930 counterpart.

4. If none of the three previous scenarios is correct it may happen that behavioral (or psychological) economics will acquire enough momentum to become a separate quasi-autonomous subdiscipline with its own courses, degrees, training programs, research funds, journals, and societies. This book already indicates that the process is under way, and it seems likely to gather momentum. Indeed it is not unreasonable to foresee that this is but part of a general movement in economics, one may that leave the core of the discipline increasingly isolated and irrelevant to contemporary affairs. This would be compatible with the widespread contemporary view that advanced economic theory and econometrics is becoming simply a branch of applied mathematics, with ever more tenuous links with the real world (for example, Morishima, pp. 51–73, in Wiles and Routh, 1984; Blatt, pp. 166–86, in Eichner, 1983).

To suggest that the resurrection of psychological economics might contribute to the decline and possibly even the death of orthodox economics is a provocative but far-fetched idea. More likely, if one may judge by past experience, is the possibility that the behavioral research program will rejuventate the orthodox tradition without – one hopes – a repetition of the resistance to change that was apparent in the post-1930 era referred to earlier.

References

Akerlof, G.A. (1984) *An Economic Theorist's Book of Tales*. Cambridge: Cambridge University Press.

Arrow, K.J. (1982) Risk perception in psychology and economics. *Economic Inquiry* 20: 1–9.

Baumol, W.J. (1982) Contestable markets: an uprising in the theory of industry structure. *American Economic Review* 72: 1–13.

Bell, D. and Kristol, I. (eds.), *The Crisis in Economic Theory*. New York: Basic Books.

Black, R.D.C., Coats, A.W. and Goodwin, C.D.W. (eds.), *The Marginal Revolution in Economics*. Durham, NC: Duke University Press.

Blaug, M. (1980) *The Methodology of Economics: or How Economists Explain*. Cambridge: Cambridge University Press.

Coats, A.W. (1976) Economics and psychology: the death and resurrection of a research programme. In Latsis, S.J. (ed.), *Method and Appraisal in Economics*. Cambridge: Cambridge University Press.

Coats, A.W. (1983) The revival of subjectivism in economics. In Wiseman, J. (ed.), *Beyond Positive Economics?* London: Macmillan.

Cross, R. (1984) Monetarism and Duhem's thesis. In Wiles, P. and Routh, G. (eds.), *Economics in Disarray*. Oxford: Blackwell.

Cross, R. (1988) in P. E. Earl (ed.) *Psychological Economics: Development, Tensions, Prospects*, Boston: Kluwer, chapter 4.

Earl, P.E. (1983a) *The Economic Imagination: Towards a Behavioural Analysis of Choice*. Brighton: Wheatsheaf.

Earl, P.E. (1983c) A behavioral theory of economists' behaviour. In Eichner, A.S. (ed.), *Why Economics Is Not Yet a Science*. Armonk, NY: M.E. Sharpe, Inc.

Earl, P.E. (1986b) *Lifestyle Economics: Consumer Behaviour in a Turbulent World*. Brighton: Wheatsheaf.

Eichner, A.S. (1983) Why economics is not yet a science. *Journal of Economic Issues* 17: 507–520.

Fischer, R. (1986) *The Logic of Economic Discovery: Neoclassical Economics and the Marginal Revolution*. Brighton: Wheatsheaf.

Gilad, B. and Kaish, S. (eds.) (1986) *Handbook of Behavioral Economics (Volume A: Behavioral Microeconomics; Voulme B: Behavioural Macroeconomics)*. Greenwich, CT: JAI Press, Inc.

Gilard, B. Kaish, S. and Loeb, P.D. (1984) From economic behavior to behavioral economics: the behavioral uprising in economics. *Journal of Behavioral Economics* 13: 1–22.

Hawtrey, R.G. (1926) *The Economic Problem*. London: Longmans.

Hirschman, A.O. (1984) Against parsimony: three ways of complicating some categories of economic discourse. *American Economic Review, Papers and Proceedings* 74: 89–96.

Hirshleifer, J. (1985) The expanding domain of economics. *American Economic Review* 75: 53–68.

Hutchison, T.W. (1938) *The Significance and Basic Postulates of Economic Science*, reprinted 1965. New York: Augustus M. Kelly.

Kamarck, A.M. (1983) *Economics and the Real World*. Oxford: Blackwell.

Keynes, J.M. (1936) *The General Theory of Employment, Interest and Money*. London: Macmillan.

Langlois, R.N. (ed.) (1986) *Economics as a Process: Essays in the New Institutional Economics*. Cambridge: Cambridge University Press.

Lekachman, R. (1976) *Economists at Bay: or Why the Experts Will Never Solve Your Problems*. New York: McGraw-Hill.

Maital, S. (1982) *Minds, Markets and Money*. New York: Basic Books.

Mirowski, P. (1986) *The Reconstruction of Economic Theory*. Boston: Kluwer.

Morishima, M. (1984) The good and bad uses of mathematics. In Wiles, P. and Routh, G. (eds.), *Economics in Disarray*. Oxford: Blackwell.

Nelson, R.R. and Winter, S.G. (1982) *An Evolutionary Theory of Economics Change*. Cambridge, MA: Harvard University Press.

O'Driscoll, G.P. and Rizzo, M. (1985) *The Economics of Time and Ignorance*. Oxford: Blackwell.

Parsons, T. (1931) Wants and activities in Marshall. *Quarterly Journal of Economics* 45: 101–140.

Parsons, T. (1932) Economics and sociology: Marshall in relation to the thought of his time. *Quarterly Journal of Economics* 46: 316–347.

Robbins, L. (1932/1984) *An Essay on the Nature and Significance of Economic Science*. London: Macmillan.

Robinson, J.V. (1932) *Economics is a Serious Subject*. Cambridge: W. Heffer and Sons.

Robinson, J.V. (1933) *The Economics of Imperfect Compitition*. London: Macmillan.

Rosenberg, A. (1979) Can economics explain everything? *Philosophy of the Social Sciences* 9: 509–529.

Schoemaker, P.J.H. (1982) The expected utility model: its variants, purposes, evidence and limitations. *Journal of Economic Literature* 20: 529–563.

Schumpeter, J.A. (1954) *History of Economics Analysis*. Oxford: Oxford University Press.

Scitovsky, T. (1985) Psychology by economists. Unpublished paper prepared for eighth annual Middlebury Conference on Economic Issues, October.

Sen, A.K. (1982) Rational fools: a critique of the behavioral foundations of economic theory. In Sen, A.K. (ed.), *Choice, Welfare and Measurement*. Oxford: Blackwell.

Simon, H.A. (1963) Economics and psychology. In Koch, S. (ed.), *Psychology: A Study of a Science, Volume 6, Investigations of Man as a Socius — Their Place in Psychology and the Social Sciences*. New York: McGraw-Hill.

Simon, H.A. (1987) Behavioural economics. In Eatwell, J., Milgate, M. and Newman, P. (eds.), *The New Palgrave*. New York: Stockton Press.

Stigler, G.J. (1965) *Essays in the History of Economics*. Chicago: University of Chicago Press.

Stigler, G.J. (1984) Economics: the imperial science? *Scandinavian Journal of Economics* 86: 301–313.

Tversky, A. and Kahneman, D. (1987) Rational choice and the framing of decisions. In Hogarth, R.M. and Reder, M.W. (eds.), (1987) *Rational Choice: The Contrast Between Economics and Psychology*. Chicago: University of Chicago Press.

Viner, J. (1925) The utility concept in value theory and its critics. *Journal of Political Economy* 33: 636–659.

Ward, B. (1972) *What's Wrong with Economics?* New York: Basic Books.

Whitley, R. (1984) *The Intellectual and Social Organization of the Sciences*. Oxford: Clarendon Press.

Wiles, P. and Routh, G. (eds.) (1984) *Economics in Disarray*. Oxford: Blackwell.

Winch, D. (1970) Marginalism and the boundaries of economic science. In Black, R.D.C., Coats, A.W. and Goodwin, C.D.W. (eds.), *The Marginal Revolution in Economics.* Durham, NC: Duke University Press.

Wong, S. (1978) *The Foundations of Paul Samuelson's Revealed Preference Theory.* London: Routledge and Kegan Paul.

Woo, H.K.H. (1986) *What's Wrong with Formalization in Economics?* Newark, CA: Victoria Press.

17 Appraising economic theories*

This bulky volume contains the revised proceedings of a conference held in Capri, Italy, from 15–18 October, 1989, funded by the Latsis Foundation. It was, in a sense, a sequel to the Lakatos Conference held in Nafplion, Greece, in September 1974, with lavish support from the same source. From the earlier occasion two volumes appeared: Spiro Latsis ed. *Method and Appraisal in Economics* (C.U.P., 1976) and Colin Howson ed. *Method and Appraisal in the Physical Sciences* (C.U.P., 1976). The first of these has been extensively cited in the economics literature. The latter, curiously enough, does not even get a mention here.

At the earlier conference about half of the fifty or so participants were non-economists – mainly historians and philosophers of science; and as Neil de Marchi recalls in his introduction: "The atmosphere was one of anticipation, and most papers had something of the air of first ventures into a promising but largely unexplored territory" (p. 18). However, this was more true of the economists than the other participants, among them some of Imre Lakatos' colleagues and students who were generally more familiar with and favorably disposed to his ideas than the economists.[1]

In the intervening decade and a half there has been a veritable explosion of new writings on economic methodology and some substantial, at times even startling, new developments. De Marchi and Mark Blaug uncovered seventy or so articles reflecting Lakatos's influence in economics, and the Capri conference was assembled to assess the current state of his contributions. As it transpired, the results were distinctly mixed, as were the editors' reactions. According to De Marchi:

> not a few participants displayed more awareness of the difficulties already encountered in settling the new land, or impatience with the things that had excited the first settlers, than they did a sense of expectancy about possibilities as yet unrealized (p. 18).

However, Blaug, in his "Afterword," was much less sanguine, for he was

> personally taken aback by what can only be described as a generally dismissive, if not hostile, reaction to Lakatos' MSRP [Methodology of Scientific Research Programs]. Of the 37 participants, I estimate that only

> 12 were willing to give Lakatos a further run for his money and of the 17 papers delivered at the conference not more than five were unambiguously positive about the value of MSRP (p. 500).

Whether this outcome constituted success or failure presumably depended on the organizers' expectations. Blaug, one of the principal initiators of the Nafplion gathering, was obviously disappointed. De Marchi, on the other hand, who has never been as deeply committed to the Lakatosian (or Popperian) approach, was more qualified, yet still sanguine, seeing

> in the Capri papers hopeful signs of Lakatosian and modified Lakatosian work to be pursued in some hitherto neglected directions, even when the authors themselves are more ready to call it a day so far as MSRP is concerned. The reader will have to judge whether my readings are unduly optimistic.[2]

Before responding to this invitation, or describing the contents of the Capri volume, let me first disclose an interest. I was present at and contributed a paper to the Nafplion proceedings, being then an enthusiastic but not uncritical supporter of Lakatos's methodology. Viewed from an history of economics perspective, MSRP seemed much more specific, and to that extent more useful than Kuhn's approach, enormously stimulating though that had been. It incorporated a temporal dimension – since research programmes could be said to emerge, develop, progress or degenerate, or even die off; and this temporal dimension offered suggestive insights and provided ample opportunities for historical investigation and interpretation. Needless to say, back in 1974 MSRP represented promise rather than performance, for there had been few attempts to apply it to economics. Yet even then I was fully aware that my own conference topic, suggested by Lakatos, was far too large, ill-defined, and sprawling to constitute an ideal case study.[3] Now I note with some satisfaction that during the Capri proceedings there were substantial differences of opinion over MSRP strategy – e.g., whether to focus on "broad" (encompassing) or "narrow" (specific) SRP's; whether to study individual SRP's or groups; and how to define their boundaries and isolate their Lakatosian components. These matters will be considered more fully later.

The table of contents of the Capri volume gives a clear general indication of the subject matter. De Marchi's introduction, "Rethinking Lakatos' precedes two unequal parts: I "The Criterion of Empirical Progress in Economics," and II "Program Identification and Program Rivalry." Each part has three subsections, as follows:

1. "Theoretical Progress and Excess Content" – papers by Jeremy Shearmur and D. Wade Hands; comments by Kurt Klappholz, Bert Hamminga, and Uskali Maki.
2. "Testing" – papers by Jinbang Kim (on Job Search Theory) and Christopher Gilbert (on Demand Analysis and Consumption Analysis); comments by de Marchi and Marjorie McElroy.

3. "Empirical Hypotheses in Game Theory and Experimental Economics" – papers by Marina Bianchi and Hervé Moulin (on Game Theory), and Vernon Smith, Kevin McCabe, and Stephen Rassenti (on Experimental Economics); comments by H.M. Collins.
4. "On Including and Excluding Lines of Enquiry" – papers by Mary Morgan (On Process Analysis in Econometrics), Roy Weintraub (On Stabilizing Dynamics); and Rod Cross (Alternative Accounts of Equilibrium Employment); comments by Roger Backhouse, Blaug, and Jan Kregel.
5. "Delineating Programmes" – papers by Rodney Maddock and Kevin Hoover (On Aspects of New Classical Macroeconomics), and a third by Backhouse (On the Neo-Walrasian Programme); comments by Alessandro Vercelli, Nancy Wulwick and Maarten Janssen.
6. "Assessing Sraffian and Austrian Economics" – papers by Ian Steedman and Don Lavoie; comments by Stefano Zamagni, Edwin Burmeister and Bruce Caldwell.

Finally, Blaug's "Afterword" is preceded by Collins's short paper on "History and Sociology of Science and History and Methodology of Economics," for which there was no commentator.[4]

To say that the main value of this volume lies in the dozen detailed studies plus comments on particular aspects or branches of recent economics (not always research programs) involves no denigration of the two useful scene-setting papers by Shearmur and Hands. The latter's penetrating dissection of "The Problem of Excess Content: Economics, Novelty, and a Long Popperian Tale" admirably prepares the reader for some of the difficulties encountered later in the book. In recent years, however, economic methodologists have increasingly recognized the need for closer examination of what economists actually do – i.e., how they go about their business – rather than looking to the philosophy of science for guidance; and from this standpoint, the Capri volume represents a substantial advance. There has, indeed, been genuine progress in knowledge and understanding since Nafplion.

Taken as a whole, the Capri essays reveal the difficulties encountered in proceeding from the high plane of Lakatosian philosophy of science to the nitty gritty details of particular research programs, including what de Marchi calls "local strategies" (p. 20). Doubtless some of these difficulties would arise in applying any general philosophy or methodology to the ideas and activities of working scholars (or, as some might prefer, proceeding in the opposite direction from particulars to generals).[5] In the present case, some participants were clearly uncomfortable with any discussion of abstract epistemological issues whatsoever, while others (perhaps most?) were unfamiliar with the full range of Lakatos's writings. This was a matter of no small significance, given his occasional vagueness and inconsistency, and the major shift of his ideas from the earlier *Proofs and Refutations* to his later MSRP. Some authors, e.g., Lavoie and Steedman, either made no serious attempt to apply MSRP or declared that it was unhelpful or irrelevant; and while conventional neoclassical economists may dismiss Austrian and Sraffian economics as fringe or deviant topics, to which MSRP may be inapplicable, the same cannot be said for econometrics (Morgan), game theory (Bianchi and Moulin) or experimental economics (Smith, McCabe and Rassenti), novel though the last of these is. The authors of the essays on these three subjects evidently did not find Lakatos helpful.[6] Hoover, after a scholarly and revealing struggle with MSRP, declared that "Lakatos's own methodology is falsified like all the others" – softening the blow somewhat by citing Lakatos's admission that: "*All* methodologies, *all* rational reconstructions can be historiographically 'falsified': science is rational, but its rationality cannot be subsumed under the general laws of any methodology" (p. 385).

Given the range and variety of material in this volume it may be helpful to present some of the principal problems schematically.

What is a research program?

A resonably clear answer to this question is essential if MSRP is to serve as a valuable tool of interpretation or appraisal. Difficulties include: the boundary problem – what is inside or outside a given program (pp. 337–8) and what are the relationships between intra-and extra-core variables (p. 445); and how to distinguish between successive variants of a given program and the emergence of a new program (a point admirably revealed in the Maddock and Hoover studies of New Classical Macroeconomics – especially pp. 337–8, 343, 352–3, 368–70, 374–5, with Hoover effectively employing the terms 'tribe' and 'family' to characterize programs).

Unfortunately Lakatos did not explain how programs emerge, or whether a program can develop in isolation or only in competition with others; and Steedman, discusssing negative contributions, asked: if program (a) is legitimately criticized from the standpoint of program (b) is that a contribution to (a) or (b) or both? (p. 443)

As noted earlier, programs can be defined either narrowly or broadly, and each approach has merits and limitations. Janssen, following Zandvoort, distinguished between 'guide' and 'supply' programs, the former determining the issues to be discussed while the latter provides the language and methods by which they must be tackled. "Roughly speaking, the guide program has a well-defined domain of issues with which it is concerned, but it does not have a method of its own. The reverse holds true for the supply program, which is characterized by a clear-cut method and a rather vague domain of intended applications" (p. 430). Of course, uniformity of interpretation is neither to be expected nor desired. Sometimes, perhaps usually, there is scope for "reasonable interpretation" (p. 132), but none of the Capri authors seemed disposed to supplement Duhem's "reasons of good sense" by incorporating "some hard Popperian standards of appraisal" (as suggested by Lakatos) even "to avoid embarrassment arising from their theories being contradicted by empirical evidence".[7]

What is a hard core?

The answer to this question is complicated by the realization that: The actual hard core of a program does not actually emerge fully armed like Athene from the head of Zeus. It develops slowly, by a long preliminary process of trial and error" (Lakatos, quoted on p. 370). During that process it can undergo articulation, hardening, refurbishment, even crumbling, prompting Hoover to liken it to "Elmer's glue, which is hard enough until it gets wet" (p. 371). Although de Marchi maintains that "putting Lakatos to work seems to *require* clear enunications of hard core and heuristics that can be tested against the historical record, just as Weintraub has taught us to do" (p. 16), he immediately adds the qualifier. "Or does it, in all cases?". Backhouse, who favors a more formal attempt to define hard cores and heuristics (pp. 267), finds it necessary to reconstruct Weintraub's version in examining the Neo-Walrasian Research Program (p. 404 ff). De Marchi warns that if hard core and heuristics "evolve and mutually inform each other," then preoccupation with the former rather than a process of discovery may lead to "misplaced concreteness" (p. 16). This, however, is but one of several pitfalls for interpreters, since Lakatos's admission that "different programs may have a common hard core and be differentiated only by their positive heuristics" (quoted by Hoover, p. 368) provides yet another occasion for disagreement between contentious critics and defenders. More generally, Maddock observes that economic research cannot easily be fitted into the Lakatosian framework because

> one can analyze the same theoretical phenomenon at a variety of different levels and in the context of encompassing research programs. In a large literature this can clearly lead to confusion; the same contributions will be assessed in quite different ways, depending on whether they are defined as being within program A or program B: one person's hard core will be another's protective belt (p. 338).

The criterion (criteria?) of progress

For historically-minded methodologists, one of the initial attractions of Lakatos's approach was his distinction between progressive and degenerating research programs; but, unfortunately, this too constituted a difficulty for the Capriciosi. As Hands notes, theoretical progress occurs with the prediction of some novel, hitherto unexpected fact, whereas empirical progress requires that this excess empirical content be also corroborated (p. 64). De Marchi stresses Lakatos's emphasis on the primacy of theory – "the relative autonomy of theoretical science"; yet he also notes Lakatos's claim that: "All propositions are theoretical, even those we call observational or 'factual'" (p. 134). Lakatos recognized progress in heuristic power, and in technical refinements, provided the resulting succession of new models involves an increase of content at each step, though apparently this may not be essential (cf pp. 133; and 135–6,11-12,16). However, Backhouse, commenting on Morgan, asserts that: "Novel facts and empirical testing can be brought in only when we consider economic ideas as well as econometric techniques" (p. 269). He doubts that research programs in such techniques constitute research programs in economics, in the Lakatosian sense, (pp. 266–7).

Novel facts, the key element in excess content (which is essential to the Lakatosian idea of research progress), cause further trouble. Lakatos offers three definitions of novel facts (p. 133) whereas Hands, who has undoubtedly "spent a great amount of time with the Lakatosian literature" confesses that he has "no idea what Lakatos 'really meant' by novel facts." His pursuit of this quarry in his "novel fact hunt" yields at least five different definitions, consequently one sympathizes with his distaste for "novel fact fetishism."[8]

Theories, empirical models, and the role of testing

The discussion of these matters, which are central to present-day technical economics, constitutes one of the most important elements in the Capri volume. But the outcome is by no means clear.

A reiterated theme is the "continuing interplay between empirical testing, theoretical modification, further testing, and so on" (Smith *et. al.*, pp. 218–9), while Hoover remarks that: "There is a division of labour in scientific research between theory and empirics with influence running in both directions. And, as any economist would expect, there are gains from trade" (p. 383). Gilbert, who, describes "testing theories as a major professional obligation," emphasizes that "economic theory seldom relates directly to data. Instead economists are required to intermediate theory and data with empirical models but we cannot directly test theories. Whether or not we may interpret these tests of models as indirectly testing theory is a more complicated question" (p. 139; cf. pp. 139–40). Whereas Morgan contends that economists test empirical models, not theories, Gilbert qualifies this assertion, adding that to concede that a theory can be tested only through an empirical model is not to argue that theories can never be tested. His paper aims to demonstrate that "in demand analysis we are only testing the appropriateness of particular empirical models, while in consumption analysis tests of empirical models are genuine tests of the underlying theory".[9] Hence, "whether or not a theory can be tested depends at least in part on the character of the theory" (p. 162), an observation he makes no effort to specify more fully.

Kim flatly contradicts the conventional interpretation of Lakatos by arguing that "few economists regard it as necessary for new empirical models to contain excess empirical content in order for them to replace earlier models.... It is therefore a category mistake always to seek for content-increasing changes in a series of empirical models" (p. 128). Moreover, two economists will seldom end up with the same empirical model even though they started with the same theory. (p. 115)

No careful reader of the Capri volume will conclude that the process of developing and testing empirical models is easy. These models may be more or less simplified than theoretical models; and: "The appropriate empirical model may have to combine implications from different theories; to acknowledge the possibility that implications of the theory under investigation may be blurred by failure of the theoretical *ceteribus paribus* conditions; and to admit nuisance parameters to account for theoretically extraneous effects" (Morgan, p. 141; cf. Kim, p. 105).

Clearly there is no consensus on the relationships between theories, empirical models, and testing; and de Marchi may be somewhat overoptimistic in concluding that despite all the conditions and qualifications the essays in Part I are still valuable by "forcing us into a subtler, richer understanding of the role of theory in economics and especially of the interactions between theoretical and empirical models, and between models, measurement and testing in the ongoing process of theory development" (p. 21). Whether this enhanced understanding could have been obtained without Lakatos's assistance, is quite another matter.

Economic methodology

Several of the conference participants explicitly dissociated themselves from any kind of methodological monism, even of the Lakatosian species. Steedman, for instance, cites Zamagni's "warnings that each science may need its proper (different) methodology, that methodology follows science rather than leads it, and that it is indeed undesirable that methodologists be permitted to prescribe what is good procedure in science" (p. 447). Likewise, Gilbert mentions the "danger that in discussing methodology one starts with a view of the way scientific activity is or should be carried out and then looks for examples which illustrate this view" (p. 137). He considers that "methodologies are to a large extent implicitly defined by the questions being asked" (p. 159). Hoover, who cites Wittgenstein and Lakatos in support, maintains that "one must discover the general principles in the particular cases.... Scientific practice, therefore, consists of groups of related and partly overlapping models and practices.... No model is primary," although: "When many variants on a model exist, any one may, for many purposes at least, serve as an exemplar" (pp. 375,373). As Wulwick acknowledges, although Lakatos tried to demarcate science from non-science, he recognized that scientific practice was in fact often unscientific (p. 395) and this should be borne in mind by those seeking to employ Lakatos's method of rational reconstruction.

Lakatos, history and the sociology of science

The Lakatosian approach to science is essentially historical (p. 25), and Lavoie suggests that the impetus Lakatos gave to intellectual history may indeed be his most valuable contribution (p. 473). Yet once again we encounter serious philosophical methodological and interpretative problems that limit Lakatos's value to historians of economics. De Marchi believes that despite all the difficulties, MSRP still "offers hints that help to make sense of what economists do and have done in the past." He strongly endorses the multiple interpretative possibilities inherent in Weintraub's constructivist approach (p. 27; cf p. 273 ff) although Weintraub himself, like Shearmur, is very critical of Lakatos's monistic view of the history of science as a story to be told exclusively in Lakatosian methodological and epistemological terms (p. 44). It ends up

> recommending as *the* historiography of science, the writing of the kind of historical account that in his view is needed for evaluative purposes.... But what is written for the purposes of theory appraisal is a strange kind of history; and it seems to me unlikely that we will gain much by treating the activities of historical agents whose concerns and criteria are different from ours as if what they were really doing was to be explained in terms of Lakatos's ideas about methodology (pp. 44–5).

Shearmur concedes that there is

> a sense in which a personal familiarity with certain kinds of problem solving under theoretical constraints can be of the greatest interest in understanding the ideas of historical figures... [Yet] some very bad history has been written by people who assume that what historical figures were *really* concerned with was the discovery of ideas with which we are familiar, or even that ideas familiar to us are to be found implicitly lurking behind their texts (p. 45)

In a hard-hitting paper, Weintraub argues that Lakatos's rational reconstruction commits the storyteller to create a rational program which becomes the main actor in the story; so that the history of science becomes an exemplar of rationality itself. This is especially clear in the case of economics, in which

> producers and consumers of the history of economics have accustomed themeselves to read the past from the present's perspective,... [leading to] a concentration on issues of precursors, harbingers, logical slips, factual errors, misuse of evidence, and all manner of past writing which illuminates the present state of economics or helps us to understand what we currently believe. (p. 279)

Of course there is nothing wrong in principle in pointing out precursors, harbingers, logical slips, factual errors, misuse of evidence etc. But Weintraub is entirely justified in pointing to Donald Walker's Presidential Address as a series of simple instructions how to do history of economics 'proper' (p. 280). Whether a constructivist approach means any one interpretation is as 'good' as any other is, however, quite a different matter, which opens a can of worms best left closed for the time being.[10]

To this reviewer, it is of particular interest that the sociology of economics (or knowledge, or science) figures much more prominently in the Capri than in the earlier Nafplion volume. In recent years we have learned that science viewed from close range, as for example, in studies of 'laboratory life', is very different from that seen through the philosopher's inverted telescope. The familiar distinction between the 'internalist' and 'externalist' approaches to the history and philosophy of science may be crude; nevertheless, several of the Capriciosi are critical of Lakatos's hostility to what he once termed "externalist rubbish". Shearmur, for instance, argues that "methodological appraisal and the study of the sociology and the rhetoric of science are not necessarily enemies, but, rather, complement each other," for there is no incompatibility between Popper's and Lakatos's concerns and an interest in "the sociology of institutions or power relationships, or perhaps even to the wider issues of political economy" (pp. 47, 45). Collins, the one *bona fide* sociologist of science featured in this volume, complains that historians of economics fail to utilize their specialist insights into the discipline as practitioners, "preferring to do the sort of history which does not require any special *understanding* of the subject".[11] Fortunately there are clear signs that this kind of misallocation of intellectual resources is nowadays gradually being rectified.

In this volume Hoover's study of the New Classical Macroeconomics and the neoclassical "family" or "tribe" is the most explicitly critical attack on Lakatos's neglect of the social aspects of research. In the case of rational expectations, Hoover argues, the program's ability

> to capture the interest of the generation of economists being trained in the 1970's was crucial to its great popularity in that decade and perhaps to the rapid exhaustion of its potential. The ability to convert was partly explained by the advertising undertaken on its behalf. There is a clear feedback from advertisement to recruitment, and from recruitment to the pace of exploitation of the positive heuristic of any program. It is an element of the sociology of knowledge rather than its logic, but the two are related in a way that lies outside Lakatos (p. 354; cf p. 347 ff).

Shearmur, more generally, emphasizes the inter-subjective element in testing (pp. 48–9; cf p. 382). The pressure for consensus is sociological, and

> if one sees the 'empirical basis' of our knowledge as the product of inter-subjective agreement – and thus of argument and negotiation between different parties: as a social construction – then clearly one should be interested in empirical and theoretical investigations of how all of this currently takes place… a *critical* sociology of knowledge… will lead us to suggest improvements in our institutions from the perspective of our pursuit of scientific knowledge (p. 50).

According to Andrea Salanti, historians of economics have accepted MSRP because of the dominant influence of 'internal' history of the kind Lakatos favored (cited on p. 28). However, that attachment may have been permanently undermined by the present volume. Despite de Marchi's editorial efforts to present the Lakatosian approach in a favourable light, he concedes that the work of Weintraub, Maddock, Klamer, Hoover and others raises pertinent questions about the social conditions of the production of 'knowledge'... which, when based on modem pragmatic philosophy's challenge to rationality as a privileged standpoint, threaten to undermine the comfortable link in MSRP between knowledge and rationality (p. 14).

Conclusion

The Capri volume is a striking testimony to Lakatos's influence on the history and methodology of economics – an influence that now clearly seems to be waning rapidly. In part this is but one manifestation of a more general movement away from the earlier fashion of applying comprehensive philosophical and methodological frameworks to economics, or indeed to other scientific disciplines.

The meticulously detailed studies of specific research programs in this volume, written by acknowledged experts and commented on by their informed critics, do not merely display Lakatos's limitations – though that may be the overwhelming impression most readers take from this collection. They also demonstrate, more constructively, how much can be learned when practicing economists take the trouble to examine critically what they and their professional colleagues have been up to, and where it may lead. This is undoubtedly a contribution of lasting value, for which the editors are to be congratulated.

Unfortunately the same cannot be said for the proofreading. In a volume of this size the dozen or so typographical errors are not excessive. But the concluding general bibliography is not complete, as readers are entitled to suppose, for a number of items cited in the text or in the bibliographies appended to most of the articles and comments are missing, while others are incorrect. One page reference (on p. 446) is meaningless – presumably it refers to the author's manuscript; the discussant mentioned in a footnote on p. 58 does not appear in the list of participants; while in commenting on Cross, Blaug cites two passages and one author that do not appear in Cross's essay. Presumably it was revised without Blaug's knowledge.

Notes

* A Review Article of: *Appraising Economic Theories. Studies in the Methodology of Research Programs.* Neil de Marchi and Mark Blaug, eds. (Aldershot: Edward Elgar, 1991) ISBN 1 85278 515 2 pp. ix + 566. £75.

1 While the Capri participants included a "sprinkling" of philosophers and sociologists of science (Cf. Blaug's Afterword), there was an overwhelming preponderance of economists. I see no evidence of the physicists who, Blaug says, were also present. Unless otherwise indicated, all subsequent page references are to this volume.

2 p. 19. De Marchi's introduction gives an excellent overview of the subject matter of the conference, together with thoughtful comments on past uses (and misuses) of Lakatos' work in the economics literature and indications of opportunities missed. While agreeing with many points in his account, I nevertheless feel that his conclusions are more favorable than an examination of the volume suggests.

3 See my "Economics and Psychology: the death and resurrection of a research programme," in Spiro Latsis, *op.cit.* pp. 43–64; and my earlier, even more exploratory

effort, "Situational determinism in economics: The implications of Latsis' argument for the historian of economics," *The British Journal of the Philosophy of Science* Vol. 25 (1974) pp. 285–8. To judge by de Marchi's Appendix, pp. 29–30, the first of these efforts was not "creative," although from my standpoint it represented an attempt to find some merit in the Lakatosian model, without being "mechanical".

4 For the provenance of Collins's paper, see p. 22.

5 For differing views on this point see, for example, pp. 18, 27, 137, 336, 364–5.

6 However, interestingly enough, in a post-conference letter to Blaug, Vernon Smith wrote: "On almost every page of Lakatos I find articulate expressions of what I have been doing as an experimentalist for years. I never got that much out of my much earlier reading of Kuhn and Popper … "(quoted by de Marchi, p. 21). Possibly others of the Capricies may have had similar afterthoughts.

7 (pp. 319–20). On pp. 24–5 de Marchi argues that "it is not the singularity of designation that makes 'research program' the appropriate unit of appraisal, but the notion of dynamically linked sequences of theories, which cohere as to research strategy (and perhaps techniques) and which share some underlying metaphysical presuppositions." It seems doubtful that many of the Capri authors would accept this rather loose interpretation.

8 (pp. 70, 94ff). As de Marchi observes, "the narrowness of the excess content (novel fact) criterion for judging progress not only causes MSRP to exclude many of the acknowledgeably best gambits of economics, but means that most of economics, indeed of all science, is irrational" (p. 26, n. 6 para 6).

9 P. 142. It should be noted that the commentator, McElroy, firmly disagrees with Gilbert's interpretation. (Cf. pp. 169,174).

10 The following remarks are both wise and constructive: "It is no news to the historian to be told that it is impossible to construct a convention-free rational history; nor, of course, to hear that all histories are constructs, and the rational is but one of many possible histories; or to read that rational history fails to portray scientific practice 'truly'. One writes methodologically self-conscious and, ideally, multiple histories for any episode, in the same spirit as a working scientist tries to be aware of the procedures he or she selects, and of the alternative procedures that might have been chosen or are in fact being used by others. This is not an instrumental defense for ignoring philosophical objections, but a pragmatic argument for proceeding anyway, dealing with the objections on the basis of the best solutions currently available." (De Marchi, p. 27)

11 (p. 496). As Steedman observes, "appraisal needs to be based on the *fullest* knowledge and understanding of a body of work" which only the 'insider' possesses; but does it necessarily follow that an insider is likely to be lenient in his or her appraisal? Admittedly, "someone who suspects, on whatever grounds, that a body of work is not that valuable, may not be motivated to acquire the requisite knowledge and understanding for adequate appraisal…. The 'insider' might be tempted to abuse Lakatos's work to glorify his own scientific allegiance, the 'critic' to abuse it to cover his own illiteracy" (pp. 442–3). In other words, as historians well know, there are no impartial, objective criteria of appraisal.

18 The influence of Veblen's methodology

> ... in whatever science there exist, among those who have attended to the subject, what are commonly called differences of principle, as distinguished from differences of matter-of-fact or detail, – the cause will be found to be, a difference in their conceptions of the philosophic method of the science.
>
> John Stuart Mill, *On the Definition of Political Economy: And on the Method of Investigation Proper to It.*

In recent years there has been a marked growth in the literature dealing with Veblen's contributions to American social and philosophical thought, and it seems clear that a more critical perspective is becoming prevalent.[1] There has, however, been no comparable growth or trend in the literature dealing with Veblen's contributions to American economics, for the only extended analysis in this period, by Professor Gruchy,[2] adopted a somewhat eulogistic tone reminiscent of certain earlier reactions to Veblen's writings. The way is now being prepared for a definitive reappraisal of Veblen's entire system of thought,[3] and the present article is submitted in the belief that methodology represents a vital but neglected aspect of his influence upon American economics.

In order to portray the essential features of Veblen's methodology, it is necessary to examine the "preconceptions" underlying his work – a procedure justified by Veblen's own technique of criticism – and to contrast them with the "preconceptions" attributed by him to the orthodox economists. In so doing, it will be possible to display the essential differences between the so-called "scientific point of view" of the classical and neoclassical writers and that proposed by Veblen for a modern, "evolutionary" science of economics.

Veblen's critique

In view of earlier discussions of Veblen's attacks on orthodox economics, no effort will be made here to review the charges in detail. In sketching the main outlines, however, some significant points neglected in earlier commentaries will be examined, particularly where these are relevant to the influence of Veblen's methodology upon his contemporaries.

As is well known, Veblen contended that classical and neoclassical economics was based upon outmoded preconceptions which he termed "animistic" and "teleological," and as a result the science was "taxonomic" and subjective in its method.[4] In brief, the term "animism" referred to the quasi-spiritual character which the economists attributed to nature itself, and "teleology" referred to their tendency to view the laws of nature as purposively oriented toward a final end or consummation. The latter feature, sometimes called the "meliorative" view of economic change, might be termed "cosmological teleology," as opposed to "individual teleology" – the view that human nature is purposively motivated – which Veblen enthusiastically advocated. With reference to human motivation, Veblen laid particular emphasis on the inadequacies of the "hedonistic" psychology, and the withering scorn which he poured on this doctrine hastened its repudiation by economists.

In Veblen's eyes the teleological view of events and the hedonistic view of human motivation were indissolubly linked, for, "given an indefeasible meliorative trend in events, man is but a mechanical intermediary in the sequence."[5] By thus associating hedonism and teleology, Veblen presumably hoped to bring down the entire structure of orthodox economic theory by undermining its hedonistic foundations, a task in which he was aided by such leading contemporary psychologists as James and McDougall. But, in so doing, Veblen was attributing to the economists not merely the vague notion that the "end" of economic development was given but also the more rigid conception that the intermediate steps in this process were also irrevocably predetermined, for it is only under such circumstances that man becomes a "mechanical intermediary," powerless to influence the course of economic change. It would be a simple task to demonstrate that no such conception was ever held by a reputable economist, even though strong traces of the looser concept of a meliorative trend are discernible, as, for example, in the writings of J. B. Clark. Thus, not only was Veblen's account of the hedonistic theory exaggerated and distorted, but its relation to his interpretation of teleology was grossly oversimplified.

Veblen's habit of pushing his criticisms to unwarrantable extremes is further illustrated by his claim that the orthodox economists were guilty of a "normalization of data." In its more innocuous form this led to "conjectural history" – the practice of distorting the past in terms of a preconceived "normal" – the outcome of which, he remarked, was, at best, "of the nature of harmless and graceful misinformation."[6] Beyond this, however, he levied a more serious charge, namely, that the economists had come to regard their theoretical constructs as realities which transcended actual experience, so that "elucidations of what normally ought to happen, as a matter of ceremonial necessity, have in this way come to pass for an account of matters of fact."[7]

There is undoubtedly an important truth underlying this contention. The orthodox economists had frequently interpreted the concepts of "competition," "normal," and "equilibrium," not merely as logical tools, designed for the purpose of analysing and explaining observed reality, but also as real properties of the economic system. In so doing, they failed to distinguish clearly between the logical and the empirical significance of their concepts. If Veblen had pursued the full methodological implications of his criticism, undertaking a study of the extent to which this omission had influenced their policy judgments, he would have performed a valuable service. Typically, however, he neglected this scholarly responsibility, for he was primarily concerned with broader considerations.

Equally sweeping, and no doubt more confusing to his followers, was Veblen's apparent dismissal of the so-called deductive and inductive methods. Veblen's attack on the former amounted to the familiar claim that the deductive theorist usually failed to put his logical system to empirical test or that, when doing so, he was often so enamored of his preconceived criteria of "relevance" that he was willing to dismiss facts not in accord with his formulas by regarding them as "abnormal cases" resulting from "disturbing causes."[8] Yet Veblen did not consistently maintain his opposition to the deductive method. In discussing the work of Karl Marx, which was affected with "Natural Rights" preconceptions similar to those of the classical writers, Veblen nevertheless observed that "it is not, therefore, to be assumed, nor indeed to be credited, that his propagandist aims have in any substantial way deflected his inquiry or his speculations from the faithful pursuit of scientific truth. His socialistic bias may color his polemics, but his logical grasp is too neat and firm to admit of any bias, other than that of his metaphysical preconceptions, affecting his theoretical work."[9]

This presents us with a notable dilemma. Are we to conclude that scientific truth can be maintained irrespective of the scientist's underlying preconceptions? If so, it would appear that the sting is removed from Veblen's attack on classical economics. On the other hand, if this interpretation is rejected on the grounds that the entire weight of his assault was directed against the preconceptions of the "pre-Darwinian" writers, how is scientific truth to be differentiated from "normalization" or propagandizing? Veblen seemed to imply that scientific truth was merely a matter of logical consistency, in which case it becomes a matter of indifference whether the conclusions bear any relation to the facts of actual life or not.

It is probable that this inconsistency in Veblen's critique was due to his sympathy for Marx's attempt to develop a theory of the cumulative change of economic institutions rather than to any sympathy for his socialistic aims. That Veblen did not regard the facts of economic life as irrelevant to the pursuit of scientific truth is evident from his dismissal of the taxonomic procedure of neoclassical economics. "Taxonomy," he said, represents mere "definition and classification" as opposed to causal analysis, and, with the taxonomic sciences, "the great truths or laws of the science remain hypothetical laws; and the test of scientific reality is congruence with the hypothetical laws, not coincidence with matter-of-fact events,"[10] that is, the facts of economic life.

If by this Veblen meant that the "hypothetical laws" of the taxonomic sciences would be validated by referring them to "matter-of-fact events," it might appear that he was merely demanding some sort of inductive test. Yet he supported no naïve appeal for an inductive science of economics; indeed, he sharply criticized the use of induction by the German historical school of economists, concluding that "the whole broad range of erudition and research that engaged the energies of that school commonly falls short of being science, in that, when consistent, they have contented themselves with an enumeration of data and a narrative account of industrial development, and have not presumed to offer a theory of anything or to elaborate their results into a consistent body of knowledge."[11]

Veblen's wholesale denunciations of familiar methods were designed to prepare the way for an acceptance of the genetic method, advocated so persistently in his writings. It cannot be doubted that his destructive attacks caused bewilderment among his contemporaries and, in so far as they were successful, tended to undermine their faith in orthodox economic theory. Unless Veblen could provide a workable alternative methodology, it was unlikely that his admirers would adhere to any systematic method whatsoever. To this extent there appears to be a serious justification for Herbert Davenport's bantering protest "that on the Judgment Day he would have to account to his Maker for having spoiled so many promising theorists."[12]

Veblen's constructive proposals

Veblen's constructive methodological proposals may conveniently be approached through his account of the differences between the evolutionary and the pre-evolutionary sciences. In essence, he claimed it was a "difference of spiritual attitude or point of view in the two contrasted generations of scientists,"[13] and this had come about through a change in the prevailing habits of life, which had induced changes in the habits of thought, including the "canons of science." Thus the modern scientific point of view was largely an outcome of the machine technology, which, he said, "inculcates thinking in terms of opaque, impersonal cause and effect, to the neglect of those norms of validity that rest on usage and the conventional standards handed down by usage."[14]

Whereas the orthodox economists analyzed their data in terms of a preconceived "normal," no such error was committed by the evolutionary scientists. "The great deserts of the evolutionist leaders," Veblen said, "… lie, on the one hand, in their refusal to go back of the colorless sequence of phenomena and seek higher ground for their ultimate syntheses, and, on the other hand, in their having shown how this colorless impersonal sequence of cause and effect can be made use of for theory proper, by virtue of its cumulative character."[15]

Veblen was not advocating the direct observation of causes, although this view has recently been attributed to him;[16] indeed, he criticized some economists for having attempted to dispense with "metaphysical premises." The central principle of modern science, "causal sequence" or continuity, "is not a fact of observation, and cannot be asserted of the facts of observation except as a trait imputed to them. It is so imputed, by scientists and others, as a matter of logical necessity, as a basis of systematic knowledge of the facts of observation."[17] In modern science this was the end of the imputation process, but in pre-evolutionary sciences, such as classical economics, there was what may be called a "second degree of imputation," namely, the resort to an "absolute or definitive ground of economic legitimacy," lying "beyond the causal sequence in which the observed phenomena are conceived to be interlinked."[18] In the last analysis this "second degree of imputation" occurred as a result of the role assigned to rationality and was expressed in terms of the principle of "sufficient reason." This principle, Veblen said, "runs by way of the interested discrimination, the forethought, of an agent who takes thought of the future and guides his present activity by regard for this future ... it is solely of an intellectual, subjective, personal, teleological character and force." By contrast, the imputation procedure adopted by modern scientists, involving the methodological principle of "efficient cause" (or "cause and effect"), "runs only in the contrary direction, and it is solely of an objective, impersonal, materialistic character and force. The modern scheme of knowledge, on the whole, rests, for its definitive ground, on the relation of cause and effect; the relation of sufficient reason being admitted only provisionally and as a proximate factor in the analysis."[19]

Veblen was anxious to minimize the independent contribution of human reason to social change, contending that "under the Darwinian norm it must be held that men's reasoning is largely controlled by other than logical, intellectual forces."[20] The clearest illustration of the Darwinian norm is provided by his rejection of Marx's theory of economic change, which was not a "consistent materialism," since it proceeded in terms of the class struggle. The Marxian standpoint is personal, not impersonal; it seeks in the facts "a continuity of reason and consequently of logic"; it "is essentially an intellectual sequence, and it is therefore of a teleological character," whereas the Darwinian scientist employs "a scheme of blindly cumulative causation, in which there is no trend, no final term, no consummation. The sequence is controlled by nothing but the *vis a tergo* of brute causation, and is essentially mechanical."[21]

Thus Veblen's system represented an extreme form of Social Darwinism, a type of social theory in which the forces of heredity and environment are given primacy over human rationality.[22] In attacking theories of cultural change that assigned the leading role to human forethought, Veblen appeared to adopt a highly deterministic view of the process of change, a view which was strangely at variance with his expressed opposition to the hedonistic concept of man as a mere "mechanical intermediary." In decrying theories imputing order or regularity to the sequence of events, he was, as Louis Schneider has pointed out,[23] attacking the very faculty of reasoning which permits the construction of scientific systems, for these are essentially based on the apprehension of uniformities and regularities amid the complex of events. In this sense Veblen's attack on human reason amounted to an attack on the very foundations of science. Moreover, it is difficult to see how a scientific theory of the process of change is conceptually possible if that process is blind, demonstrating no trend, and is thus virtually haphazard.

The central element in Veblen's proposed evolutionary methodology was the concept of "cumulative causation." "Any evolutionary science," he remarked, "... is a theory of a process, of an unfolding sequence," and the leading question to be asked is "what takes place next, and why?"[24] This analysis of the "genetic succession" of phenomena was to be not a mere narrative description of the historical sequence of events but an analysis in terms of "efficient cause." This last concept was not carefully defined, but Veblen seemed to imply that the efficient cause of any phenomenon was to be found in the immediately antecedent circumstances, and this interpretation is supported by his explanation of "cumulative causation." The process of cultural change is cumulative, he said, in the sense that "each new situation is a variation of what has gone before it and embodies as causal factors all that has been effected by what went before."[25] In other words, every institutional situation is a product of everything that has preceded it, so that any attempt to isolate individual causes is bound to fail. Thus Veblen proposed a kind of "organismic" concept of the universe as a "whole" within which everything was explained by everything else.[26] Since a time relationship was also involved, the inevitable outcome was a historical account of successive cultural changes, despite his assertion that such an account did not constitute "theory proper" in the modern evolutionary sense. For Veblen, the process of change was not merely a theoretical construct but an empirical reality; a false picture of the cultural whole would be given if any attempt were made to isolate a particular segment for separate study. This helps to explain his scornful references to the "hypothetical laws" of the "taxonomic sciences," since he apparently felt that his evolutionary science would avoid such artificial abstractions.[27]

As has often been remarked, the truly dynamic factor in Veblen's system is technological change; yet Veblen provided no adequate theory of *how* technology changed. Admittedly he discussed the incidental contributions of the nonpragmatic instinct of "idle curiosity" to technological progress, but his Darwinian preoccupation with the impact of technology upon man led to a comparative neglect of the impact of man on technology. Consequently, his theory of technological change lacked a principle of continuity, so that his account appears to be "an ever changing description of an ever changing environment," as Lewis Haney has aptly put it.[28] In part this was the result of Veblen's confusion between *trend* and *order* in the pattern of events and of his desperate desire to avoid the "teleological" error. Indeed, he sometimes conveyed the impression that under a Darwinian type of theory no constant laws are possible, and, despite his occasional assertions that science must necessarily proceed in terms of uniformities and laws, he appeared to share the view of some contemporary pragmatists that a changing body of logic is required to explain a changing universe.[29] Thus Veblen provided no scientific explanation of the nature of change, producing instead a genetic (historical) account of how changes had, in fact, taken place.

In order to comprehend the full significance of Veblen's proposed evolutionary methodology, it is necessary to look briefly at his cultural theory of knowledge. With changing technology and the resultant changes in "habits of thought," there were concomitant changes in the "canons of validity," leading to the development of new concepts of science. Although Veblen contended that this process of change was gradual, he drew from it the drastic conclusion that there was no basis of comparison between two bodies of knowledge based on different sets of metaphysical preconceptions.[30] Moreover, as the essential difference lay "in the higher syntheses, the methods of handling the material of knowledge, the basis of valuation of the facts taken up, rather than in the material of knowledge,"[31] it was clearly impossible to establish the superiority of one over another by means of any empirical test. Yet when we move from the empirical to the speculative realm, the problem of how to demonstrate the superiority of one body of knowledge over another, based on different preconceptions, is insoluble, for, as Veblen acknowledged, the central principle of his proposed evolutionary science – the concept of "cumulative causal sequence" – is "an unproven and unprovable postulate."[32]

Thus the professed superiority of Veblen's "evolutionary" methodology was not demonstrable on rational grounds; it lay merely in the broad conformity of its central preconceptions with the current stage of cultural development, a conformity which was presumably self-evident. Indeed, Veblen's entire approach represented a naïve form of *Wissenssoziologie*, according to which the validity of a proposition or a body of knowledge depends upon the circumstances under which it is formulated.[33] In his extreme relativistic model, periodic changes in the dominant cultural pattern would completely preclude the persistence of any continuous body of valid scientific knowledge. Moreover, no scientific theory could withstand criticism of its preconceptions, for, as soon as a preconception "comes to be criticized," he said, "it is in a way to be superseded by a new, more or less altered formulation; for criticism of it means that it is no longer fit to survive unaltered in the altered complex of habits of thought to which it is called upon to serve as a fundamental principle."[34] In thus providing a built-in justification of his attack on the preconceptions of orthodox economics, Veblen sealed the fate of his own, and indeed of every other, scientific system. This is surely the *reductio ad absurdum* of scientific relativism.

In concluding this analysis of Veblen's methodological proposals, some attention must be paid to his claim that, while the pre-evolutionary sciences were "subjective, personal," an evolutionary science of economics would be "objective, impersonal." To some extent this difference arose from the divergent underlying preconceptions, but the various implications of the term "objective" in Veblen's writings need to be distinguished, for they possess practical as well as logical significance.

In the first place, the distinction between "subjective" and "objective" refers to the psychological level of analysis. In line with contemporary developments in social psychology Veblen rejected the emphasis on individual "consciousness" and the (personal) introspective method, espousing instead the "objective" behavioristic approach to human nature.[35] Reference to rational action was to be subordinated to an approach based upon "habit" or "instinct," and in Veblen's system human behavior often seemed to be merely a succession of instinctive adaptations to changing external forces beyond man's control.

Second, on the methodological plane, the distinction between the "subjective" and "objective" approaches to society entails a differentiation between the "subjective" role of the social actor and the "objective" role of the scientific observer – a vital distinction emphasized by Max Weber. Veblen completely ignored the fact that the concepts and point of view appropriate to the scientific observer are quite different from those of ordinary everyday life, and he criticized the orthodox economists for employing categories different from those "under which the men at whose hands the action takes place themselves apprehend their own action at the instant of acting."[36] To limit the scientist in this way would be, for instance, to exclude many of the concepts advanced in modern theoretical physics. All the (empirical) sciences commence with the materials of everyday experience, but it is only by transcending the details of these materials that systematic scientific propositions can be made. Veblen's failure to appreciate this is further evidence of the inadequacy of his so-called "Darwinian" approach to society.

Finally, Veblen's plea for objectivity represents an attempt to escape what he considered to be the normative features of economic science, for he persistently complained that economists had failed to separate "what is" from "what ought to be." In attempting to avoid this, he introduced a fundamental epistemological dichotomy between scientific knowledge based on the instinct of idle curiosity and the pragmatic body of wordly wisdom based on the motive of expediency. Whereas the preconceptions underlying the latter type of knowledge were "animistic" and "teleogical," modern scientific knowledge was "impersonal" and "matter of fact." He appeared to think that the mere assertion that modern science was "matter of fact" was a sufficient guaranty that the modern scientist was objective, in the sense of being disinterested. Veblen's own account does not lend support to this contention. His definition of the "instinct of workmanship" was clearly normative;[37] his attack on the admittedly "unproven and unprovable" preconceptions of orthodox economics was evidently not based on "scientific" grounds; the modern scientist's imputation of the postulate of "cumulative causal sequence" was clearly a "subjective" procedure. Despite his periodic disclaimers, there is ample evidence in Veblen's writings that he did not refrain from making value judgments. One example is his assertion that economists defended the status quo as a necessary condition for the validity of their own theories.[38] This represents a hopeless confusion of the historical notion that economic theory is only relevant to the modern business situation with the idea that economists regard that situation as desirable in itself.

The significance of Veblen's methodology

As the foregoing account suggests, Veblen's methodological program was vague and incomplete, amounting to scarcely more than a few general indications of the direction in which he wished to proceed; and in consequence his admirers adopted widely differing interpretations of its nature and importance. Wesley Mitchell, for instance, apparently considered that Veblen's evolutionary method did not differ significantly from that of previous writers, adding that the distinctive features of his work arose from the premises and the conception of the nature and purpose of the subject.[39] More recently Allan Gruchy, in attempting to assess Veblen's contribution to American economics, conceded that his work suffered from the complete absence of "an analysis of the kind of method that would be most appropriate to his evolutionary economics."[40]

However, it would be a serious mistake to deny the influence of Veblen's methodology upon the subsequent development of American economics.

Although his technique of "doubting preconceptions," as practiced by Descartes, Hume, and C. S. Peirce, inspired a distaste for orthodox economics and a distrust of systematic theory, it forced economists of all shades of opinion to reconsider fundamental issues. Those who possessed a sound understanding of the nature and limitations of scientific method emerged chastened but refreshed by this ordeal; on many of the younger economists, however, especially those inadequately trained in economic theory who were impatient of abstractions and eager for "results," Veblen's diatribes exerted a disintegrating influence which took a variety of forms, according to the "personal equation" and environment of the individual.

Largely because of the lack of a comprehensible, systematic methodology of "evolutionary economics," the "institutionalists" were a heterogeneous group of Veblenian disciples, each with his own version of the gospel, instead of a cohesive school. Thus Wesley Mitchell, an admirer rather than a follower, turned to an essentially empirical and statistical study of business cycles, employing a method toward which he was drawn more by personal predilection than by Veblen's influence.[41] Mitchell's program of "quantitative economics" was basically inconsistent with the encyclopedic tendency of Veblen's system, which embraced all aspects of the cultural environment irrespective of their capacity for quantification. R. F. Hoxie, a disciple who deliberately turned away from systematic theory to more pressing practical problems, enunciated a "historical method" which was less ambitious than Veblen's, since it differed from the "ordinary method of scientific investigation" only in the character and source of its data.[42] Another leading institutionalist, W. H. Hamilton, devised a method of "organic particularism," according to which the object of study was to be examined in its relationship to the entire cultural milieu.[43] This method gave rise to the fallacious notion that such "wholes" as "labor union," "corporation," or "price system" were somehow more real than the concepts employed by the orthodox economist and led to the examination of an exhaustive (and logically infinite) list of all the "factors" or "functions" linking the given "organism" to its environment, with little or no attempt to assess the theoretical significance of the various relationships involved. Finally, J. M. Clark, an economist whose "institutional" pedigree is more difficult to define, turned to the problems of economic dynamics suggested by his father, John Bates Clark, and attempted to apply his sound grasp of scientific method to a Veblenian quest for an understanding of "the extent to which economic theory was limited by its premises."[44]

Many of Veblen's greatest admirers respected him for his brilliant insights and his devastating wit but found his philosophical range too great; and they may have suspected that some of his derogatory epithets applied with equal force to his own work. Apart from the absence of a systematic evolutionary methodology, the most important factor in Veblen's influence on American economics lay in his avoidance of policy proposals. Veblen's distaste for "maxims of expediency" or "worldly wisdom" gave no satisfaction to those disciples who wished to get "results," that is, to solve "practical" problems; but here the pragmatists, particularly the "instrumentalist" supporters of John Dewey, stepped into the breach. With policy recommendations to offer on every conceivable subject, and with an emphasis on experimentation – in the sense of "trying things out" – and social control, the instrumentalists gave purpose and content to the institutionalism of the 1920's. Veblen's hold over the movement gradually diminished; his earlier appeals for "theory proper" and nonpragmatic "idle curiosity" were perverted into "monographic atomism"[45] and "functional" or "experimental" economics.[46] Gradually the desire for and interest in a systematic "institutional economics" to replace orthodox economic theory waned,[47] and the attention of most economists was diverted into new channels suggested by the theories and problems of imperfect competition and economic fluctuations.

No attempt has been made here to assess the over-all significance of Veblen's contribution to American economics. It is clear that his work must be judged in relation to a wider background, in which the connections between his primary emphases[48] and the central doctrines of pragmatism must be underlined. From a methodological standpoint Veblen's influence is attributable to the destructive impact of his critique, the shortcomings of his constructive program coupled with his apparent detachment toward policy recommendations, and the attractiveness of the instrumentalist emphasis on the solution of currently pressing problems. In relation to the development of scientific method in economics, Veblen's contribution cannot be highly rated.

Notes

1 A useful bibliography is included in David Riesman's recent book, *Thorstein Veblen* (New York, 1953), pp. 211–14.
2 Allen Gruchy, *Modern Economic Thought* (New York, 1947), pp. 31–135.
3 A valuable contribution, neglected by Riesman, is Leo Dobriansky's unpublished thesis, "The Social Philosophical System of Thorstein Veblen" (New York University 1950).
4 Veblen's principal methodological writings appeared in articles, reprinted in *The Place of Science in Modern Civilization* (New York, 1932).
5 Ibid., p. 157.
6 Ibid., p. 184.
7 Ibid., p. 125.
8 Ibid., p. 67.
9 Ibid., p. 410.
10 Ibid., p. 164.
11 Ibid., p. 58.
12 Cited by Joseph Dorfman, *Thorstein Veblen and His America* (New York, 1934), p. 311.
13 *The Place of Science in Modern Civilization*, p. 60.
14 Veblen, *The Theory of Business Enterprise* (New York, 1904), p. 301.
15 *The Place of Science in Modern Civilization*, p. 61. The meaning of the phrases "colorless sequence of cause and effect" and "theory proper" will be explained below.
16 Stanley Daugert, *The Philosophy of Thorstein Veblen* (New York, 1950), p. 34.
17 *The Place of Science in Modern Civilization*, p. 34 n.
18 Ibid., p. 146.
19 Ibid., pp. 237–38.
20 Ibid., p. 441.
21 Ibid., p. 436.
22 See the discussion by Talcott Parsons, in *The Structure of Social Action* (New York, 1937), chap. vi. Veblen did not, of course, propose to dispense altogether with the

principle of "sufficient reason" (cf. *The Place of Science in Modern Civilization*, pp. 238–39).

23 Louis Schneider, *The Freudian Psychology and Veblen's Social Theory* (New York, 1948), p. 99.

24 *The Place of Science in Modern Civilization*, pp. 58 and 84.

25 Ibid., p. 242.

26 This is strongly reminiscent of William James's view (see *Some Problems of Philosophy* [New York, 1911], p. 192). James pointed to a parallel between his own view and that of John Stuart Mill (cf. *Logic* [8th ed.], Book I, p. 383).

27 Veblen's refusal to distinguish economic from noneconomic aspects of human behavior is another example of this misconception (see *The Place of Science in Modern Civilization*, pp. 241 and 77). The scope of Veblen's "evolutionary economics" cannot be examined here in detail.

28 See his discussion of "The Institutional Approach to Economic Theory," *American Economic Review* (Supplement), IX (1919), 320–21.

29 See Morris R. Cohen, *Reason and Nature* (New York, 1931), pp. 18–20.

30 The dichotomy between "sufficient reason" and "efficient cause" is explicitly stated in *The Place of Science in Modern Civilization*, p. 237. See also *The Theory of Business Enterprise*, pp. 343–44, for a similar view.

31 *The Place of Science in Modern Civilization*, p. 99.

32 Ibid., p. 33.

33 The fallacy underlying this view has been admirably demonstrated by Maurice Mandelbaum in *The Problem of Historical Knowledge* (New York, 1938), p. 177.

34 *The Place of Science in Modern Civilization*, p. 149.

35 The importance of the role of "consciousness" in the social sciences has been fully elaborated by Frank H. Knight in such articles as "Economic Psychology and the Value Problem," *Quarterly Journal of Economics*, XXXIX (1925), 372–409, and "Facts and Metaphysics in Economic Psychology," *American Economic Review*, XV (1925), 247–66.

36 *The Place of Science in Modern Civilization*, p. 178.

37 Veblen, *The Theory of the Leisure Class* (New York, 1934), p, 15.

38 Dorfman, op. cit., p. 365.

39 *Lecture Notes on Types of Economic Theory* (New York, 1949), pp. 234 and 252. These notes, transcribed during Mitchell's lectures, were not acknowledged by him.

40 Op. cit., p. 56.

41 *Wesley Mitchell: The Economic Scientist*, ed. A. F. Burns (New York, 1952), pp. 94–95.

42 Robert F. Hoxie, "Historical Method versus Historical Narrative," *Journal of Political Economy*, XIV (1906), 568.

43 Walton H. Hamilton, "The Development of Hoxie's Economics," *Journal of Political Economy*, XXIV (1916), 871, n. 2.

44 John Maurice Clark, *Preface to Social Economics* (New York, 1936), p. 94.

45 An expression employed by John Gambs in *Beyond Supply and Demand* (New York, 1946), p. 82.

46 See the essays by A. B. Wolfe and R. G. Tugwell in *The Trend of Economics*, ed. R. G. Tugwell (New York, 1924).

47 See, e.g., E. M. Burns, "Does Institutionalism Complement or Compete with 'Orthodox Economics'?" *American Economic Review*, XXI (1931), 80–87. John R. Commons regarded his *Institutional Economics* (New York, 1935) as a supplement to orthodox economics (p. 5).

48 The following may be regarded as Veblen's primary emphases: (*a*) change (economic dynamics and business cycles); (*b*) the genetic method; (*c*) social psychology; and (*d*) the interdependence of economics and the other social sciences.

19 The politics of political economists

Comment

Professor Stigler has raised important questions in his provocative paper on the conservative bias of political economists,[1] but his unwillingness to adopt a broad enough historical and philosophical perspective has prevented him from providing wholly satisfactory answers. There *is* a sense in which a training in economics exercises a conservative influence, but it is doubtful whether Stigler has correctly interpreted the nature and causes of this influence.

Although it would be preferable to avoid purely terminological issues it is necessary to examine Stigler's key concepts of "political economist" and "conservative" because his conclusions follow directly from his definitions of these terms. By identifying a "political economist" with a student of economic analysis, thereby ruling out "historical and sociological approaches," he automatically excludes most of the socialist, historical and institutionalist critics whose policy prescriptions differed radically from those of their orthodox opponents. Marx, we find, was no economist because he allowed his radical presuppositions to outweigh the influence of his study of economics,[2] whereas the genuine economist is one whose self-confessed reformist motives for selecting that calling did not survive the period of training. No wonder "political economists" are relatively conservative! In the absence of a more explicit criterion by which to identify an economist the whole argument assumes a tautological air. This impression is strengthened by Stigler's definition of a conservative as one who "wishes economic activity to be conducted by private enterprise, and who believes that abuses of private power will usually be checked, and incitements to efficiency and progress usually provided by the forces of competition."[3] While admitting the difficulty of defining this elusive notion and acknowledging Stigler's right to choose his own definition we must observe that it differs significantly from the one suggested by his dictionary[4] or by political theorists.[5] Radical and conservative elements were intermingled in the works of the classical economists, the first great spokesmen for private enterprise. Basing their arguments on the "radical" ideas of reason, utilitarian calculation, egalitarianism and progress, they deeply distrusted the "conservative" canons of emotion, tradition, order and privilege.

Even in Stigler's sense of the term "conservative," their conservatism was by no means unqualified. In the case of Bentham, for example – whose philosophical ideas greatly influenced the group, and who was no mean economist in his own right – there was a crucial ambivalence which has persuaded some interpreters that he was an advocate of laissez faire while others have regarded his legal and administrative doctrines as the source of late nineteenth century collectivism.[6] John Stuart Mill, the most radical member of the classical school, facilitated the parting of the ways, for his distinction between the natural laws of production and the socially-determined laws of distribution[7] enabled the economists to take the conservative road. Adopting a pose (however sincerely held) of ethical neutrality, they assumed the distribution of wealth as given – thereby avoiding the more controversial social and political issues – and concentrated their attention mainly upon problems of production and exchange. This, admittedly, may have been the most fruitful way of developing economic science.[8] But in consequence traditional micro-economic theory has tended to instil in the student a sense of the delicacy, intricacy and efficiency of the self-regulating price system. Although he may learn to recognize "the deficiencies of existing economic arrangements,"[9] the student becomes fully aware of the disruptive effects of policies that impair the operation of the co-ordinating mechanism of the market economy. Under this influence it is hardly surprising that the qualified economist becomes "an imaginative and realistic critic of economic nostrums."[10]

There is, however, another aspect of the economist's training that complicates Stigler's argument. Judging by his definition, an economist is presumably one who has undergone a lengthy and rigorous academic apprenticeship in the course of which he has learned to respect the scholarly and scientific virtues – impartiality, detachment, and a willingness to suspend judgment until the evidence has been sifted and a determined effort has been made to trace cause and effect relationships. Even if economists as a group are more conservative than other social scientists – a point which it is virtually impossible to demonstrate – their conservatism may be attributable not to any specific doctrinal influences, but to the fact that their training has made them more susceptible to the psychological constraints imposed by the academic environment.

Yet once it is conceded that a training in economics exerts a significant, if moderate, conservative influence, Stigler's assertion that "economics as a positive science is ethically – and therefore politically – neutral"[11] is seriously undermined. As Myrdal has insisted, we must recognize "the conservative predilections of economic theory and their foundations in the basic philosophies"[12] of individualism and natural law, and the influence of these philosophies on the kinds of questions asked by economists and the kinds of answers that have satisfied them. Stigler himself admits that political attitudes affect both the *direction* and *substance* of scientific work in economics.[13] Indeed, there is nowadays a surprising measure of agreement among "orthodox" economists like Myrdal, Hutchison, and Koopmans and a lone-wolf institutionalist like Ayres, that the conventional categories of "positive" and "normative" economics are by no means as distinct as has long been claimed.[14] Whereas Hutchison and Koopmans have stressed the need for more conceptual and semantic precision and have called for investigation of the foundations of economic knowledge and the possibilities of "more systematic observation and direct or indirect testing of postulates,"[15] Myrdal and Ayres have concerned themselves with the methodological and philosophical implications of the interdependence of positive and normative economics.

Whether economists have become "more conservative in recent decades"[16] or have bent before the wind "in a period when the trend of policy has been strongly anti-conservative"[17] – two statements which it seems difficult to reconcile – it is likely that the conservative influence of traditional economic theory will decline, if indeed it has not already done so. The political connotations of macro-economic theory are less favorable to private enterprise than were those of micro-economic theory, which nowadays occupies a far less important place in economic training than it once did; the preoccupation with economic growth in underdeveloped countries is emphasizing the historical and institutional limitations of the competitive market economy on which so much theorizing has been based; and there have recently been indications that the basic postulate of "methodological individualism," which has often been illegitimately associated with political individualism, is being undermined by the study of group behavior.[18] When these influences are combined with the growing awareness of the normative residue in economic theory the economists may, perhaps, abandon their pose of ethical neutrality and reveal their hitherto repressed radical tendencies!

Notes

1 George Stigler, "The Politics of Political Economists," The Quarterly Journal of Economics, LXXIII (Nov. 1959), 522–32. I wish to thank my colleague, André Gabor, for his valuable suggestions and criticism of the initial draft of this note.

2 Curiously enough, Veblen asserted (without proof) exactly the opposite. *The Place of Science in Modern Civilization* (New York: Viking, 1932), p. 410. But, of course, Veblen was no economist.

3 Op. cit., p. 524.

4 Ibid., p. 523.

5 For example, Russel Kirk, *The Conservative Mind* (London: Faber, 1954), pp. 17–19. It is no coincidence that individualism, private enterprise and competition appeared as radical and subversive doctrines in countries like Germany, where authoritarian government and the organic conception of the state prevailed.

6 Cf. T. W. Hutchison's review of W. Stark's three volume edition of *Jeremy Bentham's Economic Writings*. "Bentham as an Economist," *Economic Journal*, LXVI (1956), esp. 300–306.

7 Stigler's acceptance of this dichotomy is revealed by his remark that an economist "cannot believe that a change in the *form* of social organization will eliminate basic economic problems" (op. cit., p. 528). But this is exactly what the study of underdeveloped economies has taught us – that without a change in ideological beliefs and social organization basic economic problems *cannot* be solved in some societies.

8 It is questionable whether, as Myrdal suggests, the "theoretical superiority of conservative thinking is, of course, entirely fortuitous." G. Myrdal, *Economic Theory and Under-developed Regions* (London: G. Duckworth, 1957), p. 132.

9 Stigler, op. cit., p. 526.

10 Ibid., p. 529.

11 Ibid., p. 522.

12 This is Myrdal's chapter title, op. cit., p. 135. His approach was formulated in his early study of *The Political Element in the Development of Economic Theory*, trans. Paul Streeten (London: Routledge, 1953) in which he criticized the "naive empiricism" of

his original publication (of 1932) for the neglect of value elements in theoretical analysis (Preface, p. vii).

13 Op. cit., pp. 530–31.

14 See Myrdal's works referred to in endnote 12 above. Also T. W. Hutchison, "Desarrollos recientes de la metodologia economica," *Revista de Economia Politica*, IX (May–Dec. 1958), 349–52. T. C. Koopmans, *Three Essays on the State of Economic Science* (New York: McGraw-Hill, 1957), pp. 129ff. C. E. Ayres, *The Theory of Economic Progress* (Chapel Hill: University of North Carolina Press, 1944), Chaps. I, II. Schumpeter occupied an intermediate position, for although he emphasized the distinction between "ideologically vitiated'' and ideologically pure elements in economics, he admitted its provisional character. *History of Economic Analysis*, ed. from ms. by E. B. Schumpeter (New York: Oxford University Press, 1954), pp. 34ff.

15 Koopmans, op. cit., p. 150. On p. 141 he observes that although Robbins and Friedman defended contradictory interpretations of the ultimate basis of economic knowledge their policy conclusions were similar.

16 Stigler, op. cit., p. 524.

17 Ibid., p. 532.

18 Cf. Herbert A. Simon, "Theories of Decision-Making in Economics and Behavioral Science," *American Economic Review*, XLIX (June 1959), 253–83.

20 Value judgments in economics[1]

I

During the past half century the role of value judgments in economics has so frequently been discussed that any further excursion into this verbal jungle calls for some preliminary justification. Within the past decade or so there has been a pronounced swing towards the "positive", natural science interpretation of economic method, and a concomitant stress on the need for empirical testing and verification; but this has become so fashionable that the difficulties of attaining the "positive" ideal are being seriously underestimated, and consequently the extent of recent methodological gains is tending to be exaggerated. This contention is, of course, difficult to prove; but it gains support when one contrasts the familiar text-book versions of "positive" economics with the trend of recent work in ethics, linguistic analysis, and the history and philosophy of science. According to the text-books, economic science is ethically neutral, concerned exclusively with "what is" rather than with "what ought to be", and hence value judgments (which are usually regarded as normative propositions) have no place in the subject. On the other hand, recent discussions in logic and philosophy reveal that the relationships between factual and value judgments are far more subtle than economists generally recognise, and historians and philosophers of science have been demonstrating that value judgments play an indispensable role in the scientist's work.[2]

These conflicting interpretations can, of course, be reconciled by distinguishing sharply between the logic of science and scientific practice, and this distinction is especially pertinent to economics, for there has long been a wide gap between the economist's methodological preachings and his methodological performance. This gap is not, of course, peculiar to economics; but economists have long been conscious of their status as the most "scientific" of the social scientists, and have accordingly been sensitive to criticisms that seem to cast any aspersions on their reputation. The distinction between the logic of economic science and the practice of economists lies at the heart of the perennial dispute between the opponents and the defenders of orthodox (i.e. classical and neoclassical) economics, for while the former have been chiefly concerned with the economists' practice, the latter have presented the case for the defence largely in terms of methodological principle. Yet both parties agree that modern economic analysis had its origins in the liberal moral philosophy of the 18th century enlightenment, and it would be a matter of considerable historical and theoretical interest if this once ideologically-tainted body of doctrine had, in the fullness of time, been successfully purged of its normative features, as its modern defenders claim. Historicist, institutionalist and socialist critics of economic orthodoxy have repeatedly insisted that these normative residues persist; but their arguments have been brushed aside by the orthodox methodologists, who have usually experienced little difficulty in demonstrating that their adversaries were confused, misguided or influenced by ideological bias. Some doubt may, indeed, have persisted within the ranks of the orthodox faithful; but this may well be because they too have not always been careful enough to distinguish between principle and practice.

The problem of value judgments in economics underlies the entire controversy about the "positive" character of economic science. In logic, the distinction between judgments of fact and judgments of value can be maintained, though not always without difficulty, whereas in practice the scientist is necessarily obliged to make judgments in which factual and value considerations are intertwined. According to the conventional, "positive" view (which will be defined below), this raises no questions of principle for although the economist's personal judgments necessarily exert some influence upon his work, his methods and his conclusions are subject to scrutiny, modification and possibly rejection by his scientific colleagues, and this explains the importance attached to empirical testing and verification, for these procedures provide the means whereby the scientific wheat can be separated from the pseudo or non-scientific chaff. In practice, however, little progress has so far been made towards the successful application of these procedures to economics; large areas of economics remain untested, and are accordingly subject to disputes which cannot be settled purely on scientific grounds. From one point of view, of course, this is an argument for redoubling the effort to devise and perfect empirical tests in economics and to extend the range and variety of testable propositions, and surely no-one will deny the legitimacy of this aim. On the other hand, it would be unwise to ignore the difficulties involved in this task, and there is a real danger that economists may be tempted to devote a disproportionate amount of time and energy to the task of translating significant untested propositions into terms that render them amenable to empirical testing, but reduce them to triviality in the process.

The dangers of methodolatry – i.e. the excessive preoccupation with a single methodology – can be readily illustrated from the history of methological controversy, and not only in economics.[3] The dilemma facing the practicing economist (or scientist) is that on the one hand he cannot afford to spare much of his time and energy for methodology, on the other, he cannot afford to work in a methodological vacuum. Far too much methological discussion is conducted on an abstract plane of principle which ignores the unavoidable gap between principle and practice. The present article is necessarily somewhat general in character, but it is designed to help bridge this gap, by surveying some of the recent literature in fields outside the economist's normal purview which have a direct bearing on current methodological discussion in economics.

II

Unfortunately, methodological disagreements all too often stem from or are reducible to terminological issues, and this is especially so in the present instance. The term "positive" conjurs up associations of a long and somewhat chequered history of positivist philosophy, and of late it has become a weasel word in the literature of economics, changing its identity from writer to writer and even from context to context, occasionally appearing in guises that would be unrecognisable to many positivist philosophers.[4] In an effort to avoid these difficulties, the expression "positive economics" will be used in the following pages to denote an ethically neutral descriptive and explanatory science in which a minimal reliance is placed on statements that are not conceivably capable of empirical falsification. This is a much broader, and therefore less precise, definition than that employed by exponents of operationalism or logical positivism, who maintain that all scientific statements can be translated into or are reducible to statements directly verifiable by sensation. But the foregoing definition of "positive economics" avoids certain philosophical difficulties associated with the narrower definition, difficulties which are irrelevant to the present discussion.[5] It should, moreover, be noted that our definition implies that it is possible to make both hypothetical and descriptive ethically-neutral statements about economic affairs; and therefore if in practice economics falls short of the "positive" ideal, it is either because ethical notions are illegitimately incorporated into the analysis or, in some sense, because the *selection* and interpretation of the hypothetical or descriptive statements is influenced, whether consciously or unconsciously, by the economist's value judgments.

There is, however, another way of looking at the "positive" definition. If we regard it as a description of the actual behaviour of economists, it is demonstrably false; most economists do in fact make policy recommendations involving value judgments, despite the "positive" view that such activities fall outside the economist's proper function *qua* economist. Yet if we regard "positive economics" as an ideal rather than an actuality, the concept necessarily acquires normative overtones, and it can, in principle, be used to deny professional recognition to those whose practice fails to live up to the ideal.[6] There are, in fact, various reasons for believing that the "positive" definition of economics has been used persuasively. During the past century and a half the central corpus of economic theory has demonstrated a remarkable resistance to criticism from the most varied quarters, less, one suspects, because the validity of the theory has been convincingly demonstrated than because it has not and cannot be falsified. From time to time in the course of methodological controversy the scope of the discipline has been redefined, with the dual effects of excluding the root-and-branch critics and limiting the area of disagreement among those whom the established leaders of the subject have chosen to regard as *bona fide* economists. Yet despite their scientific pretensions, the economists have never found it easy to specify the requisite standards of scientific or technical competence in their field, and they have never developed a strong professional organization or a code of ethics. Instead, the authority of tradition, albeit a "liberal" tradition, has been relied upon as the principal means of strengthening the professional *esprit de corps* and preserving the continuity and coherence of the discipline.[7]

It is, of course, exceedingly difficult to assess the importance of these considerations; but unless they can be entirely dismissed, they tend to support the view that the modern economist's training may influence not only his technical approach to the subject but also his attachment to the liberal moral values inherited from earlier generations.[8] However, before attempting to suggest how these and other values may have influenced the contemporary approach, we must first define the expression "value judgment" for this is another key concept in the ensuing discussion.

In the present context, a value judgment will be defined *either* as a *process* of evaluation designed to determine whether an object is good, an act is right, or someone ought or ought not to do something, *or* alternatively as the *outcome* of such a process.[9] Economists generally assume that value judgments are merely arbitrary whims or preferences; but there is in fact a continuum of judgments involving personal appraisal which runs from objectively verifiable judgments of speed, height, distance at one end of the scale, to personal preferences and categorical moral imperatives at the other, and recent philosophical writings demonstrate that judgments of fact and judgments of value possess more features in common than is usually supposed. Both types of judgment may, but need not, be arbitrary; on the other hand, both may be, and often are, susceptible to rational analysis and justification. Like factual judgments, value judgments entail reference to the descriptive characteristics of the act or object in question, and when disagreements arise, appeal may be made to the standards or rules presupposed by the judgment. Provided that these standards or rules are fully specified, and the methods of computing gradings or rankings are known, the demand for "objectivity" is satisfied.[10]

Given these common features, it is hardly surprising that in practice it is often difficult to distinguish between factual and value judgments, for they are often combined in a body of argument in such a way as to mutually reinforce one another. The facile text-book distinction between "what is" and "what ought to be" ignores the fact that the terms "ought" and "should" can be used non-normatively in connection with inferences and predictions, quite apart from their normative use in evaluative or prescriptive statements. There is no special kind of value language by which normative statements can be identified; "what makes a statement the expression of a value judgment is not *which words* are used, but the ways in which and the purposes for which they are used".[11] And, as will be indicated later, there are special reasons why the terms employed by economists and the manner of their employment tend to blur the distinction between factual and value statements. However, such a blurring occurs throughout the social sciences, for as Ernest Nagel has observed, "a large number of characterisations sometimes assumed to be purely factual descriptions of social phenomena do indeed formulate a type of value judgment ... it is often difficult, and in any case usually inconvenient in practice, to distinguish between the purely factual and the 'evaluative' contents of many terms employed in the social sciences; and ... values are commonly attached to means and not only to ends".[12]

The foregoing remarks do not, of course, imply that there are no differences in logic between factual and value judgments; indeed, this difference is crucial, and is most clearly revealed by an examination of the criteria by which such judgments are justified. In the case of factual judgments, it is sufficient to consider their truth or falsity, and the general procedure for establishing this status is known as verification; in the case of value judgments, however, while verification may be possible, something more is needed, namely the procedures which have been recently termed "validation" and "vindication". For as the criteria (standards or rules) on which such judgments rest are disputable, they must themselves be justified by reference to a higher set of criteria.[13]

To examine this process in detail would take us too far beyond the scope of the present discussion; for our purpose it is sufficient to indicate the similarities and the differences between factual and value judgments and the kind of practical difficulties involved in distinguishing between them. It is, however, worth considering one further question of principle, namely what lies behind the requirement that factual (i.e. scientific) statements must be verifiable.[14] To rely upon verification presupposes that the fundamental "end" or object of scientific enquiry is the pursuit of "truth", and as truth is an ideal or "good", it necessarily follows that science, like other human activities, cannot be value-free in any absolute sense. Viewed as a whole, science is a "moral enterprise", one that is deeply influenced by the individual scientist's personal aims and interests, as well as those of the society to which he belongs;[15] and in addition to the supreme "end" of scientific endeavour there are subordinate procedural ideals or rules, some of which are purely instrumental (i.e. "positive" means to the pursuit of scientific knowledge, such as freedom of enquiry) while others are aesathetic.[16] These procedural ideals, such as "certainty", "universality", "system", "simplicity", are necessarily general in character, and their application to particular cases is therefore open to dispute. Moreover, "all formal rules of scientific procedure must prove ambiguous, for they will be interpreted quite differently according to the particular conceptions about the nature of things by which the scientist is guided".[17] This does not, of course, mean that the results of scientific work are purely arbitrary, for in principle these results are

> subject to the self-corrective mechanisms of science as a social enterprise. For modern science encourages the invention, the mutual exchange, and the free but responsible critcism of ideas; it welcomes competition in the quest for knowledge between independent investigators, even when their intellectual orientations are different; and it progressively diminishes the effects of bias by retaining only those proposed conclusions of its enquiries that survive critical examination by an indefinitely large community of students, whatever be their value preferences. It would be absurd to claim that this institutionalized mechanism for sifting warranted beliefs has operated or is likely to operate in social enquiry as effectively as it has in the natural sciences. But it would be no less absurd to conclude that reliable knowledge of human affairs is unattainable merely because social enquiry is frequently value orientated.[18]

In economics, however, where the authority of tradition is strong, where well-defined standards of technical competence are lacking, and where it is exceedingly difficult to devise conclusive empirical tests of the validity of economic hypotheses or statements, it is unlikely that "the self-corrective mechanisms of science as a social enterprise" will function effectively. And if this is so, the scope for the individual economist's personal judgments, both normative and nonnormative, will accordingly be much greater than in disciplines where more rigorous and conclusive empirical tests are possible.

III

Turning from questions of definition and general principle to more practical matters, it is convenient to distinguish three broad "stages" of enquiry in economics which may be conveniently termed the pre-scientific, the scientific, and the post-scientific respectively. These three stages are not clearly demarcated in practice: indeed, the present argument rests largely upon the fact of their interdependence. Generally speaking, proponents of positive economics would not deny that value judgments enter into the first and third of these stages; but they would deny that values play a part in the intermediate stage. Or, alternatively, they would maintain that the presence of value judgments in scientific economics proper can always be detected, and their influence discounted by the rigorous inter-subjective processes of theoretical analysis and empirical testing.

In the interests of brevity, the following discussion will be chiefly concerned with the second or intermediate stage. It should, however, be noted that extra-scientific considerations deeply influence the selection of problems for scientific study, the choice of methods of enquiry (at least within broad limits), the kinds of questions asked, and the kinds of answers or results deemed satisfactory. Moreover, as in any science, the economist is also greatly influenced by the inherited corpus of established knowledge. In addition to a toolbox of "positive" techniques,

> the student who approaches economics for the first time will find to hand a theory which reflects the earlier investigators' opinions as to which policies were worth examining and which objectives were worth pursuing. He may also find theories which show the evil effects of policies that these earlier writers disliked, as well as the methods of achieving objectives which they desired and any obstacles in the way of their achievement. But he will not find theories exposing the method by which one might achieve objectives that have never entered the heads of earlier investigators or which they have dismissed as not worthy of consideration.[19]

As the economist's theoretical and practical interests interact in this way, some methodological disagreements necessarily derive from extrascientific sources, and the scientific progress of the discipline might well be facilitated if an effort were made to develop a pre- or meta-economic science in which these matters were fully investigated.[20] Such a body of knowledge would not, of itself, eliminate methodological controversy; but it would help the disputants to determine how far their disagreements were susceptible to "positive" resolution, and how far they were metaphysical, ideological or otherwise non-scientific in character. Even the most technical branches of economics, such as econometrics, presuppose "criteria of scientific quality".[21] Indeed, the very conception of science itself rests upon a "criterion of demarcation" by which scientific statements can be distinguished from non-scientific (e.g. metaphysical) statements, and this criterion rests on

> a proposal for agreement or convention ... a decision going beyond rational argument ... scientific discovery is impossible without faith in ideas which are of a purely speculative kind, and sometimes quite hazy, a faith which is completely unwarranted from the point of view of science, and which, to that extent, is metaphysical.[22]

To say that economic science is ultimately dependent on metaphysics does not, of course, mean that all disagreements among economists are directly traceable to metaphysical sources;[23] not does it imply that all attempts to devise "positive" tests of economic statements are futile and should be abandoned. On the other hand, recent efforts in this direction have seldom gone beyond the limited, though necessary, stage of reformulating non-testable propositions in such a way as to render them conceivably testable,[24] while discussions of the basic principles involved in empirical testing (and verification) have hitherto proved to be disappointingly inconclusive.

While insistence on the need for empirical testing has become something of a fad among economists – so much so that it is sometimes offered as a panacea for all the methodological ills of the discipline – the literature is disturbingly vague about the nature of an empirical test, and there is little agreement as to precisely which statements are to be tested. Yet these are essential considerations, for empirical testability is, of itself, no criterion of the scientific importance of any given statement. Testable statements may be trivial, while non-testable statements may occupy a central place in the discipline. In this respect the current discussion of empirical testing is curiously reminiscent of the lengthy debate about measurement or quantification in economics which occurred during the 1920s; in both cases the protagonists seem to be under the influence of methodolotry, for if "the subject matter does not permit of exactness and conclusiveness then it does not suffice to be exact and conclusive about some other matter".[25] Here, as elsewhere, a study of the past may provide a salutary corrective to the excesses of the present.

The notice of scientific importance referred to in the preceding paragraph is, of course, a relative not an absolute idea – it is relative both to the problem under consideration (which may be a purely theoretical problem) and to the methodology employed. In all branches of economic science the methodological presuppositions will determine what we have called the "criteria of scientific quality", i.e. what is involved in verifying a statement. According to orthodox (non-mathematical) economics, for example, "theory" and "facts" are required to "correspond" in some sense, and therefore verification calls for "reasoned and judicious comparison between descriptive statistics and other facts of economic history and the conclusions or expectations implied by the theories held". Such a procedure cannot be either precise or incontrovertible because "economic laws or regularities are … at best statements of tendencies subject to displacement and at times outright reversal", so that verification depends on the "weight of evidence".[26] This procedure leaves a considerable scope for the individual economist's judgment of the goodness of fit between fact and conclusions and this is partly why so much emphasis has been laid on the need to devise more "objective" tests of economic propositions.[27] Such an emphasis has been especially marked in econometrics, for the theoretical concepts employed in this discipline are specifically designed to fulfil the requirements of certain statistical tests which themselves constitute the criteria of empirical validity and scientific meaningfulness.[28] There are, of course, certain obvious dangers when all scientific considerations are subordinated to certain obvious dangers when all scientific considerations are subordinated to the single aim of empirical testing, dangers that are implied in the view that "economic theories can be 'meaningful' and 'useful' only if they can be written in the form of systems of simultaneous equations specified in such a fashion as to allow their transformation into operational, statistical hypotheses in the sense of modern Statistical Inference Theory".[29] Any attempt to represent one particular method as the only useful or worthwhile method must automatically be suspect; and even in econometrics the judgment of the individual economist is not wholly eliminated, for serious technical problems arise in applying the method, quite apart from those arising in connection with the task of interpreting the meaning of results.

Thus the appropriateness of any given verification procedure is dependent upon the methodology employed, and, as we have seen,[30] the choice of a given methodology may well be determined either consciously or unconsciously by nonscientific (e.g. epistomelogical) consideration. It is therefore hardly surprising that economists differ among themselves as to the nature, methods and significance of empirical testing (or verification). To say that the debate is still unsettled, as for example in the discussion of "direct" versus "indirect" testing,[31] does not imply that the situation is hopeless. Indeed, there are parallel difficulties in the natural science, even in those disciplines to which positive economists look for their methodological ideals. For example, one recent writer has claimed that "no process yet disclosed by the historical study of scientific development at all resembles the methodological stereotype of falsification by direct comparison with nature;[32] while another maintains that "the assertion that science is simply based on experiments that anybody can repeat at will is hollow" for those philosophers who analyse the verification process "invariably choose as specimens such laws as are not in doubt", thereby understating the role of the scientist's tacit or intuitive "powers for recognising reality".[33]

In view of these and similar difficulties, those economists who believe it is possible to eliminate "the critical nature of judgment in deciding when to test a theory and what facts to test it by" are deluding themselves. To press for "rigorous attention to the letter of a theory, exposure of a theory to genuine tests wherever possible, acceptance of a refutation where it occurs, and explicit amendment of a theory in the light of empirical refutation, (rather than the introduction of vague qualifications based on judgment)" is reasonable enough;[34] but the trend of recent theoretical work in economics is not such as to facilitate this task, even if this continuous sequence of refutations and amendments were feasible in practice.[35] The question of what is to be tested has of late been complicated by the growing habit of substituting "models" for "theories" in economics, for where the change is more than simply a matter of terminology it involves the abandonment of logical chains of theoretical reasoning (which can at least be tested for logical consistency) in favour of loose combinations of theoretical and empirical statements constructed on no fixed logical principles, but merely designed to afford insights into some aspect of the real world. The explanatory value of many such models is beyond doubt; but the issue here is one of empirical testing, and as there is often no clear distinction between those components of the model that are amenable to empirical test and those that are not, it is correspondingly more difficult to falsify any given hypothesis, or to identify the sources of failure when the "results" or "predictions" of the model are not confirmed.[36] This difficulty is aggravated by the "convertibility or propositions" – the fact that in economics it is so often possible to interpret the "fundamental assumptions" either as "rules of procedure (imperative statements), definitions (resolutions), useful fictions, or 'true' empirical propositions".[37] And the verification requirements will vary according to which interpretation of the meaning of the assumptions is adopted.

The convertibility of propositions is but one of a wide variety of problems that arise from the customary use of language in economics. Like the concept of a "neutral" money which exerts no autonomous influence on the "real" economic process, an ideal scientific language may be termed "transparent" in the sense that it transmits the meaning of a message without any distortion or loss of clarity. In practice such a language is unattainable: all languages actively shape the way we perceive, describe and interpret reality; even mathematical language is less than ideal, for it can be manipulated in ways which transcend reality and yet it must eventually be "translated" back into non-mathematical terms. The contemporary economist's attachment to mathematics is, of course, fully understandable, and defensible, for his predecessors have given him a vocabulary which has oscillated dangerously between ordinary everyday language and the specialised language of science. Extra-scientific motives, especially the desire to communicate with and to influence the lay public, have made economists reluctant to abandon this vocabulary; but communicability has been purchased at what often seems to be an extraordinarily high price in terms of popular misconception and scientific disagreement.

The deficiencies of the language of economics constitute a link between the foregoing discussion of verification and the general problem of value judgments in economics. As A. N. Whitehead once observed, "there is not a sentence which adequately states its own meaning. There is always a background of presupposition which defies analysis by reason of its infinitude",[38] and this penumbra of uncertainly also extends to the problem of verification. According to a leading positivist philosopher, Richard von Mises:

> It does not appear expedient to accept verifiability as the sole criterion of a sentence's admissibility because the question of verification depends on the accepted definitions, and hence upon the linguistic rules; thus, in the last

> analysis, verifiability is determined by the fact that the sentence in question can be embedded in a totality of sentences which for it take the place of semantic rules.[39]

Such considerations as these take us to the heart of our discussion of the role of value judgments in economics, for if the concept of verifiability (or falsifiability) is itself dependent upon the chosen "linguistic rules", and it is necessary to analyse the role of a sentence or statement in a "totality of sentences", then it is clear that the task of distinguishing between factual and value statements demands a precision of language and analysis which is seldom found in the literature of the subject. It has, of course, long been recognised by economists that such terms as "utility", "equilibrium", "welfare", etc. possess normative overtones, and that great care and attention is required in order to avoid blurring the distinction between the "positive (technical) and normative (emotive) connotations of these terms".[40] Beyond this, however, there are more serious logical and philosophical difficulties which have too often been underestimated.

As we have seen, there is no special value language: the distinction between a factual and a value statement is as likely to be governed by the context as by the words used,[41] and when economic "models" or arguments incorporate a blend of logical, empirical and normative statements of different degree of precision and reliability it is hardly surprising that the role of evaluative elements is exceedingly difficult to assess. Philosophers now recognize that it is often impossible to analyse the individual statements in a theoretical system in order to assess their logical status, and one commentator surveying recent work in linguistic analysis has concluded that "we must surrender the notion that for each kind of statement there is a separate and distinct method of validation".[42] Economists have been acutely conscious of this type of problem in the field of welfare economics, where the normative implications of the theoretical analysis are especially obvious; and although the debate about welfare economics cannot be regarded as settled, there is substantial justice in I.M.D. Little's well known strictures that

> welfare conclusions are important and influential, especially among economists, although few economists are clear as to what the word means, or what the theory is about.... Welfare economics could be purged [of its normative connotations] by the strict use of a technical terminology, which, in ordinary speech, had no value implications ... [but] it would no longer be welfare economics. It would then consist of an uninterrupted system of logical deductions which would not be about anything at all, let alone welfare.[43]

Taken literally, this is an overstatement, for it implies that welfare economics must necessarily be interpreted either as pure logic or as metaphysics, whereas in fact the interpretation will depend on the uses to which welfare theory can be put. Here, as elsewhere, the economist *can* use his concepts in a strictly positive manner; but this involves a degree of self-discipline which is, unfortunately, often lacking; and not all those who suggest that the language of economics is "saturated with moral feeling" are blinded by prejudice.[44] There are many pitfalls: for example, the introduction of implicit evaluations; the use of the *ceteris paribus* clause for obscurantist purposes; the "sleight of the invisible hand" which converts the concept of "order" from a system of logical propositions to a desirable harmony of interests; and, above all, the use of concepts which assume the character of value judgments "because they have no rigid descriptive criteria of application and consequently can be used persuasively without it being possible to check whether they are being accurately used factually at all".[45] In many cases, no doubt, the economists play their professional language game according to rules which permit fellow members of their fraternity to distinguish between the evaluative and non-evaluative meanings of terms. But to judge by the protests of those who advocate more "positive" procedures, there are many shortcomings in current practice which need to be corrected; while the economists themselves may be able to distinguish clearly between the scientific and the extra-scientific "interest" of any body of argument, even the positivists are not wholly indifferent to the applicability of their theories to practice, and there are many persons ready to supply the unstated normative implications in the event that the "scientific" economist himself should hesitate to do so.[46]

IV

Two broad conclusions emerge from the foregoing discussion:

1. Economists have inherited from the past a language which makes it often difficult to distinguish between the positive and the normative implications of any given body of economic reasoning, even to distinguish between the positive and the normative implications of particular propositions; and their normal usage tends to blur, rather than to clarify, this distinction.
2. As the scope for conclusive inter-subjective empirical tests in economics is severely limited, there must necessarily be considerable room for differences of opinion among qualified economists as to whether any given hypothesis or body of conclusions has been confirmed or refuted.

Obviously these two issues are interdependent, for if satisfactory empirical tests were available, the problem of distinguishing between the positive and the normative implications of any set proposition or body of propositions would become insignificant. But in so far as the function of an empirical test is to minimise or eliminate the role of the economist's personal judgments, any deficiencies in such tests necessarily leave scope for such judgments. Not all the judgments involved are normative value judgments, but as we have seen,[47] normative and nonnormative judgments are less readily distinguishable than is usually supposed; and even the most professedly "positive" of economists may be open to the charge that his methodological beliefs and practices are influenced by normative or ideological considerations.

This is clearly the case with Milton Friedman, whose outspoken advocacy of perfect competition and the private enterprise system[48] made his essay on the methodology of "positive" economics doubly suspect, for his treatment of certain key issues was disturbingly vague and his use of terms was shifting and inconsistent. Freidman's main contention was that a theory should be tested by reference to its "results", i.e. its "predictive power" with respect to the class of phenomena which it is designed to explain; but he completely failed to specify precisely what steps should be taken in order to provide a satisfactory test of, for example, the profit maximization hypothesis, appearing to rest his defence on a combination of intuition and casual observation.[49] One commentator complained that "Friedman uses different rules–different standards of rigour–for judging the perfectly competitive and the monopolistically competitive models",[50] and although it has not been specifically stated that Friedman's own methodological preferences were dictated by ideological bias,[51] his argument was not precise enough to nullify such a possibility.

As Michael Polanyi has shown, personal judgment cannot be wholly eliminated from scientific work, even in physics,[52] and to say that economics falls far short of physics, not only with respect to the problem of empirical testing but also because the economist's data are more limited, less reliable, and require far more careful interpretation, is to say nothing new.[53] Not all the differences of opinion among economists stem from matters requiring personal judgment; and not all irrefutable statements are necessarily normative. But the influence of tradition, or professional conservatism in economics is strong, and the fact that most economists are keenly interested in the practical applications of economic theory, and especially the policy implications of their analysis, enhances the likelihood that their tacit or explicit value judgments about policy problems will exert a feedback effect upon their "scientific" work. Nor is there much hope for those who believe that the solution to the problem of value judgments in the social sciences is the adoption of a firm resolution to declare one's value commitments, for although this recommendation

> is undoubtedly salutary and can produce excellent fruit, it verges on being a counsel of perfection. For the most part, we are unaware of many assumptions that enter into our analyses and actions, so that despite resolute efforts to make our preconceptions explicit, some decisive ones may not even occur to us. But in any event, the difficulties generated for scientific enquiry by unconscious bias and tacit value orientations are rarely overcome by devout resolutions to eliminate bias.[54]

"Positive" economics is, in other words, an ideal to which economists may legitimately aspire; it is not a state of grace that has already been attained. If economists blind themselves to the gap between the ideal and the actual, between methodological principle and methodological practice, they will only exacerbate the already formidable difficulties confronting them.

Notes

1 This paper draws upon my monograph, *The Role of Value Judgments in Economics*, which was mimeographed by the Thomas Jefferson Center for Studies in Political

Economy, at the University of Virginia, in May 1964. It was completed before the publication of T. W. Hutchison's, *Positive Economics and Policy Objectives* (London, 1964), in which similar topics are treated from a different standpoint. Many former colleagues have made pungent criticisms of earlier drafts, especially Bertram F. Levin (Univ. of Delaware), James R. Schlesinger (Rand Corporation) and J. L. Mackie (Univ. of York). None of these persons is, of course, responsible for the remnants.

2 See for example the works by Baier, Corbett, Frank, Kuhn, Nagel, Polanyi, Quine, Waissman, and White cited below.

3 For example, *Infra*, p. 9, fn. 1.

4 The expression "positive" economics rapidly gained currency after the publication of Milton Friedman's essay "On the Methodology of Positive Economics", in his *Essays in Positive Economics* (Chicago, 1953), pp. 3–43. For criticisms of Friedman's ideas see, for example, Eugene Rotwein, "On the Methodology of Positive Economics", *Quarterly Journal of Economics*, Vol. LXXIII (November 1959), pp. 554–575; K. Klappholz and J. Agassi, "Methodological Prescriptions in Economics", *Economica*, N.S. Vol. XXVI (February 1959), pp. 65–69; and Ernest Nagel, "Assumptions in Economic Theory", *American Economic Review: Papers and Proceedings*, Vol. LIII (May 1963), pp. 211–219, and the ensuing discussion by Herbert A. Simon and Paul A. Samuelson, ibid, pp. 229–236.

For evidences that the "positive" nomenclature is gaining adherents in this country, see R. G. Lipsey, *An Introduction to Positive Economics* (London 1963). A revealing footnote on the distinction between "positive" and "normative" statements appears on pp. 4–5.

5 For example of these difficulties see the essays by Henry Margenau, Gustav Bergmann, Carl G. Hempel, Raymond J. Seeger, Adolf Grunbaum, and P. Bridgman in *The Validation of Scientific Theories* (ed. Philipp G. Frank) (New York, 1961), pp. 45–92.

For an attempt to apply operationalism to economics, see Donald F. Gordon, "Operational Propositions in Economic Theory", *Journal of Political Economy* Vol. LXIII (April 1955), pp. 150–161; and for a critique of this approach see Fritz Machlup, "Operational Concepts and Mental Constructs in Model and Theory Formation", *Giornale degli Economisti e Annali Di Economia* Vol. XIX (September-October 1960), pp. 1–32.

6 Lionel Robbins' famous definition in *An Essay on The Nature and Significance of Economic Science* (1st ed., London, 1932), p. 132, was subsequently criticized as being "normative as the behavior of economists" Cf. L. M. Fraser, *Economic Thought and Language* (London, 1937), pp. 37–38, 34–35.

Such "persuasive" definitions of science are common enough, and it has recently been argued that science cannot be defined simply by specifying its attributes, but only by reference to the scientific "tradition". Cf. Max Black, "The Definition of Scientific Method", in his *Problems of Analysis, philosophical Essays*, (Cornell. 1954), pp. 3–23; also W. B. Gallie, "What Makes a Subject Scientific?" *British Journal for the Philosophy of Science*, Vol. VIII (August 1957), pp. 118–139.

7 Limitations of space preclude an attempt to substantiate the claims made in this paragraph, which are derived from a general study of the history of methodological controversy in economics and the history of the principal British and American organizations of economists.

8 According to one prominent "orthodox" American economist, George J. Stigler, "the professional study of economics makes one politically conservative", that is it encourages a preference for private enterprise in economic affairs and a belief that "abuses of private power will normally be checked and incitements to efficiency and progress usually provided by the forces of competition". "The Politics of Political Economists", *Quarterly Journal of Economics*, Vol. LXXIII (November 1959), p. 524. See my "Comment", *Q. J. E.*, Vol. LXXIV (November 1960), pp. 666–669.

The most extreme exponent of the view that modern economics presupposes the values of 18th century liberalism is Ludwig von Mises, who has claimed that "no logical or scientific arguments whatsoever could or can be brought against the theories of liberalism which were developed by philosophers, economists and praxeologists of the 18th and of the first half of the 19th centuries ... only one who prefers sickness, misery, and suffering may reject the reasonings of liberalism on the ground that it is not neutral with regard to value judgments". See his *Epistemological Problems of Economics* (Princeton, 1960), pp. 189, 39, Cf. Joseph Schumpeter, *History of Economic Analysis* (Oxford, 1954), pp. 44, 394.

9 This definition is adapted from Paul W. Taylor *Normative Discourse* (New Jersey, 1961), p. 3. Taylor has provided the most systematic analysis of value judgments to appear in recent years. His definition, unlike some others, does not blur the distinction between factual and value judgments.

10 Cf. Kurt Baier, *The Moral Point of View, A Rational Basis for Ethics* (Cornell, 1958), p. 72. Chapter 2 of this book contains a useful, though sometimes misleading, discussion of the similarities and differences between judgments of fact and judgments of value. See also Taylor, op.cit., Chapter 2, and Mary Carman Rose, "Value Propositions and the Empirical", *Ethics*, Vol. LXIII (July 1953), pp. 262–275.

11 Taylor, op.cit., p. 54. Also Chapters 7 and 9.

12 Ernest Nagel, *The Structure of Science, Problems in the Logic of Scientific Explanation* (London and New York, 1961), p. 491.

On the interdependence of "means" and "ends" in economics, see Gunnar Myrdal, *Value in Social Theory* (ed. Paul Streeten) (London, 1958) especially pp. xiv-xvii, xxi-xxv, 206–230.

13 These matters are extensively discussed in Taylor, op.cit., especially Chapters 3–6.

14 Throughout this paper the term 'verification' will be used rather than Karl R. Popper's concept of falsification, because the former is more familiar. For Popper's views see *The Logic of Scientific Discovery* (New York, 1961), *passim*.

15 Cf. Bernard Barber, *Science and the Social Order* (Glencoe, III., 1952); also Michael Polanyi, *Personal Knowledge* (Chicago, 1958), *passim*.

16 For example see Morris R. Cohen, *Reason and Nature, An Essay on the Meaning of Scientific Method* (New York, 1931), p. 83; also J. W. N. Sullivan, *The Limitations of Science* (New York, 1949), chapter 7. On the role of aesthetic and ideological elements in economics see, for example, E. Ronald Walker, *From Economic Theory to Policy* (Chicago 1943); Joan Robinson, *Economic Philosophy* (Chicago, 1963), p. 61.

17 Polanyi, op.cit., p. 167. For an example of this in economics, *infra*, pp. 7,9.

18 Nagel, *The Structure of Science*, pp. 489–490.

19 Walker, op.cit., p. 216. This is undoubtedly one of the principal ways in which the value presuppositions of a group of scientists determines the content of a discipline; once established, the scientific tradition is very difficult to resist.

20 For an idea of the character of such a study see the discussion of metasociology in Paul H. Furfey, *The Scope and Method of Sociology* (New York, 1953), Chapters 2 and 4.

21 See the discussion of econometrics in Henry W. Briefs, *Three Views of Economic Method* (Georgetown UP, Washington, 1960), especially pp. 32–34. At the end of his study Briefs concludes "Each of the methodologies gives a definitive positive answer to the question: In what manner are economic phenomena conceived to exist relative to the scientific observer and what are the conditions of achieving a definite knowledge concerning them? ... there is no general standard by which the adequacy of economic doctrines can be judged [and] valid appraisals of economic doctrines are likely to be rare whenever the critic holds methodological convictions which differ fundamentally from those in the analysis to be appraised". Ibid, pp. 78–9, 91. Cf. the quotation from Polanyi cited *supra*, p. 6.

22 Karl R. Popper, op.cit., pp. 37, 38. For a similar argument applied to economics see Andreas G. Papandreou, *Economics as a Science* (New York, 1958), p. 30. Papandreou's argument has, however, been attacked by Klappholz and Agassi, op. cit., pp. 69–70.

23 One approach to economic methodology that stems directly from metaphysical ideas is "methodological individualism". The main issues involved are discussed in the

following works: F. A. Hayek, *The Counter-Revolution of Science, Studies in the Abuse of Reason* (Glencoe, Ill., 1952); May Broadbeck, "On the Philosophy of the Social Science", *Philosophy of Science*, Vol. XXI (April 1954), reprinted in E. C. Harwood, *Reconstruction of Economics* (Great Barrington, Mass., 1955), pp. 45–65; Nagel, *The Structure of Science*, op.cit., pp. 473–478, 535–546; and a number of articles by J. W. N. Watkins, Leon J. Goldstein, Maurice Mandelbaum, and K. J. Scott, which appeared in the *British Journal for the Philosophy of Science* between 1952 and 1961.

24 T. W. Hutchison's influential study, *The Significance and Basic Postulates of Economic Theory* (New York, 1960), originally published in 1938, was designed to achieve this objective.

25 Ralph Barton Perry, *Realms of Value* (Cambridge, Mass., 1954), p. 357. The discussion of quantification in economics was initially prompted by Wesley C. Mitchell's "Quantitative Analysis in Economic Theory", *American Economic Review*, Vol. XV (1925), pp. 1–12, and occupied a prominent place in the pages of that journal during the ensuing two years. This issue is discussed in Chapter VII of my unpublished PhD thesis, *Methodological Controversy as an Approach to the History of American Economic Thought 1885–1930* (Johns Hopkins, 1953).

26 Briefs, op.cit., pp. 54, 16.

27 For an impassioned outburst by a British exponent of positive economics see Lipsey, op.cit., pp. 532–533.

28 Briefs, op.cit., pp. 32–34.

29 Ibid, pp. 29–30. Briefs bases this interpretation on Haavelmo, "The Probability Approach in Econometrics", *Econometrica* Supplement, July 1944.

30 *Supra*, p. 6.

31 Fritz Machlup, "The Problem of Verification in Economics", *Southern Economic Journal*, Vol. XXII (July 1955–April 1956), pp. 1–21; T. W. Hutchison, "Professor Machlup on Verification in Economics", ibid, pp. 476–483; and Machlup, "Rejoinder to a Reluctant Ultra-Empiricist", ibid, pp. 483–493.

32 T. S. Kuhn, *The Structure of Scientific Revolutions* (Chicago, 1962), pp. 77, 143–6.

33 Polanyi, op.cit., p. 13.

34 Lipsey, op.cit., pp. 532–533. Lipsey claims that his views reflect those of a group of economists at the London School of Economics.

35 As Morris Cohen once remarked, "It is only as a last resort that we modify (as little as possible) the old ideas. If we did not hold on to our old ideas tenaciously, if we threw them away the moment they encountered difficulties, we could never develop any strong ideas and our science would have no continuity of development" op.cit., p. 27. For stronger statements of this kind see Polanyi, op.cit., p. 138, and Kuhn, op.cit. Chapter VIII.

36 Cf. Papandreou, op.cit., pp. 7–9; for the philosophical background see Carl G. Hempel, "A Logical Appraisal of Operationism", in Frank, op.cit., pp. 56–59; also the references *infra* p. 12 n. 2.

37 Machlup, "Rejoinder to a Reluctant Ultra-Empiricist", loc.cit., p. 487, fn 5.

38 See his *Essays in Science and Philosophy* (London, 1948), p. 73.

39 *Positivism* (New York, 1956), p. 76.

40 These terms "carry within their meaning some at least of the criteria by which the goodness or badness of their referents must be judged", and in such cases the temptation to draw normative conclusions from positive analysis is exceedingly difficult to resist. Cf. A. R. Montefiore "Goodness and Choice", *Proceedings of the Aristotelian Society* Supplement Vol. XXXV (1961), p. 70. For examples of the misuse of the term 'equilibrium' see Fritz Machlup, "Equilibrium and Disequilibrium: Misplaced Concreteness and Disguised Politics", *Economic Journal*, Vol. LXVIII (March 1958), pp. 1–24, reprinted in his *Essays in Economic Semantics* (ed. Merton H. Miller) (New Jersey, 1963). This volume contains many excellent illustrations of the loose usage current in economic writings.

41 *Supra*, p. 5.
42 Morton H. White, "American Philosophy" in *American Perspectives* (ed. Robert E. Spiller and Eric Larrabee) (Harvard, 1961), p. 21. Apart from the difficulty of distinguishing between the positive and normative connotations of different statements, philosophers have recently coined the repellent term "analyticity" to denote the problem of distinguishing between "analytic" (theoretical) and "synthetic" (empirical) statements. Cf. Carl Hempel, op.cit., pp. 64–66; Morton G. White, *Toward Reunion in Philosophy* (Harvard, 1956), pp. 256, 246, 251; A. C. Ewing, "Recent Developments in British Ethical Thought" in *British Philosophy in Mid-century* (ed. C. A. Mace) (London, 1957), pp. 92–94; W. O. Quine, "Two Dogmas of Empiricism" in his *From a Logical Point of View, Nine Logico-Philosophical Essays* (Harvard, 1953), pp. 42–43; and the series of articles by F. Waissman entitled "Analyticity" in *Analysis*, Vol. 10 (December 1949) to Vol. 13 (March 1953).
43 I. M. D. Little, *A Critique of Welfare Economics* (2nd ed., Oxford, 1958), pp. 3, 80. (For a contrary view see G. C. Archibald, "Welfare Economics, Ethics and Essentialism", *Economica* N.S., Vol. XXVI (November 1959), pp. 316–327).
Joan Robinson, op.cit., pp. 57–58.
45 Among recent critics of these shortcomings see Anne Martin, "How Economic Theory May Mislead", *British Journal for the Philosophy of Science*, Vol. VIII (November 1957), pp. 225–236; J. H. Corbett and Honor Brotman in a symposium on "The Concept of Welfare in Economics." *Proceedings of the Aristotelian Society* Supplement Vol. XXVI (1953), especially pp. 217, 188. For an earlier, somewhat different attack upon the use of implicit definitions, see Wassily Leontief, "Implicit Theorising: A Methodological Criticism of the Neo-Cambridge School", *Quarterly Journal of Economics*, Vol. LI (February 1937), pp. 337–351. Many other examples could be cited.
46 Walker, op.cit., Chapters II and X.
47 *Supra*, pp. 11–12.
48 See for example his collected essays, *Capitalism and Freedom* (Chicago, 1962).
49 Friedman, *Essays in Positive Economics*, op.cit., pp. 8–9. In response to Friedman's assertion that "under a wide variety of circumstances, individual firms behave as if they were seeking rationally to maximize their expected returns, and had full knowledge of the data needed in order to succeed in this attempt", one critic replied that Friedman evidently "already knows what an economist will find when he looks into a business firm and that even if he finds something quite different it does not matter for economic." Cf. Herbert Simon, "New Developments in the Theory of the Firm," *American Economic Review*, Vol. LXI, Supplement (May 1961), p. 3.
50 C. G, Archibald, "Reply to Chicago," *Review of Economic Studies*, Vol. XXX (February 1963), p. 70. This appears in a reply to criticisms by G. J. Stigler and Friedman of Archibald's article "Chamberlin versus Chicago" *Review of Economic Studies*, Vol. XXIX (October 1961), pp. 2–28. For an earlier critique of Friedman see Archibald's "The State of Economic Science, *British Journal for the Philosophy of Science*, Vol. X (May 1959), pp. 58–69. Though careful and constructive, Archibald's work constitutes no more than a prolegomena to a methodology of economic testing. It reveals how much more is still to be achieved before the aims of the "positive" economists can be fulfilled.
51 However Paul Samuelson came close to suggesting this in his sometimes facetious comment on Friedman's methodology, Cf. *American Economic Review* Supplement, Vol. LIII (May 1962), pp. 229–263.
52 *Personal Knowledge*, op.cit., passim.
53 For an early, though devastating demonstration of this point see Oskar Morgenstern, *On the Accuracy of Economic Observations* (Princeton, 1950). A new and enlarged edition of this work appeared in 1963.
54 Nagel, *The Structure of Science*, op.cit., pp. 489–490.

21 Methodology and professionalism in economics

A subordinate theme in Machlup's writings

1.

The history of economics currently appears to be undergoing a modest revival both among teachers and researchers. Nevertheless some of its important aspects and themes are still seriously neglected. This chapter is designed to link together two of those themes – methodology and professionalism – and to illustrate their interrelationships by reference to some of Fritz Machlup's writings.

The tentative and provisional character of this exercise must be emphasized at the outset, for a variety of reasons. The existing literature on these two topics is very different in size and character. The volume of general works on the methodology of economics is enormous, but it has hitherto been little used by historians of the subject, for much of it is not readily susceptible to historical analysis and interpretation.[1] By contrast there has been little or no serious effort to examine the history of the economics profession, and one of the aspects of that subject most pertinent to the present discussion – the formation and development of professional standards – is still virtually uncharted territory.

To explore these matters is no easy task, and in addition to the intrinsic difficulties of the undertaking there are the additional hazards involved in analyzing the works of the formidable analyst whose achievements constitute the *raison d'être* of this volume. Such a task can be inviting only to a member of that species which proceeds precipitately in advance of the proverbial angels; and it is to be hoped that in this instance at least the master will not be held responsible for the follies of his former students.

2.

The title of a short Machlup article published over forty years ago, "Why Bother with Methodology?"[2] provides a convenient starting point for this inquiry. The question is apt, for many distinguished economists have invested time and energy in this subject, despite the fact that methodology has usually been held in low esteem by their professional peers. What irresistible force has drawn them, seemingly against their better judgment, into this treacherous morass from which few reputations have emerged entirely unsmirched? In this, as in so many other matters, the motivations have usually been mixed, and not always pure. Individual self-interest, the desire to defend or assert the superiority of a specific method, approach, doctrine, school, or even a policy or ideology, has often been present; but there has also been a perennial desire to establish or to maintain and defend certain approved procedures or standards of professional practice. For this reason a study of the sociological aspects of methodological controversy can be enlightening. And it is also worth noting – on this occasion only in passing – that the spatial and temporal distribution of methodological discussion in economics is also a subject of considerable interest, one that still awaits systematic investigation.[3]

Methodological writings in economics usually have two distinct dimensions: the cognitive and the regulative. From the cognitive standpoint they are concerned, whether explicitly or implicitly, with such questions as: what is knowledge in economics and what are its limitations? How is it attained? What are the criteria and tests of valid knowledge? From a regulative standpoint, however, somewhat different questions arise, such as: how can correct standards of scientific practice be established and maintained? How are knowledge-seeking processes best organized and controlled? How is knowledge most efficiently accumulated, preserved, and disseminated? While many writers on the methodology of economics have recognized the existence of both the cognitive and the regulative aspects of their discipline, and have appreciated that methodological debates usually raise questions of professional values and standards as well as questions of logic and scientific method, they have rarely chosen to consider the regulative aspects directly or in depth.

From the professional standpoint, values and standards are invariably involved when methodological discussion occurs. If, as is usually claimed, economics is a science, it must be acknowledged that science is a "moral enterprise," one that is deeply influenced by the individual scientist's personal aims and interests as well as those of the society to which he belongs.[4] Like other human activities, science cannot be value free in any absolute sense: in addition to the supreme "end" or value of scientific endeavor – the pursuit of "truth" – there are also subordinate procedural ideals or rules, some of which are purely instrumental (i.e., positive means to the pursuit of scientific knowledge, such as freedom of inquiry), while others are aesthetic.[5] These procedural ideals, such as "certainty," "universality," "simplicity," "system," are necessarily general in character, and their interpretation and their applicability to particular circumstances and cases is accordingly liable to dispute. Moreover, "all formal rules of scientific procedure must prove ambiguous, for they will be interpreted quite differently according to the particular conceptions about the nature of things by which the scientist is guided."[6]

This does not, of course, mean that the results of scientific work are purely arbitrary, for in principle at least these results are

> subject to the self-corrective mechanisms of science as a social enterprise.... It would be absurd to claim that this institutionalised mechanism for sifting warranted beliefs has operated or is likely to operate in social enquiry as effectively as it has in the natural sciences. But it would be no less absurd to

> conclude that reliable knowledge of human affairs is unattainable merely because social enquiry is frequently value orientated.[7]

In economics, however, where the authority of tradition is strong, where well-defined standards of technical competence are lacking, and where it is exceedingly difficult to devise conclusive empirical tests of the validity of economic hypotheses or statements, there are serious obstacles to the smooth functioning of the "self-corrective mechanisms of science as a social enterprise." As this is so, the scope for the individual economist's personal judgment is much greater than in disciplines where technical and professional standards are more rigorous and uniform.

3.

The foregoing remarks suggest the possibility of viewing methodological discussion as part of the overall process of scientific advance, a process which has a number of facets: logic; personality; human interaction; the formation, preservation, and development of scientific standards and traditions; the interaction of one set of standards or tradition with another; and the interaction of the members of the scientific community with the wider society of which they form a part. Against this background the concept of professionalization falls into place.

The attempt to define a profession and the process of professionalization has in the past absorbed a considerable amount of scholarly time and energy. For the present purpose, however, it is sufficient to mention certain characteristics or traits that seem especially relevant to the present discussion.[8] To a greater or lesser extent the members of a profession possess a common sense of identity and purpose; a set of shared values and standards; a high degree of generalized, systematic knowledge; a common language, which is understood only partly by outsiders; a measure of control over the selection and training of recruits, which is also a socialization process; and a system of rewards, both monetary and honorary, which primarily symbolize work achievement. There are, of course, in any profession various subcommunities or subspecialisms and there is never perfect unanimity or harmony, if only because the individual members usually possess a high degree of personal independence and autonomy. Nevertheless, even in a controversial and rapidly changing subject like economics, where there are no effective controls over entry and no accepted codes of ethics, it is not difficult to recognize many of the characteristic features of a professional community.

4.

It is now time to consider some aspects of the interrelationships between methodology and professionalism as revealed in some of Fritz Machlup's writings, even though limitations of space and the author's competence make it impossible to do justice to the subject.

To what extent do these issues appear in Machlup's work, and in what form? As is well known, Machlup has been an enormously prolific and wide-ranging author, and in addition to his career as an economist his role in professional matters has been prominent both within the American Economic Association and in the American Association of University Professors. Although the concept of professionalism does not appear as such in the methodological writings reviewed for the purposes of this chapter, it is nevertheless a recurrent underlying theme, for Machlup is an unusually self-conscious economist, highly sensitive to matters of language, method, and philosophy, and in addition concerned with economic theory and its applications to policy. Consequently, his writings contain many revealing insights into his conception of professional standards and values. Much of Machlup's methodological writing has been motivated by dissatisfaction with "the scientific attitude of a generation of economists contemptuous of 'philosophical' reflection and impatient to get on with the business of measuring."[9] Economists should "bother with methodology" simply because it is both important and unavoidable. Admittedly, methodological discussion is usually inconclusive, for the issues in dispute "cannot be settled either by empirical tests or by formal logical demonstration."[10] But there is no easy way out. Reliance on "authority" is dangerous, while to imagine that methodology – or, for that matter, metaphysics – is avoidable is a delusion. Those who turn away from the subject are often unaware of the limitations of their own method and neglectful of the gap between their methodological prescriptions and their practice. Even if he makes no explicit reference to methodoological or philosophical issues "the researcher in economics cannot avoid using a method and implicitly accepting an epistemological position on how to distinguish the knowable from the unknowable, the true from the false, the probable from the improbable."[11] Current standards of professional practice are frequently lax. "Too often researchers do not question the meanings of the terms with which they work; they are diving into third-rate statistical data which they believe, or assume, to be suitable proxies for the vague or ambiguous theoretical concepts with which their supposedly first-rate models are finished."[12]

Central to Machlup's own methodological position is his opposition to certain fashionable and influential currents in mid-twentieth century thought which threaten to create "a scientific orthodoxy which in turn (a) tends to block the development of new methods, (b) tends to exclude many problems from the jurisdiction of science, and (c) tends to make scientists 'safe' rather than 'daring.' "[13] These tendencies can be summed up in the word "scientism" – the fundamental belief that natural science methods can be applied directly to the social sciences without due regard to the special characteristics of their subject matter and to the distinctive problems with which they are concerned. In economics scientism appears in a number of different guises – for example positivism, operationalism, behaviorism, mathematization, quantification – not all of which are inherently dangerous, but each of which is liable to be pushed to extremes by some of its proponents. Thus, while acknowledging that there are several varieties of empiricism, Machlup especially attacks what he terms radical empiricism or ultra-empiricism: the doctrine of those who "refuse to recognize the legitimacy of employing at any level of analysis propositions not independently verifiable."[14] His views on these matters have been the subject of considerable scholarly debate, which cannot be reviewed again here.[15] But while acknowledging an element of exaggeration in the statement of his views, which is deliberately designed to warn his fellow economists of the dangers of extremism, it is important to emphasize Machlup's profound and persistent antiauthoritarianism, whether in matters of terminology, philosophy, method, theory, or policy. Even in Machlup's methodological writings there is, of course, an unavoidably prescriptive element, for correct standards must be upheld and errors exposed and eliminated. Nevertheless, he has repeatedly stressed the need to preserve the analyst's freedom to choose his terms, problems, methods, and models as he deems appropriate. A few of his innumerable appeals for professional toleration will suffice to illustrate the point: "I shall not attempt to tell other people in which problems they should be interested or from which problems they should turn away"; "the semanticist may analyze, but not dictate"; "no theorist is appointed or ordained to speak in the name of theory."[16] To those who seek to make economics an exclusively mathematical discipline he has appealed on behalf of "polylingual scholarship," even though he concedes that reluctance to make "the serious effort required in learning new languages" may explain "the common preference for vague and ambiguous terms."[17]

So profound is Machlup's hostility to scientific orthodoxy, with its concomitant restrictions on the scientist's freedom of choice, that he sometimes appears to carry toleration to extremes, with the result that his methodological prescriptions seem vague or eclectic. For example, despite repeated pleas for precision of language he admits that catchall words like "model" are "a boon, not only for sloppy thinkers and writers, but also for thoughtful ones when they have a good reason for postponing commitment to a definite idea."[18] Hence, "without wishing to restrict the freedom of choice of those who formulate definitions, I submit that the choice should be appropriate to the purposes for which the concept is used" – an injunction which hardly provides specific guidance.[19] Somewhat similar difficulties arise from his statements that "models of different degrees of realism and complexity will be adequate for different problems"; that "any well constructed model furnishes precisely the results the constructor wants it to furnish"; or that as there are twenty-one different concepts of the firm to be found in the literature of business and economics it is "pointless" to argue "which is the most important or the most useful."[20]

As positive guides to correct methodological practice these observations can hardly be regarded as helpful, and it is easy to understand why they have been described as "conventionalist stratagems,"[21] given Machlup's persistent and persuasive arguments in favor of "the legitimacy and usefulness of abstract theorizing on the basis of unrealistic assumptions, or perhaps on the basis of assumptions regarded as 'reasonable' though not universally true."[22] His conception of the functions of economic theory strikes many economists as unduly modest. Its "sole purpose and value," he maintains, "is to deduce logically necessary conclusions"; contrary to widespread opinion its value "is not measured in terms of its immediate applicability to policy making but, instead, in terms of the improved insight and better understanding of complex relationships."[23] In an age dedicated to social engineering, both piecemeal and wholesale, Machlup's personal feelings are revealed in his remark that "there are instances, thank God, in which the investigator selects his project out of sheer intellectual curiosity and does not give 'two hoots' about the social importance of his findings. Still to satisfy curiosity is a value too, and indeed a very potent one."[24]

Machlup's reluctance to specify precise rules of procedure is perhaps best illustrated by his well-known essay on verification, a subject on which he admits that "my own views are so decided that I cannot see how intelligent people can still quarrel about them, and I have come to believe that all good men think as I do, and only a few misguided creatures think otherwise."[25] It is presumably the nature of the subject, rather than evasiveness, that leads him to say that his analytical machine helps us to select an "adequate" cause for an observed change, and to find the "probable" effect. Although we cannot get reliable figures, and our statistical concepts may not be exact counterparts of our analytical concepts, "we cannot be too fussy, and must be satisfied with what we can get." Any attempt to establish "a rigid verification requirement would be out of place"; nevertheless the analyst's judgment will usually be sufficient, "even if he cannot support it with more than the most circumstantial evidence or mere 'impressions'."[26]

Whether Machlup's treatment of verification is "adequate" for its purpose is a question beyond the scope of this essay, although it is appropriate to remark that there is much to be said in favor of methodological agnosticism, as against those who make excessive claims for their own methods and base dogmatic assertions on weak reasoning and unsubstantial evidence. More directly relevant to the present purpose, however, is the extent to which Machlup has acknowledged the role of personal judgment and values in scientific affairs, a matter that has been increasingly acknowledged in the recent literature of the logic and philosophy of science. In the course of a detailed discussion of the relationships between normative and positive economics, Machlup provided a list of a dozen different kinds of values and value references of concern to the economist, four of which-his own values as an analyst and as an adviser and persuader – are of direct relevance to this discussion.

1. Values of the economist as analyst that influence him in the choice of his research projects, of the problems to be analyzed and of the hypotheses to be entertained and examined.
2. Values of the economist as analyst that influence him in the choice of his research technique and analytical procedures, in the weights he attaches to various types of evidence, in the elegance of his logical demonstrations, and in his eagerness to subject his findings to suitable empirical tests.
3. Values of the economist as analyst that influence him in the choice of his terminology and in the acceptance of available statistical data as magnitudes adequately reflecting his theoretical constructs (such as national product at market prices, with the given distribution of income).
4. Values of the economist as adviser or persuader that influence him in substituting his own value judgments chiefly for those of his actual or symbolic clients but without deliberate falsifications of his data or conscious bias in his findings.[27]

Once again, a few examples must suffice to illustrate the recognition of personal values in Machlup's own work. In terminological matters, for example, while making strenuous efforts to awaken his professional colleagues to the need for linguistic precision and consistency he concedes that "standards of clarity are not uniform ... I cannot be sure whether, when I complain about vagueness, my perception is too poor, my sense of discrimination too fine, my insistence on unambiguous expression too pedantic – or whether the writings in question were just too wooly."[28] Moreover, he acknowledges that his own biases may well influence his interpretations, for "my suspicion is aroused by the strange coincidence that I have found crypto-apologetic meanings of structure only in pleas for policies which I do not like: restrictions of competition, price and allocation controls, import barriers, exchange restrictions. Have I perhaps failed to notice similar aberrations in policies I happen to like? ... to grasp an argument that leads to conclusions hitherto rejected is much more difficult than to grasp an argument supporting a preconceived conclusion. Where I do not like the results, I am more eager than otherwise to question the validity of the premises, the consistency of the argument, the clarity of the concepts.... Aware of these influences of one's political philosophy upon one's understanding of concepts, I must concede the possibility that my judgement has not attained the degree of fairness to which I aspire."[29]

Many economists have admitted the influence of value judgments on their views on policy matters. Few, however, have been as full and explicit as Machlup in acknowledging the influence of personal values on the selection of analytical methods and terms. In his analysis of the relationship between macro- and microeconomics, for example, Machlup denied that there is a *logical* link between methodological individualism and ethical or political individualism, but he conceded that "there are psychological associations between them. An economist who has become accustomed to assign great importance to individual choices as elements in the explanation of economic phenomena may easily have developed a bent of mind hospitable to ideas of individual freedom of choice in economic, political, and social affairs in general."[30]

Whatever the direction of the causal relationship in Machlup's own case, there is no denying the compatibility of his professional and his political beliefs. Is it surprising that this staunch and eloquent advocate of individual freedom in academic and political affairs should be so insistent upon the economist's right to individual freedom in the choice of assumptions, models, and theories? He has, admittedly, prescribed some moderate rules designed to limit freedom of choice in terminological matters; but it is no exaggeration to say that much of his methodological writing has been designed to assert the economic theorist's right to exist professionally. Machlup has expressed his preference for "daring" rather than "safety" in scientific work, and has defended the dissemination of "hunches and impressions" as a "necessary first step on the route to more securely warranted beliefs"[31] – presumably because he ultimately has faith in the ability of the scientific community to devise and apply the established "mechanism for sifting warranted beliefs."

This faith is, however, neither blind nor naive. His well-known reservations about the limitations of statistical data and empirical research stem from an acute awareness that overconfidence and dogmatism are seldom absent, even from the community of professional scholars. While enjoining honesty in the exposure of value judgments, and declaring that "as a rule we probably will indicate which value position we regard as the most 'reasonable.' Most of us will do this in a rather unmistakable way, since we are usually convinced that our own ethical values are more ethical than others"[32] – he is nevertheless only too well aware of the influence of unconscious bias. Moreover, in his "customs officer" analogy he recognizes not only the "norms" the peripatetic economist knows to be in his personal baggage, but adds that "he cannot declare those values that he will work out or develop only long after settling down, when he finds that he has to make choices for which none of the evaluations that he had ever thought about are relevant."[33]

Nevertheless, despite all his warnings and reservations, Machlup is not pleading that the economist should refrain from making policy statements-merely that he should express them with due caution and recognize their limitations. "For while economics can well serve to criticize policies, by showing that the reasoning on which they are based is faulty, inconsistent or woefully incomplete, economic analysis will rarely be complete enough to permit unambiguous conclusions from it to be drawn in the form of positive prescriptions for the governments of nations." This does not diminish the importance of economic theory, but "merely urges caution in its application."[34] More than one policy recommendation can be drawn from a given theory, if only because "economic theory is not derived solely from economics, but from a complex of considerations involving several fields of knowledge and also numerous value judgments." Beyond this, a fertile theorist can usually "think of countless alternatives in any problem of economic policy" as, for example, in Machlup's case, when he enumerated forty-one different types of measures "capable of removing or reducing the U.S. payments deficit."[35]

5.

Fritz Machlup's work forms part of a long and vigorous liberal-ideological tradition in economics dating back at least as far as Carl Menger and the late nineteenth century Austrian school. The term liberal is, of course, elusive, and in dealing with such a dedicated semanticist it is fitting to cite his own definition of the word, as "one who values liberty above all social goals and who will never consent to the restriction of any freedom, economic, political, or intellectual, except as the price to be paid for the fuller realization of other freedoms."[36] Although the foregoing review of his views on methodological and professional matters has been limited and selective, enough has been said to reveal the compatibility between his preaching and his practice. While he has not been loath to express his opinions on a wide range of issues of professional and public concern, he has displayed a remarkable tolerance of variety in scholarly matters. This toleration has not, however, been complete. He has been persistently hostile to abuses of scholarship whether in the form of dogmatism, obscurantism, or laxity of standards. As a persistent defender of abstract theory he has been especially impatient with loose reasoning, and has always insisted on the "demands of logic," distinguishing between "reasonable" and other theories, asserting that "analysis requires" that certain distinctions be explicated, and protesting that "it is hopeless to argue where one side flouts logic."[37] Describing himself as a "compulsive pedagogue" with a "love for language," "a fascination with matters of exposition, composition, style, rhythm, and sound," he has displayed an inveterate "propensity to sort things out, clarify terminology, and remove ambiguities."[38] Even if he had made no significant contributions to the advancement of economic theory or to the understanding of economic policy problems, this would in itself have been a significant contribution to the maintenance and elevation of professional standards.

As a persistent and eloquent spokesman for general economic theory – in line with such distinguished allies as Ludwig von Mises, Friedrich A. von Hayek, Frank H. Knight, and Milton Friedman – Machlup has been consistently swimming against the tide of mid-twentieth century empiricism in economics. While acknowledging the need for the hypotheses with empirically fertile implications, and recognizing the value of empirical research, he has nevertheless insisted that "the *chief condition* for improved research is a thorough understanding of the theories to be tested." Familiarity with the relevant technical and institutional conditions, and a grasp of the relevant research techniques employed are "supplementary" prerequisites.[39] Doubtless Machlup believes that given the preoccupations of the age these supplementary requirements are unlikely to be neglected. In an era dedicated to Beherrschungswissen (knowledge for the sake of control, power or action) he believes it is essential to preach the value of *Bildungswissen* and *Erlösungswissen* (knowledge for the sake of knowledge, and for the sake of salvation).[40] In the last analysis the basic values of professional scholarship are honesty and humility, for "the faster we learn, the more we appreciate the incompleteness of our knowledge, and the more doubtful we become of its definiteness."[41]

Notes

1 There have, however, been some valuable contributions to this subject. See, for example, T. W. Hutchison, *'Positive' Economics and Policy Objectives* (London: Allen and Unwin, 1964).

2 *Economica*, New Series Vol. 3 (1936), pp. 39–45.

3 For a preliminary study of one aspect of the field see the chapter author's unpublished Ph.D. thesis, *Methodological Controversy as an Approach to the History of American Economics, 1885–1930* (Johns Hopkins, 1953). Under the influence of nostalgia it seems appropriate to quote Machlup's remark that Johns Hopkins provided "what probably was the best climate for graduate study in economics that had existed anywhere," from an unpublished paper, "Reminiscences without Regrets," delivered at the American Economic Association Meetings in December 1974.

4 See Bernard Barber, *Science and the Social Order* (Glencoe, Ill: Free Press, 1952); also Michael Polanyi, *Personal Knowledge* (Chicago: University of Chicago Press, 1958).

5 For example, see Morris R. Cohen, *Reason and Nature: An Essay on the Meaning of Scientific Method* (New York: Harcourt, 1931) p. 83, also J. W. N. Sullivan,

The Limitations of Science (New York: Viking Press, 1949), chapter 7. On the role of aesthetic and ideological elements in economics see, for example, E. Ronald Walker, *From Economic Theory to Policy* (Chicago: University of Chicago Press, 1943); Joan Robinson, *Economic Philosophy* (Chicago: Praeger, 1963), p. 61.

6 Polanyi, *Personal Knowledge*, p. 167.

7 Ernest Nagel, *The Structure of Science, Problems in the Logic of Scientific Explanation* (London and New York: Routledge, Kegan, and Paul; Harcourt Brace, 1961), pp. 489–90.

8 See, for example, William J. Goode, "Community within a Community; the Professions," *American Sociological Review*, Vol. 22 (April 1957), p. 194; Bernard Barber, "Some Problems in the Sociology of Professions," *Daedalus*, Vol. 92 (1963), p. 672.

9 From the Introduction to *International Mobility and Movement of Capital*, Fritz Machlup, Walter Salant, and Lorie Tarshis, eds. (New York: National Bureau of Economic Research 1972), p. 4.

10 "Homo Oeconomicus and His Class Mates," in Maurice Natanson, ed., *Phenomenology and Social Reality. Essays in Memory of Alfred Schutz* (The Hague: Nühoff, 1970) p. 125.

11 "Operationalism and Pure Theory in Economics," in Sherman Roy Krupp, Ed., *The Structure of Economic Science: Essays in Methodology* (N.J: Prentice-Hall, 1966), p. 54; "Issues in Methodology," *American Economic Review, Papers and Proceedings*, Vol. 42 (1952), p. 34.

12 Machlup, et al., *International Movement and Mobility of Capital*, p. 4.

13 Quoted, with approval, from Arnold M. Rose, *Theory and Method in the Social Sciences* (Minneapolis: University of Minneapolis Press 1954), p. 254, in *American Economic Review*, Vol. 65 (1955), p. 395.

14 "The Problem of Verification in Economics," *Southern Economic Journal*, Vol. 22, (July 1955), p. 7.

15 See, for example, T. W. Hutchison, "Professor Machlup on Verification in Economics," *Southern Economic Journal*, Vol. 22 (April 1956), pp. 476–83; Jack Melitz, "Friedman and Machlup on The Significance of Testing Economic Assumptions," *Journal of Political Economy*, Vol. 73 (February 1965), pp. 37–60; Spiro J. Latsis, "A Research Programme in Economics," in Latsis, ed., *Method and Appraisal in Economics* (Cambridge: Cambridge University Press 1976), especially pp. 9–14.

16 "Issues in Methodology," p. 70; "Positive and Normative Economics: An Analysis of the Ideas," in Robert L. Heilbroner, ed., *Economic Means and Social Ends, Essays in Political Economics* (Englewood Cliffs, N.J.: Prentice-Hall 1969), p. 100n.; "Concepts of Competition and Monopoly," *American Economic Review, Papers and Proceedings*, Vol. 45 (1955), p. 483.

17 "Issues in Methodology," p. 71 ; *Involuntary Foreign Lending* (Stockholm: Almguist and Wicksell, 1965), p. 81n.

18 "Operational Concepts and Mental Constructs in Model and Theory Formation" in *Giornale Degli Economisti*, Vol 19 (September-October, 1960), p.19.

19 *Essays on Economic Semantics* (Englewood Cliffs, N.J. : Prentice-Hall, 1963), p. 251.

20 "Issues in Methodology," p. 70. He added "To expect that one theory of the firm should serve all purposes is almost like expecting one all-purpose theory of man or a panacea that cures all ills from sore throats to broken noses." See also "Situational Determinism in Economics," *British Journal for the Philosophy of Science*, Vol. 25, (September 1974), p. 283; and "Theories of the Firm: Marginalist, Managerial, Behavioral," *American Economic Review*, Vol. 57 (March 1967), p. 28.

21 See, for example, Latsis, "A Research Programme in Economics"; also T. W. Hutchison, "History and Philosophy of Science and Economics," in Latsis, *Method and Appraisal in Economics*, especially pp. 195–6.

22 "Theories of the Firm: Marginalist, Managerial, Behavioral," p. 2.

23 "Operationalism and Pure Theory in Economics," p. 61; and *International Trade and The National Income Multiplier* (Philadelphia, Pa.: Blakiston, 1943), p. 218.
24 "On the Alleged Inferiority of the Social Sciences," in Leonard 1. Krimerman, ed., *The Nature and Scope of Social Science. A Critical Anthology* (New York: Appleton-Century Crofts, 1969), pp. 171–2.
25 "The Problem of Verification in Economics," p. 5.
26 Ibid., pp. 12, 13, 15.
27 "Positive and Normative Economics: An Analysis of the Ideas," p. 114.
28 *Essays on Economic Semantics*, p. 82. Nevertheless, on semantic questions Machlup has prescribed a number of procedural rules. For example, the unnecessary coining of new terms is to be "castigated" as a sign of lack of humility, and a practice liable to be positively confusing. Terms that have degenerated should be abandoned and the economist has a "moral duty" to distinguish the different meanings of terms and concepts, especially when they can be used either in an analytical, descriptive, or evaluative manner. Persuasive definitions are dangerous, because they can be used to convey the impression that logical necessity also implies political or moral necessity. Yet "the real ground for objection" to persuasive definitions – for example of "equilibrium" – is not so much the disguised politics but the fact that the concept itself "becomes less useful, if not useless in the analysis of most problems." This practice consequently involves the "sabotage of economic analysis." Ibid., pp. 71–2.
29 Ibid., p. 96.
30 Ibid., p. 143.
31 "The Illusion of Universal Higher Education," in S. Hook, P. Kurtz, M. Todorovich, eds., *The Idea of A Modern University* (Buffalo, N.Y.: Prometheus Books, 1974), p. 10.
32 "Positive and Normative Economics: An Analysis of the Ideas," p. 124. Elsewhere he notes that value judgments, "even if they cannot be refuted, can be debated, defended, criticized." "The Illusion of University Higher Education," p. 16.
33 "Positive and Normative Economics: An Analysis of the Ideas," p. 129.
34 *International Trade and the National Income Multiplier*, p. 218. Earlier on the same page Machlup acknowledged that the policy of more generous foreign lending which he advocates "has not naturally grown out of the body of economic analysis contained in these passage, but was rather arbitrarily appended to it." However, he added, this is "common more or less to all policy recommendations." Ibid.
35 "Positive and Normative Economics: An Analysis of the Ideas," p. 127. Such intellectual refinement is, of course, wholly inappropriate when the economist is required to give specific advice on urgent policy problems, for example, as an adviser to government or business. Machlup is, however, well aware of this fact of life, having been actively involved in national and international policy-advising bodies.
36 "Liberalism and the Choice of Freedoms," in Erich Streissler, ed., *Roads to Freedom: Essays in Honour of Freidrich A. von Hayek* (London: Routledge and Kegan Paul, 1969), p. 145.
37 *Essays on Economic Semantics, pp. 268, 287.*
38 "That's the way it was – I think", pp. 4, 23.
39 *Essays on Economic Semantics*, p. 190 (emphasis supplied). This is from the conclusion to his famous essay, "Marginal Analysis and Empirical Research."
40 These terms are from Max Scheler. See Machlup, "Do Economists know Anything?" *The American Scholar*, Vol. 22 (Spring 1953), p. 179. This is one of several essays in which Machlup provides a persuasive case for the social sciences against those – including many social scientists – who consider them to be inferior to the natural sciences. See "On the Alleged Inferiority of the Social Sciences."
41 "Do Economists Know Anything?" p. 182.

22 Comments

Against 'Against convergence'

(*with S. Thompstone*)

As teachers of a course on the comparative economic development of Russia and the USA, we read Michael Ellman's article 'Against convergence' (1980) with genuine interest. While agreeing that the convergence 'theory' (his terminology) has both 'positive' and 'negative' features, we found his argument against the theory so poorly specified, confused and misdirected that we feel it should not go unchallenged.

Although Ellman discussed both Tinbergen's original conception of the convergence process and a later version advanced by his pupil, van den Doel, we shall concentrate exclusively on the former, for we accept that Ellman has conclusively demonstrated the inadequacy of van den Doel's variant. The central issue is the methodological and historical status of Tinbergen's theory, and the grounds on which it should be accepted or rejected. As we shall show, this is a far more complex question than Ellman seems to appreciate, and it involves a general issue of considerable importance to historians and social scientists.

We begin with Ellman's loose and vague description of Tinbergen's conception of convergence, according to which 'a movement was taking place away from the polar opposites of communism and free … economies as each system adopted elements of the other' (p. 199). He acknowledges that the 'wide international discussion' of this theory has 'played a healthy role in reducing cold war hysteria' – a consideration entirely irrelevant to the issue of its historical and scientific validity – and admits that it has been 'fruitful' from 'a scientific point of view' (whatever that may mean). Nevertheless, while recognising the 'huge and growing number of facts which "confirm" the convergence theory', Ellman rejects it on the grounds that:

(a) 'many of the "observations" made in the light of the theory are wrong';
(b) it tends to belittle important and persistent differences between the systems;
(c) it ignores the extent of divergence; and
(d) it fails to deal with changes in the geographical relations between the two systems.

In the following paragraphs we shall ignore point (d) as irrelevant to the main issue, and treat (c) simply as a reformulation of (b).

Ellman dismisses the 'huge and growing' accumulation of evidence in favour of Tinbergen's theory with the casual remark that 'Nevertheless, as all good Popperians know, the existence of confirmations is not decisive for the scientific standing of a theory' (p. 199). We have no desire to introduce semantic quibbles about the meaning of the terms 'decisive' and 'standing', but it is clear that Ellman himself is no 'good Popperian'. According to Popper theories are 'conjectures' which, if scientific, are subject to refutation or falsification; and there have been complex and protracted discussions among methodologists and philosophers of science as to the precise conditions under which falsification can be achieved (Popper, 1959, 1969, 1972; Schlipp, 1974; Lakatos, 1970). However, both Popper and his followers accept that an accumulation of evidence which appears to confirm a theory constitutes *prima facie* grounds for increased confidence in its validity. Proof, in the strict sense, may be unattainable, but differences in the 'degree of corroboration' are of major importance in determining the status of a theory until it has been conclusively refuted or falsified.

Ellman's methodological confusion is apparent in his concluding summary, where he remarks that 'the original convergence theory is an inductive generalisation about the world economy' (p. 209). Apart from the fact that 'good Popperians' do not regard an 'inductive generalisation' and a 'theory' as equivalent, this statement raises the crucial question: what more can one ask of such a generalisation than that it be supported by 'huge and growing' confirmations? Surely Ellman does not regard the convergence theory as a synthetic universal proposition which can be falsified by a single negative instance?[1] All that is required is a judicious weighing of the evidence for and against the theory, yet Ellman makes no effort to show that there is an even greater and more rapidly growing body of evidence sufficient to outweigh the substantial confirmations. We are not in fact concerned here to defend the convergence theory against all comers; we are merely addressing ourselves to the issues of principle at stake.

Unfortunately for Ellman an inductive generalisation is potentially falsifiable (and therefore 'scientific' in Popper's sense) only if it is expressed in precise and definite terms, and subject to specific constraints of time and space, whereas Tinbergen's theory, as Ellman presents it, is couched in such loose and vague language as to be incapable of conclusive falsification. Even a falsifiable inductive generalisation may not be falsifiable in practice if, for instance, it proves impossible to devise conclusive tests, or if it takes an infinity of time to carry them out. But this does not mean that Tinbergen's theory (or, for that matter any other non-falsifiable inductive generalisation) is necessarily valueless as a source of historical insight or understanding for it may provide useful criteria by which to organise and evaluate the relevant evidence.

Further evidence of Ellman's confusion arises in his remark that 'many of the observations made *in the light of* (Tinbergen's theory) … are wrong' (p. 209, italics added). Although the vagueness of the italicised words makes it difficult to attach any precise meaning to this statement it suggests that Ellman is a 'naïve falsificationist', to cite Imre Lakatos's expressive term (Lakatos, 1970,

p. 106ff), that is, one who believes that a theory can be refuted simply by direct confrontation with 'the facts'.[2] In practice supposedly 'wrong' observations derived from a theory may be due not only to defects in the theory itself but also to observational errors – for example where the observer uses defective instruments, misinterprets his readings, or, more seriously, cites 'irrelevant' observations because he has failed to comprehend the meaning or range of applicability of the theory. If, as in Ellman's account of Tinbergen's theory, the theory is poorly specified, how can we determine the 'relevant' observations by which it is to be tested? What observations will confirm or refute 'a movement away from the polar opposites of communism and free ... economies', especially when it is admitted that each may be adopting 'elements of the other'? What if the movement towards convergence is intermittent, or even temporarily reversed?

While it is easy enough to demonstrate the inadequacies of 'naïve falsification' it is by no means easy to specify the precise meaning and applicability of 'sophisticated falsification'. Nor is this the appropriate place to attempt a comprehensive summary of the philosophy and methodology of the social sciences, a subject that currently appears to be in a considerable state of confusion. In addition to the general reaction against the naïve positivism of the period from about the 1930s to the 1960s there is also some evidence of a reaction against Popper's earlier anti-inductivist views. While one may sympathise with Popper's objections (1959, p. 82) to the 'defensive stratagems' employed by conventionalists,[3] who protect their theories from refutation by adopting *ad hoc* modifications or by redefining and reinterpreting key terms, it is impossible, if not pointless to try, to formulate falsifiable *theories*, and by no means easy to devise *significant* falsifiable hypotheses in the social sciences. Moreover the significance of any hypothesis which has withstood repeated efforts at falsification still has to be *interpreted* in the light of the theoretical framework or paradigm of which it forms a part.

Conclusion

The preceding paragraphs may unfortunately convey the impression that we are using a sledgehammer to crack a nut. But the central issue is important, and extends far beyond the particular case under discussion. Hypotheses and theories come in all shapes and sizes and serve a variety of widely differing purposes. As Barrington Moore (1966, p. xiv) has remarked, generalisations are like maps and there is no single criterion of theory-choice.[4] Hence it is impossible to dispose of the convergence theory, or any other general hypothesis, merely by citing isolated facts or by casually invoking bands of 'good Popperians'.

Ellman correctly observes that the convergence hypothesis (we prefer this term to the more precise, and less applicable term 'theory') forms 'one of the basic elements in contemporary analysis of comparative economic systems' and acknowledges its value in directing attention to 'the similarities of the rival systems' (p. 199). What more need one ask? Like any other hypothesis it suggests questions with which to approach the 'facts', and in this as in other cases one must of course look for disconfirmations as well as confirmations. Ellman himself does not hesitate to distort the historical record in saying (in support of his point (c)):

> It is easy to make out a case for the two systems being further apart today than they were 55 years ago during the period of the New Economic Policy. At that time the USSR had an extensive private sector, there was unemployment, price-market relations played a key role in the economy and there was no central economic planning. Similarly, comparing the UK and the USSR, it is easy to see that their economic systems, quite similar during the second world war, have since become more dissimilar. Furthermore, the end of the great postwar boom in the capitalist world has re-emphasised important differences between the systems (e.g. state socialist countries have maintained full employment and job security) previously masked by the boom. (p. 201)

Notwithstanding the uncertainties and inconsistencies in the attitude of Lenin and the Bolshevik Party towards the NEP, it was ideologically unacceptable to all groups within the party and in our view the balance of argument is strongly in favour of regarding the NEP as a temporary aberration. Nor can the war periods in the UK and Russia be regarded as typical in either case. If the convergence hypothesis has any value at all it must be utilised broadly as a basis from which to compare general trends rather than exceptional short periods. Ellman's method is roughly equivalent to the practice of measuring a statistical trend from the trough of a depression to the peak of a boom, or *vice versa*. Neither the NEP nor World War II are in any sense typical or representative periods.

Ellman justly reproves van den Doel for employing 'a holistic concept of a single Chinese society' (p. 204) yet he himself reifies 'Third World Countries' in precisely the same terms, saying: 'They evidently see important differences between the systems and regard state socialism as superior' (p. 201). How far these 'countries' – i.e. their people, their government, their leaders? – actually 'see' the available 'choices' between 'systems', is a debatable point.

Notes

1 For the distinction between 'analytic' and 'synthetic' propositions of various types see Kaufmann (1944).
2 See, for example, Ellman's remark on p.202 where he implies that non-observance of a trend towards convergence in the period 1970–85 would necessarily constitute a refutation of the van den Doel theory.
3 For a recent useful discussion of conventionalist, pragmatist, and instrumentalist theories in economics, see Boland, 1979, pp. 503–22. A broadly Popperian presentation of the background literature is provided in Blaug, 1980, especially Chs.1 and 4.
4 The essential point is that the kind of map (theory) required by an airline pilot is somewhat different from that required by a hiker, and must be judged accordingly.

Bibliography

Blaug, M. 1980. *The Methodology of Economics, or How Economists Explain*, Cambridge

Boland, L. 1979. A critique of Friedman's critics, *Journal of Economic Literature*, vol. 17, June

Ellman, M. 1980. Against convergence, *Cambridge Journal of Economics*, vol. 4, no. 3, September

Kaufmann, F. 1944. *Methodology of the Social Sciences*, London

Lakatos, I. 1970. The methodology of scientific research programmes, in Lakatos, I. and Musgrave, A. (eds), *Criticism and the Growth of Knowledge*, Cambridge

Moore, B., Jnr. 1966. *Social origins of Dictatorship and Democracy*, Boston

Popper, K. R. 1959. *The Logic of Scientific Discovery*, Oxford

Popper, K. R. 1969. *Conjectures and Refutations, the Growth of Scientific Knowledge*, London

Popper, K. R. 1972. *Objective Knowledge, an Evolutionary Approach*, Oxford

Schlipp, P. A. 1974. *The Philosophy of Karl R. Popper*, Schlipp, P. A. (ed.), La Salle

23 The methodology of economics

Some recent contributions

> 'Methodology is like medicine We tolerate it because it is supposed to be good for us, but secretly despise it. We would rather prescribe it for others than use it ourselves. The study of methodology takes place in a shadowy other-world, and its few participants are accepted as eccentrics. Only occasionally do our philosophical norms and our day-to-day practice clash head-on. For the most part we are too busy pushing out the frontiers of knowledge to question whether those frontiers are of any significance.[1]

To say that methodology is once again in *vogue* in economics may be an overstatement; but there has certainly been a marked recent surge of interest in the subject which has led to the publication of a considerable number of periodical articles and several books designed for students and practising economists. The purpose of this article is to review some of these contributions, with the aim of both indicating their principal features and merits and placing them in an appropriate historical and intellectual context.

Forty-five years ago Fritz Machlup, one of the most prolific contributors to this literature, published an article entitled 'Why Bother with Methodology?,'[2] and as Evan Jones's above-quoted remarks reveal, the question is still relevant. Most professional economists are too preoccupied with more immediate and mundane matters to concern themselves with what they regard as abstract, even metaphysical issues. Nevertheless, as several recent authors have insisted, the study of methodology has a directly practical value, quite apart from its perennial fascination for those attracted to more fundamental and esoteric problems. This is obviously not the place to discuss the importance of methodology. For the present purpose it is sufficient to note that, like it or not, many economists evidently cannot resist the temptation to engage in methodological controversy, notwithstanding their customary disdainful neglect and professed indifference; and predictably, those who play with fire without adequate preparation or forethought are liable to be burnt.

There is, of course, a perennial need to raise the standards of professional understanding and practice. But this apart, any attempt to review and evaluate the methodology of economics is especially welcome at the present time. Since the beginnings of modern economics in the mid-eighteenth century, methodological controversy has waxed and waned under a variety of influences, both exogenous and endogenous to the discipline, and these vicissitudes would, incidentally, repay systematic historical investigation. Now, however, given recent widespread reports that economics is in a state of 'crisis,'[3] the swelling flood of methodological publication is most readily explained as a response to (some cynics might even say a symptom of) the unsettled and uncertain condition of the discipline and its practitioners. For whenever efforts to resolve basic disagreements over theoretical, empirical, and policy issues prove unavailing there is a natural urge to return to fundamentals in an effort both to expose the roots of current controversies and in the hope of establishing more solid and reliable foundations for subsequent work.

Whether the discussion of methodological principles can serve so constructive a purpose, and if so how, is a matter of opinion on which some will be more sceptical than others. In addition to the hardy perennials of methodological debate there have been novel features in the recent situation, especially those arising from the professionalization of economics and the increasing prominence of economists in public policy issues. And there have also been approximately concurrent developments in the philosophy of science, including the social sciences, which have contributed to the disintegration (though by no means the complete destruction) of the positivist hegemony of the first two postwar decades.[4] The ideas of Popper, Kuhn, Lakatos, Feyerabend[5] and others have led to the reopening of hitherto supposedly settled questions about the similarities and differences between the natural and the social sciences. Far from having gone through its Newtonian Revolution, as Popper once maintained, it is the limitations of the economist's knowledge which now seem to merit special emphasis.[6] While recognizing these limitations there must be no abandonment of serious efforts to maintain and improve scientific procedures and standards, and it is appropriate to ask how far recent literature on economic methodology sheds any new light on these fundamental issues.

Mark Blaug is by far the most widely known of the three authors of the methodological survey volumes considered here.[7] As might be expected of a leading historian of economic analysis, his reviews of the relevant background literature are especially valuable and should, indeed, be compulsory reading for all economics graduates. The first two chapters on 'What you always wanted to know about the philosophy of science but were afraid to ask' are outstanding, by far the best introduction to the recent literature known to this reviewer; and they are followed by three almost equally valuable chapters on the history of economic methodology dealing, successively, with: 'the verificationists, a largely nineteenth-century story'; 'the falsificationists, a wholly twentieth-century story'; and, more conventionally, 'the distinction between positive and normative economics'. Several of these titles aptly convey Blaug's relaxed, almost chatty, style which combines an effortless grasp of a wide range of esoteric and technical writings with a refreshing ability to provide a lucid account of essential issues without becoming bogged down in unnecessary details.

It is, however, Part III of Blaug's volume, entitled 'A methodological appraisal of the neo-classical research programme', that is most likely to attract the attention of practising economists and apprentices to the profession (many of whom will welcome it in preparing for graduate exams). Within the space of roughly 100 pages he confidently and succinctly evaluates a large volume of recent literature on nine topics in economic theory: consumer behavior; the firm; general equilibrium; marginal productivity; 'switching, reswitching, and all that'; the Heckscher-Ohlin theory of international trade; Keynesians versus monetarists; human capital; and the new economics of the family. As he explains in his preface, the purpose of these case studies is 'not to settle substantive questions on which economists now disagree among themselves but rather to show how every controversy in economics involves questions of economic methodology' [p. xiii]. On many of these topics Blaug is highly critical of the current state of economic knowledge, though his basic approach is 'internalist' – to use an expression now familiar among historians and philosophers of science[8] – for he has only very limited sympathy with heterodox critics of neo-classical economics. But before amplifying these comments with reference to the current state of economic methodology, let me first consider the volumes by Drs. Stewart and Katouzian.

Ian Stewart's aim is less ambitious than Blaug's, although he too has both a practical and didactic intent since his book originated in, and is designed primarily for, undergraduate teaching. While he presupposes a basic knowledge of economics on the reader's part, he traces the relevant philosophical concepts 'from the ground up'. After three chapters on deduction (17 pp.), induction (7 pp.), and the hypothetico-deductive method (39 pp.: the distribution of space is significant), he proceeds to apply these methods to such topics as: the distinctive features of economic data; economic theory and reality; the job of the applied economist; accuracy and error in applied economics; sense and nonsense in econometrics; and the survey method. This volume is therefore both an introduction to the formal logic of economics – for, like Blaug, Stewart emphasizes the essential distinction between 'methodology' and 'methods' – and something approaching a guide to its practical applications. The scope of the study is deliberately restricted because the author concentrates on 'the day-to-day process of investigation and research' [p. 153], with special emphasis on the limitations of economic statistics and econometric measurement and testing. While he endeavours to be impartial in discussing conflicting methodological fashions it is possible to detect his underlying preference for what he terms the 'analytical school' which, he maintains, most nearly approximates 'a 'correct" reconstruction of what is actually done in economic science' [p. 125], As befits his purpose Stewart has consciously tried 'to put things in a conversational way', rather than in 'conventional scientific prose' [p. viii], and the resulting text is crystal clear, comprehensible, and readable. The student is skilfully conducted across difficult terrain with frequent signposts to matters he is likely to have encountered in other economics courses, and there are helpful lists of discussion topics, reading guides, and a glossary.

Whatever their differences of scope and level, both Blaug and Stewart may be said to view economic methodology as insiders, for while neither is by any means complacent or uncritical of the *status quo*, they take the contemporary professional economist's aims and practices largely for granted. By contrast

Homa Katouzian, though he too is an established member of an English university department of economics, writes essentially from the standpoint of an outsider whose dissatisfaction with the profession is decidedly stronger, more personal, and passionately committed. Like Blaug, he devotes considerable space to the history of economic ideas and recent literature on the philosophy of science, but he does so not because he is interested in philosophy for its own sake, but because he considers it the essential basis on which to account for the present condition of economics which he depicts in sombre, some might even say alarmist, terms. Both Stewart and Blaug would doubtless accept much of the substance of Katouzian's concluding protest that today's professional economists too often display 'a parochial vision combined with technological formalism', an 'uncritical commitment to existing theories and methods', and a 'preoccupation with little abstract puzzles as opposed to great and real problems' ([p. 210] – though they would probably cavil at the undefined terms 'great' and 'real'). Indeed, Stewart has already publicly expressed his support for the substance of Katouzian's penultimate chapter 'Unto this Last: Some Evidence From Current Research', in which he 'analyses a number of articles from the journals to illustrate the kind of puzzle solving which "professional academic" economists get up to.'[9] But it is doubtful that either Stewart or Blaug would fully endorse Katouzian's description of the present state of economic science in terms of 'the ever-increasing complexity of its formal edifice; and the never-ending poverty of its substantial achievements' [p. 210]. While Stewart seeks to inculcate in his students an awareness of the diversity of methodological approaches, their respective strengths and limitations, and the need for healthy scepticism towards the more exaggerated claims of mathematical economists and econometricians, Blaug's principal complaint is that economists all too seldom practise what they preach: their ostensible commitment to a Popperian-type methodology, with its concomitant requirements of rigorous testing and determined efforts to falsify hypotheses is, at best, no more than a pious aspiration or a delusion and, at worst, merely a professional smokescreen designed to protect their findings from decisive refutation.[10]

Katouzian's diagnosis of the current deficiencies of economics goes well beyond either Blaug's or Stewart's for in addition to presenting 'a comprehensive and critical study of the logic and methods of economic science' he also proposes to encompass 'the moral, ideological and sociological characteristics of its progress or stagnation' and to provide 'a framework within which the roots of the real crisis of economic science may be discovered' [p. 8]. His study deserves special attention not only because it goes further than Blaug's and Stewart's in accepting some of the more strongly anti-positivist implications of recent writings in the philosophy of science, but also because it serves as a bridge between the 'internalist' approach to economic methodology and that adopted by more heterodox writers, whose views get short shrift from Blaug and Stewart.

Like Blaug, Katouzian deplores the fact that professional economists fail to practice what they preach, and the central and most original feature of his book is his effort to account for this state of affairs in historical and socio-psychological, rather than in logical or philosophical terms. Building on Kuhn's key distinction between 'normal' and 'revolutionary' periods in the development of science he draws a parallel between attitudes towards methodology and the resistance to paradigm change in a period of 'normal' science. Being for the most part uninterested in methodology per se economists found no difficulty in switching their allegiance without a concomitant change of practice from Robbins' *pre-war a prioristic* views to Positive Economics which, though incompatible with Robbins' ideas, was all the rage in the postwar period. But they could not dispense entirely with methodology, which has an ineradicably prescriptive element, because it is necessary to provide a persuasive rationalization and justification for 'how we do things in economics' [p. 46], and the leaders of the disciplinary profession were able to exercise control over would-be members of their segment of the scientific community, for

> The established "majority" has the power of appointing and disappointing members of the economic profession, and controlling the content of the learned journals ... This is the ''normal' scientific attitude [p. 7].

Katouzian's positive (*i.e.* non-normative) sociological theory of the growth of knowledge is designed to reveal the similarities and differences between the social influences on the behaviour of practitioners in an immature science like economics and a mature science like physics. Their theories may not be amenable to conclusive empirical tests; but economists do profess belief in the need for self-contained and consistent theories. Nevertheless, Katouzian maintains, 'logic on its own can be pretty powerless even in the best of circumstances – i.e. when the critics' reputations have already been established' [p. 119], and he cires the example of the neoclassical economists' failure either to dispose or take full account of Joan Robinson's exposure of a fundamental logical inconsistency in orthodox capital theory.[11] Katouzian concentrates his attention on certain influential social, historical and institutional phenomena of modern academic life rather than ideology – which has been a traditional component of so much literature on the sociology of knowledge – because he wishes to identify the conditions influencing 'the amount of knowledge gained, and the rate of its discovery' *within* any given ideological vision [p. 115], This objective is compatible both with recent tendencies in the philosophy of science and with the efforts of heterodox commentators and some independent-minded orthodox economists.[12]

Katouzian's sociological model is presented in two chapters: 'Big Science versus Great Science. A contribution to the Sociology of the Academic Profession', and 'Value Judgements and Ideology: Morality and Prejudice in Economic Science'. He argues that the modern professional academic, who wishes to succeed in his career, is obliged to specialize narrowly on problems dictated and approved by the leaders of his discipline, rather than 'real' problems of genuine intellectual or social importance. Few can resist this pressure; moreover, few have the necessary intellectual equipment to transcend the limitations of their situation. The pressure is especially strong in large scale, relatively mature disciplines that are either technologically useful or otherwise socially significant. The large scale modern university, which now virtually monopolizes professionalized intellectual activities, has induced both social- and self-alienation among academics who, unlike factory workers, cannot even see a visible final product to which they have contributed. They cannot fully comprehend the existing gigantic socio-technical structure of modem society, let alone criticize, direct and reconstruct it. They may be called on for diagnosis and prescription when there is a total breakdown, but they are then ill equipped to do so, 'morally, intellectually and professionally' [pp. 129, 130/131, 133]. Unfortunately, Katouzian can offer no ready solution to this problem, though his avowed ideal is the Renaissance or Enlightenment type of 'unprofessional' vocational type of scholar who was prepared to risk his life in the effort to solve 'real' problems.

For the present day unprofessional scholar the choice is either to abandon resistance and join the profession; to stand by his principles and take the moral and material consequences, or quit the profession – in which case he will be admitting 'defeat in defending those very intellectual ideals to which *ceremonious* homage is regularly paid by all' [p. 122, italics in original]. Contrary to Lakatos' contention that Kuhn's account of the behaviour of the scientific community entails the advocacy of 'mob rule', Katouzian claims that there exists an 'iron rule of a few learned respectable oligarchs over the disciplinary profession' [p. 123].

Like this reviewer, many readers of this journal may feel that Katouzian's description of the current academic scene is exaggerated; but there is an undeniable core of truth in his account. Specialization is obviously unavoidable, given the explosion of knowledge in the twentieth century, hence a return to Renaissance or Enlightenment versatility is inconceivable; but this is not to deny the disadvantages of excessive specialization. Likewise the absence of a substantial leisure class makes professionalization – and the concomitant dependence on the professional hierarchy for recognition and promotion – unavoidable. Indeed, Katouzian's claim that insecurity of academic tenure prevails, despite impressions to the contrary [pp. 127, 225], has increasing plausibility at the present time when the university sector is contracting. And many readers will sympathize with his attack on the mathematisation of economics – he coins the term mathemature, to describe the current displacement of literature – as the prime example of the prevalence of trivial puzzle solving over 'real' problems (or, as he quotes Popper, the victory of Big Science over Great Science).[13]

Katouzian's sociological interpretation of the shortcomings of current economics may be viewed as a bridge, or half-way stage between the internalist critique of positivist methodology (as in Blaug and Stewart) and more extreme radical or institutionalist heterodoxies. To the present reviewer, however, the most significant and promising recent trend in economic methodology is towards a narrowing of the gap between orthodox and heterodox approaches. It would be over-optimistic to speak of an emerging consensus or synthesis: no-one familiar with the long history of methodological controversy is likely to anticipate the disappearance of disagreement. But there have been welcome signs of an enhanced understanding of and sympathy towards divergent and even incompatible approaches, without going as far as Feyerabend's proposed anarchistic theory of knowledge.

This bold contention can be illustrated, though certainly not proved, by examining the treatment of value judgments and the relationship between 'positive' and 'normative' economics in the three volumes under review. There are, of course, significant differences of terminology and emphasis on this thorny issue among our three authors. But they apparently agree that:

(1) there is a fundamental logical distinction between positive and normative propositions or statements in economics;
(2) this distinction is not, however, as clear-cut, either in theory or in practice, as many textbook writers imply;
(3) value judgments are normative propositions, but they are not all of the same type – e.g. mere matters of personal opinion;[14]
(4) any unnecessary blurring of the distinction between positive and normative statements is a source of confusion, and therefore to be deplored;
(5) whether economics is a positive or a normative science is largely a matter of definition, and not an issue worth arguing about.

Needless to say, this is by no means an exhaustive catalogue. But if there is to be a reconciliation, or even an armistice, between the perennially warring camps, this last point is of crucial importance, although it has often been obscured by semantic disagreements. Radical, marxist, and institutionalist critics have usually held that orthodox (e.g. neo-classical) economics is ideologically biased in favour of capitalism (or market solutions to economic problems), but unless we are prepared to deny even the possibility of objective knowledge there is no logical escape from the conclusion that all opinions count equally. As Blaug notes, the heterodox contention that

> absolutely all propositions about sociological phenomena are value impregnated and hence lack "objectivity" ... proves too much, it is either uniquely exempt from the charge, in which case there is at least one objective statement that can be made about social questions, or it is itself value loaded, in which case we are locked into an infinite regress and are driven towards extreme subjectivism [p 134].

The only way out of the dilemma is to formulate some methodological rules or norms that will limit the role of subjectivity, and this involves consideration of the actual procedures of the scientific community. To Blaug, whose treatment of this problem is by far the most explicit of the three, the positive-normative distinction functions as 'a clarifying and therapeutic convention ... yet another Popperian norm peculiarly relevant to a policy science like economics' [pp. 150, 130]. While the logical distinction between is- and ought-statements is basic,

> the acceptance or rejection of is-statements is not a very different cognitive process from the acceptance or rejection of ought-statements, my contention is that there are no empirical descriptive is-ought statements that do

> not rely on a definite social consensus that we "ought" to accept that is-statement [p. 131].

Blaug's acknowledgement of the role played by the social (or, more properly, the scientific or professional) consensus in the process of validating, testing or falsifying knowledge undoubtedly reflects recent anti-positivist tendencies in the philosophy of science. But while Katouzian would doubtless agree that

> Ideological biases and special pleading of all kinds are a universal feature of scientific work
>
> (Blaug [p. 152])

his deep dissatisfaction with the existing professional establishment would hardly permit him to accept Blaug's conclusion that

> the only remedy is the public cuticism of other scientists relying on the shared professional standards of the subject (ibid.).

Katouzian does not, however, offer any practicable way out of this impasse.

Whatever may be the tendency towards a convergence between orthodox and heterodox economists on specific methodological issues, there are still likely to be continuing irreconcilable differences with respect to professional aims and standards and the concomitant methodological norms or criteria. A revealing feature of Blaug's frank and penetrating discussion is his admission that there are deep-seated intellectual and professional resistances to effective falsification among orthodox professional economics.

> ... there are special biases to which economists are prone that have no parallel in the physical sciences. ... every economist feels in his bones that the invisible hand theorem is not just an abstract proof of hypothetical significance in the stratosphere of ideas. Somehow, it seems just as relevant to socialism as to capitalism, coming close indeed to providing a universal justification for the price mechanism as a rationing device in literally any economy. ... No wonder then that intellectual tenacity in the face of empirical refutations, the tendency to protect falsified theories by ad hoc immunizing stratagems, ... has loomed and continued to loom so large in the history of economics [p. 153].

Surely this is simply what generations of heterodox critics have been saying at least ever since Thorstein Veblen's penetrating essays on 'The Preconceptions of Economic Science[15]'? Moreover, faced with this massive resistance to change on the part of orthodox economists what is the likelihood that they will respond to Blaug's justified plea for more determined efforts 'to produce theories that yield unambiguously refutable implications' and to 'confront those implications with the facts' [p. 254]. As Blaug himself knows only too well, it is now generally acknowledged that such confrontations seldom if ever prove decisive: to believe that they do is the 'naive falsificationist' error that Lakatos and others have so effectively exposed. Again, what if it proves to be not merely difficult but impossible to produce a significant number of such theories in economics that are non-trivial – i.e. relevant to the solution to real-world situations, rather than mathematicians' or econometricians' pastimes equivalent to 'playing tennis with the net down' (to cite Blaug's own phrase [p. 256]).

Under these circumstances there is a real danger that Blaug's wise and balanced, if limited, methodological prescriptions will go unheeded by orthodox economists, while his heterodox critics will merely interpret his volume as confirmation of their existing conviction that the neo-classical research programme is hopelessly inadequate. And, in a separate publication embodying essentially the same message, Blaug has emphasized the hopeless degeneracy (in Lakatos' sense) of the Marxist research programme.[16] Needless to say, there is no easy solution to present difficulties, but it is nevertheless regrettable that Blaug has evidently failed to appreciate the significance of certain constructive advances in methodological insight and understanding in recent heterodox, especially institutionalist, economic literature, while our other two authors have entirely ignored them.

This is not the place to embark upon a detailed evaluation of this heterodox literature. But it deserves recognition here for it is entirely in harmony with the recent anti-positivist tendencies in the philosophy of science referred to earlier, and also fully compatible with Blaug's explanation of the reasons why orthodox economists have clung so tenaciously to their competitive model, despite its widely acknowledged deficiencies. To cite Benjamin Ward, an author whose critique of orthodox methodology has earned Blaug's warm commendation:

> The fundamental message of the breakdown of falsifiability is the interaction between theory-belief systems and data, an interaction that is only partly mediated by induction. The reason the investigation is unwilling to accept the evidence is that he has other reasons for believing the hypothesis These reasons are partly tied to the body of theory from which the hypothesis came, some parts of which at least he believes because of then empirical status. Partly also they are tied to colligation, to the more informal and intuitive set of beliefs he and other scientists have about the way the world functions. These deductive and colligative reasons are treated by the investigator as if they were partial corroborations of the hypothesis, even though they contain no directly relevant data.[17]

Given the orthodox economists' consistent failure to undertake rigorous systematic tests Ward recommends two alternative practices, systematic 'storytelling' – 'the attempt to give an account of an interrelated set of phenomena in which fact, theory, and values are all mixed together in the telling', and 'colligation' – a species of idea-formation that is 'strictly neither induction or deduction' but rather the use of 'intuition engaged in the process of making some thesis or data relevant: that is, of tying the thesis to things that are already known.'[18] A related approach, not mentioned by Ward but briefly referred to by

Blaug, is 'pattern modelling' a term derived from the philosopher and methodologist Abraham Kaplan and applied to economics by the institutionalists Charles Wilbur and Robert Harrison.[19] According to Blaug, 'pattern modelling' is

> A methodological standpoint that seeks to "understand" events of actions by identifying their place in a pattern of relationships that is supposed to characterize a particular economic system [pp. 266/267]

As might be expected, Blaug's reaction to these approaches is brief, and essentially negative. The pattern modelling institutionalists are dismissed because they do not 'share a common methodology, that is, a common method of validating their explanations', and storytelling is inadequate because it lacks rigour or a definite logical structure, and is consequently 'all too easy to verify and virtually impossible to falsify. It is or can be persuasive precisely because it never runs the risk of being wrong' [pp. 126/127]. There is, of course, substantial truth in both these contentions; but they do not thereby dispose of the central issue between the orthodox and heterodox (institutionalist) economists. Given the manifest inadequacies of the positivist emphasis on the crucial importance of falsification is it not time to acknowledge defeat, at least for the time being, and to seek other methods of *supplementing* the methodological armoury available to contemporary economists? If the determined and persistent efforts to make economists a 'hard' science have failed,[20] at least largely if not totally, is it not time to acknowledge (as, indeed Blaug, Ward, and many others do) the wide gap that exists between preaching and practice, and do something to bridge it? Of course, it is true that many heterodox economists – including institutionalists, Marxists, radicals, Post-Keynesians, and others – view their respective approaches as substitutes for, rather than complements of orthodox methodology; but these differences are perennial and inescapable components of methodological debate in economics. It is true, as Blaug maintains, that institutionalists do not adopt the same 'method of validating' their explanations as that preached, but not usually practiced, Katouzian calls the established 'invisible college'. But the persistence of and increasing support for these alternative approaches is recognized by Blaug, by some leading orthodox economists, and by some outstanding mavericks or heterodox authors like Kenneth Boulding, J. K. Galbraith, and Gunnar Myrdai. Among these options the most promising, to the present reviewer, is the so-called neo-institutionalist approach reiterated in various forms in *The Journal of Economic Issues* during the past decade or so.[21] The distinction between the economist's and the physicist's data – especially the historicity[22] and complexity of the former – is increasingly acknowledged. But this does not mean, as Von Mises and others have argued, that fundamentally different methods are required in the social as against the natural sciences. At the same time the need to avoid foisting natural science methods on the social sciences – the error termed 'scientism' by Hayek – is increasingly recognized.[23] It is precisely because orthodox economists especially mathematical economists and econometricians – have sacrificed understanding and relevance to the pursuit of formalist rigor that the pendulum of professional opinion has been swinging in favour of looser, and more flexible approaches. There is no reason to suppose that existing methods will be readily abandoned the influence of the professional hierarchy is far too strong for this to be a likely outcome, even if it were desirable. There is, however, a more tolerant and flexible attitude now than that prevailing twenty years ago. How far there will be genuine convergence and reconciliation of differences remains to be seen.[24]

Notes

1 Evan Jones, 'Positive Economics or What?', *The Economic Record*, Vol. 53 (1977), pp. 350–363.

2 Reprinted in his collected essays, *Methodology of Economics and the Social Sciences*, New York: Academic Press 1978, pp 63–73. This includes a valuable hitherto unpublished introductory essay, 'What is Meant by Methodology A Selective Survey of the Literature', pp. 5–62 and several linking passages, containing interesting retrospective comments on the literature.

3 See, for example, my survey of this issue in 'The Current "Crisis" in Economics in Historical Perspective', *Nebraska Journal of Economic and Business*, Vol. 16 (1977), Summer, pp. 3–16, and the symposium by 12 authors 'The Crisis in Economic Theory', *The Public Interest*, Special Issue (1980). The most widely discussed concept of crisis is, of course, that advanced by Thomas S. Kuhn in *The Structure of Scientific Revolutions*, Chicago 1962; 2nd ed. 1970.

4 The literature on positivism and 'positive' economics (*à la* Milton Friedman) is vast. The volumes by Blaug, Katouzian and Stewart cited below have useful bibliographies and, in addition to Jones's article cited in *footnote I supra*, the following are especially recommended: Bruce Caldwell, 'Positivist Philosophy of Science and the Methodology of Economics', *Journal of Economic issues*, Vol 14 1980), March, pp 53–76, Laurence A. Boland, 'A Critique of Friedman's Critics', *Journal of Economic Literature*, Vol. 17 (1979), June, pp. 503–522; and A. Coddington, 'Positive Economics', (*Canadian Journal of Economics*, Vol. 5 (1972), February, pp. 15.

5 The principal works are Karl R. Popper, *The Logic of Scientific Discovery*, London 1959, *Conjectures and Refutations. The Growth of Scientific Knowledge*, London 1972, *Objective Knowledge. An Evolutionary Approach*, London 1972. Kuhn, op. cit, Imre Lakatos, *The Methodology of Scientific Research Programmes Philosophical Papers*, edited by J. Worrall and G. Currie, Cambridge I978, Vols. 1 and 2, Paul Feyerabend, *Against Method. Outline of an anarchistic theory of knowledge*, London 1978. There is an excellent review of this and other relevant recent literature on the philosophy of science in the first two chapters of Mark Blaug, *The Methodology of Economics, or how economists explain*, Cambridge: Cambridge University Press 1980, pp. xiv and 296.

6 Emphasis on the limitations of the economist's knowledge has been a major theme in the powerful recent writings of T. W. Hutchison. See, especially, *Knowledge and Ignorance in Economics*, Oxford 1977, *On Revolutions and Progress in Economic Knowledge*, Cambridge 1978, and *The Limitations of General Theories in Macroeconomics*, Washington D. C., American Enterprise Institute for Public Policy Research 1980 See also his '*Positive*' *Economic and Policy Objectives*, London 1964, and *Economics and Economic Policy in Britain, 1946–1966*, London 1968. Popper's reference to a 'Newtonian revolution' in economics appears in The *Poverty of Historicism*, 2nd ed., London 1960, pp. 1 and 16.

7 They are Mark Blaug, *The methodology of economics, op. cit*., Ian M. T. Stewart, *Reasoning and Method in Economics*, London: McGraw Hill (UK 1979,

pp. x and 238, and Homa Katouzian, *Ideology and Method in Economics*, London and Basingstoke 1980, pp xiii and 248. In the following paragraphs page references to quotations from these volumes will be placed in the text. Other recent contributions to economic methodology will be referred to later.

8 The term 'internalist' is used here not in the technical sense employed by Imre Lakatos (of Blaug, p. 27) but more loosely, as a description of an approach to the history and philosophy of science, including the social sciences, which explains intellectual developments primarily or exclusively in terms of conditions internal to the discipline. There is undeniably a residue of ambiguity in this usage which cannot be adequately explored here.

9 In his review of Katouzian, *Economic Journal*, Vol 90 (1980), September, p. 672.

10 Blaug argues that current orthodox methodology is 'highly protective of economic theory' and 'ultrapermissive with respect to the rules of the game' (p. 128). Mainstream neoclassical economists rarely employ rigorous empirical tests, preferring analytical elegance and simplicity to predictability and policy significance (p. 259). Although 'economists engage massively in empirical research ... unfortunately, much of it is like playing tennis with the net down. Instead of attempting to refute testable predictions, modern economists all too frequently are satisfied to demonstrate that the real world conforms to their predictions, thus replacing falsification, which is difficult, with verification, which is easy' (p. 256).

11 This controversial example is discussed in Blaug, Chapter 10.

12 For a discussion of these matters see below, pp. 319–321.

13 Katouzian devotes two chapters to 'Economic Theory and Mathematical Economics. Abstraction and Generalization in Economic Science', and 'Unto this Last: Some Evidence from Current Research', which includes a brilliant caricature of orthodox economic theory and method entitled 'The Quantity Theory of Drink: A Restatement' by O. L.Covick from *Australian Economic Papers* (1974), December. Katouzian's attack on mathematical economics is not original, but it is nonetheless effective. He argues that 'Economic science cannot afford the professional hegemony of mathematical economics especially if this is effected by a combination of chauvinism and professional power politics' (p. 172). Curiously enough, this last contention, which may strike some readers as extreme, has recently been endorsed in almost identical language by no less a figure than Nicholas Georgescu-Roegen, who regards it as evidence of the corruption of the economics profession, at least in the U. S. A. cf. *Journal of Economics Issues*, Vol 15 (1981), March, p. 191.

For Popper's distinction between Big Science and Great Science see Katouzian pp. 131/132, citing Popper's 'Reason or Revolution' in *The Positivist Dispute in German Ideology*, London 1976, pp 288–300.

14 While Katouzian distinguishes between moral judgments or ethical statements and policy judgments or prescriptive statements (p. 141), Blaug distinguishes between basic and non-basic, or pure and impure value judgments – adding that the latter (i.e. impure) type predominate (pp. 133/134). For a valuable attempt to provide an exhaustive analysis of the relevant issues see Machlup, 'Positive and Normative Economics', *Methodology of Economics*, op. cit., pp. 425–450

15 Originally published in *The Quarterly Journal of Economics (1899–1900);* reprinted in *The Place of Science in Modern Civilization*, New York 1919.

16 *A Methodological Appraisal of Marxian Economics*, Amsterdam: North Holland 1980 (p. 82). It contains three lectures 'Marx and Marxists on the Nature of Profits', 'Marx and Marxists on the Future of Capitalism', and 'Marx on the History of Economic Thought'.

17 *What's Wrong with Economics*?, London: Macmillan 1972 pp. 166/1973 of the passage from Blaug, p. 153 cited earlier.

18 Ward (pp. 180, 164) he cites Michael Polanyi, *Personal Knowledge,* Chicago: University of Chicago Press 1958, N. R. Hansen's *Patterns of Discovery,* Cambridge: Cambridge University Press 1958, and Kuhn op. cit. as relevant background works.

19 Blaug (p. 126), see also Kaplan, *The Conduct of Inquiry: Methodology for Behavoral Science*, San Francisco: Chandler Publishing Co. 1961. Chapter 9, also C. K. Wilber and R. S. Harrison. 'The methodological basis of institutional economics: pattern model, storytelling, and holism', *Journal of Economic Issues* Vol 12 (1978), March, pp. 61–89 This article contains the best single recent survey of the institution list approach to methodology.

20 Blaug cites the constructive proposals designed to strengthen the claim of economics to be a 'hard' science, in Thomas R. Mayer, 'Economics as a hard science realistic goal or wishful thinking', *Economic Inquiry*, Vol. 18 (1980), April, pp. 165–178, but does not report Mayer's conclusion that the quest for hardness has been harmful because it encourages exaggerated claims to policy makers and members of the public. 'In addition, the stress on using advanced mathematical tools allows us to have a good conscience while ignoring some very elementary rules of good research procedure. Much of the published research consists of taking a new technique out for a walk rather than of really trying to solve a problem' (pp. 176/177). Cf. Blaug (pp. 261/262). The parallels between Mayer's view and those of Katouzian, Hutchison and Ward need hardly be emphasized.

21 The most recent Symposium on Methodology appeared in the *Journal of Economic Issues*, Vol. 13 (1979), December, and Vol 14 (1980), March. For earlier collections with various articles on methodology and related matters see Warren J. Samuels (Ed.), *The Chicago School of Political Economy*, East Lansing: Michigan State University 1976 (reviewed in this journal), and Warren Samuels, *The Methodology of Economic Thought*, New Brunswick, U.S.A.: Transaction Books 1980. Both volumes contain useful editorial introductions. The latter is subdivided into the following sections 'Heterodoxy vis a vis Orthodoxy', 'Methodology', 'The Development of Economics Thought', 'Critique of Economic Theory as Social Control and a Guide to Policy', 'Toward a Meaningful Political Economy'.

22 See, for example, John Hicks, *Causality in Economics*, Oxford: Basil Blackwell 1980 (passim)

23 Cf. *The Counter-Revolution of Science Studies in the Abuse of Reason*, Glencoe, Ill.: Free Press 1952 (p. 15). In a penetrating paper, 'Austrians on the Philosophy and Method of Economics', to be published in a forthcoming volume of essays entitled *The Politics and Philosophy of Economics: Marxists, Keynesians and Austrians*, Oxford: Basil Blackwell 1981. T. W. Hutchison has shown how Hayek's views have changed radically since the early 1930s. He is now much closer to Popper's falsificationism than Mises' *a priorism*.

24 For a hopeful prognostication, not entirely incompatible with that outlined above, see the paper by J. F. G Shearmur, 'Subjectivism, falsification and positive economics' delivered at the meeting of Section F British Association for the Advancement of Science in September, 1981. This is to appear in Jack Wiseman (Ed), *Beyond Positive Economics*, London: Macmillan 1982.

24 Economic methodology

Theory, practice, and the current state of economics[1]

The past decade has witnessed a veritable flood of literature on economic methodology and on the parlous state of economics as a scientific discipline and a profession. Strictly speaking these two subjects are distinct, for while methodology *proprement dit* is a branch of philosophy mainly of interest to specialists rather than to practising social scientists, concern about the state of economics embraces much broader issues, such as the methods of training new recruits, the allocation of resources within the discipline, the organisation, control and reward system in the profession, and its public reputation – which is, of course, especially affected by the economists' performance in the policy arena. There are, however, direct links between the broader and the narrower issues, for many of the economists most concerned about the state of their subject attribute its deficiencies to features and problems of the kind that figure prominently in methodological writings. Needless to say, these matters are far too varied, complex, and intractable to be treated adequately in a review article. Nevertheless, the volumes under scrutiny here touch on, and in some instances examine in detail, so many of the topics currently in dispute that they provide a suitable vehicle for some general reflections on the discipline's present state and prospects.

Methodological controversy in economics can be traced back at least to the early nineteenth century classical economists[2], and the anthologies edited by Caldwell and Hausman provide a valuable introduction to the subject for economics and philosophy of science students, practising social scientists and philosophers, and intelligent laymen, especially if Hausman's substantial editorial introduction is read in conjunction with one or more recent general books.[3] Hausman's collection covers a longer time span than Caldwell's, beginning with passages from John Stuart Mill, John Neville Keynes, Max Weber, Karl Marx, Thorstein Veblen and Lionel Robbins: both authors include excerpts from the writings of Terence Hutchison, Fritz Machlup, Milion Friedman, and Mark Blaug; and both provide extensive bibliographies revealing the sheer volume of recent contributions to the subject. Beyond this the anthologies diverge somewhat. Hausman publishes pieces on ideology and values, special topics such as econometrics, economic model construction, methodological individualism, and the differences between neo-classical and institutional economics, and concludes with a section on new philosophical directions, including the 'interanimation' of micro and macro economics, the explanatory status of general equilibrium theories, and paradigms versus research programmes in economics.[4] Some of these topics also appear in caidwell's collection, which is especially suitable for class discussion since he groups together papers on the testability and realism of assumptions, Friedman's 'positive' economics, the maximisation hypothesis, meta-methodology (i.e., falsification and the rhetoric of economics), and concludes with articles on Chicago style economics, micro-micro theory, the Post-Keynesian research programme, and econometrics[5].

Readers of this journal need no reminder of the deep and persistent methodological disagreements in economics and the low esteem methodology is usually accorded by practising economists. Hausman, a philosopher with credentials in economics[6], welcomes the recent convergence of the two fields as more economists read the history, philosophy and sociology of science, and as more philosophers focus their attention on the problems of specific disciplines. Like Caldwell, an economist specialising in methodology, he believes that economists familiar with the methodological literature are less likely to engage in fruitless and destructive controversy, and more likely to recognise the nature and limits of their knowledge, with beneficial effects on their professional performance[7]. This does not mean that economic methodologists either can or should prescribe precise rules for their colleagues to follow as some extremists claim they do[8]: nor, however, should it on the other hand prevent methodologists from analyzing economists' practice and passing on to students the lessons of past experience. After all, if there are neither examples nor criteria of good and bad practice in economics what right have economists to claim professional status, together with the privileges, employment opportunities and emoluments pertaining thereto?

Johannes Klant offers his volume not as a philosopher's or logician's attempt to prescribe 'rules' but as a practising economist's effort to solve basic problems in his field, such as: How do economists prove *(sic)* their theories? How do they decide whether to accept or reject theories? Do they base their decisions on intersubjective tests, as in empirical science; or on rational discussion of plausibility, as in speculative philosophy; or on the outcome of deductions from axioms, as in formal science? (p. ix). In a series of densely packed chapters he reviews economists' and philosophers' views on empirical science, and apriorism, pure theory, positivism, specific and general theories, and his concluding observations or 'rules' are designed as a description of 'how economic theories are'[9], rather than as statements about how economic theories should be and how they can be improved. However, those who seek to go beyond Klant's austerely self-denying ordinance can certainly find constructive guidance in his conclusions.

Like many other contemporary economists, Klant critizes economists' methodology and their pretensions, and his twelve rules (pp. 184–187) are designed to expose the extent of common ground between those who seek only to 'understand' the world and those who aim to predict. These rules, too complex to be summarised adequately here, embody a carefully qualified acceptance of Popper's falsificationist program as an ideal likely to be attainable in practice only within narrow limits and under the most stringent conditions. Owing to 'the rapid historical changeability in the domain of research and the instability of many human behavioural patterns' Klant doubts that any 'universal numerical constants' will be found, consequently economists will be unable to avoid using 'explanation sketches' and non-falsifiable 'explanatory schema' to supplement the few limited empirically refutable scientific theories available to them (p. 186). Like many critics of neo-classical economics, Klant acknowledges that the subject comprises a variable combination of empirical science, metaphysics, purely formal theory, and 'philosophies on individual freedom and social justice and analyses which serve purely to fashion its tools. In economics proof must usually be furnished in rational discussions on the *plausibility* of hypotheses' (pp. 184–185). This explains how the methodologist can play a constructive role in sorting out, identifying and exposing the various ingredients in the mixture, and why recognition of the limits of his scientific knowledge should be a cardinal principle in the economist's code of professional ethics.[10]

Whether volumes of the kind edited by Eichner, Wiles and Routh help to raise the average level of the economists' scientific performance and promote methodological understanding and consensus, rather than simply exacerbating existing divisions within the professional ranks, is debatable. Possibly the frequency, insistence, and occasional ingenuity with which the dissidents press their assaults on the neo-classical citadel will at least keep the defenders on the alert and dispel the mists of complacency within the professional establishment Many of the critics' contentions are cogent and persuasive, even though few are unfamiliar to students of methodology or the history of economics. Indeed at times one wonders about the market for such collective jeremiads as these? Are the authors merely indulging themselves in preaching to the converted, or do they occasionally succeed in converting (or perhaps subverting) the young, driving away prospective new recruits, or – more likely – finding enthusiastic readers among the profession's mavericks, outsiders, or the large and important corps of trained economists employed outside the universities? Surely some enterprising publisher should undertake systematic market research on the matter.

Eichner's is much the more coherent of the two collections in tone, style, and content, partly because the contributors share a common, broadly Post-Keynesian standpoint[11]. By contrast, most essays in the Wiles-Routh volume are followed by one or more comments by relatively orthodox critics, a requirement imposed by the Royal Economic Society as a condition of financing the Oxford conference from which most of the papers emanated[12]. This arrangement has the merit of giving the reader some impression of the neo-classical economists' defence of their principles and procedures. It also adds considerably to the variety, entertainment, and confusion of the proceedings for several of the authors disagree among themselves and/or reply to their critics, while Terence Gorman, an eminent ex-econometrician, who was originally assigned to provide a general assessment of the conference, contributes a lengthy, provocatively idiosyncratic and opinionated paper. Indeed at times there is an almost farcical tone, for example where Gorman's protest that only one speaker discussed econometrics 'which is, after all, the existing methodology of economics, tailored for the subject, and taught as such to graduate students almost everywhere' (p. 261), elicits Wiles's retort that 'Methodology, after all, is about personalities. ... Econometrics .. is not even the methodology of econometricians'[13]. The contrast between this knockabout stuff – which is admittedly not characteristic of the volume – and Klant's sober analysis could hardly be sharper.

Despite marked differences in their individual backgrounds, interests and emphases, the principal contributors to the Eichner and Wiles-Routh volumes broadly agree about the deficiencies of neo-classical economics. Orthodox theory rests on weak epistemological foundations, employs highly unrealistic assumptions, and is therefore incapable of generating significant empirically falsifiable predictions or serving, as a reliable guide to policy-making. While paying lip service to empirical scientific procedures, too many economists are preoccupied with refinements and elaborations of abstract general theories that have no relevance to any known or likely state of affairs. Instead of seriously trying to devise refutable hyposes, and to refute them, econometricians are too often satisfied with weak confirmations. When confronted with inconvenient evidence or anomalous findings they either fudge their results, make ad hoc adjustments or devise immunizing stratagems to protect their theories from falsification[14]. In extreme cases they ignore serious inconsistencies or flat contraditions in their theoretical structures[15]. The primary source of these shortcomings is their disregard and disrespect for facts Graduate training and professional advancement emphasize command of esoteric mathematics and sophisticated quantitative techniques[16], whereas knowledge of the economy and painstaking empirical work receive little recognition, even when the latter sheds essential new light on problems of acknowledged importance to the disciplinary community[17] The charge that neoclassical economics is ideologically biased, though forcefully argued by Wiles in both volumes, and mentioned by others in Eichner (pp. 10, 6lff.. 148, 228: cf. Wiles-Routh, 294ff.), figures less prominently than would have been the case had the collections included radical or Marxist authors. A more clearly marked feature, one that differentiates recent from earlier methodological and protest writing on economics, is the space devoted to the organisational and social structural defects of economics both as a discipline and a profession[18]. These aspects deserve more attention than the familiar complaints cited earlier in this paragraph.

Research on the sociology of science has made considerable strides during the past decade or so, and as several contributors to Eichner and Wiles-Routh suggest, economics is certainly a suitable case for analysis and treatment. Many of the subjects' worst features are attributable to or exacerbated by the prevailing mode of professional training, especially in the USA, where

> tenured members of leading economics departments, continue to exercise tight control over the training, promotion and research activities of their younger faculty members and, by means of peer review, of the senior members as well The methods used to maintain intellectual disciplines in this country's most influential economics departments can occasionally remind one of those employed by the Marines to maintain discipline on Parris Island[19]

This complaint emanates not, as might be expected, from a neglected and embittered minor dissident, but from *Wassily Leontief*, a Nobel prizewinner, past President of the American Economic Association, and long-term member of the Harvard faculty. His views received wide publicity in the American magazine, *Science*, and they are endorsed here, with substantial supporting evidence, in the paper by Canterbery and Burkhardt on the concentration of disciplinary control in the United States[20]. Wiles agrees, quoting extensively from Benjamin Ward's thoughful book *What's wrong with Economics ?* (1972), an early example of the professional protest genre, while Peter Earl, in an original and skilfully elaborated essay, uses a behavioral model to demonstrate why individual economists have such strong incentives to conform to the prevailing *déformation professionnelle*[21]. Academic promotion and appointments committees, like journal editors, find it comparatively easy to judge candidates and publications by purely technical standards, and despite their differences on other matters Morishima and Gorman agree that mathematization and the quest for rigor and even consistency have been carried too far (Wiles-Routh, pp. 64, 69–70, 77). Gorman attacks the (American) idea that there is only one way to produce good economists, maintaining, on the contrary, that economists nowadays are too homogeneous, so that professional single-mindedness is 'the besetting sin' of modern economics (ibid., pp. 282, 284, 286).

As might be expected, there are sharp differences of opinion about possible remedies for the discipline's sickness. Given the prevailing power structure, incentive system, and organisational inertia Eichner, despite his professed optimism, addresses his collection to the lay public who suffer from the profession's failures, and to the younger generation of economists, who may yet see the light (p. xiii). Neild – in a paper Wiles had to fight to include (Wiles-Routh, p. 292; against whom, one wonders?) – advocates demolishing economics and reconstructing it 'from scratch' (ibid., p. 42), an absurd notion, while Routh proposes a sweeping reform of the curriculum with a scheme that his critic, Morris Perlman, has no difficulty in demolishing[22]. Several authors in both volumes stress the importance of historical perspective and understanding, institutional knowledge, and willingness to learn from other disciplines as essential components of the professional economists' equipment.

Unfortunately most of the references to these matters amount to little more than well-meaning *obiter dicta*, citations from recognised authorities such as Schumpeter and Keynes, or pious platitudes. Indeed, more might have been expected from Eichner's volume, considering the oft-repeated Post Keynesian complaint that orthodox economists neglect 'real' or 'historical' time. In these circumstances it is a pity that Klant did not devote more space to the discussion of explanation sketches (p. 173ff.) or the broadly similar methods of 'storytelling' or 'pattern modeling'[23] on which economists must rely more heavily given the limitations of falsification procedures, which force them back on to the plausibility criterion (Klant, pp. 184–185). To suggest that economists have anything to learn from such humble folk as historians may be unseemly, and wildly unpractical, given the profession's current prestige hierarchy. Nevertheless, a study of historians' ways of handling their problems, taken in conjunction with detailed, methodologically sophisticated historical studies of particular examples of professional work in economics[24], may well represent the most promising way out of the present impasse. Moreover, work of this kind could easily be fitted into the existing graduate framework, in combination with instruction in recent economic history and the history of economics[25]. Together with the Caldwell, Hausman, and Klant volumes, four of the chapters in Wiles-Routh would provide useful reading for such a course, namely, Marsden on 'Homo Economicus and the Labour Market'; Dennis Mueller 'Further Reflections on the Invisible Hand Theorem', which focuses on the stock market; and the two essays on the Full Cost Principle by Wiles and Frederic Lee.

It is, perhaps, appropriate to conclude with a consoling thought from Terence Hutchison, a distinguished elder historian and methodologist

> A 'crisis' (in economic theory) may constitute a much healthier intellectual condition than the preceding 'boom', with its excessive pretensions and pretences, and even fantasies, of knowledge, and of the power to plan and regulate Economics, or political economy, is perhaps a subject which is only in a healthy condition when it is in a pretty profound depression, that is, when the time extent of ignorance becomes more apparent (Wiles-Routh, pp. 1–2).

Notes

1 Bruce J Caldwell (ed) *Appraisal and Criticism Economics azA Book of Readings* (Boston, Allen & Unwin, 198400).

Daniel M Hausman (ed) *The Philosophy of Economics An Anthology* (Cambridge Cambridge University Press. 1984).

Johannes J Klant *The Rules of the Game The Logical Structure of Economic Theories* (Cambridge, Cambridge University Press, 1984) Translated by *Ina Swart* from the Dutch original of 1973 and 1979.

Alfred S Eichner (ed) *Why Economics in not yet Science* Armonk/New York M E Sharpe, 1983) Peter Wiles and Guy Routh (eds) *Economics in Disarray* (Oxford Basil Blackwell. 1984).

2 For examples of earlier debates see A W Coats (ed) *Methodological Controversy in Economics Essays in Honor of T W Hutchison* (Greenwich, Conn J A 1 Press. 1983) also T W Hutchison *'Positive' Economics and Policy Objectives* (London Allen and Unwin, 1964) and idem. *On Revolutions and Progress in Economic Knowledge* (Cambridge, Cambridge University Press, 1978).

3 Ian M T Stewart *Reasoning and Methods in Economics* (London McGraw Hill, 1979), Homa Katouzian *Ideology and Method in Economics* (London Macmillan. 1980); Mark Blaug *The Methodology of Economics or How Economists Explain* (Cambridge, Cambridge University Press, 1980). Lawrence A Boland *The Foundations of Economic Method* (London Allen & Unwin, 1982). Bruce J Caldwell *Beyond Positivism Economic Methodology in the Twentieth Century* (London Allen and Unwin, 1982) The first three volumes were discussed in my review article in this journal The Methodology of Economics Some Recent Contributions'. Vol 35 (1982), pp. 310–321.

4 In addition to those already cited in the text, the authors represented are Frank H Knight, Herbert Simon, Gunnar Myrdal, Joseph Schumpeter, Kurt Klappholz, Jacob Marshak, John Maynard Keynes, Ludwig M Lachmann, William Dugger, Alexander Rosenberg, and the editor.

5 In addition to those already cited in the text the authors represented are Ernest Nagel, Paul Samuelson, Alan Musgrave, Brian Loasby, Rod C Ross, Donald McCloskey, Melvin Reder, Harvey Lubinstein, E Roy Weintraub, Sheila Dow, Elba Brown, Edward Leamer, and the editor.

6 Cf his *Capital, Profits and Prices: An Essay in the Philosophy of Economics* (New York, Columbia University Press 1981).

7 By contrast Boland, op at, pp 56 rejects a time series explanation of current practice, preferring to concentrate on a 'cross-sectional' analysis.

8 For example, Donald McCroskey 'The Rhetoric of Economics, *Journal of Economic Literature*, Vol 21 (June, 1983), pp. 481, 517. This provocative paper is included in Caldwell's collection but neither the 'Comment' by Caldwell and Coats, nor McCloskey's 'Reply' ibid Vol 22 (June 1984), pp 575–580.

9 There is now a substantial history, philosophy, and sociology of science literature on scientists rules procedures norms, and values as revealed in scientists practice and it has a counterpart in specialist studies of how economists do economics. For example, Part III, pp. 159–249 in Blaug, op cit. Also S Wong. *The Foundations of Paul Samuelson 'sRevealed Preference Theory* (London Routledge and Kegan Paul, 1978).

10 This is a major theme in T W Hutchison's recent writings especially *Knowledge and Ignorance in Economics* (Oxford Blackwell, 1977).

11 The authors in Eichner's collection are, in order of appearance, E Ray Of Canterbury and Robert J Burkhardt, James A Swanbey and Robert Premus, Peter Wiles, Peter B Earl, Richard X Chase, John Blatt, J Ron Stanfield, and the editor Wassily Leontief's much quoted letter to *Science* (1982) on the state of economics is reprinted as an introduction.

12 In addition to the editors, the principal authors in Wiles and Routh are Terence Hutchison, Robert Nield, Michio Morishima, Rod C Ross, David Marsden, Dennis Mueller, Hiroyuki Odagiri and Frederic Lee. The critics are Martin Hoills, Mark Blaug Oliver Hart, Brain McCormik, Andrew Haripopp, David Heathfield Louis Levy-Garbola, Austin Robinson, Morris Perlman, and W M Gorman, whose lengthy and idiosyncratic contribution provoked pungent replies from Peter Wiles and other authors.

13 Wiles-Routh pp 289, 290. There must surely be few, if any, more amusing exchanges in the literature of economic 'methodology'. However neither protagonist maintains the essential clear distinction between 'method' and 'methodology'. See, for example, Wiles, in Eichner, p. 63 Cf Fritz Machlup, *Methodology of Economics and other Social Sciences* (New York Academic Press 1978) p. 6ff also Blaug, op cit, pp xi.

14 In support of Cross (Wiles-Routh, p. 93ff.), Wiles maintains that 'Econometricians do not respect fact, they do not look at institutional data, they do treat their own wild assumptions as facts, they do show a perverse reluctance to abandon them because of their computational convenience, their elegance or their uniformity to this or that traditional *economic* theory. The magnificent testing apparatus is hardly ever used on orthodox theories' (ibid, p. 290). In recent years several highly competent econometricians have been making similar complaints. A major issue, however, one mentioned by Gorman and others, is the need to distinguish between good and bad econometric practice, a distinction too rarely made in general methodological debates.

15 For example. Wiles and Lee cite the marginal versus full cost pricing literature (Wiles-Routh, especially p. 221. also Lee. pp. 233–239, and Robinson's comment on Wiles, where he refers to the 'contemptible nonsense that is represented by the discussion of these problems in almost any textbook of economics', p. 231), and several authors in the Eichner volume cite the Cambridge capital controversy (e g, pp. 6, 7, 106, 107, 149, 160, 171).

16 See, for example, the persuasive papers by two highly competent authors Morishima, The Good and Bad Uses of Mathematics' (Wiles-Routh, pp. 51–73) and Blatt, 'How Economists Misuse Mathematics' (Eichner. pp. 166, 186) Blatt, who focuses mainly on

optimal control theory (a chapter he had apparently been 'forced to leave out of a book' on the subject, Eichner p. XIII) cites Keynes's warning against reliance on a maze of pretentious and unhelpful symbols'(*General Theory*, p. 298) while Morishima,. who also cites Keynes, uses the *Econometrica* 1954 Report of the Evaluation Committee to similar effect. Evidently *plus ça change, plus c'est la meme chose* Morishima also refers to the experienced of Japanese *wasan* Mathematics over two centuries as a 'salutary lesson' to contemporary mathematical economists See below, pp. 113–114. for discussion of the professional implications of this state of affairs.

17 It is noteworthy that among a score or so of Nobel Prizes in economics only one has been awarded for major empircal contributions, i e that to Simon Kuznets.

18 As far as 1 am aware, the pioneering treatment of these matters in the English language methodological literature is in Chapter 5. 'Big Science versus Great Science A Contribution to the Sociology of the Academic Profession in Katouzian. op cit. pp. 114–134.

19 Eichner, p. xi, from Leontief's Foreword Wiles refers to a 'delicate balance of terror' between the younger and older generations, the latter being technically better equipped, and 'a spiralling "arms race" in economic methodology' (Wiles-Routh, p. 292 (f p. 299 Wiles means 'style', i e, methods, not methodology) Elsewhere he refers to the generation conflict between the innovativeness of the young and 'the great *law of sunk intellectual capital.* What has been learned in youth will be taught in age' (p. 296) Italics in original).

20 They especially cite the concentration of Ph.D output in a few American universities, the narrow range of institutional affiliations of the authors of articles in leading economics journals, and certain organizational features of the American Economic Association (An international comparative study of these features would be illuminating).

21 Wiles in Wiles-Routh pp. 299–300, Earl in Eichner, pp. 90–125 Earl focuses on economists' motivations and decision-taking processes in relation to their personal and professional goals, scientific research strategies, and the screening of contributions to economic knowledge. Like several of his fellow authors he notes that 'The signals most economists receive are that mathematical tractability is to be rated above realism of assumptions, or 'presently available' testable predictions' (p. 121).

On the other hand, in commenting on the uniqueness' of economies in the history of science, and the relationships between theory and the social structure of the discipline, Wiles argues that in all disciplines the prestige hierarchy favours theory, and that those who write on methodology generally have inferior minds (pp. 296–302, 308 ff).

For a different perspective on 'the historically unique pathology of economics' (Wiles, p. 322) see the fascinating typology of the sciences in Richard Whitley *The Intellectual and Social Organisation of the Sciences* (Oxford The Clarendon Press, 1984), which provides a comparative perspective on economics.

22 Wiles-Routh, pp. 240–259 See also Gorman's views on teaching, ibid., p. 277ff .

23 See, for example, Charles Wilbur with Robert S Harrison 'The Methodological Basis of Institutional Economics Pattern Model, Storytelling, and Holism'. *Journal of Economic Issues*, Vol XII (March. 1978), pp. 61–90. This article has an extensive bibliography including, especially, Abraham Kaplan *The Conduct of Inquiry Methodology for Behavioural Science* (San Francisco Chandler Publishing Co, 1964), Paul Diesing *Patterns of Discovery in the Social Sciences* (Chicago Aldine Atherton, 1971), idem. Science and Ideology in the Policy Sciences (New York Aldine Co, 1982) and Ward, op cit, Chapter 9.

24 For example S Wong *The Foundations of Paul Samuelson's Revealed Preference Theory* (London Routledge and Kegan Paul. 1978), Daniel M Hausman *Capital, Profits and Prices An Essay in the Philosophy of Economics* (New York Columbia University Press. 1981) The recent founding of a new journal. *Philosophy and Economics* is an encouraging sign.

25 Benjamin Ward's *The Ideal Worlds of Economics Liberal Radical and Conservative Economic World Views* (New York Basic Books, 1979), would provide instructive background reading. For an original attempt to apply a somewhat different trichotomous approach to undergraduate teaching, in terms of conflicting value theories, see Ken Cole, John Cameron and Chris Edwards *Why Economists Disagree the Political Economy of Economists* (London Longmans, 1983).

25 Reflections on the Austrian/institutionalism symposium

The continuing prominence and vigor of contending schools of economic thought has been one of the more distinctive features of the discipline's recent history, a feature inconsistent with the powerful pressures to professional conformity. Naturally enough, mainstream (neo-classical?) economists view these rival positions with mixed feelings – indifference, contempt, hostility, or at best condescension – either denying their significance (like the reviewer who claimed over 90 percent of economists are neoclassical, as though numbers were the relevant criterion), or dismissing them for failure to produce a viable alternative paradigm or intellectual framework.

Whether this state of affairs is peculiar to economics or characteristic of the social sciences generally and, perhaps all other intellectual disciplines (including the so-called 'hard' sciences) need not concern us here. The point is that despite the incentives to professional conformity and the belief that agreement on fundamentals is the hallmark of a genuine 'science',[1] dissident and heterodox streams of economic thought have persisted throughout most of the discipline's history and show no signs of withering away. On the contrary, there is clear evidence – which cannot be presented in detail here – that the divisions among economists are not merely surviving but also beginning to penetrate the subject's basic textbooks,[2] which have long been central agents for the preservation and dissemination of the conventional wisdom.

Broadly speaking, in methodological, doctrinal, and policy terms, economics has been in a markedly transitional and unsettled phase, both as a discipline and as a profession, during the past decade or two. To pessimistic critics the situation has been one of crisis, whereas optimistic defenders (Heller 1975; MacDougall 1974) have viewed it bravely as evidence of healthy scepticism towards received doctrine and exceptional openness to new ideas and approaches. There is, indeed, some truth in both these perspectives. Mainstream economists are nowadays generally far more conscious of the limitations of their science than in the 1950s and 1960s, and somewhat more sympathetic towards the traditional heterodox criticisms. Many are reaching into neighbouring fields for concepts, models, and research findings which can be applied to theoretical and applied problems treated earlier either as irrelevant to economics or beyond the discipline's boundaries. While economistic imperialists have been vigorously colonising problem areas hitherto regarded as belonging to other disciplinary domains, specialists in those and other cognate disciplines have been taking a sustained and intelligent interest in economists' concepts and models, even trying them out in their own fields. As yet the promise of these developments may be said to exceed the achievements – the interactions between economics and politics (Frey 1978, 1983), and between economics and psychology (Earl, 1988; Hogarth and Reder, 1987) are two conspicuous examples. Nevertheless, the portents are good.

Against this background, exploration of the commonalities and differences between two strong and durable dissenting traditions – Austrian and Institutional economics – is to be welcomed, especially if, as seen likely, there are prospects of fruitful collaboration and even convergence between them. This symposium is therefore a useful starting point for more systematic and detailed research into the AE/IE relationship, and the following comments are designed to highlight matters that would repay investigation in an effort to extend rather than simply to repeat arguments put by the other symposiasts.

Warren Samuels' useful ground-clearing paper is essentially taxonomic and his emphasis on the heterogeneity of the views and individuals associated with each 'school' (if, indeed, that is an appropriate term) offers an immediate entry point. He perhaps wisely sidesteps the difficult task for differentiating between the essential and the inessential elements within each school; yet this task cannot be postponed indefinitely. It is not enough to catalogue features: we need either measures of central tendency or a clear identification of the filiation of ideas within each camp before crucial similarities and differences can be assessed. This is no easy task, and it may be advisable to approach the matter historically, identifying the key individuals and leading doctrines in each case before attempting to determine which are integral to each movement. For example, on the Austrian side it seems clear that Menger was not only the founder, but also the key figure in the first generation. Then how far do Wieser's views belong in the same general category? (Böhm-Bawerk is no doubt a much less difficult individual to 'place'.)

In what may loosely be termed the middle generation, what are the characteristically Austrian features that unite such leading disparate figures as Hayek, Machlup, Mises, Morgenstern and Schumpeter? The last named, it is often held, cannot properly be viewed as a member of the 'school' given, for example, his eclectic methodological views and the variety of work he produced, though business cycles has been a unifying topic of study in all five cases, presumably (in part) because of their native country's experiences. Mises and Hayek are obviously key figures, the former because of his exceptionally strong views and his enormous influence on the American revival of interest in Austrian economics after World War II. His pedagogical influence via his seminars was crucial; yet his vigorously expressed methodological a priorism has been repudiated by many who admired other aspects of his work, and has even been regarded as a source of embarrassment. Of Hayek, none will deny his intellectual eminence or the remarkable impact he made at the LSE during the 1930s; but of course his later economic work, especially after his impenetrable *Pure Theory of Capital*, has proved to be a dead end, and the Austrianism of his later methodological views is now the subject of direct and profound disagreement among the experts. According to some he has revealed disconcerting Popperian sympathies, and even if he has not undergone major shifts of methodological allegiance, as has been claimed, he is certainly no Misesian. Nor can Machlup's or Morgenstern's Austrian lineage be viewed as pure, although both have made significant contributions to methodology and economic theory, and both share many of the familiar Austrian ideological views.

It is, however, with the recent (mainly) American Neo-Austrian revivalists that the greatest problems of classification arise. Directly or indirectly influenced by Mises as most of them have been, they nevertheless disagree sharply both with the master and among themselves. As noted by other symposiasts, Menger is the forefather who commands the greater respect, but was he in any sense typical? And what are the similarities and differences between Menger and Mises? However defined, they are certainly substantial. Some of the new Austrians can be unequivocally characterised as "true believers," especially Rothbard; but others deviate so strongly from earlier views that one feels that either they should be excluded from the "school" or that the membership is so heterogeneous as to cast doubt on the descriptive value of that term. Whereas Rothbard, for example, is clearly an outsider as far as mainstream neo-classical economics is concerned, Kirzner, whatever his designation, is widely recognized as a perceptive and important contributor of suggestive new ideas. Perhaps the later generation of neo-Austrians is too varied and independent minded to be usefully classified as such, and the characterisation is further blurred by the inclusion (by some commentators) of older generation figures such as Lachmann (undeniably Austrian), Shackle (possibly, but less assuredly) and Hicks (perhaps least convincing). And when we get into the difficult issue of the relationships between Austrian economics and subjectivism, the possibility of identifying a unifying central tradition and its branches becomes remote.

It has seemed appropriate to cite the Austrian case first because the elements of unity and continuity among writers usually included under this rubric – with respect to their philosophy, methodology, theory, policy, and ideology – have usually been taken for granted by economists who have not seriously studied their works. Even now I do not wish to deny that such unity and continuity may exist, but merely to emphasize that on closer inspection the case appears much weaker and more difficult to establish than appeared at first sight.

By contrast, with the institutionalists there have long been fewer doubts about their right to be viewed as a "school." Their common characteristics have often been depicted as negative – i.e., a matter of polemical orientation, or point of view, rather than matters of constructive aims or doctrine. Peter Boettke's reservations aside, Veblen did not have any literal disciples, though many were influenced by him; whereas Ayres, in some ways undoubtedly a disciple, developed idiosyncratic views and, while exercising a deep influence on undergraduates, generally failed to inspire postgraduates or younger faculty to take up and develop his ideas into a research programme (using that term in a non-technical sense). They tended to repeat Ayres's views parrot fashion, or to apply them to some specific topic in a more-or less mechanical fashion. Of the other members of the original institutionalist triumvirate, Mitchell founded a great research institution and an approach to the study of central economic issues, but he did not found a doctrinal school. Nor, indeed, did Commons, despite his great personal influence on his Wisconsin "Friday Nighters" and others who came under his spell. A great practitioner who taught many other successful practitioners, no doubt he was; but not the founder of a theoretical tradition.

In this, as contrasted with the Austrian case, there is a considerable and useful secondary literature on the relations between the ideas of Veblen, Mitchell, Commons and Ayres and other later economists with declared institutionalist learnings. But as with the Neo Austrians the difficulties mount rapidly as we enter the post 1945 world. Allan Gruchy utterly failed to identify and characterise members of the so called "neo-institutionalist" persuasion (school is hardly the proper word here). Common ideas and interests there certainly are, as Warren Samuels (1977, 1978) showed in two survey articles in the Journal of Economic Issues. The problem here is rather to identify the unifying beliefs and practices, and to deal with the problem that many "applied" economists accept (perhaps only in moments of weakness) the institutional label, without any very clear or intentional commitment to membership of a school.

Perhaps one simple conclusion from this meandering discourse is that the term "school" has relatively little value – too little concreteness and far too much flexibility – to be of much use to the analyst or historian of the discipline.

Notes

1 For example, Milton Friedman (in Breit and Spencer 1986, p. 90) has argued, on a number of occasions that, "If scientific issues are separated from policy and value issues, there is widespread agreement among economists whatever their political views." More than fifty years ago Joseph Schumpeter (quoted in Schneider 1975, p. 40) argued, "there is no room for schools in our discipline. As a matter of fact we do find a great convergence of the really leading and capable brain workers in our discipline," Controversy between schools is a waste of energy, he continued, for, "There is no use fighting something which life will sooner or later eliminate anyway. Unlike business and politics, just what matters in science is not monetary success. All we can say is that if in science something wins through it will have proved its right to exist, and if the thing is not worth anything it will surely wither."

In recent years there have been a number of systematic efforts to assess the degree of consensus among economists. Broadly speaking it appears to be significantly greater on micro than on macro economic issues.

2 For example, Cole, Cameron and Edwards 1983 and Dow 1985. These texts incorporate divisions among economists into the pedagogical process. There arc of course a number of one-line dissident texts, for example, by Marxists, Radicals, Post Keynesians, and Institutionalists.

References

Breit, William, and Roger W. Spencer, eds., (1986) *Lives of the Laureates*. Cambridge: MIT Press.

Cole, Ken, John Cameron, and Chris Edwards, (1983) *Why Economists Disagree: The Political Economy of Eonomists*. London: Longmans.

Dow, Sheila, (1985) *Macroeconomic Thought: A Methodological Approach*. New York: Basil Blackwell.

Earl, Peter, ed. (1988) *Psychological Economies*. Norwell, MA: Kluwer Academic Publishers.

Frey, Bruno, (1978) *Modern Political Economy*. Oxford: Martin Robertson.

——, (1983) *Democratic Economic Policy. A Theoretical Introduction*. Oxford: Martin Robertson.

Heller, Walter W., (1975) "What's Right With Economics," *American Economic Review*, March, *65*, 1–26.

Hogarth, Robin, and Melvin Reder, eds. (1987) *Rational Choice: The Contrast Between Economies and Psychology*. Chicago: University of Chicago Press.

MacDougall, Donald., (1974) "In Praise of Economics," *Economic Journal*, December, *84*, 773–786.

Samuels, Warren J., (1977) "Technology vis-à-vis institutions in the JEI: A Suggested Interpretation," *Journal of Economic Issues*, December, *11*, 871–895.

——, (1978) "Information Systems, Preferences, and the Economy in the JEI," *Journal of Economic Issues*, March, *12*, 23–41.

Schneider, Erich, (1975) *Joseph A. Schumpeter: Life and Work of a Great Social Scientist*. Translated by W. E. Kuhn. Lincoln: Bureau of Business Research, University of Nebraska.

26 Economics as a profession

> Every profession lives in a world of its own. The language spoken by its inhabitants, the landmarks familiar to them, their customs and conventions can only be learnt by those who reside there.
>
> (Carr-Saunders and Wilson 1933: iii)

1. Introduction

Most economists see themselves, and wish to be seen by others, as professionals, although if pressed many would find it difficult to say precisely what that designation means. This is understandable, for the terms 'profession' and 'professionalization' have long been the subject of dispute among specialists, most of whom are sociologists and therefore not taken seriously by economists. Moreover, as noted later, there are specific reasons why the economics profession is difficult to define and identify. What is less understandable, indeed inexcusable, is the dearth of serious research on the nature, historical evolution and significance of the professionalization of economics, whether by economists or other scholars. Of course, there has been considerable discussion of the profession's problems, especially during and since the so-called 'crisis' of the late 1960s and early 1970s (e.g. Heller 1975; Coats 1977; Bell and Kristol 1981 among others), but most of this has been either occasional, personal partisan or mainly methodological. There is no full-scale published study of the growth of the economics profession in the United Kingdom or the United States, the two leading countries in the development of modern economics; and comparative work on the subject is still in its infancy[1] – although there has been some promising, but essentially preliminary, research on the role of economists in government that is referred to below. Consequently, given the current state of our knowledge, the following account must perforce be sketchy and impressionistic.

Some things, however, are indisputable. During the past half-century or so the number of trained economists has increased remarkably by comparison with the rest of the period since Adam Smith published *The Wealth of Nations*, and this is attributable both to supply and demand forces. Prior to the late nineteenth century in the United Kingdom and the United States, and much later still in most other countries, there was little or no formal training in economics as we know it today.

When the social sciences eventually emerged as a group of identifiable specialized disciplines, economics was in the vanguard, partly because it was a subject of obvious public interest and significance, but mainly because it was based on a well-developed and recognizable corpus of theoretical knowledge. The latter feature is nowadays seen as the *sine qua non* of a 'modern' science-based profession, as contrasted with such traditional professions as the church, the law and the military.

In the extraordinary global expansion of higher education after the Second World War economics was by no means the least of the disciplinary beneficiaries, and naturally enough this process called for a rapid growth in the numbers of academic teachers and researchers. However, this was but an extension of a much earlier and broader process of economic and social change – namely, the growth of specialization and division of labour in modern urban industrial communities. As one thoughtful sociologist has pithily observed; 'an industrializing society is a professionalizing society' (Goode 1960: 902). Another has claimed that:

> The development and strategic importance of the professions probably constitutes the most important change that has occurred in the occupational structure of modern societies. The growth of the professions has brought to prominence a set of occupations which never figured prominently in the ideological thinking that, after having crystallized in the late nineteenth century, has tended to dominate public discussion in the twentieth.
>
> (Parsons 1968: 536)

The weasel word 'ideological' is pertinent here in at least two distinct but interrelated senses. The first and more obvious of these is political. Thus radical, Marxist, institutionalist and other dissenting economists have argued that orthodox mainstream neoclassical doctrine explicitly or implicitly involves an acceptance of the socio-economic status quo. For example, marginal analysis focuses attention on small-scale incremental adjustments of present discontents, thereby discouraging more fundamental questioning of the existing order, and it is certainly true that when marginalism was gaining acceptance among academic economists around the turn of the century there was a concomitant narrowing of the discipline's scope (symbolized by the terminological shift from 'political economy' to 'economics'), a move that enabled economists to delegate to other social science specialists such troublesome issues as the distribution of income and wealth, the power structure and social justice. Such a contraction of scope is a familiar feature of the professionalization process. Of course, some critics strenuously resisted this constriction of their subject matter. However, the change was facilitated by the practice of distinguishing sharply between the 'science' (i.e. theory or analysis, sometimes referred to as economics 'proper') and the 'art' of political economy (i.e. the discussion of current economic problems and policies), so that the adept economist could both have her cake and eat it, i.e. she could participate as a detached impartial expert in public policy debates without thereby compromising her scientific purity.[2] How far the laity acknowledged this differentiation of roles is another matter.

More recently, with the growth of non-academic employment opportunities in business, banking, local, regional and national government, and international agencies, an increasing number of economists have entered policy-making positions, and the consequent politicization of the subject has made the distinction between the science and the art more and more difficult to sustain in practice. Especially during and since the Second World War – although the process was already well under way in some countries from the Great Depression of the early 1930s – professionally trained economists have occupied prominent positions as heads of state, cabinet ministers, principal official advisers to government, chief executives of large corporations and so on. They have been outspoken in public debates on contentious policy issues in many different forums at a variety of levels, and they played a major part in the construction and operation of the international economic organizations that have become so integral a part of the post-war world.

All this makes it difficult to maintain that economics is an essentially technocratic and apolitical subject. Indeed, one perceptive economist critic has persuasively argued that there are not one but three distinct professional economic ideologies or world views – the conservative, liberal and radical versions – each with its own ideological assumptions, theories and policy preferences, and that by his definition the majority of academic economists are liberals (Ward 1979). This seems entirely appropriate, given the discipline's eighteenth-century liberal moral philosophical antecedents.

However, there is a second meaning of the word ideological that is particularly relevant here. This is the concept of professional ideology – the set of ideas, beliefs, values, standards and behaviour patterns that differentiates one category of professionals from others. As noted in the opening epigraph, a professional ideology is an integral part of the common culture shared by the workers in any reasonably well-defined field. It is circumscribed by the group's accepted aims, conventions and methodological rules; it is reinforced by the development of an esoteric language inaccessible to laymen; and it also usually embodies elements of 'tacit' knowledge which even experienced practitioners find difficult to articulate fully. In the economist's case a central tenet of this ideology is the conception of the neutral objective scientific expert which underlies the above-mentioned distinction between 'science' and 'art', or between 'positive' and 'normative' economics, to use the current jargon (Hutchison 1964). In the economics community the academic ideal, namely that of the pure research truth-seeker, the detached non-partisan expert, outweighs any more pragmatic conception of professionalism or public service; and when this ideal is transported into the non-academic realm it often takes the form of partisan advocacy of efficiency and market methods (Nelson 1987) which, according to some critics, are given unwarranted priority over considerations of equity – an emphasis facilitated by the efforts at the turn of the century to sever the links between political economy and ethics. These professional values are deep rooted, firmly stressed in the standard textbooks and inculcated, both tacitly and explicitly, in the initiation, training and socialization of new recruits to the field. And however remote from reality the conception of professional neutrality may seem, it has exercised a potent force in the creation and maintenance of the economists' collective professional identity.[3]

Of course, the subjective components of professional ideology count for little without the external dimension of public recognition of the occupation's cultural status, which takes the form of specialized appointments, above- average remuneration, the delegation of responsibility and authority, and social esteem. Command of esoteric knowledge and skills is usually certified by the award of degrees, diplomas and other qualifications, for which a lengthy period of training is required; and controls over entry, whether through the training process or direct regulation by a body issuing credentials, or both, serve to limit the supply of new recruits and thereby to maintain the profession's privileged status.

A profession is not a static phenomenon, identifiable simply by a fixed list of traits.[4] Professions grow and develop over time, and professionalization is a dynamic process that involves

> an attempt to translate one order of scarce resources – specialized knowledge and skills – into another – social and economic rewards. To maintain scarcity implies a tendency to monopoly: monopoly of expertise in the market, monopoly of status in the system of stratification.
>
> (Larson 1978: xvii)

Against the cynical view that the essence of professionalism is power – a species of conspiracy against the laity – there is the contrasting belief that the professional has a distinctive moral obligation to his or her clients, or to society at large – for instance in the obligation to use expertise responsibly in the service of others.[5] Whichever of these standpoints is preferred, it is clear that economists have not attained full professional status; indeed, they may not have seriously tried to do so. They have traditionally been ideologically opposed to monopoly, and this has led them to question the merits of professionalism more openly and persistently than other social scientists (Johnson 1972: 15).[6] How far they have sought detachment from the market-place, another characteristic associated with the professions, is a nice question (Herman 1982).

Although academic economists necessarily influence entry into the profession through their control of the degree process, they have consistently opposed any kind of formal professional accreditation. The leading British and American learned societies or professional organizations rely solely on the economic criterion, for they are open to anyone willing to pay the requisite membership fee, and economists have made no collective effort to prescribe standards of professional conduct, whether in universities or elsewhere. Even now, when the level of technical sophistication of PhD students from so-called elite graduate departments has reached heights that to older professionals seem dizzyingly abstract, there is often still no clear occupational discrimination in the non-academic world between (a) those with advanced rather than undergraduate degrees, (b) those with joint or mixed rather than single honours undergraduate degrees (Towse and Blaug 1988) and (c) those in higher management or civil service positions with no formal training whatsoever in economics. Sceptics may argue that it is not ideological distaste grounded in an inherited liberal moral philosophy that explains the reluctance to enforce strict controls over entry, a code of professional ethics or procedures for excommunicating those who fail to maintain acceptable standards of behaviour or performance. Rather, it is the wisdom of recognizing that that species of professionalism is simply unenforceable, perhaps even undefinable, in economics.[7]

Underlying this situation is a troublesome epistemological question: exactly what do economists 'know' (i.e. that other professionals do not)? Of course, trained economists can be expected to 'know' the corpus of economic analysis enshrined in innumerable conventional textbooks (which, incidentally, display a remarkable degree of uniformity). Presumably, they understand the nature and operations of the price mechanism far better than non-economists do; and also the functioning and interdependence of markets at home and abroad, the significance of scarcity and opportunity costs, the nature and functions of money, banking, finance etc., and so on. Yet many of the economist's fundamental ideas are elementary and very general, albeit with wide applicability. Do they suffice as a foundation for claims to expertise in non-academic settings?

Judging by half a century's experience of economists' employment in government the question can confidently be answered in the affirmative. After all, despite the well-publicized conflicts and disagreements within the profession, the demand for economists in the public service has been remarkably sustained, and although much less is known about their successes and failures in the private sector, no doubt the same answer applies there also. However, there are important reservations to be made which cannot be fully explained and justified here.

With respect to government employment, attention has usually been focused on the economists' role in the higher-level advisory or decision-making positions, whereas in demand terms activities within the bureaucratic machine are obviously more significant, albeit less glamorous. These activities vary enormously, and sweeping generalizations must therefore be suspect. Nevertheless, the nature, extent and effectiveness of the economists' work will obviously depend on such factors as the range and variety of the government's economic and social policies (*laissez-faire* is not good for the profession), the political climate (a degree of stability is essential), the character of the bureaucracy (corruption, politicization and inefficiency are obvious impediments) and the readiness to acknowledge the authority of the economist's expertise (which is dependent on the society's culture, the educational system and the degree of consensus within the economics community) (cf. Coats 1981, 1986; Pechman 1989). Economists can perform many different functions in many different contexts, but they are usually more effective in departments or agencies with a relatively clear economic purpose and responsibility. They may be temporary or permanent employees, working either in segregated specialist units (for example, as model-builders and forecasters) or as isolated free-floating individuals in close day-to-day contact with generalist administrators or with other specialists or professionals (and in such cases conflicts of professional values and ideologies may become significant). Much of the lower-level work consists of routine data collection, presentation and analysis, calling for little or no input of the economist's specialist knowledge and equipment. And as government work, like economics itself, has become more and more quantitative, partly in response to the almost insatiable demand for economic and social statistics, economists often find themselves working alongside other numerate specialists such as statisticians, mathematicians, operations researchers or accountants. It is in these situations that the economists' product can and must be differentiated, for in addition to their quantitative, technical and mathematical abilities they also possess a distinctive intellectual apparatus or 'way of thinking' that is unfamiliar to most (but not all) non-economists.[8] The value of this basic, seemingly elementary, mental equipment has repeatedly been stressed by senior professional practitioners reflecting on their experience in government. They have frequently been agreeably surprised by their ability to pose penetrating and effective questions that others were either unable or unwilling to ask. In this context, overemphasis on quantitative methods can be professionally as well as intellectually debilitating, for the solutions to complex policy problems can rarely be reduced to quantitative terms.

As is clear from comparative studies of national governments and international agencies, the tasks performed by a government economist will largely depend on the scale, structure and responsibilities of the organization in which he or she works. Many are employed within the several levels between the top official advisers and policy-makers and the humbler toilers in the bureaucratic vineyard, many of whom are mere number-crunchers. Policy proposals may originate anywhere within the government machine, or from outside, but much of the essential policy formulation and implementation occurs in the middle levels. Proposals are usually modified, refined and reshaped repeatedly – i.e. if they are not abandoned – while moving through the official channels; and once a firm decision has been made, implementation often necessitates its adaptation and interpretation to fit specific circumstances that were not envisaged by the original drafters and decision-makers. Economists contribute to all these activities.

Experienced government economists have learnt that if they are to be effective they must accept the facts of bureaucratic and political life. As Robert Nelson has observed in a valuable recent survey of a large literature, they cannot function simply as undeviating partisan advocates for efficiency. In practice they

> must also tailor their advocacy of market methods, efficient resource use, and other economic approaches to the political environment … modify proposals to make them attractive in terms of equity, or to avoid infringing on real or perceived 'rights'… recognize that they are members of an organization with which they must conform to some degree … [and] develop and exercise skills in bureaucratic and political tactics, which are necessarily interwoven with their exercise of economic experience.
>
> (Nelson 1987: 50)

In official life personality, intuition, imagination, communication skills, speed and stamina may count for more than logic and technique, and the implications of these requirements for graduate training in economics will be considered later. What is clear at this point is that adherence to a strict form of professionalism, which tends to assume the omnipresence of rationality, may be positively harmful.[9] There are many complaints that much of the trained economist's hard-earned professional capital is useless or actively misleading in government work, while the academic emphasis on the value of originality is out of place in an organizational setting where teamwork is essential. Some prominent economists, like the late Harry G. Johnson, have claimed that good economists do not go into government, or, if they do, they do not stay good for long, since they rapidly suffer from professional obsolescence. Others believe that government work is necessarily corrupting, even if only mildly so, because of the unavoidable compromises involved.

2. Passages in the historical development of the economics profession

Given the difficulties of definition, the history of the economics profession has no unambiguous starting point.[10] While the French Physiocrats may be seen as the first modern 'school' of economists in the intellectual rather than the sociological sense of that term, it is convenient to begin with the Ricardians, the first group of British economists to regard themselves, and to be recognized by important segments of the public, as experts in economic affairs. To a remarkable extent this status was attributable to the personal influence of David Ricardo himself, a retired stockbroker, the very epitome of the scientific intellectual, whose work drew upon and developed Adam Smith's ideas. Ricardo became widely acknowledged as the leading economic authority of the day because of the skill, lucidity and disinterestedness with which he analysed the hotly contested technical and policy problems of the currency, banking and international trade, both in his published writings and in his House of Commons speeches. At that time 'economist' was not yet a recognizable occupational category, and although scholars have suggested that either T. R. Malthus or J. R. McCulloch should be described as the first British professional economist, since each derived most of his income from economic teachings or writings, there was no clear demarcation between those who were qualified to write on economic subjects and those who were not. Despite Thomas Carlyle's familiar jibe about 'the gloomy professors of the dismal science', most of the leading economists spent a limited proportion, if indeed any, of their time in academic employment, and as academic instruction in political economy was woefully inadequate there was no reliable source of prospective new recruits. The Political Economy Club of London, founded in 1821, provided an organizational centre for the discussion and propagation of 'sound' doctrines, particularly free trade. However, it was but one of many such private clubs at home and abroad, and the other prerequisites of professionalization were lacking. The Ricardians' influence derived from their claim to scientific authority which they strenuously asserted in books, pamphlets, magazines, newspapers, official enquiries and parliamentary debates. For the present purpose, however, the most distinctive feature was their effort to distance themselves, as experts, from the amateurs, especially the despised 'practical' men. As Ricardo's ally, James Mill, confidently proclaimed: 'a reasoner must be hard pressed when he is driven to quote practical men in aid of his conclusions. There cannot be a worse authority, in any branch of political science, than that of mere practical men' (Mill 1824, cited by Coats 1964: 90). Mill insisted that: 'Among those who have so much knowledge on the subject as to entitle their opinion to any weight, there is wonderful agreement', despite some disputation 'on the minor questions involved' (Mill 1836, cited by Coats 1964: 90), while a few years later Robert Torrens, a fringe member of the Ricardian group, was confident enough to assert that an economist should be appointed to the Board of Trade because

> it partakes of the nature of a professional appointment, requiring a peculiar course of study, and knowledge of an almost technical nature.... Though the time may not have actually arrived, yet it is rapidly approaching, when it will be deemed as necessary to select the members of the Board of Trade from the Economists, as it is to take the Bishops from the Church, or the Law Officers from the Bar.
>
> (Torrens 1826, cited by O'Brien 1965: 32)

Needless to say, this forecast was wildly overoptimistic. Yet it illustrates the trend of opinion among the spokesmen for classical economics, which soon hardened into a rigid orthodoxy in the hands of popularizers and propagandists. Conceivably the intellectual groundwork for professionalization had been laid, but until the late nineteenth century the academic preconditions were insufficient to provide a significant supply of trained economists clearly differentiated from the many amateur practitioners, some of whom carried considerable weight with both the public and the professors.

The marginal revolution of the 1870s was a watershed in the development of the modern economics profession, a complex process that involved changes both within the discipline itself (for example, the shift from political economy to economics noted earlier) and in the higher educational system, which became the principal source of new recruits. In the late nineteenth and early twentieth centuries the essential institutional conditions for academic specialization were being established, such as degree courses, the shift of emphasis away from teaching towards research, the launching of new journals devoted exclusively to economics and the founding of new learned societies that eventually acquired quasi-professional status, even though they were open to all comers.[11] Among these organizations, the American Economic Association (1885) and the British Economic Association (1891, later the Royal Economic Society) were particularly significant (Coats 1960, 1968b). Both had a very heterogeneous membership, especially initially; both were effectively dominated by academics; and both served as models for similar bodies in other countries.

In an original and penetrating book, John Maloney (1985) has examined the influence of the Marshallian paradigm on the professionalization process in the

United Kingdom. He distinguishes between a primary professional orthodoxy 'based on a theoretical paradigm capable of supporting a programme of research, uniting economists who have its partisanship, regular use and comparative mastery', and secondary professional orthodoxies that

> though dependent for their effect on the primary ones, feature a consensus on some policy question which, because it involves non-economic arguments, admits of a distinctively limited 'professional view'. This implies that the purely technical questions of economic policy, because they impose the same strictly economic terms of discourse on everyone, have less power to create genuine professional orthodoxies.
>
> (Maloney 1985: 230–1)

In the United States the primary professional orthodoxy was slower to emerge and to attain hegemonic status for a variety of reasons including the sheer size and diversity of the territory; the far greater number, heterogeneity and competitiveness of the higher educational institutions; the persistence of heterodox economic ideas, in part a legacy of the German historical school; and a culture far less deferential to intellectual and scientific authority than its British counterpart (Coats 1980). In both countries there was an influential secondary professional orthodoxy based on free-trade ideas, which serves as a reminder of the intimate interdependence of theory and practice in the development of professional economics.

This interdependence was strikingly revealed in the United Kingdom during the intense public controversy over tariff reform in the early years of this century. In 1903 fourteen leading economists signed a letter to *The Times* opposing Joseph Chamberlain's reform proposals and voicing their concern at 'the prevalence of certain erroneous opinions' in favour of protection, a doctrine which, they asserted, had been discredited 'partly for reasons of the same kind as those which, as now universally admitted, justified the adoption of free trade' (*The Times*, 15 August 1903, cited by Coats 1964: 100). Here is a prime example of orthodoxy at work: presumably the 'sound' doctrine propagated earlier by the Political Economy Club and subsequently 'universally admitted' should have been sufficient to counter the resurgence of protectionism, despite markedly changed historical conditions.

Unfortunately, the letter from the fourteen professors not only brought predictable howls of protest from Chamberlain's supporters, but also provoked a number of dissenting letters to *The Times* from reputable academic economists who either opposed or were not fully committed to free trade, whether as a scientific doctrine or as a policy. Some of them firmly objected to the attempt to bring the weight of scientific authority to bear on this controversial political issue (Coats 1964: 100–3).[12] Alfred Marshall, the most influential British economist of the day, soon bitterly regretted his participation, which breached his customary practice of cautious detachment from contentious public issues, and undoubtedly the public's reaction taught other economists the need to exercise individual and collective discretion, and to avoid exposing their deeper disagreements to the laity.

In the United States during this formative period the prevalence of serious threats to academic freedom provided an additional powerful incentive to self-restraint, and in due course, after considerable heart-searching, a kind of professional consensus emerged among the leading economists with respect to the proper forms and limits of professional participation in public affairs (Furner 1975). In neither country was there any concerted effort to devise a formal code of professional behaviour designed to protect the disciplinary practitioner. Yet in both cases, and especially in the United States, there was a growing sense of professional community born of the desire to combine the scientist's intellectual prestige and occupational security with the reforming urge to make a constructive impact on the discussion and solution of contemporary economic problems.

The Keynesian revolution of the late 1930s and 1940s was another major watershed in the professionalization of economics, as it was in the development of economic ideas and policy. Although both Keynes's ideas and his policy proposals proved to be deeply controversial, the conjunction of macroeconomic analysis and major advances in the supply of official statistics gave economists the wherewithal to demonstrate their potential value to society, and on this basis the expansion of the non-academic, especially government, economics profession gained substantial momentum. There had, of course, been many earlier examples of governments, public commissions, banks and businesses employing expert economic advisers, usually on an occasional or even personal basis, but sometimes more formally and permanently. Had the American participation in the First World War been more lasting, the number of economists in the federal service would surely have continued to grow apace, and the permanent complement of peacetime civil service economists might well have remained high. Indeed, it was in the early 1920s that American agricultural economists first became established in the federal administration, and it is no coincidence that their transatlantic counterparts became the first group of permanent economic specialists in British government, roughly a decade later (Coats 1976; McDean 1983). The Great Depression marked a new low in the profession's public esteem, for the economists' response to the urgent and widespread demand for explanations and solutions to the crisis proved to be confusing, often contradictory and therefore deeply disappointing to politicians and the general public alike. But the recovery and approach of war radically changed the climate of opinion.

During the 1940s the global centre of economics, both as a science and as a profession, shifted decisively and permanently from Europe, especially the United Kingdom, to the United States, and within that country in wartime Washington became the intellectual as well as the governmental centre of economists' ideas and activities (including, temporarily, the editorship of the leading professional journal, the *American Economic Review*). Keynes's theoretical ideas and policies dominated academic economics during the first two post-war decades, although never to the same degree in the United States as in the United Kingdom, and, indeed, the multi-centred distribution of academic resources in the United States and the challenge of dissenting orthodox and heterodox doctines combined to sustain the subject's intellectual vitality.

In retrospect it appears that America's post-war leadership was inevitable, in economics as in many other academic disciplines, given the country's overwhelming superiority in material and human resources – the latter's having been disproportionately strengthened by the influx of European emigrés, many of whom had crossed the Atlantic to escape Nazi persecution. The list of Presidents of the American Economic Association provides evidence of the recognition that some of these individuals evidently earned, and the presence of Paul Samuelson, Milton Friedman and George Stigler in the roster of Nobel Prizewinners testifies to the emergence of a cohort of distinguished Americans trained in their native universities during the 1930s who came to professional maturity in the ensuing decade.

This is not the place to examine post-1945 developments in economic doctrines. In the present context the most important consequence of the Americanization of economics (and, gradually, its internationalization also) has been that American methods of advanced training, theories and techniques, intellectual values and professional standards have become increasingly acknowledged and adopted throughout the world, obviously with varying time lags and degrees of resistance.[13] This process was enormously facilitated by a number of factors including the growth and acceleration of global communications; the movement of large numbers of foreign students who studied and obtained their professional credentials in the United States and, to a lesser extent, in the United Kingdom and Western Europe; the veritable army of American and British professors who have taught, studied and undertaken research or advisory work in foreign countries; the proliferation of international conferences, scholarly organizations and study groups; and, less conspicuously, the emergence of small but influential global networks of economic specialists (for example, in development economics, international trade and monetary affairs) and a cadre of economists employed by foreign governments, international agencies and other para-statal bodies. Another major force in the internationalization of economics, as in some other disciplines, has been the increasingly widespread and efficient distribution of research monographs, professional journals, official reports and, especially, relatively standardized elementary and advanced teaching texts and related materials. Of course, the flow of ideas, methods, techniques and various species of hardware and software has by no means been all one way, and there is some danger of overstating the extent of uniformity, especially if we focus on the conventional contents of the standard macroeconomics and microeconomics curriculum. However, as noted at the beginning of this chapter, in the present state of our knowledge we have embarrassingly little systematic data on the precise nature and differences of national 'styles' in training, research and publication (Johnson 1973).

3. Recent developments and concerns

For a variety of historical and cultural reasons that cannot be explored adequately here, Americans have long been more fascinated (and worried) than their European counterparts by the nature, growth and influence of the professions.

Consequently, matters of this kind have attracted more controversy and research in the United States than elsewhere.

Needless to say, much of the activity in this area stems from dissatisfaction with the status quo, and in the case of economics it is hardly surprising that the euphoria of the Keynesian era (*c.* 1945–65) was followed by a reaction both within and outside the economics community. The doctrinal challenges to Keynesian ideas from monetarists, post-Keynesians, Marxists, radicals, institutionalists and neo-Austrians were reinforced by the manifest inability of mainstream 'neoclassical' economists to cope with the problems associated with 'stagflation'. But the most distinctive feature of this particular 'crisis' was the extent to which it exposed the widespread and deep-seated loss of professional self-confidence. This was manifested in a veritable orgy of public self-flagellation led by some of the profession's most respected figures in a series of presidential addresses and invited public lectures (Heller 1975; Coats 1977). The critics focused on some of the familiar negative features of professionalism, such as rigidity, conformity, resistance to innovations (other than those of an approved species), the maintenance of tight disciplinary boundaries, the exclusion and/or denigration of dissenters, and excessively centralized control over access to resources, training and employment opportunities.

It is pertinent to note that professional standards, like methodological rules, have prescriptive and regulative as well as cognitive functions, and the quest for scientific truth or community service can easily be sacrificed to the interests of maintaining and advancing special privileges, securing higher remuneration, and protecting the field from encroachments by charlatans and those operating in closely related or overlapping disciplines or occupations.

These and many other features of the sociology of economics have been analysed and documented in a large, contentious, and often entertaining and insightful body of literature that is far too large to be cited extensively here. Not all of this outpouring can be dismissed, as some critics have been wont to do, as the work of cranks, dissidents and incompetents; some of it emanates from acknowledged leaders of the profession.[14] Some, indeed, regard these criticisms not as pathological, but rather as evidence of vigorous health (Heller 1975). Nevertheless, there is general recognition that too much well-publicized disagreement, especially with respect to fundamentals, may undermine the discipline's scientific status in the public's eyes.

Many of the most outspoken critics of the state of economics complain that the profession is too hierarchical and elitist, and that it is dominated by a relatively small contingent of orthodox neoclassical economists centred in a few leading departments. As one President of the American Economic Association has declared, there is nowadays

> a new despotism. That consists in defining scientific excellence as whatever is closest in belief and method to the scholarly tendency of those who are already there. This is a pervasive and oppressive thing not the less dangerous for being, in the frequent case, both righteous and unconscious.
>
> (Galbraith 1973)

The professional establishment is said to control directly or indirectly the selection of officers of the American Economic Association, the editors and editorial boards of the Association's publications and other leading professional journals, the winners of the principal honours and awards, and the allocation of major research funds through the peer review system employed by the National Science Foundation and the principal private grant-giving agencies. Members of this elite also determine the basic requirements of core courses in the elite graduate schools, thereby controlling the means of certification, the entry of new recruits into the profession and their career prospects through both the informal communications network that influences most appointments and the publication process that so heavily shapes the individual's subsequent career. There are, of course, many specialist subgroups, invisible colleges, schools and networks, and occasionally an exceptional individual who has had the misfortune to be trained or appointed at one of the lesser institutions is spotted, like a star athlete, and recruited by a major league team. But for the most part the students of the leading graduate schools remain within the elite circuit, if they can, and in due course produce their own progeny who help to perpetuate the system.

Various useful studies have been undertaken to document this state of affairs. In particular, the journals network, which reveals both the core of the profession's reputational system and the processes whereby new ideas are generated and disseminated, has been extensively examined. Among the topics covered are the use of citation indexes to trace the institutional affiliations of authors of articles in the leading periodicals in an effort to determine how far there is a closed community of the elite; the prestige ratings of various journals; the earnings and career implications of publication in a leading journal; the mathematical and technical content of articles; the extent to which authors seriously endeavour to refute and/or empirically test their findings; the number of publications by 'star' economists; fashions, trends and cycles in the literature; and so on.[15]

Of course, every human organization, not least every academic discipline, necessarily has its leaders and followers, its superior performers and its mediocrities, and disputed scientific findings, evaluations and decisions cannot be settled by conventional democratic processes, even within the community of the competent. Moreover, it is natural for those in the establishment who have already achieved success to approve of the system in which they have attained their eminence, since their own virtues and abilities have been so fittingly recognized and rewarded. A telling example of this perspective is the complacent analysis of the process whereby private foundation grant allocations purportedly facilitate the concentration of research and talent in the already acknowledged 'best' university departments, thereby reinforcing their members' existing ability to attract able colleagues, hire research assistants, obtain any requisite equipment and produce more successful work, thus enhancing their department's visibility and prestige rating in the economics community (Stigler 1967).

Whether this system works well or badly depends on the alternative possibilities – a matter rarely considered, since it involves a massive counterfactual that not even the most ambitious exponent of the new cliometric history would undertake lightly. In practice professional inertia is likely to preclude any dramatic changes: most scientists are reformers, not radicals. Unfortunately both critics and defenders of the status quo too often base their assessments on personal experience and hearsay rather than reliable evidence, and there are underlying differences of professional values and standards, if not incommensurable paradigms.

Rather than elaborating on this subject by citing individual economists' views, which are hardly detached, it is more illuminating to turn to an impartial sociologist of science, Richard Whitley, who has reviewed modern economics from the standpoint of his ambitious comprehensive typology of the natural and social sciences. Whitley treats scientific fields as reputational systems of work organization and control in terms of specific key variables deriving from their individual histories and subject content. Against this background, Anglo-Saxon economics emerges as a unique case (Whitley 1984, 1986).[16]

As in physics, the theoretical core of economics dominates textbooks, training programmes, the communication system and academic posts and honours, but economics is distinct from other fields in that, unlike physics, there is a marked division between theoretical and empirical work. This is partly due to the lack of technical control over empirical work which limits the applied economist's dependence on the theorist (unlike the situation in physics), and also because of the existence of other audiences outside the theoretical establishment and the scientific or professional community. Competition by producers within the central core, although intense, is restricted to technical refinements and extensions of the analytical scheme to novel problems that can be tackled with existing techniques. The dominance of the established theoretical goals, and the degree of impersonality and formalization of coordination and control procedures, vary as between empirical specialisms because the relatively intractable and unpredictable nature of empirical phenomena restricts the extent to which systematic comparison and validation of task outcomes can be accomplished through the formal communication system. The heterogeneity of applied fields is limited by 'rigid delimination' of the types of problems deemed legitimate and important; on the other hand, deviations on the periphery can be largely ignored by the intellectual elite who control the dominant communications media and training programmes.

This analysis is compatible with many of the familiar complaints from those dissatisfied with the state of the discipline, especially the excessive emphasis on a high level of abstraction, mathematization and formalization in advanced training programmes (cf. Bauer and Walters 1975; Hutchison 1977; Blatt 1983; Morishima 1984; Grubel and Boland 1986; Woo 1986) and the irrelevance of much of this work to contemporary problems and especially policy issues. The fact that one major school of economists based in Chicago has endeavoured to extend its 'imperialistic' sway (Stigler 1984) by applying a standardized analysis to a whole range of problems formerly thought to lie outside the economist's domain merely confirms the arguments of those who complain of the tendency towards uniformity in the discipline.

There are, of course, other contending approaches within mainstream economics that challenge the Chicagoans' approach. But this does not necessarily reflect a happy state of affairs, as suggested by the distinguished ex-Chicago economist who reported, sadly:

> What generates in me a great deal of scepticism about the state of our discipline is the high positive correlation between the policy views of a researcher (or, what is worse, his thesis director) and his empirical findings. I will begin to believe in economics as a science when out of Yale there comes an empirical thesis demonstrating the supremacy of monetary policy in some historical episode – and out of Chicago, one demonstrating the supremacy of fiscal policy.
>
> (Patinkin 1972: 142, cited by Hutchison 1977: 61)

Another recent critic, also with strong earlier Chicago associations, has outspokenly protested at the exaggeration of internal divisions within the discipline:

> The typical economist, alas, is harshly if unreflectively dogmatic, demanding that students or colleagues be members in good standing of this or that church. Sales people for university textbooks in the United States complain that an economics professor simply will not look at a text that does not come from the right church: he asks, shamefully, is the book monetarist or neo-classical or Marxist or Keynesian? … the extent of real disagreement among economists … is in fact exaggerated … [this] makes all the more puzzling the venom they bring to minor disputes.
>
> (McCloskey 1985: 184)

What this discloses about the character of textbooks, the extent of disagreements among economists, and their values – professional or other – cannot be further explored here.

Continuing concern about the state of economics as a discipline and a profession has led to recent official investigations sponsored by the Royal Economic Society and the American Economic Association – inspired in the latter instance by a disturbing study of graduate training in elite departments (Colander and Klamer 1987, 1989). The British study is complete, and can be considered more briefly because the major findings appeared in the March 1990 issue of *The Economic Journal*. It is broader in scope than its American counterpart for it focuses on the stock, supply, demand and patterns of employment of British economists, as well as some characteristics of economics departments in British universities and polytechnics (Dolton and Makepeace 1990; Towse and Blaug 1990). To a historian, the surprising thing is that no previous study of this kind has been undertaken (but cf. Booth and Coats 1978), whereas studies of the market for economists, their salaries and employment opportunities have quite frequently appeared in the United States, usually in reports initiated by or papers presented to the American Economic Association at the annual meetings. American labour economists have often taken an interest in these matters.

Among the findings of the Towse-Blaug study, the most striking are the limited size of the total flow demand for economists and the prediction that it will decline in the foreseeable future. Despite the loss of university posts (especially professorships) since the 1981 university cuts there is apparently still an excess supply of professional economists, so that reports of the 'dire straits' of economics departments have been exaggerated. The spectacularly high salaries attached to certain posts in the City of London are untypical, and there has been no mass exodus of academic economists to that centre. Unlike the United States, many non-academic economists in the United Kingdom have only an undergraduate degree, often of a non-specialized kind, although the reporters firmly insist that 'there is no warrant whatever for thinking that an undergraduate course in economics is a vocational preparation for a world of work in which the graduate will normally be called upon to use his economic expertise' (Towse and Blaug 1990: 98). On the other hand there are conclusions that would certainly strike a responsive chord across the Atlantic. For example, 'the constant complaint of virtually every employer of professional economists that new recruits lack familiarity with data sources, and have never been taught national income accounting' (Towse and Blaug 1990: 98), and the view widely held both inside and outside higher education that 'economics degrees are too theoretical, too impractical, too unrelated to the possible uses of economics in business and government … [and that] teaching is indifferent to the actual pattern of employment of economics graduates' (Towse and Blaug 1990: 99).

Given the scale of the economics profession in the United States, the investigation conducted by the American Economic Association's Commission on Graduate Education in Economics is necessarily much larger than its British counterpart, although its terms of reference are narrower.[17] Of particular interest is the fact that the Commission has surveyed not only the six so-called elite departments but also other tiers of departments covering nine, fifteen, twenty and forty-two additional PhD programmes. No such systematic comparison has ever been undertaken previously.

Despite the loud and persistent chorus of complaints about the state of contemporary American economics, some of which have already been noted, and the general desire for changes in economics PhD programmes expressed by faculty, graduate students and recent PhDs in response to the survey, there was a large consensus in favour of the weights currently attached to various types of knowledge in the curriculum, according to which economic theory is given priority followed by econometrics, empirical economics, applications, institutions, history and literature. With respect to skills, it was generally acknowledged that the following were currently emphasized in PhD programmes, in descending order of importance: analytics, mathematics, critical judgement, applications, computation, creativity and communications. However, there was much less agreement that this was the way things should be. In agreement with many of the profession's public critics, it was felt that mathematics and computation were overrated and creativity was undervalued, and when recent PhDs were asked about the importance of various skills in their current jobs, whether in graduate economics programmes, business or government, they again ranked mathematics lower and communications skills and creativity higher than the weights assigned to them in current graduate teaching. Thus, as is probably the case in the United Kingdom, 'both faculty members and graduate students' sense that 'the mix of needed skills differs from the skills being developed in graduate training' (Hansen 1990). Departments offering PhD programmes tend to continue to appoint new recruits with much the same skills as already emphasized, rather than those more highly valued by prospective employers, but whether this is evidence of professional inertia or *faute de mieux* (the absence of suitable alternatives) is unclear. As Robert Solow argued in his comments, the results display more satisfaction with what is taught and the teacher's ability to teach it than what should be taught in a better, if not an ideal, world: 'If I knew how to teach creativity and critical judgment, I guess I would do it. I know how to recognize them [i.e. like pornography?], and can even offer examples, but that is very far from being able to teach them' (Hansen 1990: 448–50). On the whole, he felt, the survey results were 'predictably bland'.

Of course, by any standards the Commission's members constitute part of the profession's elite, so that radical proposals for change are hardly to be expected, especially given the strong practical sense that such ideas are hardly likely to be implemented. It is much too early to predict the outcome of this investigation, other than the Commission's recommendations, which will no doubt be vigorously discussed with a wide variety of reactions. The supplementary studies to appear later will undoubtedly add substantially to the accumulating, although uneven, body of data on the economics profession in the United States. And, in line with the opening paragraph of this chapter, we may conclude with the hope that other organizations and scholars will be encouraged to undertake serious research on the history, current condition and future prospects of the profession.

Notes

1 In their classic volume Carr Saunders and Wilson (1933: 2) observe that: 'An adequate study of the rise of one of the great professions with its roots deep in the past would be the work of a lifetime'.

2 Furner (1975) provides a valuable analysis of this issue in which the economists figure prominently. Unfortunately there is no comparable study for a more recent period, or for the United Kingdom.

3 Professional ideology can, of course, be defined narrowly, as in Joseph Schumpeter's pertinent distinction between the ideology of the mathematical mind and that of the mind allergic to mathematics (Schumpeter 1949: 351). This particular ideological divide is nowadays much more significant in economics than it was forty years ago, for mathematical competence is now virtually a precondition of entry into the economics profession and an indispensable weapon in the early stages of a career. This is serious, notwithstanding jocular references to the 'spiralling "arms race" ' in econometrics and the intergenerational 'balance of terror' between established incumbents and their technically sophisticated young colleagues (Wiles 1984: 292). From a huge relevant literature the following citations must suffice: Bauer and Walters (1975) and Woo (1986). There are valuable remarks on the professionalization-mathematization link in other disciplines in Whitley (1977, 1984).

4 Many such listings have been proposed. One multivariate analysis identified six elements and twenty-one subelements (Jenkins 1970: 59).

5 Some analysts regard the service or fiduciary ideal as a middle-class rationale reflecting the professionals' self-deception, rather than any deliberate effort to deceive the lay

public. Much of the literature vacillates between viewing professions as a broad educational and cultural stratum or as a distinctive species of occupational organization. Historically, the format is more applicable to the continental European so-called 'public' professions and the latter to the Anglo-American 'free' professions, although with the development of bureaucracy and the welfare state the distinction between them has become blurred.

6 The literature on professions and professionalism is vast, conflicting and sometimes even sensational. In a fascinating survey, a leading expert in the field, Walter Metzger, has coined the term 'professionism' to cover 'all systematic attempts to attribute historical trends – especially undesirable ones – to the rise of the professions or to the foibles of professionals' (Metzger 1987: 13). No doubt the economists too have suffered from the general decline of deference towards expertise.

7 There may indeed be some consolation in the Victorian dictum that a gentleman needs no code of ethics, whereas no such code will make a gentleman out of a crook!

8 Rhoads (1985) gives a perceptive political scientist's conception of the strengths and limitations of the professional economist's intellectual apparatus.

9 Commenting on the irrational elements in policy-making, a very experienced British ex-government economist remarked that 'the atmosphere of a large Government department is frequently almost indistinguishable from that of the loony bin. I use the term in no pejorative sense; it is simply one of the facts of official life' (Cairncross 1970). For fascinating and illuminating stories of American economists' experiences in government service see Allen (1977).

10 According to one scholarly historian of economics the Sophists were the first 'professional instructors' in the subject (Gordon 1975: 2, 15).

11 Broadly speaking professional organization preceded doctrinal consolidation in American economics, whereas the opposite was true in the United Kingdom.

12 The editor of *The Times*, which supported Chamberlain's proposals, poked fun at 'the spectacle of these fourteen dervishes emerging from their caves and chanting their venerable incantations against the rising tide of inquiry … the day has gone by when the professors of political economy can impose opinions upon the country by the weight of authority…. A more scientific conception of their own science, which pretends to be, but never is, an experimental science, would save the professors from the painful discovery that they convince nobody who stands in need of conviction' (*The Times*, 18 August 1903, cited by Coats 1964: 101). Coats (1968a) gives a more extended account.

13 There is a perceptive, and at times amusing, analysis of the Americanness of American economics in a neglected article by Johnson (1977b).

14 The critics include J. K. Galbraith, N. Georgescu-Roegen, H. G. Johnson, T. Koopmans and W. Leontief in the United States, and P. Bauer, P. Deane, F. Hahn, T. W. Hutchison, E. H. Phelps Brown, G. D. Worswick and A. A. Walters in the United Kingdom. For examples of the sociologically oriented critical literature see Leontief (1971, 1982), Ward (1972), Leijonhufvud (1973), Johnson (1977a, b), Stanfield (1979), Katouzian (1980), Canterbery and Burkhardt (1983), Earl (1983, 1988), Wiles (1984), Coats (1985), Burkhardt and Canterbery (1986) and Tarascio (1986).

15 From a large output the following items must suffice: Bronfenbrenner (1966), Siegfried (1972), Lovell (1973), Eagly (1974), Stigler (1982a, b) and Liebowitz and Palmer (1984).

16 According to Whitley the key variables in any scientific field are the degrees of functional and strategic mutual dependence among scientists and the degrees of technical and strategic task uncertainty.

17 I am most grateful to my colleagues Anne Krueger, the Commission's Chairman, and Lee Hansen, its Executive Director, for making available the unpublished preliminary report, and also the additional comments by Commission members Alan S. Blinder, Claudia Goldin and T. Paul Schultz, and by Robert Solow. The final report is now available in the *Journal of Economic Literature* (Hansen, forthcoming).

References

Allen, W. R. (1977) 'Economics, economists, and economic policy: modern American experiences', *History of Political Economy* 9: 48–88.

Bauer, P. T. and Walters, A. (1975) 'The state of economics', *Journal of Law and Economics* 8: 1–23.

Bell, D. and Kristol, I. (eds) (1981) *The Crisis in Economic Theory*, New York: Basic Books.

Blatt, J. (1983) 'How economists misuse mathematics', in A. S. Eichner (ed.) *Why Economics is Not Yet a Science*, pp. 166–86, Armonk, NY: M. E. Sharpe.

Booth, A. and Coats, A. W. (1978) 'The market for economists in Britain (1945-1970)', *Economic Journal* 88: 436–54.

Bronfenbrenner, M. (1966) 'Trends, cycles, and fads in economic writing', *American Economic Review* 56: 538–52.

Burkhardt, J. and Canterbery, E. R. (1986) 'The orthodoxy and legitimacy: toward a critical sociology of economics', in W. J. Samuels (ed.) *Research in the History and Methodology of Economics 4:* 229–50.

Cairncross, A. K. (1970) 'Writing the history of recent economic policy', unpublished, quoted by permission.

Canterbery, E. R. and Burkhardt, J. (1983) 'What do we mean by asking whether economics is a science?', in A. S. Eichner (ed.) *Why Economics is Not Yet a Science*, pp. 15–40, Armonk, NY: M. E. Sharpe.

Carr Saunders, A. M. and Wilson, P. A. (1933 *The Professions*, Oxford: Clarendon Press.

Coats, A. W. (1960) 'The first two decades of the American Economic Association', *American Economic Review* 50: 555–74.

——. (1964) 'The role of authority in the development of British economics', *Journal of Law and Economics* 7: 85–106.

——. (1968a) 'Political economy and the tariff reform campaign of 1903', *Journal of Law and Economics* 11: 181–229.

——. (1968b) 'The origins and early development of the Royal Economic Society', *Economic Journal* 78: 349–71.

——. (1976) 'The development of the agricultural economics profession in England', *Journal of Agricultural Economics* 27: 1–11.

——. (1977) 'The current crisis in economics in historical perspective', *Nebraska Journal of Economics and Business* 16: 3–16.

——. (1980) 'The culture and the economists: American-British differences', *History of Political Economy* 10: 298–314.

——. (ed.) (1981) *Economists in Government: An International Comparative Study*, Durham, NC: Duke University Press.

——. (1985) 'The American Economic Association and the economics profession', *Journal of Economic Literature* 23: 1697–727.

——. (ed.) (1986 *Economists in International Agencies. An Exploratory Study*, New York: Praeger.

Colander, D. C. and Klamer, A. (1987) 'The making of an economist', *Journal of Economic Perspectives* 1: 95–111.

——. and ——. (1989) *The Making of an Economist*, Boulder, CO: Westview Press.

Dolton, P. J. and Makepeace, G. H. (1990) 'The earnings of economics graduates', *Economic Journal* 100: 237–50.

Eagly, R. V. (1974) 'Contemporary profile of conventional economists', *History of Political Economy* 6: 76–91.

Earl, P. E. (1983) 'A behavioral theory of economists' behavior', in A. S. Eichner (ed.) *Why Economics is Not Yet a Science*, pp. 90–125, Armonk, NY: M. E. Sharpe.
——. (1988) 'On being a psychological economist and winning the games economists play', in P. E. Earl (ed.) *Psychological Economics. Development, Tensions Prospects*, pp. 227–42, Boston, MA: Kluwer.
Furner, M. O. (1975) *Advocacy and Objectivity: A Crisis in the Professionalization of American Social Science 1865–1905*, Lexington, KY: University of Kentucky Press.
Galbraith, J. K. (1973) 'Power and the useful economist', *American Economic Review* 63: 1–11.
Goode, W. (1960) 'Encroachment, charlatanism, and the emerging professions: psychology, sociology, medicine', *American Sociological Review* 25: 902–14.
Gordon, B. S. (1975 *Economic Analysis Before Adam Smith. Hesiod to Lessius*, London: Macmillan.
Grubel, H. G. and Boland, L. A. (1986) 'On the efficient role of mathematics in economies: some theory, facts and results of an opinion survey', *Kyklos* 39: 419–42.
Hansen, W. L. (1990) 'Educating and training new economics Ph.D.'s: how good a job are we doing?', Commission on Graduate Education in Economics, Preliminary Report, *American Economic Review, Papers and Proceedings* 80: 431–50.
——. (forthcoming) 'The education and training of economics doctorates: major findings of the American Economic Association's Commission on Graduate Education in Economics (report and tables), Madison, WI, January 1991', *Journal of Economic Literature*, to be published.
Heller, W. W. (1975) 'What's right with economics?', *American Economic Review* 65: 1–26.
Herman, E. S. (1982) 'The institutionalization of bias in economics', *Media, Culture and Society* 4: 275–91.
Hutchison, T. W. (1964) *Positive Economics and 'Policy' Objectives*, London: Allen & Unwin.
——. (1977) *Knowledge and Ignorance in Economics*, Oxford: Basil Blackwell.
Jenkins, H. G. (1970) 'Professional organizations', in J. A. Jackson (ed.) *Professions and Professionalization*, pp. 53–107, Cambridge: Cambridge University Press.
Johnson, H. G. (1973) 'National styles in economic research: the United States, the United Kingdom, Canada, and various European countries', *Daedalus* 102: 65–74. Reprinted in Johnson, H. G., *On Economics and Society*, Chicago, IL: University of Chicago Press, 1975.
——. (1977a) 'Methodologies of economics', in M. Perlman (ed.) *The Organization and Retrieval of Economic Knowledge*, pp. 496–509, Boulder, CO: Westview Press.
——. (1977b) 'The American tradition in economics', *Nebraska Journal of Economics and Business* 16: 17–26.
Johnson, T. J. (1972) *Professions and Power*, London: Macmillan.
Katouzian, H. (1980) *Ideology and Method in Economics*, London: Macmillan.
Larson, M. S. (1978) *The Rise of Professionalism: A Sociological Analysis*, Berkeley, CA: University of California Press.
Leijonhufvud, A. (1973) 'Life among the Econ', *Western Economic Journal* 11: 327–37.
Leontief, W. (1971) 'Theoretical assumptions and non-observed facts', *American Economic Review* 71: 1–17.
——. (1982) 'Academic economics', *Science* 217: 104–5. Reprinted in Eichner, A. S. (ed.) *Why Economics is Not Yet a Science*, pp. vi–xi, Armonk, NY: M. E. Sharpe, 1983.
Liebowitz, S. J. and Palmer, J. P. (1984) 'Assessing the relative impacts of economic journals', *Journal of Economic Literature* 22: 77–88.

Lovell, M. C. (1973) 'The production of economic literature: an interpretation', *Journal of Economic Literature* 11: 27–55.

McCloskey, D. (1985) *The Rhetoric of Economics*, Madison, WI: University of Wisconsin Press.

McDean, H. C. (1983) 'Professionalism, policy, and farm economists in the early Bureau of Agricultural Economics', *Agricultural History* 37: 64–82, 83–9.

Maloney, J. (1985 *Marshall, Orthodoxy and the Professionalization of Economics*, Cambridge: Cambridge University Press.

Metzger, W. P. (1987) 'A spectre is haunting American scholars: the spectre of "profes-sionism"', *Educational Researcher* 16: 10–19.

Mill, J. (1824) 'War expenditure', *Westminster Review 2:* 45.

Morishima, M. (1984) 'The good and bad uses of mathematics', in P. Wiles and G. Routh (eds) *Economics in Disarray*, pp. 51–77, Oxford: Basil Blackwell.

Nelson, R. H. (1987) 'The economics profession and the making of public policy', *Journal of Economic Literature* 25: 49–91.

O'Brien, D. (1965) 'The transition in Torrens' monetary thought', *Economica (N.S).* 32: 269–301.

Parsons, T. (1968) 'Professions', in D. Sills (ed.) *The International Encyclopedia of the Social Sciences*, vol. 12, pp. 536–47, New York: Macmillan.

Patinkin, D. (1972) 'Keynesian monetary theory and the Cambridge School', *Banca Nationale del Lavoro Quarterly Review* 25: 138–58.

Pechman, J. A. (1989) *The Role of the Economist in Government: An International Perspective*, Washington, DC: Brookings Institution.

Rhoads, S. E. (1985) *The Economist's View of the World. Government, Markets, and Public Policy*, Cambridge: Cambridge University Press.

Schumpeter, J. (1949) 'Science and ideology', *American Economic Review* 39: 345–59.

Siegfried, J. J. (1972) 'The publishing of economic papers and its impact on graduate faculty ratings, 1960–1969', *Journal of Economic Literature* 10: 31–49.

Stanfield, R. J. (1979) 'The social structure of the economics community', in R. J. Stanfield, *Economic Thought and Social Change*, Carbondale, IL: Southern Illinois University Press.

Stigler, G. J. (1967) 'The Foundations and economics', in W. Weaver (ed.) *U. S. Philanthropic Foundations, Their History, Structure, Management and Record*, pp. 276–86, New York: Harper.

——. (1984) 'Economics: the imperial science?', *Scandinavian Journal of Economics* 86: 301–13.

Stigler, G. J. and Friedland, C. (1982a) 'The pattern of citation practices in economics', in G. J. Stigler (ed.) *The Economist as Preacher and Other Essays*, pp. 173–91, Chicago, IL: University of Chicago Press.

——. and ——. (1982b) 'The citation practices of doctorates in economics', in G. J. Stigler (ed.) *The Economist as Preacher and Other Essays*, pp. 192–222, Chicago, IL: University of Chicago Press.

Tarascio, V. J. (1986) 'The crisis in economic theory: a sociological perspective', in W. J. Samuels (ed.) *Research in the History of Economic Thought and Methodology* 4: 283–95.

Torrens, R. (1826) Letter to Wilmot Horton, 7 November.

Towse, R. and Blaug, M. (1988) *The Current State of the British Economics Profession*, London: Royal Economic Society.

——. and ——. (1990) 'The current state of the British economics profession', *Economic Journal* 100: 227–36.

Ward, B. (1972) *What's Wrong With Economics?*, London: Macmillan.
——. (1979 *The Ideal Worlds of Economics. Liberal, Radical, and Conservative Economic World Views*, New York: Basic Books.
Whitley, R. (1977) 'Changes in the social and intellectual organization of the sciences: professionalization and the arithmetic ideal', in E. Mendelsohn, P. Weingart and R. Whitley (eds) *The Social Production of Scientific Knowledge*, pp. 143–69, Dordrecht: Reidel.
——. (1984 *The Intellectual and Social Organization of the Sciences*, Oxford: Clarendon Press.
——. (1986) 'The structure and context of economics as a scientific field', in W. J. Samuels (ed.) *Research in the History of Economic Thought and Methodology* 4: 179–209.
Wiles, P. (1984) 'Epilogue: the role of theory', in P. Wiles and G. Routh (eds) *Economics in Disarray*, pp. 293–325, Oxford: Basil Blackwell.
Woo, H. K. H. (1986) *What's Wrong With Formalization – in Economics? – An Epistemological Critique*, Newark, CA: Victoria Press.

27 The past, present and future of economics

Preamble

The title of this lecture is intentionally sweeping, over-ambitious, and, I hope, provocative. Few, if any, individuals are qualified to provide an authoritative general survey and evaluation of late twentieth century economics[1] and I certainly am not one of them. The discipline is far too large, complex, fragmented, changing and, in many of its branches, sophisticated and technically difficult. Fortunately, however, one need not aim that high.

From time to time most historians of economics are tempted to stand back from their reading and research and consider where the discipline has come from, how it has developed, what is its present condition, and where is it headed. In this lecture I shall venture to make my general reflections public.

Contemplating the future is, of course, the most dubious part of this exercise. As the great American baseball catcher, Yogi Berra, once observed: "Prediction is difficult; predicting the future is especially difficult," and most historians wisely avoid that uncharted terrain. Nevertheless, in this instance I am emboldened by the number of predictions recently offered by a series of leading economists largely inspired by the centenary of the Royal Economic Society.[2] So, if my prognostications are wildly inaccurate I may, at least, be in good company.

Needless to say, knowledge of history, however comprehensive and profound, is no substitute for omniscience and perfect foresight; and with a huge subject such as this, the subjectivity inherent in all historical selection and interpretation is more patently obvious than when dealing with more modest and conventional topics. On the other hand, the degrees of freedom are correspondingly greater; and I am prepared to accept the risks involved – especially as I am on a fleeting visit to an unfamiliar region, and can expect to make a safe getaway well before the dust has settled!

Whatever limited qualifications I may have for this venture stem from my career-long interest in the history, methodology, sociology, and professionalization of economics, particularly with reference to the United States and Britain. I have also looked beyond those countries in organizing international comparative studies of the role of economists in national government, and in international agencies[3] and I am currently engaged in organizing a large-scale comparative study of the post-1945 global internationalization (Americanization?) of economics.

As an economic historian, I have necessarily been an outside observer and commentator, rather than a practicing professional economist – an economist-watcher, somewhat akin to a bird watcher. One can be a bird watcher without being a bird, though the perspective is obviously different! In doctrinal terms, I have never been fully committed to either the orthodox classical/neoclassical tradition or any of the leading dissenting schools of thought. But the changing relationships among these various intellectual currents, both in the past two decades or so, and in prospect, strike me as especially fascinating, even portentous. At this point, however, I wish to make a brief introductory general comment on the development of economics as an intellectual discipline over the past two centuries or so.

A brief historical conspectus

One of the most striking features of the history of economics is the continuity of its central core – the theory of economic equilibrium via the market mechanism[4] – which has survived virtually intact from the mid-eighteenth century to the present. Of course this theory has undergone innumerable modifications, reformulations, elaborations, and extensions over the decades, changes which cannot be described here. Some years ago, when 'growth of knowledge' theories were fashionable among historians and philosophers of science, many attempts were made to identify Kuhnian-type revolutions in economics, of which the so-called marginal and Keynesian revolutions were the leading candidates. Though frequently instructive, these efforts were ultimately unsatisfactory – which is hardly surprising, given the difficulties of defining and indentifying paradigm changes in any discipline. Certainly, none of the supposedly revolutionary episodes in economics could be shown to entail a clear break with the past, though the Keynesian revolution undoubtedly seemed dramatic to many who lived through it, especially Keynes's younger disciples. Even so, after long and tortuous discussions and reinterpretations there is still no general consensus as to the precise nature and significance of the *General Theory*. How far this continued dissensus is ideological rather than scientific is a matter for further debate.

Continuities and discontinuities are the very stuff of history, and it would indeed be strange if they failed to attract the historian's attention. Yet there is another enduring element in the history of economics that has not, in my view, received the attention it deserves, namely, the persistence of a dissenting tradition (or perhaps traditions) alongside the mainstream which can be traced right back to the early nineteenth century. This comprises a heterogeneous cast of characters, some of them totally ignorant of or unreasonably hostile to classical or neoclassical ideas, whereas others have advanced penetrating criticisms of the received doctrines that have still not yet been satisfactorily answered. Despite the vigourous, effective, ingenious, and sometimes brutal arguments and tactics employed by defenders of the orthodox tradition, dissent, heresy and heterodoxy continue to thrive.[5] And one of my principal claims is that in some respects these ideas seem more potent and threatening now than at any previous time.

Of course the defenders are wont to assert that if there had been a superior alternative theory, approach, paradigm, or body of doctrine, it would already have displaced the established tradition. However, matters are not so simple in the history of ideas. Recent work in the history, philosophy, and sociology of science emphasizes the difficulties of falsification and demonstrates that crucial experiments, radical breakthroughs, and clear-cut paradigm shifts rarely occur, especially in the social sciences. And if they did, it would be a considerable time before their significance was fully recognized. The "principle of tenacity" that protects inherited intellectual capital works very effectively.

There are, indeed, many reasons why the critics of mainstream economics have not been, and perhaps cannot be silenced or exorcised.[6] Not least is the fact that many of their arguments are correct, and unanswerable. One category of reasons for the remarkable durability of the established tradition is sociological, rather than intellectual, especially in more recent decades as the discipline has become more tightly organized. Challengers have to confront not only a long-established body of ideas, but also a hierarchical disciplinary and professional power structure of the kind that exists in most developed sciences or intellectual fields. Methods of economic education and training have become relatively standardized, serving to perpetuate the ruling beliefs and practices in the subject. There are controls over entry, publication outlets, access to research resources, and the reward structure. There is, in short, a well entrenched professional ideology and value system.

This does not mean that under present conditions all innovation is stifled, or all dissent suppressed. It does, however, mean that creativity tends to be channeled in certain approved directions, and that there are serious obstacles to the emergence and spread of any radically new research programme. Also, that if the ruling doctrines and the underlying theory and methods are seriously challenged and undermined, they will not quickly succumb. Too much "sunk" intellectual capital has been invested; the "Kuhnian losses" involved would be too great; the existing "reputational system" is too strong;[7] and the prevailing pedagogical practices powerfully reinforce the *status quo*.

The present situation

For the purposes of this lecture I shall define 'the present' arbitrarily, as beginning in the later 1960s and early 1970s, the first period marked by widespread discussion of a so-called "crisis" in economics. Before that time during the so-called Keynesian hegemony, the economics profession enjoyed a phase of rare consensus and confidence. Of course there were dissenting voices; and as Peter Hall and his collaborators have demonstrated, the acceptance of Keynesian economics was far from complete even in the advanced industrial non-communist countries.[8] Nevertheless, as fears of a post war slump faded in the 1940s and early 1950s, many economists displayed what now appears as a naive and unwarranted faith in the efficacy of their professional ideas and equipment, and concomitant confidence in the efficacy of economic management in the modernized economies and economic planning in the underdeveloped countries. Sad to relate, the situation is very different now. One of the most experienced and wisest of British post war economists, Sir Alec Cairncross, probably exaggerated when he remarked recently that:

> belief in the magical touch with which the [economics] profession was credited in the days of full employment and the glory that was Keynes, has long departed, and no one [now] pays much attention to what economics has to say.[9]

Nevertheless, a statement of that kind by a leading economist would have unthinkable, or at least highly eccentric, in the early or mid 1960s.

The crisis in economics, which, arguably, has still not been resolved, was a complex phenomenon involving a combination of theoretical, empirical, policy and sociological issues, resulting from an interaction of internal and external pressures.[10] From an historical standpoint, the most remarkable feature was the collective loss of professional self-confidence manifested most clearly in the volume of public breast-beating by a number of leading economists with impeccable credentials, few of whom were usually noted for their dissenting opinions. Among the most common complaints – few of them novel; most of them still to be heard – were: the overdevelopment of formal mathematical theorizing; the preoccupation with technique; the irrelevance of much theoretical research; the lack of interest in and low prestige of empirical research; the weakness of the discipline's empirical foundations; the prevalence of training that was actively unhelpful in preparing graduates for non-academic work (notwithstanding the increasing employment of economists in business, banking, local, regional and national governments, international agencies, private foundations and para-statal organizations, etc.); and a perverse reward system that perpetuates the *status quo*.[11]

Prospects for change

Against this background, and making due allowance for intellectual and professional inertia, is there any reason to think that matters are any different now than twenty years ago; or that the situation is likely to change in the forseeable future?

These are two interrelated, but entirely distinct questions, and it is obviously more hazardous to predict than to assess the significance of recent changes. I shall therefore concentrate on the latter, while acknowledging the unavoidable subjective judgments involved.

First, it would be unlikely, and indeed, deeply depressing, if twenty years of penetrating and informed (and, of course, also much uninformed) criticism and self-examination had left absolutely no trace on the subject. Admittedly, during the initial crisis phase there was some exaggeration of the discipline's plight, doubtless an over-reaction against the unwarranted claims and professional hubris of the pre-crisis era. Yet the fallout proved lasting. In doctrinal terms, monetarism emerged as a serious counterrevolution against the dominant Keynesianism: and this was but one of a number of intellectual challenges, most of them with long historical antecedents, such as neo-Austrianism, Marxism, radical economies, and institutionalism. Also there soon appeared various novel variants on Keynesianism, or the economics of Keynes. Significantly enough, all these bodies of ideas still have their adherents, usually equipped with their own publications and periodic conferences. This is one consequence of the sheer growth of the number of economists. which makes it easier to assemble a critical minimum group with shared, interests, grievances and perhaps even goals.

In policy terms, there was a conspicuous loss of faith in Keynesian-type measures, especially for dealing with the problem of stagflation. More generally, inflation quite rapidly replaced full employment and economic growth as the primary policy problem. (In 1994 we may, incidentally, be seeing the beginnings of a reverse shift of policy priorities in the forseeable future). How far the profession led rather than followed political and public opinion and historical events on these matters is debatable. But the combination of doctrinal and policy changes contributed to enhance the profession's awareness of the limits of its science, a desideratum strongly and repeatedly urged by some commentators – for example the distinguished methodologist and historian of economics, Terence Hutchison.[12] To him, it was as much a matter of professional ethics, as of scientific humility or realism.

Reference to science and methodology leads directly to my second point, the remarkable transformation in the treatment of the philosophy of economics which has occurred during the past two or three decades, associated with the writings of Popper, Kuhn, Lakatos, Feyerabend, Laudan, and others. Admittedly it is debatable how far this literature percolates down to the average practicing economist, for most economist, profess indifference or hostility to the discussion of these fundamentals. Nevertheless, the transformation in the post-positivist philosophy of science, which of course extends well beyond economics, has gone far towards undermining the earlier complacent image of the economist as an objective, neutral and detached expert working in the hardest of the so-called 'soft' sciences. Controversies over deductivism, empiricism, falsificationism, instrumentalism, 'revolutionary' as against 'normal' science, not to mention such exotic ideas as rhetoric, discourse, deconstruction, structuralism, and constructivism, appear with increasing frequency and intensity in economic journals and books.[13] To dismiss this as merely froth on the discipline's surface would be a mistake for it is a symptom of an underlying malaise, and, as such, it is compatible with the doctrinal and policy disagreements mentioned earlier. All three constitute evidence of a loss of scientific and professional confidence.

Thirdly, in recent years there have been a wide variety of important innovative efforts to strengthen the central corpus of equilibrium theory in at least three distinct but interrelated ways:

1. by incorporating such complex but inescapable features of economic life as uncertainty, expectations, imperfect information, and the limits to human ability to make rational calculations;[14]

2. by breaking away from conventional static analysis and developing various types of nonlinear dynamics, incorporating path dependency, 'real' historical time and irreversible processes, evolutionary change, and chaos;[15] and
3. by breaking down the barriers between economics and its neighbor disciplines – e.g., by developing links or 'interfaces' with psychology, politics, ethics, sociology, anthropology, biology, etc.[16] This does not simply mean what has become known as economic imperialism – i.e., the direct and uncritical application of standard neoclassical economic analysis to subjects conventionally regarded as noneconomic, on the grounds that economics is the only truly scientific social science and therefore should presumably swallow up all the others![17]

Economic imperialism has been most vigorously applied – carried to extremes, some critics would aver – by the recently en-Nobeled Chicago economist, Gary Becker. Becker's work is undoubtedly ingenious, and the source of some intriguing conclusions – and some amusing extensions too, for example an article (not by Becker) on the economics of brushing teeth! But in my view it is of little constructive value as compared with genuinely comparative research, which is much more time-consuming and much less misleading, especially when the Chicagoan approach is glibly and ignorantly applied to remote historical periods or non-Western cultures. As Daniel Hausman has warned in his recent valuable survey of economic methodology, theorizing without due respect for evidence is inherently dangerous. This may be an old fashioned view; yet the problem of evidence is seldom treated seriously, if at all, by economic methodologists, despite the innumerable complaints from orthodox and heterdox economists alike, that economists generally display a profound disrespect for 'facts'.[18]

This is but one example of what contemporary economists can learn from historians, for it has been aptly said that whereas historians tend to complain that a work is under-researched, not that it is under-analyzed, with economists the relationship is usually reversed. Historians tend to adopt an eclectic, pragmatic approach to problem-solving, pursuing their enquiries wherever they lead with little concern for disciplinary boundaries or the methods deemed 'proper' to a specific field.

Economics is nowadays in the process of being transformed from a 'separate' science – as John Stuart Mill and Daniel Hausman have depicted it – into a more interdisciplinary one. How far this process will go is by no means clear. It seems unlikely that a new Kuhnian type of paradigm change will lead to the displacement of neoclassical economics; but there is a distinct possibility that the orthodox tradition will atrophy, and be left behind as economics disintegrates into an increasing number of specialized compartments, and its more creative and lively practitioners reach out to other disciplines for the solution of problems incapable of being handled with the conventional economist's ideas and techniques.

At the present time a number of non-orthodox approaches are flourishing as never before, such as institutionalism (both "old" and "new"),[19] evolutionary economics (especially the Schumpeterian variety),[20] game theory (which is undermining the orthodox conception of rationality), public choice theory (or the "new political economy"),[21] and socio-economics.[22] All these movements represent efforts to break out the restrictive confines of mainstream neoclassical economics. Each has its band of adherents, usually international in scope, and organized conferences, associations, journals, and other publications, many of which are devoted to surveys of recent work and estimates (usually glowing) of future prospects.

It is obviously impossible for me to review and evaluate all these various streams of thought owing to limitations of time and knowledge. I shall therefore confine myself to a brief account of the relations between economics and psychology (or what has become known as behavioral economics), for this not only illustrates what the distinguished anthropologist, Clifford Geertz, has called "the blurring of genres"; it also represents a trend directly contrary to the elementary assumptions about economic motivation enshrined in the classical and neoclassical economic literature.

The antecedents of behavioral economics can be traced back at least to the attacks on the early nineteenth century classical economists' concept of economic man as primarily motivated by self interest (notwithstanding Adam Smith's emphasis on the role of sympathy in his *Theory of Moral Sentiments* 1759). In one form or another these attacks were repeated and elaborated in the next century or so, especially by the German Historical School and the American Institutionalists, but also by various critics of Benthamite hedonistic psychology. Efforts to incorporate developments in instinct or behaviorist psychology into economics proved unsuccessful, and by the 1930s the remnants of utilitarianism had been largely exorcised and a depsychologised economic theory based on the logic of choice became dominant.

However the intellectual situation is very different now. Recent writings on economic methodology emphasize the need for:

a) more "realistic" assumptions compatible with observed behavior, and consistent with the findings of other disciplines including psychology.
b) a shift of focus away from general abstract theories towards more specific, low- or middle- level empirically-grounded theories which may be testable.
c) more systematic research, as a basis for sound empirical generalizations.
d) more dynamic theories, incorporating changes in incomes, tastes, expectations, new commodities, etc.
e) a broadening of the scope of economic theory to take account of such influences on economic behavior as habit, custom, social emulation, advertising, etc., and
f) studies of the influence of market and non-market forces on economic and social welfare.

The development of the interrelations between economics and psychology are directly relevant to all the items in this list, and recent research in the field striking illustrates the exciting possibilities of two-way interpenetration and mutual learning – by economists working on psychological problems, and vice versa.[23] The problem of preference reversals,[24] which goes to the very heart of the neoclassical economist's basic analysis, perfectly exemplifies the limitations of the conventional microeconomic concept of rationality. Despite various efforts to explain it away, or to deny its significance, it is perhaps the most striking example of the potential longterm implications of research in behavioral economics.

The substantial centenary symposium in the *Economic Journal* cited at the beginning of this lecture contains a wealth of impressions of the current state of economics and its long term prospects. It is impossible to summarize the results in a few words, but it is sufficient to say that they are broadly compatible with the list of needs provided earlier. Many of the criticisms of neo-classical economics made during the crisis period referred to earlier[25] are still to be heard, sometimes from Nobel prizewinners as well as less eminent economists.

Economics may be disintegrating into an increasing number of partially segregated compartments, but it is unlikely to disappear in the forseeable future. Given the power of professional inertia, as revealed in recent lively discussions of the education of economists, it will not be easy to reform the *status quo* radically.

Notes

1 It is noteworthy how many of the official commentators on the achievements of winners of nobel prizes in economics admit their lack of competence to evaluate all aspects of a given laureate's work.
2 My scholarly disinclination to speculate about the future has been offset by the recent essays in the *Economic Journal's* symposium on the next century in economics (Vol. 101, January 1991 pp. 1–155), and the collection edited by Horst Hanusch and Horst Claus Recktenwald, *Ökonomische Wissenschaft in der Zukunft. Ansichten führender Ökonomen* (Dusseldorf: Verlag Wirtschaft and Finanzen Gmbh, 1992).
3 A. W. Coats, ed., *Economists in Government*. An International Comparative Study (Durham, NC: Duke University Press, 1981): also in History of Political Economy, Vol. 13 (Fall 1981): *Economist in International Agencies*. An Exploratory Study (New York: Praeger Special Studies, 1986).
4 Of course this core concept can be expressed in various ways. For example, underlying equilibrium theory are philosophical ideas such as: natural law. "*the* invisible hand," the harmony of interests and the emergence of a spontaneous social order as a result of the unplanned and unintended consequences of individual actions.
5 For a stimulating but controversial review of these concepts see "The Underworld of Economics: Heresy and Heterodoxy in Economic Thought," by Meghand Desai, in G.K. Shaw ed., *Economics, Culture and Education, Essays in Honour of Mark Blaug* (Aldershot: Edward Elgar 1991) pp. 53–63.
6 For a fascinating general discussion of the protection of belief, i.e., the defense mechanisms employed, consciously or unconsciously, by defenders of orthodoxy, see Eduardo Giannetti Da Fonseca. *Beliefs* in *Action. Economic philosophy and social change.* (Cambridge: Cambridge University Press. 1991) Chapter 13. Most of Part II of the volume is relevant.
7 The concept of a reputational system is developed in Richard Whitley. *The Intellectual and Social Organization of the Sciences* (Oxford: Oxford University Press, 1984).
8 Peter Hall, *The Political Power of Economic Ideas. Keynesianism Across Nations* (Princeton: Princeton University Press, 1989).
9 "In Praise of Economic History." *Economic History Review* Vol. 42 (1989) p. 178.
10 See, for example my essay, "The Current 'Crisis' in Economics in Historical Perspective," originally published in the *Nebraska Journal of Economics and Business* (Summer 1977), and reprinted in A. W. Bob Coats. *On the History of Economic*

Thought. British and American Economic Essays. Vol. 1 (London: Routledge, 1992) pp. 459–471.

11 Ibid, p. 464, where some of the authours of these and other complaints are identified.

12 For example, in his *Economists and Economic Policy in Britain,* 1946–1966 (London: Allen and Unwin, 1968); *Knowledge and Ignorance in Economics,* (Blackwell, 1977); *On Revolutions and Progress in Economic Knowledge* (Cambridge: Cambridge University Press, 1978); *Changing Aims of Economics* (Oxford: Blackwell, 1992).

13 It has been estimated that more than fifty books on economic methodology were published in English between 1970 and 1990. Heaven knows how many journal articles! Cf. Deborah Redman, *Economics and the Philosophy of Science*, (New York: Oxford University Press, 1991) p. 91. In addition to Redman's useful but incomplete survey see also the review article by Bill Gerrard. "On Matters Methodological in Economics," *Journal of Economic Surveys*. Vol. 4 (1990) pp. 197–219. The flow of publications in this field continues unabated, and a new *Journal of Economic Methodology* has just been launched.

14 The problem of rationality is fundamental and has been the subject of an immense and complex literature that cannot be listed or discussed here. However, it is directly linked to the expanding field of behavioral economics which is briefly considered later.

15 As an economic historian I have a special interest in these matters from a non-technical standpoint. See, for example, my "Explanations in History and Economics," *Social Research*, Vol. 56 (Summer 1989) pp. 331–360: and my unpublished paper: "Autopoiesis, Dissipative Structures, and Historical Processes in Economics," and the sources cited therein. The term autopoiesis mean self-production or self organization. For a recent discussion of the relevance of this idea to economic see John Foster, "Economics and the Self-Organization Approach: Alfred Marshall Revisited," *Economic Journal,* Vol. 103 (July 1993) pp. 975–991.

A profoundly influential book by a non-economist is Ilya Prigogine and Isabelle Stengers, *Order Out of Chaos, Man's New Dialogue with Nature* (Toronto: Bantam, 1984). A powerful critique of economists' preliminary efforts to treat chaos as a minor variant of conventional problems of economic dynamic is Philip Mirowski's "From Mandelbrot to Chaos in Economic Theory," *Southern Economic Journal* Vol. 57 (October 1990) pp. 289–307. A crucial question is whether non-linear dynamic systems with irreversible processes and human learning capacities can be treated in statistical terms.

16 For a useful recent survey of some of the possibilities see Ulf Himmelstrand ed., *Interfaces in Economic and Social Analysis* (London and New York: Routledge, 1992).

17 See, for example, George J. Stigler, "Economics – the Imperial Science?", *Scandinavian Journal of Economics,* Vol 86 (1984) pp. 3101–13; and the essays in Peter Bernholz and Gerard Radnitizky eds., *Economic Imperialism: The Economic Approach Applied Outside the field of Economics,* (New York: Paragon House, 1987).

18 Daniel Hausman, *The Inexact and Separate Science of Economics,* (Cambridge: Cambridge University Press, 1992).

For a discussion of these matters see my "Explanations in History and Economics," op.cit..

19 For a balanced survey of this literature see Malcolm Rutherford: *Institutions in Economics. The Old and the New Institutionalism,* Cambridge University Press).

20 In addition to a series of recent books and articles on Schumpeter's life and work there is now a Schumpeter society and a new Journal of Evolutionary Economics, reflecting a Schumpeterian approach. See also Lars Magnusson, *Evolutionary and Neo Schumpeterian Approaches to Economics* (Boston, Dordrecht, London: Kluwer, 1993).

21 For a survey of work reflecting this approach, which is especially associated with the ideas of James M. Buchanan, see Dennis Mueller ed., *Public Choice* II (Cambridge: Cambridge University Press, 1989).

22 Socio-economics (or social economics) has a long and somewhat chequered history. For recent attempts to survey the field see: Mark A. Lutz, *Social Economics,* (Boston, Dordrecht, London: Kluwer, 1989); also Neva R. Goodwin, *Social Economics*: An *Alternative Theory*. Vol. 1 *Building Anew on Marshall's Principles* (London: Macmillan, 1991).

23 For an account of this process see my: "Economics and Psychology: the Death and Resurrection of a Research Programme," in Spiro Latsis ed., *Method and Appraisal in Economics* (Cambridge: Cambridge University Press, 1976) pp. 43–64. The account is further developed in my "Economics and Psychology: A Resurrection Story" in Peter E. Earl ed., *Psychological Economics: Development, Tensions, Prospects* (Boston/Dordrecht: Kluwer, 1987) pp. 211–225.

24 The best single introduction to recent research in these fields is Peter E. Earl, "Economics and Psychology: A Survey," *Economic Journal* Vol. 100 (September 1990) pp. 718–55. See also his collection of articles, *Behavioral Economics* 2 Vols. (Aldershot: Edward Elgar, 1988).

25 There is a valuable discussion of the nature and significance of this issue in Hausman op.cit. Chapter 13.

28 Fusfeld and economic methodology

In the present era of excessive intellectual specialization, Dan Fusfeld stands out as an unusually versatile, wide-ranging and erudite economist. His work cannot be neatly compartmentalized, for an incomplete list of his writings and interests includes: the history of economic ideas and policy, economic history (from primitive societies to the modern corporation), labor economics, urban problems, race and the ghetto, and economics education. Like his successful introductory textbook, *Economics* (1972, 1976),[1] his research publications reveal his strong sense of values, and his conception of economics as a normative discipline with a distinctive ideological background and clear policy implications. Never just a cloistered academic, Fusfeld has participated actively in public affairs at the national, state and local levels; and he is an old-fashioned economist in the best sense of that term, since he regards his subject as a means to the improvement of the human condition, rather than simply a 'good game', to cite John Hicks's expression (1979: viii). In this respect, he is at odds with the main thrust of contemporary academic economics.[2]

Judging by his own fourfold classification of radical economists, Fusfeld is first and foremost an intellectual and secondarily an activist; he is neither a lifestyle nor a utopian radical (Fusfeld 1973). And as a persistent and penetrating but undoctrinaire critic of economic orthodoxy and contemporary society he is centrally located in that amorphous and ill-defined but vigorous movement known as American institutionalism. His election as president of the Association for Evolutionary Economics in 1971 testifies to his standing in that community.

Given his broad intellectual predilections, it is hardly surprising that Fusfeld cannot be regarded as a specialist in economic methodology – a subdiscipline latterly so vigorous and so narcissistic as to be virtually self-sustaining. Yet, although he is not usually regarded as a methodologist, Fusfeld was the inaugural chairman (from 1989) of the newly founded and now flourishing International Network for Economic Method. In a short paper published in *Methodus*, the network's bulletin, he linked 'Economics, Science and Society' in a manner explaining why he could not contemplate treating methodology (and perhaps anything else!) in splendid isolation (1990b). A few brief passages will make the point:

> We cannot achieve a pure science independent of the social order and the preferences of the scholar [or, for that matter, the scholarly/ scientific community]. (ibid.: 32)

Scientific inquiry

> is a mixture of objective analysis (the logic and verifiability of theories), subjective judgment, and the relative position of the scholar in the spacetime continuum.
>
> (ibid.)

Beyond this, however, there is the radical corollary that

> scientific inquiry is fundamentally subversive of things as they are … [The extension of knowledge] enables everyone to act in the new ways that would not be open to them in the absence of increased knowledge.
>
> (ibid.: 30)

Whether the resulting changes will in fact have subversive or radical consequences is, of course, open to question. But one could hardly have a clearer example of the institutionalist-instrumentalist (i.e. Deweyite) conception of the relationship of knowledge to action.

In this chapter attention will be focused on Fusfeld's long essay 'The Conceptual Framework of Modern Economics' (1980), not only because of its intrinsic interest but also because he has announced his intention of producing a further, and presumably extended, treatment of the same subject (see Fusfeld 1990a: 355). This will be no easy undertaking, for the literature of economic methodology has expanded at a dizzy pace since 1980, with an estimated thirty-one books (in English) during the 1980–91 period, and heaven knows how many journal articles (Redman 1991:91).[3] Nor is this merely a question of numbers. There has also been a startling proliferation of contending viewpoints, approaches and philosophies applied to economics.[4]

'The Conceptual Framework'

After a brief introduction, Fusfeld's article (1980) is subdivided into three major parts:

1 *Scientific Method* – mainly a critique of logical empiricism, with discussion of mathematical models and symbolic logic, and the question of a value-free science.
2 *The breakup of General Equilibrium Theory* – its logical structure; the problem of production theory; market imperfections; chance and indeterminacy; the theory of the second best; behavioral assumptions; and the present dilemma.
3 *New Approaches* – pattern models and formal models; open and closed models; processes of change; verification, objectivity, and worldview.

It is obviously impossible to comment on all these topics in detail. Instead, attention will be focused on those features of Fusfeld's argument that seem especially effective, or amenable to constructive elaboration or improvement.

Section 2 demonstrates how the old world metaphysical viewpoint embodied in general equilibrium theory has been virtually destroyed from within, mainly by criticisms from thoughtful orthodox (neoclassical) economists working on the frontiers of theory with the aim of strengthening its defenses or modifying it to make it more plausible, or more relevant to real world economic problems. As Fusfeld himself puts it (1980:27):

> Space, time, information, chance, and market imperfections cause determinate results to fade into indeterminacy, orderly adjustment to become disorderly, and equilibrium nonequilibrium. As the limiting assumptions that lead to determinate equilibrium are dropped, we move not merely into a more complex world with a larger number of variables, but into a qualitatively different world in which the very nature of the outcomes is changed from the Panglossian rationalism of the eighteenth century to the existential dilemmas of the twentieth.

Characteristically, while demonstrating his grasp of the significance of recent theoretical developments, Fusfeld is not content with exploring the inherent weaknesses of recent fashionable so-called good games.

> Any social theory that interprets events as the outcome of a social process of rational individual behavior leading to a social optimum clearly does not make sense of the events of our time. In some respects the foremost problem of social philosophy in this century is why and how purposive and presumably rational human behavior can lead to massively irrational outcomes. Its vision of the world is one of order, determinate results, and social good.
>
> (ibid.: 26)[5]

Section 3 is the most stimulating and challenging part, since it contains Fusfeld's proffered solution for economic theory's present discontents. It must be emphasized at the outset, however, that his proposals are neither dogmatic nor overconfident. Moreover, they are somewhat lacking in specificity, and become more promising when set against some recent methodological trends that were not clearly apparent when the paper was written. According to Fusfeld's summary formulation:

> Methods that were more intuitive than systematic twenty years ago are now undergoing careful development and analysis. Briefly, the new methods involve pattern (*Gestalt*, holistic) models that remain open and changing … and are therefore able to deal with such phenomena as chance, historical development, wide varieties of individual and social behavior, and indeterminacy as integral parts of the analysis. They lead to explanations that might be termed 'understanding' rather than 'knowledge', although this difference is often murky. Prediction is a secondary goal, while policy guidelines are emphasized. There is no assumption that normative

> conclusions are unscientific or that the social sciences should have a positive emphasis.
>
> (ibid.: 28)[6]

In his account of 'new approaches' Fusfeld attaches special importance to the role of pattern (*Gestalt*, holistic) models, which, he contends, constitute 'the [*sic*] appropriate method for economic and social theory' (ibid.: 43), although he acknowledges their limitations and flaws. Unlike the formal models employed by orthodox economists, which proceed in an essentially linear fashion from premises to conclusions (utilizing a chain of logical deductions based on mathematical formulations), pattern models move 'by logical analysis from one element to another, backward, sideways, up and down, until a general pattern or framework is brought together by logical connections' (ibid.: 29). In one sense a pattern model is 'analogous to a jigsaw puzzle: It involves putting pieces together to form a meaningful whole' (ibid.).[7] A more 'descriptive' term that Fusfeld evidently prefers is *Gestalt* model, derived from *Gestalt* psychology, according which

> learning takes place by a process of integrating new ideas and information with other ideas and information in a pattern of relationships meaningful *to the individual*. Each part of the pattern is understood not as an isolated unit but as part of the whole. This emphasis on 'wholes' has sometimes led to use of the phrase 'holistic' to characterize these models. *Gestalt* psychologists argue that even [*sic*] perception of facts is colored by the *Gestalt* within which perception occurs: For example, a coin resting on a table and seen from an angle is perceived as round, even though it is actually seen as an ellipse, and an artist drawing it would draw it as an ellipse.
>
> (ibid.: 29; emphasis added)

This passage has been cited at length because it gives some indication of the bewildering variety of terms employed by authors seeking to specify *the* distinctive methodology employed by institutionalist economists, and it draws attention to Fusfeld's unusual emphasis on the *Gestalt* approach. Alternative terms used by economists, not all of them heterodox, include: 'storytelling', 'appreciative theory', 'process theories' and 'path-dependent analysis', and 'orientation theories' or 'pattern predictions'.[8] In Fusfeld's paper, however, the subjective element in pattern and/or *Gestalt* models is emphasized because 'some people are able to perceive and understand larger and more complex patterns than others' (ibid.: 31). *Gestalt* psychology demonstrates that

> the interpretation of a pattern depends on the background, experiences, and state of mind of the observer. Differences in those influences on the individual – position in the space-time continuum, place in the social order, previous psychological influences, and so forth – result in differences in perception and understanding... The general principle is that different

> individuals, observing the same data, will derive different understandings and identify different relationships within the whole.
>
> (ibid.)

However, unless there are significant elements in common in these understandings and perceptions of relationships, intersubjective agreements among observers will be unattainable.

Turning away from exposition, at least for the time being, Fusfeld's essay raises two immediate questions. Do pattern (*Gestalt*, holistic) models constitute the identifiable core of a distinctive institutionalist economic methodology? Does the subjectivity inherent in these models, especially the *Gestalt* version, render them 'unscientific' in some sense of that weasel word? Conflicting answers to both these questions can easily be found in the literature.

Wilbur and Harrison, for example, argue somewhat equivocally that pattern models constitute 'the methodology implicit in' institutional economics; they form its 'methodological basis'; but this does not necessarily mean that pattern models should be the methodology of institutionalism (1978:61–61).[9] Warren Samuels is similarly cautious, maintaining that institutionalists lack 'a shared body of theory' but nevertheless have 'a common model of explanation'. They have

> only a way of investigating with some important guides to inquiry. I think that institutional economics does involve more than this but am prepared to recognize that substantively it may be closer to an investigatory mode than a corpus of knowledge comparable to other schools of thought.
>
> (Samuels, quoted in Wilbur and Harrison 1978:72–72)

Fusfeld, too, does not commit himself unequivocally. Yet this seems to be implied in his essay, and at one point he asserts that pattern modeling based on twentieth century *Gestalt* psychology is '*the* appropriate method for economic and social theory' (1980:43; emphasis added).

By contrast, according to Mark Blaug, one of the foremost contemporary economic methodologists, there is no essential difference between the processes of validating storytelling (or pattern models) and the hypothetico-deductive explanations employed in orthodox economics. 'Storytelling lacks rigor, or a definitive logical structure. It is all too easy to verify, and virtually impossible to falsify. It is or can be persuasive because it never runs the risk of being wrong' (1980:127).[10] Yet he concludes with a major concession: 'Perhaps economic problems are so intractable that storytelling is the best we can do'.[11] A somewhat similar admission was made by Johannes Klant, an austere, unusually clearheaded Dutch methodologist, who argued that in economics 'proof must usually be furnished in rational discussions of the *plausibility* of hypotheses' (1984:184; emphasis added).[12] But while plausible general themes were not unattainable in principle, in practice the prospects of attaining them were not great.

> The rapid historical changeability in the domain of research and the instability of many human behavioral patterns lead one to suspect, however, that we

> shall never succeed and that numerical constants will never be discovered. As a rule, theories are therefore more in the nature of explanation sketches.
>
> (ibid.: 186)

This comment is significant, for the concept of 'explanation sketches' was introduced by Carl Hempel, who distinguished between this looser type of explanation employed by historians and the genuine 'Nomological Hypothetico-Deductive' explanations produced by natural scientists. Whether or not this distinction is accepted, Klant's conclusion points, once again, to the underlying similarities between explanations in history and in economics (see Coats 1989, 1993/4).

Bruce Caldwell, another leading economic methodologist, is more favorably disposed than Blaug towards pattern models (treating them as equivalent to 'holistic explanations'). Such models embody

> a grand and ambitious vision. Indeed, by comparison standard economic analysis seems terribly restrictive, static, narrow, even pedestrian... That their program has independent support from a growing research tradition within the philosophy of science also counts favorably

– an argument reinforced by developments in economic methodology in the decade or so since Caldwell's book was published (1982: 203).[13] However, few institutionalists have tried to construct concatenated models – 'of the type linking validated hypotheses or themes in a network or pattern' (as contrasted with 'the hierarchical, formal models employed by positivist philosophers and economists') (ibid.: 202). This is partly because of the difficulties involved. The institutionalists' lack of an explicit theoretical base, like their rejection of a general theoretical structure,

> rules out theory choice on non-empirical grounds, that is, criteria like theoretical connectedness, logical consistency, elegance, and the like cannot be applied. Yet, on their own admission, empirical criteria are not well-suited for deciding among competing paradigms.
>
> (ibid.: 203)[14]

Turning to the question whether the subjectivity inherent in pattern or *Gestalt* models renders them unscientific, Fusfeld argues that, while there are subjective elements both in pattern models and in formal models of the kind employed by orthodox economists, in the former category these elements 'are often [but not invariably?] readily apparent and identifiable', whereas in the latter they are 'often [but not always?] hidden under the camouflage of seemingly value-free logic' (1980:32). Such concealment is apparently much more difficult with pattern models. This, however, does not go far enough. In order to achieve a reasonable degree of consensus within the relevant part of the scientific community systematic *intersubjective* comparisons or tests are required, a point Fusfeld does not consider. Matters are made more complex by his admission that all the components of pattern models, and the phenomena under investigation, change over time, including the parameters as well as the variables. 'The subject-matter, its component parts, and the relationships among them change as the analysis develops' (ibid.: 37). Hence, if a degree of intersubjective consensus is achieved it is likely to be only transitory.[15] This recalls the early, caustic characterization of institutionalism as 'an ever-changing description of an ever-changing environment'. Fusfeld does, in fact, acknowledge that there are relatively static or slowly changing elements in any social system, but does not explain how to combine the analysis of these with the analysis of more volatile elements.

The 'wholes' that pattern modelers choose to study may be large or small scale, but [Fusfeld] does not discuss the latter species.[16] As examples of 'wholes' he instances Marx's analysis of capitalism, the totality of Galbraith's *oeuvre*, and his own analysis of the American corporate state.[17] Indeed, pattern models represent *'the* [*sic*] style of inquiry adopted by the great thinkers of the past' (Fusfeld 1984: 684), surely a sweeping and controversial statement. In these configurations the part-whole relationships can be extraordinarily complex. 'The theory of pattern models tells us that the functioning of the social system at any one time is affected by all of its history' (Fusfeld 1980: 37), hence changes in parameters must be taken into account as well as changes in variables. However, as Malcolm Rutherford, a sympathetic critic, has pointed out (though without specific reference to Fusfeld), if the advocates of pattern models

> mean simply that the part should always be analyzed within its broader context, and that those factors that create the organization, structure and evolution of the whole should be objects of study, then the claim is not objectionable, but also not necessarily inconsistent with the use of abstract or formal techniques. Alternatively, the statements can be interpreted as the argument that the social scientist should be trying to capture the whole in its *total* complexity.
>
> (1994:19; emphasis added)

That, however, is impossible.

Fusfeld does not explicitly consider the role of history in pattern modeling, and he does not use the term 'storytelling', which has been more widely adopted since his essay was published. He does, however, observe that in the notorious late nineteenth century *Methodenstreit* Schmoller's recommended procedures for an historical economics constituted 'an early version of the *Gestalt* method and the use of pattern models' (Fusfeld 1987:454–5).[18]

Like the Austrian economists, pattern modelers are more concerned with 'understanding' (*verstehen*) than with explanation according to the hypothetico-deductive model. According to Fusfeld, understanding involves 'a subjective weighting of the various elements' in the model.

> While each part of the pattern may be verified in the sense that is consistent with historical fact and empirical evidence, and the subsidiary causal

> explanations do not lead to falsified hypotheses, the overall configuration is validated by the judgment of the investigator.
>
> (1980:40–1)

This reference to judgment is interesting, given Hayek's recognition of the problem of analyzing very complex phenomena. In such cases

> the *recognition* of the conditions to which the theory applies may often require the ready perceptions of patterns or configurations which demand a special skill which few acquire. The selection and application of the appropriate scheme thus becomes something of an art where success or failure cannot be ascertained by any mechanical test ... [and] this constitutes no more than a distinction of degree from the physical sciences.
>
> (Hayek 1967:18)[19]

This paragraph reveals a certain eclecticism in Fusfeld's methodological and epistemological views. Consistency with 'historical fact and empirical evidence', and references to 'falsified hypotheses' and 'validation', clearly distance him from some of the more extreme forms of anti-empiricist post-positivism to be found in current methodological writings in economics. These are complex and controversial matters, to be approached with caution in analyzing Fusfeld's methodology.

Fusfeld can certainly be exonerated from the charge recently leveled at some exponents of the 'old' institutionalist economists, namely their

> almost total rejection of any and all formal techniques, even where these could play an illuminating role (as in the case of game theory), and in the overly empiricist view of the way in which pattern models should be developed and constructed.
>
> (Rutherford 1994:19)

But while he does not reject formal methods, Fusfeld does not provide a satisfactory account of the interaction between formal and informal elements in pattern models, and the relationship between causal explanations and understanding in their formation.

Fusfeld's treatment of change

Viewed retrospectively, the least satisfactory aspect of Fusfeld's 'Conceptual Framework' essay is his treatment of change, in the section concerned with new approaches. This contention may at first sight seem strange, even perverse, given his work as an economic historian and historian of economic ideas, and his manifest interest in the long-run development of large-scale socio-economic systems. Yet it is a measure of the extent to which economic methodology has advanced since 1980, both among orthodox and heterodox economists. Of course Fusfeld's essay does not ignore intertemporal relationships, the role of 'real' historical (as against analytical) time, and the interaction of rapid as against slowly changing (e.g. institutional inertial) elements in society; and his concept of a 'cone of causation' is vivid, albeit presented only in very general terms (1980: 35). His attempt to distinguish between dialectical change – resulting from 'the interaction of opposing or contradictory forces, which creates a new situation' – and evolutionary change, is unclear, for the latter is depicted as 'also dialectical in nature, resulting from some form of conflict, contradiction, or disparity within existing configurations of social processes and institutional structures'. Indeed, he maintains that from the standpoint of 'the pure theory of pattern models, the distinction between dialectical and evolutionary change does not appear to be a fruitful one' (ibid.: 38, 39).

During the past decade and a half there has been a tremendous growth of interest in, and literature on, processes of change in economic and social systems, together with a concomitant deepening of understanding and analytical sophistication. This has been manifested among American institutionalists, their European counterparts in the recently founded European Association for Evolutionary Economics, among supporters of the revival of interest in Schumpeter's economics, and among orthodox economists sensitive to the problems Fusfeld exposed in Section 2 of his essay. Needless to say, this extensive and complex intellectual terrain cannot be examined in detail here, but an indication of the intellectual possibilities and excitement of much of this work can be conveyed by reference to Paul David's article on 'Path Dependency', mentioned earlier (1993).

According to David, an American economic historian at one time associated with the so-called 'new' economic history, there is currently a highly promising reemphasis on the character of economics as an historical social science. Mainstream economics, he argues, has had a restrictive effect by ignoring events, causal explanations involving sequential actions, and 'the disequilibrium foundations that must underlie any predictively useful theories'. And this has contributed directly to the disjuncture between theoretical and empirical research programs (ibid.: 36–7).[20] More recently, however,

> there has been an alteration in the general climate of thought, which has accorded new significance to details of historical sequence – a development associated with the growth of interest in non-linear dynamics across many disciplines and the consequent emergence of the so-called 'sciences of complexity'. This intellectual ferment may be eroding the basis of the former stability of the ahistorical path on which our discipline has remained trapped (all too self-contentedly, it should be said) for well over a century. But equally, if not more, decisive will be the attainment of a 'critical mass' among the subset working on problems of positive feedback within the discipline of economics.
>
> (ibid.: 36–7)

Of particular interest to the historian of economics is David's enigmatic comment that

> our altered ability to discern positive feedback mechanisms at work in the world about us may have as much to do with the internal social dynamics of our science, and the external intellectual environment formed by developments in other disciplines, as it does with the technological and institutional and transactional phenomena we are seeing.
>
> (ibid.: 31)

Conclusion

Obviously no single article, however perceptive and broad in scope, can convey the variety, depth and range of current research and discussion of the processes of economic and social change. But in an essay dedicated to Dan Fusfeld it seems especially appropriate to cite the work of a thoughtful, analytically sophisticated economic historian that is in harmony with the general tone of his 'Conceptual Framework'. Other, among many, possible examples of developments since that essay are the partly parallel, but in certain respects fundamentally different characteristics and trends in the so-called 'old' and 'new' institutional economics,[21] and the intensive exploration of evolutionary theories of economic and social change, especially those linking economic and biological processes. It is to be hoped, and indeed it is highly likely, that when Fusfeld publishes his prospective methodological volume he will draw upon, and modify and extend this literature.[22]

Notes

1 For interesting comments on Fusfeld's teaching style see Brazier (1962:242–3, 248–9).

2 For a powerful critique of the current state of affairs in academic economics see, for example, Hutchison (1992), especially chapter 2.

3 Redman (1991) estimates that more than fifty books on economic methodology were published in the 1970s and 1980s, and the flood has not yet abated. No wonder Hutchison observed that 'this last decade of the century probably should be, and just conceivably might be, the methodological decade' (Hutchison 1992:x).

4 The following list, which extends back beyond 1980, includes: anarchism, antifoundationalism, causal holism, confirmationism, constructivism, conventionalism, critical rationalism, critical realism, deconstruction, descriptivism, discourse analysis, empiricism, fallibilism, falsificationism (naive or sophisticated), growth of knowledge theories, hermeneutics, holism, instrumentalism, logical empiricism, logical positivism, methodology of scientific research programs, modernism, naturalism, positivism, postpositivism, postmodernism, pragmatism, predictivism, realism, and rhetorical analysis. Needless to say, these categories overlap, and I do not intend to repeat Redman's mistake by claiming 'to represent as many methodological positions as possible' (1991: vii). Fortunately, as will appear later, many of the more recent variants are inapplicable to Fusfeld's eminently sensible approach. His 'Conceptual Framework' is not treated here merely as a standpoint from which to view the current Babel of economic methodology.

5 The fundamentally normative character of orthodox economic theory is widely recognized, especially by institutionalist and radical economists. For a cogent statement of

the same broad conclusion by a 'hard-nosed' philosopher of economics see Rosenberg (1992:216–217), who argues that general equilibrium theory can be interpreted as a species of contractarian political philosophy.

6 A number of statements in this passage are certainly contestable; but to examine them in detail would not be fruitful, given the broader objective of this chapter. Exposition rather than dissection is appropriate at this point.

7 However, this analogy seems unfortunate, given that the individual parts of a jigsaw puzzle are rigid, unlike the elements in a pattern model, and the size and shape of the completed 'whole' are predetermined, before the exercise begins.

8 On storytelling, see Ward (1972: chapter 12) and McCloskey (1990). On 'appreciative theory' see Nelson and Winter (1982). Process or 'processual' theories are widely discussed in the old and new institutionalist literature, for example in Langlois (1986:7 n). For a perceptive discussion of 'path-dependent economic analysis' see David (1993); also Hodgson (1993:203–210). Hayek employs the terms 'orientation theories' and 'pattern predictions' in his essays 'Degrees of Explanation' and 'The Theory of Complex Phenomena' (1967: 3–21, 22–42). For the advocacy of 'pattern models' in economics see the widely quoted article by Wilbur and Harrison (1978). Earlier discussions of pattern models occur in Kaplan (1964) and Diesing (1971). The philosophy of holism derives from the philosopher-statesman Smuts (1926). For its application to economics see Gruchy (1947:18–28). Gruchy also provides extensive discussion of the concept of process. In this account I have drawn on my earlier papers; see Coats (1989, 1993/4).

9 However, at one point they come close to saying that Diesing's participant observer approach is *the* methodology of institutionalist economics. One recent author, after analyzing a series of articles in the leading institutionalist journal, has concluded that there is no such thing as a special set of institutionalist methods (Lind 1993). Ramstadt endorses this view (1986).

10 'How does one validate a particular piece of storytelling? One asks, of course, if the facts are correctly stated; if other facts are omitted; if the lower-level generalizations are subject to counter examples; and if we can find competing stories that will fit the facts. In short, we go through a process that is identical to the one that we regularly employ to validate the hypothetico-deductive explanations of orthodox economics' (Blaug 1980:127).

11 Blaug immediately adds, however: 'But if such is the case, it is odd that we should actually recommend the safe method of storytelling and deplore the risky methodology of falsificationism. Surely the more falsificationism, the better?' (1980:127). In the decade and a half since the first edition of Blaug's book appeared the case for and against falsificationism has been vigorously debated, with the current balance of expert opinion against.

12 For a careful examination of the concept of plausibility see Nooteboom (1986).

13 Caldwell's entire account of institutionalist methodology is valuable (1982: 200–5). Recent developments in economic methodology and the philosophy of science discussed in the *Journal of Economic Issues* include hermeneutics, critical theory, rhetoric, methodological pluralism and postmodernism. No wonder there are said to be 'competing paradigms' in institutionalist economics.

14 On concatenated theories see Wilbur and Harrison (1978:80–1); these authors treat the concatenated structure of holistic theories as equivalent to pattern models (ibid.: 71–83). Fusfeld's concept of pattern models seems more complex than Kaplan's (1964) concept of concatenated structures, since he refers to logical analysis in these models moving 'backwards, sideways, up and down' (Fusfeld 1980:29).

15 In the case of *Gestalt* psychology this is an especially significant problem, for the perception of patterns differs not merely between individuals but at different times, possibly even frequently, for a given individual. This is true, for example, of the well-known figure-ground example in which the relationship between an object and its background appears to vary according to the observer's perception.

16 Small-scale wholes form the basis of Diesing's analysis, which emphasizes the role of the participant observer, who must 'allow himself to be socialized and accept the point of view and ideology of his hosts'. How this is possible when 'studying a whole human system in its natural setting' is unclear. He also argues that the concepts employed in the pattern model must be 'relatively concrete and particularized, close to the real system being described', a point Fusfeld would doubtless accept (quoted in Rutherford's excellent discussion in 1994:16–14).

17 See Fusfeld (1980:28), where he provides a more extended list of 'grand schemes' or 'great integrative configurations', and 'smaller constructs'. See also Fusfeld (1984:684).

18 The question of the historicity of pattern models, *Gestalt* models, and story-telling cannot be fully explored here. According to McCloskey (1990:64) 'most economics is saturated with narration'. Fusfeld recognizes that pattern models embody an amalgam of 'logical relations and historical reality: real types rather than ideal types'. But while 'ideal types are constructs of pure logic … real types have a historical aspect as well' (1980:36).

19 The role of pattern recognition in the natural sciences is perceptively discussed by an eminent physicist in Ziman (1978). The role of tacit knowledge, a form of 'art', is examined extensively in Polanyi (1957, 1967).

20 As examples, reflecting his main interests as an economic historian, he cites the comparatively recent recognition of local or global positive feedbacks, endogenous technical progress through learning-by-doing and learning by using, habituation affecting tastes and behaviors, and adaptive cognitive processes (such as Bayesian information processing) affecting the formation of expectations.

21 For an authoritative review of the literature see Rutherford (1994). A selective list of articles on the process of change from the *Journal of Economic Issues* includes the following: Carrier (1992); Dopfer (1986, 1988, 1991a,b); Poirot (1993); Radzicki (1988, 1990); and Setterfield (1993). There is, of course, a very large and highly technical orthodox literature on non-linear dynamics and disequilibrium systems.

22 See, for example, the comprehensive treatment of recent work in Hodgson (1993). Also see Witt (1993).

References

Blaug, M. (1980) *The Methodology of Economics, or how Economists Explain*, Cambridge: Cambridge University Press.

Brazier, M. C. (1982) 'The Economics Department at the University of Michigan: A Centennial Retrospective', in S. H. Hymans (ed.) *Economics and the World around It*, Ann Arbor: University of Michigan Press.

Caldwell, B. (1982) *Beyond Positivism. Economic Methodology in the Twentieth Century*, London: Allen & Unwin.

Carrier, D. (1992) 'A Methodology for Pattern Modeling: Nonlinear Macroeconomic Dynamics', *Journal of Economic Issues*, 26: 221–42.

Coats, A. W. (1989) 'Explanations in History and Economics', *Social Research*, 56: 331–60.

——. (1993/4) 'What Can we accomplish with Historical Approaches in an Advanced Discipline such as Economics?', *History of Economic Ideas*, II: 227–65.

David, P. (1993) 'Historical Economics in the Long Run: Some Implications of Path Dependence', in G. D. Snooks (ed.) *Historical Analysis in Economics*, London: Routledge.

Diesing, P. (1971) *Patterns of Discovery in the Social Sciences*, Chicago: Aldine Atherton.

Dopfer, K. (1986) 'The Histonomic Approach to Economics: Beyond Pure Theory and Experience', *Journal of Economic Issues*, 20: 989–1010.

——. (1988) 'Classical Mechanics with an Ethical Dimension: Professor Tinbergen's Economics', *Journal of Economic Issues*, 22: 675–706.

——. (1991a) 'The Complexity of Economic Phenomena', *Journal of Economic Issues*, 25: 39–76.

——. (1991b) 'Toward a Theory of Economic Institutions, Synergy and Path Dependency', *Journal of Economic Issues*, 25: 535–50.

Fusfeld, D. R. (1972 *Economics*, Boston, MA: D. C. Heath.

——. (1973) 'Types of Radicalism in American Economics', *American Economic Review*, 63: 145–6.

——. (1976 *Economics*, 2nd edn, Boston: D. C. Heath.

——. (1980) 'The Conceptual Framework of Modern Economics', *Journal of Economic Issues*, 14: 1–52.

——. (1984) 'John Kenneth Galbraith', in H. W. Spiegel and W. J. Samuels (eds) *Contemporary Economists in Perspective*, Vol. I, Part III B, Greenwich, CT: JAI Press.

——. (1987) 'Methodenstreit', in J. Eatwell, M. Milgate, and P. Newman (eds) *The New Palgrave Dictionary of Economics*, Vol. 3, London: Macmillan.

——. (1990a) 'Economics and the Determinate World View', *Journal of Economic Issues*, 24: 355–9.

——. (1990b) 'Economics, Science and Society', *Methodus*, 2: 30–2.

Gruchy, A. G. (1947 *Modern Economic Thought: The American Contribution*, New York: Prentice Hall.

Hayek, F. (1967 *Studies in Philosophy, Politics and Economics*, Chicago: University of Chicago Press.

Hicks, J.R. (1979 *Causality in Economics*, Oxford: Basil Blackwell.

Hodgson, G.M. (1993 *Economics and Evolution: Bringing Life Back into Economics*, Cambridge: Polity Press (Blackwell).

Hutchison, T.W. (1992 *Changing Aims in Economics*, Oxford: Basil Blackwell.

Kaplan, A. (1964 *The Conduct of Inquiry: Methodology for Behavioral Science*, San Francisco: Chandler Publishing Co.

Klant, J. (1984 *The Rules of the Game: The Logical Structure of Economic Theories*, Cambridge: Cambridge University Press.

Langlois, R. (ed.) (1986) *Economics as a Process*, Cambridge: Cambridge University Press.

Lind, H. (1993) 'The Myth of Institutionalist Method', *Journal of Economic Issues*, 27: 1–17.

McCloskey, D.N. (1990) 'Storytelling in Economics', in D. Lavoie (ed.) *Economics and Hermeneutics*, London: Routledge, 61–72.

Nelson, R. and Winter, S. (1982 *An Evolutionary Theory of Economic Change*, Cambridge, MA: Belknap Press of Harvard University Press.

Nooteboom, B. (1986) 'Plausibility in Economics', *Economics and Philosophy,* 2: 197–224.

Poirot, C.S., Jr (1993) 'Institutions and Economic Evolution', *Journal of Economic Issues*, 27: 887–907.

Polanyi, M. (1957) *Personal Knowledge: Towards a Post-critical Philosophy*, London: Routledge.

____ (1967) *The Tacit Dimension*, London: Routledge.

Radzicki, M. (1988) 'Institutional Dynamics: An Extension of the Institutionalist Approach to Socioeconomic Analysis', *Journal of Economic Issues*, 22:633–65.

____ (1990) 'Institutional Dynamics, Deterministic Chaos, and Self-organizing Systems', *Journal of Economic Issues,* 24:57–102.

Ramstadt, Y. (1986) 'A Pragmatist's Quest for Holistic Knowledge: The Scientific Methodology of John R.Commons', *Journal of Economic Issues,* 20:1067–105.

Redman, D. (1991) *Economics and the Philosophy of Science*, Oxford: Oxford University Press.

Rosenberg, A. (1992) *Economics–Mathematical Politics or Science of Diminishing Returns?*, Chicago: University of Chicago Press.

Rutherford, M. (1994) *Institutions in Economics: The Old and the New Institutionalism*, Cambridge: Cambridge University Press.

Setterfield, M. (1993) 'A Model of Institutional Hysteresis', *Journal of Economic Issues,* 27:755–74.

Smuts, J. C. (1926) *Holism and Evolution,* New York: Macmillan.

Ward, B. (1972) *What's Wrong with Economics?*, London: Macmillan.

Wilbur, C. K. and Harrison, R. S. (1978) 'The Methodological Basis of Institutional Economics: Pattern Model, Storytelling, and Holism', *Journal of Economic Issues,* 12:61–98.

Wise, G. (1980) *American Historical Explanations: A Strategy for Grounded Enquiry*, Minneapolis: University of Minnesota Press.

Witt, U. (ed.) (1993) *Evolutionary Economics*, Cheltenham: Edward Elgar.

Ziman, J. (1978) *Reliable Knowledge: An Exploration of the Grounds for the Belief in Science*, Cambridge: Cambridge University Press.

29 The progress of heterodox economics

Chairman's opening remarks (somewhat modified)

The central theme of this session is the changing relationship between "orthodox" (i.e., mainstream, neoclassical) and "heterodox" economics, especially in the USA, during the past two or three decades. Economics is such a large and heterogeneous discipline that it cannot be characterized both briefly and accurately. Alongside the growth of formalization and mathematization, and the high degree of uniformity in the undergraduate and graduate curricula and in the leading textbooks, there are also within the subject a number of dissenting or deviant doctrinal schools, rival methodological approaches, and innovative developments designed to remedy its defects and/or overcome its limitations. Moreover, many of the outspoken criticisms of the status quo, proposed remedies, and innovations, originate with or are endorsed by prominent economists with impeccable professional credentials. Indeed, in some cases their contributions threaten the discipline's foundations and can, therefore, be considered a species of "orthodox subversion."

A significant number of the recent innovative developments in economics are changing, or seem likely to change, economics in ways compatible with ideas, proposals, and objectives long associated with heterodoxy, in particular the so-called "old" institutional economics. Thus innovation, especially "orthodox subversion," can be said to contribute, albeit unintendedly, to the "progress" of heterodox economics. This can occur either in the form of orthodox or heterodox inputs, or some combination of the two.

The key terms in this discussion: "orthodox," "heterodox," and "progress," are widely and variously used in the economics literature, but rarely defined precisely. For the present purpose, the following rough guidelines may be helpful.

Orthodox

According to Richard Nelson and Sydney Winter (1982), the theoretical orthodoxy in economics provides "a narrow set of criteria that are used as a cheap and simple test for whether an expressed point of view is worthy of respect." This orthodoxy is "quite widely enforced." It appears especially in the leading textbooks used in: "Relatively standardized undergraduate intermediate macroeconomics courses designed to provide background for more advanced applied work... [and] essentially the same ideas also appear at more advanced level courses, although with more mathematical tools.[1]

Heterodox

The term is interpreted broadly here as encompassing all nonorthodox ideas and approaches. (Of course the borderline between heterodox and orthodox is unclear, and changing over time.) A conventional list of heterodox groups or schools would normally include all or most of the following: "old" institutionalist; neo-Austrian; post-Keynesian; Sraffian; radical; Marxian; evolutionary (including neo-Schumpeterian); experimental; behavioral; social, etc.

The following distinguished individuals are among those whose research is, at least in part, heterodox (i.e., idiosyncratic, maverick, or deviant, but not necessarily dissident): George Akerlof, James Buchanan, Paul Davidson, Jon Elster, Robert Frank, Nicholas Georgescu-Roegen, Albert Hirschman, Daniel Kahneman, Harvey Leibenstein, Brian Loasby, Mancur Olson, Thomas Schelling, Tibor Scitovsky, Amartya Sen, Vernon Smith, Richard Thaler, Amos Tversky, Douglas Vickers, and Oliver Williamson. This roster could, of course, be extended, but it is sufficient to indicate the immense diversity of recent and contemporary economics.

Progress

This has recently been analyzed by Roger Backhouse (1997, chapter 8; also chapters 10 and 13). The following is a condensed version of his enumeration:

1. Five broad features – increased agreement; closer approximation to the truth; increasingly reliable knowledge; improved explanatory power; irreversible change.
2. Theoretical Progress – increased generality, scope, precision, rigor; the elimination of error or inconsistency; increased simplicity (or beauty).
3. Empirical progress – increase in the number and quality of empirical generalizations; increased predictive success and/or corroboration; successful prediction of novel facts; improved problem-solving ability; establishing facts and testing theories.

(Some of these criteria overlap, are contestable, and require careful specification).

The above-mentioned non-orthodox or anti-orthodox innovations are far too numerous to be considered in detail here. I shall, therefore, mention only four broad areas of work in economics in which fruitful – indeed sometimes startling – new developments are taking place.

First, we have seen the emergence of a far richer, more varied, and complex conception of human nature than that proposed in the *homo oeconomicus* stereotype. Herbert Simon's concept of bounded rationality, which emphasizes the limitations of the individual's calculative capacity, is venerable; but it has been supplemented and strengthened by experimental evidence of the defects of expected utility theory, and by a recognition of the significance of "framing" and preference reversals, which undermine the orthodox assumption of stable preferences. The role of novelty, uncertainty, and various forms of "irrationality" are now being taken into account, together with non-deliberative types of behavior such as habit, custom, conventions, and routines. Economists are also currently exploring the implications of such motives as altruism, trust, fairness, commitment, reciprocity, status, and the emotions (such as happiness). How far these various elements can be incorporated into economic theory is not yet clear.

A second major area of work centers on various conceptions of change in economic systems, emphasizing process rather than equilibrium, and dynamic rather than static analysis. Time is now seen as an essential feature—i.e., "real" historical time, as opposed to mere logical time; irreversible rather than mechanically repetitive changes; and the roles of path-dependency, hysteresis, non-ergodic sequences, non-linear dynamics, complexity, and chaos. Needless to say, uncertainty and imperfect information can be incorporated into analyses of these kinds, but the difficulties are formidable, and future developments are still unclear.

Third, significant and highly promising efforts are now being made to overcome the barriers to interdisciplinary research, especially with respect to the interconnections between economics and the other social sciences, but also between economics and history, language, literature, and law. The exemplary case is economics and psychology (more than half a century since economic theorists adopted isolationist tactics), as indicated above. In economic history there has been a fruitful (if at times overly aggressive and polemical) rapprochement with the economists, especially in studies of long-run economic growth and development, while economics and law are currently more intimately involved than ever before. Collaborative research in these and other disciplines calls for serious study and understanding of the other specialist's discipline and its problems, by contrast with the so-called "economic imperialism"[2] that largely consists of imposing conventional static utility maximization analysis on conventionally "non-economic" subject-matter, without due sensitivity to the differences in content and the theoretical and empirical problems involved. As it has been wisely remarked, a science (or theory) that purports to explain everything, ultimately explains nothing.[3]

It is tempting to add economic methodology, as a heterodox field or subdivision within economics, which has been undergoing rapid expansion and dramatic changes during the past two or three decades. "Positivism," in its various, often ill-defined and confusing forms, has been discredited and displaced by a bewildering variety of alternative conceptions and approaches too numerous to itemize.[4] Of more general interest to working economists is the fact that the days of total immersion in (or mere flirtations with) fashionable philosophies of science (especially Kuhn, Popper, Lakatos, *et al.*) are largely gone, and the current (welcome) vogue is the study of how economists actually work, invent theories, and (perhaps) test them. The watchword is "the recovery of practice"; sophisticated doctrines such as hermeneutics, deconstruction, constructivism (perhaps) nowadays have few exponents. An intermediate case is rhetoric, which is fashionable, stimulating, and close to practice, but is not yet a persuasive theory, even as a colorful anti-methodology.

Notes

Roundtable Session: History of Economics Society Conference, Greensboro, NC June 27, 1999. This roundtable is a by-product of the Chairman's keynote address to the European Association of Evolutionary Political Economy in Athens, November 1997, under the same title. It appeared in the conference proceedings: *Evolution and Path-dependence in Economic Ideas: Past and Present*, Pierre Garrouste and Stavros Ioannides, eds., Edward Elgar, 2000. The roundtable participants had received copies of this address.

1 Nelson and Winter (1982 pp. 6–7; also pp. 7–8). The orthodox elements in basic economic theory include: the preoccupation with equilibrium; the definition of competition; the strict version of the concept of economic rationality, including stable preferences, individual maximizing behavior, perfect information, the ability to calculate a wide range of options, certainty. For a heterodox caricature of economic orthodoxy, see Gruchy (1972, p. 295). Many informed commentators have remarked on the slipperiness of the term orthodox and/or neo-classical economics.

2 The term "economics imperialism" is preferable, as it minimizes confusion with the economic imperialism of J. A. Hobson, V. I. Lenin, et al.

3 This remark is attributable to Alexander Rosenberg (source can be supplied).

4 In a recent article I enumerated almost thirty different species of current economic methodology. However, several of the individual items overlap. Cf. Coats 1997.

References

Backhouse, Roger E. 1997. *Truth and Progress in Economic Knowledge*. Cheltenham, UK: Edward Elgar.

Coats, A. W. Bob. 1997. "Fusfeld and Methodology." In Nahid Aslanbeigui and Young Back Choi, eds., *Borderlands of Economics: Essays In Honor of Daniel R. Fusfeld*. London: Routledge, pp. 32–46.

Gruchy, Alan G. 1972. *Contemporary Economic Thought: The Contribution of Neo-Institutional Economics*. Clifton, NJ: Augustus M. Kelley.

Nelson, Richard R. and Sydney G. Winter. 1982. *An Evolutionary Theory of Economic Change*. Cambridge, MA: Belknap Press of Harvard University.

Rutherford, Malcolm. 1994. *Institutions In Economics: The Old and the New Institutionalism*. Cambridge: Cambridge University Press.

Witt, Ulrich. 1991. "Reflections on the Present State of Evolutionary Theory." In Geoffrey M. Hodgsonand Ernesco Screpanti, eds., *Rethinking Economics: Markets, Technology and Economic Evolution*. Aldershot: Edward Elgar.

30 The professionalization of American social science

Mary O. Furner's *Advocacy and Objectivity: A Crisis in the Professionalization of American Social Science* [1] treats, from an historical standpoint, a number of interrelated fields – the history of ideas, the growth of higher education, the changing relationship between scholarship and society, and the professionalization of the social sciences – a group of modern disciplines in which American theories and their applications have come to dominate Western thought. The emergence of economics, sociology and politics as distinct academic disciplines, each with its own identifiable personnel, university departments and degrees, learned society, and scholarly periodicals, is an important episode in American intellectual and cultural history, one that cannot be fully comprehended without reference to contemporary economic and social conditions. As an historian, the author naturally appreciates this fact; but as she is not an economist, her book suffers from certain limitations since economics figures more prominently than the other social sciences.[2]

The professionalization of the social sciences in the United States took place in an economic, social, and institutional context that was being decisively transformed by an exceptionally rapid process of modernization, a term which both embraces and transcends the more familiar concepts of industrialization and urbanization. Much that occurred in post-Civil-War America had already occurred, or was concurrently taking place, in Britain and Western Europe; but the sheer speed and scale of American development had the effect of compressing and dramatizing conflicts of ideas and interests that were concealed or muted in those older, more slowly evolving communities of Europe, built on generations of tradition and protected by entrenched institutional constraints. In the United States, by contrast, new values, standards and institutions had to be created, often *ab initio*, and adapted to cope with immediate and pressing needs. Not that the process was either purely or uniquely American: certain features of European academic life were consciously imitated across the Atlantic, while such contemporary European ideas as British classical economics, German historicism, and various brands of social evolutionism entered directly and sometimes decisively into the American intellectual milieu. Nevertheless, late nineteenth-century Americans, especially the younger generation, were often sceptical of the European heritage, embracing it selectively, and often modifying and adapting what they took to fit the exigencies of their situation.[3] Given the absence of generally recognised standards and criteria of relevance, discussion and disagreements were inevitable, and many solutions bore a distinctively hybrid character.

One of Furner's major themes is the rise and subsequent decline of the generalist amateur social scientist, whose institutional embodiment was the American Social Science Association (1865-1909), and his replacement by the specialist academic social scientist, as represented by the American Economic Association (1885), the American Political Science Association (1903) and the American Sociological Society (1905).[4] The professionalization of academic life is but one aspect of the modernization process which generated – at least until recently – a seemingly insatiable demand for new skills and techniques. Unlike the natural scientist, the social scientist finds it virtually impossible to insulate himself from the pressures and temptations of everyday life, especially in the United States, where the public clamour has frequently disrupted the peace of the ivory tower. The social role of the man of knowledge has been the subject of continuing criticism and attack in the United States,[5] and the late nineteenth-century emergence of the professional social scientist was accordingly an uncertain, occasionally painful, and usually self-conscious process. The relevant historical and institutional context was complex and rapidly changing. Even Furner treats this subject too summarily, omitting or failing to elaborate certain matters of direct importance to her central theme – such as the increasing bureaucratization of the universities; the significant differences between state and privately financed institutions; and the changing attitudes and influence of college presidents, trustees and alumni with respect to the professional academics.

In the post-Civil-War era American higher education underwent a revolution, in response to the changing demands of a rapidly industrializing society.[6] The old style liberal arts college, modelled largely on the Oxbridge pattern, gradually gave way to the modern university in a movement which has been aptly described as a broadening of the base and a narrowing at the top. Both tendencies directly affected the social sciences. The introduction of the elective system widened the students' range of subject choice and gave the social scientists an opportunity to infiltrate into the conventional college curriculum, which had hitherto been dominated by the classics, mathematics and moral philosophy. Concurrently, the shift of emphasis from teaching to research, and the introduction of graduate training – largely under German influences – created new academic employment opportunities for specialists in a wide variety of disciplines, including the social sciences. Meanwhile, the growth of population and urbanization was accompanied by a rapid expansion in the number of institutions and academic teaching and research posts, and there was intense inter-institutional – and, to a lesser extent, interregional – competition, which facilitated the emergence of an academic elite. Nevertheless the conditions were by no means ideal. As Furner notes, the new professional social scientists were in an anomalous position:

> As professors, they depended for livelihood on sources of financial support which they did not control. As scholars, they conducted investigations and developed critical theories which could adversely affect the very interests

> that supported them. Thus they were caught in a situation that inevitably produced conflict. As professionals, they wanted to defend colleagues against community pressure. Yet they needed to place reasonable restraints on restless performers who persisted in undermining community support (p. 145).

The inevitable conflicts to which Furner alludes appeared most obviously, and in a heightened form, in the academic freedom "cases" which figure so prominently in her pages. These cases – which Richard Hofstadter once referred to as the pathology of academic freedom – performed a catalyctic function, exposing significant divisions within the academic community and raising basic questions about professional rights and responsibilities. As is well known, in this century problems of academic freedom in America came to a head during the McCarthy period – though they had been present well before that time.[7] Less well known, however, is the rich scholarly literature provoked by these episodes, a literature that has no counterpart in the United Kingdom[8] – not simply because academic life has been more peaceful in Britain but also, one suspects, because British scholars seem to have regarded systematic critical analysis of the academic community as either uninteresting or unseemly. In the United States academics have generally been more professionally self-conscious and more present-minded,[9] and Furner's study, which originated in an investigation of American intellectuals' reactions to the McCarthy charges also has relevance to the ferment of the 1960s, when "radical caucuses attempted to control the meetings of social science associations and to commit their professions to policy positions against American involvement in South-east Asia or in favour of increased opportunities for minority groups in American society" (p. 8).

Twenty years ago Hofstadter and Metzger noted that in the later nineteenth century, as denominational colleges gave way to modern-type universities as the representative species of American higher educational institution, there was a parallel change in the focus of academic freedom disputes. Religious heresy declined in importance, being replaced by new secular forms, especially those arising within the social scientists' field. It is no coincidence that this shift of focus occurred at a time when clerical influence on boards of trustees was declining, and the representation and power of businessmen was growing apace, a process arousing fears in some quarters that the universities would, like the great industrial corporations, be swallowed up by the robber barons.[10] As the economists appreciated, when they concentrated on abstract deductive theories the public and the trustees were uninterested, and correspondingly disinclined to interfere. But when they made public statements about such controversial issues as the currency, tariffs, public utilities, trusts, or labour unions, they were liable to offend some individual or vested interest. As George Howard, the Stanford historian, declared in 1900, "The economist, the sociologist, and to some extent the historian deal with questions that are near the battle line;"[11] and it is on this basis that Richard T. Ely and other besieged academics argued the right, on the grounds of their professional competence and expertise, to advocate reforms as well as merely to investigate contemporary economic and social problems.

The central dilemma confronting the later nineteenth-century American social scientist was: how to demonstrate the relevance of his knowledge to contemporary life without at the same time endangering his reputation for scientific detachment and objectivity – and possibly also risking dismissal from his academic post. The economic and social position of the professoriat was much less comfortable and assured in America than in Europe, and the numerous young scholars who undertook graduate studies in Germany soon became vividly aware of this discrepancy on their return home. In the 1870s and early 1880s the number of academic appointments was still small, and the more aggressive among the "young Turks," as Ely called them, were deeply dissatisfied with the low emoluments, broad and arduous teaching duties, poor library and research facilities, and insecurity of tenure existing in all but a few wealthy and prestigious colleges and universities. They were determined to prove that society was undervaluing their services, not merely in purely academic terms but also by more crudely utilitarian standards. Most of them were first generation academics from rural farming or small town business backgrounds, and they could appreciate what William James later referred to as the "cash value" of ideas. Moreover many, especially those from devoutly religious families, felt a strong moral duty to contribute to social progress by devising solutions to current economic and social problems. The conventional American college professor had, more often than not, also been a clergyman, and the new generation of social scientists often found it tempting to assume this role together with their academic robes, even though moralising became recognised as somewhat at odds, if not directly incompatible, with a scientific approach. It was, after all, natural enough that a man like Henry Carter Adams, who had been unwilling to follow his father into the ministry, notwithstanding his strong filial loyalty, should turn first to the prospect of reform political journalism and then to economics as a means of assuaging his guilt. And though his personal history was unique, the pattern of his career was in many respects typical of the American social scientists of his generation.[12]

The dangers of reformist zeal and unrestrained advocacy were epitomized in the career of Richard T. Ely, the influential founder-member and first Secretary of the American Economic Association. Ely was a tireless popularizer of ethical economics and mildly interventionist policy proposals, and the academic and lay reactions to his efforts were often so hostile that they threatened the prospects of unity among the small but potentially influential corps of rising young economists. The response to Ely's activities focussed attention on issues of professional conduct which might otherwise have lain dormant, or at least inadequately formulated and collectively appreciated, for some time; and during the seven turbulent years of his Secretaryship there emerged the rudiments of a consensus about the limits of permissible advocacy. In this consensus moderation tended to become equated with objectivity and scholarly merit (p. 91), and this involved a trend away from radicalism towards conservatism. However it was less a movement towards *political* conservatism than towards *professional* conservatism, although there tended to be some correlation between the two.

The attainment of a recognizable consensus about professional behaviour and standards was delayed until the early years of this century, which is hardly surprising given the variety of individual backgrounds, the heterogenity of contemporary academic conditions, and the absence of developed scholarly values. But by an uneven and painful process there eventually emerged a dominant

> small, highly professionalized elite which determined a model for younger, less self-conscious academics to follow.... Out of all the cases there emerged a rudimentary discipline which identified the degree and type of advocacy that was entitled to collective security. Within the limits where agreement could be reached on goals and tactics, the economists had exchanged the capricious discipline provided by powerful external opponents for the more steady influence of national professional control.... The academic freedom cases cut two ways. They established more autonomy than professional social scientists had enjoyed before. They also demonstrated the negative results of partisanship. For better or worse, these troubles taught many academics to conserve their image, and preserve their institutions, to prepare to defend themselves but avoid the necessity, to exert influence quietly as experts rather than noisily as partisans. (pp. 257–58)

Although there were conspicuous earlier encounters involving social scientists in the 1880s and 1890s – for example, Henry Carter Adams at Cornell; President Elisha Benjamin Andrews at Brown; Edward W. Bemis at Chicago; and Richard T. Ely at Wisconsin – it was the Ross case at Stanford, in 1900, that eventually provoked the economists into collective, if still informal, action. Edward Alsworth Ross, a prominent economist (former Secretary of the American Economic Association) and sociologist, was dismissed from Leland Stanford Junior University on the insistence of its powerful benefactor and sole trustee, Mrs. Jane Lathrop Stanford. Ross was an able and contentious individual who had nearly been fired in 1896 because of his active intervention during the election campaign on behalf of William Jennings Bryan and free silver (although thirty-two other Stanford professors declared for McKinley without, apparently, causing offence). After stern warnings, a sabbatical leave, and a transfer from economics to social science, and Mrs. Stanford's ban on political activity by all Stanford professors, Ross's position seemed secure until he advocated the transition from private to public ownership of all public utilities, praised racial purity and condemned the supporters of coolie immigration. As Leland Stanford had built his railroads with cheap oriental labour even strong support from President David Starr Jordan could not shield Ross from Mrs. Stanford's wrath. He departed, with maximum publicity, and was followed by several of his social scientist colleagues, seriously damaging both the functioning and reputation of the institution and provoking a reaction not only in the press, but also in the report of an informal investigative committee endorsed by fifteen leading economics professors.

It was the economists who took the lead in the professionalization process not only because their discipline was more frequently in the firing line, but also because it was the most venerable and intellectually secure of the social sciences. As in reality, the role of political science and sociology figures much less prominently in Furner's study, though the emergence of these two disciplines from the social science umbrella of the 1860s is an integral part of the story. And it is no coincidence that economists played a leading part in the formation of the American Association of University Professors in 1915, an organization which was to devote a considerable proportion of its efforts to the defence of academic freedom.

Advocacy and Objectivity is a well-written, carefully researched, thought-provoking study of a topic of interest to all American Studies specialists. One might wish that Furner had concentrated somewhat less heavily on conditions within the social science community: doubtless she assumed her readers would already be familiar with such broader background themes as the changing role of the scholar in American society, the nature and extent of anti-intellectualism, and the general history of higher education and the professions. Adopting a sociological approach, she displays some tendency to impose an overall pattern on a chain of events in which chance and personality played a major part, although at one point she concedes that the outcome of particular "cases" depended more on "how the game was played" (p. 204) than on the nature of the game *per se*. Again, while she devotes considerable space to personal biographies, it is worth noting that the number of "cases" may be too small to justify confident generalizations about the process of professionalization for, as she acknowledges, a somewhat different picture might be revealed were it possible to study the academic rank and file: "If scholarly opinion in colleges and universities had been polled in 1897, as many social scientists as not would probably still have thought of their own positions as political sinecures where advocacy that conformed to local expectations was properly expected" (p. 228). There are numerous points in the story where this insight into the gap between the leaders and the led might have been elaborated.

The emergence of collective self-consciousness in any group is seldom easy to document, and at times Furner's use of the elusive terms "profession" and "professionals" is a source of confusion. For example, did the "crisis" of the 1880s and 1890s occur within an existing academic profession or among a group of scholars who were in the midst of an incomplete or on-going *process* of professionalization, one in which the academic freedom cases played a crucial *formative* role? A reading of the abundant correspondence of the *dramatis personae* suggests that some of them were less clear and far-sighted about the nature and significance of professional issues than Furner suggests. In the case of economics, which figures so prominently in her pages, questions of method, doctrine, and policy recommendations were usually more important than the problems of professional conduct and responsibility which came to a head in crisis periods.

It would, however, be unjust to end on a carping note. Historians of the social sciences in Britain have reason to be envious of the rich archival resources which Furner has mined so skilfully, for there are few counterparts on this side of the Atlantic. It is to be hoped that her book will inspire British Americanists to be more adventurous in their exploration of multi-disciplinary themes which can be used as foundations for a more coherent and systematic approach to American Studies.

Notes

1 Mary O. Furner, *Advocacy and Objectivity: A Crisis in the Professionalization of American Social Science* (Lexington, Kentucky: the Univ. Press of Kentucky, 1975, $17.50). Pp. xv, 357.

2 The dilemma is, ultimately, inescapable. But it is impossible to endorse the compartmentalist doctrine advanced by a distinguished (economist) historian of economics, "that it takes an economist to read an economist" and that "the correct way to read Adam Smith is the correct way to read the forthcoming issue of a professional journal." See George J. Stigler, "Does Economics Have a Useful Past?" *History of Political Economy*, 1 (Fall 1969), 219, 221.

3 As F. W. Taussig wrote to H. C. Adams, "We must look to the Germans for suggestions, but must work out our salvation in our own way – a fact which some of our friends are apt to overlook" (Furner, p. 91).

4 It is worth noting that Furner barely mentions the American Historical Association (1884), which formed part of the same general movement, presumably because she does not regard history as a social science, although it has been included within the domain of the (US) Social Science Research Council. Incidentally, the date of formation of a scholarly society is an unreliable guide to the professionalization of the discipline in question. History in America was dominated by amateurs until the early years of this century. See John Higham, *History: The Development of Historical Studies in the United States* (Englewood Cliffs, New Jersey, 1965).

5 For a lively, but not altogether satisfactory, survey see Richard Hofstadter, *Anti-Intellectualism in American Life* (New York, 1962).

6 Laurence R. Veysey, *The Emergence of the American University* (Chicago, 1965) is an excellent general introduction to the subject. See also Frederick Rudolph, *The American College and University* (New York, 1962).

7 The pioneer work is Richard Hofstadter and Walter P. Metzger, *The Development of Academic Freedom in the United States* (New York, 1953). This was subsequently republished, under the respective authors' names, as *Academic Freedom in the Age of the College*, and *Academic Freedom in the Age of the University*.

8 In addition to the Hofstadter and Metzger study cited in the preceding footnote the main general works are Robert MacIver, *Academic Freedom in Our Times* (New York, 1955); and Paul Lazarsfeld and W. Thielens, *The Academic Mind, Social Scientists in a Time of Crisis* (Glencoe, 111., 1958).

9 See, for example, Theodore Caplow and R. McGhee, *The Academic Marketplace* (New York, 1958).

10 It is noteworthy that Thorstein Veblen's famous indictment of the influence of business, and the emergence of a new style of " captains of erudition," does not appear in Furner's bibliography. See Veblen, *The Higher Learning in America: A Memorandum on the Conduct of Universities by Businessmen* (New York, 1918). This study was published about twelve years after it was written. The conspiracy thesis is discussed in Metzger, Chap. 4.

11 Furner, p. 240. One wonders why she did not pursue this reference to history.

12 See my article, " Henry Carter Adams: A Case Study in the Emergence of the Social Sciences in the United States, 1850–1900," *Journal of American Studies*, 2 (Oct. 1968), 177–97.

31 The rhetoric of economists

A comment on McCloskey*

(*with Bruce J. Caldwell*)

In "The Rhetoric of Economics," Donald McCloskey (1983) argues for a new approach to the methodology of economics. The official methodology is "modernism," which consists of "an amalgam of logical positivism, behaviorism, operationalism, and the hypothetico-deductive model of science" (p. 484). But modernism is a poor method because it is "obsolete in philosophy" (p. 486), has not been followed in other sciences (pp. 491–93), runs into problems of application in economics (pp. 487–88); indeed, is itself "impossible" (p. 488). If this were not enough, *any* method is arrogant and pretentious; (p. 490). Economists need not worry, however, because our unofficial methodology, *what economists actually follow*, is rhetoric – honorable but unexamined (p. 493). Praised earlier as "disciplined conversation" (pp. 482–83), rhetoric is a literary matter (p. 499), heavily metaphorical, which comprises a poetics of economics (pp. 502–05). Various examples of such rhetoric are offered (pp. 495–508) and the benefits of its study are enumerated (pp. 512–15).

We are in qualified agreement with many parts of McCloskey's witty and provocative article. For example, though more careful and accurate (but less entertaining!) reviews of the demise of positivism are in the literature (e.g. Frederick Suppe, Mark Blaug, Bruce Caldwell), few would question McCloskey's main thesis that modernism is in eclipse.[1] Also, it is widely agreed that the main problem with modernism is that no science, inducting economics, has ever followed; or could ever follow its prescriptions. (Only Paul K. Feyerabend would assent to his claim that any method is arrogant and pretentious, however.) Finally, McCloskey's appeal to "see what economists actually do" is not only laudable, but a common cry among contemporary philosophers of science (e.g., Daniel Hausman, 1981, pp. 215–26; Larry Lauden, 1977).

But there are serious problems with McCloskey's piece, due to his having ignored the rather sizeable post-positivist literature that developed within the methodology of economics. McCloskey does not seem to be aware of this literature. How else can one explain the rather bizarre notion, implicit in his article, that the collapse of modernism entails the end of methodology (p. 483, especially note 1)? Of course, he has it exactly wrong: the crumbling of the philosophical foundations of positivist methodology has caused a tremendous increase in the amount of methodological work, in economics as well as in other disciplines.[2]

Researchers in economic methodology are currently grappling with a number of profound and troubling questions engendered by the decline of modernism. If science can no longer be distinguished from other human enterprises by its method, how can it be distinguished? What *is* science? Does it have specific defining characteristics? Are there many types of science? Is there progress in science? How is it measured? What about the rationality of science? Why do various research programs emerge, change, and wither away? Is the rational appraisal of theories possible, ex ante? These are broad, far-ranging questions that go beyond the boundaries of economics to philosophy, history, sociology, and other fields. Far from being dead, methodology has dramatically increased its scope in the past few years.

McCloskey deals with at least some of these questions in his own way. He argues that if we look at what economists really do we will see that they argue using the tools of rhetoric. This is certainly one way of responding to the collapse of modernism. But McCloskey fails to realize that it is only one of many possible responses, each of which has its own strengths and limitations.

What other responses are possible? Some economists insist that modernism can and should be replaced by another prescriptive methodology, such as falsificationism or instrumentalism. The merits and weaknesses of these and other prescriptive methodologies have provided grist for numerous recent debates. Other economists eschew particular prescriptions and urge that some form of methodological pluralism be followed, which usually blends prescription and description. Still others believe, with McCloskey, that description is the best we can do, and they have turned to methodological analyses of the practice of economists.[3]

Each of these responses has its own virtues and, more important, its limitations. Prescriptive approaches to methodology are too often strict and confining, and McCloskey is justified in leveling this charge against modernism. The danger of a pluralistic approach is that its prescriptive content may be reduced to "anything goes." And the problem with a purely descriptive approach is, though the author may insist that his is simply an honest, objective description, his own prescriptive biases are inevitably injected into the analysis.

As Donald McCloskey the economic historian knows very well, this problem always exists when one attempts to describe something: reality is everywhere dense. Observation thus requires selection. All description is from a point of view. McCloskey's description of forms of argumentation in economics is novel and suggestive, but it is only one of many such possible and plausible descriptions.

But, we would like to raise an additional and more serious objection to McCloskey's piece. He argues: "any method is arrogant and pretentious" and that at no time should methodology be allowed to "interfere with" practice (p. 490). Apparently, then, methodological articles should avoid offering prescriptions. Yet we find that McCloskey's article is filled with proposals for improving economists' practice! These cover such matters as the improvement of writing, teaching, foreign relations, science, and personal dispositions (p. 512 ff.); the inculcation of enhanced self-consciousness – a familiar methodologist's prayer – with respect to rhetoric, the use of metaphor, and the grounding of arguments (pp. 482, 502, 507); and repeated reference to desirable "standards" (pp. 496–97, 499, 509).

In one valuable section he provides instructive examples of unsatisfactory practice, designed, presumably, to serve as warnings and to raise "standards" (pp. 495–99). If McCloskey believes that methodological prescriptions are arrogant and pretentious, why does he include so many? If, on the other hand, he believes that there is a difference between good and bad practice, why doesn't he tell us which criteria he is using to distinguish between them?

We believe strongly that good methodological work includes, of necessity, both prescriptive and descriptive elements, and that discovering the best blend of the two is one of the most perplexing yet significant tasks facing methodologists today (Caldwell, 1982, Ch. 11). Despite his disclaimer that prescription in methodology is pretentious and arrogant, McCloskey apparently believes (to his credit!) that there is a difference between good and bad rhetoric, that practice can be prescribed. But he never answers satisfactorily the fundamental question: How do we tell good rhetoric from bad?

His nostrums that "well-educated participants" should know the difference and that the "justly influential" will show us the way (p. 512) are uncharacteristically conservative. Feyerabend, whom he praises, would gag at the suggestion that such decisions be left to the justly influential! But, more important, such answers beg all of the major questions. Who are the justly influential? What distinguishes them from the unjustly influential, or the unjustly non-influential? Even if we could identify the justly influential (e.g. nobel laureates or presidents of the American Economic Association), what if their views are as diverse as those of Milton Friedman and Paul Samuel-son, Gunnar Myrdal and F. A. Hayek?

If McCloskey replies, "The justly influential are those whose views are *most* persuasive over time," that would simply apply the survivalist thesis to methodology, and it has as little content here as elsewhere in economics. For, the question remains: What sorts of arguments persuade economists, and why? And *that is* the age-old problem as to which weights should be given to various criteria of theory appraisal. For example: Is generality more important than simplicity? Is explanatory power more important than predictive power? Such issues have occupied methodologists for decades, although McCloskey has added an interesting new twist by describing the criteria in literary terms.

McCloskey is writing a book on the rhetoric of economics, and this last point may help him in his efforts – our contribution to "better science" and "better dispositions." A number of recent methodological studies conclude that the theory choice problem is insoluble (Blaug, 1980, p. 27; Boland, 1982, pp. 17–26; Caldwell, 1982, Chs. 11, 12). This has caused some economists to turn to the sociology of science to see whether it helps to explain how theories develop in economics. Of particular interest is the "Strong Program" in the sociology of knowledge, now developing at Edinburgh University, which has a certain similarity to McCloskey's approach.[4] This program examines how scientists argue in order to discover what causal conditions bring about their beliefs. Perhaps more important, the Strong Program does not concern itself with the truth of beliefs, but with how particular beliefs come to be shared by a scientific community (whether they are true or false). Such an approach might support McCloskey, allowing him to avoid the conundrums of the theory- appraisal problem. But it leaves unexplained the critical issue: How to distinguish between true and false beliefs and, more specifically, how to distinguish between reasoning patterns in science as against other disciplines.

To conclude: McCloskey is right in claiming that modernism is dead. He is wrong in maintaining that methodology is dead. Indeed, his article is part of the growing tide of post-positivist literature in methodology. Had he paid closer attention to that literature, he would have realized that his but one of many possible responses to the decline of modernism, and he would have been more cognizant of the limitations of his approach. In particular, though his reinterpretation of the traditional criteria of theory appraisal in terms of the canons of rhetoric is novel, he does not deal adequately with the theory-appraisal problem of identifying which rhetorical tropes are most persuasive. One possible way out of this dilemma is for McCloskey to incorporate contributions from the sociology of science, an approach which bears some similarities to his own.

Notes

* Valuable comments were given by Ken Snowden, but we are responsible for accuracy.

1 Without wishing to get bogged down in semantics, we must nonetheless register our objection to McCloskey's startlingly idiosyncratic, use (at least among economists) of such terms as "modernism," "rhetoric," and "conversation." We cannot ignore this issue, because these terms are central to his argument but are only vaguely defined. The first two are evidently borrowed from recent, especially poststructuralist, debates in literature, linguistics, and sociology. Such importation is not objectionable in principle, but consistency and clarity in their usage is essential, and this McCloskey has not provided. Thus, the precise relationship between "modernism" and "positivism" (itself, admittedly, often a weasel-word) is obscure. "Rhetoric" is used in at least seven different ways, varying from the derogatory (e.g. "mere" rhetoric, p. 482) to the salutory (p. 483), from a narrow version which stresses its classical roots to a broader version that is virtually co-extensive with reason itself. And the term "conversation," even in its "disciplined" form, is simply vague.

2 Ironically, McCloskey seems better informed about developments in other fields than in his own (pp. 491–93). For the record, at least nineteen books and collections of reading have been published on economic methodology since 1975. (They are listed in the References.) The number of articles on methodology presented at the History of Economics Society's (HES) annual conferences has increased dramatically in recent years. (Titles and abstracts are printed in the summer issue of the HES bulletin each year.) Finally, about a dozen economists offer surveys of the field in the 1984 edition of the annual, *Research in the History of Economic Thought and Methodology*.

3 For four very different views of these subjects, compare the finid chapters of Blaug, (1980); Lawrence Boland, (1982); Caldwell, (1982); and Hausman, (1981).

4 Though this list is not exhaustive, some important works include Barry Barnes (1974, 1977, 1982), Barnes and David Bloor (1982), Bloor (1976) and Steven Shapin (1982). Many of these works contain substantial bibliographies.

References

Barnes Barry. *Scientific knowledge and sociological theory*. London: Routledge & Kegan Paul, 1974.

——. *Interests and the growth of knowledge*. London: Routledge & Kegan Paul, 1977.

——. *T. S. Kuhn and social science*. NY: Columbia U. Press, 1982.
——. and Bloor, David "Relativism, Rationalism and the Sociology of Knowledge," *in Rationality and relativism*. Eds.: Martin Hollis, and Stevens Lukes. Cambridge, MA: MIT Press, 1982, pp. 21–47.
Blaug, Mark *The methodology of economics*. Cambridge: Cambridge U. Press, 1980.
Bloor, David. *Knowledge and social imagery*. London: Routledge & Kegan Paul, 1976.
——. "The Strengths of the Strong Program," *Philosophy of the Social Sciences*, June 1981, *11*, pp. 199–213.
Boland, Lawrence A. *The foundations of economic methodology*. London: Allen & Unwin, 1982.
Caldwell, Bruce J. *Beyond positivism: Economic methodology in the twentieth century*. London: Allen & Unwin, 1982.
Hahn, Frank and Hollis, Martin eds. *Philosophy and economic theory*. Oxford: Oxford U. Press, 1979.
Hausman, Daniel. *Capital, profits and prices: An essay in the philosophy of economics*. NY: Columbia U. Press, 1981.
——. ed. *The methodology of economics*. Cambridge: Cambridge U. Press, Forthcoming.
Hollis, Martin and Nell, E. J. *Rational economic man: A philosophical critique of neoclassical economics*. Cambridge: Cambridge U. Press, 1975.
Hutchison, Terence W. *Knowledge and ignorance in economics*. Oxford: Basil Blackwell, 1977.
——. *On revolutions and progress in economic knowledge*. Cambridge: Cambridge U. Press, 1978.
——. *The politics and philosophy of economics: Marxians, Keynesians and Austrians*. Oxford: Basil Blackwell, 1981.
Katouzian, Homa. *Ideology and method in economics*. NY: NYU Press, 1980.
Latsis, Spiro, ed: *Method and appraisal in economics*. Cambridge: Cambridge U. Press, 1976.
Lauden, Larry. "The Sources of Modem Methodology," in *Historical and philosophical dimensions of logic, methodology, and philosophy of science*. Eds.: Robert Botts and Jaakko Hintikka. Dordrecht, Holland: D. Reidel, 1977, pp. 3–19.
Machlup, Fritz. *Methodology of economics and other social sciences*. NY: Academic Press, 1978.
Mackay, Alfred. *Arrow's theorem: The paradox of social choice: A case study in the philosophy of economics*. New Haven: Yale U. Press, 1980.
Marr, William and Raj, Baldev, eds. *How economists explain: A reader in methodology*. Lanhma, MD: U. Press of America, 1983.
McCloskey, Donald. "The Rhetoric of Economics," *Journal of Economic Literature*, June 1983, 1(2), pp. 481–517.
Rosenberg, Alexander. *Microeconomic laws: A philosophical analysis*. Pittsburgh: U. of Pittsburgh Press, 1976.
Shapin, Steven. "History of Science and its Sociological Reconstructions," *History of Science*, 1982, *20*, pp. 157–211.
Stewart, Ian. *Reasoning and method in economics: An introduction to economic methodology*. London: McGraw Hill, 1979.
Suppe, Frederick, ed. *The structure of scientific theories*. 2nd. ed. Urbana: U. of Illinois Press, 1977.
Wiseman, Jack, ed. *Beyond positive economics:* NY: St. Martin's Press, 1983.
Wong, Stanley, *The foundations of Paul Samuel son's revealed preference theory: A study by the method of rational reconstruction*. London: Routledge & Kegan Paul, 1978.

32 Further comments on McCloskey's argument

A. W. Coats

It is difficult to summerize McCloskey's argument briefly and fairly, given the wide range of topics he covers and the distinctiveness and force of his literary style. The conscientious critic faces the task of separating the grains of cognitive wheat from the polemical and declamatory chaff; of exposing and assessing the central argument without being unduly distracted by the accompanying rhetorical embellishments and the parade of sources and authorities unfamiliar to many methodologists, let alone humble workaday practising economists.

The interpretative problem posed by McCloskey's recent publications is to distinguish among three interrelated targets of his attack:

1. The more extreme manifestations of "modernism" proposed by certain philosophers and specialist methodologists, which are now generally discredited;
2. the crude misuse or abuse of modernist claims by illiterate economist practitioners seeking a weapon against their professional opponents and other 'softer' social scientists;
3. the best predominantly anti-positivist current literature in economic methodology. It is currently in a state of flux owing to the loss of confidence in economics as a science, and recent controversies in the philosophy, history and sociology of science.

On a sympathetic reading, it seems that McCloskey is mainly concerned with (ii), while devoting most of his polemic energy to attacking (i) – largely a dead horse – and unintentially or deliberately misrepresenting (iii). In so doing he is diverting attention from the current stimulating and constructive work in economic methodology, thereby undermining his professed aim of promoting good disciplinary conversation. Statements of the kind that "all talk of causes is [merely?] metaphorical" or that "philosophical consistency" is merely an "appeal to a figure of speech" (pp. 80, 101) gloss over or obscure matters that require much more thorough discussion.

A major point that deserves further development is McCloskey's contention that "the standards of 'good' reasons and 'warrantable' belief and 'plausible' conclusions" are, in a sense, immanent since they come from

> the conversations of practitioners themselves, in their laboratories or seminar rooms or conference halls. It is the sort of evaluation that economists and other dealers in ideas do anyway, by professional habit (p. 29).

Such conversations are at least partly closed to outsiders, for "if you are not familiar with the history of a conversation, you will misunderstand the remarks made in it, and if you are bold, you will make remarks of your own that do not bear on the issue" (pp. 130–1). While all conversations, whether in science or elsewhere, have common features that the rhetorical approach emphasizes, each field has its 'special topics' which are only known to the cognoscendi. And although he does not explicitly say so, perhaps the best argument against orthodox methodology, especially in its more rigid and dictatorial manifestations, is that the outsider is incapable either of understanding or evaluating what is going on among the practitioners. But if this is what McCloskey is really getting at he could have done so much more clearly and directly. Indeed, his frequent allusions to the role of the audience and the social character of knowledge, science and scholarship, lead directly into the existing rich and rapidly growing literature of the history and sociology of science. Whether this literature eliminates the need for epistemological or methodological analysis and interpretation, as for example advocates of the Strong program maintain, is still unsettled. Unfortunately McCloskey does not discuss how to distinguish between "well-educated participants in the conversations of our civilization and of our field" (p. 46) and the rest of mankind. Nor does he shed any light on the structure and internal functioning of the scholarly and scientific communities who engage in disciplined conversations. Perhaps here is a function for the methodologist-cum-historian-cum-sociologist.

Beyond this, I believe, contrary to McCloskey, that a study of the recent literature of economic methodology, far from being inhibiting or constricting, is actually liberating – albeit confusing – given the wide variety, controversial character, and even incompatibility of current views, not to mention their transitional elements. The significant constraints and inhibitions in contemporary economics derive not from methodological literature, which has never exerted great influence, but from the organization and structure of the economics profession. Of particular importance, especially in the U.S.A., seem to be the relative homogeneity of economics textbooks; the standardization and narrowness of training, especially at the advanced level; and the influence of economic orthodoxy on such matters as the choice of suitable dissertation topics, professional placement and promotions (especially in the so-called elite academic institutions), and the management of the leading professional journals, learned societies, conference programs, and the award of prizes and honors. There is a growing professional protest literature focused on these matters, and many of McCloskey's legitimate complaints can be brought under this umbrella. Unfortunately professional inertia is such that no significant change is likely in this state of affairs.

33 Economic rhetoric

The social and historical context

I

By comparison with the situation in literary studies, the discussion of economic rhetoric or discourse (the terms will be used interchangeably here) is still in its infancy. In this respect economics clearly lags behind other branches of science studies,[1] which is hardly surprising, considering economists' general lack of interest in cognate fields of inquiry and their manifest disdain for the history of their own discipline. Notwithstanding the pretensions of some of its proponents, it is still too early to judge whether the study of economic discourse will eventually grow up to become a mature research program with a recognized place and influence on its parent discipline, The preliminary results are promising, even exciting, and as budding research programs require nurturing, it is appropriate at this stage to focus on the constructive possibilities.

To the present writer this self-denying ordinance imposes severe constraints, for the Klamer/McCloskey (KM) agenda incorporates a number of negative features that constitute serious impediments to a balanced appraisal of its implications for an understanding of the development and functioning of economics as an academic discipline and a profession. The KM campaign is based on, and actively propagates, a currently fashionable radical epistemology (or antiepistemology) that directly conflicts with widely accepted views of the nature and purposes of the scientific enterprise. In particular. Mc Closkey's exaggerated and misdirected attack on economic methodology (rather than the abuse of it) – in which he has lumped together and caricatured various intellectual positions under the blanket label "modernism" – is both "alarming"[2] – (as he intends) and confusing. He willfully blurs the distinction between familiar and useful categories, for instance, declaring. "Economics is a collection of literary forms, not a science. Indeed, science is a collection of literary forms, not a science. And literary forms are scientific." Moreover, lest the reader should infer that economics (like science) is not a science, he adds helpfully a page later, that "economics *is* science, a successful sort at that. "Elsewhere he also terms it "a peculiar variant of social history. "humanism," equivalent (identical?) to "sociology," and "literary too."[3]

No doubt these terminological maneuvers are designed to have a shock effect, to disturb the reader's complacency prior to changing the conventions of established economic discourse, and, indeed, the initial impact may well be salutary. Whether in the long run this practice promotes "good" disciplinary conversation – that is, mutual comprehension as a basis for intersubjective agreement in the advancement of knowledge – is another matter.

Unfortunately the concepts of "rhetoric," "conversation," and "persuasion" that figure so prominently in the KM campaign are not sufficiently clear, precise, and comprehensive to provide a basis for understanding the distinctive character, operation, and social significance of economics or any other intellectual discipline. The initial applications of discourse and rhetorical analysis in case studies of rational expectations, economics textbooks, the use of statistical significance tests, and the writings of Muth Fogel, et al., have undoubtedly been illuminating, providing a useful addition to the repertoire of concepts and techniques already available to serious students and practitioners of the discipline. Whether the techniques of literary criticism can significantly enhance our knowledge and understanding of the substance of a purportedly "scientific" discipline remains an open question.[4] It is appropriate to recall the intellectual historian's quip that "text without context is pretext." and to suggest that the KM campaign has so far lacked the depth of insight and evidential richness to be found in numerous recent history and sociology of science studies.

Critics of the KM program who sense that the preoccupation with rhetoric and discourse is, indeed, "mere" conversation, that it lacks adequate contextual substance or "thick description" (in Clifford Geertz's sense), are unlikely to be reassured by the accompanying all-out attack on empiricism and the moderate realist interpretation of science. Among other controversial claims. KM reject the philosopher's concept of a demarcation criterion by which to differentiate science from other species of knowledge, they appear to deny the possibility of any "objective" knowledge of the world, and they dismiss or belittle the notion that truth is the (or a) goal of scientific research. These views faithfully reflect the uncertain and volatile postpositivist state of the philosophy of science and economic methodology, raising questions too fundamental and far-reaching to be treated adequately here. Nevertheless they demand some attention, however brief. before turning to the more mundane purpose of this chapter, which is designed to suggest how a more direct and conventional sociological approach can add depth and content to the KM campaign.

II

One obstacle to good conversation between KM and their critics is the coexistence of conflicting concepts of discourse, currently a topic of active discussion among historians and sociologists of science. According to the so-called Anglo-Saxon view, discourse is epiphenomenal and clearly distinguishable from actual scientific practice *(praxis)*, whereas KM, in conformity with continental authors like Foucault, deny or seek to dissolve the distinction between language and action. To Foucault. for instance, discourse is *constitutive* : While it does not actually prohibit a distinction between a thing and what is said about a thing (which is crucial for realists), it insists that the distinction is actively created rather than an inescapable feature of reality.[5] KM apparently view knowledge simply as an ongoing, ever-changing product of conversation that can be usefully studied virtually without reference to what is "out there" in the world. Nevertheless it is entirely possible to accept the constructivist's account of knowledge as an active, creative process without at the same time denying the existence of "reality." To the historian and sociologist the concepts of language-community and speech-community, cited by Klamer, are useful in analyzing past and present economic "schools" (as will be suggested below in part VI), and the same applies to Clifford Geertz's ethnographic approach[6] which recalls Axel Leijonhufvud's light-hearted but brilliantly incisive anthropological account of the economics tribe.[7] The concepts of initiation rites and the socialization of new recruits into economics are familiar, but they have not been systematically utilized.[8] Yet when Klamer goes on to approve Geertz's argument that scholarly disciplines are not simply "coigns of vantage," but also "ways of being in the world ... forms of life ... or varieties of noetic experience." and Nelson Goodman's idea of the "multiple actual worlds" presupposed indifferent conversations, it is time to plant our feet more firmly on the ground and reemphasize the subject matter (i.e., content) variations between (and indeed within) disciplines.[9]

Curiously enough, the aura of philosophical (or literary) abstraction in some parts of the KM writings sharply contrasts with much recent research in science studies. At one time sociologists of knowledge (for example, Karl Mannheim) were justly accused of dealing in vague general categories that were not amenable to historical research. Nowadays, however, the focus has shifted markedly as the effort to discover "what scientists actually do" has led to a preoccupation with minutiae, so that the broader purposes of the undertaking are obscured by the details. While one may warmly endorse Richard Rorty's claim on behalf of community "solidarity, "expressing "the desire for as much inter-subjective agreement as possible,"[10] it does not follow that this solidarity "is threatened by the pursuit of objectivity which values a relationship with something outside the community above relationships within."[11] On the contrary, Rorty puts the cart before the horse. It is the collective quest for "reliable" intersubjective knowledge that has created the broader scientific community, giving it special, historically identifiable, characteristics.[12] Nor is it necessary (or desirable?) to deny the existence of "one world" simply because there are multiple ways of perceiving and interpreting it. As Mary Hesse observes, in a critique of radical conventionalism (an approach apparently favored by KM):

> Science does not depend on algorithmic rules of methodology, nor on necessary and sufficient conditions for what counts as replicability, and in general, science need not be supposed to exhibit one-to-one correspondence with objects and regularities in the world independently of human categories and classifications.[13]

Nevertheless, science exhibits "order," which reflects the order of the natural world. It stems from the scientists' collective interest in "predictability and control in the natural environment" hence their preoccupation with such matters as "confirmation, falsifiability, instrumentality, objective respectability, technical interest," and so on. The view that these social habits are purely conventional, and do not reflect some actual order in the world, is unnecessarily destructive. The belief in that order is the basis on which we conduct our daily lives; without it there would be personal (psychological) and social disintegration. To Hesse:

> Without the assumption that social habits have grown to reflect some order in the world ... [we cannot] explain the general success of the expectations we have to rely on for everyday practical needs. Some biological needs are common to all cultures, and would explain why many inductive assumptions are the same in all cultures in similar environments. In other respects different cultures may have different needs and correspondingly different linguistic classifications.[14]

III

The so-called Strong Program (SP) in the sociology of knowledge, a radically relativist conception that asserts the primacy of sociological over all other interpretations of scientific knowledge and procedures, has much in common with the KM interpretation.[15] SP advocates question the supposedly universal and immutable correct principles that have usually figured so prominently in methodology and philosophy of science writings, emphasizing instead the local, contingent, and context-dependent character of scientists' beliefs and activities and arguing that the explanation of beliefs is independent of their status, whether true or false, scientific or nonscientific. They focus on the "internal" sociology of knowledge, arguing that the methodological rules, heuristic principles, basic norms and conventions adopted by any scientific group have no absolute, unique, or universal validity and significance. The language employed, systems of classification, logical conventions and procedures inferences, and judgments are all learned within the relevant segment of the scientific community. Instead of defining a theory in the conventional manner as "a system of statements perhaps or a formal mathematical structure from which particular solutions are deduced or logically derived ... the tables are turned, and a theory ... is defined by its applications: it is simply the cluster of what are called its 'applications' " or problem solutions.[16]

According to the SP – as can be the case with the rhetorical or discourse approach – there is a general correspondence between knowledge and reality," but reality can be perceived, described, and interpreted in a variety of different ways. There is no single criterion of truth acceptable in all cultures, and scientific concepts, theories, paradigms, tests, judgments, and so on are simply conventions approved by the scientific community. However, this does not mean that these conventions are either arbitrary or lax: On the contrary, they derive from stringent rules and procedures that cannot easily be mastered or changed. Science is based on order, continuity, authority and control, and while it is neither rigid nor inflexible the scope for novelty and innovation is strictly limited by the recognized conventions (tradition) and by the specific circumstances of the scientist's field.[17] Tradition governs the accepted theories. methods, and techniques in any discipline, and also the selection, training. qualification, and socialization of recruits.

This account, which in many respects resembles Kuhn's description of "normal" science, provides the context for disciplinary "conversation" and the persuasive deployment of techniques and forms of argumentation a state of affairs that depicts "many characteristics of cognition and culture which it is difficult to imagine could be otherwise."[18] Radical criticism is possible "only where there are more than one set of standards and conventions and more than one conceivable definition of reality.''[19] This does not mean that normal disciplinary conversation is static. On the contrary, acceptable usage and procedure is "developed step by step in a succession of on-the-spot judgments. Every instance of use, or proper use, of a concept must in the last analysis be accounted for separately, by reference to specific, local, contingent circumstances,"[20] and "there is no basis for validation superior to the collective contingent judgment of the paradigm-sharing community itself."[21]

Needless to say, several features of the SP are highly controversial. Critics complain of the overemphasis on sociological determinants, the particularistic description of scientific work, and the relativistic denial of an epistemological distinction between science and other forms of knowledge, making it difficult to explain why modern science has developed as a peculiar and crucially important species of knowledge. The tendency to treat the social process of knowledge production as chaotic makes the eventual emergence of agreement on results appear mysterious or inexplicable; hence it is necessary to provide a more generalized and comprehensible account of scientific work and its significance both for the growth of knowledge and for society at large. An impressive step in that direction has been taken by Richard Whitley, who insists on the interdependence of the content of science at any stage and the concepts, propositions, reasonings and methods employed by the relevant group of scientists. Whereas the SP treats scientists' judgments and scientific change merely as epiphenomena of material causes and interests. Whitley claims that these interests and scientific beliefs are reciprocally interrelated, so that

> ... the sociology of knowledge should concern itself with the configuration of relations linking beliefs, rationalities, social structures, and the organization of knowledge production. Sociological accounts of the genesis, elaboration and acceptance of scientific beliefs ... need to reconstruct the procedures and practices through which it made sense to particular groups to believe one theory or set of statements rather than another.[22]

IV

McCloskey's conception of rhetoric as a complex blend of literary devices and styles, persuasive arguments, and modes of communication can, in principle, be applied systematically to the structure of audiences for the economist's output, in combination with Klamer's analysis of "levels" of discourse. In his stimulating book, *Conversations with Economists*, Klamer identified the principal components of economic conversation as comprising

1. Core claims
2. Various types of arguments, including
   a. Theoretical
   b. Empirical
   c. Epistemological (methodological)
   d. Philosophical (ideological)
   e. Commonsense
   f. Metaarguments
3. Personal and social factors.[23]

This list is formidable, and perhaps overly subtle. Applied in conjunction with the various types of audiences it offers an irresistible challenge to mathematical manipulators. Without attempting to be exhaustive, a necessary classification of audiences would have to include the following:

1. Undergraduates – differentiating between elementary and advanced students
2. Graduates – including specialists (prospective recruits to the economics profession) and students in other fields (e.g., business, law, engineering, public policy)
3. Professional economists
   a. Academics (in a variety of special fields and doctoral schools, possibly differentiating between elite and nonelite academics)
   b. Nonacademic economists, for example, in business, banking, governments (federal, state, and local), international agencies, and so on
4. Noneconomist academics, for example, deans, promotion committees, research grant committees
5. Nonacademic audiences, including "experts" in other fields; government and international agency bureaucrats; business persons, bankers, politicians, journalists; foundation boards; and members of the lay public (intelligent and otherwise)

How far it would be either practicable or fruitful to study these various combinations of economic arguments and audiences is a question that need not concern us here. Some groupings are clearly more feasible and promising than others, being instructive in analyzing the spread of economic ideas, a long neglected topic that is now beginning to attract serious scholarly attention.[24] Rather than pursuing this line of inquiry, however, the remainder of this chapter will focus on some issues in the KM agenda that have been considered in earlier economic literature. While pointing to contextual matters that have previously been considered, sometimes inadequately, the following examples may suggest topics for future investigators armed with the new rhetoric and discourse (r&d?) apparatus.

V

One of the economist's greatest assets – the fact that his discipline deals with questions of obvious public interest and importance – has also been a major source of vulnerability, for economists have rarely been able for long to enjoy the measure of insulation from external pressures considered essential to sustained intellectual and scientific inquiry. In other words, the internal and external sociology of economics have invariably overlapped and interpenetrated in various ways. Consequently economists have long recognized that open disagreements within their ranks, especially those involving fundamental issues of principle and policy, were bound to impair their individual and collective reputations as scientists or experts, and they have accordingly proposed various means of reducing, suppressing, or eliminating unnecessary controversy. The nature of these means has obviously varied contextually, according to the state of the discipline, the number of practitioners, and their relations with the general public.

Richard Whitley has recently provided a systematic analysis of scientific fields in terms of the degree of their "reputational autonomy" from competing organizations and the wider social structure over such matters as the setting of performance standards, the assessment of problems, and the development of research strategies.[25] Fields can be characterized by references to their domain, problems, and descriptive language, and the last of these is especially pertinent to economics and the KM campaign. As Whitley has observed:

> ... the topics which economics purports to deal with are important everyday issues and the terminology of economic analysis is close to ordinary language even if technical definitions of these terms are quite distinct. Profit, for example, has a technical meaning in microeconomics which is not the same as usages in conventional accounting – which themselves vary. In their internal discussions and rankings of intellectual significance of contributions economists use their technical concepts and their own standards of evaluation, yet they also make policy pronouncements and seek to intervene in everyday debates and discussions where terms are not technically defined and they do not control usages. Indeed, it seems unlikely that economics could receive so much financial support if it was not thought that its subjects and problems were strongly connected with everyday phenomena. Thus, within the professional fraternity, performance and significance standards, and technical terminology, are fairly strongly controlled by the reputational elite but there is also considerable overlap with common sense terms and concerns which legitimates public support and sometimes affects standards. As with the problem of demonstrating effective technical control over phenomena, this difficulty is resolved to some extent in economics by separating analytical economics by fields of application and elevating the former to a position of dominance and insulating it from external influences to a very high degree. Thus economics is a hybrid science in which divergent features are combined so that the core exhibits different characteristics to the peripheral subfields.[26]

Early nineteenth-century British economics provides a wealth of examples of economists' desire for unity, the difficulties of achieving it, and their concern to protect the intellectual authority of the *cognoscenti* against criticism from the lay public.[27] There was at that time virtually no formal training in economics and no clear demarcation between those who were qualified to write or speak on economic topics and those who were not. Most of the leading economists, "the gloomy professors of the dismal science," as Thomas Carlyle termed them, spent only a small proportion of their lives in academic chairs if that, and their decision to found the Political Economy Club of London in 1821, to disseminate "sound" ideas, can be viewed both as a professional and political act. Most of the club's members shared common values about the ends of economic activity, as well as other liberal moral philosophical ideas, and although the boundaries of the "scientific community" were blurred, there was at least a clear distinction between the economists and their most articulate opponents, the literary critics-interestingly enough, at a time when the emergence of a distinct literary "profession" is clearly discernible.[28] The question whether economics was a purely logical discipline, as Robert Torrens implied in claiming that its arguments constituted "proof amounting to strictly mathematical demonstration," or a science of "fact and experiment," as John Ramsay McCulloch argued, need not detain us.[29] But the interdependence of methodology and professionalism, a much neglected theme in the history of economics, clearly underlay s James Mill's insistence on the need to establish "the criteria and tests of a science" in his essay on the usefulness of political economy. Mill claimed:

> Among those who have so much knowledge on the subject as to entitle their opinion to any weight, there is wonderful agreement … A reasoner must be hard pressed when he is driven to quote practical men in aid of his conclusions. There cannot be a worse authority, in any branch of political science. than that of merely practical men.[30]

Mill grudgingly conceded the existence of some dispute "on the minor questions involved." but the economists' desire for collective solidarity was such that another member of the Political Economy Club, Thomas Robert Malthus, whose differences with Mill and David Ricardo were by no means minor, was also concerned to minimize damaging public dissension. In his *Definitions in Political Economy* (1827),[31] the first work of its kind in English, he made a sustained attempt to prescribe rules designed to eliminate purely verbal disagreements among economists on the following grounds:

> Till some steadiness is given to the science by the greater degree of care among its professors not to alter [terminology] without improving – it cannot be expected that it should attain that general influence in society which (its principles being just) would be of the highest practical utility.[32]

Malthus acknowledged that the frequent complaints about "the differences of opinion among political economists" might be reduced by introducing "a new and more perfect nomenclature." thereby enabling that subject to approach more closely "to the strict science of mathematics." but he also conceded that a change "would not be submitted to" in a science like morals and politics. "where the terms are comparatively few, and of constant application in the daily concerns of life."[33]

Needless to say. Malthus failed to achieve his objective, and the same is true of innumerable later schemes, including the American Economic Association's early action in establishing a committee to explore ways of reaching agreement on the use of terms, and the recent proposals to standardize the use of symbols in economic models.[34] To cite a different type of activity, the refusal of American journal editors to agree on uniform conventions (e.g., in the use of citations and footnotes), so that an author could send a rejected typescript to a succession of periodicals without extensive revisions, is testimony to the strength of individualism in a discipline traditionally hostile to all forms of collusion and monopoly practice. Professional solidarity obviously has distinct limits.

The basic defect of schemes to standardize language on some French Academy – type model, was acknowledged in Lindley Fraser's classic *Economic Thought and Language* (1937), namely:

> If economists as a whole were to adopt a corpus of technical terms, each one with an unalterable meaning and content, there would be a real danger of their being left behind by the march of events. A static terminology is not well suited to the study of dynamic phenomena.[35]

It was also vital to maintain contact with "ordinary life," to cite Alfred Marshall's self-consciously pedestrian expression. Nevertheless, like many of his contemporaries and predecessors, Fraser was keenly aware of the errors and confusions resulting from uninhibited individualism in terminological usage, some of which reflect deliberate authorial efforts to differentiate a theoretical product. Oddly enough, his attempt to demonstrate "the frequency with which economists have not merely misunderstood each other's arguments but have even failed to grasp the implications of their own contentions"[36] was published during a major controversy over the terms *savings* and *investment*, which John Maynard Keynes had defined in the *General Theory* (1936) in direct contradiction to the definitions he had used six years earlier in his *Treatise on Money*. How far the differences were "merely" terminological rather than substantive and theoretically significant was a question actively debated in the leading economic journals.

In recent decades the most assiduous and perceptive student of economic language has undoubtedly been Fritz Machlup. whose collected *Essays on Economic Semantics* were published a quarter of a century-ago.[37] Machlup was not only concerned with terminological inconsistencies, vagueness and similar sources of misunderstanding, focusing on targets like kaleidoscopic and weasel words, jargon, and misplaced concreteness, he was also eager to expose the unintentional or deliberate employment of persuasive definitions and disguised politics lurking behind a cloak of scientific respectability. Machlup was anything but authoritarian, insisting that "the semanticist may analyze, but not dictate."

and against those who sought to make economics an exclusively mathematical discipline he pleaded on behalf of "polylingual scholarship."[38] With respect to the choice of language he was pragmatic, acknowledging that the selection of definitions must be "appropriate to the purpose" at hand.[39] and while strenuously appealing for linguistic precision and consistency he conceded that

> ... standards of clarity are not uniform.... I cannot be sure whether, when I complain about vagueness, my perception is too poor, my sense of discrimination too fine, my insistence on unambiguous expression too pedantic – or whether the writings in question were just too wooly.[40]

Machlup was acutely sensitive to the role of personal values and judgments in economics, not simply in terminological matters. In an exceptionally self-revealing passage he confessed:

> ... my suspicion is aroused by the strange coincidence that I have found crypto-apologetic meanings of structure [one of the fashionable terms he analysed in detail] only in pleas for policies which I do not like: restrictions of competition, price and allocation controls, import barriers, exchange restrictions. Have I perhaps failed to notice similar aberrations in policies I happen to like? ... [To] grasp an argument that leads to conclusions hitherto rejected is much more difficult than to grasp an argument supporting a preconceived conclusion. Where I do not like the results, I am more eager than otherwise to question the validity of the premises, the consistency of the argument, the clarity of the concepts.... Aware of these influences of one's philosophy upon one's understanding of concepts. I must concede the possibility that my judgment has not attained the degree of fairness to which I aspire.[41]

VI

The KM approach offers rich possibilities for a deeper analysis of the nature, content, and historical significance of doctrinal or professional schools in economics. As Schumpeter observed in his classic *History of Economic Analysis*, the scholarly or scientific workers in any particular field

> ... tend to become a sociological group ... [with] other things in common besides the interest in scientific work.... The group accepts or refuses to accept co-workers also for reasons other than their professional competence or incompetence.... In economics this group took long to mature, but when it did mature it acquired much greater importance than it did in physics.[42]

Schumpeter did not attempt to justify or document this intriguing claim, but he was particularly impressed by the cohesion and durability of the group that emerged in late nineteenth-century Cambridge under Marshall's leadership. This economic "profession," he noted

> … developed attitudes to social and political questions that were *similar also for reasons other than similar scientific views*. The similarity of conditions of life and social location produced similar philosophies of life and similar value judgments about social phenomena.[43]

In this passage Schumpeter appears to favor a crudely deterministic sociological interpretation of Marshall's remarkable influence on British economics in the half century or so following his inaugural, in 1885.[44] The explanation is, of course, more complex than this; it involves factors like his quality as a deep and original thinker, his personality, the state of the discipline, and the position of his university at the time. Marshall's deference to the authority of the British tradition in economic thought, his reluctance to claim priority for his own contributions or to acknowledge his contemporaries' originality, and his efforts to shield his pupils and colleagues from disturbing foreign influences, combined with the architectonic character of his own system to establish him as the embodiment and culmination of the wisdom of the past. Of particular interest here, however, is his insistence on the careful use of language in economics, and his development of a distinctive mode of argumentation that created unusual problems of interpretation both for his associates and for later generations of commentators and critics.

As is well known, Marshall emphasized the limitations of pure theory and mathematical reasoning in economics, and attached great importance to the economist's ability to communicate effectively with the laity, especially businessmen. Special significance therefore attaches to his contention:

> Continuity of tradition is important everywhere; it is nowhere more important than in our use of terms; while in our use of terms it is even more important as regards the *tone* or *flavor* which they connote, than as regards the boundaries marked out by them.[45]

The sociological significance of this distinction between the connotation and the denotation of economic terms can only be fully appreciated by reference to other distinctive Cambridge characteristics. For example the "oral" tradition, which has been described as "quite unique in the history of economics,"[46] developed largely because Marshall's own ideas were familiar locally long before they were published, and access to this insider's knowledge directly contributed to his pupils' and colleagues' sense of privilege and intellectual superiority. Beyond this, indoctrination into the subtle connotations of Marshallian language played an integral part in the training of novitiates, training that could hardly be acquired without personal contact with the fount of wisdom and insight. For the uninitiated, Marshall's terminology was full of pitfalls. resulting from his efforts to combine the linguistic precision required by the expert with the comprehensibility demanded by the layman.

Some of the implications of the Marshallian approach have been explicated in Wassily Leontief's critique of "implicit theorizing" and Lawrence Fouraker's discussion of the "Cambridge didactic style." Leontief focused on the distinctive mode of reasoning that, he complained, enabled Cambridge economists to defend themselves against accusations of error by adopting subtle shifts of meaning or by employing illegitimate modes of argument.[47] Fouraker demonstrated that this procedure was a calculated method of disseminating subtle, technically complex arguments in a form accessible to a wider audience.

> Instead of leading the reader through the intricate processes that their own minds had traversed ... [the Cambridge economists, following Marshall's lead] would provide a short cut, in the form of an assumption whose purpose was to eliminate consideration of the intricate problem they had solved.
>
> This is an admirable method for bringing the fruit of intellectual labor to the attention of the largest number of people in the shortest time. It has a major shortcoming however. The most capable of one's [non-Marshallian] professional colleagues may point to the bypassed terrain and question whether that path leads to the same conclusion as the short cut. Marshall and Keynes covered this contingency with a bit of literary gamesmanship. Their major works are infested with oblique passages that the novice dismisses as manifestations of a poor writing style. It is only after he has seized upon some apparent flaw in the system and followed its implications that such passages lose their opaque quality. They are then recognized as admirably constructed defenses of the author's flank, indicating that he has already considered and resolved the objection. Many a criticism of the *Principles of Economics* and *The General Theory* has been transformed into an interpretation of some obscure paragraph by a rereading of the pertinent chapters....[48]

whence the well-known Cambridge dictum that "it's all in Marshall" (or in Keynes, as the case might be).

Fouraker's exercise in literary deconstruction represents a telling example of the difficulties of designing a language suitable for communicating simultaneously with two or more very different audiences. To the sociologist of science, the Cambridge didactic style is but one of several practices that combined to create a sense of intellectual solidarity and communion among the *cognoscenti*.[49] As Michael Polanyi has convincingly argued, scientific training calls for the acquisition of semi-intuitive skills, "tacit knowledge" and "connoisseurship," as well as more conventionally explicit kinds of comprehension.[50] The Marshallian style can be maddening to economists who value logical rigor over realism, whose ideal in economics is mathematical formalization, complete specification of all terms and steps in the argument, and conclusive empirical tests.[51] No wonder they prefer the precision and apparent completeness of general equilibrium analysis rather than Marshallian partial equilibrium analysis, the successful application of which depends on the analyst's skill in distinguishing relevant from irrelevant variables, and in knowing how far to pursue the implications of a given problem.[52]

It is no coincidence that Keynes fully appreciated the nature of Marshall's method and the difficulties "contained in the concealed crevices of that rounded globe of knowledge which is Marshall's *Principles.*"[53] Many of the same qualities appear in Keynes's own writings, especially in his *magnum opus*, which has been the joy and exasperation of generations of students and full-fledged professional economists. As Don Patinkin has so effectively demonstrated. Keynes displayed an ambivalent attitude toward mathematical analysis in economics, substantial reservations about the use of econometrics, and a "genuine concern with integrating his theoretical analysis with the data of the real world ... [and] strong intuitive feelings for the proper orders of magnitude of the various data."[54] Keynes was, of course, a genius and arguably *sui generis*. Nevertheless the beliefs he shared with Marshall suggest the importance of a continuing scholarly and scientific tradition, one that was fully in harmony with the cultural heritage and the prevailing conception of the economist's role in British society.

VII

The standpoint adopted in this paper is that the study of the discourse (or rhetoric) of any scientific or scholarly discipline is and should be treated as subordinate to the study of its intellectual content and the social and historical context in which it occurs.[55] In other words, the so-called Anglo-Saxon approach (referred to earlier) is accepted here, according to which there is a clear and essential distinction between content and discourse (or form), although the interrelationships between these elements are subtle, varied, and changing over time.

This is not to deny either the validity or the value of the KM agenda. Indeed, its value is enhanced by the general neglect of economic rhetoric in the past although, as the two immediately previous sections of this chapter demonstrate, questions of language, types of argumentation, and audience have by no means been entirely ignored. The examples provided here are of course merely illustrative. A search of the literature armed with some of the KM tools could be highly illuminating. The Cambridge tradition, as briefly sketched[56] above, is but one unusually revealing case. How far it is exceptional is yet to be determined. And it seems clear that, for example, a comparative analysis of orthodox and heterodox versions of economics on KM lines would add much to our understanding of the past development and current functioning of the discipline.

As is so often the case with innovations, the KM campaign has been accompanied by exaggerated claims; it is still much too early to assess its long-term value. In this connection the experience of historians and sociologists of science may be helpful, for a number of scholars in these closely interrelated fields have approached scientific research from the standpoint of how scientists construct accounts of what is going on during the research process. In conformity with the current tendency to treat this process as problematic, they contend that "reality" cannot be distinguished from the scientist's account of it, and that by analyzing scientific discourse they can not only shed new light on such familiar topics as the nature of discovery, theory choice, scientific consensus, and the role of norms in scientific work, but also provide insights into neglected topics, such as accounts of error, the structure of formal texts, the use of pictorial representations, the practical applications of scientific knowledge, and even the role of scientific jokes.[57] The similarities to the KM agenda are clear, but this suggests a much richer range of possibilities than has been tried out in economics. As in some other contemporary work, this so-called social-accounting approach emphasizes, as do KM, the substantial gap between how scientists go about their work and how they present it as finished, public knowledge. We are all familiar with the expression "writing up" research, and this phase of the operation has acquired added depth and significance through studies emphasizing that scientific knowledge does not emerge spontaneously in a pristine, objective, neutral form, but is consciously *constructed* in accordance with the researcher's aims, interest, and conception of conventionally acceptable procedures and results.

Some proponents of scientific discourse analysis go further, making an unwarranted epistemological claim by viewing it as a means of circumventing the interpretative difficulties arising from the remarkable variety to be found in scientists' accounts of their actions and beliefs. This, of course, is mistaken: There are no grounds for assigning privileged status to discourse or, indeed, to any other species of data, and the problem of interpretation is inescapable.[58] An even more radically empiricist and relativist approach to scientific work in Karin Knorr-Cetina's "constructivist" program, which involves microscopic internalist studies of scientists' behavior on the grounds that research is essentially idiosyncratic, contingent, and context dependent. However it should be noted that this program is designed not simply as an end in itself, but as a means to a deeper – and eventually presumably more general – understanding of the nature and processes of scientific knowledge production.[59]

Needless to say, like the KM agenda, none of these approaches has privileged status. Moreover, pace McCloskey, all have epistemological and methodological implications, and there is need for scholarly cooperation even, may it be suggested, with modernists!

Notes

1 See, for example, the discussions of scientific discourse in various volumes of *Social Science Information* and *Social Studies of Science*. Also, especially, the references in note 5, infra.

2 Donald McCloskey, *The Rhetoric of Economics* (Madison: University of Wisconsin Press, 1985), 51: also p. 4. For criticism of McCloskey's treatment of methodology, see Bruce Caldwell and A. W. Coats. "The Rhetoric of Economists: A Comment on McCloskey," *Journal of Economic Literature* 22 (June. 1984): 575–8: also see my "Why Bother with Methodology?" (forthcoming), being a revision of a paper delivered at the History of Economics Society's 1986 meetings in New York.

3 McCloskey, *The Rhetoric of Economics*, 55–7, italics in original. Also Donald McCloskey, "Economics as an Historical Science." in *Economic History and the Modern Economist*, ed. William R. Parker (Oxford: Basil Blackwell. 1986), 69; "Thick and Thin Methodologies in the History of Economic Thought," mimeographed, to be published in de Marchi volume (December. 1985), 15, 17.

4 In *Rhetoric of Economics*, 57, McCloskey cites Charles Bazerman, "What Written Knowledge Does: Three Examples of Academic Discourse," *Philosophy of the Social Sciences* 11 (September, 1981): 361–87, as evidence that "the workaday methods of economic scientists ... are literary," But Bazerman's analysis focuses on the *differences*, rather than the similarities, between the critical methods appropriate to the analysis of imaginative literature, as contrasted with those appropriate to the natural and social sciences. However, a sample of three hardly constitutes a sufficient basis for generalization.

5 For example, Steve Woolgar, "On the Alleged Distinction Between Discourse and Praxis," *Social Studies of Science* 16 (1986): 309–17, and the sources cited therein. Also Ellsworth R. Fuhrman and Kay Oehler, "Discourse Analysis and Reflexivity," *Social Studies of Science* 16 (1986): 293–307.

6 Cited by Arjo Klamer, "As If Economists and Their Subjects Were Rational," in John S. Nelson. Allan Megill, and Donald N. McCloskey (eds.), *The Rhetoric of Human Sciences* (Madison: University of Wisconsin Press, 1987), 165.

7 Axel Leijonhufuud, "Life Among the Econ" (1973), reprinted in his *Information and Coordination: Essays in Macroeconomic Theory* (Oxford: Oxford University Press, 1981), 347–59.

8 For a revealing pioneering study, see David Colander and Arjo Klamer, "The Making of an Economist." *Journal of Economic Perspectives* (Fall 1987): 95–112.

9 Cited by Klamer, "As if economists ...," 165; also see his "Economics as Discourse" (December 1985), 20–1 (to be published in de Marchi volume).

10 Cited by Klamer, "Economics as Discourse," 25.

11 Ibid., Klamer's paraphrase of Rorty.

12 See, for example, John Ziman's admirable study, *Reliable Knowledge: An Exploration of the Grounds for Belief in Science* (Cambridge: Cambridge University Press, 1978), passim. For his comments on the socialization of recruits into physics see pp. 128–30. The idea that science is a unique cultural institution with unequalled cognitive authority has been forcefully argued by Robert Merton and his followers.

13 Mary Hesse, "Changing Concepts and Stable Order," *Social Studies of Science* 16 (1986): 725. Her review of Harry Collins's *Changing Order: Replication and Induction in Scientific Practice* (1985) argues that Collins's radical conventionalist interpretation of scientists' activities conflicts with his "realist" conception of science in general. Such an inconsistency is not unusual nowadays.

14 Hesse. "Changing Concepts." 717, 723.

15 The following section is based largely on my "The Sociology of Knowledge and the History of Economics." published in Warren Samuels, ed., *Research in the History of Economic Thought and Methodology*, vol. 2 (Greenwich. Conn.: JAI Press, 1984), 211–34. The principal differences are that the SP is based on a more elaborate and explicitly relativistic epistemology than the KM program, which focuses more narrowly on literary styles and modes of argument. Proponents of the SP have undertaken more detailed, sociologically and historically rich empirical studies of past and present science, dealing with both "internal" and "external" influences on its development.

16 Barry Barnes, T. S. *Kuhn and Social Science* (New York: Columbia University Press, 1982), 121.

17 Cf. W. B. Gallie, "What Makes a Subject Scientific?" *British Journal for the Philosophy of Science* 8 (August, 1957): 118–39.

18 Barnes, *T. S. Kuhn and Social Science*, 57.

19 David Bloor, *Knowledge and Social Imagery* (London: Routledge and Kegan Paul, 1976), 38.

20 Barnes, *T. S. Kuhn and Social Science*, 30–1.

21 Thomas S. Kuhn. *The Essential Tension: Selected Studies in Scientific Tradition and Change* (Chicago: University of Chicago Press, 1977), 51.

22 Richard Whitley, "From the Sociology of Scientific Communities to the Study of Scientists' Negotiations and Beyond." *Social Science Information* 22 (1983): 694. See also ibid., 687–94, and Whitley's general study, *The Intellectual and Social Organization of the Sciences* (London: Oxford University Press, 1984.)

23 Arjo Klamer, *Conversations with Economists: New Classical Economists and Opponents Speak Out on the Current Controversy in Macroeconomics* (Totowa, N. J.: Rowman and Allanheld, 1983), especially Ch. 13. An earlier, less complex clarification appeared in his "Levels of Discourse in New Classical Economics," *History of Political Economy* 16 (1984): 263–90.

24 A conference on "The Spread of Economic Ideas." organized by David Colander, was held at Middlebury College, Vermont, in October 1986. The papers presented are being prepared for publication.

25 Cf. Whitley, *Intellectual and Social Organization of the Sciences.*

26 Ibid., 225–26. On the problem of the influence of "lay images" in the social sciences, see Cornelis Lammers, "Mono- and Poly-paradigmatic developments in natural and social sciences," in Richard Whitley, ed. *Social Processes of Scientific Development* (London: Routledge and Kegan Paul. 1974) 123–47.

27 For a more extended treatment of this topic, see my "The Role of Authority in the Development of British Economics." *Journal of Law and Economics* 10 (1966): especially 85–95.

28 Raymond Williams, *Culture and Society* (London: Chalto and Windus, 1958). 49.

29 Robert Torrens, *On Wages and Combinations* (London. 1834), 73; John Ramsay McCulloch, *A Discourse on the Rise, Progress, Peculiar Objects and Importance of Political Economy* (London, 1824), 9.

30 James Mill, "Whether Political Economy Is Useful?" *The Westminster Review* 30 (1836): 553, 554. The last passage is from his "War Expenditure." *The Westminster Review 2* (1824): 45.

31 The full title was *Definitions in Political Economy. Preceded by an Inquiry into the Rules Which Ought to Guide Political Economists in the Definition and Use of Their Terms, With Remarks on the Deviations from These Rules in Their Writings* (London, 1827). Republished in *Reprints of Economic Classics* (New York: Kelley and Millman, 1954). Malthus's rules are stated in Chapter 1. He was not alone in his concern, Nassau W. Senior, in *An Outline of the Science of Political Economy* (London, 1936), declared: "If Economists had been aware that the Science depends more on reasoning than observation, and that its principal difficulty consists not in the ascertainment of its facts, but in the use of its terms, we cannot doubt that their principal efforts would have been directed to the selection and consistent use of an accurate nomenclature" (p. 5). He regarded this as a major reason for the slow progress of political economy.

32 Ibid., p. 124. Curiously enough, this appeared at the end of a severe criticism of McCulloch's usage, hardly an indication of professional solidarity!

33 Ibid., 3–4.

34 Cf. the early *Publications of the American Economic Association.* Also, see J. Mars, "A Note on a Problem of Notation." *Economic Journal* 73 (June, 1963): 226. Contrasting economics with the natural sciences. Mars argued that "the curse of Babel still hangs over the social sciences." But although the *Journal's* editors invited readers to comment on this "important" issue, no further discussion occurred.

35 Lindley Fraser, *Economic Thought and Language* (London: A&C Black, 1937), vii–viii.

36 Ibid., 20.

37 Fritz Machlup, *Essays in Economic Semantics* (New Jersey: Prentice-Hall, 1963).

38 Machlup, "Issues in Methodology." *American Economic Review. Papers and Proceedings* 42 (1952): 70–1; "Positive and Normative Economics: An Analysis of the Ideas," in Robert L. Heilbroner, ed. *Economic Means and Social Ends, Essays in*

Social Economics (New Jersey: Prentice-Hall, 1969). 100n; "Concepts of Competition and Monopoly." *American Economic Review, Papers and Proceedings* 45 (1955): 483.

39 Machlup, *Essays on Economic Semantics*, 251.

40 Ibid., 82. He nevertheless proposed a number of procedural rules on semantic matters on pp. 71–2.

41 Ibid., 96.

42 Joseph A. Schumpeter, *History of Economic Analysis* (New York: Oxford University Press, 1954), 47.

43 Ibid. Italics in original.

44 For general background see my "Sociological Aspects of British Economic Thought (ca. 1880–1930)." *Journal of Political Economy* 75 (October. 1967): 706–29. Also the recent, brilliant study by John Maloney. *Marshall, Orthodoxy and the Professionalization of Economics* (Cambridge: Cambridge University Press. 1985).

45 Alfred Marshall, "Distribution and Exchange." *Economic Journal* 8 (March, 1898: 43. At that time there was much terminological product differentiation in the theories of value and distribution in a number of different countries.

46 Ben B. Seligman, *Main Currents in Economics, Economic Thought Since 1870* (New York: The Free Press, 1963), 457.

47 Wassily Leontief. "Implicit Theorizing: A Methodological Criticism of the Neo-Cambridge School." *Quarterly Journal of Economics* 51 (February, 1937): 337–51.

48 Lawrence A. Fouraker, "The Cambridge Didactic Style." *Journal of Political Economy* 66 (February, 1958): especially 67. He illustrates his general case by analyzing Marshall's concept of consumer's demand, and Keynes's concept of the propensity to consume.

49 Other aspects include agreement with respect to the important questions for study, and distaste for purely theoretical and methodological discussion.

50 See, for example, Michael Polanyi, *Personal Knowledge: Towards a Post-Critical Philosophy* (Chicago: University of Chicago Press, 1958), especially Ch. 4 and 5.

51 For a penetrating general critique of these "modernist" tendencies see, for example, Henry Woo. *What's Wrong with Formalization in Economics* (Newark, Calif.: Victoria Press. 1986). Also Nicholas Georgescu-Roegen on the urge to make economics an "anthropomorphic" science, in his *The Entropy Law and the Economic Process* (Cambridge, Mass.: Harvard University Press, 1971), Ch. 11.

52 Henry W. Briefs, *Three Views of Economic Method* (Washington. D. C.: Georgetown University Press, 1960), 13–17, provides shrewd comments on this type of analysis.

Colander-Klamer, "The Making of an Economist," a study of graduate training in economics, reinforces the impression that prevailing practice both attracts and helps to form "convergent" mental attitudes unsuitable for developing the kind of judgment required in dealing with practical problems. This is one reason for stressing the historical dimensions of economics. The helpful distinction between "convergent" and "divergent" minds is elaborated in Liam Hudson. *Contrary Imaginations: A Study of the English Schoolboy* (London: Methuen, 1966).

53 Quoted by Fouraker. "The Cambridge Didactic Style." 67, from Keynes's classic memorial essay on Marshall.

54 Don Patinkin, "Keynes and Econometrics: On the Interaction Between the Macroeconomic Revolutions of the Interwar Period" (1974), reprinted in his *Anticipations of the General Theory? And Other Essays on Keynes* (Chicago: University of Chicago Press. 1982), 238. Patinkin adds that Keynes was "indeed, so strong and so confident that he did not hesitate to pit these feelings against the systematic estimates made by the specialists in the field. Not unrelatedly, it shows him as a person who was not too meticulous in his handling of data, and who sometimes succumbed to the temptation to bend the data to fit his preconceptions … not exactly a phenomenon which has since disappeared from the face of the earth" (pp. 238–9).

55 It would, for example, be worth examining the components of knowledge production in economics in terms of training employment reputational assessment and funding, as Whitley suggests in *Intellectual and Social Organization of the Sciences*.

56 This term is employed deliberately. An adequate treatment of any such tradition would require much more depth and detail.

57 Cf. for example Michael Mulkay and G. Nigel Gilbert. "What Is the Ultimate Question? Some Remarks in Defence of the Analysis of Scientific Discourse." *Social Studies of Science* 12 (1982): 309–19; also their earlier "Contexts of Scientific Discourse: Social Accounting in Experimental Papers," in Karin D. Knorr, Roger Krohn, and Richard Whitley (eds.), *The Social Process of Scientific Investigation, Sociology of the Sciences Yearbook* vol. 4 (1980) (Dordrecht. Holland: D. Reidel, 1981). 269–94; and "Joking Apart: Some Recommendations Concerning the Analysis of Scientific Culture." *Social Studies of Science* 12 (1982): 585–613.

58 This issue has been extensively discussed in *Social Studies of Science*, especially in the 1982 and 1984 volumes.

59 Cf. Karin Knorr Cetina's *The Manufacture of Knowledge: An Essay on the Constructivist and the Contextual Nature of Science* (Oxford: Pergamon Press, 1981); also her "The Constructivist Program in the Sociology of Science: Retreats or Advances?" *Social Studies of Science* 12 (1982): 323;

For criticism see, for example, Thomas F. Gieryn, "Relativist/Constructivist Programs in the Sociology of Science: Redundance and Retreat," *Social Studies of Science* 12 (1982).

Part II

Book reviews

1 *History of economic analysis*

By J. A. Schumpeter

Oxford University Press, New York. George Allen & Unwin Ltd. 1954
pp. xxv + 1,260

Economists in general, and historians of economics in particular, have long awaited the publication of the late Professor Schumpeter's monumental *History of Economic Analysis*. Ever since the appearance of his *Epochen der Dogmen – und Methodengeschichte* in 1912,[1] he had taken a direct interest in the history of economics, and the present volume is the outcome of a lifetime's thought, research and teaching.

Drawn on an ambitious scale, the *History* is designed to portray "the Filiation of Scientific Ideas – the process by which men's efforts to understand economic phenomena produce, improve, and pull down analytic structures in an unending sequence" (p. 6). But while this statement accurately describes the purpose of the volume, in executing this purpose Schumpeter ventures far beyond the limits of economic analysis *per se*, and this feature effectively "individuates" the performance. For each of the four periods considered – Part II, The Beginnings to 1790 (325 pp.); Part III, 1790 to 1870 (371 pp.); Part IV, 1870 to 1914 (and later) (382 pp.); and Part V, Conclusion, a Sketch of Modem Developments (45 pp.) – a conscientious attempt is made to paint the "Intellectual Scenery" and the "Socio-Political Background" and to outline the main historical events affecting economic thought. In addition Part I deals with Scope and Method (pp. 3–47), touching upon the Techniques of Economic Analysis, Contemporaneous Developments in other Sciences, and the Sociology of Economics.

The distinctive features of the *History* are demonstrated in Part I, where Schumpeter presents the conceptual skeleton that is to be clothed in the subsequent pages. Few, if any, economists were better equipped to display the historical development of economic analysis against such a broad background of ideas and events, and while the historical sketches are inevitably terse and somewhat over-simplified, they invariably illuminate the main story and arouse the reader's respect and admiration for the author's immense scholarship.

The work bears throughout the unmistakable stamp of Schumpeter's personality to an extent recalling the Wesley Mitchell *Lecture Notes*, published in 1949.

The personal element is present not only in the characteristic verbal felicities – such as the references to "methodological hypochondria" (p. 534), Roscher's "fricassee" (p. 741), Wagner's "rabies systematica" (p. 851), and to Dupont de Nemours' talents as "those of the pianist and not those of the composer" (p. 226) – and in the way that the reader is taken into the author's confidence, but also in a deeper sense. Schumpeter claims that whereas "there is no objective meaning to the term progress in matters of economic or any other policy" (p. 40), progress in scientific economics is clearly identifiable; yet he concedes that in making "evaluations of analytic quality" value judgments are both "permissible and unavoidable in a history of scientific economics" (p. 348).

These personal evaluations are evident in his comments on the nature of scientific achievement. In no other history of economics have such effective methodological distinctions been drawn between the various aspects of scientific work. "Low standards of rigour and sloppiness of thinking have been worse enemies of scientific economics than has been political bias" (p. 233), he says, adding that confusion between the scientific and ideological features of a given performance has frequently prevented the recognition of analytic merit. Mere technical skill is not enough, for "precisely the strongest achievements in science proceed not from observation or experimentation and orderly logic-chopping but from something that is best called vision and is akin to artistic creation" (pp. 113–4). Absence of vision or "lack of imagination", he asserts, is "much worse than defective technique" (p. 684), and by contrast with the classical economists, whose theory of economic development suffers from "a complete lack of imagination" (p. 571), Marx's vision of the economic process receives high praise.

The most important contribution a theorist can make to the advance of scientific economics is through his perception of system. "This all-pervading interdependence [of economic phenomena] is the fundamental fact, the analysis of which is the chief source of the additions that the specifically scientific attitude has to make to the practical man's knowledge of economic phenomena... The history of economic analysis or, at any rate, of its 'pure' kernel, from Child to Walras might be written in terms of this conception's gradual emergence into the light of consciousness" (p. 242). This explains Schumpeter's verdict that Walras is the greatest of all pure theorists; and it also accounts for the importance he attaches to the Cantillon-Quesnay model of the economic system.

On general matters of interpretation, the passages most likely to provoke controversy in this country are those dealing with British economic thought since 1776. The overall picture which emerges will, however, be no surprise to readers familiar with Schumpeter's earlier writings. The spotlight is directed away from the established stars – especially Smith and Ricardo – towards some of those usually regarded as supporting players. Schumpeter clearly demonstrates the extent to which the *Wealth of Nations* is an 18th- century product, maintaining that it "does not contain any single *analytic* idea, principle, or method that was entirely new in 1776" (p. 184). Due acknowledgment is paid to Ricardo's "priceless gift of leadership" (p. 473), and to his "engine of analysis" as a "decisive advance" (p. 474), but two major weaknesses are stressed in an endeavour to reduce the analytic importance of his contribution to its "proper proportions" (p. 475). The first, termed the "Ricardian Vice", refers to "the habit of piling a heavy load of practical conclusions upon a tenuous groundwork, which was unequal to it yet seemed in its simplicity not only attractive but also convincing" (p. 1171), and this, when reinforced by the "Art of Triviality … leads the victim, step by step, into a situation where he has got either to surrender or allow himself to be laughed at for denying what, by the time that situation is reached, is *really* a triviality" (p. 653, n.). The second defect is called the Ricardian "detour", an expression reminiscent of Jevons' famous indictment. Schumpeter contends that Ricardo led his followers away from the more profitable study of "the problem of distribution as a problem of valuation" and "the factors that explain the size and rate of change of the Social Product" (p. 568) to a study of the "labour-quantity theory of value" (p. 560). Moreover, he adds that this implies "that Ricardo was completely blind to the nature, and the logical place in economic theory, of the supply-and-demand apparatus and that he took it to represent a theory of value distinct from and opposed to his own. This reflects little credit on him as a theorist" (p. 601).

These are grave charges which will inevitably provoke discussion. Here it must suffice to say that Schumpeter's estimate of the continental utility-distribution analysis and its British exponents is in full accord with recent research. Although personal evaluations play a part, there is ample evidence of Schumpeter's readiness to acknowledge a wide variety of contributions. Economists specially commended include Serra, Misselden, Botero, Galiani, Turgot, Cournot, Moore, and Fisher. Ricardo's immediate supporters emerge with credit, John Stuart Mill's reputation is enhanced, and Marshall's greatness as an economist is generously praised. Leaders of the Austrian School, on the other hand, are severely admonished for the technical inadequacies which led them up blind alleys (pp. 916–7), although Böhm-Bawerk's errors are treated somewhat indulgently.

Schumpeter's treatment of mediæval literature merits special attention, for it far surpasses any previous examination of this period in histories of economics. To Marshall's remark that "it is all in A. Smith", Schumpeter is tempted to reply "it is all in the scholastics" (p. 309). It may justly be said that he draws too freely upon the wisdom of hindsight, and he sometimes expresses unnecessary surprise at the slow development of suggestive ideas. But he draws a fruitful distinction between "objective" and "subjective" originality in the works reviewed.

On first acquaintance Schumpeter's *History* may disappoint professional economists. The pedagogical purpose of the volume (p. 4), however, explains its textbook characteristics, the "exercises" provided for the reader, and the "jejune" quality of some of the explanatory comments. It might be said that the book is designed for an unusually learned undergraduate. If the theoretical discussions lack novelty it is partly because Schumpeter's views are well known, and partly because he relies heavily on previous studies by established authorities, such as Cannan, Hayek, Marget, Stigler, and Viner. In the text he frequently glosses over difficulties, sometimes elaborating them in footnotes but often failing to dispose of them adequately. This is the price paid for the extensive background material, and to some readers it will appear excessive. The volume is either too short or too long, depending on the point of view.

In conclusion, a tribute must be paid to the magnificent editorial task performed so devotedly by the late Mrs. Schumpeter and her eminent collaborators. Some imperfections were inevitable. The indexes and cross-references are inadequate; there are a few misprints and minor inaccuracies; and the different kinds of type are occasionally misleading. But these deficiencies are too slight to detract significantly from the volume as a whole. It is an outstanding memorial to Schumpeter's career, and will long remain a classic.

Note

1 Recently translated by R. Aris, under the title *Economic Doctrine and Method.*

2 *The meaning and validity of economic theory: A historical approach*

By Leo Rogin

New York: Harper. London: Hamish Hamilton. 1956
pp. xvii + 697

This posthumous publication is an unorthodox and stimulating contribution to the history of economics. The individuality of Professor Rogin's study, as with the works of Wesley Mitchell and Joseph Schumpeter in this field, arises mainly from the author's conception of the nature and functions of economic theory, which is vigorously stated at the outset. This initial statement gives a distinctively personal quality and unity to the remainder of the volume. The reader's verdict as to the success or failure of this venture will probably be governed by his methodological views, for, as J. S. Mill once remarked, differences between scientists on matters of principle usually stem from this source. But whatever the verdict, one cannot fail to be stimulated both by the novelty and boldness of the author's judgments, and by his efforts to encompass the diversity of the past within a single unified framework.

Professor Rogin's methodological position is closer to Mitchell's broad institutionalism than to Schumpeter's strict identification of economic science with theoretical analysis, for he is chiefly concerned "with the objective and hence readily demonstrable correspondence between theory and policy" (p. 13). The "objective meaning" of a theory represents its public significance – the use to which it is put, rather than the theorist's motivation – as evidenced by its orientation to certain "strategic factors" in the contemporary social situation. The validity of the theory, i.e. its relevance to the empirical situation "at the time of its original projection", must also be tested by reference to this situation. Thus the criterion is pragmatic and positivistic ; the purpose of science is prediction, not merely explanation which is the task of "philosophers" (p. 480). But while historical and institutional factors must obviously be taken into account in assessing the relevance of theory to policy, Professor Rogin recognises that the key question is not one of the legitimacy of abstraction *per se* – that red herring pursued by the historicists and the institutionalists – but of "significant" abstraction (p. 482).

There are many difficulties inherent in this approach, and the author is obviously more at ease when dealing with classical and neo-classical writers, whose policy orientation is fairly readily indentifiable, than with writers like Walras and Menger, whose policy interests are subordinated or disguised. Though he proposes to avoid references to motivation, he often fails to live up to this ideal. Professor Rogin attacks the "sterile" pursuit of "objectivity" in social theory (p. 12) and claims that it usually ends in support for the *status quo*, whether intentionally (as with Jevons' theory of capital, which was designed to resolve the conflict between capital and labour, pp. 467–8) or not (as with Menger). Conversely he applauds Senior's progress from pure theory to policy in recognition of the fact that a neglect of "sound" principles (p. 246) can have serious practical consequences, though he exaggerates Senior's fear of the "economics of the poor" (pp. 251–9). There is a fruitful discussion of Böhm-Bawerk's failure to exclude institutional (i.e. juridico-historical) influences from his theory of capital. But Walras' general equilibrium theory is summarily dismissed: it is not general, since it postulates private property in land and capital goods (can any theory be general in this sense?); its technical and institutional assumptions are too far removed from the realities of modem capitalist society – and this applies to all modern theories of equilibrium under perfect competition; and, being incapable of verification, it is unscientific.

Even when he is dealing with writers demonstrating an avowed interest in policy matters Professor Rogin's approach raises many difficulties, partly because he narrows his perspective unduly when identifying the "strategic factors" to which their theories are orientated. Though he considers such problems as short-term fluctuations (Malthus), the Corn Laws (Ricardo), and unemployment (Keynes), his discussion often boils down to the issue: does the writer in question accept or reject capitalism and the institution of private property? At one stage (p. 366) Professor Rogin even remarks that economic theory has usually been a by-product of the theorist's conception of the state. This is an appropriate standpoint from which to examine Marx's theory, or the relationships between J. S. Mill's socialist programme and his economic doctrines; and there is an illuminating discussion of the correspondence between Marshall's "practical gradualism" and his theoretical conservatism, though the attempt to link this with his use of the differential calculus (p. 566) is obviously far-fetched. But in general the task of identifying the policy orientations of any theory is far more complex than Professor Rogin implies.

Enough has been said to indicate the objectives and some of the distinctive features of this volume. Judging the author by his own pragmatic standards, he has clearly failed to shed much new light on the criteria for selecting economic principles relevant to the present day. As he himself admits, it takes a generous measure of hindsight to identify the "strategic factors" in any situation; and the attempt to develop theory with direct reference to these factors would result in an intolerable constriction of the theorists' perspective. But by concentrating on the policy implications of economic doctrines Professor Rogin has provided a welcome change from the usual preoccupation with the development of pure theory. In recompense one can almost excuse his narrow and doctrinaire methodological conceptions.

3 *A history of economic ideas*

By Robert Lekachman

New York 1959. Harper
pp. xiii + 427

Histoire de la pensée économique et analyse des théories contemporaines

By Andre Piettre (Précis Dalloz.)

Paris 1959. Dalloz
pp. 517

Although these volumes are designed to provide a broad introductory survey of the history of economic throught, they differ so radically in scope and method that the differences can only be explained by reference to the respective academic traditions of which they are the product. Whereas the former is intended to meet the needs of American students specialising in economics, either at an advanced undergraduate or preliminary graduate stage, the latter has been prepared for second year French students in the faculty of law – that faculty in which study of political economy has long flourished in France. Given these circumstances it is no surprise to find that Professor Lekachman's text covers fewer writers and a narrower range of topics than Professor Piettre's, in which considerable space is allotted to social thought and to the historical context. Yet Lekachman's work is less technical in content and less assured in tone, and in these respects his *History of Economic Ideas* reflects the somewhat tenuous status of his subject in the American social science curriculum. In particular, his approach reveals the influence of Wesley Mitchell and the eclectic tradition of Columbia University, where institutionalism and empiricism have obtained a more respectful reception than has usually been the case in most leading English-speaking institutions of higher learning. Like Mitchell, and in contrast with Schumpeter, Professor Lekachman believes that "economics tries to be a pure science at the peril of barrenness and intellectual gamesmanship" and that economists do best when they concentrate on the solution of pressing social problems. However the author's practice fails to live up to his preaching, for while doing "penance for these unscientific leanings" (p. xiii) be slights the mercantilists and only briefly discusses economic heterodoxy and applied economics. In all, three quarters of his space is devoted to classical, neo-classical and modern economics, with a conventionally heavy emphasis on theory and technical matters, and while this allocation is by no means reprehensible, it is hardly what we are led to expect in the preface. The treatment of writers and doctrines is generally sound if pedestrian, and the author's attempt to be fair to the theorists is exemplified by his defence of the marginalists (pp. 263/264, 296/297). The strongest part of the book is the account of the Ricardians, apart from his serious underestimate of Nassau Senior – who is, incidentally, casually dismissed by Piettre as a minor vulgariser (p. 71 n.). Finally, while Lekachman's comments on individual writers are often reinforced by his sociological insights, there are some notable lapses of judgement – as, for example, when he compares the English economists' distaste for metaphysics with "the embarrassment of a well-bred man in the presence of a bounder" (p. 300).

When we open Piettre's volume we are immediately transported into a different world – a world of colourful images, magnificent vistas, and heroic generalisations. At the outset sweeping parallels arc drawn between the stages of economic thought and the (numerically equivalent) stages of economic evolution, and the ensuing 230 pages leading up to the analysis of contemporary theory come under the headings: I'économie de service; l'économie de liberté; and l'économie d'intervention. This Gallic zest is infinitely refreshing to a reviewer suffering from a surfeit of conventional Anglo-Saxon texts. But occasionally, it must be confessed, the atmosphere becomes too rarified, for the author does not hesitate to summon Sombart's "Geist" or Professor Nef's suggestive, if highly debatable, distinction between "qualitative" and "quantitative" economies to give substance to his generalisations. This is unfortunate, for some of his insights are penetrating. For instance, most economists would deny that protectionist policies are determined by national character (p. 223), but the claim that the prevailing type of theory (l'esprit d'analyse) reflects the nation's "mental structure" (p. 441) is worthy of investigation.

Generally speaking, Part I of this study is too ambitious in scope and too sketchy in treatment to give the reader an adequate grasp of the subject. Despite the author's erudition and his ability to capture the spirit of an age or the essence of a doctrine in a vivid phrase, his paragraphs too often consist of little more than a parade of ideas and personalities. By contrast, Part II contains a thorough and occasionally rigorous account of contemporary economics, under the headings mechanistic, functional and dynamic analysis. This part will undoubtedly serve as a valuable supplement to an intermediate or advanced course in economic theory, and, in the best continental manner, the international scope of the survey is especially commendable. Many English economists would benefit from an acquaintance with the writings of many of the lesser-known figures included here. The distinction between "la dynamique des forces", and "la dynamique des structures" which underlies the last two chapters is both novel and suggestive, and may serve as an example of the author's procedure.

4 *Founders of American economic thought and policy*

By Virgle Glenn Wilhite

New York: Bookman Associates, 1958
pp. 442

To compile a volume of extracts from the writings of a group of defunct economists and offer it as a contribution to the history of economic thought is a comparatively easy process, and one which becomes more attractive as economic research becomes increasingly technical. Yet in this as in other fields of scholarship genuine excellence calls for a combination of rare qualities, including painstaking research, freshness of vision, mature judgment, interpretative skill, and independence in the choice of subject or method of approach. Given the scarcity of these attributes, the superficial attractiveness and the deceptive simplicity of the process of compilation results in a volume of publication distinguished only by its dullness and its irrelevance to current activities. In this state of affairs it is hardly surprising that the field is so generally neglected by practicing economists and graduate teachers.

The title of Professor Wilhite's volume inspires the hope that his study will prove an exception to what is fast becoming the rule, for a careful examination of the relationships between the ideas of the founding fathers of American economics and subsequent policy measures, if based on an intimate knowledge of contemporary economic and social conditions, would have been of perennial interest. For we know far too little about the way in which ideas influence events. But once again we are doomed to disappointment, for the author is content to retrace familiar ground and provide the reader with a wholly conventional review of the intellectual furniture and the policy issues of the time. He is apparently unaware of the existence of Professor Dorfman's two volumes dealing with this period, and is consequently led to exaggerate both the extent of our ignorance of the field and the usefulness of his own contribution.

Not only are these sound reasons for questioning the importance of the author's self-appointed task, there are also legitimate grounds for objecting to the manner of his performance. The amount of space actually devoted to the ideas of the "near-economists" who form the subject of this study is so small that one is led to suspect that what began as a specialist's monograph was subsequently inflated in an endeavor to attract a wider audience. The book begins with a readable and comparatively unexceptionable account of the theological, philosophical and economic ideas that formed the colonists' cultural inheritance. But this introduction occupies almost one third of the total space and the chapters dealing with the "near economists" contain an excessive amount of additional background material, repetition and summary restatement. To cap it all, there is an extraordinary forty-page chapter of resumé and conclusions, in which Professor Wilhite not only reiterates points already made repeatedly in the text, but actually reproduces (word for word, with some inaccuracies) paragraph after paragraph of commentary already printed in earlier chapters (cf. pp. 303–7 and 405–9 ; pp. 357–63 and 410–14). This might be regarded as the result of gross carelessness on the part of the printer, were it not for the fact that the order of treatment in the final chapter differs capriciously from that of its predecessors, and that some comments and even quotations appear in the resumé but not in the text (cf. pp. 343 and 401–2).

Apart from these bizarre features, there are many statements that hardly bear close examination. Gallatin, we are told on p. 369 "probably was thinking more of the Europe of his day than the America of our generation"; Franklin was not impressed by the British factory system (which scarcely existed in his day); on pp. 350–1 we learn that Hamilton's advocacy of protectionism was not shaken by the contrary doctrines of David Ricardo (which appeared alter his death); and so on. Nor does it help to make naive and superficial comparisons between eighteenth and twentieth century ideas, as in the comment that Gallatin's thought "shows strains of… marginal utility analysis and institutionalist ideas; likewise a bit of Keynesianism" (p. 426). In general Professor Wilhite does not seem to be at home with economic analysis; his analysis is often blurred and sometimes confusing. Finally, the errata slip does not cover all the errors of the text.

5 *The economic mind in American civilization, Vols. IV and V: 1918–1933*

By Joseph Dorfman

New York: Viking Press, 1959
pp. lxxxviii + 776

With the publication of these two volumes Professor Dorfman has brought to a successful conclusion the most ambitious survey of the history of economic thought in a single country ever undertaken; he has thereby placed not only economists but also historians and other social scientists deeply in his debt. There is ample justification for thinking that the final instalment of his self-appointed herculean labor will prove even more valuable than its predecessors. It not only provides an indispensable account of the content and context of economic thinking in the United States in the period 1918–33; it also has a vital, if indirect, relevance to any assessment of the current state of systematic economics and to a wide range of recent and current policy issues.

J. M. Clark, whose work occupies more space in these volumes than that of any other economist, once described the 1920s as a decade in which economic heterodoxy was so widespread that it virtually became the new orthodoxy. Dorfman's approach is well calculated to reveal this facet of the period, for he has a sympathetic understanding of the efforts then being made to bring economic theory into closer touch with reality, and an unrivaled knowledge of the activities of the growing number of economists who were dealing directly with public problems, whether they were employed by universities, government agencies, research institutes, or business organizations. He not only describes their work but also shows how pragmatist philosophy, wartime experiences, and the new demands placed on the economics profession by the expanded opportunities for public service combined to produce the impression that the inherited corpus of economic doctrine was disintegrating under the strain. Whatever the justification for this impression, subsequent experience has revealed that even the shock of the great depression did not prove fatal, and these volumes constitute a mine of information for those who seek to account for the ensuing renascence and the current high prestige of abstract theory. Dorfman provides many clues to the explanation of both the sorry state of orthodox economics in the 1920s and its subsequent revival – in substantially modified form – in the 1930s. His procedure may be likened to that of Wesley Mitchell, his former teacher and colleague, whose method of "analytic description" has frequently been criticized for being unduly descriptive and insufficiently analytical. Just as Mitchell sought to lay the foundations for the explanation and control of the business cycle by a laborious selection, compilation, and analysis of data, so Dorfman has endeavored to demonstrate by a similar process the interdependence of economic ideas, conditions, and policy. In so doing, he far transcends the conventional boundaries set by academic books and journals. Most readers will use his work for reference purposes and may find that the author's conclusions often seem unduly restrained, if not actually colorless. Yet the reader who has the time and persistence to examine the entire study will find that the whole is greater than the sum of its parts and, it may be added (by one who has made intensive use of Dorfman's earlier volumes), the style conceals many insights and shrewd comments that will be overlooked by the casual reader.

As with the earlier volumes, the scope of the undertaking is truly remarkable and so is the author's sureness of touch. In addition to his clear, succinct, and impartial account of the careers and works of the leading economists of every school and persuasion, he provides extremely well-balanced surveys of the postwar, "new era" prosperity and the depression settings in which they lived and had their being. Some readers will doubtless cavil at the amount of space allocated to their particular heroes, schools, or subdisciplines; and the author at times appears overgenerous to his Columbia colleagues as, for example, in his reference to the consistency of Mitchell's thinking (p. 376). Yet his over-all assessment of economic heterodoxy of the orthodox tradition, and of the relationships between economics and the other social sciences is eminently sound, and few scholars have had greater success in their efforts to be just and impartial. Some chapters are unduly condensed (e.g., chap. xxi surveying the public reaction to the depression; and chap. xix dealing with special areas of research), and yet they provide essential and reliable information. In particular, the treatment of what may loosely be termed "applied economics" is excellent, for example, in the areas of monetary economics, where many important but neglected personalities and proposals are described. This part of the study will be of interest to all students of economic policy.

With the passage of time there has been a bewildering proliferation of the topics, techniques, and personalities that must be included in a history of economic ideas, and there is a correspondingly enhanced need for a reliable guide to the mass of books, articles, reports, speeches, etc., that constitute the historian's raw material. It is, therefore, a source of considerable regret to me that Dorfman has announced his unwillingness to continue his researches into the post-1933 period. Most historians appreciate the scholar's difficulty of obtaining full data and of preserving his perspective when dealing with recent periods (p. x); yet Dorfman has demonstrated an almost unique capacity for overcoming these difficulties. And while any piece of historical writing is necessarily incomplete, the comprehensive examination of the economic writing of the depression era that forms the latter half of Volume V leaves the reader anxious for a comparable portrayal of professional reactions to the experiences of the 1930's. We are currently witnessing several attempts to reinterpret the New Deal epoch, and economists have need of such a worthy champion to record their contributions and to protect them from misinterpretation.

6 *The economic mind in American civilization, Vols. IV and V, 1928–1933*

By Joseph Dorfman

New York: Viking Press, 1959
pp. lxxxviii + 776

If the majority of intellectual historians have their way, the mysterious diffusion process whereby ideas are transmitted from seminal minds through the works of disciples and imitators until they come to play a vital role in the climate of opinion influencing policy formation is likely to remain a mystery. For too many practitioners in this field are content to undertake minute studies of the works of great thinkers, or to make ingenious efforts to thrust greatness upon (often justly) neglected minor figures, while the fascinating and important task of tracing the influence of ideas goes by default. At first sight it might appear that Professor Dorfman's monumental survey of American economic thought, the two final volumes of which were published last summer, merely provides a catalogue of names and notions that does nothing to repair the deficiencies of previous studies. He is primarily concerned to record the ideas of a host of major and minor contributors to the flood of American economic ideas, and he goes to considerable lengths to avoid imposing his personal judgments and interpretations upon the reader. Not only has he decided to terminate his study in 1933 because of the difficulty of preserving a clear perspective when dealing with recent periods but his affiliation with Columbia University, and his admiration for Wesley Mitchell, in particular, lay him open to the charge of transferring the "National Bureau" method of "description without theory" from the field of economic statistics to that of the history of ideas. Yet there are many reasons for strongly recommending Professor Dorfman's work to all serious students of American economic and social thought and conditions. No man is infallible, and time will undoubtedly reveal omissions and shortcomings in his selection of writers and his interpretation of their works; but, for the present generation of scholars at least, his researches are definitive, and the thoroughness, completeness, and accuracy of his volumes makes them an indispensable reference source. Beyond this, it is apparent to those who look below the surface that they contain innumerable judgments and insights that are indispensable to those who seek to assess the influence of ideas on events.

The author is especially sympathetic to the heterodox elements that form so important a part of modern American economics. If he occasionally slights the academic theorists, he more than makes amends by his abundant use of the less accessible writings of journalists, jurists, businessmen, bankers, farmers, politicians and trade unionists. Moreover, Professor Dorfman is not content merely to record and interpret ideas; he provides masterly surveys of the essential background to his principal themes in chapters on postwar, new-era prosperity, boom and slump conditions, and in revealing accounts of the impact on the economics profession of pragmatist philosophy, wartime experiences, and opportunities for public service. These surveys will be of particular value to readers of this journal, whose interest will undoubtedly centre upon Part II of volume five, which covers the public and professional reaction to the Depression and the impact of economic ideas upon public policy. It is, of course, well known that opinions differed widely both as to the causes and the solution of the most momentous slump in American history. But as an economist of sorts, the reviewer cannot forbear to mention that these pages make both the opinion and the disagreements among contemporary economists seem much more reasonable than has generally been supposed.

7 *Types of economic theory, from mercantilism to institutionalism, Vol. 1*

By Wesley C. Mitchell

Edited with an introduction
by Joseph Dorfman
New York: Augustus M. Kelley, 1967
pp. xi + 608

This volume is part of a greatly enlarged edition of the famous lecture course on "Types of Economic Theory" given by Wesley Mitchell at Columbia University for over thirty years. An earlier mimeographed version – based on (hitherto privately circulated) students' notes and never formally recognized by Mitchell – was published in 1949, and was soon highly regarded by historians of economics. Now Mitchell's former pupil and colleague, Joseph Dorfman, the leading expert on American economic ideas, has combined a variety of materials – including various versions of Mitchell's lecture notes, transcripts, abstracts, outlines made throughout his professional life, excerpts from his published writings, and lecture notes compiled by the editor and others – to produce a fittingly erudite monument to Mitchell's scholarship.

These lectures inevitably invite comparison with Schumpeter's massive posthumous *History of Economics Analysis*. Both men were outstanding economists whose writings bore indelible traces of their personalities, and both transcended the usual limitations of works in the field. Yet, their preconceptions were fundamentally different, for while Schumpeter regarded the progress of theory as his primary theme, Mitchell dismissed *dogmengeschichte* as an approach that "satisfies no one who is himself awake" (p. 535), one that interests only those who believe the theory to have "permanent validity" (p. 25). He considered that students "will never have any adequate appreciation of what role the social sciences can play in life unless they look at the thing as something broader, something more active, than a discussion of a set of varied, abstract problems conducted on the basis of analysis of imaginary conditions" (p. 373). The history of economics was, to him, "part of humanity's struggle to deal with the problems that evolving social life has brought" (p. 25). Hence, the purpose of his course was instrumentalist and present-minded, since he wished "to help students to become better constructive workers by understanding more clearly the relation between cumulative economic changes and economic theory" (p. 10).

History is called upon to perform many tasks, of which this is but one – and perhaps not the most vital; but, given his intention, Mitchell executed it with clarity, consistency, insight, and erudition. He emphasized the social aspects of the development of ideas, especially the interaction of intellect and environment, for "social conditions may not affect the birth rate of genius, but they do affect the problems which interest genius, and they determine what type of genius shall get a hearing" (p. 171). As with Schumpeter's *History*, this volume contains many shrewd comments on the sociology of economics, a topic that has been unduly neglected by historians of the discipline. For example, Mitchell described the emergence of political economy as an independent specialism; its methodological peculiarities as a science; its development as "a way of thinking about things rather than an organized body of steadily growing ascertained knowledge ... [that is, by] excogitation rather than investigation" (pp. 146–47); the rise and fall of schools of thought; the growth of academic posts and professional self-consciousness; the role of intellectual authority; the changing public reputation of the discipline; and the vital part played by practical rather than purely intellectual interests. Naturally the treatment of these matters reflects Mitchell's personal predilections as, for example, in his preference for Malthus' empirical method rather than Ricardo's deductive method, and in the great importance he attached to the psychological foundations of classical political economy. His view of Bentham and utilitarianism is well known, and his institutionalist leanings appear in his periodic references to the role of money in society, cumulative change, and the pecuniary culture. Indeed, the very title betrays his conviction that "economics is in a rather rudimentary stage as a science. It exists not as a single body of theory; but as several types of theory. A critical appreciation of these different types ... is of use to a person who wishes to know what economics can accomplish and particularly to a person who wishes to remain or become critical of his own ideas" (p. 13).

Given its size, the chronological and geographical range of Volume I is comparatively limited, for despite the word "mercantilism" in the subtitle ("institutionalism" will appear in Volume II) it is mainly devoted to Britain between 1750 and 1850. A revealing introduction "On the Study of the Economic Classics" leads to chapters on "Adam Smith and How Political Economy Came to be Systematized in England"; "Jeremy Bentham and the Utilitarian Creed"; "Thomas Robert Malthus and the Empirical Trend"; "David Ricardo and the Making of Classical Political Economy"; "The New Social Sciences at Work: The Philosophical Radicals"; "Political Economy in the Days of Its Triumph"; and "John Stuart Mill and the Humanization of Classical Economics."

Two main factors determine the scale of the project: the range of issues Mitchell considered relevant to "the social history of classical political economy" (p. 484) and sheer repetition – which is largely a matter of editorial policy. Mitchell's interests were catholic, for he concerned himself with the "type of problems the man attacks, his way of formulating them, what materials he had to work with, the general method he employed, the things he took for granted without inquiry, the grounds for the confidence he felt in his results, what use he put these results, to their acceptance or rejection by his contemporaries and the reaction of his scientific work upon social processes" (pp. 6–7). As he recognized, this approach made the history of economics appear "far more complex than it seemed to our predecessors" (p. 5) and presented difficult organizational problems and decisions about the proper boundaries of any given discussion. As the reviewer is fundamentally sympathetic to Mitchell's intention, believing that more historians of economics should place their work within such a broad framework, it is the more painful to report that he often went into far more detail than his argument required. Admittedly his treatment of the historical setting of classical political economy and the interactions of ideas and policy have stood the test of time remarkably well, despite the wealth of subsequent research and post-Keynesian reinterpretation. Nevertheless, too much space is devoted to the growth of democracy and the minutiae of contemporary politics, and there are too many biographical sketches of minor personalities who, however colorful and interesting in themselves, tend to distract attention from the main story. Moreover, the editor's zeal and scholarship have emphasized these features, for he has added much (valuable and well-chosen) supplementary information and has reproduced Mitchell's comments and summaries, some of which, however appropriate to his audiences, seem superfluous in a work of this size.

So skillfully has the editor connected the various tissues that one is sometimes, perhaps unjustifiably, in doubt as to where Mitchell ends and Dorfman begins; and the scale of the project is so vast that it seems likely that its readership will be unduly restricted. It might, therefore, eventually be worth considering the publication of an abridgement containing the quintessence of Mitchell's message.

8 *Events, ideology and economic theory: The determinants of progress in the development of economic analysis*

Edited by Robert V. Eagly

Detroit, Wayne State University Press, 1968
pp. 206

This volume is of exceptional interest to those scholarly brokers who have been seeking to arrange a match between the history of economic thought and the sociology of knowledge. The fruit of a symposium held at Wayne State University, in May 1966, it contains six papers and comments (authors of the latter are listed in brackets): Robert V. Eagly, "The Swedish and English Bullionist Controversies: A Comparative Study of the Impact of Events on Ideas" (Allen); Ronald L. Meek, "Ideas, Events and Environment: The Case of the French Physiocrats" (Spengler); William R. Allen, "The Position of Mercantilism and the Early Development of International Trade Theory" (Kurihara); Paul M. Sweezy, "Karl Marx and the Industrial Revolution" (Meek); Kenneth K. Kurihara, "The Dynamic Impact of History on Keynesian Theory" (Sweezy); Joseph J. Spengler, "Exogenous and Endogenous Influences in the Formation of Post-1870 Economic Thought: A Sociology of Knowledge Approach" (Eagly).

As a group, the symposiasts admirably combine unity of theme with variety of viewpoint and method. Despite the subtitle, they examine the relationships between ideas and the environment, rather than the environmental determinants of intellectual progress. As the editor notes in his introduction, the contributors eschew "the 'extreme' historical relativist position that considers the meaning and validity of ideas to be ephemer 1 and relevant only to specific historic time and place", for they recognise that "environmental determinants do not play the same pervasive role in all periods". Thus while Eagly, in a comparative study of a particular case, endeavours to show (not altogether successfully, in the view of his critic, and this reviewer) that "largely identical events and environment gave rise to largely identical analytical advances in economic theory", Allen's essay suggests that contemporary events "dictated the particular questions discussed by seventeenth century mercantilist writers" but not "the analytical response". Both these authors start with fairly precise questions derived from the history of economic theory: Eagly with the monetary theories of Pehr Niclas Christiernin and Henry Thornton, and Allen with a preconceived (and necessarily post-mercantilist) notion of international trade theory. A comparison between Meek's and Sweezy's papers suggests that this is a more fruitful procedure than one starting from broader, historically less manageable questions. Meek's examination of the links between Quesnay's *Tableau Economique* and the condition of the French economy yields more definite conclusions than Sweezy's stimulating, but somewhat amorphous account of the influence of Marx's view of the industrial revolution on his theory of economic development. One reason, of course, is that Sweezy is concerned less with the details of Marx's theories or predictions than with his "vision" of the capitalist process, and it is no easy task to relate this to the contemporary background. However his essay provokes Meek's response that "one of the most compelling intellectual tasks of the present day" is to apply "Marxian methods of analysis and criticism to the work of Marx himself" – a remark that might, *mutatis mutandis*, serve as a text for this volume, given Marx's status as a founding father of *Wissenssoziologie*.

The last two essays in the volume differ both from one another and from their predecessors. Kurihara surveys post-Keynesian macro-economic theory, including a number of very recent (and indeed current) theoretical models; but he is preoccupied with the endogenous development of theories, and makes only casual references to the relationship between ideas and events. Spengler, like Kurihara, considers that endogenous factors have become dominant in recent decades, and his densely-packed essay – which should be read in conjunction with his recent article on "Economics: its History, Themes Approaches", *Journal of Economic Issues* Vol. II (1968) pp. 5–30 – contains an instructive commentary on the "relativist" and "absolutist" approaches to the history of economics, an outline of major elements in the sociology of economics, and a lengthy review of the endogenous and exogenous (direct and indirect, intellectual and non-intellectual) influences on the discipline since 1870. Characteristically, the range of his citations is vast, and the paper contains numerous penetrating remarks on the professionalization of economics. Also suggestive are Eagly's broad concluding comments on the sociology of the economics profession, which, though brief and generalized, constitute a preliminary analytical foundation for the study of the leading differences between (roughly speaking) the pre- and post-1870 processes of production of economic knowledge.

Among historians of economics, only the most rigid "absolutists" can fail to profit from this volume, while those interested in the sociology of knowledge will find various constructive hypotheses and illustrative examples. Eagly's essay, for instance, poses a "specification" problem – that is (as his commentator notes), were economic conditions and developments in fact "strikingly similar" in essentials in mid-eighteenth century Sweden and early nineteenth century England? Was monetary theory "substantially the same" in the two cases, and were the advances in theory "largely identical in nature"? Was there a causal connection or merely a correlation between ideas and events; and did the stimulus of events merely provide the topic, or did it also actually determine the content of analysis? "If events are so significant in determining analysis, why is it that the *same* circumstance... does not call forth uniform – or at least clearly dominant and hopefully superior – analysis"? (Allen, pp. 33–5 ; cf. Spengler on the "core" and "shell" of economics, p. 187). In his own essay, Allen concedes that real world conditions undoubtedly "played a dominating role in determing the questions and problems of the mercantilist writers" (p. 73), but he has a low opinion of their analysis partly because (as his commentator observes) he considers they lacked an adequate price theory, and "without price theory, there can be no theory of international trade" (Kurihara, a Keynesian, calls this an "idiosyncratic view", and concludes that Allen may have failed to grasp the "historical role of mercantilism", p. 82). There are, of course, semantic difficulties here (what is a "theory"?), as well as questions of "goodness of fit", quite apart from the causation/correlation issue. Meek, while rejecting the extreme "relativist" thesis, argues that environments "can and do set fundamental problems", adding that in the physiocratic case "the selection of the particular relations which were to be regarded as the 'key' ones and the particular economic categories which were to be generalized in the basic model was obviously subject to the influence of the kind of factors which we usually label 'accidental' or 'arbitrary'" (pp. 45, 47). He adopts an eclectic explanation of the content and purpose of Physiocratic doctrine which embraces Quesnay's personal genius, the influence of improvements in farming in northern France, and the concept of the circular flow – which "was evolved not for its own sake, but rather for the light which the Physiocrats believed it could help throw on certain burning policy issues of their times" (p. 50). Environmental influences explain some of the peculiar features of Physiocratic doctrine (e.g. the unimportance of foreign trade, and the "sterility" of manufacture) while "policy considerations were largely instrumental in preventing the Physiocrats from making greater efforts than they in fact did to overcome these conceptual difficulties", and from giving "proper weight to certain new economic facts" (pp. 54–5).

Clearly there is no single or simple relationship between events, ideology and economic theory. But this volume demonstrates that the problem is not only worth studying, but is indeed of critical importance to historians of economics.

9 *Economic theory in retrospect (Revised edition)*

By Mark Blaug

Homewood, Illinois 1968. Richard D. Irwin
pp. xxiv + 710

This is a new and substantially revised version of a textbook which first appeared in 1962. The author's aim is 'to write a history of economic analysis which pictures it as evolving out of previous analysis, propelled forward by the desire to refine, to improve, to perfeet, a desire which economists share with all other scientists' (p. xi), and he is well aware of the dangers inherent in this approach. In a stimulating introduction he contrasts the 'absolutist' and 'relativist' styles of intellectual history, and although he is broadminded enough to appreeiate the virtues displayed by such moderate relativists as Wesley Mitchell or Alexander Gray, he relentlessly follows the logic of his position. His intention is 'to teach contemporary economic theory' by presenting its antrecedents in a manner 'undiluted by entertaining digrressions or biographical coloring' (p. ix), and the questions he seeks to answer are: 'What do economists know? How much does economics explain? What are the standards by which economic theories have been accepted or rejected? What features have characterized endurable economic ideas? What practical use is economic knowledge?' (p. 8).

As Professor Blaug acknowledges, the historian who resists the lure of ancestor worship runs the risk of patronizing his predecessors; and even his title suggests the dangers of an undue reliance on the wisdom of hindsight. Certainly his tone is confident – at times, indeed, downright assertive, and he readily passes summary judgments on matter which have in the past been the subject of protracted and heated controversy. Yet this is but a small price to pay for the most acute, intelligent, and methodologically self-conscious general survey of the progress of economic theory since Schumpeter.

Beginning with a brief review of 'Pre-Adamite Eeonomics', the author proceeds through the classieal economists, Marx, the early marginalists, Marshall, and the Austrians, to the marginal produetivity and general equilibrium theories, and Keynesian analysis. The structure of the present book and the chapter titles closely follow the original edition, and the additional eighty odd pages in the revised version are fairly evenly spread throughout – apart from a substantial expansion of Chapter 11 on the Marginal Productivity Theory of Distribution.

Despite passing references to many individuals, Professor Blaug concentrates on the leading figures. His present-mindedness is reflected in the disproportionate share of space devoted to the past hundred years, and (in the new edition) in the additional material on such currently fashionable topics as activity analysis, economic dynamics, welfare economics, growth models, and technical ehange. The incisive concluding '*Methodological PostScript*' has also been extended, and conspicous among the book's many virtues are the seventeen valuable critical bibliographical '*Notes on Further Reading*' and the seven detailed Readers Guides to the major works by Smith, Ricardo, Mill, Marx, Marshall, Wicksteed and Wicksell. Denying the deistical imputation that these Guides are 'heaven-sent cribs' rather than 'stimuli to consult the original writers', Professor Blaug warns that they are 'neither summaries nor précis; they are running commentaries, and more concemed with what the great economists might have meant than with what they actually said' (p. xii). However, he need have no fear that critics will accuse him of pandering to his readers. No other history of economics text known to this reviewer contains so much mathematics. In addition to both symbolic and diagrammatic translations of verbal theories, there are several novel symbolic reformulations of earlier analyses (e.g. Quesnay's *Tableau* as a three-sector closed Leontief model) which are designed to appeal to the present, mathematically sophisticated generation of graduate students.

This is a long, densely packed book, and no conventional review can convey an adequate impression of the richness of its contents. At many points the informed reader will disagree with the author's judgments, interpretations, and facts. As a confirmed (but, one hopes, moderate) relativist, this reviewer cannot help wondering whether the student who first encounters the history of economics in these pages will be encouraged to examine for himself the context and the historical significance of even the classics – not to mention the cranks, and the minor contributors to the literature of economics, since he may feel that all the answers are here. If he does pursue the subject he will encounter some surprises, for even the advanced student will find it difficult in these pages to distinguish between the contributions of the original author, his crities and his commentators – including Professor Blaug himself! One may legitimately ask whether this is the best way to learn either contemporary theory or the history of economics. On the other hand, given the author's viewpoint and intentions, his book contains a considerable amount of non-analytical material, much of it perceptive, and this feature is doubtless due to the fact that Professor Blaug is a recognised economic historian. Although he virtually ignores the historicists and non-Marxian socialists, the new edition includes a brief, and not wholly unsympathetic, commentary on the American institutionalists – presumably because of their contemporary relevance. In his postscript, Professor Blaug admits the validity of many of the fundamental arguments advanced by the anti-positivist critics of economic orthodoxy, and he does not conceal the detours, blind alleys, prejudices, and follies which have so often impeded the pursuit of scientific truth in economics. Can one reasonably expect more from a self-confessed absolutist?

In conclusion, it should be noted that most of the innumerable misprints which marred the first edition have now been eliminated.

10 *J. R. McCulloch: A study in classical economics*

By D. P. O'Brien

London 1970. George Allen & Unwin
pp. 452

Historians of economics have long regarded McCulloch as the least rewarding member of the British classical school. The original for Carlyle's caricature of 'the gloomy professors of the dismal science', textbook writers have usually depicted him as Ricardo's most rigid and slavish disciple. His statistical compilations have, admittedly, been appreciated by economic and social historians, and close students of classical economics have recognised his importance as a propagator of Ricardian ideas. But his low reputation and the sheer volume and repetitiveness of his writings have discouraged scholars from investigating this aspect of his contribution. Consequently the conventional view of his life and work has survived largely unaltered for a Century or more.

Now, however, as a result of Dr. O'Brien's detailed, comprehensive, and scholarly research, McCulloch appears in an entirely new light. Not only was he a distinctive and forceful personality who lived a vigorous and effective life; he was also an original and independent-minded economic theorist who owed more to Adam Smith than to Ricardo himself. At times he was a severe critic as well as a disseminator of Ricardian doctrine. Hence Dr. O'Brien's study undermines the conventional view of Ricardian economics as a unified body of doctrine rin which its exponents unwaveringly applied to contemporary policy problems.

After a brief introduction and biographical outline, Dr. O'Brien devotes three chapters to McCulloch's career as 'the first professional economist in the sense of one who lived by means of his learning on the subject'. He was an energetic journalist, an extraordinarily effective teacher (who gave his audience a simplified and pragmatic version of economics), a prolific author, an advisor to leading statesmen (especially Sir Robert Peel), and a civil servant. Although economists were unpopular in many quarters, McCulloch was socially acceptable, and was eventually awarded a pension for his services 'to the Science of Political Economy' (p. 111).

McCulloch's economics followed the Hume-Smith tradition, 'with its mixture of fact and analysis, of theoretical and empirical considerations. Although he did not have the incisive analytical powers of Ricardo or Torrens, he did have wide powers of synthesis, and an enormous command of factual and institutional analysis' (p. 16). Dr. O'Brien rightly rejects Professor Blaug's view that there was 'a complete divorce between fact and theory in the work of McCulloch and his contemporaries' (p. 96), and cites a number of theoretical and policy issues on which McCulloch markedly changed his views as a result of experience and observation (e.g. government debt policy, poor laws, the Malthusian population thesis, diminishing returns in agriculture, and corn law repeal). Nor was he lacking in independence or flexibility on basic theoretical questions. In his value theory – one of the areas in which his limitations have usually been emphasized – Dr. O'Brien reveals the differences between Ricardo and McCulloch, and shows how the latter's views developed with the passage of time. In monetary matters he owed more to Hume than to Ricardo; and in international trade theory he followed Smith rather than the Torrens-Ricardo-Mill analysis. (This re-interpretation does not really enhance McCulloch's reputation, and here Dr. O'Brien puts McCulloch in too favourable a light.) He was more concerned with economic growth than distribution, and placed considerable emphasis on the productivity of capital and the role of knowledge and inventions. His treatment of public finance was more comprehensive than any of his predecessors' and he was an ability-to-pay theorist, not a benefit theorist as usually supposed – a position that made him a staunch opponent of Gladstonian financial policy.

On policy questions McCulloch displayed genuine independence, and Dr. O'Brien reveals him as much less pig-headed than had hitherto been supposed. Although he was politically conservative, and greatly concerned for the security of property and the stability of the social order, he was no Tory. Moreover, he was a sincere friend of the working man, displaying more sympathy and insight into the labourer's condition than any of his classical contemporaries.

This book is the product of immense research of a high order, but it is not easy to read or to digest. The style is unexciting, the predominantly topical organisation entails some repetition and much cross-referencing (which is inadequately signposted), and the footnoting is cumbersome and sometimes excessive. But while general readers may be deterred, specialists will be delighted, and they will be exploring its treasures for many a decade.

11 *The correspondence of Lord Overstone*

Edited by Denis P. O'Brien

London 1971. Cambridge University Press. 3 vol
pp. lxxxi + 1,548

In recent decades scholars in economics, economic history, and related disciplines, have become increasingly indebted to the Royal Economic Society for its sponsorship and financial support of a variety of outstanding editorial, bibliographical and archival ventures. Most conspicuous among these, of course, are the great collected editions of Ricardo's and Keynes's works. But Professor O'Brien's three substantial volumes of Lord Overstone's Correspondence form part of a larger series of projects which includes the current four-volume edition of Jevons' Correspondence, and the Guide to Archive Sources for the History of British Economic Thought.

Not even Professor O'Brien would contend that Overstone ranks as an economist with Ricardo, Jevons and Keynes. And there will undoubtedly be some unkind spirits who question, especially before purchasing these expensive books, whether Overstone merits such dedicated and extensive treatment. In an effort to silence this doubt two answers can be offered: one general, one specific. The first is that if a thing is worth doing, it is worth doing well; and no one who handles these volumes will doubt that it has been most excellently done. The second is to direct readers to Frank Fetter's magisterial (though admittedly,comparatively slim) study of *The Development of British Monetary Orthodoxy,* which demonstrates the importance, both theoretical and practical, of the achievements of leading nineteenth century members of the banking community. Amid this distinguished company Overstone, originally Samuel Jones Loyd (1796–1883), was undeniably outstanding, both as a contributor to the oft-studied controversy between the so-called Banking and Currency schools, and as one of the chief architects of the Bank Charter Act of 1844, one of the major items of nineteenth century British economic legislation. Discerning critics, like Viner and Schumpeter, have recognized his intellectual strength and perspicacity, and his contributions to early business cycle theory have been appreciated, if inadequately. But hitherto it has been difficult to do him justice.

Professor O'Brien discovered a rich hoard of Overstone papers while engaged on the research for his distinguished study of J. R. McCulloch (reviewed in Vol.24 [1971] 3 of this journal). His 130 page editorial introduction successfully places Overstone in his context as a man, a thinker, and a decisive influence on policy-makers, and his career reveals more of those fascinating connections between economic ideas and events which have recently become the object of systematic study. In addition, O'Brien has provided all the essential scholarly apparatus, including some 850 biographical sketches of *dramatis personae,* a substantial index, and nineteen appendices comprising 170 pages of unpublished documents by Overstone and his contemporaries. These documents supplement and amplify subjects covered in the introduction and correspondence. They include items on currency, fiscal and commercial topics by G. W. Norman (the influential director of the Bank of England, and grandfather of Montagu Norman) C. Wood (later Lord Halifax, who was Chancellor of the Exchequer during the 1847 financial crisis) and Mcculloch. The most substantial group of appendices covers the discussion of decimal coinage proposals which Overstone, as a member of the Royal Commission of 1856–9, was largely instrumental in defeating.

The main body of material consists of 923 letters, both incoming and outgoing, covering the period 1804–1833. Overstone's letters have been supplemented by material from other collections where they formed the other half of correspondence. They fall into fourteen subject-categories, including: personal and social, politics, pauperism and distress, London University, Political Economy Club, limited liability, statistics, and the obvious currency, financial and fiscal topics. The biggest single group is from Overstone to Norman, and there are many letters between Overstone and Wood. But among other correspondents are most of the major and minor economic writers of the period – apart from David Ricardo – with Torrens especially prominent. Among leading politicians are Lord John Russell, (to whom Overstone was an important adviser), Gladstone (to whom he was continuously hostile), Robert Lowe, Lord Monteagle and Disraeli; but the list is too long and too rich to be fully enumerated. Political historians. Even those uninterested in monetary matters, will find these volumes a rich source of information and insight into political connections and parliamentary affairs, while social historians and students of nineteenth century biography will also find much of interest. This is especially so in the case of Overstone himself, described in the *Times* obituary as 'a representative man... the greatest living authority on all matters connected with trade and finance', and his principal correspondent. G. W. Norman, who has hitherto been a rather shadowy figure.

These bulky volumes are, of course, essentially reference works rather than contributions to narrative history, though the epistolary style of the period makes them enjoyable reading as literature. But they are, above all, the most important single addition to the published source materials on British nineteenth century monetary history for many decades.

12 *The structure of classical economic theory*

By Robert V. Eagly

New York, London and, Toronto 1974.
Oxford University Press
pp. 142

The classical economists

By D. P. O'Brien

London 1975. Clarendon Press.
Oxford University Press
pp. 306

During recent decades there has been a remarkably sustained interest in the nature, significance and development of classical economics, and the secondary literature on the subject has been enriched by a variety of approaches and interpretations. These two volumes exemplify that variety, for while they deal with essentially the same period and subject matter, they could hardly be more different. Professor Eagly is the dissecting anatomist: his short, austere, severely abstract analysis is designed to expose the theoretical skeleton concealed beneath the complexity and diversity of the classical writings. By contrast, Professor O'Brien is the comprehensive historian: his much longer, more general treatise encompasses not merely the whole range of classical economic theory, but also the historical and intellectual context, the personalia, and the policy issues. Both authors address a wide audience: Eagly appeals to non-specialists seeking 'a concise and integrated survey of the development of economic theory' as well as specialists in quest of 'an encompassing analytical framework for research in classical economics', whereas O'Brien's book is designed for the economic historian and the economist interested in the history of economic thought. Both works are ambitious, but they must have imposed quite different demands on their authors. Eagly's effort to distil the essence of classical economics. 'to elaborate the conceptual framework or gestalt of the system' called for heroic simplification, rigorous logic, and a determined refusal to be distracted by mere empirical impediments. His study is convergent to the point of distortion – and, no doubt some critics will think, well beyond that point. By contrast, O'Brien's book required a more judicious balance of the conceptual and the empirical, a massive erudition combined with a disciplined command of a bewildering array of writers and topics. While his approach frequently entails the deployment of modern analytical techniques, and a mastery of some recent severely mathematical forays into the history of economic theory, his acknowledged preference for verbal argument ensures that his book is much more readable than Eagly's.

Confronted by two such dramatically contrasting studies the reviewer must choose his standpoint carefully, and in the interests of objectivity it is appropriate to admit a personal predilection for O'Brien's concrete historical treatment. A further problem arises from the difficulty of criticizing Eagly's work without appearing pedantic, for its strength lies in the whole, the *Gestalt*, rather than the individual parts. Fortunately, however, his message is clear and easy to summarize.

The key to Eagly's interpretation of classical economics is the concept of capital: its 'centrality ... cannot be overemphasized'. It 'defined a new scientific frontier', became the central preoccupation of 'generations of practitioners', and provided the 'analytical schema around which the component parts of classical economic theory are built' (p. 3). After a brief glance at mercantilist theory and the transition to classical economics (circa 1720–1759), Eagly examines the so-called Quesnaysian Revolution, which represented the break-through to modern economics. Quesnay prepared the ground for the dominant classical theme that 'commodities are produced by commodities' and the concept of capital as 'prior accumulated goods which constituted the all-inclusive input into the reproduction process' (p. 127). Quesnay recognized that output was a function of capital which was divisible into fixed and variable categories, and Marx's subsequent rearrangement of these categories was merely a slight variation on the same dominant theme (ibid.). The basic classical model was 'period-analytic', with distinct 'production' and 'exchange' periods, and Say's law was just a simplifying device designed to dispose of the possibility that capitalists might fail to reconstitute their capital stock at the end of the exchange period. No significance was attached to the money supply since it was held that monetary exchanges were unlikely to affect the economy's total capital stock – and classical theory was preeminently aggregative.

Walras' general equilibrium model marked the end of the system, although it was initially merely 'a natural extension of the classical analysis' (p. 6). In Walras' *Elements* the two 'activity periods were explicitly tied together' by establishing equilibrium simultaneously in commodity exchange and in the allocation of factor inputs. Thus in retrospect Walras' work 'constituted the last truly monumental contribution to the structure of classical theory' (p. 7), while at the same time striking the 'decisive blow' against it by posing new problems. As a result price gradually replaced capital as the central economic concept. It was Walras' redefinition of capital, not J. S. Mill's recantation, that killed the wages-fund doctrine. Wage income was 'transformed into a flow from current productive activity rather than a division of an already accumulated capital stock for current production', and this paved the way for the marginal productivity theory. Thus the Walrasian Synthesis led to the elimination of the classical allocation problem and the period-analytic approach. 'Capitalists, who carried the classical economy on their shoulders, were pushed into the background, and economic analysis no longer relied upon the *noblesse oblige* of the capitalist class; the oligarchic rule of the classical world was replaced by the participatory democracy of the post-Walrasian world in which the preferences and utility curves of everyman were taken into consideration' (p. 8).

This lapse into socio-political rhetoric is uncharacteristic, although the same sentiments are reiterated in even more grandiose terms in the concluding chapter (pp. 135–137). In between, Eagly develops his argument confidently, consistently and unswervingly. Successive chapters deal with 'The Basic Classical Model'; 'The Analytical Role of Money' (with an 'Appendix on the Thornton-Wicksell Theory of Credit Creation') ; 'Malthusian Aggregative Analysis'; and 'Business Fluctuations in the Classical System: Karl Marx's Real Endogenous Cycle'. Citations from classical writings designed to buttress the argument are provided, usually in footnotes, but references to scholarly commentaries and interpretations of classical economics are comparatively sparse.

In a normal-sized review it is clearly impossible to attempt an adequate appraisal of the historical validity of Eagly's interpretation, for this would require detailed textual exegesis. Moreover, his approach poses all the usual problems encountered in applying systematic modern ideas to the efforts of more primitive writers. Parts of his story are familiar enough; but in developing his main theme he deliberately ignores or deals summarily with so many of the individuating characteristics of classical economics that it is hardly surprising if his 'gestalt' fails to provide the requisite 'shock of recognition', to use Edmund Wilson's expressive phrase. As an exercise in theoretical ingenuity Eagly's 'encompassing analytical framework' has a certain attraction, and the influence of Schumpeter and Sraffa, especially the latter, is obvious enough. Yet it seems doubtful that either would admit paternity, while more humble readers will inevitably miss so many of the vital theoretical and empirical issues which engaged the attentions of the classical economists and their commentators.

O'Brien's opus is less daringly original than Eagly's; but his effort to cover the entire classical literature in a single volume is certainly not wanting in ambition. While he extends the classical period back to 1750 – thereby embracing Hume, who is dismissed by Eagly as a mercantilist – he excludes Quesnay and Walras, who are so conspicuous in Eagly's gestalt, and omits Marx, as an offshoot from the main stem. Even so, some readers will consider O'Brien's tastes too catholic, for his list of classical 'personnel' is much longer than is usual. By comparison with earlier accounts he pays particular attention to McGulloch (who appears but once in Eagly's index) and Torrens (who appears not at all), and this shift of emphasis reflects recent historical scholarship (notably the work of O'Brien himself, and Robbins). As might be expected, the distinguished editor of Overstone's correspondence provides a thorough analysis of classical monetary theory, and there are equally conscientious chapters on value theory, distribution, international trade, and public finance – the last of which, as he remarks, has too often been neglected hitherto. These chapters comprise nearly two-thirds of the volume, and they display sound judgment, clarity of thought and expression, and careful attention to deviations from the mainstream of classical ideas. O'Brien also draws effectively upon the vast secondary literature of commentaries and interpretations. He would probably agree with Eagly that 'the task of economic theory is a matter of pulling out the most central variables and connecting them together in a concise theoretical structure' and that 'the transition to classical economics… was characterized by developments in the analysis of interdependence or interconnectedness among participants in the market economy' (op,cit., pp. 16–17). But he goes beyond this to show the limitations as well as the logic of economic theory, and specifically warns that undue concentration on the basic functional relationships serves to obscure the complexity, richness, and empirical relevance of classical writing. (Cf. for example, pp. 211–214 on Smith's theory of economic growth.) In his first three chapters on 'The Classical Economic Stage', 'The Roots', and 'The Characteristics and Preconceptions of Classical Economics', O'Brien places the classical personnel and topics squarely in their historical context, and an admirable chapter on 'Policy Prescriptions' rounds off the volume.

In embracing so wide a field some compression and oversimplification is unavoidable, and no reviewer will endorse all O'Brien's judgments. In this writer's opinion he somewhat underrates the influence of mercantilist, Physiocratic and Benthamite ideas on classical economics. In giving McCulloch and Torrens more prominence than usual, and perhaps more than their due, he somewhat undervalues Ricardo, and he overpraises J. S. Mill's theoretical contributions. Specialist economic historians will find his treatment of their subject-matter rather sketchy, but sound enough, while the concluding chapter on policy matters contains a comprehensive and judicious treatment of many controversial points. There are valuable bibliographies at the end of each chapter.

Taken as a whole, the book is a considerable achievement – the nearest thing we have to an authoritative survey of the field. Specialists will find it instructive; teachers of the history of economics will find it indispensable; and it is to be hoped that many economists conscious of their profession's prevalent 'provincialism in time', to use Lord Robbins' apt phrase, will consult it in an effort to broaden their horizons.

13 *The emergence of professional social science: The American Social Science Association and the nineteenth-century crisis of authority*

By Thomas L. Haskell

Urbana: University of Illinois Press, 1977
pp. xii + 276

Once upon a time the question whether economics is a science provoked heated controversy, whereas nowadays it arouses comparatively little response among economists, not because their discipline is in a healthy, settled condition – far from it! – but because the issue it poses seems merely semantic and irrelevant to current problems and needs. Nevertheless, fundamental questions of this kind rarely fade away for long, especially in an unsettled subject; and when they reappear, they usually assume a different shape.

In recent years the fashionable form has been sociological rather than epistemological. Studies of the development and status of economics as a science have been giving way to investigations of the professionalization process, and although this change of focus has by no means eliminated the semantic difficulties, the new formulation is attracting a wider scholarly audience. Consideration of economics as a profession is not merely of interest to methodologists and philosophers of science; it is also of interest to historians, sociologists, and all those active practitioners of the discipline who recognize its bearing on the range of their employment opportunities and their emoluments.

Economics may or may not be a science; but it is certainly recognized as a profession, in terms of all but the most traditional and stringent definitions of that weasel word. Admittedly economists lack the statutory powers of licensing and self-regulation exercised by such traditional professions as law and medicine; and they have neither a formal code of ethics nor powers of excommunication. But they possess all the other essential attributes, including effective control of training and initiation rites; incomes broadly commensurable with those of other acknowledged professions; a considerable and probably growing measure of professional self-consciousness; and substantial public recognition in its most pertinent and tangible form – specialized employment opportunities. Moreover, with reference to the last point, they enjoy increasing participation and influence in the highest councils of state.

The professionalization of economics during the late nineteenth and early twentieth centuries was an integral part of the modernization process, and its precise nature and significance can be expressed in a variety of ways. On one level, it was simply a by-product of the increasing specialization and division of labour among the educated cadres. Beyond this, it reflected the egotistic middle-class drive for status and power; and it represented a threat to the old established elites, the last generation of amateurs, as the new groups used their cognitive skills to capture and control the extended markets for their services. In intellectual terms it involved a crisis of authority among both the older and the newer generations; and for the latter, it posed a sensitive problem of the relationship between advocacy of social reform and the assertion of authoritative claims to neutrality and scientific objectivity. A somewhat similar process was, of course, under way in Europe about the same time. But in the United States the rate of change was much more rapid, and the absence of an entrenched intellectual class and well-established institutions of higher education meant that the emergence of a new professional elite was more dramatic, and conflicts of outlook and interest correspondingly more pronounced.[1]

In his ambitious and provocative new book Thomas Haskell breaks new ground by examining these conventional aspects of professionalization in relation to the underlying epistemological foundations, where he detects a "profound change in the conditions of adequate explanation" (p. vi). His central theme – the rise and fall of the American Social Science Association (ASSA), 1865–1909 – is familiar to students of American intellectual history, but Haskell sets it in a much broader context than usual.

The ASSA was formed under the sponsorship of the Massachusetts State Board of Charities by a group of New England gentlemen educators and men of affairs who wished to study and find solutions to various contemporary social problems, especially those resulting from rapid urbanization and immigration. For some time this group had been trying to establish a "community of the competent" designed to raise standards of scientific inquiry, and they were reinforced by a number of prominent or rising educators eager to reform American higher education. By the 1880s the ASSA had expanded, not without difficulty, to the point where the activities of its several "departments" embraced most of today's social science disciplines, and it began to give birth to a number of specialized learned societies, most notably the American Historical Association (1884) and the American Economic Association (1885). Given the explosive growth of knowledge and the revolution in higher education then under way, the ASSA could not hope to control its expanding bailiwick indefinitely. Leadership in the establishment of authoritative sources of knowledge passed from the gentlemen founders of the ASSA to the new university professionals, and the organization gradually lost even its coordinating function. Before this time the ASSA's leaders had been uncertain whether to concentrate their efforts regionally or to aim at a national membership, but the question was really an academic one, in the pejorative sense of the term, for even the new specialized societies with their growing nucleus of university members and institutional affiliations initially found it difficult to overcome the problems of geography and poor communications.

The emergence of the modern social sciences in America has been viewed as a drive for cultural consolidation comparable to the trust movement in American business (cf. John Higham, cited by Haskell, pp. 63–64). It was inspired by a "heroic enthusiasm" for the construction and reinforcement of professional institutions. The epistemological foundation of professionalization, Haskell claims, was the movement

> to establish or reestablish authority in the face of profoundly disruptive changes in habits of causal attribution, in the criteria of plausibility, in the relation of the man of knowledge to his clientele – [and] finally, changes in the very notion of truth itself [p. 65].

The paradigm or "interpretative keystone" in terms of which the professionalization process can be grasped is the concept of "interdependence" which, according to Haskell, represented for John Dewey and his generation

> an intellectualization of the objective conditions of their society – or, more accurately, an intellectualization of the *direction* in which objective conditions were changing.... As long as life remained within the intimate confines of family, sect, and village, sensitivity to the interdependence of human relationship in time and social space was not a critical matter. It was plausible enough to construe each individual as self-reliant master of his own fate, and to construe society as an artificial and even ephemeral aggregate of human wills.
>
> But as society became increasingly interdependent, the conditions of adequate explanation and prediction changed. Dewey and his generation were the first to adopt the habits of mind appropriate to an interdependent society. Social thinkers who clung to older habits of mind, appropriate to a simple society, became implausible and faded into obsolescence. The main point of cleavage between the professional theorists... and the declining amateur theorists studied in these pages is the recognition of, or the failure to recognize, the objective fact of social interdependence and its larger theoretical implications [p. 15].

This passage reveals the breadth and boldness of Haskell's main thesis; but it cannot adequately suggest the skill with which he has woven his account of the ASSA's fortunes into his interpretive framework. One of the climaxes in his story is the (hitherto unknown) abortive attempt to merge the organization into the newly established Johns Hopkins University, an episode of great symbolic and historical interest. The decisive figure in this episode, Hopkins's brilliant President, Daniel Coit Gilman, is depicted as standing "on the very edge of the transition from amateur to professional social science" (p. 160), and his rejection of the scheme probably sealed the ASSA's fate, though the "death blow" was delayed until 1909, when the American Political Science Association was launched. Another central individual in the story, one who has too often been neglected by previous scholars, is Frank Sanborn (1831–1917), whose career as the indefatigable secretary of the ASSA also straddled the transition from amateur to professional and directly contributed both to its initial success and its subsequent demise.

Haskell's capable handling of these and other parts of his subject-matter cannot, however, conceal the difficulties posed by his main argument. His ambitious attempt to synthesize the epistemological and sociological planes of discourse is plausible and suggestive but, ultimately, unconvincing, and his central concept of "interdependence" is too fuzzy and imprecise to provide a criterion for distinguishing between gentry-amateur and academic-professional modes of explanation in the social sciences. The shift of intellectual authority between the two groups was neither as clear-cut nor as decisive as he claims. At a number of important points, Haskell makes sweeping or simplistic generalizations, for example about the pre-Civil War crisis of the professional class (pp. 77–78); the dramatic shift of cultural mood in mid-century (p. 57); the psychological differences between mid- and late-century anxieties (p. 45); and the shift from consensus to competition among men and ideas for positions of authority in the 1870–90 period (p. 161). As with other sociological studies of the professionalization of the social sciences, his approach is predominantly "externalist," and he is distinctly ungenerous towards Mary Furner's valuable contribution,[2] which somewhat overemphasized conditions within the various academic disciplines. More directly relevant to economics is his debatable contention that the departmental divisions within the ASSA (i.e. Education; Public Health; Economy, Trade, and Finance; Jurisprudence and the Administration of Laws) conformed roughly with the tripartite division of labor of the classical professional class (pp. 87, 104). Economics was, in fact, well represented in the ASSA before 1885 (a Department of Social Economy was created in 1873–74); and Haskell's tendency to strain the evidence for the sake of symmetry is also evident in his effort to play down the role of reform in the early years of the American Economic Association (cf. pp. 178, 182, but also 187) and to gloss over the prominence of amateurs in the American Historical Association long after 1884. However he gives valuable attention to the significant but unduly neglected clash between Henry George and the academic economists at the 1890 ASSA meeting, and his account of late-nineteenth-century American sociology, though not novel, will be suggestive to all historians of economics prepared to compare it with concurrent developments in their own field.

Of course, it is easy to detect flaws on a canvas as broad as Haskell's. Nevertheless, as the length of this review indicates, his book represents an important new departure in the literature on the sociology of the social sciences. It deserves careful attention from all broad-minded historians of economics.

Notes

1 These matters are discussed in Burton J. Bledstein, *The Culture of Professionalism. The Middle Class and the Development of Higher Education in America* (New York, 1976); and Mary O. Furner, *Advocacy and Objectivity: A Crisis in the Professionalization of American Social Science, 1865–1905* (University Press of Kentucky, 1975). For my review article on the latter work, which contains valuable material on the development of American economics, see *Journal of American Studies*, 12:227–33. There is a stimulating comparison of British and American conditions in Magali Sarfatti Larson, *The Rise of Professionalism: A Sociological Analysis* (Berkeley, 1977).

2 See n. 1 supra.

14 *Beyond Adam Smith's economics*

By Donald Winch

One clear conclusion to be drawn from the flood of publications occasioned by the *Wealth of Nations* bicentennial is that although studies of Adam Smith's economic analysis encountered rapidly diminishing returns some time ago, there is still ample scope for original and illuminating research into other aspects of Smith's intellectual achievement.[1] During the past two decades or so the close interdependence between Smith's *Theory of Moral Sentiments* and the *Wealth of Nations* has been acknowledged by all but extreme 'absolutist' historians of economics, and the unity and comprehensiveness of his mental outlook is nowadays widely appreciated. Doubtless it is too much to hope that Smith's departed spirit will ever be entirely released from the tortures devised by ingenious mathematical economists seeking to force his subtle insights into their own sadistic conceptual apparatas.[2] But there is consolation for the humanists in the two important publications under review[3] – one an austere major addition to the limited available corpus of Smith's own writings, the other a suggestive interpretative essay which will undoubtedly both stimulate and provoke the *cognoscenti*.

One's pleasure in perusing the latest addition to the excellent Glasgow edition of Smith's *Works and Correspondence* is seriously marred by knowledge of the sad, recent, and unexpected death of its principal editor, Ronald Meek, a world ranking authority on eighteenth century British and French economic thought. Students of the Scottish Enlightenment have been eagerly awaiting the recently discovered lecture notes which amount to more than double those published in 1896 by Edwin Cannan as *Lectures on Justice, Police, Revenue and Arms, Delivered at the University of Glasgow by Adam Smith*. The Cannan material, herein comprising 157 pages reprinted under the title 'Report of 1766' and referred to by Meek and his co-editors as *LJ(B)* is now supplemented by 390 pages of additional material, entitled 'Report of 1762–3' and referred to as *LJ(A)*. The new material was acquired by auction in 1958, by Professor John M. Lothian, together with a set of notes on Smith's lectures on Rhetoric and Belles Lettres, which Lothian published in 1963. (A newly edited version of that transcript will also appear in the Glasgow series.)

In their forty-two page introduction Professor Meek and his collaborators deliberately refrain from attempting a general evaluation of the new material. They provide an exact description of the manuscripts, an estimate of the dating based on a meticulous reconstruction of Smith's lecture time-table, and an analysis of the substantial differences in the content and structure of *LJ(A)* and (*B*). In collating the two sets, they note the consequential advances in our knowledge of Smith's sources, the striking additional parallels with Francis Hutcheson's Glasgow Lectures, and – reflecting Meek's own special interest – further evidence of the significance of Smith's 'fourstage' conceptual framework. Other noteworthy points are the links between *LJ(A)* and the *Moral Sentiments* in Smith's explanation of the natural right to property by occupation; his stress on the contemporary 'dangers' to English liberty; the attention given to the detrimental effects of slavery on population; and his generalization of the idea that institutions harmful to society may have originally been necessary and even convenient to it. As the section of *LJ(A)* devoted to 'police' is incomplete, it adds less to our knowledge of Smith's economic thought than might have been expected. Nevertheless, it sheds additional light on his reliance on Hume's specie-flow theory, the development of his division of labour concept, and, more tentatively, his views on the role of capital, the rate of profit, and the notion of profit as a category of class income.

Study of the notes and text reinforces the editors' judgment that *LJ(A)* and (*B*) differ more in arrangement than content. (*A*) proceeds through property and other rights to domestic law, government and police, whereas (*B*) treats government, domestic law, property and other rights, and police, in that order. The volume contains a clear and effective technical apparatus, and its value is enhanced by the inclusion of the so-called 'Early Draft' of Smith's *magnum, opus* and two 'Fragments' on the Division of Labour dating from the 1760s, previously published by W. R. Scott.

Economists whose knowledge of Smith is derived solely from history of economic theory texts or selections from the 'economic' parts of the *Wealth of Nations* will be astonished by the sheer range of subject matter covered in the *Lectures on Jurisprudence*, which will undoubtedly be a gold mine for serious students of the period. Moreover, given the vigorous current interest in economic aspects of law, property rights, and public policy, many other professional economists will find relevant material therein. Indeed, Smith's concept of justice has already attracted attention among bicentennial essayists,[4] and it is intimately related to Donald Winch's central theme.

Drawing freely upon a large and important recent body of research on eighteenth century British and American political ideas – a literature which is, not surprisingly in this age of academic specialization, almost entirely unknown to historians of economics – Professor Winch seeks to reinstate Smith's coneption of *homo politicus* (or, more precisely, *homo civicus)* alongside the more familiar *homo socius* of the *Moral Sentiments* and *homo oeconomicus* of the *Wealth of Nations*. Previous authors, he argues, blinded by their teleological preconceptions of Smith's significance for later generations, have failed to grasp his *intention*. The nineteenth century Whig interpretation of his work is not merely anachronistic, but positively misleading, as is the now discredited view of Locke as the ideological progenitor of modern parliamentary democracy.

Smith's politics has often hitherto been regarded, not without justification, as elusive, obscure, and confusing, and Winch's disarmingly modest, but elegant, learned, and forceful 'historiographical revision' is likely to prove controversial. He effectively dismisses George Stigler's Chicago-style analysis of Smith's neglect of self-interest in political affairs by stressing the role of 'opinion' as well as 'interest' in his system.[5] This reflects Smith's intellectual milieu, especially his debt to Hume, and provides the basis of an illuminating reinterpretation of Smith's intriguing and much-debated observations on the future of the American colonies. Winch also presents a constructive reappraisal of Joseph Cropsey's influential account of Smith's conception of the interdependence of 'commerce' and 'freedom'[6] and one regrets that he did not analyse in detail Smith's treatment of the relationship between the 'commercial' stage of socio-economic development and the 'mercantile system' – especially the latter's prospective future in an imperfect world.[7] Winch sheds valuable light on such obscure or neglected aspects of Smith's work as the machinery of government, the influence of political factions, the functions of the legislator (though here the links with Sir James Steuart and the later mercantilists need to be explored), the political and social role of the 'natural aristocracy', the significance of defence and a standing army or militia (which have direct implications for Smith's view of the Navigation Acts and the effects of the division of labour on the 'martial virtues'), and his conception of the general progress of civic society.

Viewed as a whole, Smith's politics was modern, moderate, centrist, sceptical, pessimistic, and realist. It was neither nostalgic, utopian, nor unoriginal. Contrary to the conventional wisdom among historians of economics, Winch maintains, Smith did not encourage the severance of political economy from its eighteenth century intellectual framework. In accordance with the work of Alec Macfie, Dennis O'Brien, and Terence Hutchison, he emphasizes the gap between the Smithian Scottish tradition of economic thought and the Bentham-Ricardo tradition of rationalistic analysis which has been so dominant in twentieth century professional economics.

Perhaps it is not over-optimistic to suggest that the recent return to Adam Smith may contribute something to the shift from narrowly technical economics to the broader type of political economy which is nowadays so urgently needed if professional economists are to make constructive contributions to the solution of current and prospective problems.

Notes

1 Compare, for example, the first and second parts of the especially commissioned Glasgow *Essays on Adam Smith*, edited by Andrew S. Skinner and Thomas Wilson, Oxford 1975.

2 For example, Paul Samuelson, 'A Modern Theorist's Vindication of Adam Smith', American Economic Review, Papers and Proceedings, Vol. LXVII (February, 1977), p. 42, which has a substantial mathematical apparatus. Also, his 'The Canonical Classical Model of Political Economy', Journal of Economic Literature, Vol. XVI (December, 1978), pp. 1415–1434. Admittedly Samuelson does warn against simple

codifications and stereotypes involving 'distortions that both improve on (sic and distort the originals', p.1415.

3 *Adam Smith, Lectures on Jurisprudence*, edited by R. L. Meek, D. D. Raphael, P. G. Stein, Oxford: Clarendon Press 1978, pp. viii +42 4 610, and Donald Winch, *Adam Smith's Politics: An Essay in Historigraphic Revision,* Cambridge: Cambridge University Press 1978, pp. xi + 206, Paperback.

4 Cf: James M. Buchanan, 'The Justice of Natural Liberty', and Leonard Billet, 'Justice, Liberty and Economy', in: Fred R. Glahe (Ed,), *Adam Smith and the Wealth of Nations. 1776–1976 Bicentennial Essays*, Boulder, Colo. 1978, pp. 61–81, 83–109.

5 On a related theme see Albert O. Hirschman, *The Passions and the Interests*, Princeton: Princeton University Press 1977.

6 Joseph Cropsey, *Polity and Economy. An Interpretation of the Principles of Adam Smith*, The Hague 1957.

7 Cf: A. W. Coats, 'Adam Smith and the Mercantile System', in: Skinner and Wilson, op. cit., pp. 218–236, for an exploratory discussion of these matters.

15 *The organization of knowledge in modern America, 1860–1980*

Edited by Alexandra Oleson and John Voss

Baltimore and London: The Johns Hopkins University Press, 1979
pp. xxi + 478

American academics then and now

By Logan Wilson

New York: Oxford University Press, 1979
pp. 309

During the past decade or so, largely under the influence of such powerful and controversial thinkers as Karl Popper, Thomas Kuhn, and Imre Lakatos, scholars in a variety of disciplines have been vigorously exploring the nature and causes of the growth of knowledge. The most novel feature of this movement has been the practice of bringing together in various combinations three levels of discourse which, in more traditional treatments of the history of ideas, have usually been kept apart – namely, philosophy, history and sociology. Starting out with an emphasis on the development of the natural sciences – especially physics, which has conventionally been regarded as the paradigmatic case of valid, tested knowledge – the discussion quickly spread to the social sciences, especially economics, and thence even to the humanities. But while this enquiry has aroused keen, at times almost obsessive, interest among those who are at home on a high plane of abstraction, there is a dearth of more specific, empirically grounded, studies of particular disciplines and epoches which can test the generalisations that have figured so prominently in this literature.

This substantial volume of essays edited by Alexandra Oleson and John Voss is the second instalment of a trilogy devoted to the institutional history of American intellectual activity commissioned by the American Acadamy of Arts and Sciences. (The first volume, edited by Oleson and Sanborn C. Brown and published in 1976, was entitled *The Pursuit of Knowledge in the Early American Republic: American Scientific & Learned Societies from Colonial Times to the Civil War*.) As the title reveals, the scope of the enterprise is ambitious. The nineteen chapters include: an editorial introduction and two *tours d'horizon*, by John Higham ("The Matrix of Specialization") and Edward Shils ("The Order of Learning in the United States"); seven case studies of groups of disciplines and some of their applications; five essays on organizations – including the Carnegie Institution of Washington, the National Academy of Sciences, libraries, and the Boston Society of Natural History; and three concluding chapters of comparison and commentary – by Fritz K. Ringer ("The German Academic Community"), Neil Harris ("The Lamp of Learning: Popular Lights and Shadows"), and Charles Rosenberg ("Toward an Ecology of Knowledge: on Discipline Context and Knowledge"). The disjointedness and unevenness so often found in collections of this kind have been largely avoided by the organizers' and editors' careful planning, which included the discussion of earlier drafts at a symposium designed to focus on points of comparison and contrast among fields and institutions, and between the American organization of learning and that in other Western Systems.

During the six decades under review there was a remarkable growth in the number and diversity of institutions devoted to the production and distribution of knowledge, in the degree of financial support they received from both public and private sources, and in the size of the community they served and employed. The pace of development, so much faster than in Europe, necessarily generated powerful tensions in the form of "sometimes contradictory and sometimes complementary dualisms: teaching and research, abstract learning and the practical arts, liberal culture and specialized research, amateurism and professionalism, the push for centralized leadership and the pull of decentralized authority" (p. xiv).

In so far as there is a single theme underlying this process it is *specialization*, rather than what the editors, following Rosenberg, term "such superficial and overschematized concepts as modernization and professionalization," which tend to obscure the "fine structure" of specific developments in knowledge (p. xviii). (Incidentally, Rosenberg has some reservations about specialization too – viz. p. 441.) According to Higham's brilliantly effective keynote address, "the multiplication and differentiation of bodies of esoteric knowledge made the new professions possible," and he claims that "the rampant growth of specialization … is so ubiquitous that historians have taken it for granted, as if it were one of the constants of nature, like the speed of light, rather than one of the riddles of history" (p. 4). Doubtless there is some rhetorical overstatement in this passage. But as one who has already got some mileage out of the concept of professionalization it is only fair to acknowledge the force of Lawrence Veysey's attack on that intellectual weapon in his perceptive account of "The Plural Organized Worlds of the Humanities." The mixed bag of subjects usually classified under this banner "took on a more or less clear shape only *after* the self-conscious arrival of the social sciences" (p. 57). Contrary to John Dewey's view, in 1910, that the humanities had been reduced to a "humble and apologetic role," Veysey contends that they were actually vigorous and expanding. This process did not involve "the creation of professions from scratch" but, rather, a "transition from an older, long-existing professional outlook and mentality to newer, more specalized versions ... at the end of the nineteenth century." Notwithstanding the humanists' tendency to preach the elitist virtues of a generalized "culture" or "civilization," as distinct from the more egalitarian, scientistic, and utilitarian claims of other disciplines, the humanities too experienced intellectual segmentation and the standardization, structural hierarchy, and bureaucratic procedures associated with the formation and maintenance of academic departments. Veysey holds that the term professionalization has only a limited value as a description of the process since it presupposes a false dichotomy between the lay individual's self-interest and the trained professional's sense of community interest and responsibility, thereby excluding from knowledge-producing occupations "a third independent source of interest that may frequently be the most compelling of all – the fascination with a particular kind of subject-matter" (p. 60). As Rosenberg observes, "it is the discipline that ultimately shapes the scholar's vocational identity.... Like the ethnological fieldworker, historians of knowledge must integrate formal intellectual content with social and institutional organization, systems of economic support, and finally, the values that sanction and reward the career choice of members of a particular intellectual subculture" (pp. 444, 447).

The subjects represented in this volume include physics, mathematics and chemistry; biology, with special reference to the career of T. H. Morgan; the agricultural sciences; and the application of science to industry. Reviewer's privilege, nay prejudice, justifies a strong recommendation on behalf of Dorothy Ross's chapter on the social and behavioral sciences – psychology, anthropology, economics, sociology, and political science – for these subjects are directly relevant to, but unduly neglected by, practitioners of American Studies. Their history is especially revealing because they either emerged, or were transformed (as in the case of political economy) in this period. They were directly dependent on the rise of the modern university and were, at the same time, closely associated with contemporary social reform movements, often to the embarrassment if not danger of their more outspoken participants. The concept of professionalism is less potentially misleading here than in the case of the humanities, but as Ross acknowledges, the academic pioneers were already members of an existing profession of college teachers even though they did shift their attention towards specialized research and scientific "objectivity." Ross somewhat overstates the distinction between the older generation of traditionalists and the new more "militant" professionals, but her chapter provides a valuable introduction to the works of Mary Furner, Thomas Haskell, and a host of earlier cultivators of this fruitful field.

During the period covered by this volume European, especially German, ideas and institutions played a significant role in the U.S.A. Nevertheless most contributors draw attention to the distinctive national social and cultural roots of the processes under investigation. Higham, for example, stresses the shift from early nineteenth-century suspicion of specialization because it entailed dependence on established authorities, as against "the American ideal of the untrammelled individual and its corollary, the Jack-of-all-trades" (p. 4), to the later enthusiasm captured in the delightful quotation from a Johns Hopkins graduate of the 1880s: "vive la specialization! Go to, let us centrifugate" (p. 7). A number of mechanisms were devised in an attempt to reconcile "the elitist tendencies of intellectual specialization with the egalitarian requirements of American society" (p. 16), of which he singles out four: a standard entrance requirement; the university department as a society of equals; multipurpose agencies to sponsor research; and rule by reference works. A more extensive analysis of these mechanisms – including the use of quantitative methods to set standards in a large and widely dispersed society lacking an established "mandarin ideology" (cf. Ringer, p. 412) – is one of many stimulating research possibilities suggested by this collection. Another is the relationship between "high" academic and popular culture, although that receives only limited attention.

The contributors to the Oleson and Vos collection are primarily concerned with ideas and institutions, whereas Logan Wilson, a distinguished ex-academic and university administrator has focussed his attention on the academic producers and disseminators of knowledge, who are also, of course, among its principal consumers. In the earlier period, as Veysey and Rosenberg noted, the academic humanists sought, among other things, "a collegial atmosphere of like-thinking peers whose devotion to the same scholarly vocation served to forge a bond of emotional affinity in a world frequency lacking in such ties for the sensitive and introspective" (p. 450). But times have changed, even since Wilson published his well-known book on *The Academic Man* (1942), and throughout his new volume he draws telling comparisons and contrasts between *Then and Now*, to cite his subtitle.

One of the most dramatic transformations in American higher education has been due to a factor Wilson hardly thought worth mentioning in the 1940s, the role of the federal government, which helped to ensure that universities were a growth industry in a period of demographic expansion. Now, however, some readers will find only depressingly familiar, even ominous, his prediction that "under conditions of heightened institutional competition" we must expect to see "the rise in influence of students as consumers, of governments as suppliers of financial support, and of administrators who will be held more strictly accountable for the allocation and expenditure of moneys. These circumstances unquestionably will impose tighter controls on faculties in the economic aspects of their jobs, no matter what may happen in collective bargaining" (p. 189). Chapters on "Professional Recruitment," "Status Appraisal," "Professional Status," "Economic Status," "Academic Profiles and Social Status," and "Individual Prestige and Competition" constitute over half of the volume, and reveal the persistent dynamism and heterogeneity of American higher education despite the enormous pressures towards uniformity and standardization.

Viewed as a whole, Wilson's book gives a balanced, stimulating and very informative picture of the American academic landscape. It is written in a lively, no-nonsense style; each chapter begins with a series of relevant questions which the author proceeds to answer; and there are numerous statistics and citations from a wide range of published studies. There are also five Appendices on such matters as faculty tenure and contract systems, Carnegie Commission recommendations on Academic Governance, salaries, and rankings of institutions and graduate faculties.

16 *Beyond positivism: Economic methodology in the twentieth century*

By Bruce Caldwell

London: Allen & Unwin, 1982

Given the currently confusing and depressed condition of the dismal science and its gloomy professors it is hardly surprising that economic methodology is nowadays flourishing; and as the literature of the subject expands apace, the need for a thorough and reliable survey of the field becomes increasingly urgent.[1] Professor Caldwell is too modest to claim that his book meets this need, for it is not designed to be comprehensive. Nevertheless it is a distinctive and a distinguished contribution, which will become compulsory reading for specialists and an invaluable guide and handbook for any practising economist bold or foolhardy enough to venture into these stormy and treacherous waters.

The most immediately striking feature of this volume is the fascinating eighty page detailed, but highly relevant, analysis of selected issues in twentieth century philosophy of science, in Part I. This will be invaluable for non-specialists, and as Caldwell convincingly demonstrates in Part II, which contains 'Some Essays on Positivism and Economic Methodology', much scarce intellectual energy and economic journal space could have been saved, and much unnecessary confusion and controversy avoided, if writers on economic methodology had taken the trouble to familiarize themselves with the relevant technical and background literature. Methodological controversy in economics almost invariably lags behind the philosophy of science frontiers, which is hardly surprising, and it is characteristically ironic that the heyday of 'positive' economic methodology almost exactly coincided with the decline of its philosophical and logical counterpart, as the result of sustained critical attack by specialists in that field. In his Introduction, Professor Caldwell is careful to acknowledge that philosophers of science have no inherent right to tell practising economists how to go about their business. But those who do rush impulsively into the methodological lists need to beware of the pitfalls in their path, especially when – as is so often the case – they prescribe procedures and principles for others to follow. As Caldwell notes: 'Many economic methodologists borrow phrases, terms and concepts from the philosophy of science' and then disagree about their meanings.

> A study of economic methodology from a philosophy of science perspective may help one to clarify, unify, categorize, and explicate debates in the former field. But it will not provide ultimate grounds for arbitrating among well-developed and well-argued alternative positions. Fortunately, there is a sufficient number of poorly-developed and badly-argued cases to keep us busy (p. 3).

Caldwell describes his own position as 'methodological pluralism', a position that enables him to criticize various positions both internally (i.e. on their own terms) and externally (i.e. from other methodological standpoints). In so doing he applies the material in Part I – which contains chapters on: logical positivism; logical empiricism; the philosophical attack on that doctrine (including the work of Popper); and the contemporary growth of knowledge tradition (Kuhn, Feyerabend, and Lakatos) – to the case studies in Part II. These include chapters on: 'Robbins *versus* Hutchison – The Introduction of Positivism in Economic Methodology'; 'Hutchison *versus* Machlup-On Indirect Testing and the Rationality Postulate'; 'Friedman's Methodological Instrumentalism'; and 'Samuelson – Operationalism, Descriptivism, and Explanation in Economics'. Caldwell's analysis is incisive, his writing lucid and crisp, and the results of his case studies are highly illuminating.

In Part III, Caldwell cautiously proposes a series of 'Provisional Answers to Some Unsettled Questions', and his chapter on 'Prescription, Description, and Theory Appraisal' is especially instructive. He fully appreciates that his pluralistic position will be too eclectic, tolerant, and even evasive for some tastes, but he modestly offers it merely as an attempt to prescribe 'some common-sense procedural norms' for the methodology of economics, rather than a 'systematic philosophy of science' (p. 252). To the present reviewer this approach is both more satisfying intellectually, and more appropriate to the current limitations of our knowledge, than Mark Blaug's courageous, but narrow adherence to Popperian falsificationism, which seems to be largely self-defeating.[2] (The treatment of institutionalist 'pattern-modeling' in the two volumes provides an instructive contrast. Caldwell is far more sympathetic, yet still highly critical.)

Somewhat like economics, though far less publicly, the philosophy of the natural and especially the social sciences seems currently to be in a state of transitional un-certainty. Positivism has lost most of its appeal, yet there is a profound and proper reluctance to embrace subjectivism. Popper's falsificationism may have proved to be a disappointment, but to abandon his Critical Rationalism would be a grave mistake. At such a time one can only welcome the efforts of those who, like Caldwell, endeavor to apply cool, open-minded, and reasoned critical judgement to the elucidation of difficult problems.

Notes

1 See for example A. W. Coats, 'The Methodology of Economics Some Recent Contributions', *Kyklos*. Vol 35, 1982 (Fasc. 2), pp. 310–321 Also the review of Lawrence Boland, *Kyklos*, Vol 36, 1983 (Fasc. 2), pp 317–318.

2 See his *The Methodology of Economics, or How Economists Explain* (Cambridge, 1980) reviewed in Coats, op. cit.

17 *John Maynard Keynes, hopes betrayed 1883–1920 (volume one)*

By Robert Skidelsky

London/Basingstoke: Macmillan, 1983
pp. xxiii + 447

Keynes died in 1946. Five years later Roy Harrod published his authorized biography[1] which has had no competitors, despite the veritable torrent of scholarly, journalistic and polemical literature on the man and his works, especially on the sources, development, and impact of his economic ideas. In that quarter century prospective biographers have doubtless been deterred by the sheer range and scale of the undertaking, and also by the inaccessibility of some of Keynes's personal papers and correspondence, and the lengthy process of compiling and editing his *Collected Writings*. Now, however, all is revealed in this first instalment of Robert Skidelsky's *magnum opus*, and he warns us that there may be one or even two more rival biographies in the pipeline.

Skidelsky's book is a 'study of Keynes's life as distinct from the study of Keynesian economics or Keynes as an economist' (p. xv), and it focuses on a period when economics seems to have been less important to him than philosophy. Keynes undoubtedly struggled much longer and harder with his *Treatise on Probability* (1921) than with his *Economic Journal* editorial work or his two economics books: *Indian Currency and Finance* (1913) and the internationally sensational *The Economic Consequences of the Peace* (1919), with which this volume closes. Nevertheless Skidelsky possibly exaggerates the point, which is crucial to the interpretation of the relationship between Keynes's life and the development of his economics. It is therefore appropriate to illustrate his argument with a few quotations.

Given the primitive state of the economics *Curriculum* in England when Keynes was an undergraduate it is no surprise to find that his total professional training came to little more than eight weeks' preparation for the 1906 Civil Service Examination. By comparison with his earlier remarkable examination performances his results were poor. He came second overall to Otto Niemeyer (later a distinguished Treasury official) and only seventh in the economics papers. Subsequently, in his Cambridge lectures, which displayed no more than 'a firm understanding of a fairly limited range of theory', he failed to 'develop the Marshallian apparatus of thought in any significant way, and in some respects did not carry it as far as Marshall had done'. This was partly because he did not consider any 'important innovation in economic theory was needed', but also because 'he regarded it as an inferior branch of knowledge – inferior to philosophy in which he still hoped to make an original contribution to thought'. Unlike Marshall, he saw no direct link between economics and ethics, and lacking 'a strong intellectual or ethical stimulus, Keynes's capacity for original thought had to be evoked by some practical problem'. He 'was not an instinctively original economist, like an economic theorist who is fascinated by intellectual puzzles, regardless of whether they have any practical importance ... although some parts of the subject gave him real intellectual pleasure without taking up an excessive amount of time.' He was interested in the problem of induction in economics and in the improvement of economic statistics; 'but his views on the use of mathematical and statistical methods were mainly critical and destructive'. There were, however, compensating advantages from having learnt economics mainly on the job.

> His low ranking of economics as an intellectual pursuit protected him from intellectual superfluity, always a great temptation for the brilliant puzzle-solver; his lack of ethical ambitions in the subject help to ensure that his later interests were narrowly focused on problems of statecraft rather than being dissipated over the whole field of social reform (p. 229).

[Previous quotations in this paragraph from, in order, pp. 116, 206, 217, 209, 228–9, 211, 229.]

It is, of course, too early to judge whether Skidelsky's interpretation of Keynes's economics sheds any new light on the origins and background of the *General Theory*. But even at this stage the book makes a major impact on the much-debated question of the role of biography on the history of economics.[2] Keynes was inevitably a prime candidate in that controversy, for he was much more than a mere academic, and the style, manner of presentation, content, and timing of his economic writings so directly reflected the idiosyncratic relationship between the man and his times. Skidelsky's study is both significant and shocking, not simply because it contains numerous references to Keynes's energetic and sordid homosexual exploits and his scatological language – which could not be suppressed once Michael Holroyd had published his powerful biography of Lytton Strachey in 1967 – but chiefly because he so effectively exposes the grave shortcomings of Harrod's biography, on which we have had to rely for so long. Needless to say, Harrod wrote under the eyes of Keynes's family, including his widow, parents, and his formidable brother, Geoffrey. Nevertheless Skidelsky justifiably indicts him on two counts: failure to make explicit the conventions and limitations he was adopting; and for 'writing about Keynes's private life and the Bloomsbury milieu at length' as though 'he was telling the whole story, whereas much of it is an exercise in covering up and planting false trails' (pp.xix – xx).

Skidelsky considers that Harrod's 'most shocking biographical stratagems' occurred in his concealment of Keynes's conscientious objection to World War I, which Elizabeth Johnson disclosed in the *Economic Journal* in 1960. Harrod's response was weak, for whether it was discreditable or not, this episode revealed Keynes's complex attitudes towards the war and to his friends, and it had a direct bearing on *The Economic Consequences of the Peace*. Harrod's refusal to pry into the affairs of the Apostles society – a less reputable body than it once appeared to be – led him to suppress a dozen of Keynes's papers to that group which afford important new insights into the connections between his ethics, his ideas on probability, and his economics. Also, in toning down, omitting, or even altering the wording of certain passages in the correspondence he depicted Keynes as less passionate and 'much smoother and blander that he was', in conformity with a well-established tradition of biographical writing about great men. Even if the suppression of references to Keynes's homosexuality was unavoidable, the consequence was

> a severely impoverished account of Keynes's feelings, his values, his friendships, and his cultural milieu ... and while no one would want to argue that a knowledge of Keynes's sexual and emotional leanings gives one a better understanding of Keynes's economic theory, there are interesting connections between his economic outlook and what Schumpeter calls his 'childless vision', which Harrod precludes himself from exploring (p.xvii).

Only those dreary economists who regard economic theory and measurement as the sum and substance of their discipline will fail to derive great pleasure or instruction from this fascinating, wide-ranging and well-written volume. Skidelsky has drawn skilfully on the voluminous biographical and historical studies published since Keynes's death, and on the invaluable documentation so devotedly compiled by the editors of Keynes's *Collected Writings*. This book reminds us once again what an extraordinary man was the author of the most influential single economics work published this century. Keynes's wit, arrogance, remarkable verbal and literary fluency, enormously varied interests and knowledge, powerful prejudices, exceptional stamina, unusual powers of intense concentration allied to an ability to shift rapidly to a new subject, complacently melioristic social philisophy, exaggerated revolt against supposedly false Victorian values combined with surprising ability to gain acceptance in the highest establishment circles – the list is almost endless. One can only speculate whether any individual will again exert so profound an influence on the discipline, its theory and its practice. This biography is a must.

Notes

1 *The Life of John Maynard Keynes* (London: Macmillan, 1951).
2 The most useful discussion of this problem is in Walker, Donald A.: 'Biography and the Study of the History of Economic Thought' in Warren J. Samuels (ed.)., *The Craft of the Historian of Economic Thought. Research in the History of Economic Thought and Methodology*, Vol. 1 (Greenwich, Conn., JAI Press Inc., 1983), pp. 41–59.

18 *The intellectual and social organisation of the sciences*

By Richard Whitley

Oxford: Clarendon Press, 1984
pp. 319

From knowledge to wisdom: A revolution in the aims and methods of science

By Nicholas Maxwell

Oxford: Basil Blackwell, 1984
pp. vi + 298

At first sight these two books seem not simply ill-assorted, but downright incompatible bedfellows – the one analysing the social and intellectual organisation and functioning of the 'sciences' as the crucial species of knowledge production in the modem world, the other questioning the value and purposes of the entire scientific enterprise. Yet they traverse much common ground, for Whitley follows continental European practice in defining his subject to include the 'human,' 'social,' and 'natural' sciences, while Maxwell's powerful appeal for 'wisdom' stresses the paramount importance of the humanistic values so often ignored or repressed by uncritical proponents of scientism. Moreover, in asserting that "problems of knowledge and understanding need to be tackled as rationally subordinate to intellectually more fundamental problems of living" (p. 3), Maxwell appreciates that if the shift of emphasis from knowledge to wisdom is to be accomplished – a mammoth task, as he concedes – then changes in the basic aims, social structure, and intellectual organisation of the sciences will be required. This objective may indeed seem utopian, yet it is presented with great vigour, logic, and persuasiveness which effectively counteracted this reviewer's initial scepticism. And while Whitley's study is of great value to all students of the history and sociology of the social sciences, Maxwell's addresses problems of much broader, even transcendental global significance.

Of the two books, Whitley's is obviously more directly relevant to readers of *HOPE*, not only because his ambitious general typology of the sciences includes a substantial treatment of economics as exemplifying the species "partitioned bureaucracies." The "disjunction between theoretical analysis and empirical research ... and the lack of reliable, visible and stable results in empirical work in economics" (p. 183) are of course familiar to students of the discipline; but these characteristics appear in an entirely fresh light when viewed from Whitley's systematic and historically informed sociological perspective. Like some recent partisan critics of economic orthology, he recognizes that "the dominant theoretical framework" is

> well entrenched in the major graduate schools, the central journals, and the international prestige system. Tight control is exercised over intellectual priorities, the selection of 'real' problems, and the sort of analysis which is admissable in contributions to economic knowledge. Of especial note in this respect is the domination of undergraduate and postgraduate instruction in economics by a small number of textbooks which inculcate a distinct and rather rigid set of intellectual practices [p. 184].

Applying to economics T. S. Kuhn's account of the role and characteristics of textbooks in the natural sciences. Whitley argues that the training process produces

> a high degree of uniformity in the analytical skills and outlook of economists, strong consciousness of the boundaries of economics and what are, and are not, economic problems, a highly rule-governed set of research practices which are strongly orientated to theoretical and analytical goals and a highly formal symbol system for communicating and coordinating task outcomes. However, coupled with this coherent body of doctrine and practices in theoretical economics is considerable confusion and disputes about its relationship to economic 'realities,' as witnessed by the seemingly interminable methodological debates in the 'theory of the firm' and macroeconomics. The price paid by the insistence on analytical coherence and restriction has been the increasing difficulty of using economic theory to explain empirical phenomena [pp. 184–85].

As suggested earlier, these views are not novel, for like any good intellectual historian engaged in comparative analysis Whitley draws on reputable and well-informed specialist sources. But his views merit special consideration both because his systematic typology obliges us to recognise just how unusual a subject economics is. While reticent on epistemological issues (no doubt to the relief of some readers!), Whitley's broad comparative historical and sociological approach invites us to ask how and why economics got to be this way. Was any other course of development possible? And if so, why wasn't it adopted by the influential leaders in the discipline? If not, what specific intellectual and social forces determined that development? And for present-day Cassandras and crystal-gazers, now that there are such widespread doubts about the subject's validity and viability, is its social and organisational structure significantly prejudicing its intellectual future?

Needless to say, Whitley does not indulge in futurology, nor does he presume to prescribe necessary and desirable changes in economics or any other scientific field. His primary concern is to present the modem sciences as "reputational work organisations" and occupational systems, and to examine the patterns of control, organisational structure, contexts, and interrelationships between various scientific fields. Unfortunately it would take a lengthy review article to do justice to his skillful development of his two central concepts: the degree of functional and strategic dependence between scientific researchers; and the degree of technical and strategic task uncertainty in various scientific fields. Nor would it be helpful to list the component parts of his typology, which includes some curious and unfamiliar nomenclature. It is, however, worth noting that Whitley's approach sheds new light on familiar debates about the relationships between the natural and the social sciences.

To those historians of economics who are sceptical of the sociology of knowledge (science), it is important to stress Whitley's ability to demonstrate connections between the *content* of any scientific field and its organisational structure and functioning. Such connections within and between social science disciplines have been seriously neglected in the past. Students of economics, in particular, will find attractive Whitley's view of scientific research as involving a special kind of work organisation and control that combines continual novelty production "with strong coordination of task outcomes through access to rewards being controlled by reputations based on the utility of results for colleagues' research" (p. 33). How far, for example, has there been a tendency in recent decades towards the homogenization of intellectual commitments and standards in economics? Have such perceptive critics as the late Harry G. Johnson been justified in expressing concern at the harmful effects of the increasing integration of "the production of intellectual innovation[s] with their dissemination and the inculcation and certification of research skills"? (Whitley, p. 74). Whitley's treatment of differences in the degree of autonomy of scientific fields pinpoints the neglected possibilities for research into the changing relations between economists and the public; while the actual and potential significance of the spread of knowledge production in economics from academia into banks, industrial and commercial enterprises, government departments, and international agencies can be more fully appreciated against the background of Whitley's systematic analysis.

To lazy readers reluctant to venture into unfamiliar pastures, let me add that Whitley provides succinct summaries to each chapter, though they cannot, of course, begin to convey the richness of his study. He draws extensively on a wide range of literature in the history, philosophy, and sociology of science, and his book should be studied carefully by all who presume to make general observations on the state of economics as a discipline and a profession.

Whereas Whitley, a sociologist, sets out to explain the current organisation and structure of the sciences (in itself no mean undertaking), Maxwell, a philosopher, pleads the case for a radical change in the aims and methods of "the academic enterprise" as a means of contributing to the development of a more rational social world. Emphasising the close interrelationship between problems of knowing and problems of living, he argues that the dominant "philosophy of knowledge" wrongly and harmfully dichotomises the two in its pursuit of objective knowledge, whereas the "philosophy of wisdom" assigns "absolute priority to the intellectual tasks of articulating our problems of living, proposing and criticising possible solutions, possible and actual human *actions*" (p. 65; italics in original). Maxwell is not a social reformer. His primary focus is on cognitive processes, not value objectives; and his central purpose is to develop "a kind of inquiry that is devoted, in a genuinely rational way, to enabling people to realise what is of most value to them in living" (ibid.). The shift to what he terms "aim-oriented rationality" – which focuses not on truth in general, but with that species of explanatory truth that will enhance our understanding of the world – is needed precisely because it is so difficult to determine what is actually and potentially valuable to individuals, and how it is to be achieved in practice. Like Whitley, though more explicitly, Maxwell appreciates that the dominant philosophy of enquiry exerts a profound influence on the entire structure and functioning of the academic system, and on the content and organisation of intellectual disciplines (cf. pp. 44–45, 127 ff, 152–53), and he argues that the philosophy and sociology of science are neither separate disciplines nor parasites feeding on the main body, but integral to science. He fully appreciates that his proposals for revolutionary change may seem utopian, and that any attempt to supplant the philosophy of knowledge will encounter a fierce resistance from the scholarly and scientific establishment. Nevertheless, his critique of that philosophy – including the "standard empiricism" of Karl Popper, for whom he displays considerable respect – is impressive; so too is his defense of the philosophy of wisdom. Social inquiry, he claims, is more fundamental than natural science because it is directly concerned with the problems of living (p. 72); but the social sciences are not sciences at all, merely "social methodologies" or "social philosophies". They are

> concerned to articulate, and to criticise diverse actual and possible aims and methods for our diverse personal and institutional endeavours. What (aim-oriented) *scientific methodology* is to science so economic methodology is to actual *economic endeavour* in the real world.... On this view the *sociology of science* is precisely the same thing as the methodology of science (or the philosophy of science) [p. 108; italics in original].

While the philosophy of wisdom emphasises the role of "person-to-person understanding" both in science and in life generally, as against the impersonal scientific understanding – which is central to the philosophy of knowledge – Maxwell repeatedly denies that the former entails either value subjectivism or relativism. He repudiates Paul Feyerabend's methodological anarchism, and his sensitivity to the role of personal elements in scientific and humanistic knowledge is reminiscent of Michael Polanyi, while his treatment of cultural evolution and the role of "love" in society recalls the work of Kenneth Boulding.

Maxwell's approach is probably too radical and idiosyncratic to win many converts. But like Whitley, he raises major questions about the nature of the academic and scientific enterprise, and this is a healthy corrective to academic and intellectual complacency.

19 *Economic history and the modern economist*

Edited by William N. Parker

Oxford: Basil Blackwell, 1986
pp. xi + 105

Like historians of economics, most economic historians consider themselves undervalued by economists, and with good reason. In Britain during the 1980s, as a direct consequence of severe government financial constraints, the number of independent university departments of economic (or economic and social) history and posts in the subject has diminished substantially, partly because university administrators, under pressure to increase the average size of departments, believe it properly belongs under history or economics. As a result, a once-proud and vigorous scholarly tradition has been seriously weakened.[1]

In the United States economic history has not been organized as an autonomous discipline. Owing to the combined influence of German historicism and institutionalism it has always been linked to economics rather than to history, and this was a boon after World War II, during the glorious so-called mathematical/quantitative revolution. In those halcyon years the links were reinforced by the rise of "cliometrics" in the later 1950s[2] – a movement designed, so it was said, to put American economic history on "a sound quantitative foundation," thereby hopefully ensuring it parity of esteem with its more scientifically prestigious parent. Needless to say, despite the concurrent preoccupation with problems of economic growth in both developed and underdeveloped countries, this goal remained elusive. Moreover, now that the academic boom has ended on both sides of the Atlantic, economics itself is no longer in robust health, and the essayists in the volume under review argue that a substantially larger dose of historical input into the economics curriculum would not merely improve the quality of graduate training, but might also help to restore some of the economists' diminished prestige and public influence.

This volume is frankly partisan. It comprises revised versions of four papers delivered by Kenneth Arrow, Robert Solow, Paul David, and Peter Temin, at the 1984 meeting of the American Economic Association under the apt title Economic History: A Necessary though not Sufficient Condition for an Economist. The comments by Donald McCloskey and Gavin Wright on that occasion have been supplemented by short papers by W. W. Rostow and Charles Kindleberger, who was President of the AEA in 1985. His co-organizer, William N. Parker, has provided an editorial Preface; an Historical Introduction describing "how economics grew up in British and American universities, and how it came to neglect history, politics, and even the problems of economic policy in the pursuit of theory and measurement" (p. x); and an Afterword pleading the case for requiring economics graduates to undergo "a generous exposure" to economic history.

Given their background, the contributors' insistence on the value of history in the training of economists is predictable; so too is their dissatisfaction with contemporary economics. Parker and Rostow complain that contemporary economic theory is too narrow and technical; Kindleberger believes much of international economics is "bankrupt" (p. 85); Solow declares that "economic history is as much corrupted as enriched by economic theory" (p. 21); Wright doubts whether economics and history "can hope to have a congenial, complementary relationship" (p. 77); and McCloskey concludes, somewhat mischievously: "Economics does not merely have a lot to learn from history: history is what it is" (p. 69). The papers by David: 'Undertaking the economics of QWERTY: the necessity of history,' and Temin, 'Is history stranger than theory? the origin of telephone separations,' are excellent examples of the subtle interactions of theory and history in research.

In his Afterword Parker enumerates history's five contributions to the training of economists, it is a body of data on which theories can be tested; a source of important background information; a delightful occupation of the mind; a mine of examples of past errors; and a "broader view of life and a certain wisdom and sophistication that both protects and sensitizes them [i.e., students] for the economic world in which they are to spend their professional lives" (pp. 95–97).

Taken as a whole, the collection provides a valuable compendium of arguments that historians of economics can exploit in pressing their own case. Economic historians can and should be our allies, for we can acquire leverage from the widespread dissatisfaction with the current state of economics and the growing post-positivist awareness of the historicity of the social scientists.

The volume is, unfortunately, marred by a serious gaffe in Parker's truncated sketch of the history of economics. He should know better than to declare that whereas economic history is "an endangered species," the history of economic thought "is now almost completely defunct"! Clearly he has not attended a recent History of Economics Society annual conference, only one of a number of such gatherings around the world. Defunct, indeed; we have witnessed the resurrection!

Notes

1 For historical background see the Introduction to N. B. Harte, *The study of economic history: collected inaugurals 1893–1970* (Southampton, Hants.: Cass, 1974), and the symposium, What Is Economic History? in *History Today* 35 (Feb. 1985): 35–43.

2 Cf. A. W. Coats, 'The historical context of the new economic history,' *Journal of European Economic History* 9 (Spring 1980): 185–207. Two more recent publications are also directly relevant: Alexander J. Field, ed., *The future of economic history* (Boston, 1986); and Donald Coleman, *History and the economic past: the rise and decline of economic history in Britain* (Oxford, 1987).

20 *Before Adam Smith: The emergence of political economy, 1662–1776*

By Terence Hutchison

Oxford: Blackwell, 1988
pp. x + 469

Terence Hutchison's magisterial survey of British and European economic ideas from Petty to Smith is a fitting climax to a long and distinguished career of dedicated, independent, and at times lonely scholarly endeavour. Although he has not previously produced an extended study of the 'pre-Adamite' era, he has made several valuable contributions to the period and the central interpretative stand of this major opus will be readily recognizable to those familiar with his earlier publications. There have, of course, been significant developments in Hutchison's views both with respect to methodology (which is directly relevant here) and doctrinal history, as he acknowledges in his penultimate chapter on Adam Smith. Moreover, as will be noted later, these developments are of direct interest to economic historians as well as to students of *dogmengeschichte* since they involve an overall reappraisal of the 'Smithian revolution' and the gains and losses to economic knowledge and policy consequent upon the remarkable success of nineteenth-century British political economy. However, this reappraisal emerges from, rather than dominates the main body of *Before Adam Smith*, which is preeminently European rather than Anglo- Saxon in its focus and compass. This, too, is a long-established feature of Hutchison's writings, which have usually been more cosmopolitan in tone and content than the vast majority of English language studies of the history of economic ideas.

Hutchison's volume is subdivided into five parts. It is a feast, both for the cognoscenti and for all those willing to look beyond the British Isles. According to Hutchison, the writers on political economy of 'the highest interest and quality' in the 1662–1776 period were: 'Petty, Locke, Boisguilbert, Mandeville, Cantillon, Galiani, Hume, Quesnay, Turgot, Steuart, and Smith', an array of talent partly justifying Louis Salleron's claim 'that this was the most brilliant period in the history of the subject' (p. 9). But the output was uneven in quantity, and the sources were varied. In the seventeenth century Italy was in the lead; then England emerged on top in the 1690s, to be followed in the early decades of the eighteenth century by a widely scattered array of contributions that nevertheless displayed a convergence of ideas and the emergence of 'a new kind of systematization'. Thereafter France reigned supreme in the 1750s, and then Scotland. More generally, there was a 'great international efflorescence' from the 1740s, 'in which all the leading countries were represented, with varying degrees of distinction,' (pp. 185–6). Economic historians, in particular, should note that:

> there hardly seem to have been any sufficiently important external events and problems in the preceding decade or so which could have stimulated, or brought to a head, such a remarkable burst of intellectual advance. No external stimuli, in the form of pressing policy problems, such as had existed in England in the 1690s, seem to have been present in any sufficiently significant form. ... The mid-century efflorescence of economic theorizing must have been created and shaped more by the internal condition of the subject, (p. 187)

So much for the economic historian's belief that the development of pre-Smithian economic ideas was normally or invariably determined by short-term economic events.

A major theme of *Before Adam Smith*, calculated to appeal to readers of this *Review*, is the importance Hutchison attaches to the historical approach and to empiricism in economic thought. Without seeking to denigrate economic theory, except perhaps in its more abstract formalistic garb, he contends that 'impressive gains in the form of analytic rigour and persuasive power' were made in the post-Smith era at the expense of 'the historical-institutional methodological approach and its rich mature political and psychological component' (p. 370) as found, for example, in Montesquieu, Hume, and Smith. This may be seen as another indirect swipe at the Ricardo-Mill 'methodological revolution', which figured so prominently in his 1978 book. His assessment of Quesnay's and the Physiocrats' contribution, for example, is qualified by the consideration that 'what *is* highly important is the quality of the political and philosophical understanding with which any technical analysis is applied (p. 295), and of course this also applies *mutatis mutandis* to the twentieth-century 'age of technique' in economics.

Hutchison is a disciplined sceptic seeking balanced interpretations, and he is critical of those historians of economics who generate unnecessary controversy whether by arguing that only a single interpretation of a given author or episode is valid 'partly because they insist that economists maintain unrealistically, or unnecessarily, high standards of consistency', or because they make 'an excessively rigid and exclusivist use of the categories "mercantilist" and "*laissez-faire*"' (p. 125). Like others, Hutchison is uneasy about the concept of mercantilism, which he regards as not 'so fatally confusing as to be completely unusable' (p. 4); and, indeed, he employs it cautiously throughout, while insisting on the variety of circumstances – economic, political, constitutional, and philosophical – under which policy was formulated and implemented. Some of the great figures of the period, such as Petty, Mandeville, and Steuart, fall clearly within the 'mercantilist' rubric, while others, like the genius Cantillon, can be described as simultaneously mercantilist, physiocrat, and classical liberal, though 'not fully committed in any of those directions' (p. 178). On occasion Hutchison's own ideological vision colours his assessments, as for example his high praise of Tucker's skilful linkage of economic freedom with freedom of thought (pp. 233–4) and his contention that 'it is not too much to maintain that a subjective concept of utility is essential and fundamental to the case for, and explanation of, a pluralist and free society' (p. 363).

Enough has been said to indicate the range and richness of this volume. Each significant writer is presented in his biographical and historical context, and in relation to his precursors and successors, and this alone will make *Before Adam Smith* an invaluable work of reference for non-specialists. As in Hutchison's other writings, the literary style is clear and graceful, and the array of up-to-date secondary, as well as primary, sources is impressive. In short, the book is strongly recommended for all those interested in the development of economic ideas, their interrelations with events, and their bearing on policy both before and after Smith.

21 *The Popperian legacy in economics: Papers presented at a symposium in Amsterdam, December 1985*

Edited by Neil De Marchi

Cambridge, New York, and Melbourne: Cambridge University Press, 1988
pp. xii + 280

This is a valuable collection for all economists seeking to understand the current state of economic methodology, a much misunderstood but frequently maligned subject that has progressed substantially since the publication of T. S. Kuhn's classic *The Structure of Scientific Revolutions* in 1962. Admittedly, economic methodology is nowadays considerably more complex, controversial, and open-ended; but it is also far more relevant to an understanding of the discipline's past history, current condition, and future prospects.

The volume derives from a conference held to mark Joop Klant's retirement from the University of Amsterdam's Chair of History and Philosophy of Economics. Appropriately enough, the editor is Klant's successor, and his co-authors and their discussants include a significant proportion of the leading English-speaking writers in the field. There are five parts to the collection: 1) Popper as a philosopher of science (with papers by Daniel M. Hausman and J. J. Klant); 2) Popper among the economists (D. Wade Hands and N. De Marchi); 3) Falsification and trying to do without it (T. W. Hutchison and Mark Blaug); 4) The missing chapter: empirical work and its appraisal (Mary Morgan and E. Roy Weintraub); 5) Non-Popperian perspectives on economics (Bruce J. Caldwell, Donald N. McCloskey, and Arjo Klamer). Part I is preceded by a useful editorial introduction and a 45-page edited version of the discussion, with authors' summaries of their papers. This novel arrangement entails some unnecessary repetition and obliges the conscientious reader to turn repeatedly back and forth between paper and discussion. Unfortunately it may also discourage some readers from studying the papers which, given their quality, would be regrettable. Moreover, given the interdependencies within the collection the index is inadequate.

Whatever it is, this volume is certainly not uncritical hagiography. Hausman's persuasive introductory appraisal of Popper's methodology is devastating. His repeated emphasis on *logical* falsification, Hausman maintains,

> is irrelevant to any important questions concerning science. On the other hand, Popper's relevant views concerning falsification as a methodology or a policy are unfounded and unacceptable.... I doubt that an enterprise that functioned according to Popper's methodology could exist. It would be a poor tool for acquiring knowledge and of no use in practice, (pp. 65, 83)

Of course, most of the contributors are less destructive, and Popper has at least three defenders in the company, Klant, Hutchison, and Blaug, who provides a relentless exposé of Hicks' methodological views. The editor admits that "there is no substantial Popperian legacy in economics," at least with respect to his "rules of the practice of 'good' science" (p. 12). In "Popper and the LSE economists," a veritable gem of historical reconstruction, he argues that Popper knew little about economics (despite some confident pronouncements on the subject), and that the economists in his own institution, for all their short-lived enthusiasm for his ideas, neither understood nor had close contact with him. (His aversion to smoking deterred Popper from attending their seminars!) Nevertheless, Popper's influence reinforced "their desire to remake economics as a rigorous empirical science," even though they were neither willing nor able to follow his "quite specific rules of procedure" (pp. 28–29). Popper's philosophy of science disabused

> economists of the idea that they could establish truth and could rest content with criteria for theory acceptance such as plausibility based on introspection, or logical consistency. Quantification, rigor in formulation, explicitness in establishing conditions for rejection – these things were given a fillip. (p. 13)

There is an important lesson here, which highlights one of the book's central themes: methodology and/or philosophy of science is of limited value either to working economists or to students of the discipline unless it is closely geared to past or present practice. A clear mark of progress in the field is that this lesson is now being heeded by a growing number of researchers in economic methodology and the history of economics, whose findings will in due course filter through to the profession at large.

In addition to De Marchi's paper, two further excellent examples of such work are Morgan's analysis of early econometrics, revealingly called "Finding a satisfactory empirical model," and Weintraub's case study of household decision and allocation models, entitled "The neo-Walrasian program is empirically progressive," which concludes with an appeal for more careful studies of applied economics. Both these papers effectively utilize general as well as specific methodological ideas, from Popper and Lakatos respectively, while Hands' thoughtful exploration of "Ad hocness in economics and the Popperian tradition" provides another, yet different type of answer to those who deny the value of methodological enquiry. This is not the place to argue whether "rhetoric" or "discourse" – represented here by McCloskey and Klamer, their two prominent spokesmen – constitute rival or antimethodologies, or merely suggestive supplementary aids to understanding what economists do. How much they can deliver in practice remains to be seen. In the present instance their principal value may be in demonstrating how far the discussion of economic methodology has come since the logical empiricists.

Curiously enough, despite the crucial role of falsification in his writings Popper had comparatively little to say about empirical testing. He repeatedly emphasized the need for a critical approach to theories, and this is a major feature of Caldwell's spirited reaffirmation of "The case for pluralism" – to which Hutchison responds tartly that "criticism without empirical testing is merely a matter of likes and dislikes ... empty" (p. 55; cf. Hausman, p. 83). To an economic historian the importance attached by several contributors to evidence and background knowledge in the development and appraisal of economic theories is entirely welcome.

Taken as a whole the portrait of economics presented herein is far less flattering than that depicted by the self-described economic imperialists, who claim it can and should take over the other social science disciplines. To cite the honoree:

> In economics it is almost only metatheoreticians and historians, who write not about the world but about theories, who permit themselves skepticism and neutrality. The real theoreticians, when they present their speculative solutions, are as a rule very sure of themselves.... They have more about them of prophets or mathematicians than of careful, empirical scientific researchers. (p. 112)

Elsewhere we are told that basic economic theories are neither objective nor falsifiable, and the preference for heuristic over theoretical or empirical progress in economics may explain the paucity of "novel facts" produced by economists (p. 134).

As Terence Hutchison once sardonically observed, perhaps a state of crisis in the discipline is healthy if it has the effect of sensitizing its practitioners to the limitations of their knowledge. From this standpoint the Popperian legacy is valuable, for by setting up an ideal standard it has encouraged serious economists to undertake severe critical self-examination – an indispensable precondition of scientific progress. To the impatient the beneficial results may seem a mighty long time coming. But by now we know that scientific revolutions, if they occur at all, are few and far between, and not readily recognized if and when they happen.

22 *Economists and the economy: The evolution of economic ideas, 1600 to the present day*

By Roger Backhouse

Oxford and New York: Basil Blackwell, 1988
pp. x + 224

Economic ideas have helped to shape the opinions and lives of millions, but the study of their evolution, relevance, and impact will remain a minor, selfcontained, and self-absorbed academic discipline so long as its practitioners neglect their broader responsibilities to other members of the academic community (especially to economists, historians, and philosophers) and to the general public. The history of economic ideas is too important to be left to the specialists. But unfortunately the dearth of really first-rate studies of the linkages between economic ideas, their historical setting, and their influence on society, is eloquent testimony to the difficulties inherent in that undertaking. Neither Wesley Mitchell nor Joseph Schumpeter, both outstanding economists with wide-ranging scholarly interests and abilities, was able to master the mass of material he covered, whereas Leo Rogin's still stimulating and instructive history illustrates the dangers of adopting too specific and narrow a criterion by which to organize the data. Now a younger and equally bold contender has entered the lists, apparently undaunted by the difficulties despite his awareness of the pitfalls in any comprehensive effort to combine economic history and economic ideas.

Roger Backhouse has already published a well-received *History of economic analysis* (1985) which, he claims, "is the only book which provides anything like a systematic coverage of the history of twentieth century economic thought, including developments since 1945" (203). This large claim will not be examined here. In the present volume he tackles a much longer period and is still mainly concerned with economic ideas, the economic history being "selected to fit in with this" (ix). A perfectly legitimate choice, of course; but it obviously runs the risk of displeasing the economic historians, who will, I suspect, legitimately express dissatisfaction with the limited subject range of the four central chapters on, respectively, growth and development; the regulations of trade and industry;

money and inflation; and employment and economic fluctuations. Backhouse recognizes the problem, warning the reader that his account is meant to be illustrative rather than exhaustive. For instance, among the great economists Marshall has been slighted (although he is cited generously in the concluding chapter), and among the historical topics public finance has been omitted, although it "has been an important stimulus to economic thought" (ix). And there are other, at least equally eligible topics, such as population and poverty, which are not featured, and the historical focus is too Anglocentric to provide a general treatment of the interaction of economic ideas and conditions. For all his balance in discussing absolutist and relativist approaches in his introductory chapter, Backhouse is essentially a conventional neoclassical economist primarily interested in the evolution of economic theory, and this is a further limitation. His introduction, and the two concluding chapters on the theory of a market economy (which is really focused on the history of the concept of economic equilibrium) and the discipline of economics, can be welcomed: indeed they should be required reading for all serious students of economic history who wish to be well-informed of the current state and limitations of economics as a predictive science. Nevertheless there is a need for a chapter on the economic role of government (Backhouse's references to laissez faire, for example, are far too casual) and on the relations between economic theory and policy, two topics mentioned but inadequately covered elsewhere.

Changing the focus, one wonders what the book would have been like had the author started out from a reliable but conventional economic history text, rather than the history of economic ideas. In some of his topics – e.g., money and inflation, and employment and economic fluctuations – the task of relating economic ideas to conditions (or vice versa) is not so difficult as with others. Everywhere, however, Backhouse has to generalize on complex matters owing to self-imposed limits on space; thus it is hardly surprising that he makes many statements to which exception can legitimately be taken. Nevertheless, as a whole the exercise is worthwhile: a brave pioneering foray into treacherous terrain. Although the economic history is often oversimplified, it is generally sound and up-to-date; and it is difficult to believe that an economic historian unwise enough to tackle the history of economics would emerge with so few critical wounds. Few historians of economics could fail to learn some useful economic history from these pages.

23 *The state and economic knowledge: The American and British experiences*

Edited by Mary O. Furner and Barry Supple

Washington, D. C., Cambridge, England, and New York: Woodrow Wilson International Center for Scholars and Cambridge University Press, 1990 pp. xiv + 477

In July 1930 Keynes wrote to the prime minister, Ramsay MacDonald, recommending the establishment of an Economic Advisory Council:

> It may be that economics is enough of a science to be able to produce useful fruits .... I think it might be given a trial, and that we might assume for a moment, if only as a hypothesis, that it can be treated like any other science, and ask qualified scientists in the subject to have their say (pages 189–90).

This uncharacteristically modest statement, cited in Peter Clarke's exemplary essay on 'The Treasury's analytic model of the British economy between the wars', aptly conveys one of the central motifs in this splendid volume. The Council was established, and may indeed have had some influence in taming the notorious 'Treasury View', a possibility that has been the subject of much careful and illuminating historical, economic and administrative research during the past two decades or so. However, 'influence', especially the influence of economists' ideas, has proved to be far more difficult to identify and assess than most economists or historians of the discipline generally appreciate. This is one reason why the twelve British and American case-studies in *The State and Economic Knowledge* are so instructive. Taken together, they constitute a scholarly landmark in the understanding of the interrelations between economic thought and policy.

The volume opens with two pertinent and constructive scene-setting chapters: the editors' 'Ideas, institutions, and state in the United States and Britain', and Donald Winch's 'Economic knowledge and government in Britain: some historical and comparative reflections.' At the Wilson Center conference from which this volume emanates, Robert Cuff proposed certain categories of economic knowledge which the editors have reformulated as: professional or disciplinary knowledge; informed opinion or practical knowledge; and cultural beliefs and values regarding the economic order (page 12). At the present time, when the serious deficiencies of advanced training in economics are being effectively exposed by qualified critics on both sides of the Atlantic, this classification serves as a timely reminder that the policymaker's world is far more complex than classroom model builders' constructions suggest, even the simpler ones. Thus if a review, and much better still, a reading of this volume can persuade a few economists to consult the past in pursuit of enhanced understanding of their discipline's functions and limitations, it will have served its purpose.

The case-studies herein are far too varied and rich in historical and institutional insight and detail to be easily summarised. Apart from John Lauritz Larson's 'Liberty by design: freedom, planning and John Quincy Adams's American System', which examines the struggle over the federal government's role in internal improvements, they focus on the period of emerging professionalised economics since the later nineteenth century. Thus, in most instances, they fall chronologically between the scholarly literature on classical economic policy and the mass of writings on recent micro- and macroeconomic policy, some of which appears on undergraduate and postgraduate reading lists. Unfortunately, few of these works are the product of serious historical research, so that the literary critic's quip applies: 'text, without context, is pretext'. *The State and Economic Knowledge* is a powerful response to this challenge.

The case-studies are evenly balanced nationally. In addition to Clarke's above-mentioned contribution there is George C. Peden on the Treasury and Keynesian economics in the 1940s and 1950s; Barry Supple on official enquiries into Britain's industrial decline, from the 1880s to the 1930s; Leslie Hannah on post-1945 economic ideas and government policy on industrial organisation; José Harris on economic knowledge and British social policy; and Jay M. Winter on the economists' contributions to the Royal Commission on Population 1944–49. These last two essays, incidentally, provide chastening evidence that informed opinion and policymakers may entirely ignore economic theory. On the American side, together with Larson's essay, there is Mary O. Furner on late-nineteenth and early-twentieth-century investigations of the labour question; W. Eliot Brownlee on the economists' role in tax policy during and after World War I; Ellis W. Hawley on antistatist corporatism and positive statism in the 1920s; William J. Barber on economics in the Roosevelt era; and Robert M. Collins on economic growthmanship in the Truman years. All these subjects deserve attention, not merely because they are fully researched, well-written and argued, but also because they make such effective use of the voluminous secondary literature.

The State and Economic Knowledge is important both as a substantial collective contribution to scholarship in its own right, and because it reveals some of the various ways in which the implementation of economic knowledge depends on the interactions of ideas, individuals and institutions. As the editors note, institutions can serve as contexts for social learning, mechanisms for state building, and vehicles for the mediation of ideas between persons and groups within and outside official circles (pages 27 ff.). Winch, in his magisterial survey of British nineteenth- and twentieth-century economic thought and policy (regrettably there is no comparable treatment of the American literature), offers stern warnings against oversimplified accounts of ideas and influence, distinguishing between: rhetoric and reality, persuasion and proof, opportunistic versus sincere uses of knowledge, and the 'clarificatory' as against the 'sociotechnic' models of governmental deployment of the social sciences. As the case-studies reveal, at times policy is knowledge-driven, as intellectuals suppose, whereas at others, especially in crises and in wartime, knowledge is policy-driven. This is particularly so where, as often occurs, data essential for policy decisions is inadequate or lacking. Public inquiries, and the less-publicised investigations conducted within government departments, contribute in subtle, indirect, and slow ways to the accumulation and dissemination of economic knowledge, for as Hugh Heclo has observed, governments 'puzzle' as well as 'power ', and '"collective puzzlement" may go on for years even decades' (pages 28–9). Academic economists need to be constantly reminded that their contributions, and not merely their theories, are often held in contempt by economists in government as well as by politicians, civil servants, and so-called 'practical' persons. One minor lesson of this volume is that 'institutionalist' economics frequently looms much larger in the policy process than more formal economic doctrines, and 'insider learning' can be of crucial significance. Ideological commitments and visions, including those held consciously or unconsciously by disciplinary professionals, operate alongside 'do it yourself' amateurism through filters of bureaucratic obstructionism and political prejudice. In short, the would-be economic policymaker's lot is not always a happy one.

24 *More heat than light. Economics as social physics: Physics as nature's economics*

By Philip Mirowski

Cambridge: Cambridge University Press, 1989
pp. xii + 450

During the past century or so, while asserting their claim to be recognized as the most scientific of the social scientists, mainstream economists have ritually compared their subject to physics, the 'icon of scientificity', notwithstanding the obvious and profound differences between the two disciplines, and the fact that physics is by no means a typical 'hard' science. Heterodox economists, on the other hand, have repeatedly emphasized these differences, both when attacking classical and neoclassical doctrines and methods and in advocating alternative approaches. In so doing, they have had ample support from a miscellaneous band of academics (including some distinguished natural scientists), journalists, literary figures, and other intellectuals; and in the current post-positivist era the critics' armoury has been substantially reinforced by new concepts, arguments and findings from the history, philosophy and sociology of science.

Philip Mirowski has drawn effectively on this background in his brilliant, original, and ambitious enterprise. (There are more books to come, he informs us). The range of his sources is remarkable, consequently few reviewers (the present writer included) will be fully equipped to follow him throughout his detailed 87 page history of the energy concept, in Chapter 2; the extended discussion of the body/motion/value simplex (or 'primal metaphor'), in Chapter 3; his novel interpretation of nineteenth and twentieth century economic thought, in Chapters 4 to 7; and his generous utilization of the history of mathematics, including the formalisms of Lagrange multipliers and Hamiltonian mechanics, without which, we are told, *'there can be no understanding of modern neoclassical economics'* (p. 30; italics in original). Mirowski's handling of all these topics is thorough, but perforce selective; and as his argument is couched in sweeping terms it is tempting, and easy, to find fault with some of the details, for he is nothing if not confident in his claims. However, this temptation must be resisted, for his challenge deserves to be assessed on its own level, whereon he is seeking 'a higher plane of synthesis, one that uncovers the unity of dicourse behind the quotidian barriers of fields or disciplines, or indeed, betweeen the social and the natural' (p. 107). Given its style, as well as its scope, *More Heat than Light*, more than most books, needs to be reviewed as far as possible in the author's own terms, subject of course to space limitations and editorial indulgence.

As his subtitle reveals, Mirowski focuses on the links between economics and physics, two disciplines whose relationship has been so intimate as to be 'scandalous'. Thus: 'the importation of physical metaphors into the economic sphere has been relentless, remorseless, and unremitting in the history of economic thought' (p. 395). In classical, neoclassical, and Marxian economics 'the theory of value, the very core of the explanatory structure, has been dictated by the evolution of physical theory'; and the domination of these schools of thought is itself 'due to their emulation of physical explanation and their resonance with the primal metaphors of body/motion/value' (p. 396), the three interrelated components of the energy concept. In the classical period, Samuel Bailey stood out as an exception to the rule. But whereas he went too far in questioning the significance, or indeed even the existence of value or any other economic invariants through time, most of his contemporaries were preoccupied with the analysis and elaboration of a substance theory of value. By contrast with Bailey, 'the progenitors of neoclassical economic theory boldly copied the reigning physical theories in the 1870s term for term, and symbol for symbol' (p. 3). The concepts of energy in physics and utility in economics performed 'many of the same explanatory functions in their respective contexts, evoking many of the same images and emotional responses, not to mention many of the same mathematical formalisms' (p. 4). Most of the intellectual traffic was from physics to economics; but it was by no means all one way, as Mirowski demonstrates with various telling quotations. While the physicists drew analogies with economics rather than borrowing its metaphors, there was nevertheless 'an economic core to Western physical theory, one encased in metaphor and analogy, specific to a particular configuration of economic relationship, molded firmly within the energy concept' (p. 100). Indeed, at one point he suggests there was a connection between the mid-nineteenth century 'discovery' of energy conservation and 'the rise of the world mercantile economy and the institution of the world industrial economy' (p. 119), a startling conjunction which he does not elaborate.

Mlrowski's account is directly relevant to several crucial episodes in the history of economics, and it will be both stimulating and provocative to specialists in the field. For example, while ackowledging the continuing urge to imitate physical theory, he nevertheless contends (contra Blaug and Hollander) that the marginal revolution constituted a sharp break with the past, for several reasons (cf. pp. 194–197). In particular, the discontinuity in physical theory made the discontinuity in economics *'inevitable'* (p. 196; italics supplied) as the concept of economic value was reconceptualized as a relation or 'field' (cf. p. 29, 66 f.f, in physics; p. 218, 231 f.f in economics), rather than an embodied substance (p. 202; cf. Chapter 4: 'Science and substance theories of value in political economy to 1870').

Whereas a substance theory stipulates: 'the conservation of value in exchange (i.e. the trade of equivalents); a productive/unproductive distinction; production defined as the locus of the augmentation of value; the external residence of value in the commodity and as such conserved through time; some naturalistic justification of value by means of tautologies such as: "You are what you eat" (physiocracy), "Things are valuable because people made them" (Marx) (p. 399), a field theory stipulates: 'virtual conservation of preferences plus endowment, either jointly or severally; the law of one price a market-clearing conception of equilibrium; the specification of a conservative vector field suffused throughout an independently given commodity space; the locus of value in the field and not in the commodities; some justification of value by means of the tautology that 'things are valuable because people think they are' (ibid).

Unfortunately, according to Mirowski, the shift from substance to field theories of value in economics was incomplete, and there was subsequently a regression as neoclassical economics remained 'wedded to a straw man of a physical metaphor of vintage circa 1860, with some minor alterations' (p. 374), and this continues to constrain economists activities to the present day (p. 197). Through the development of indifference curve analysis and revealed preference theory the neoclassical program 'has misled generations of students by suggesting that it has relinquished all attachment to theories of value', whereas 'in fact the theory of value patterned on a conservative vector field is the only thing that holds the programm together' (p. 399; cf. p. 308). As many friendly and unfriendly critics of mainstream economics have argued, it is a very rigid discipline with respect to fundamentals, having (according to Mirowski) failed to incorporate the implications of such profound innovations in physics as thermodynamics (with its attendant concept of irreversibility and path dependency), quantum mechanics, relativity, unified forces theory, and chaos theory. Some heterodox writers have made considerable efforts to incorporate some of these more up-to-date metaphors (p. 358, note the joint dedication to Veblen and Georgescu-Roegen), but hitherto with only limited success – although Mirowski is still optimistic (cf. p. 10; and Chapter 8).

Among early neoclassical economists Irving Fisher was the first, and the last, to explore the physics metaphor in any detail in his attempt 'to implement a vector characterization of an economy' (p. 223 ff); and Mirowski provides a fascinating analysis of 'Fisher's Translations'. Even more telling, however, is his lengthy dissection of Paul Samuelson's work, especially his practice of referring to modern physics 'in superficial and theoretical ways while persistently misrepresenting both its content and its relationship to neoclassical theory' (p. 379). Despite some impressive sounding article titles, and various fleeting references to physics, the actual physics content in Samuelson's ceuvre is 'paltry'; while at the same time 'avoiding any direct acknowledgement of the fact that utility is functionally identical to potential energy (p. 380), he was pursuing incompatible objectives. Thus, Mirowski concludes, Samuelson's defense of the neoclassical program managed to dodge all the substantive issues, such as the wisdom of the appropriation of the original proto-energetics metaphor, the uneasy coexistence of such a nineteenth century social physics with twentieth century physical theory, and the impact of mathematical formalism upon the substance of twentieth century economic thought (p. 383).

These grave and far-reaching charges are based on Mirowski's detailed knowledge of the history of physics and mathematics, which he deploys with a combination of technical facility and a witty and colorful literary style – one that is too lighthearted and exhibitionist for some tastes, and too heavily seasoned with highly esoteric words. Of course, Mirowski's general case does not stand or fall on his dramatic demystification of Samuelson's influential work. His powerful extended analysis of neoclassical production theory in Chapter 6, under the heading: 'The corruption of the field metaphor, and the retrogression to substance theories of value' is both learned and closely reasoned; and it includes such topics as the 'battle of metaphors' in the notorious Cambridge Capital Controversy; a briefer reference to the 'quixotic search' for the microfoundations of macroeconomics', and an effective expose of the production function concept. The classical concept of production, Mirowski asserts, simply refused to die because 'the very concept of production rests so uneasily within the ambit of a field metaphor (p. 285; cf. p. 280).

By this time some readers may be wondering why Mirowski attaches so much importance to the energetics metaphor (Chapter 2) in particular, and metaphorical reasoning in general. What does it matter, they may ask, if economics has drawn on illchosen or inadequately analysed metaphors? Like some other contemporary philosophers of science, Mirowski maintains that 'most scientific reasoning is metaphorical' (p. 277), and despite certain unavoidable risks in their use metaphors constitute 'a method of theory construction' (p. 278; italics in original). By contrast with literary metaphors, which often serve only ornamental purposes, 'much of normal scientific activity can be interpreted as an attempt to render unseemly aspects of metaphors intelligible and pedestrian. A hallmark of scientific metaphors is the fact that they are deemed failures if they can muster only temporary impact and do not become the object of pedantic explication and elaboration.... Scientific metaphors should set in motion research programs... [because they] provide guidance and structure in the process of inquiry, which might otherwise be even more rife with rampant individualism and random research than is already the case' (pp. 278–279).

Mirowski believes the crucial role of the physics metaphor in economics cannot be overstated. In the absence of the metaphor of utility as upon nineteenth century potential energy, there is no alternative theory of value, no heuristic guide to research, no principle upon which to base mathematical formalism, no causal invariant in the Meyersonian sense, and most threatening, no basis for the claim that economics has finally become scientific (p. 368).

Enough has been said to cover the nature, force, and potential significance of Mirowski's book, which has the curiously old fashioned feature of restoring the theory of value to the central place it once occupied in the history of economics canon. Whether the history of any venerable and well-developed discipline can be adequately portrayed in terms of a single theme or Ariadne's thread (p. 222), however important, is another matter. Has he achieved 'the clarification of the entire history of economic thought' that he announces with such assurance (p. 142); or does the preoccupation with one facet of a rich and complex story necessarily obscure or detract unduly from other significant aspects? The central argument is too novel to be accepted uncritically at first reading, yet at the same time too well documented and penetrating to be dismissed out of hand. No previous writer has made such a sustained and determined effort to explore the undeniably important conceptual links between economics and physics; and this alone is a landmark contribution of importance to all economists, not merely to specialist historians of the discipline.

25 *The inexact and separate science of economics*

By Daniel M. Hausman

Cambridge: Cambridge University Press, 1992
pp. xi + 372

Economic methodology is an unloved, but heavily cultivated terrain. Indeed, in recent years the literature on this subject has proliferated so rapidly that Terence Hutchinson, one of the leading contributors, has suggested that the 1990's may become known as the methodological decade. Some economists will doubtless be horrified by the prospect. Yet it is well known that despite methodology's low reputation, many of their professional colleagues seem to find it irresistible.

Daniel Hausman's new book is designed both as a reference work and as an advanced text for economists and economics graduates, and it is to be warmly welcomed on all these counts. As co-editor of the successful journal *Economics and Philosophy*, he is admirably positioned to survey the territory. In addition to covering much of the relevant recent methodological literature, he also provides a substantial introduction to the philosophy of science, which will be invaluable for students and instructive to all but the best educated specialists. Beyond this, the volume can be strongly recommended to all those non-economists, especially social scientists, who have been attracted, baffled, or repelled by this so-called imperial science.

Hausman's title is both apt and provocative for it echoes John Stuart Mill, and may suggest to some cynics that there has been little or no progress in economic methodology during the past century or so. He depicts economics as a discipline whose practitioners labour under special handicaps and have devised fascinating and successful strategies for overcoming them. Hausman concedes that his approach may seem old fashioned, since he claims that: 'The method of economics is deductive', and confidence in its implications 'derives from confidence in its axioms rather than from testing its implications' (p. 1). Defending his position against the views expressed in a number of recent methodological monographs, he maintains that: 'many of the basic principles of economics can be regarded as inexact laws, and the methods of theory appraisal that economists employ in practice are scientifically acceptable' (ibid). However the commitment to economics as a 'separate science' is indefensible, and leads to stagnation.

The volume is in three parts. The first, 'Introduction, Structure and Strategy' covers: rationality and utility theory; demand and consumer choice; theory of the firm and general equilibrium; equilibrium theory and economic welfare; models and theories; the structure and strategy of economics; and a case study of overlapping generations models. Part. II, 'Theory Assessment', tackles the problem of inexactness in economic theory, and reviews – for the most part unflatteringly – the ideas of various well-known economist methodologists and the Popperian and Lakatosian approaches. The argument is drawn together in a chapter on 'Economics as an inexact and separate science', and followed by a fascinating case study of preference reversals, entitled: 'On dogmatism in economics'. Here, as with the treatment of overlapping generations, Hausman's account is in accordance with the welcome current tendency for methodologists to examine what economists actually do, rather than simply applying the latest philosophical fashion to basic, abstract and general issues. Part III contains a general review of economic methodology and a chapter of conclusions.

At the outset Hausman characterises his book as 'an extended argument for a particular vision of economic methodology' (p. 8). Yet its great virtues lie less in the originality of that vision, than in the vigour, freshness and balanced judgment with which it is presented. Economics, Hausman contends, is a one theory science, and that theory is equilibrium, not general equilibrium, as some have claimed. Economists that is to say orthodox neoclassical microeconomists (for Hausman has comparatively little to say about macroeconomics or non-orthodox approaches) – tacitly assume.

> That every good economic theory must, like the accepted theory, have both comprehensive scope and a compact or parsimonious theoretic core … and any alternative to accepted theory must preserve a peculiarly "economic" realm to be spanned by a single unified theory (pp. 235–6).

The economists' professional value system (or ideology) gives extraordinary weight to 'mathematical elegance', and 'comparatively small attention' to 'experimentation, data gathering, and testing … and policy relevance' (p. 84). Yet

> one of the most striking problems of theory appraisal in economics is that equilibrium theory is full of "Laws" that are, if taken literally, false, and further false assertions are made when the theory is applied to specific problems (p. 121).

To cope with this situation, economists have devised strategies for beating phenomena into methodologically tractable shape (data massaging, etc?). Without knowing these strategies one does not know economics. Furthermore economists also have heuristic commitments against regarding aspects of human social life as significant causal factors in economics (p. 84) and inevitably this severely limits their ability to explain some economic phenomena. For example,

> economists eschew additional behavioral postulates unless they have wide scope, and are compatible with rational choice explanation, consumerism, and equilibrium (p. 98).

Yet, as the case of preference reversals demonstrates, this practice can lead to a refusal to accept relevant but inconvenient evidence, and thence to dogmatism.

In Hausman's view:

> If unfamiliar forms of explanation can be well tested and can command empirical support, they should be pursued. Economic theory has not been successful enough to justify theoretical or methodological purism (p. 98).

In other words, the possibility of discovering errors in the 'Laws' of equilibrium theory may be foreclosed by the inadequacies in the data and the limitations of economic knowledge, but they cannot be foreclosed by 'methodological fiat' (p. 204).

To congratulate a philosopher on his sound common sense may seem a back-handed compliment, especially coming from an historian; but in this instance it is sincere. He acknowledges that economists often have good reasons for clinging to the inherited corpus of neoclassical microeconomics despite specific anomalies or apparently disconfirming evidence. The anomalies may be 'cast up by largely uncontrolled observation of complicated market phenomena', while disconfirmation may be attributable to the 'failure of the (unavoidable) simplifications and ceteribus paribus assumptions' (p. 207). Indeed: 'So long as the data consist of noisy economic statistics, I doubt that the sacrifice' of the basic theory 'could ever appear worthwhile' (p. 225).

Like many other contemporary observers, Hausman recognizes that the scientific and professional dice are loaded against empirical workers in economics.

> The obstacles in the path of empirical success in economics are so profound and the costs of empirical research so high that standards of excellence in economics, such as mathematical process, can persist indefinitely regardless of whether they contribute to or hinder progress in the discipline (p. 262)

Nevertheless he still considers 'economists desperately need better data in order to advance their theoretical knowledge and a serious direction of efforts … is called for' (p. 253).

The ideal of general theory may have to be abandoned. And he inserts the thin edge of a potentially subversive wedge by asking, innocently enough, whether the profession would do better 'to develop a variety of different theories with smaller domains and a larger repertory of causes' (p. 225), thereby making it less 'separate'. In the long term, Hausman believes, there is scope for change with the development of experimental economics, increasingly sophisticated field research, and – most radical – more extensive reliance on 'the sorts of theories favoured by institutionalist economics' (p. 225–6; cf. pp. 254–5).

Hausman makes no effort to develop this suggestive hint. His comments on institutionalism and other non-orthodox approaches are tentative and circumspect, which is hardly surprising given his intended audience and his acknowledgement of his outsider status. Yet despite his devastating, possibly overstated, criticism of the Popperian and Lakatosian philosophies of science, he still makes a strong claim for the philosopher's contribution to economics (p. 268). To Hausman: 'What is wrong with economic theorizing is not what economists are doing but what they are not doing and what they refuse to do' (p. 255).

Hausman's book is an important contribution to the philosophy and methodology of economics, and to the education of economists, currently a topic of intense interest and concern. His proposals for reform are fully compatible with recent constructive suggestions which, if adopted, would make economics a more legitimate, pedagogically effective, and socially valuable science.

26 *The making of an economist – a review*

By Arjo Klamer and David Colander

The coauthors of this fascinating, entertaining, and pioneering volume deserve a vote of thanks from the economics profession, for several reasons. The first, and potentially most important, is that in its original published form – as an article in the *Journal of Economic Perspectives* (1987) – their research provoked the American Economic Association (AEA) to undertake a systematic review of graduate education in economics in the United States, with the aid of a substantial grant from the National Science Foundation. The full results of that investigation, the first of its kind since the Bowen Report in the 1950s (Bowen, 1953)[1], are not yet available, and whether they will lead to any significant changes in the aims and content of that education remains to be seen. Nevertheless, even at this early stage, the preliminary findings and report of the AEA's Commission on Graduate Education in Economics (Cogee) suggest that its work will, at the least, provide ample fuel for discussion and food for thought for years to come.[2]

Beyond this, the Klamer-Colander (K/C) volume is rich in professional (or, strictly speaking, preprofessional) opinion and gossip among graduate students which affords revealing insights into, and raises serious questions about, the current state and functioning of part of the economics profession. The COGEE project extends that investigation into the various strata of graduate education in economics "below" the elite departments examined by K/C; and it suggests to this reviewer that a horizontal extension of the research into the international domain would prove highly instructive. The idea that world economics has to some degree been Americanized since 1945 has often been mooted, but, as yet, never seriously investigated empirically. Moreover, at a deeper intellectual level, it seems conceivable that K/C plus COGEE could mark the beginning of a much-needed effort to synthesize and develop existing research on the relationships between the sociology, methodology, and history of economics.

K/C, it must be said at once, do not envisage any such grandiose international scenario. But, given the more ambitious possibilities their study opens up, it deserves to be taken seriously – more seriously, perhaps, than they seem to appreciate, judging by their frequently offhand style and commentary.[3] Sociological analysis of the kind attempted in this volume is not, generally speaking, highly esteemed by professional economists; hence, it is all the more important that it should be undertaken carefully and systematically, and presented in a rigorously scholarly manner. With this in mind, the remainder of this review will, perhaps ungenerously, concentrate on the more obvious shortcomings of *The Making of an Economist*.

For a start, since K/C are primarily concerned, appropriately enough, with the "Academic Professional" (sic), a more fitting title would be *The Making of an Academic Economist*, for their brief references to "the profession" seem at times both confusing and inconsistent. They note that only 20 % of economists are academics (admittedly a rough estimate) and refer fleetingly to the other major branches of the profession, observing that almost half (47 %) of the graduate students in their survey plan nonacademic careers and that most of the demand for economists comes from the business sector (pp. 7–8, 15). Nevertheless, they maintain that academic economics has not only come "to dominate economics organizations" (i.e., learned societies?), which seems reasonable enough, but also "to define the nature of economists" (p. 4), which is quite another, more debatable, matter. Academic economists, we are told, do not take "vows" (p. 182), but in dealings within the profession they "follow a code" which consists of: "Helping out colleagues, writing recommendations, traveling long distances to serve on panels" (pp. 4–5). This hardly amounts to a professional code as defined by specialist students of the professions. Moreover, K/C's comparisons between economists and medical doctors do not help matters. On the one hand, economists are said to be quite unlike doctors, "who are a species of prototype professionals" (p. 181), yet the AEA is described as the "equivalent" of the American Medical Association (God forbid!) in that it "confers legitimacy on economists" (p. 5). What that "legitimacy" amounts to, and how far it is recognized outside the elite groves of academe, is unclear.

Part, but only part, of the problem here is whether K/C are simply summarizing or reflecting the views expressed by their respondents, or presenting their own, presumably more considered and authoritative, opinions on the state of the profession. Their book, they claim, "is no 'profscam' story. It is more objective, more balanced, than the peek people got into academia in Sykes's book *Profscam*" (p. xiv). Well, this reviewer wonders, after reading some of the following K/C statements, which are either flatly wrong, exaggerated half-truths, or, at worst, representative of a very blinkered conception of the profession.

> Once having entered the profession one stops asking questions about its nature (p. xiv).
>
> Untenured academics who "venture into the public realm … simply do not become tenured" (pp. 6–7), whereas tenured academics who do so thereby put their tenure and professional standing at risk" (p. 182).
>
> Government economists … do not write articles [i.e., in professional economic journals? This qualifier is omitted] (p. 8).
>
> [S]erious economists do not go out and apply their skills to improve the lives of others … [they] are academics" (p. 182).

> Downgrading in academic prestige "awaits economists" who "trespass on the domain of other departments in the pursuit of knowledge ... incorporating anthropological theory or psychological theory as an economist is a taboo in *most* economics departments" (p. 7, emphasis supplied).
>
> The ultimate purpose in life [for the Academic Professional is] the production of scientific papers (p. 183).

Maybe there are economists who hold these views, but they are incompatible with (to take the first) a considerable literature on the state of economics, some of it written by presidents of the AEA and Nobel Prize winners, and (to take the second and third) with more than forty years' experience with the President's Council of Economic Advisers and their staff, who include others of the same august standing. These generalizations simply undermine one's confidence in the author's "Academic Professional" contribution. Similar misgivings arise in connection with their handling of historical data – for example, the implication that after the founding of the AEA in 1885, economics ceased to be "a field open to anyone" (p. 176), or that Wesley Mitchell, a staunch advocate of the use of trained intelligence in society, believed that "extensive contact with the outside world compromises the scientific inquiry about that world" (p. 5). Of course, as K/C demonstrate in their citation, he recognized the dangers; but from their reference to him, no uninformed reader would gather that Mitchell's conception of economics was instrumentalist, both in the popular and the technical philosophical sense of that term, and directly opposed to that of the ivory tower Academic Professional depicted by K/C.

While K/C do not exaggerate either the scale or the representativeness of their survey of graduate-student opinion, the casual reader of this volume might easily overlook its severe limitations. For example, there were significant variations in the timing and method of distribution of the questionnaires, and some replies had to be eliminated where the response rate was too low. In the cases of Harvard and Columbia, two cohorts of students were interviewed together, whereas in other instances, separate interviews were held with each year. Sometimes only one coauthor conducted the interviews; at others, both were present. Thus, whether "the survey and the questionnaire effectively show us graduate education in economics at elite universities" (p. 187) is not beyond dispute, especially as the findings are "not unexpected" – that is, compatible with their preconceptions.

As *The Making of an Economist* is aimed at the lay public as well as aspiring and established economists, it is regrettable that one of the leading questions bearing on the students' perceptions of success was so poorly specified. To judge by the students' reactions to questions about problem sets, problems, and problem solving, they seemed in no doubt as to the meaning of "being smart" in the sense of being "good at problem solving"; but the reader is given no examples of these problem sets. This could be a handicap for any specialist in education interested in the survey. Another minor regret is that the outcome of contacts with George Mason students is mentioned only en passant, as this would seem to be another group worthy of comparison with the Chicago "true believers."

As K/C fully appreciate, their conversations with graduate students convey a disturbingly depressing picture of their education, one that is far removed from the complacent tone of the preliminary COGEE findings referred to earlier.[4] The students seem overworked, discouraged, and cynical about their graduate experience and the profession. For example, one complains of being obliged "to spend a lot of time ... learning stuff that is either not interesting or not true" (p. 88). It is said that they "have to do what they tell you to do" (p. 91), and are socialized to ignore problems that cannot be handled in terms of constrained optimization. Several complain that "alternative approaches" are not discussed (pp. 81, 90, 124, 138, 144) so that they do not hear arguments counter to the views presented in class, or "get anywhere near a fair perspective" (p. 90). Attention is concentrated solely on recently published work, and some professors discuss only their own writings and ridicule views they disagree with (pp. 92, 93, 124, 128). No wonder some students feel they are undergoing a brainwashing which leaves them "completely malleable" (p. 94), though others deny this. We are told that Chicago faculty have "a fixed view of the world" (p. 128) and a strong methodological and professional ideology, which some Chicago students evidently welcome. More generally, given the emphasis on technical training, which many deplore, one sees economics as "a field in which there isn't a lot of just thinking to be done," as for example, by comparison with the philosophy of law (p. 81).

K/C refrain from drawing joint general conclusions from their study, preferring instead to close with two independent interpretative chapters: "A Case of Mistaken Identities" and "Workmanship, Incentives and Cynicism." In the former, Klamer considers the tensions between the realities of graduate education and student ideals, in terms of the various "characters" or ideal types – Academic Professional, Teacher, Intellectual, and Social Activist. In the final chapter after some brief, oversimplified comments on the current state of economic methodology – a subject far too complex to be dismissed in a few lines – Colander correctly observes that: "Many, if not most, of the interesting questions in economics are not empirically testable with econometrics," and complains with justification that "graduate economics programs are not teaching students the craft of economics" – that is, "alternative methods of choosing among theories, of informally processing nonformal empirical evidence, of integrating institutional knowledge with their formal analysis" (pp. 190, 191). How this is to be done is not entirely clear. Even less clear, however, is his advocacy of *"the* sociological approach" (emphasis supplied), which "accepts that empirical testing is an art and cannot be used as a decision rule for many hypotheses" (p. 191).

Unfortunately, Colander's vague comments on what he calls "sociological methodology," with its distinction between "formal empirical conventions" and the required "set of conventions to guide students so they can deal effectively with a wider range of empirical evidence" (p. 194), are far too sketchy to be helpful.[5] All well-established social groups have conventions. What distinguishes the economists' conventions from those accepted by, say, other social scientists, natural scientists, and nonacademic professionals, including business and government economists? There is, in fact, some literature on this not cited here, but it is seriously inadequate and needs to be developed more comprehensively and systematically.

Nevertheless, Colander's suggestions, such as they are, seem to be on the right lines as a corrective to the present, unquestionably unacceptable state of affairs. Time will tell whether the COGEE initiative will lead to any substantial reform of graduate economics education in the United States.

Notes

1 Though sponsored and published by the AEA, Bowen's report and recommendations were not, in accordance with the Association's customary practice, given its "official sanction" (Bowen, 1953, p. iii).

2 The preliminary report by W. Lee Hansen, the Executive Secretary, and a discussion of the findings by three of the Commission's members, and by Robert M. Solow, were published in the *American Economic Review (*1990). The full report, presented at the Atlanta meetings in December, 1990, will appear in the *Journal of Economic Literature*. Anne O. Krueger of Duke University chaired the Commission. The term Commission suggests that the Report is somewhat more "official" than is usual with the reports of AEA subcommittees.

A substantial body of data and supplementary material is to be published or otherwise made available by the Commission's Executive Secretary, W. Lee Hansen, of the University of Wisconsin. A number of other related or supplementary studies were prepared for the Commission. (see Krueger et al (1991)).

3 David Colander has responded to this comment with the following delightful, but so far untraceable comment attributed to Sydney Smith: "Because I am witty you must not imagine I am frivolous and I will not imagine that because you are serious you are therefore pompous."

4 The full report, though guarded, is a good deal less complacent. It is, after all, a consensus view of the members of COGEE.

5 Colander elaborates these comments in his book, *Why Aren't Economists as Important as Garbagemen?* (1991).

References

American Economic Association – Commission on Graduate Education in Economics. 1990. "Papers and Proceedings." *American Economic Review* 80(May): 437–450.

Bowen, Howard R. 1953. "Graduate Education in Economics." *American Economic Review* 43(September): Part 2, pp. xv, 223.

Colander, David. C. 1991. *Why Aren't Economists as Important as Garbagemen?* Armonk, NY: M. E. Sharpe.

Colander, David C., and Arjo Klamer. 1987. "The Making of an Economist." *Journal of Economic Perspectives* 1(Fall): 95–111.

Krueger, Anne O. et al. 1991. "Report of the Commission on Graduate Education in Economics." *Journal of Economic Literature* 29(3): pp. 1035–53.

27 *Economics – mathematical politics or science of diminishing returns?*

By Alexander Rosenberg

University of Chicago Press, 1992
pp. xvii + 266

In the disarmingly frank preface to his latest book, Alexander Rosenberg provides a valuable personal perspective on the perplexed and perplexing condition of the philosophy of economics over the two decades since the publication of his Microeconomic Laws: A Philosophical Analysis (1976). He continues to regard microeconomic theory as 'a body of contingent laws about choice behavior, its causes and consequences', but he now believes that 'this conclusion takes us only a very little way towards understanding the nature of economic theory' (p. xiii). Indeed, he doubts that anyone really understands the cognitive status of that theory. His own views have remained 'permanently unsettled', partly as the result of contemporary discussions in the burgeoning literature of economic methodology and the philosophy of science, which have forced him to change his mind on important issues more than once. Now, however, he believes his thinking has 'found an area of local stability' (p. xiii). He still focuses on the question of whether economic theory 'is to be understood and assessed for adequacy along the lines of theories in the sciences – physical, biological, behavioral'[1], because the issue is crucial to the problem of the relevance of economics to public policy.

> If economics is a science, if its theories are composed of improvable regularities about human behavior and its aggregate consequences, then its bearing on policy is as evident as the study of physiology is to human health. If not, confidence reposed in it will be repaid by frustration at best. (p.xii. Italics supplied)

Needless to say, methodological empiricists like Terence Hutchison and Mark Blaug have made this point repeatedly and Rosenberg endorses Wassily Leontief's claim that economics has made little or no progress in this respect over the past century or so. 'The theory has not been increasingly accommodated to data it has led us to uncover, it has not even motivated much augmentation of data. Leontief's arguments can hardly be treated as expressions of impetuousness' (p. 65; cf pp. 79, 84, 230, 235–6).

This is familiar stuff; but Rosenberg goes further than most critics in asserting that 'economics is not an empirical science at all' (p. 236). The basis of this disturbing conclusion is the discipline's dependence on 'folk psychology', the concepts of belief, desire and preferences, which 'function as part of a heuristic device, an instrument useful up to a point in organising our every day experience, but incapable of improvement beyond the predictive powers reflected in our every projection of people's actions' (p. 148). Economics cannot dispense with folk psychology because:

> The conclusion that beliefs and desires don't explain behavior just seems inconceivable. Introspection alone assures that our actions are caused by our beliefs and our desires, and no amount of predictive failure on the part of a social scientific theory is going to shake this conviction among ordinary people and among economists, (p. 151; cf p. 234)

Unfortunately the discipline's explanatory power and scientific status are seriously weakened by its inability to 'identify its causal variables independently of the effects they bring about' (p. 181), so that economists are limited to producing 'generic' (or 'qualitative') predictions which constitute an insufficient basis either for policy purposes or for producing improvable regularities.

> By refusing to take seriously the psychological states it attributes to individuals, economics ends up by treating the economic agent as just a complicated and highly discriminant teleological system, one whose behavior is highly appropriate to its biological needs, given its environment. (p. 175)

Needless to say, economists make little or no effort to investigate either those needs or the relevant environment. Slow and laborious empirical research of the kind so long powerfully advocated by Leontief, Herbert Simon, and other luminaries carries comparatively little weight in the economists' professional (and 'scientific'?) value hierarchy. Instead, economists – especially those of orthodox or neoclassical persuasion – rely on 'extremal theories', according to which 'a system's behavior always minimizes or maximizes variables [e.g., utility] reflecting the mechanically possible states of the system' (p.231). Like all such theories, economic theory is committed to 'explaining' everything within its domain, a territory that economics imperialists seem to regard as indefinitely extensible. Nevertheless, Rosenberg argues, the theory cannot be preserved by revising the auxiliary assumptions about test conditions, or by adding new antecedent clauses to its generalizations. Either the auxiliary hypotheses must be rejected or the theory itself (p.232).

In developing his argument Rosenberg provides penetrating critiques of a number of recent authors familiar to readers of this journal. For example, in Chapter 2, 'Two Dead Ends in the Philosophy of Economics,' he juxtaposes Hollis and Nell's advocacy of rationalism as a foundation for Marxian-Ricardian economic theory with McCloskey's rhetorical approach, which is dismissed in a lengthy éxpose as illogical, riddled with confusions, over-hasty generalisations, inconsistencies, false and misleading comparisons, and other deficiencies. If McCloskey is right, Rosenberg argues, 'economists will have to stop doing economics', thereby abandoning their longstanding hope of exerting a constructive influence on policy',[2] or else consign their discipline to the status of a genre, a stylistic tradition in literature, like the heroic couplet or the stream of consciousness novel' (p. 31).

Chapter 5, 'Neoclassical Economics as a Research Program', contains an extended (and respectful) dissection of Weintraub's effort to interpret the neo-Walrasian program as both theoretically and empirically 'progressive', and therefore 'scientific'. Unfortunately, Weintraub's commitment to Lakatos now seems far less persuasive than it did ten or fifteen years ago, for as Rosenberg observes, the Lakatosian concepts of 'empirical content, novel fact, and corroboration are among the most vexed ones in the philosophy of science. By and large philosophers have given up trying to make sense of them in a way that will shed any light on the problem of demarcation' between science and non-science.[3] Rosenberg questions Weintraub's claim of empirical progressiveness arguing, as earlier in the book, that only generic predictions emerge, and that these are inadequate for the applied or policy-making economist's purposes. Moreover, partly under McCloskey's influence, Weintraub has more recently abandoned the Lakatosian program in favour of adopting a species of 'general cultural criticism' which treats economics simply as an 'interpretive community'. This has taken him 'down the slippery slope' to McCloskey's anti-methodology epistemology. However, economists have much graver responsibilities to society than literary critics, since 'jobs, fortunes, and even lives, are at stake' in the advice they give to policymakers (pp. 110, 111).

Chapter 6, 'Could Economics be a Biological Science?', provides a surprisingly glowing account of Becker's effort to circumvent the problem of intentionality in his new theory of consumers' choice which, Rosenberg terms, 'the most important, influential and empirically powerful reformulation of the theory of economic behavior since ordinal utility replaced marginalism'.[4] Recent work in human capital influenced by Becker 'comes close to being a revolution in economics', and Rosenberg even endorses Becker's grandiose claim that his approach 'provides a valuable unified framework for understanding *all* human behavior' (p. 155. Italics in original). This is flatly contradictory to his earlier assessment.

There are, however, serious defects in Becker's theory. 'His simple expedient of assuming that every agent has exactly the same set of lifelong tastes for the same set of quite specific goods as any other agent' (p. 161) conceals, as Becker himself acknowledges, 'an inability to explain tastes behind the camouflage of a production function' (p. 163), that is, the consumer's ability to combine 'market goods together with his time in accordance with techniques available to him' (p. 161). The deficiencies of Becker's theory could be partly remedied by interpreting stable preferences as human needs, making 'tastes exogenous, by naturalizing them as the explicable expression of biologically expressible human needs' (p. 170). For this purpose the role of information in a disaggregated extensional form is crucial.

> What the new theory needs is an account of belief in general, which will explain how agents come to have different beliefs about their own needs and

> available productive techniques, and an account of the economics information, as it affects markets, industries and whole economies. (p. 171)

This is indeed a tall order, and Rosenberg's analysis of the problems involved in constructing such an economics concludes that it would still be limited to generic prediction, owing to the lack of information and the role of uncertainty. Nor would 'biologizing' economic theory, that is, treating it as a claim about biological needs, solve the problem, for those economists who seek support form Darwinian theory fail to recognize that it constitutes a 'remarkably inappropriate model' for their discipline one that is, still, limited to generic predictions (pp. 177–8). Rosenberg provides a lengthy treatment of Friedman's and, especially. Alchian's efforts to draw upon the theory of evolution in explaining economic phenomena, but finds them seriously wanting. Indeed, the outlook for efforts to treat the theory of rational choice as a theory about biological systems is bleak. And, 'together with the economists' resolute commitment against taking psychology seriously, there seem no avenues along which to link it [i.e., economic theory] with the rest of science – social or natural' (p. 199).

In his last two chapters Rosenberg argues that economics is both a part of political philosophy – an area of debate in social contract theory[5] – and a species of applied mathematics. Whether economics is in fact a science is a moot point, for in the present unsettled state of the philosophy of science 'it is hard to know exactly what science is'. Rosenberg is willing to endorse the economists' claim that 'their theories [are] the best and most powerful explanatory and predictive devices there are among the social sciences'. However there is little cause for hubris given 'the theoretical impoverishment of the other social sciences' (p. 228). While many economists view the development of general equilibrium theory as the pinnacle of their discipline's intellectual achievement, the theory's cognitive status is perplexing. As it is not explanatory – for equilibrium is not a fact to be explained – its attraction must be normative. It constitutes a body of prescriptions how to be rational; and

> ... economists continue to lavish attention on general equilibrium theory ... not because they think it can be improved in the direction of a descriptively and productively accurate explanation of economic activity, but because they believe it is already part of the best contractarian argument for the adoption of the market as a social institution and, more important, stands a chance of becoming an even better one, as its assumptions are weakened, changed and varied (pp. 219–20).

General equilibrium theory fascinates economists because it appeals to their urge to emulate physics ('physics envy') and biology, two disciplines in which equilibrium theory has had considerable success. But alas, the comparison is misleading for, unlike those sciences, economics has produced nothing to rival 'the physicists' discovery of new planets or of new technologies by which to control the mechanical phenomena Newton's law systematized', nor independent insights 'to rival the biologists' understanding of macroevolution and its underlying mechanism of adaptation and heredity' (p. 234). Like other applied mathematicians, economists are relatively unconcerned about the factual application of their most central theoretical achievement, and the influence of general equilibrium theory has helped to make modem economics increasingly abstract and non-empirical. Nothing will persuade them to abandon the extremal and intentional approach they have employed for well over a century, and although some economists are interested in 'applying their formalism to practical matters, this formalism does not really have the aims, nor does it make the claims, of an unequivocally empirical theory' (p. 236).

Economics – Mathematical Politics or Science of Diminishing Returns? is hardly calculated to encourage complacency among economists, should any of them deign to read it. Among economic methodologists it will certainly provoke controversy, for the author is well known as a serious and intelligent philosopher who has spent much of the past two decades thinking and writing books and articles on economics and the social sciences. Whether the 'area of local stability' he now occupies is adequately defended against external shocks, remains to be seen. Rosenberg's definition of science is surely too narrow for some tastes, as is also his emphasis on prediction and the need for the discipline to demonstrate improvable empirical regularities. To this reviewer, the reminder that economics is a policy science as well as a 'good game' for ivory tower applied mathematicians is especially welcome. Whether Rosenberg's analysis can advance the cause of scientific economics is another matter. The debate will undoubtedly continue.

Notes

1 p.xii. This was a central theme in his book, *The Philosophy of Social Science* (1988).
2 Terence Hutchinson's *Changing Aims in Economics* (1992) contains a forceful discussion of this point, together with a severe critique of McCloskey's approach.
3 For a major effort to assess the status of Lakatos' philosophy in economics see the valuable papers and critiques in N. de Marchi and Mark Blaug, (eds.), *Appraising Economic Theories, Studies in the Methodology of Scientific Research Programs* (Elgar, 1991). Cf my review article in *History of Economics Review* (Australia) 1993, pp. 46–56.
4 p.155. Italics in original. In an earlier book, *Sociobiology and the Preemption of Social Science* (John Hopkins University Press, 1980) Rosenberg gave a much more critical, though in many respects similar, account of Becker's theory, arguing that it had 'the same defects as the theory it was erected to supercede', and concluding that it 'may be neither an *economic* theory, since it does not explain behavior in terms of rational choice properly understood, nor a theory of distinctively *human* behavior, since its lack of interpretation makes it formally applicable to behavior which is not peculiarly human. Nor, in the end, may it turn out to be a theory, as opposed to one of an indefinitely large number of axiomatic formalisms whose lack of interpretation makes them compatible with any occurrence at all, and thereby deprives them of any real explanatory power at all' (pp. 81, 88. Italics in original). At that time Rosenberg believed the adoption of methods and concepts form the natural sciences, especially biology, would overcome some of the defects of conventional social science.
5 (p. 228). There is a suggestive discussion of Buchanan's 'constitutional economics' in the section on general equilibrium and the social contract, pp. 215–24.

28 *Economic thought in communist and post-communist Europe*

Edited by Hans-Jürgen Wagener

London & New York: Routledge, 1998
pp. xii + 388

This volume is the fruit of a major research project managed by the Frankfurt Institute for Transformation Studies at the University Vadrina. Frankfurt (Oder), under Professor Wegener's direction, and it is both fascinating and highly important. It contains six substantial studies of post-1945 economic thought and practice in Central and Eastern European countries – Soviet Union (pp. 33–79), Poland (pp. 80–157), Hungary (pp. 158–212), Czechoslovakia (pp. 213–263), East Germany (pp. 264–328), subsequently referred to as the GDR): and Yugoslavia (pp. 329–361). Apart from Russia, these countries are largely unknown to English-speaking and Western European specialists in our field; and the book provides penetrating insights into the personal, intellectual, and professional problems encountered by economists (and to a lesser extent, other social scientists and public servants) working under the constraints of an authoritarian, doctrinaire politico-economic regime. The country studies are preceded by Wegener's excellent editorial introduction (pp. 1–32) under the apt title: 'Between conformity and reform: economics under state socialism and its transformation.' The editor has also provided helpful notes on the eleven contributing authors and an appendix of brief biographies of nineteen eminent East European economists, including such luminaries as Kalecki, Kantorovich, Kornai, Lange, and Varga. As the size of the volume indicates, the individual chapters are substantial and detailed, in the best sense of those terms. Nevertheless, the editor and several other authors acknowledge that their contributions are by no means exhaustive, and they mention a number of topics that have been omitted because of space and time limitations. Most of the chapters have extensive bibliographies.

Wegener's concluding summary remarks effectively characterize the volume's main theme:

> At its best economics under communism was a policy-oriented science, tinkering, within the given limits, with the economic order, and analysing alternative development strategies. Such an approach is highly contingent

upon the historical situation. It does not lend itself to elegant abstract theorizing. Hence, the protagonists are country specific, and their fame remains within the historical boundaries ... these were not the boundaries of the socialist system as a whole, but rather national ones. What is called the invisible college in the West, supported by an international infrastructure of learned journals, publishing houses and scientific conferences, never existed in the East. There was, at most, an informal rather private, exchange of views, above all between Hungarian, Czechoslovak and Polish economists (p. 362).[1]

Given the importance of the changing historical (i.e. mainly political) situation the editor provides a useful list (somewhat abbreviated here) of key events affecting the development of economic thought and policy in the six countries, including:

1948–9	the transition to full Stalinism
1953	the death of Stalin; the East German uprising
1956	Kruschev's revelations on Stalin and Stalinism; the Hungarian uprising
1962–3	the East German New Economic System
1964	the ousting of Kruschev
1968	Czechoslovak reform: the Prague Spring, and its suppression; the New Economic Mechanism in Hungary
1970 & 76	political crises in Poland Solidarity in Poland, followed by martial law
1985	Gorbachev and perestroika
1989	the fall of the Berlin Wall (and the aftermath)

Most of these events led to significant, sometimes dramatic changes in policy, and in the prevailing climate of opinion, necessitating substantial, often painful adjustments on the part of the economics community. Needless to say, only a few examples of these policy shifts and their human consequences can be considered here. But their widespread, repeated, and sometimes cumulative effects on efforts at economic reform, reveal the unstable and sometimes dangerous situations faced by economists and public officials in the Euro-communist world.

In his reader-friendly editorial introduction Wegener provides a Lakatosian-type analysis of the political economy of socialism, 'which was supported by the dogmatic school of Marxism-Leninism and taught at universities all over the region' (p. 9). He also lists seven propositions that constituted the core 'paradigm' of Stalinist doctrine.[2] These propositions are not, he emphasizes, a caricature of socialist economics. Indeed, on the basis of this paradigm it was possible to develop a huge body of literature, to feed an army of university teachers and to govern an economy which supported the second world power (p. 12).

The ruling paradigm was subjected to severe criticism at one time or another in every European communist country. But the core issues – such as ownership, the principle of planning, and the primacy of the party – could not be questioned.

Economists were providing interesting and valuable diagnoses of various pathologies, but the investigations were superficial. There was 'systemic optimism or implicit acceptance of the superiority' of the system. To blame the system for its failure was 'taboo'; hence there must be a possibility of making it perfect (ibid.).

Throughout most of the 1945–95 period covered by Wegener's volume the economists' efforts were focused on the possibilities of significant reforms of the system. However the opportunities for radical change were limited to the transformation period (i.e. the late 1980s and early 1990s). Wegener suggests seven reasons why the socialist economic system proved to be unreformable earlier, including: the primacy of politics; soft (i.e. lax) budget constraints; state monopoly of foreign trade; the subordinate role of money and finance; the unity of economic activity and social policy; the closed shop system of *nomenklatura*; and reliance on paternalism. Thus:

> The essence of unreformability lies in a certain power structure sticking to an ideology which it considers essential for survival. If there are no endogenous forces, like reform politics supported by reform thinking breaking up the locked-in situation, stagnation and decline will become endemic. There may also be exogenous forces causing or speeding up the collapse of the inefficient system (p. 14).

It would be wrong to assume that the economists in communist countries had no room for intellectual manoeuvre or originality. But over time 'the quality of economic science deteriorated due to enforced constraints, aprioristic judgements or taboos in choices of objects for study, in methods applied and in basic values taken implicitly or explicitly in appraisals' (p. 85: re Poland). During the early post World War II years the operation and the future of the socialist system were discussed against the background of the failure of market economies in the inter-war period. In Czechoslovakia, for example, a species of 'mixed economy' emerged with the coexistence of public and private property, and a combination of market and planning elements. This evolved 'as a gradual outcome of disputes, controversies and compromises, and in an environment of some political pluralism (which weakened under the increasing influence of the communists)' (p. 214). After the Prague Spring (1968) the authorities clamped down, and there were serious purges of economists and others viewed as opponents of the regime.[3] During the 1970s and early 1980s there was growing criticism of the command-type system partly underground and partly by groups organized informally, until by the end of the latter decade it was increasingly argued, even in published studies and articles, that only the transformation from a command to a market system would reverse the decline of the Czech economy (pp. 250–2).

In the GDR, which emerged from the Soviet Occupied Zone (SOZ) in October 1949, there was initially only limited controversy over alternative conceptions of economics and their relationship to society. Soviet socialist doctrine was generally accepted.

Subsequently, however, the attempt to devise new solutions to the economy's fundamental problems sparked off the so-called 'revisionism' debate, in which 'certain principles of Marxist-Leninism' were denied under the flag of 'free' scientific dispute and the struggle against dogmatism' (p. 289). The author of the chapter, Gunter Krause, observes that the 'revisionism' dispute in the 1950s concerning commodity production and the law of value began as 'a relatively autonomous scientific discussion' but eventually became 'one of the most shameful events dominated by party and power politics in the history of science in the GDR.' (p. 287). The controversy had a dramatic effect on the development of economic theory, for despite revealing the potential for innovative thinking in economics it also demonstrated the power of official economics to repress change. 'When the party ruled on science to the detriment of competent economists and convinced Marxists, it did more than depress the whole fraternity of economists. It ended their willingness to work productively' (pp. 290–91). As the editor observes in his introduction, 'Being a scientific economist under communism was a politically sensitive job' (p. 18).

The Wegener project raises the question, given the absence of freedom of science teaching and research, 'whether any cognitive process can proceed and bring about successful results in terms of scientific progress?'[4]

He cites the Polish economist, A. Lukaszewic, who defined intellectual sovereignty as equivalent to intellectual sincerity, to which Gligorov, author of the Yugoslavian chapter, added that 'autonomous science relies on the authority of the argument, rather than the argument from authority' (p. 330) Wegener comments:

> In a hierocratic system, where holy writs, fundamentalism or partisanship (partinost) prevails, the argument from authority cannot easily be put aside. *As long as scholars have internalised the ideology, by definition they can be sincere: they are true believers*. Where this is not the case, either exit, external or internal emigration, or cynicism, a distorted form of loyalty – the voice often being precluded – is the alternative. It has not been as bad as that all the time and in all places.[5]

Wegener reports that Yugoslavia was added to the original roster because that country's doctrine and practice of self-management was 'the source of important systemic and theoretical developments with considerable influence all over the region' (p. xi), in Hungary, the GDR, Russia (where there were a few advocates in the transformation era), and especially in Poland (cf. Pp. 52–3, 288). It also attracted considerable attention in the West. By the early 1970s self-management had become the unchallenged ideology in Yugoslavia, swamping other reform ideas, and most of the economists there sincerely believed in it as a means of combining the advantages of decentralized decision-making with more general collectivist commitments (pp. 9, 334–5). It was considered to be more efficient, more just, and more in accordance with Yugoslavia's specific political and social configuration. There were, however, varying degrees of commitment to self-management in different parts of the country, and there were various schools of thought within the self-management paradigm – for example the more orthodox socialists versus the professional economists with a more or less pragmatic and technocratic outlook (pp.336, 345, 346–7). Over time:

> the institutional and ideological controls were increasingly decentralized and relaxed … [and] specialization developed with the scientific interest being increasingly detached from the more dogmatic one. Yugoslav economics was converging with the economics taught in the West, with which it was communicating, though it was not integrated in it and the level of its professionalism was increasing all the time. The system of external and internal norms … evolved with the authority structure becoming looser and with methodological collectivism giving way either to positivism or to individualism. Thus, there was significant progress in the level of intellectual freedom. Still, the institutional and ideological control was always present (p. 332).

The economics of socialism in central and eastern Europe was by no means monolithic, either within a given country or over the region as a whole. This could lead to a paradoxical situation where, as in Russia during the 1960s,

> the fundamental ideas for change were developed by one group of economists. Normative documents were prepared by another group, generally of more moderate persuasion. The practical implementation was carried out by yet another group, a number of whom were out-and-out opponents of the central ideas of the reform (p. 6l).

In Poland a decade earlier, to cite another example:

> the issue of decentralization was difficult not only for politicians (wishing to keep their totalitarian power), but also for many economists who were conscious of various pathologies and failures of centralism but who, at the same time, were convinced that one must keep some version of central control with consciously planned allocation as inherent to socialism. Recalling that many other pathologies and failures were present also in the capitalist market economy and democracy, they rejected concepts that would lead reforms in the direction (p. 91).

Disagreements about the meaning of key terms: such as 'state' versus 'market' or 'plan', and the difficulty of excluding non-Marxist language such as: normal (or equilibrium) price, profits, and Western monetary categories, helped to complicate and intensify controversies about policy problems, while it was said that the development of 'quasi- codes' that served as protection against official disapproval and intervention 'destroyed clarity' (pp. 83–4). Formalist language and quantitative subject-matter – as in mathematical economics, econometrics and statistics – could be viewed as scientific, and therefore apolitical, while certain fields, such as business management, macroeconomics (but not microeconomics), economic history, and history of political economy, also seemed relatively free from ideological taint. National or local conditions could further muddy the intellectual waters. In Czechoslovakia, for instance, it was claimed that because of the country's high level of industrial development, a centrally controlled economy could not be efficient: 'decentralization and indirect regulation of economic processes' was required (pp. 2–21). In the GDR, discussions of the nature and proper scope of private ownership covered 'state ownership, socialization, nationalization and transformation into public ownership, private and capital ownership, state and communal ownership and cooperative and personal ownership' (p. 270), and there were comparable disputes over the various species of markets and their role in a socialist economy. Differences in the historical situations of the different countries meant that language and concepts had to be adapted to specific circumstances, in the interests of descriptive accuracy and the avoidance of capricious official scrutiny. Teaching in the universities was especially vulnerable to political interference, particularly where the professor was unwilling to teach orthodox Marxist doctrine, or introduced unwarranted deviations from the conventionally accepted line. Such interference continued, to some extent, even after the transformation of the early 1990s. At that time in Russia some teachers

> Stuck to Marxist orthodoxy; others created mixtures of Marxist and economic theory; a third group argued that both should be taught, but separately; while a final group argued for replacing Marxism with economics. For may teachers job maintenance is the primary concern. They often also argued for a peculiarly Russian variety of economics – obviously something they would be able to teach (p. 73).

Given this background, it is hardly surprising that first-rate students were said to prefer to work in research institutes (including the various Academies of Science) and government departments, rather than the universities, where the academic staff were conservative.

Economists in Central and Eastern Europe (CEE) countries were not, of course, entirely ignorant of the ideas and activities of their counterparts elsewhere, whether within the region or further afield. In most cases there were Emigrés[6], or involuntary economic exiles, even among members of the younger generation, who were still in communication with their former compatriots. Some returned home either occasionally or even permanently, whether formally to give lectures or conference papers, or informally – for example to visit family members or former professional colleagues. Russian and GDR economists were much more tightly restricted than their Polish, Hungarian, Czechoslovak and Yugoslav counterparts, who generally enjoyed freedom to travel abroad (except when the authorities were reacting against domestic political unrest). These opportunities were highly prized by the beneficiaries, many of whom were in the early stages of their careers. Foreign funds were made available, for example by the Ford Foundation or government bodies, either for short trips or periods of study abroad, and 'these

'American Boys', as they were called in Hungary, were definitely lost to ideological indoctrination, and they pushed for curriculum reforms' when they returned.[7] The availability of language laboratories was of special importance in facilitating comprehension of foreign literature. Generally speaking, Hungarian and Polish economists had far greater linguistic skills than their Russian and GDR counterparts, especially when they were able to attend international conferences or spend a period of study or teaching abroad.

Of course, access to foreign economics books and other relevant published materials constituted by far the most important means of keeping abreast of foreign economists' ideas and activities. While there was no invisible college or regular participation in a CEE or Western-type international network or learned journals, the combined output of CEE publications was immense, and of great significance for practical policy as well and academic and professional (scientific) purposes. The most frequently cited non-CEE authors were Von Hayek, Keynes, Kalecki and Samuelson – the last named especially for his famous textbook.[8] Ideological and partisan control by journal editors within the six countries was often more savage than the censorship exercised by party officials (p. 238). Fear of official disapproval encouraged collaborative publications, thereby giving the individual authors some protection from censors.

Given their unavoidable preoccupation with economic policy and system reform, rather than abstract theory, considerable numbers of CEE economists inevitable became directly or indirectly involved in policy-making and implementation processes, whether as government employees, advisers to ministers and other policy-makers, or members of official or unofficial expert teams.[9] This meant that these economists became 'an integral part of the political structure' and, for example in the GDR, 'this instrumentalization category included treating the economist as a political functionary, a party worker at the theoretical front who had to deliver what policy dictated' (p. 265). In consequence of this intimate relationship, the failures of the socialist system covered in Wegener's study were damaging to the reputation of the economics profession as a whole, as well as the individual economists directly involved. He concludes that '[almost] nothing is left' of the efforts of

> The large group of able and sincere economists in Central and Eastern Europe who: endeavoured to get to grips with the model and the practice of central planning ... On the whole it seems that the contribution of Soviet [and Yugoslav] to economics was, above all, negative in establishing the counter-argument of more successful market capitalism (pp. 24, 25).[10]

Notes

1 Some of the intra-communist interactions, and links with economists outside the region will be mentioned.

2 The propositions (somewhat abbreviated) are:

a) under socialism there are no contradictions between productive forces and productive relations because the latter are always in advance of the former.

b) There are no fundamental conflicts between individual, collective and social needs.
c) In socialist production labour has a direct social character due to planning. A market transforming individual into social labour is redundant.
d) Collective social production is superior to all other (cooperative, individual) forms of production. From this follows the hierarchy of ownership forms.
e) Planning is not coordination of independent economic subjects [i.e. workers], but conscious organization from above.
f) Individuals' utility functions contain only material arguments. Hence, the economic system can be separated from the social, cultural and emotional system, and can be organized from above.
g) Really existing socialism is scientific: the level of knowledge is sufficient for conscious order and planning (p. 11).

3 The chapter on Czechoslovakia (5) contains a vivid and detailed account of the strict exercise of party controls over economics – university appointments, publications, the arrest of those whose work incurred official disapproval, the closing of academic departments of economics, and the banning of contacts with émigré economists (regarded as a form of betrayal). 'Any piece of paper meant for publication was carefully scrutinized' (p. 235), and in the 1980s the authorship of textbooks was 'as a rule collective, thus minimizing the risk for individuals of falling into disgrace with the party authorities, (p. 236. See also pp. 216–8, 220–1, 228 et seq., 233ff). There were periods of relaxation and subsequent reassertion of control. In the Soviet Union professorships of economics were open only to party members. Yet the intellectual climate there was generally less restricted than in Berlin or Prague (pp. 18, 20).

4 Wegener does not attempt to define either 'science' or 'profession', key terms in his study. His project, he states, is concerned with the history of thought.

As there are few contributions to economic theory proper he will not treat the history of economic analysis a la Schumpeter, but 'the history of economic thinking … This includes aspects of management of economic theory as a science, its institutional organization, and its representation in teaching. It also includes some aspects of the sociology of science' (p. 5). On this matter see, especially, the chapter on Yugoslavia (pp. 330–3).

5 P.5. Italics supplied. The terms 'exit', 'loyalty' and 'voice' refer to the thoughtful book of that title by Albert O. Hirshman.

6 Especially Germans, many of whom left the GDR for the Federal Republic in the early postwar years. Few returned home later. (The GDR was, of course, the creation of Soviet Power).

7 P. 20. For an account of foreign economic thought in Czechoslovakia see pp. 230–2, which was, in many respects, closer to Poland and Hungary than to Russia or the GDR. Yugoslavia can be viewed as an intermediate case owing to the distinctive influence of self-management ideas and practice. 'It was neither a centrally planned economy nor a market economy. But it was not simply a mixture of the two' (p. 334ff.).

8 The most frequently cited CEE authors in Wegener were F. Behrens, W. Brus, J. Knorai, O. Lange, N. Petrakov, O. Sik, J. Stalin and P. Sutela.

9 The six chapters provide numerous examples of the economists' official activities and positions, which cannot be considered in this already lengthy review. One interesting example may be cited, when a major research project on the long-term prospects of the Czech economy to 2010 was suppressed because its conclusions were so gloomy. The secret report was leaked to Radio Free Europe and subsequently published, together with all the background papers, in a leading journal. Some of these papers were much more radical than the forecast (p. 246).

10 Each country chapter in Wegener has an account of the transformation process in 1989–92. (In Yugoslavia the process began gradually in the 1960s).

Considerations of space have precluded an adequate account of this process which is, of course, central to Wegener's larger project.

Index

For Product Safety Concerns and Information please contact our EU representative GPSR@taylorandfrancis.com
Taylor & Francis Verlag GmbH, Kaufingerstraße 24, 80331 München, Germany

www.ingramcontent.com/pod-product-compliance
Ingram Content Group UK Ltd.
Pitfield, Milton Keynes, MK11 3LW, UK
UKHW020025200926
475702UK00014B/2060
* 9 7 8 1 1 3 8 2 4 3 7 6 7 *